1 MONTH OF
FREE
READING

at

www.ForgottenBooks.com

By purchasing this book you are eligible for one month membership to ForgottenBooks.com, giving you unlimited access to our entire collection of over 1,000,000 titles via our web site and mobile apps.

To claim your free month visit:

www.forgottenbooks.com/free1254847

ISBN 978-0-428-63250-2
PIBN 11254847

REPORT

OF THE

PENNSYLVANIA
HOME TEACHING SOCIETY

AND

FREE CIRCULATING
LIBRARY
FOR THE BLIND

(INCORPORATED)

1905

THE PENNSYLVANIA
HOME TEACHING SOCIETY AND FREE CIRCULATING
LIBRARY FOR THE BLIND.

ESTABLISHED 1882.   REORGANIZED 1898.
INCORPORATED 1901.

President:
HON. WILLIAM N. ASHMAN, 4400 Spruce Street, Philadelphia.

Vice-Presidents:
DUNDAS T. PRATT, 128 S. 19th St., Philada.
JOHN P. RHOADS, Bible House, 7th and Walnut Sts., Philada.
JOHN E. BAIRD, 1705 N. Broad St., Philada.
BENEDICT GIMBEL, 9th and Market Sts., Philada.
JOHN H. CONVERSE, LL. D., Broad and Spring Garden Sts., Philada.

Treasurer:
FRANK READ, 827 Drexel Building, Chestnut St., Philada.

Secretary:
ROBERT C. MOON, M. D., 1319 Walnut St., Philada.

BOARD OF MANAGERS.

Prof. Edward Ellis Allen,
Institution for the Blind, Overbrook.

Hon. William N. Ashman,
4400 Spruce Street.

John E. Baird,
1705 N. Broad Street.

John H. Converse, LL. D.,
Broad and Spring Garden Streets.

Rev. Edgar Cope,
Lehigh Avenue and 9th Street.

Rev Alfred L. Elwyn,
1422 Walnut Street.

Benedict Gimbel,
9th and Market Streets.

Robert C. Moon, M. D.,
1319 Walnut Street.

Rev. James Morrow, D. D.,
Bible House, 7th and Walnut Streets.

J. Rodman Paul,
505 Chestnut Street.

Dundas T. Pratt,
128 S. 19th Street.

Frank Read,
Rosemont.

Wm. H. Richardson,
3717 Lancaster Avenue.

John P. Rhoads,
Bible House, 7th and Walnut Streets.

Richard H. Thomas, Jr.,
Bible House, 7th and Walnut Streets.

John Thomson,
Free Library of Philadelphia.

John J. Wilkinson,
4024 Spring Garden Street.

Mrs. Edward Ellis Allen,
Overbrook.

Mrs. Charles R. Colwell,
Weymouth, N. J.

Mrs. Samuel Dickson,
901 Clinton Street.

Mrs. Louis Estel Fagan,
470 Locust Avenue, Germantown.

Mrs. Margaret Morris Moon,
Ardmore Avenue, Ardmore.

Mrs. Thomas B. Morris,
241 S. 21st Street.

Miss E. R. Neisser,
Free Library of Philadelphia.

Miss Sarah Nicholson,
Haddonfield, N. J.

Mrs. Beulah M. Rhoads,
Haddonfield, N. J.

Ophthalmologist—ROBERT C. MOON, M. D.,
1319 Walnut St. (Witherspoon Building), Philadelphia, Penna.

PHOTOGRAPHED FROM DR. MOON'S EMBOSSED ALPHABET FOR THE BLIND.

INSTRUCTIONS.—In teaching the Alphabet, care should be taken to explain the alterations made in the letters, as indicated by the dotted lines (see the note above the Alphabet). The first line of reading is read from left to right, and the second from right to left, to prevent the reader from losing his place; the brackets guide the finger from line to line. Words ending in *ing, ment, tion,* and *ness* have the last letter put for the whole syllable, as: *g* for *ing*; *t* for *ment,* etc.; two dots one above the other giving notice of the contraction. The first letters of *LORD, GOD, JESUS,* and *CHRIST* always stand for those holy names. Two dots side by side are used for a full stop, a single dot for any shorter stop. Verses are divided by two short lines one above the other. — stands for *th* and *the.*

REPORT OF THE BOARD OF MANAGERS

OF THE

PENNSYLVANIA HOME TEACHING SOCIETY AND FREE CIRCULATING LIBRARY FOR THE BLIND.

READ AT THE ANNUAL MEETING

HELD IN THE WITHERSPOON BUILDING, PHILADELPHIA, PA.

JANUARY 19, 1905.

HON. WILLIAM N. ASHMAN IN THE CHAIR.

IT has been the custom of this Society, from the time of its inauguration in 1882, to promote home teaching of the blind throughout the United States, and to respond to applications for embossed literature from the most distant parts of the Union, as readily as those from Philadelphia and its neighborhood. In accordance with this time-honored practice, the Board of Managers realized that the opportunity presented during the past year, at the World's Fair at St. Louis, to make home teaching for the blind more widely known than ever before on this continent, ought not to be neglected. The Exposition authorities cordially responded to the Society's request for space, and our exhibit of embossed books in the Moon type, as well as maps, diagrams and pictures in relief, designed by the late Dr. William Moon, of Brighton, England, was carefully prepared and dispatched to St. Louis in time for the opening of the Exposition.

During the months of September and October, one of the Society's blind teachers, Mr. James W. Moore, was present at the Exposition to explain the exhibit, and to answer the questions of inquiring visitors who had come from every State of the Union, from Hawaii, the Philippines, Mexico, Brazil, Japan, and many European countries. A large number of them, who had blind relatives and friends, eagerly sought for information about the reading, and carried away alphabets and specimen pages of reading, in the hope of being able, upon returning to their homes, to instruct the blind persons in whom they were interested.

It is most gratifying that the jurors of the Section, devoted to the education of the blind at the World's Fair, awarded a gold medal to this Society for its interesting and attractive exhibit.

sition, which has now passed into history, was a universal institution of instruction, and the members of this Society may well feel pleased and satisfied with the success which has attended its exhibit at the World's Fair.

This special enterprise at St. Louis, the expense of which was, to a considerable extent, defrayed by special contributions for that purpose, has, however, not been allowed to interfere with the prosecution of the work in our own city and State.

The two teachers at present employed have had 117 new pupils under instruction during the year, and have paid 2843 visits to them and various other blind persons in private houses and public institutions, for the purpose of instructing them in reading and furnishing them with an exchange of books. When to these are added 71 names of persons who have been enrolled during 1904 at the Free Library of Philadelphia, the total number of new blind readers during the year is 188. After allowing for those who have died, there are 774 names upon the roll of blind readers. During 1904 no less than 5284 volumes of embossed books were issued from the Department for the blind in the Free Library of Philadelphia, 1954 of which were distributed by our teachers, and 1352 were sent out of the city to distant places in the United States, and even to blind persons in the Philippine Islands.

In the Report for 1903 of the Free Library of Philadelphia, the following reference is made to the 4819 embossed volumes issued during that year from its Department for the Blind, to readers, who are persons of all ages, using the five embossed types:—

"The distribution, according to types, has been as follows: Braille, 480 volumes; American Braille, 467 volumes; New York Point, 85 volumes; Line Letter, 159 volumes; Moon Type, 3628 volumes; total, 4819 volumes.

"The large preponderance of Moon type over the other types circulated, is due to the fact that the majority of the readers are those who have become blind in adult life. Many at this age are not readily able to master a point system, and for them the Moon system has proved a blessing."

One of the memorable features of the year's progress has been the enactment by Congress of a law providing for free transportation through the mails of embossed reading matter, when loaned to the blind. The agitation for such free postage, which has been kept up for several years by this Society and many of the friends of the blind, has thus resulted in a concession, which will confer a boon upon 80,000 blind persons in the United States and its various possessions; and as this beneficent arrangement becomes more generally known, there will doubtless be an increased demand from distant places for embossed books from the Society's library.

The Board of Managers desires again to express its grateful appreciation of the continued hearty and harmonious co-operation of the Free Library of Philadelphia, which so efficiently conducts the distribution of the embossed books from the library. It is no uncommon thing to see, at one time, in the Department for the Blind, several large packages of books ready for mailing, and addressed to various towns in the State of Pennsylvania, as well as to places in distant States, such as Texas, California, Colorado, Georgia and Maine, and also to Alaska. These represent a large amount of work in addition to the regular issuing of books to the blind of the city of Philadelphia. The latter is conducted by the Free Library without any charge, but the clerical and packing expenses connected with the forwarding of books beyond the boundaries of the city have to be met by this Society.

In addition to the contributions of the annual subscribers, the Managers thankfully acknowledge the receipt of $500 from the estate of Hannah W. Gadsden, through the kindness of the executor, John B. Moffitt, Esq., and also of $1000 from the estate of Hiram J. Brooke,

DR. WILLIAM MOON.

Inventor of Moon's Type for the Blind.

through the executor, The Fidelity Trust Company of Philadelphia. These contributions have greatly aided them in their efforts to extend the knowledge and usefulness of this beneficent work for the blind. To Mr. Frank Read, the Treasurer of this Society, they are also indebted for three complete copies of "Barriers Burned Away," which form a valuable addition to its library of embossed books in the Moon type. Whilst it is a cause for deep thankfulness that the efforts of this

5

Society, on behalf of the blind, have been so abundantly blessed, there are thousands of the blind, in Pennsylvania alone, who need to be sought out and taught to read. This is not only a philanthropic but an educational work, which is most worthy of aid from the State, and it is to be hoped that a generous appropriation toward its support may, ere long, be granted by the Legislature of Pennsylvania. The schools for the blind provide efficiently for those under twenty-one years of age, but hardly 500 are at the present time under instruction in the schools for the blind in Pennsylvania, whereas the total population of blind in the State is more than 6000. Of these, 82 % are over twenty-one years of age, so that the adults, who are so greatly in the majority, could not enter the schools if they would ; and it may well be supposed that but few would become inmates of them, if they could. The plan of home teaching is therefore a necessity for the adults, and employment could easily be found for a dozen more teachers, to search out and teach the blind of Pennsylvania alone.

This Society devotes its efforts, free of charge, to the blind of all classes, without distinction of age, sex, color, nationality, or religion. It is found that by means of the easily felt Moon type, a very large proportion of the blind can become good readers, notwithstanding that their sense of touch is oftentimes impaired, either from hardened fingers, or from diseases affecting the nervous system, which further make it impossible for them to decipher complicated characters, or commit a multitude of contractions to memory, as found in other embossed types.

The lot of the blind is indeed a sad one! Added to their affliction, oftentimes, is a dependence upon friends or relatives for support ; and it is no uncommon experience that blind persons have literally to sit in darkness and solitude, with nothing to occupy them but their own thoughts.

But a change comes o'er the scene when the embossed type is handed to the blind ones by the home teacher, who comes with a word of cheer—

> " Lighting up the darkness,
> Scattering the gloom."

Despondency gives way to hope and joy soon follows, as they trace the simple embossed characters, and, after one or two lessons, are able once more to read for themselves.

To aid in such a work may well be deemed a privilege, for such a ministry is

> "twice bless'd,
> It blesseth him that gives and him that takes."

PUBLICATION FUND.

At the Annual Meeting of this Society, held in 1902, it was resolved that an effort should be made to raise a Publication Fund of $100,000, the interest of which should be devoted to defraying the cost of stereotyping new and interesting books in the Moon type for the blind. A larger number and a greater variety of books are much needed for our readers. They ask for more books of an entertaining, instructive character, such as their sighted friends enjoy; and to meet this demand, the Board of Managers hopes that fresh impetus may now be given to the efforts for raising the Publication Fund.

6

The Managers thankfully acknowledge the receipt of $100 from Mr. John H. Converse and $100 from Miss Phœbe Anna Thorne, and promises from Mr. Frank Read, Mr. John E. Baird, and Mr. Benedict Gimbel of contributions of $100 each toward the Publication Fund.

Not long ago this Society contributed $150 toward the cost of "John Halifax, Gentleman," which was stereotyped by the Moon Society for Embossing Books for the Blind, in Brighton, England, and the Managers earnestly hope that the proposed permanent fund may speedily be raised, so that the Society may be in a position to render further and larger assistance in increasing the literature for the blind. Our blind friends have pathetic claims upon our love and

MISS MOON.

Miss Moon is Successor to her father, Dr. William Moon, in conducting his Work for the Blind, at Brighton, England.

sympathy, and such an effort as this on their behalf cannot fail to appeal to the generous impulses of a high-minded and enlightened community. Let us enrich and broaden their lives, by opening up for them fresh channels of communication through the writings of the greatest authors and brightest thinkers of this and every other age. Thus, the blind throughout the world will ultimately be benefited; and perchance some darkened souls may be so illumined with "celestial light," that, like the immortal poet, they will be privileged to
"see and tell
Of things invisible to mortal sight."

ROBERT C. MOON, M.D., *Secretary.*

THE EXHIBIT OF

THE PENNSYLVANIA HOME TEACHING SOCIETY
AND FREE CIRCULATING LIBRARY
FOR THE BLIND

WHICH WAS AWARDED A GOLD MEDAL IN THE SECTION
DEVOTED TO THE EDUCATION OF THE BLIND AT
THE LOUISIANA PURCHASE EXPOSITION

ST. LOUIS, MO.

1904

ON THE SHELVES OF THE BOOKCASES ARE SEVERAL VOLUMES EMBOSSED IN
THE MOON TYPE FOR THE BLIND.

THE CLOSED CABINETS CONTAIN SPECIMENS OF EMBOSSED MAPS, DIAGRAMS,
PICTURES, PORTRAITS, ETC., MOUNTED IN SWINGING FRAMES

REPORT UPON THE EXHIBIT

OF THE

PENNSYLVANIA HOME TEACHING SOCIETY AND FREE CIRCULATING LIBRARY FOR THE BLIND,

AT THE

LOUISIANA PURCHASE EXPOSITION,

St. Louis, Mo., 1904.

By ROBERT C. MOON, M. D., *Secretary.*

IN accordance with a resolution passed by the Board of Managers of this Society at its last n eeting, the n ale teacher, Mr. Janes W. Moore, on August 31st, started fron Philadelphia to act as den onstrator of the exhibit, which had, earlier in the year, been prepared and forwarded to the World's Fair at St. Louis. I accon panied hin, to see that he was properly installed and satisfactorily provided for during the eight weeks he was to spend at the Exposition.

We arrived in St. Louis, Septen ber 1st, in tin e to reach the Fair in the afternoon. We found our exhibit in the Palace of Education, respectably located in an alcove, with the exhibits of the Overbrook and Maryland Institutions for the blind on the one side, and those of the Missouri, New York and Boston Institutions on the other. The schoolroon s, or large booths, in which blind children were going through their exercises, opened upon the n ain aisle, which passed the end of the alcove in which our exhibit was located. I soon sought out Mr. Alvin E. Pope, the Superintendent of the Section devoted to the blind and deaf. He gave us a warn reception, and directed us to the dormitory in which Mr. Moore was to be lodged during his stay. We were also provided with provisional passes for entering the World's Fair grounds. Mr. Moore could not receive his pern anent pass until he had been photographed, for which a charge of two dollars was n ade.

During a long conversation with Mr. Pope, I was able fully to explain the character of the hon e-teaching work, and how it differed fron the work of the schools for the blind. He saw at once that the en bossed type we used could be felt by the blind of all ages, whilst the dotted types required very sensitive fingers for their deciphern ent. As scon as I reached the Education Building, on the following n orning, Mr. Pope cane to n e and offered for the exhibit one of the schoolroon s n easuring 12 by 13 feet and opening upon the n ain aisle, if I could n ake use of it. I gladly accepted it, as it was in a very conspicuous location, and at once en ployed a signwriter to paint son e large placards representin the Moon alphabet and a line of reading. These were fastened acrosg the back wall of the schoolroo n , and our cabinets and photographic portraits were brought fro n the alcove and arrranged, as shown in the photograph of the exhibit.

The nu n ber of persons who stopped to inspect the exhibit and listen to Mr. Moore's explanations and de n onstrations of reading was, in the new location, n uch larger than it had been in the alcove ; and hundreds, during each day that I was there, clustered around the booth to learn about the ho n e-teaching work, and to carry away a copy of the circular, which, by direction of this Board, had been prepared for free distribution.

During n y stay at the Fair, I endeavored to interest several influ- ential persons in ho n e teaching for the blind of St. Louis, and, on Septe n ber 10th, I delivered, in the Lecture Hall of the Palace of Education, an address upon the subject of e n bossed types and ho n e teaching for the blind.

Professor Ja n es M. Ball, a celebrated oculist of the city, who was present, asked n e for n y address, for the purpose of publishing it in the ''Annals of Ophthal n ology,'' of which he is the chief editor. As this in portant publication reaches oculists all over the world, the n essage I had the honor to deliver will thereby reach a far larger audience than that at the World's Fair. As Dr. Ball very properly re n arked, oculists, in general, know too little of this n eans of an eli- orating the condition of the blind, and he thought this was a fine opportunity for n aking the n better acquainted with it.

. The ti n e of our arrival at the Fair could not have been n ore oppor- tune, for, on the very day we transferred our exhibit to its new quarters, the Juries of Award asse n bled, to co n n ence their inspection of the various exhibits, and it was n y privilege to converse with each of those who constituted the Jury of Award for the special depart n ent devoted to the blind and deaf. I was introduced to the n by Mr. Pope, and I lost no ti n e in giving one of the n — Professor Green, the Superinten- dent of the Missouri School for the Blind — a correct i n pression as to our work. I pointed out that our work in no way conflicted with the grand and efficient instruction which is given in the schools, but we dealt with the adults, who n they were unable to receive. He was n ost courteous, and fully realized that our work was the co n ple n ent of the school work, and that we endeavored to do what they did not or could not do. The other jurors. one of who n was a Japanese, grasped the sa n e thought i n n ediately, and all of the n n ade a care- ful exa n ination of our exhibit, with its e n bossed books and the cabi- nets of n ounted speci n ens kindly furnished by the Moon Society in England, which included e n bossed reading in 419 languages, as well as pictures, diagra n s, astrono n ical and geographical n aps in relief, as designed by the late Dr. Willia n Moon, for the use of the blind. It was n y good fortune to be present at the ti n e the n en bers of the jury n ade their first tour of inspection.

Mr. Pope kindly introduced n e to Miss Mary E. Perry, a lady who is so pro n inently connected with philanthropic work in the city, that she is styled the ''Helen Gould of St. Louis.'' I explained to her the character of our exhibit, and expressed a hope that it n ight be pos- sible to for n a Society in St. Louis si n ilar to ours in Philadelphia. She at once n anifested an interest in it, especially as one of her sisters,

Miss Laura Perry, has been blind for several years. Miss Perry communicated with Mr. Frederick M. Crunden, the Librarian of the Public Free Library of St. Louis, and arranged a time for us to meet, to discuss the question of his receiving and distributing the embossed books, which should be committed to his care by any organization which might be formed for home teaching of the blind. Mr. Crunden entered cordially into the plan, and said that he could promise, on behalf of his trustees, that the library work for the blind should be taken up in St. Louis as it was being conducted by his friend, Mr. John Thomson, in Philadelphia, who, by the way, had also kindly furnished me with an introduction to Mr. Crunden. I should also mention that I am greatly indebted to Professor Allen, of Overbrook, for a special introduction to Professor Green, of the St. Louis School for the Blind.

I remained in St. Louis twelve days, and left for Philadelphia on the night of September 12th, having had the pleasure of seeing Mr. Moore fully installed at the exhibit, and comfortably lodged and cared for in one of the dormitories within the World's Fair grounds. During the latter part of my stay I was, by the courtesy of Mr. Pope, also accommodated with lodging in the same dormitory.

Whilst I was at the Fair, the Illinois School for the Blind, at Jacksonville, was represented by several of its scholars, who occupied neighboring booths to our own. The scholars read from embossed books, wrote on typewriters, played on various musical instruments, and sang very sweetly. In a booth near to us, Lottie Sullivan, an interesting blind, deaf and dumb girl, was on exhibition. She was a pupil from the Colorado School for the Blind, and could read the dotted type, write letters on the typewriter, and sew with the sewing-machine. Mr. Moore readily taught her, and all the scholars from the Jacksonville School, to read by the Moon type; and Dr. Freeman, the Superintendent of that school, with whom I frequently conversed, asked many questions, and became deeply interested in our work. He expressed his determination to start a similar method of teaching the adult blind in his own city. He saw that our method, and the type we used, solved a problem about the adults and their reading which had puzzled him before.

I also had the pleasure of seeing and conversing with Miss Sarah A. Draper, the Director of the Musical Department of the Illinois School for the Blind.

After the pupils of that school had concluded their stay at the Fair, large numbers of the scholars of the Missouri School for the Blind, in charge of Miss Reese, Assistant Principal, took their places in the schoolrooms and gave interesting exhibitions illustrating the method of instruction pursued in that institution; and Mr. Moore was informed, before he left St. Louis, that all of them had learned to read the Moon type in a very short time, and were delighted with it.

It was fresh news to many, that the United States Congress had granted free postage for embossed books loaned to the blind. Indeed, this is the first opportunity we have had of announcing to this Board, that on the 2d of June the Postmaster General issued an order to all postmasters in reference to an act of Congress, passed April 27, 1904, which granted, under certain regulations, free transportation through the United States mails of embossed books, when loaned to blind persons, from the public libraries or institutions. When this good news becomes more widely known, there is no doubt that the circulation of the books from our own library, in Philadelphia, will be largely increased.

Before I left St. Louis, the Jury of Award had completed its deliberations, and one of the jurors told me that we should have no reason to be disappointed when we heard of its decision in reference to our exhibit. I have learned since, that we have been awarded the Gold Medal, and that New York has been awarded the Silver Medal. This is no small honor, and New York is surprised at the award, as the first prize was awarded New York at the Paris Exposition of 1900. But, then, it must be borne in mind that at Paris, the Pennsylvania Home Teaching Society for the Blind was not represented by an exhibit!

It was my privilege to have a long and delightful interview with Miss Laura Perry, the blind lady to whom I have already referred. Notwithstanding her blindness, I found her a very gifted lady. She told me that she remembered, with gratitude, that soon after losing her eyesight, she learned the Moon type, and received embossed books from the Bible Society in Philadelphia. She warmly embraced the idea of trying to reach and teach the adult blind in St. Louis, and expected to enlist the co-operation of her intimate friend, Miss H——, the daughter of a Cabinet Minister at Washington. Since my return to Philadelphia I have learned that she proposes to undertake some home teaching on her own account. I may here mention that she is a sister-in-law of Governor Francis, the President of the Exposition, and I think, that under such auspices, with Professor Green as adviser and Mr. Crunden as librarian, there is a good prospect of the work making headway in the city of St. Louis.

Oftentimes during my stay at the Fair I lamented the fact, that our blind friends, who were present there to enlighten the world as to the means provided for ameliorating their own condition, could not themselves behold the wonderful scenes by which they were surrounded. It was a world in itself—a fairyland, a dream. Everything was on a stupendous and magnificent scale, and all the varied objects and structures were so well proportioned, that the colossal buildings harmonized with the most pleasing effect.

But whilst the scene was grand by day, it was bewitchingly enchanting at night, when every building and every statue became suddenly outlined by the faintest of lights, which gradually grew in strength and splendor, until the whole picture, from Festival Hall to the Plaza of St. Louis, was bathed in glorious light, issuing from hundreds of thousands of incandescent bulbs.

In conclusion, I think we have abundant cause to be gratified by the success which has attended the exhibit made on behalf of this Society at the World's Fair. Thousands of persons from every State and Territory of the Union; from Mexico, Canada, Australia, Japan, and many European countries have been, and still are being, thereby made acquainted with home teaching and embossed reading for the blind, of which they had neither seen nor heard anything before their visit to the Fair.

On October 17th Mr. Moore received a telegram from Boonville, Mo. It was addressed to him at our exhibit, in the Palace of Education, and read as follows:—

"You renenber I was talking to you last Friday about ny father who is blind. If we will pay all your expenses will you cone here before you go East and teach hin to read? Distance two hundred niles—tine seven hours on Missouri, Kansas, Texas. You can take sleeper. Our expense. W. H. A ᴧ Es."

As this telegran reached Mr. Moore at the beginning of "Helen Keller Week," and he was likely to find it the nost fully occupied one of his visit, it was in possible for hin, personally, to respond to the sun nons. He however sent on the necessary papers for the instruction of Mr. Anes's blind father. This is but one of the nany instances of visitors to the Fair carrying hone to their afflicted friends the glad tidings of an easily acquired type for the blind.

I cannot refrain fron expressing ny grateful appreciation of the uniforn courtesy and kindness shown to your representatives by the officials of the Departnent of Education, especially fron Dr. Howard J. Rogers, the Chief, and Mr. Pope, Superintendent of the Section devoted to the blind and the deaf.

Mr. Moore con pleted his stay of two nonths at the Fair on Friday, October 21st, and returned on Sunday last to resune his work in Philadelphia. At the World's Fair he has taught very nany blind persons, and has given instruction to nany sighted persons, so that, upon their return to their hones, they can teach their blind relatives and friends to read fron the enbossed papers with which they were provided. Many thousands of circulars, giving a condensed account of the work of this Society, with a copy of the enbossed alphabet attached, have been distributed and carried away to enlighten people in far-distant hones, upon the subject of reading for the blind. Already several applications have cone to us for enbossed alphabets and first lessons, fron persons who heard of the type for the first tine through their friends who visited the World's Fair at St. Louis. And the end is not yet, for I fully believe the results will be farther reaching and nuch nore lasting than we can possibly now in agine.

THE SOCIETY'S BLIND MALE TEACHER GIVING ONE OF HIS PUPILS A LESSON IN THE MOON TYPE FOR THE BLIND.

The blind pupil here represented is afflicted with spinal trouble, and is unable to walk, but she finds unfailing entertainment in reading the embossed books.

TESTIMONIES OF THE BLIND.

The following are but a few of many interesting communications recently received from the blind :—

OFFICE OF
LANCASTER COUNTY HOME AND INSANE ASYLUM.

LANCASTER, PA , January 1, 1905.

MR. JOHN THOMSON, Librarian, 1217-1221 Chestnut St., Philadelphia.

DEAR SIR:—With much pleasure Mr. Fluchard and myself desire by this to express to yourself, the officials, and each member of the Pennsylvania Home Teaching Society and Free Circulating Library for the Blind, our heartfelt thanks and high appreciation of your kind and generous efforts of the past year to make cheerful the dreary hours of two lowly and humble ones as ourselves; we also join in wishing you all a happy and prosperous New Year. And we sincerely ask that in return the reward to each of you shall be God's richest and Heavenly blessings. We remain, dear sir,

Very sincerely yours in loving remembrance,

CHARLES H. GRAHAM,
PHILIP FLUCHARD,
County Hospital, Lancaster, Pa.

PENSAUKEN, N. J., January 11, 1905.

DEAR DR. MOON:—Per request of Mr. John Clift, my uncle, 621 N. Franklin, Philadelphia, I write the following, as per his dictation —:

"Since my sixty-third year, now three years past, I have been totally blind. Kind friends suggested that I learn to read by the raised alphabet. Dr. Moon promptly sent Mr. Moore, a most patient teacher, to instruct and assist me in the system, and I am overjoyed in being able to say that I can now read the finest print with but little trouble. Before this great help was brought to my attention, I was fearfully troubled with insomnia. Now, however, I have restful and peaceful slumbers. I have every reason to be most grateful for such a companion to assist in profitably spending my declining years. The best authors are now open to me. Science, religion, etc., are truly at my fingers' ends. Possibly none but the blind truly realize the awful reality of not being able longer to recognize the faces of dear ones and kind friends; the loneliness of our position can be *felt*, but with the ability to read, and that reading of the very best, from the great Book, God's Word, followed by the writings of earth's scientific master-minds, I can bask in pleasant thoughts and reasonings. Truly it is dense darkness *without*, but, thank God, light within. With many, many thanks to you and your kind assistants and ever praying for your Society and welfare, I remain,

Very truly and respectfully,

JOHN J. CLIFT,
621 N. Franklin, Philadelphia, Pa.

Per
The REV. EDWARD R BAXTER,
525 E. Park Ave.,
Pensauken, N. J.

FAC-SIMILE OF CHARTER OF INCORPORATION.

Balance, General Fund, January 20, 1904 . . . . $151 40

RECEIVED.

From Annual Subscriptions	$480 50	
From Direct Contributions	290 13	
	$770 63	
From Hannah W. Gadsden Estate	500 00	
From Hiram J. Brooke Estate	1000 00	
Books purchased by Free Library from England . . .	6 20	
From Free Library ¼ importation charges on books bought ., . . .	2 08	
From books sold to Pennsylvania Institute	40 78	
From books sold by Free Library	73 33	
From readers by Free Library for postage, expressage, etc.	29 44	$2,422 46
Total Receipts		$2,573 86

DISBURSED.

Male teacher's salary and traveling expenses, postages, etc., by the hands of Dr. R. C. Moon, Secretary	$550 00	
Books purchased Moon Society, Eng.	180 33	
Ketterlinus Lith. Mfg. Co., printing 1904 reports, programmes, circulars, invitation cards, etc.	200 65	
Contribution to Free Library on account of clerical services for the years 1903 and 1904	200 00	
Teacher's expenses to St. Louis Exhibition	213 45	
T. J. Priestly, Jr. Co., printing labels, postals, etc., used by Free Library . .	41 65	
J. L. Vaudiver, entry charges on books imported	20 65	
Advertisement in City Mission Directory	5 00	
T. H. Grigg, writing boards	12 00	
Postage used by Treasurer	6 13	
By Free Library for expressage, postage, etc., on books sent to readers 1904 .	83 96	
Books bought from Bible House by F. L. P.	64 00	
Total Disbursements		$1,577 82
Balance, General Fund, January 17, 1905		$996 04
Balance, Publication Fund, January 17, 1905		233 50
Balance, Female Teacher's Fund, January 17, 1905 . . .		113 12
Balance in Treasury, January 17, 1905		$1,342 66

PUBLICATION FUND

Balance, January 20, 1904 . . . . $100 00

RECEIVED.

1904				
Feb. 11,	Contribution from Miss Martha E. Howland			$5 00
Feb. 11,	"	"	Mr. Thomas Elder	5 00
Feb. 11,	"	"	Miss Margaret Elder	1 00
Mch. 10,	"	"	Miss Phoebe Anna Thorne	100 00
1905				
Jan. 10,	"	"	Mr. Israel Morris	5 00
Jan. 10,	"	"	Mr. Chas. D'Invilliers	1 00
Jan. 11,	"	"	Miss Marie E. Santee	10 00
Jan. 14,	"	"	Mr. C. D. Ritchie	5 00
Jan. 17,	"	"	Miss Carrie B. Beans	1 50
			Balance, January 17, 1905	$233 50

FEMALE TEACHER'S FUND.

Balance, January 20, 1904 . . . . $107 47

RECEIVED.

1904				
June 6,	Contribution, "B. M. R,"		$50 00	
Oct. 19,	"	Mrs. Beulah M. Rhoads	25 00	
1905				
Jan. 11,	"	Mr. D. T. Pratt	100 00	$175 00
				$282 47

DISBURSED.

Paid Dr. Moon, Secretary, on account of lady teacher's salary, expenses, etc.		$169 35
Balance, January 17, 1905		$113 12

ST. LOUIS EXHIBIT FUND.

Balance, January 20, 1904 . . . . $7 50

RECEIVED.

1904				
Jan. 26,	Contribution, Mr. Elliston P. Morris		$20 00	
Mch. 24,	"	Cash	5 00	
Apr. 27,	"	Mr. Frank Read	25 00	
Apr. 29,	"	Mr. D. T. Pratt	25 00	
May 2,	"	Mr. John E. Baird	25 00	$100 00
				$107 50

DISBURSED.

1904			
Apr. 29,	Paid Geo. Malcomson, picture frames, lettering, boxing, etc.	$20 25	
Apr. 29,	" lander & Taylor, mounting prints, lettering, etc.	17 70	
Apr. 29,	" Sabbague & Darbois, wall cabinets, installation, etc.	50 00	
Aug. 24,	Balance paid Dr. Moon on account of expenses of teacher at Exhibition	19 55	$107 50

($213.45 in addition paid from General Fund.)

The undersigned have audited the accounts of the Treasurer and find them to be correct.

JNO. J. WILKINSON,
ROBERT C. MOON, M. D.

January 18, 1905.

PETTY CASH ACCOUNT OF SECRETARY

JANUARY 20, 1904, TO JANUARY 18, 1905.

1904.

Jan.	20, By Cash in hands of Dr. Moon, . .	$20 78
Feb.	2, By Cash from Mr. Frank Read,	50 00
"	2, By Cash from Mr. Frank Read,	12 25
"	24, By Cash from Mr. Frank Read,	50 00
Mar.	10, By Cash from Mr. Frank Read,	16 25
"	23, By Cash from Mr. Frank Read,	50 00
Apr.	5, By Cash from Mr. Frank Read,	17 64
"	27, By Cash from Mr. Frank Read,	50 00
May	3, By Cash from Mr. Frank Read,	13 13
"	25, By Cash from Mr. Frank Read,	50 00
June	4, By Cash from Mr. Frank Read,	13 14
"	29, By Cash from Mr. Frank Read,	50 00
July	1, By Cash from Mr. Frank Read,	13 03
"	23, By Cash from Mr. Frank Read,	50 00
Aug.	2, By Cash from Mr. Frank Read,	12 85
"	24, By Cash from Mr. Frank Read,	50 00
"	30, By Cash from Mr. Frank Read,	13 00
Oct.	6, By Cash from Mr. Frank Read,	22 27
"	5, By Cash from Mr. Frank Read,	50 00
Nov.	22, By Cash from Mr. Frank Read,	50 00
"	22, By Cash from Mr. Frank Read,	22 64
Dec.	9, By Cash from Mr. Frank Read,	13 15
"	23, By Cash from Mr. Frank Read,	50 00
		$740 13

To hire of Hall for Annual Meeting, ... $6 25

To Postage and Express charges, ... 75 59

Salaries of Visiting Teachers and their Traveling Expenses, ... 574 09

To Typewriting, ... 30 38

To Stationery and Printing, 21 13

To Photographs and Half-tones, ... 21 65

To Sundries, ... 8 14

To Cash in hands of Dr. Moon, January 18, 1905, 2 90

$740 13

The undersigned has audited above account and finds it to be correct.

JNO. J. WILKINSON.

January 18, 1905.

ANNUAL SUBSCRIBERS.

1904
Jan.	22,	Rev. R. Marshall Harrison, D. D.,	$5 00
"	22,	Mr. C. A. Blakesley,	50
"	22,	Mrs. Susan Y. Foulke,	1 00
"	26,	Mrs. Adan Everly,	1 00
"	27,	Mrs. Sanuel Dickson,	5 00
Feb.	4,	Mrs. M. E. Austin,	2 00
"	18,	Mr. Charles G. Jessup,	5 00
"	20,	Miss Sarah Lewis,	5 00
"	20,	Mr. Louis Gerstley,	5 00
"	20,	Mr. Sanuel S. Fleisher,	5 00
"	20,	Mr. Albert Wolf,	5 00
"	20,	Mr. Edward Stern,	5 00
"	20,	Mr. B. Wassernan,	5 00
"	22,	Mr. Louis Wolf,	5 00
"	23,	Mr. Sanuel Snellenburg,	10 00
Mar.	2,	Mr. H. M. Nathanson,	5 00
"	4,	Mr. Moyer Fleisher,	5 00
"	4,	Mr. Joseph H. Ruhin,	5 00
"	8,	Mr. Charles Platt,	5 00
"	12,	Dr. Wn. C. Powell,	10 00
"	19,	Mr. H. L. Hall,	10 00
"	24,	Mr. Edward Wolf,	5 00
"	24,	Mr. R. H. Thonas, Jr.,	3 00
May	6,	Mr. Isaac Silvernan,	5 00
"	6,	Mr. Isidore Langsdorf,	5 00
"	6,	Mrs. Beulah M. Rhoads,	25 00
"	10,	Mr. W. A. Stern,	5 00
"	16,	Mr. Isaac Ginbel,	5 00
"	24,	Mr. Thonas Scattergood,	5 00
"	24,	Rev. Alfred L. Elwyn,	6 00
"	24,	Miss Enna R. Neisser,	5 00
June	9,	Miss Enily Dutilh, in nenory of Mrs. C. E. Frye,	10 00
Oct.	28,	Mr. Charles R. Snith,	5 00
Nov.	21,	Mr. Elliston P. Morris,	10 00
Dec.	21,	Miss Skirving, in nenory of Mrs. C. H. Skirving,	2 00

1905
Jan.	4,	Mr. John E. Baird,	50 00
"	4,	Mrs. Janes S. Biddle,	2 00
"	10,	Mr. John Story Jenks,	10 00
"	10,	Hon. W. N. Ashnan,	10 00
"	10,	Mr. Wn. H. Richardson,	5 00
"	10,	Mr. Albert Wolf,	5 00
"	10,	Mrs. Kate L. Brooks,	2 00
"	10,	Mr. Charles Platt,	5 00
"	10,	Mr. Ellis D. Willians,	5 00
"	11,	Mrs. Adan Everly,	1 00
"	11,	Miss Jane Janison,	2 00
"	11,	Mr. T. Broon Belfield,	10 00
"	11,	Miss Sarah Lewis,	5 00
"	11,	Mr. Harry G. Jungherr,	1 00
"	11,	Miss Marie E. Santee,	10 00
"	13,	Miss Fanny Rosengarten,	5 00
"	13,	Mr. Frank K. Hipple,	5 00
"	13,	Mrs. Susan Y. Foulke,	1 00
"	13,	Mrs. Sanuel Dickson,	5 00
"	13,	Mr. Felix Isman,	5 00
"	13,	Miss Frances A. Roberts,	10 00
"	14,	Mr. John H. Converse,	25 00

19

1905

Jan.	14,	Miss Catherine W. Morris,	$2 00
"	14,	Mrs. E. H. Taylor,	2 00
"	14,	Miss E. H. Thomas,	5 00
"	14,	Mr. W. E. Stering,	5 00
"	17,	Mr. Edward Stern,	10 00
"	17,	Mr. George C. Thomas,	25 00
"	17,	Mrs. Effingham B. Morris,	5 00
"	17,	Mr. Gustav Daniel,	5 00
"	17,	Miss Sarah Nicholson,	10 00
"	17,	Mr. Daniel B. Wieguer,	1 00
"	17,	Mr. Frank Read,	25 00
"	17,	Dr. and Mrs. Moon,	5 00
"	17,	Sarah A. Swain,	1 00
			$480 50

DIRECT CONTRIBUTORS.

1904

Jan.	22,	Mrs. Augusta E. Justi,	$1 00
"	22,	Mr. Charles Platt,	5 00
"	22,	Miss Mary L. Govers,	1 00
"	22,	Mr. Wm. W. Justice,	5 00
"	22,	Mr. S. W. Colton, Jr.,	10 00
"	22,	Mr. Henry Jones,	1 00
"	22,	Miss J. A. Cooper,	1 00
"	26,	Mr. C. C. Savage,	50 00
Feb.	2,	Mrs. W. Graham Tyler,	2 00
"	2,	Miss Julia Kneedler,	2 00
"	3,	Mr. Walter Sonneberg,	1 00
"	11,	Mr. J. R. Wilson,	1 00
"	23,	Cash,	5 00
Mar.	19,	Mr. Jas. F. Murphy,	1 00
"	19,	Holy Trinity Memorial Chapel,	30 00
April	4,	Miss Mary Bacon,	1 00
May	24,	Mr. Ben Gimbel,	15 00
"	31,	"B. F.,"	5 00
"	31,	Mr. W. K. Ramberger,	5 00
June	13,	Young Friends' Ass'n George School,	5 00
Sep.	15,	Cash,	2 13
"	16,	Miss Anna Stewart,	1 00
"	16,	Mrs. Timbrock,	1 00
"	19,	Mrs. Campbell,	15 00
"	25,	Mrs. L. D. Ames,	3 00
Nov.	1,	Miss Rebecca Nicholson,	5 00
"	22,	Mr. C. A. Longstreth,	3 00
Dec.	24,	Mrs. R. McM. Colfelt,	5 00
"	29,	Rev. Alfred L. Elwyn,	1 00

1905

Jan.	10,	Mr. J. L. Ketterlinus,	5 00
"	11,	Major Wm. H. Lambert,	10 00
"	11,	Mr. Wm. W. Justice,	5 00
"	11,	Hon. J. Willis Martin,	10 00
"	13,	Mr. E. P. Borden,	5 00
"	13,	Hon. I. P. Wanger,	3 00
"	14,	Mr. C. C. Savage,	50 00
"	14,	Dr. E. S. Sheldon,	1 00
"	17,	Mr. Clarence Sill,	1 50
"	17,	Mrs. Theodore H. Morris,	5 00
"	17,	Mr. Jno. H. Atwood,	10 00
"	17,	Miss Carrie B. Beans,	1 50
			$290 13

CHARTER OF THE PENNSYLVANIA HOME TEACH-ING SOCIETY AND FREE CIRCULATING LIBRARY FOR THE BLIND.

To the Honorable the Judges of the Court of Common Pleas, No. 1, for the County of Philadelphia :—

The petition of the undersigned,

respectfully represents : That they have associated themselves together for the purpose and upon the terms and by the name herein stated under the provisions of an Act of the General Assembly of the Commonwealth of Pennsylvania, entitled "An Act to provide for the incorporation and regulation of certain corporations," approved the twenty-ninth day of April, 1874, and the several supplements thereto, and that in accordance with the requirements of said Act they do set forth and declare that :

I.   The name of the corporation is "The Pennsylvania Home Teaching Society and Free Circulating Library for the Blind."

II.   The purpose for which the corporation is formed is the instruction of the blind in the art of reading by means of books printed in embossed or raised Moon type or other characters, at their homes and elsewhere, and to establish and operate by itself or through the medium of others a free circulating library, or libraries, of books printed in said type or other characters for the use of the blind.

III.   The business of the corporation is to be transacted in the State of Pennsylvania and elsewhere in the United States, and its principal office is to be in the city of Philadelphia.

IV.   The corporation shall exist perpetually.

DEPARTMENT FOR THE BLIND IN THE FREE LIBRARY OF PHILADELPHIA.

V.   The corporation shall have no capital stock.

VI.   The nanes and residences of the subscribers, three of whon, at least, are citizens of the Connonwealth of Pennsylvania, are as follows :—

WILLIAM N. ASHMAN, 4400 Spruce Street, Philadelphia.

JOHN P. RHOADS, Church and Chew Streets, Gernantown.

ROBERT C. MOON, 617 S. 48th Street, Philadelphia.

FRANK READ, Rosenont, Penna.

JOHN E. BAIRD, 1705 N. Broad Street, Philadelphia.

DUNDAS T. PRATT, 128 S. 19th Street, Philadelphia.

VII.   The business of the corporation shall be nanaged by a Board consisting of not less than twelve nenbers of the corporation, as nay be fixed by the By-Laws; a President, four or nore Vice-Presidents (the nunber to be fixed by the By-Laws), a Treasurer, and a Secretary; and the two latter offices nay be filled by one or two persons, as the corporation shall designate. The nanes and residences of the officers who have been chosen for the first year are as follows, viz. :—

President :

HON. WILLIAM N. ASHMAN, 4400 Spruce St., Philadelphia.

Vice-Presidents :

DUNDAS T. PRATT, 128 S. 19th Street, Philadelphia.

JOHN P. RHOADS, Church and Chew Streets, Gernantown.

JOHN E. BAIRD, 1705 N. Broad Street, Philadelphia.

FERDINAND J. DREER, 1520 Spruce Street, Philadelphia.

Secretary :

ROBERT C. MOON, M. D., 617 S. 48th Street, Philadelphia.

Treasurer :

FRANK READ, Rosenont, Penna.

VIII. Membership shall be open to all persons of lawful age and good moral character, who shall subscribe to the objects of the corporation and be elected by the Board of Managers by ballot ; a majority of the members voting shall be necessary to an election.

Members shall have the right and privilege of voting at elections for the Board of Managers and other officers of the corporation, and shall be qualified to vote thereat only in case they shall have paid the annual subscription fixed by the By-Laws.

IX. The yearly income of the corporation other than that derived from realty, shall not exceed the sum of twenty thousand dollars. The funds of the corporation are to be raised by subscriptions from the members and contributions by the friends of the corporation, as well as from gifts, devises and bequests of the general public, with such aid and endowment as it may receive from other sources from time to time. Such funds shall only be applied to the purposes of the corporation as expressed in this charter.

WITNESS our hands and seals, at Philadelphia, the twenty-ninth day of January, A. D., 1901.

W. N. ASHMAN,	[SEAL]
JOHN P. RHOADS,	[SEAL]
JOHN E. BAIRD,	[SEAL]
ROBERT C. MOON, M. D.,	[SEAL]
FRANK READ,	[SEAL]
DUNDAS T. PRATT,	[SEAL]

STATE OF PENNSYLVANIA, } *ss.*
CITY AND COUNTY OF PHILADELPHIA, }

Before me, the subscriber, a Notary Public of the Commonwealth of Pennsylvania, in and for the City and County of Philadelphia, personally appeared William N. Ashman, John E. Baird and Dundas T. Pratt, three of the subscribers to the above and within certificate of incorporation, and in due form of law acknowledged the same to be their act and deed for the purposes therein mentioned.

WITNESS my hand and notarial seal this twenty-ninth day of January, A. D., 1901.

ARCHER McLEARN,

[SEAL]   *Notary Public.*

DECREE.

AND now to wit, this eighth day of March 1901, the foregoing Certificate of Incorporation having been on file in the office of the Prothonotary of said Court since the seventh day of February, 1901, the day on which publication of notice of intended application was first made, as appears by the Certificate thereon, and due proof of said application having been therewith presented to the Court, I do hereby certify that I have perused and examined said instrument and find the same to be in proper form and within the purposes named in the first class of corporations specified in Section 2 of the Act of April twenty-ninth, 1874, and that said purposes are lawful and not injurious to the community : It is therefore ORDERED AND DECREED that the said CHARTER be approved, and is hereby approved, and upon recording of the said Charter and its endorsements, and this Order in the office of the Recorder of Deeds in and for Philadelphia County, it is now hereby ordered that the subscribers thereto and their associates shall thenceforth be a corporation for the purposes and upon the terms and under the nane therein stated.

CRAIG BIDDLE,

[SEAL]

Judge.

FORM OF BEQUEST.

I give and bequeath unto " The Pennsylvania Home Teaching Society and Free Circulating Library for the Blind," the sum of   *Dollars.*

FORM OF DEVISE.

I give, devise and bequeath unto " The Pennsylvania Home Teaching Society and Free Circulating Library for the Blind," and its successors :

(DESCRIBE REAL ESTATE.)

BY-LAWS.

1. The title of this Society shall be "The Pennsylvania Home Teaching Society and Free Circulating Library for the Blind."

2. The objects of the Society shall be: (1) To provide a teacher or teachers to find out and visit the blind at their homes. (2) To provide a free circulating library of embossed books in the Moon type for the blind, the volumes of which shall be exchanged by the teacher, or teachers, as often as necessary. (3) Volumes may be sent to blind readers at distant points, where there are no local libraries of such books.

3. The management of the Society shall be vested in a President, Vice-Presidents, a Treasurer, a Secretary, and a Board of Managers (of not less than twelve), to be elected annually at a general meeting of the members of the Society, which Board of Managers shall have power to fill all vacancies for the unexpired term.

4. Members of the Society may be elected at any stated meeting of the Board of Managers, and upon the payment of $2 or upward shall be qualified to vote for officers.

5. The Annual Meeting of the Society shall be held on the fourth Wednesday in January, to receive the Annual Report of the Board of Managers and Officers, and to elect officers for the ensuing year.

6. The Board of Managers shall meet on the fourth Wednesday of every month (with the exception of June, July, August and September). Five members to constitute a quorum. Special Meetings may be called at the request of five members.

The Pennsylvania Home
Teaching Society and Free Circulating
Library for the Blind.

ESTABLISHED 1882. - REORGANIZED 1898
INCORPORATED 1901.

THIS Society was founded in 1882, with the object of providing a library of enbossed books in the Moon type, and sending teachers to the hones of the blind for the purpose of teaching then to read, and periodically exchanging their books. For sixteen years the work was nost successfully carried on in Philadelphia, under the superintendence of Mr. John P. Rhoads, the Treasurer of the Philadelphia Bible Society; but in order to place it upon a nore pernanent basis, the Society was reorganized in 1898, and it is with nuch pleasure that the nanagers of the Pennsylvania Hone Teaching Society and Free Circulating Library for the Blind announce, that the Trustees of the Free Library of Philadelphia have undertaken to co-operate with then, by taking charge of the library of enbossed books belonging to this Society for the blind, as well as consenting to super-intend the loaning of the books to the blind upon the Society's roll of readers, all expenses connected with the hone teaching part of the work and the circulation of books outside of Philadelphia being borne by the Hone Teaching Society.

The library of Enbossed Works has been transferred to the Free Library, 1217-1221 Chestnut Street, Philadelphia, where the books are kept in a roon especially set apart for the purposes of this work. The roon is also open to the blind as a reading-roon, and such persons are welcone to the free use of the library. Those who live in Philadelphia or its vicinity are taught at their hones, without charge, by the visi-tors engaged by the Hone Teaching Society for that special purpose.

Eighty per cent. of the blind are over twenty-one years of age, and nany of then have lost their eyesight fron exhausting diseases, fron accidents, or fron causes which shatter the nervous systen; so that, when they are learning to read, they should have as few obstacles as possible put in their way. For this reason the books adopted by this Society are in the easily acquired enbossed type of the late Dr. Willian Moon, of England, who, with his daughter, Miss Moon, visited Philadelphia in 1882, and advocated the adoption of the hone teaching systen for the adult blind. Dr. Moon, being hinself blind, knew well the requirenents of his fellow-sufferers, and his enbossed books are especially adapted to the needs of those who have becone blind since youth, or whose sense of touch has become blunted by laboring with the fingers.

In addition to its work in Philadelphia, this Society has loaned hundreds of volunes to blind persons who live at distant points, far away fron the city, and has thus brought light and confort to nany a benighted dwelling.

Contributions to the funds of "The Pennsylvania Hone Teaching Society and Free Circulating Library for the Blind," will be thankfully received by the Treasurer, Mr. Frank Read, 827 Drexel Building, Chestnut Street, Philadelphia, Pa.

Correspondence regarding the Society should be addressed to

DR. ROBERT C. MOON, *Secretary*,
Witherspoon Building,
1319 Walnut Street, Philadelphia, Pa.

APPLICATIONS FOR LOANS OF EMBOSSED BOOKS should be nade to

JOHN THOMSON,
Librarian of the Free Library of Philadelphia,
1217-1221 Chestnut Street, Philadelphia, Pa.

An enbossed alphabet and a first lesson sheet will be forwarded upon application.

Books selected fron the accon panying catalogue will be nailed to any part of the United States, to be returned in a nonth or sooner, and exchanged for others.

FREE POSTAGE FOR BLIND READERS

When the books are returned through the mails, they should be directed to the same address, and to secure free transmission care should be taken to comply strictly with the regulations prescribed in the following Order of the Postmaster General, which has recently been issued:

ORDER OF THE POSTMASTER GENERAL

OFFICE OF THE POSTMASTER GENERAL,

Order No. 541.   Washington, D. C., June 2, 1904.

Chapter 2, Title III. of the Postal Laws and Regulations is hereby amended by the addition of the following subdivision:

V.—READING MATTER FOR THE BLIND.

Sec. 518½. Books, pamphlets, and other reading matter in raised characters for the use of the blind, whether prepared by hand or printed in single volumes, not exceeding ten pounds in weight, or in packages not exceeding four pounds in weight and containing no advertising or other matter whatever, unsealed and when sent by public institutions for the blind, or by any public libraries, as a loan to blind readers, or when returned by the latter to such institutions or public libraries, shall be transmitted in the United States mails free of postage, and under such regulations as the Postmaster General may prescribe. (Act of April 27, 1904.)

2. Reading matter in raised characters for the use of the blind, to be entitled to transmission in the mails free of postage, must not contain any advertising or other matter whatever, and must in every case be sent by or returned to a public library or public institution for the blind.

3. When mailed by a public library or public institution for the blind, the matter must be sent as a loan to a blind reader. When mailed for return to a public library or public institution for the blind, the sender must be a blind reader.

4. The matter must be wrapped so that it may be easily examined.

5. No package is to weigh more than four pounds, except in case of a single volume, and it must not exceed ten pounds in weight.

6. On the upper left hand corner of the envelope or wrapper containing the matter the name and address of the sender must appear, and on the upper right hand corner the word "Free" over the words "Reading Matter for the Blind."

Note.—Letters written in point print or raised characters used by the blind are not included in the reading matter entitled, under the provisions of this section, to free transmission in the mails. (See Section 475.)

H. C. PAYNE, Postmaster General.

Friends of the blind are asked to send to the Secretary of the Society the nanes and addresses of any blind persons of whon they know, and they will be pronptly visited by one of the teachers.

List of Books in Moon's Type for the Blind.

BIBLE.

	Hf.-Bd.			Hf.-Bd.
Genesis, 2 vols.,	$2.25		Jeremiah, 3 vols.,	$2.85
Exodus, 2 vols.,	2.27		Ezekiel, 3 vols.,	2.95
Leviticus, 2 vols.,	1.87		Daniel,	.90
Numbers, 2 vols.,	2.35		Hosea to Obadiah,	.85
Deuteronony, 2 vols.,	2.05		Jonah to Malachi,	1.10
Joshua,	1.12		Matthew, 2 vols.,	1.70
Judges,	1.12		Mark,	1.07
1 Sanuel, 2 vols.,	1.90		Luke, 2 vols.,	1.87
2 Sanuel, 2 vols.,	1.67		John,	1.00
1 Kings, 2 vols.,	1.87		Acts, 2 vols.,	1.65
2 Kings, 2 vols.,	1.82		Ronans,	.70
1 Chronicles, 2 vols.,	1.72		1 and 2 Corinthians,	1.00
2 Chronicles, 2 vols.,	2.00		Galatians to Philemon,	1.15
Ezra to Esther, 2 vols.,	1.90		Hebrews to Jude,	1.10
Job,	1.05		Revelation,	.90
Psalms, 3 vols.,	2.85		Old Testament. Conplete in 43	
Proverbs,	1.05		vols.,	42.68
Ruth to Lanentations,	.92		New Testanent. Conplete in 13	
Isaiah, 2 vols.,	2.25		vols.,	12.14

Chapters and Psalms.

1 Kings, chap. 18,	$0.16		John, chap. 6,	$0.17
2 Kings, chap. 4,	.16		John, chap. 7,	.12
2 Kings, chap. 5,	.12		John, chap. 8,	.16
Psalns 20, 25, 90, 116 and 121,	.16		John, chap. 9,	.11
Psalns 32, 51, 130 and 143,	.12		John, chap. 10,	.11
Psalms 34, 86 and 96,	.12		John, chap. 11,	.15
Psalns 40, 42 and 84,	.12		John, chap. 12,	.12
Psalns 91, 139 and 147,	.13		John, chap. 13,	.11
Psaln 119,	.26		John, chap. 14,	.12
Proverbs, chap. 8,	.10		John, chap. 15,	.11
Isaiah, chaps. 35 and 49,	.13		John, chap. 16,	.12
Isaiah, chap. 40,	.13		John, chap. 17,	.11
Isaiah 53, Psalns 23 and 125,	.10		John, chap. 18,	.12
Isaiah 55, Psalns 27 and 103,	.13		John, chap. 19,	.12
Sernon on the Mount,	.25		John, chap. 20,	.11
Mark, ch. 11 and 12 (snaller type),	.15		John, chap 21,	.10
Luke, chap. 1,	.17		Acts, chaps. 1 and 2,	.18
Luke, chap. 2,	.13		Acts, chap. 9,	.12
Luke, chap. 11,	.17		Romans, chaps. 5 and 6,	.12
Luke 15 and Ephesians, chap. 2,	.16		Ronans, chap. 8,	.12
Luke, chap. 18 and 24, each,	.12		1 Corinthians, chap. 15,	.16
John, chap. 1,	.17		2 Corinthians, chaps. 5 and 6,	.12
John, chap. 2,	.10		Hebrews, chaps. 11 and 12,	.18
John, chap. 3,	.12		1 Peter, chaps. 1 and 2,	.15
John, chap. 4,	.12		Revelation, chaps. 1 to 5 (snaller	
John, chap. 5,	.12		type),	.18

BEGINNERS' WORKS.

Alphabet and Lord's Prayer, . . .	$0.04
Spelling Lessons, 1 and 2, . . .	.02
Readings in Wide lines, No. 1, . .	.13
" " " 2, . .	.13
" " " 3, . .	.15
Reading Cards, Nos. 1–13, each, . .	.02
Golden Casket, Nos. 1 and 2, or packets of cards with texts,	.15
John, chaps. 1, 3, 14, 15, 16 and 17. Wide lines, ...	
Life of Christ in Scripture words. Wide lines; 3 vols., . St'd, $1.35,	2.00
First Lesson Book, ...	.11
He Died for Me, ...	.17

The following are for the Aged and such as have very hard hands :—

Alphabet, ...	$0.02
Cards with texts. Nos. 1–3, each, .	.02
Psalm 103, ...	.17
Psalm 51, ...	.17
Psalms 25 and 115, ...	.17
Psalms 34 and 86, ...	.17
The Crucifixion. Matt. 27, ...	.37
The Resurrection and Ascension. Matt. 28, ...	.30
Romans, chap. 8, ...	.20
Hymns : "Sun of my Soul," etc.,	.12
" I've Found a Friend,"	.10

BIOGRAPHY.

Albert, Prince Consort of England, Early years of H. R. H., the late,	$1.05
Arkwright, Sir Richard, ...	.17
Bacon, Nicholas, ...	.10
Bloomfield, Robert, ...	.23
Branah, Joseph, . . . St'd, $0.37,	.57
Brown, John, ... St'd, .23,	.41
Bunyan, John, ...	.67
Carey, William, ...	.20
Caxton, William, ...	.16
Clarke, Adam, ...	.17
Columbus, Christopher, 3 vols., . .	2.10
Cook, Captain, 2 vols. St'd, $0.70,	1.05
Cooter, Eliza, ...	.27
Cranmer, Thomas, Last Days of, .	.13
Davis, John, ...	.30
Davy, Sir Humphrey, ...	.27
Eade, William, ...	.23
Ferguson, James, ...	.25
Franklin, Benj., 2 vols., St'd, $0.80,	1.20
Garfield, James Abram, 20th President of U. S., 2 vols., each, . . .	1.10
Garibaldi, 3 vols., each, ...	1.12
Gilbert, Miss, 2 vols., each, ...	.95
Gladstone, William Ewart, 2 vols., each, ...	1.35
Gordon, Charles George, Memoir of General, ...	.55
Grey, Lady Jane, . . St'd, $0.37,	.57
Guthrie, Rev. T., D. D., ...	.60
Gypson, Mrs., Last Hours of, from a Diary, ...	.60
Hall, John Vine, ...	.30
Havelock, General Sir H., ...	1.12
Havergal, Miss Frances R., ...	.80
Herschel. Sir William, ...	.22
Jenner, Edward, ...	.11
Lincoln, Abraham, 16th President of U. S., 2 vols., ...	1.95
Livingstone, David, 5 vols., each, .	.67

Lowther, Sir C. H., Bart. With Illustrations, ...	$0.90
Luther, Martin, 3 vols., each, . . .	1.05
Maudslay, Henry, ...	.72
Metcalf, J., ... St'd, $0.40,	.60
Minton, Herbert, ...	.10
Moon, Dr. William. Labors for the Blind, ...	1.05
Morehead, Rev. R., D. D. With Illustration, :·	.65
Murray, Alexander, ...	.18
Nansen, Fridjof, 2 vols., each, . .	1.35
Nelson, Horatio, Viscount, ...	.67
Newton, Sir Isaac, ...	.20
Our Gracious Queen, ...	.75
Paton, Rev. J. G., D. D., 5 vols., each,	1.35
Peel Family, . . . St'd, $0.23,	.41
Peter the Great, ...	.72
Pollard, Harriet, ...	.17
Polycarp, St., Last Days of, ...	.13
Prince and the Prayer. St'd, $0.37,	.57
Queen's Journal : —	
First Visit to Scotland, ...	.77
Life in the Highlands, 2 vols., . .	2.00
Visit to Blair Athole, and West Tour, ...	.80
Sharples, James, ...	.25
Spurgeon, Rev. C. H., 2 vols., each,	1.35
Stephenson, George, ...	.27
Stephenson, Robert, ...	.15
Victoria Alexandrina, Queen of England, Life and Reign of, . .	1.05
Washington, George, 1st President of U. S., ... St'd, $0.35,	.53
Watt, James, ...	.30
Wedgwood, Josiah, ...	.17
Wedlock, William, ...	.22
Wesley, John, 2 vols., each, . . .	1.35
Whitefield, George, 4 vols., each, .	.75
Zisca, ... St'd, $0.35,	.50

EDUCATIONAL.

Euclid (conplete), 2 vols., each,	$0.72
First Illustrated Reader, 2 vols.,	
each, ... St'd, $0.27,	.45
First Spelling Book, . St'd, 30,	.47
Iufant Reader, Grades 1 and 2, . .	.37
" " Grade 3, ...	.40
Moon. Astronony, ...	1.05
Moon. Biblical Dictionary, 12 vols.,	
each, ...	1.05
Moon. Dictionary of the English	
Language, 10 vols. :	
Vol. 1–9, each, ...	1.05
Vol. 10, ...	1.20
Moon. English Grannar, ...	1.05
Moon. Geography, 2 vols., each, .	1.05
Moon. Natural History, 8 vols.,	
each, ...	1.05
Moon. School Dictionary (arranged	
to serve as a spelling book, with	
meanings), 3 vols., each, . . .	1.05

Nelson's Priner, . . . St'd, $0.22,	$0.37
Nelson's Royal Reader, No. 1 ;	
2 vols., each, . . . St'd, $0.27,	.45
Nelson's Royal Reader, No. 2 ;	
4 vols., each, . . . St'd, $0.40,	.62
Nelson's Royal Reader, No. 3 ;	
3 vols., each, ...	1.05
Nelson's Royal Reader, No. 4 ;	
6 vols :	
Vol. 1–5, each, ...	1.05
Vol. 6, ...	.60
Nelson's Royal Reader, No. 5 ;	
8 vols., each, ...	1.05
Public School Priner, ...	.22
Reading Books, 1 and 2, each, . .	.16
Shakespeare. Merchant of Venice,	1.15
Shakespeare. The Tenpest, . . .	1.05

HISTORY AND TRAVEL.

Daybreak in Britain, ...	$1.05
Dodds. Fifty Years' Struggle of	
the Scottish Covenanters, 6 vols.,	
each, ...	1.10
Drunnond. Tropical Africa,	
2 vols., each, ...	1.05
Fiske. History of the United	
States, 6 vols., each, ...	1.35
Fitchett. Deeds that Won the Em-	
pire, 5 vols., each, ...	1.35
Mackenzie. History of Scotland,	
7 vols. :	
Vol. 1–6, each, ...	1.05
Vol. 7, ...	.90
Moon. Ancient Britons, ...	1.05
Moon. Ancient History : Greece,	
4 vols., each, ...	1.00
Moon. Ancient History : Rone,	
4 vols., each, ...	1.05

Moon. Ancient History, 5 vols. :	
Vol. 1. Egypt, ...	$1.05
Vol. 2. Assyria and Babylonia,	.80
Vol. 3. The Persian Enpire,	.90
Vol. 4. The East under Greek	
and Ronan Rule, ...	.82
Vol. 5. The African Nations,	.70
Moon. Early Discovery of Anerica,	
by Norsenien, ...	.16
Moon. History of England, 22 vols.,	
each, ...	1.05
Moon. Outlines of the History of	
Scotland, ... St'd, $0.35,	.53
Moon. Saxon Heptarchy, 3 vols.,	
each, ...	1.05
Moon. Siege of Rone in 1849, . .	1.05
Spanish Arnada, ...	.75
With Kitchener's Arny, 3 vols.,	
each, ...	1.27

POETRY.

Abide with Me, ...	$0.16
Aged Believer at the Gate of	
Heaven, etc., ...	.12
All is Known to Thee, ...	.11
All-sufficient God, etc., ...	.12
Ashaned of Jesus, ...	.16
Beautiful Hone, ...	.12
Bright and Sunny, etc., ...	.12
Bull's Hynns, 3 vols., each, . . .	.75
Burns' Poens (selections), vol. 1, .	.77
Changed Cross, etc., ...	.12
Children's Hynns, ...	.12
Christ our Example, ...	.12

Cotter's Saturday Night, ...	$0.18
Evening Hynns, ...	.17
Father's Message to his Blind Child,	
etc., ...	.12
Four Centuries of Poetry (selec-	
tions from various authors), vol. 1,	1.05
Good Physician, ...	.12
Havergal. Loyal Responses, . . .	.75
Herbert & Quarles. Selections . .	.20
Hours of Sorrow, ...	.13
How the Lord Sustains, etc., . . .	.13
Hymn of the Blind, ...	.16
Hynnal Conpanion, 7 vols., each,	1.05

POETRY—Continued.

Hymns on Resignation,	$0.16
I am Waiting for the Answer, etc.,	.15
Keble's Christian Year (selections),	.22
Little Talk with Jesus, etc.,	.17
Little Will,	.18
Longfellow. Evangeline,	.95
Longfellow. Miles Standish,	.80
Longfellow. Poems (selections):	
Vol. 1,	.50
Vol. 2,	.67
Milton. Paradise Lost, book 1,	.67
Morning Hymns,	.17
Need of Jesus,	.12
None Other Name,	.15
Old, Old Story,	.16
Precious Promises,	.12
Prose and Poetry, for Recitation, vol. 1,	1.05

Reality, etc.,	$0.12
Revival Hymns, parts 1 and 2, each,	.20
Rose of Sharon, etc ,	.15
Sacred Poetry, parts 1 and 2, each,	.20
Safely Home, etc.,	.13
Sankey's Hymns (selections), 2 vols., each,	.67
School Life,	.12
Scott. Lady of the Lake, 2 vols.,	2.00
Scottish Hymnal (selections),	.62
Solitary Way, etc.,	.15
Starless Crown,	.15
Stranger at the Manse,	.15
Tennyson. Selections,	1.05
When to Trust Jesus, etc.,	.12
Willis. Poems (selections). St'd, $0.28,	.50
World in the Heart,	.26

RELIGIOUS WORKS.

Blood that Saveth,	$0.18
Church Catechism, St'd, $0.18,	.35
Collects,	.67
Coming Events,	.20
Communion with God,	.16
Daily Prayers and Promises from the Holy Scriptures,	1.05
Epistles in Liturgy, 2 vols., each,	.82
Eternity—Where Will You Spend It?	.12
Evening Portions (Bogatzky's),	.18
Faith Healing, vol. 1,	.50
False Hopes,	.17
Fill the Men's Sacks,	.17
Glory of God,	.17
God's Love,	.23
God's Tithes,	.55
Grace and Truth Under Twelve Aspects, 5 vols., each,	1.05
Great Error Detected,	.21
Haslam. Leaves from My Note-book, 3 vols., each,	1.35
Hele's Morning and Evening Prayers (Selections from),	.17
Holy Communion,	.67
How the Lost Are Saved. St'd, $0.25,	.47
How to Find Peace, etc.,	.12
Important Questions Answered,	.18
Jesus Only,	.17
Jottings of Precious Truth, 2 parts, each, St'd, $0.27,	.45
Life Through the Living One, 2 vols., each,	.90
Lord's Supper (Preparatory Exercises),	.20
Lowest Place,	.17
Maria's Three Names,	.16
Millenium,	.65

Morning and Evening Prayers and Litany,	$0.65
Morning Portions (Bogatzky's),	.20
Morning Watches, 3 vols.,	2.05
Pilgrim's Progress, 5 vols., each, { Christian, Vols. 1 and 2. { Christiana, Vols, 3, 4 and 5.	1.10
Prayer Before Communion, etc.,	.12
Prayer-book Psalms, 3 vols., each,	1.10
Rejoice, etc.,	.12
Resting Place,	.60
Resting Post,	.15
Safety, Certainty and Enjoyment,	.60
Saviour for You.	.60
Scotch Metrical Psalms, 4 vols., each,	1.05
Scotch Paraphrases,	.95
Scripture Truths,	.25
Search the Scriptures, etc.,	.17
Shorter Catechism,	.62
Sighs Turned to Songs,	.12
Silent Comforter,	.25
Sinner's Friend, 2 vols. St'd, $0.90,	1.35
Smith, Rev. J. Daily Remembrancer (selections for one month,)	1.05
Spurgeon, Rev. C. H. Sermons:	
Vol. 1,	.80
Vols. 2, 3, 4, 5, 6, each,	1.05
Stalker, Rev. Dr. James. Imago Christi, 3 vols., each,	1.35
Subjects for Daily United Prayer,	.11
Sunbeams for Human Hearts,	.17
Sunday Rest,	.12
Telling Jesus,	.22
Tenfold Blessings Be Yours,	.11
Texts of Consolation,	.17
Thoughts of God, in 4 parts, each,	.17
Who Gave Him Liberty?	.12

SCIENTIFIC AND GENERAL.

Atlantic Telegraph, . . .	$0.17
Ball. Hundred Million of Suns, 2 vols., each, ...	.72
Baroneter, ...	.17
Cast Steel, ...	.55
Early English Iron Manufacture, .	.55
Earthquakes, ...	.18
Induction Coil, etc., ...	.21
Iron and Civilization, ...	.75
Iron Smelting by Pit Coal, . . .	.57
Lockyer. Astronomy (science primer), ...	.55
Mundell. Stories of the Lifeboat, 3 vols., each, ...	.97

Proctor. Lectures:	
Vol. 1, On the Sun, ...	$0.23
Vol. 2, Comets and Meteors, .	.22
Vol. 3, Birth and Death of Worlds, ...	.22
Swedish and Botallack Mines, . . .	.22
Thunderstorns, etc., ...	.23
Uses of Difficulty, ...	.16
Volcanic Eruptions, ...	.23
Volcanoes Under Water, ...	.20
Wonders of Coal, ...	.18
Wonders of Digestion, ...	.18
Wonders of Light, ...	.30
Wonders of the Magnet, ...	.23

TALES AND ANECDOTES.

Anecdotes of Dogs, ...	$0.17
Beggar's Prayer, etc., ...	.13
Beside the Bonnie Brier Bush, by Ian Maclaren, 3 vols., each, . . .	1.35
Blind Beggar, ...	.16
Blind Irishman, ...	.26
Blind Man of Chak Tu, etc., . . .	.18
Bob, the Cabin Boy, ...	.18
Brave Enperor, etc., ...	.13
Bristol Merchant, etc., ...	.13
Condenned Soldier, etc., ...	.13
Dairyn an's Daughter, 2 vols., each,	1.28
Debt is Paid, ...	.13
Destruction of a Madrid Inquisition,	.23
Dirk Willemzoon, ...	.12
Disinterred Ponpeians, ...	.16
Dying Robber, ...	.21
Eyes and Ears, ...	.18
Falls of Niagara, ...	.16
Frank Harvey and George Farner,	.12
Guarded House, etc., ...	.13
Highland Kitchennaid, ...	.15
I'n Never Unhappy, ...	.16
Innkeeper's Family, etc., ...	.13
Irreverence Rebuked, etc., ...	.13
Jesus Met in Todnorden Vale, . .	.25
John Halifax, Gentlenan, by Miss Mulock, 8 vols., each, ...	1.35
King of Toobow, etc., ...	.13
Learning to Pray, etc., ...	.13
Let Him Be Spared, etc., ...	.13
Loss of Fanily Prayer, etc., . . .	.13
Lost Prayer Book, ...	.15
Luke Heywood, ...	.27
Mary Jones and Her Bible, 1 vol., .	1.05
Murderers Overawed, ...	.13
Negress and Her Nurse, etc., . . .	.13

Negro Servant, ...	$1.05
Only Nineteen, ...	.12
Patchwork Quilt, ...	.17
Paying for Praying, ...	.13
Persecuting Father, etc., ...	.13
Philip Henry's Pronise, etc., . . .	.13
Pious Teacher, ...	.18
Prayer for a Lunatic, etc., ...	.13
Prayer for Fine Weather, etc., . .	.13
Prayer-Meeting Abandoned, etc., .	.13
Praying Mother, etc., ...	.13
Praying Willys, ...	.32
Publican's Joint (A Tenperance Anecdote), ...	.15
Rab and His Friends, ...	.62
Sabbath Breaking, ...	.12
Sagacity of a Lioness, ...	.17
Sam, the Converted Sailor, ...	.23
Saved Garrotter, ...	.16
Seanan's Leap for Life, ...	.16
Soldier of Lucknow, ...	.17
Son's Admonition, etc., ...	.13
There is Roon for You, ...	.35
Three Renarkable Diamonds, . .	.18
Tiger Hunt, etc., . . .	.15
Time Enough Yet, . . .	.16
To Right the Wrong, by Edna Lyall, 8 vols., each, ...	1.35
Too Late, ...	.15
Two Praying Wives, etc., ...	.13
Vessels Saved by Prayer, etc., . .	.13
Workhouse Lad, etc., ...	.13
Written Prayer, etc., . .	.13
Yeddie's First and Last Connunion, ...	.15
Young Cockle Dredger, ...	.32
Young Cottager, ...	1.42

The foregoing are the reduced prices at which the Books are sold to Hone Teaching Societies and the Poor.

The Pennsylvania
Home Teaching Society and Free Circulating
Library for the Blind.

LIST OF BOOKS IN MOON'S TYPE FOR THE BLIND
RECENTLY ISSUED.

Fry, Mrs. Elizabeth, ... $1 05
Quorm, Daniel, 4 vols., each, ... 90
Charles. Alfred the Deliverer and the King, 2 vols., each, ... 1 05
Charles. Lights and Shadows of Early Dawn, ... 1 05
Aytoun. Lays of the Scottish Cavaliers, 5 vols., each, ... 75
Scott. Marnion, 2 vols., each, ... 1 05
Scott. Ivanhoe, 8 vols., each, ... 1 05
Stalker, Rev. Dr. Life of Christ, 3 vols., each, ... 1 05
Spurgeon, Rev. C. H. John Ploughnan's Talk, 3 vols., each, ... 97
Longfellow. Tales of a Wayside Inn, 2 vols., each, ... 1 05
Britain's King and Queen, 3 vols., each, ... 1 05
Cowper. Diverting History of John Gilpin, ... 18
Roe, Rev. E. P. Barriers Burned Away, 6 vols., each, ... 1 05
Connor, Ralph. Sky Pilot, 2 vols., each, ... 1 05
Hamilton, Rev. Dr. F. J. The Best Book of All and How it Came to Us, 1 05
Hay, Hon. John. William McKinley—Memorial Address, ... 60
Macmillan, Rev. Hugh. Bible Teachings in Nature, 5 vols. (in hand),
Hooker, Thomas. Poor Doubting Christian, 2 vols., each, ... 1 10
Whittier, John G. Poems (Selections), Vol. 1, ... 67
The Day of Trouble, ... 18
Holy Communion (American Version), ... 67
Instrument of Ten Strings, ... 18

The following for the aged, and such as have very hard hands :—

Psalms 117 and 121, Isaiah 12 and 35, ... 19
John, chap. 14, ... 17
   "   " 15, ... 19
   "   " 16, ... 22

Application for any of the books in the foregoing catalogue can be made to

MR. JOHN THOMSON, *Librarian,*
Free Library of Philadelphia,
1217-21 Chestnut St., Phila., Pa.

All the books of the SACRED SCRIPTURES can be obtained at the Bible House, 7th and Walnut Sts., Philadelphia, and the Psalms, Proverbs, The Gospels and Acts can be obtained of the American Bible Society, Bible House, Astor Place, New York.

PROCEEDS OF CRIME ACT 2002*

(2002 c. 29)

Contents

---

* Annotations by D.A. Thomas Q.C., LL.D; Dr Alastair Brown, Solicitor (Scotland, England and Wales); Andrew Mitchell Q.C.; Linda Saunt, Furnival Chambers (assisted by Abigail Barber, Fiona Jackson, Caroline Haughey and Ivan Pearce); John Walters, Q.C., Gray's Inn Tax Chambers; Rudi F. Fortson, LL.B(Hons.), Barrister; Professor Thomas Gibbons, School of Law, University of Manchester; Professor David Milman, University of Manchester; Donna W. McKenzie Skene, Senior Lecturer in Law, University of Aberdeen.

PART 3

CONFISCATION: SCOTLAND

PART 4

CONFISCATION: NORTHERN IRELAND

CHAPTER 3

SCOTLAND

An Act to establish the Assets Recovery Agency and make provision about the appointment of its Director and his functions (including Revenue functions), to provide for confiscation orders in relation to persons who benefit from criminal conduct and for restriant orders to prohibit dealing with property, to allow the recovery of property which is or represents property obtained through unlawful conduct or which is intended to be used in unlawful conduct, to make provision about money laundering, to make provision about investigations relating to benefit from criminal conduct or to property which is or represents property obtained through unlawful conduct or to money laundering, to make provision to give effect to overseas requests and orders made where property is found or believed to be obtained through criminal conduct, and for connected purposes.   [24th July 2002]

PARLIAMENTARY DEBATES
   Hansard, H.C. Vol. 372 col. 32 (1R); Vol.373, col.757 (2R); Vol.380, col.715 (3R); Vol.389, col.1050 (LA Con.); Vol.389, col.478 (LA Con.)
   H.L. Vol.631, col.1542 (1R); Vol.633, col.12, 44 (2R); Vol.633, col.530 (MfA); Vol.634, cols.10, 96 (Comm.); Vol.635, cols.23, 97, 1051 (Comm.); Vol.636, col.491 (MfA); Vol.636, col.1205, 1290 (Rep.); Vol.637, col. 839 (3R); Vol.638, col.42 (CCA)

INTRODUCTION AND GENERAL NOTE
   This Proceeds of Crime Act 2002 (c.29) ("this Act") provides for the confiscation of the assets of persons convicted of criminal offences. It will largely replace the English Drug Trafficking Act 1994 , the Criminal Justice Act 1988 and corresponding legislation in Scotland and Northern Ireland.
   Part 1 of the Act creates an Assets Recovery Agency which will be responsible for initiating confiscation proceedings and enforcing confiscation orders made by the courts. Parts 2, 3 and 4 provide for the making of confiscation orders. Part 2 of the Act applies to England and Wales, Pt. 3 to Scotland and Pt.4 to Northern Ireland. Part 5 of the Act introduces a new system of "civil recovery" under which property obtained through unlawful conduct may be recovered from a person holding the property, notwithstanding that he has not been convicted of any offence with reference to the property. Part 6 provides for the exercise of revenue functions by the Director of the Assets Recovery Agency. Part 7 creates offences in connection with money laundering, and Part 8 provides for the investigation of matters related to confiscation. Part 9 deals with insolvency, Part 10 with the use of information by the Director of the Assets Recovery Agency, and Part 11 with the enforcement of confiscation orders in different parts of the United Kingdom. Part 12 makes miscellaneous and general provisions.
   The Act will come into force in accordance with provision made by the Secretary of State (see s. 458(1). The Act contains no transitional provisions; these matters will be dealt with by statutory instrument (see s. 459(2)).

COMMENCEMENT
The Proceeds of Crime Act 2002 (c.29) received Royal assent on July 24, 2002.

ABBREVIATIONS

"ARA"	:	Assets Recovery Agency
"NCIS"	:	National Criminal Intelligence Service
"STR"	:	suspicious transaction reports
"the 1995 Act"	:	Proceeds of Crime Act 1995 (c.11)
"the 1998 Act"	:	Criminal Justice Act 1988 (c.33)
"this Act"	:	Proceeds of Crime Act 2002 (c.29)

PART 1

ASSETS RECOVERY AGENCY

INTRODUCTION TO PART 1

Part I of the Act creates the Assets Recovery Agency and provides for the appointment and powers of the Director of the Agency. The principal functions of the Agency will be to initiate confiscation proceedings and to enforce confiscation orders made by the Crown Court.

The staff of the Agency are to be appointed by the Director, and any member of the Agency staff, if authorised by the Director to do so, may exercise any of the powers or duties of the Director.

Schedule 1 provides for the tenure of office of the Director and staff of the agency, the financing of the Agency.

Part 1 applies to England and Wales, Scotland and Northern Ireland (see s.461).

1   The Agency and its Director

(1) There shall be an Assets Recovery Agency (referred to in this Act as the Agency).

(2) The Secretary of State must appoint a Director of the Agency (referred to in this Act as the Director).

(3) The Director is a corporation sole.

(4) The Director may—
   (a) appoint such persons as members of staff of the Agency, and
   (b) make such arrangements for the provision of services,
   as he considers appropriate for or in connection with the exercise of his functions.

(5) But the Director must obtain the approval of the Minister for the Civil Service as to the number of staff appointed under subsection (4)(a).

(6) Anything which the Director is authorised or required to do may be done by—
   (a) a member of staff of the Agency, or
   (b) a person providing services under arrangements made by the Director,
   if authorised by the Director (generally or specifically) for that purpose.

(7) Schedule 1 contains further provisions about the Agency and the Director.

GENERAL NOTE

Part I of the Act creates the Assets Recovery Agency and provides for the appointment and powers of the Director of the Agency. The principal functions of the Agency will be to initiate confiscation proceedings (s.6(3)(a)) and to enforce confiscation orders made by the Crown Court (see s.34). The agency will not have exclusive powers in either respect; confiscation proceedings may be begun by the prosecutor or by the Crown Court on its own initiative (s.6(3)(a) and (b)) and the Crown Court is not necessarily bound to appoint the Director as the enforcement authority (s.35) although it must do so if any of the conditions mentioned in s.34 apply. The Director is also authorised to initiate appeals against decisions of the Crown Court in connection with confiscation orders (s.31).

The staff of the Agency are to be appointed by the Director, and any member of the Agency staff, if authorised by the Director to do so, may exercise any of the powers or duties of the Director.

Schedule 1 provides for the tenure of office of the Director and staff of the agency, the financing of the Agency (which is to be out of monies provided by Parliament), and requires the Director to prepare each year an annual plan setting out his objectives, performance targets, priorities, expected financial resources and proposed allocation of resources. The plan is subject to approval by the Secretary of State. The Director is also required to submit an annual report.

For other provisions relating to the staff of the Agency, see ss.449 and 450, authorising Agency staff to adopt pseudonyms in appropriate circumstances.

Part 1 applies to England and Wales, Scotland and Northern Ireland (see s.461).

2   Director's functions: general

(1) The Director must exercise his functions in the way which he considers is best calculated to contribute to the reduction of crime.

(2) In exercising his functions as required by subsection (1) the Director must—
   (a) act efficiently and effectively;
   (b) have regard to his current annual plan (as approved by the Secretary of State in accordance with Schedule 1).

(3) The Director may do anything (including the carrying out of investigations) which he considers is—
   (a) appropriate for facilitating, or
   (b) incidental or conducive to,
   the exercise of his functions.

(4) But subsection (3) does not allow the Director to borrow money.

(5) In considering under subsection (1) the way which is best calculated to contribute to the reduction of crime the Director must have regard to any guidance given to him by the Secretary of State.

(6) The guidance must indicate that the reduction of crime is in general best secured by means of criminal investigations and criminal proceedings.

GENERAL NOTE

Section 2 sets out the general objectives with reference to which the Director must exercise his functions. The principal object of the Agency is the reduction of crime by means of criminal investigation and criminal proceedings. The Director must have regard to the current Annual Plan (as approved by the Secretary of State) and to any guidance given to him by the Secretary of State. The guidance given by the Secretary of State must indicate that the reduction of crime is in general best secured by means of criminal investigations and criminal proceedings.

It is significant that the section does not mention the recovery of the proceeds of crime as a principal object of the Director and the Agency. It appears that the Agency is not to be seen as a revenue gathering agency. If the Director were to perceive any conflict between the overriding purpose of the "reduction of crime" and the recovery of the proceeds of crime, the statute appears to require him to give priority to the reduction of crime over the recovery of the proceeds of crime.

3   Accreditation and training

(1) The Director must establish a system for the accreditation of financial investigators.

(2) The system of accreditation must include provision for—
   (a) the monitoring of the performance of accredited financial investigators, and
   (b) the withdrawal of accreditation from any person who contravenes or fails to comply with any condition subject to which he was accredited.

(3) A person may be accredited—
   (a) in relation to this Act;
   (b) in relation to particular provisions of this Act.

(4) But the accreditation may be limited to specified purposes.

(5) A reference in this Act to an accredited financial investigator is to be construed accordingly.

(6) The Director may charge a person—

(a) for being accredited as a financial investigator, and
(b) for the monitoring of his performance as an accredited financial investigator.
(7) The Director must make provision for the training of persons in—
(a) financial investigation, and
(b) the operation of this Act.
(8) The Director may charge the persons who receive the training.

GENERAL NOTE

Section 3 requires the Director to establish a system for the accreditation of financial investigators and permits the Director to charge a person for being accredited as a financial investigator. The Director is required to make provision for the training of persons in financial investigation and the operation of the Act.

Accredited financial investigators are given specific functions by s.42 (application for a restraint order) and s.68 (appeals).

See also s.453, which authorises the Secretary of State to provide by order that a reference in this Act to an accredited financial investigator is a reference to such an investigator who falls within a specified description.

4   Co-operation

(1) Persons who have functions relating to the investigation or prosecution of offences must co-operate with the Director in the exercise of his functions.
(2) The Director must co-operate with those persons in the exercise of functions they have under this Act.

GENERAL NOTE

Section 4 places on those who have functions relating to the investigation or prosecution of offences a duty to co-operate with the Director of the Agency in the exercise of his functions. The persons concerned are principally Chief Officers of Police, the Director of Public Prosecutions, the Commissioners of Customs and Excise, and other bodies concerned with prosecution, such as the Inland Revenue. The Director is placed under a corresponding duty to co-operate with those persons in the exercise of their functions under this Act, but not under any other legislation.

5   Advice and assistance

The Director must give the Secretary of State advice and assistance which he reasonably requires and which—
(a) relate to matters connected with the operation of this Act, and
(b) are designed to help the Secretary of State to exercise his functions so as to reduce crime.

GENERAL NOTE

This section places on the Director a duty to give the Secretary of State advice and assistance which the Secretary of State reasonably requires relating to matters connected with the operation of the Act and which are designed to assist the Secretary of State to exercise his functions so as to reduce crime. It appears that the statutory obligation is restricted to general matters and would not extend to details of specific investigations in individual cases.

PART 2

CONFISCATION: ENGLAND AND WALES

INTRODUCTION TO PART 2

Part 2 of the Act provides for confiscation orders in England and Wales. It will eventually replace the Drug Trafficking Act 1994 (c.37) and the Criminal Justice Act 1988 (c.33). In many ways, the new provisions reflect the existing ones. The most significant changes made by the new Act are that the distinction between drug trafficking offences and other offences largely disappears. Virtually all powers connected with confiscation orders, in particular the power to make restraint orders and the power to appoint receivers, previously exercised by the High Court, will now be exercised by the Crown Court. Similarly the power to order a defendant to serve a term of imprisonment in default of payment will normally be exercised by the Crown Court rather than by the magistrates court as under the existing legislation.

The Act introduces a new concept of "criminal lifestyle." An offender has a "criminal lifestyle" if he has been convicted of one of the offences specified in Sched.2, if his offence constitutes conduct forming part of a course of criminal activity, or if the offence was committed over a period of at least six months and the defendant has benefited from the conduct. If the defendant has a "criminal lifestyle," the court will be required to make certain assumptions, similar to those made under the Drug Trafficking Act 1994, unless the assumption is shown to be incorrect or there would be a serious risk of injustice if the assumption was made.

The period during which a confiscation investigation may be postponed in the absence of exceptional circumstances is increased from six months to two years and the Act provides that a confiscation order must not be quashed only on the ground that there was a defect or omission in the procedure connected with the application for or the grant of the postponement.

Confiscation orders

6   Making of order

(1)   The Crown Court must proceed under this section if the following two conditions are satisfied.

(2)   The first condition is that a defendant falls within any of the following paragraphs—

   (a)   he is convicted of an offence or offences in proceedings before the Crown Court;

   (b)   he is committed to the Crown Court for sentence in respect of an offence or offences under section 3, 4 or 6 of the Sentencing Act;

   (c)   he is committed to the Crown Court in respect of an offence or offences under section 70 below (committal with a view to a confiscation order being considered).

(3)   The second condition is that—

   (a)   the prosecutor or the Director asks the court to proceed under this section, or

   (b)   the court believes it is appropriate for it to do so.

(4)   The court must proceed as follows—

   (a)   it must decide whether the defendant has a criminal lifestyle;

   (b)   if it decides that he has a criminal lifestyle it must decide whether he has benefited from his general criminal conduct;

   (c)   if it decides that he does not have a criminal lifestyle it must decide whether he has benefited from his particular criminal conduct.

(5)   If the court decides under subsection (4)(b) or (c) that the defendant has benefited from the conduct referred to it must—

   (a)   decide the recoverable amount, and

   (b)   make an order (a confiscation order) requiring him to pay that amount.

(6)   But the court must treat the duty in subsection (5) as a power if it believes that any victim of the conduct has at any time started or intends to start proceedings against the defendant in respect of loss, injury or damage sustained in connection with the conduct.

(7)   The court must decide any question arising under subsection (4) or (5) on a balance of probabilities.

(8)   The first condition is not satisfied if the defendant absconds (but section 27 may apply).

(9)   References in this Part to the offence (or offences) concerned are to the offence (or offences) mentioned in subsection (2).

DEFINITIONS
"benefited": s. 76
"criminal lifestyle": s. 75
"criminal conduct": s. 76
"defendant": s. 88(3)
"sentencing Act": s. 88(5)

GENERAL NOTE

Section 6 provides the basic framework for making a confiscation order in the Crown Court. It is derived from the provisions of the Drug Trafficking Act 1994, s.2, and the Criminal Justice Act 1988 s.71 (as amended by the Proceeds of Crime Act 1995), but with significant differences from both earlier provisions.

To qualify for a confiscation order, the defendant must either have been convicted of an offence or offences in proceedings before the Crown Court, have been committed to the Crown Court for sentence in respect of an offence or offences under the Powers of Criminal Courts (Sentencing) Act 2000 ss. 3, 4 or 6, or have been committed to the Crown Court under s.70 of this Act.

Section 3 of the Powers of Criminal Courts (Sentencing) Act 2000 allows a magistrates court to commit for sentence a defendant who is convicted summarily of an either way offence in respect of which the magistrates' court considers that their powers of punishment are insufficient. Section 4 provides for the committal for sentence of a person who has indicated an intention to plead guilty to an either way offence in accordance with the Magistrates Courts Act 1980, s.17A and who is committed for trial for one or more related offences. Section 6 authorises a magistrates court to commit for sentence an offender who has been convicted of any offence punishable with imprisonment, or any offence punishable with disqualification from driving, or who is liable to be dealt with in respect of a suspended sentence by the committing court, if the offender is also committed for sentence under some other provision (normally s.3 or 4). Section 70 of this Act requires a magistrates court to commit a defendant for sentence if the prosecutor asks the court to commit the defendant to the Crown Court with a view to the consideration of a confiscation order. There is an overlap between s.3 of the Powers of Criminal Courts (Sentencing) Act 2000 and s.70 of this Act. Under s.3, the magistrates court may in its discretion commit a defendant for sentence if it considers that it would be appropriate for a confiscation order to be made by the Crown Court, as a magistrates court has no power it make a confiscation order. Section 70 imposes a mandatory obligation on a magistrates' court to commit for sentence if the prosecutor makes an application under the section. In addition, under s.70 the magistrates' court must (on application by the prosecutor) commit a defendant convicted of a summary offence, in respect of which he could not be committed under the Powers of Criminal Courts (Sentencing) Act 2000, s.3.

So far as confiscation proceedings in Crown Court are concerned, the power under which the defendant has been committed for sentence appears to make no difference, but it will affect the powers of the Crown Court in respect of the principal sentence for the offence.

If the defendant absconds after conviction, he does not qualify for an order under this section (see subs.(8)), but the Court may proceed under s.27 instead. It is not clear how this subsection applies in the case where the offender absconds after confiscation proceedings have begun but before they have been concluded. It is submitted that once confiscation proceedings have begun, they are not affected by a subsequent failure of the defendant to appear. If a defendant who has been committed for sentence on bail, or who has been bailed after conviction, fails to surrender and is arrested on bench warrant, it is submitted that he is not to be treated as an absconder for this purpose. The object of the provision appears to be to provide for a defendant who is not present at the beginning of the confiscation proceedings.

Provided the defendant falls within one of these paragraphs (and the vast majority of defendants appearing before the Crown Court will do so) the court must proceed with a view to a confiscation order if it is asked to do so either by the prosecutor or by the Director of the Assets Recovery Agency, or if the court believes "it is appropriate for it to do so." As under the legislation replaced by the Act, confiscation proceedings are mandatory if an application is made; if no application is made, the court may in its own discretion initiate confiscation proceedings. The mandatory aspect of this section is qualified by subs.(6) which in affect allows the Crown Court not to make the decisions required by subs. (5) if believes that any victim of the offence has initiated, or intends to initiate, civil proceedings against the defendant.

Where the Crown Court embarks on confiscation proceedings, it must first decide whether the defendant has a "criminal lifestyle" as defined by s.75.A person has a "criminal lifestyle" if either he is convicted of one of the offences specified in Sched.2 of the Act, or the offence constitutes "conduct forming part of a course of criminal activity," or if the offence was committed over a period of at least six months and the defendant has benefited from the conduct. "Course of criminal activity" is further defined in s.75(3). Schedule 2 lists a large number of offences, including offences under the Misuse of Drugs Act 1971, offences under the Customs and Excise Management Act 1979 connected with drugs or firearms, facilitating illegal entry, various offences connected with prostitution, blackmail, counterfeiting and certain copyright offences.

If the Court decides that the defendant has a "criminal lifestyle" it must decide whether he has benefited from his "general criminal conduct." "General criminal conduct" is defined by s.76(2) as "all his criminal conduct," and the definition provides that it is immaterial whether conduct occurred before or after the passing of this Act or whether property constituting a benefit from conduct was obtained "before or after the passing of this Act." In making this decision, the Court must make any of the assumptions required by s.10 which apply, unless the assumption is "shown to be incorrect" or there would be a "serious risk of injustice" if the assumption were made. If the Court decides that the defendant does have a criminal lifestyle and has benefited from his general criminal conduct, it must determine the "recoverable amount" for the purposes of s.7 by taking the benefit from the general criminal conduct as the starting point for calculation, making any reduction required by s.7(2).

If the court decides that the defendant does not have a "criminal lifestyle", the Court must then decide whether the defendant has benefited from his "particular criminal conduct." "Particular criminal conduct" is defined in s.76(3) as "all his criminal conduct" which "constitutes the offence or offences concerned", or "constitutes the offences of which he was convicted in the same proceedings as those in which he was convicted of the offence or offences concerned", or "constitutes offences which the court will be taking into consideration in deciding his sentence for the offence or offences concerned." It is clear that this definition does not include uncharged offences which are represented by specimen or sample counts in an indictment, unless those offences are specifically listed and the court is asked to take them into consideration under the conventional procedure for doing so.

The benefit from the defendant's particular criminal conduct forms the basis of the calculation of the "recoverable amount" for the purposes of s.7. In determining whether the defendant has benefited from his "particular criminal conduct" the Court may not make any of the assumptions mentioned in s.10, which apply only in "criminal lifestyle" cases, but the Court may order the defendant under s.18 of the Act to give the Court "information specified in the order". If the defendant fails to comply with such an order, the Court may "draw such inference as it believes is appropriate" (s.18(4)).

Any question arising in connection with whether the defendant has a criminal life style or whether he has benefited from his general or particular criminal conduct must be decided on a "balance of probabilities" (subs.(7)). This expression differs from that found in the Criminal Justice Act 1988, s.71(7A), and the Drug Trafficking Act 1994, s.2(8), both of which refer to the standard of proof "applicable in civil proceedings".

7   Recoverable amount

(1) The recoverable amount for the purposes of section 6 is an amount equal to the defendant's benefit from the conduct concerned.
(2) But if the defendant shows that the available amount is less than that benefit the recoverable amount is—
  (a) the available amount, or
  (b) a nominal amount, if the available amount is nil.
(3) But if section 6(6) applies the recoverable amount is such amount as—
  (a) the court believes is just, but
  (b) does not exceed the amount found under subsection (1) or (2) (as the case may be).
(4) In calculating the defendant's benefit from the conduct concerned for the purposes of subsection (1), any property in respect of which—
  (a) a recovery order is in force under section 266, or
  (b) a forfeiture order is in force under section 298(2), must be ignored.
(5) If the court decides the available amount, it must include in the confiscation order a statement of its findings as to the matters relevant for deciding that amount.

DEFINITIONS
"confiscation order": s. 88(6)
"criminal conduct": s. 76
"defendant": s. 88(3)
"property": s.84

GENERAL NOTE

This section substantially reproduces the effect of the Drug Trafficking Act 1994, s.5 and the Criminal Justice Act 1988, s.71(6) (as amended by the Proceeds of Crime Act 1995.) The Court must make an order for the amount which it has assessed to be the defendant's benefit, unless either it exercises the discretion given by s.6(6) in a case where it believes that a victim of the offence has started or intends to start civil proceedings against the defendant, or the defendant shows that the "available amount" is less than the benefit. "Available amount" is defined by s.9. It includes the total of the values of all "free property" held by the defendant at the time the confiscation order is made, and the total value of all "tainted gifts". ("Free property" is defined in s.82; "tainted gifts" in s.77.)

Where the court exercises the discretion given by s.6(6) in a case where a victim is believed to be instituting civil proceedings, the amount of the confiscation order is such amount "as the court believes is just," but the amount must not exceed the amount of the defendant's benefit. It appears to be permissible for the Court to make an order equal to the full amount of the defendant's benefit, and to disregard the civil proceedings if it considers it appropriate to do so.

If the defendant shows that the "available amount" is less than his benefit, the amount of the confiscation order ("the recoverable amount") is either the "available amount" itself, or a nominal amount. If the defendant shows that he has no assets and there are no "tainted gifts", the court must nevertheless make an order in a nominal amount.

If the Court decides the "available amount", it must include in the confiscation order a statement of its findings as to the matters relevant to deciding that amount. This statement will be of particular importance if an application is subsequently made under ss.22 or 23 for a reconsideration of the "available amount."

As in the case of the legislation replaced by this section, the Court has no discretion in determining the amount of the confiscation order once it has determined the amount of the defendant's benefit and the "available amount". Discretion arises only in a case where s.6(6) applies (civil proceedings instituted by a victim). The discretion given by the Criminal Justice Act 1988, s.74(10) to disregard a "gift caught by this Act" is not reproduced in this Act.

Subsection (4) might more logically have been included in s.6. It requires that any property which is subject to a recovery order under s.266 ("civil recovery") or s.298(2) (cash forfeited by a magistrates' court on application) should be disregarded in calculating the defendant's benefit.

8   Defendant's benefit

(1) If the court is proceeding under section 6 this section applies for the purpose of—

    (a) deciding whether the defendant has benefited from conduct, and

    (b) deciding his benefit from the conduct.

(2) The court must—

    (a) take account of conduct occurring up to the time it makes its decision;

    (b) take account of property obtained up to that time.

(3) Subsection (4) applies if—

    (a) the conduct concerned is general criminal conduct,

    (b) a confiscation order mentioned in subsection (5) has at an earlier time been made against the defendant, and

    (c) his benefit for the purposes of that order was benefit from his general criminal conduct.

(4) His benefit found at the time the last confiscation order mentioned in subsection (3)(c) was made against him must be taken for the purposes of this section to be his benefit from his general criminal conduct at that time.

(5) If the conduct concerned is general criminal conduct the court must deduct the aggregate of the following amounts—

    (a) the amount ordered to be paid under each confiscation order previously made against the defendant;

    (b) the amount ordered to be paid under each confiscation order previously made against him under any of the provisions listed in subsection (7).

(6) But subsection (5) does not apply to an amount which has been taken into account for the purposes of a deduction under that subsection on any earlier occasion.

(7) These are the provisions—
  (a) the Drug Trafficking Offences Act 1986 (c. 32);
  (b) Part 1 of the Criminal Justice (Scotland) Act 1987 (c. 41);
  (c) Part 6 of the Criminal Justice Act 1988 (c. 33);
  (d) the Criminal Justice (Confiscation) (Northern Ireland) Order 1990 (S.I. 1990/2588 (N.I. 17));
  (e) Part 1 of the Drug Trafficking Act 1994 (c. 37);
  (f) Part 1 of the Proceeds of Crime (Scotland) Act 1995 (c. 43);
  (g) the Proceeds of Crime (Northern Ireland) Order 1996 (S.I. 1996/1299 (N.I. 9));
  (h) Part 3 or 4 of this Act.
(8) The reference to general criminal conduct in the case of a confiscation order made under any of the provisions listed in subsection (7) is a reference to conduct in respect of which a court is required or entitled to make one or more assumptions for the purpose of assessing a person's benefit from the conduct.

DEFINITIONS
  "benefited": s. 76
  "confiscation order": s. 88(6)
  "criminal conduct": s. 76
  "defendant": s. 88(3)
  "property": s.84

GENERAL NOTE
  This section deals with two separate aspects of the calculation of the defendant's benefit under s.6(5).
  Subsection (1) and (2) apply whether the Court is proceeding under the "criminal lifestyle" provisions or otherwise. Its effect is that the Court must take account of any conduct occurring before the decision on the question of benefit is made, or any property obtained up to that time. If the defendant obtains property from his criminal conduct after he has been convicted but before the confiscation order is made, that property must be taken into account in determining the "recoverable amount."
  Subsections (3) to (8) apply only where the court is proceeding under the "criminal lifestyle" provisions, and the defendant has been subject to an earlier confiscation order. If the previous order was made under the "criminal lifestyle" provisions of this Act, the amount assessed to be the benefit from his "general criminal conduct" on that occasion must be treated as his benefit from his "general criminal conduct" at that time. If the previous order was made under earlier legislation which permitted or required the court to make assumptions, the benefit assessed for the purposes of that order is to be treated for the purposes of this section as benefit arising from the defendant's "general criminal conduct" (subss. (7) and (8)).
  It appears that this amount may be included in the calculation of the defendant's benefit from general criminal conduct for the purposes of the latest order. The Court will presumably be required to calculate the defendant's benefit from general criminal conduct arising since the original order was made, and add the two figures together to produce the new figure.
  The Court must then deduct from that figure the amount ordered to be paid by any previous confiscation orders in respect of "general criminal conduct", either under this Act or any of the provisions mentioned in subs.(7). The effect of subs.(8) seems to be that a confiscation order made under earlier legislation, in which the concept of "general criminal conduct" was unknown, is to be treated as having been made in respect of "general criminal conduct" if the court was empowered or required to make assumptions for the purpose of determining the defendant's benefit.
  Although subs.(7) includes the Criminal Justice Act 1988, Pt.6 in the list of provisions concerned, it should be remembered that a court had no power to make any assumptions under the original version of that Act in any circumstances, and under the version of the Act as amended by the Proceeds of Crime Act 1995, has the power to make assumptions only in the circumstances set out s.72AA. A confiscation order made under the Criminal Justice Act 1988 may be treated as having been made in respect of the defendant's "general criminal conduct" only if it was made under s.72AA of that Act.

The practical effect of this section appears to be that where a court is proceeding to make a confiscation order under the "criminal lifestyle" provisions in respect of an offender who was subject to a confiscation order made on an earlier occasion under the Drug Trafficking Act 1994, the Court must include the value of the defendant's proceeds of drug trafficking as assessed on that occasion under the Drug Trafficking Act 1994, s.4 in the calculation of the benefit from his "general criminal conduct" on the current occasion, but must deduct from the calculation any amount ordered to be paid under the earlier confiscation order. Where the earlier confiscation order was made under the Criminal Justice Act 1988 (other than under s.72AA), it seems that the order must be ignored for both purposes, although it may affect the calculation of the "available amount" under s.7(2) by virtue of s.9(2)(a).

9   Available amount

(1) For the purposes of deciding the recoverable amount, the available amount is the aggregate of—

    (a) the total of the values (at the time the confiscation order is made) of all the free property then held by the defendant minus the total amount payable in pursuance of obligations which then have priority, and

    (b) the total of the values (at that time) of all tainted gifts.

(2) An obligation has priority if it is an obligation of the defendant—

    (a) to pay an amount due in respect of a fine or other order of a court which was imposed or made on conviction of an offence and at any time before the time the confiscation order is made, or

    (b) to pay a sum which would be included among the preferential debts if the defendant's bankruptcy had commenced on the date of the confiscation order or his winding up had been ordered on that date.

(3) "Preferential debts" has the meaning given by section 386 of the Insolvency Act 1986 (c. 45).

DEFINITIONS
    "confiscation order": s. 88(6)
    "defendant": s. 88(3)
    "free property": s. 82
    "property": s.84
    "tainted gift": s. 77

GENERAL NOTE
    Section 9 elaborates the definition of "the available amount." The section substantially reproduces the effect of the Drug Trafficking Act 1994, s.6 and the Criminal Justice Act 1988, s.74. The "available amount" is the sum of two calculations.

The first calculation is the total value at the time the confiscation order is made of all the "free property" held by the defendant, minus the total amount payable in pursuance of "obligations which then have priority". Obligations which have priority are defined in subs.(2). They are essentially obligations to pay orders made by criminal courts upon conviction such as fines, compensation orders or earlier confiscation orders, which were made before the current confiscation order was made, and obligations to pay any sum which would be included among the preferential debts of the defendant if he had been made bankrupt on the date on which the confiscation order was made. Other general debts of the defendant, whenever contracted, are not "obligations which then have priority," but a debt which is secured on the defendant's property by way of mortgage is to be taken into account in determining the value of the property by virtue of s.79(3), so that the practical effect is much the same. Unsecured debts will not count for this purpose.

The second calculation is the value of all "tainted gifts" (as defined in s.77).

10   Assumptions to be made in case of criminal lifestyle

(1) If the court decides under section 6 that the defendant has a criminal lifestyle it must make the following four assumptions for the purpose of—

    (a) deciding whether he has benefited from his general criminal conduct, and

(b) deciding his benefit from the conduct.

(2) The first assumption is that any property transferred to the defendant at any time after the relevant day was obtained by him—

(a) as a result of his general criminal conduct, and

(b) at the earliest time he appears to have held it.

(3) The second assumption is that any property held by the defendant at any time after the date of conviction was obtained by him—

(a) as a result of his general criminal conduct, and

(b) at the earliest time he appears to have held it.

(4) The third assumption is that any expenditure incurred by the defendant at any time after the relevant day was met from property obtained by him as a result of his general criminal conduct.

(5) The fourth assumption is that, for the purpose of valuing any property obtained (or assumed to have been obtained) by the defendant, he obtained it free of any other interests in it.

(6) But the court must not make a required assumption in relation to particular property or expenditure if—

(a) the assumption is shown to be incorrect, or

(b) there would be a serious risk of injustice if the assumption were made.

(7) If the court does not make one or more of the required assumptions it must state its reasons.

(8) The relevant day is the first day of the period of six years ending with—

(a) the day when proceedings for the offence concerned were started against the defendant, or

(b) if there are two or more offences and proceedings for them were started on different days, the earliest of those days.

(9) But if a confiscation order mentioned in section 8(3)(c) has been made against the defendant at any time during the period mentioned in subsection (8)—

(a) the relevant day is the day when the defendant's benefit was calculated for the purposes of the last such confiscation order;

(b) the second assumption does not apply to any property which was held by him on or before the relevant day.

(10) The date of conviction is—

(a) the date on which the defendant was convicted of the offence concerned, or

(b) if there are two or more offences and the convictions were on different dates, the date of the latest.

DEFINITIONS

"benefited": s. 76

"confiscation order": s. 88(6)

"criminal lifestyle": s. 75

"criminal conduct": s. 76

"defendant": s. 88(3)

"property": s.84

"started": s. 85

GENERAL NOTE

Section 10 is derived from the Drug Trafficking Act 1994, s.4, and the Criminal Justice Act 1988, s.72AA (as inserted by the Proceeds of Crime Act 1995). Section 10 applies only where the court is proceeding under the "criminal life style" provisions of s.6(4).

Where the court has decided that the defendant has a "criminal lifestyle" it must make the four assumptions for the purpose of deciding whether he has benefited from his general criminal conduct, and the amount of his benefit. The Court has no discretion to decide whether or not to make an assumption (as it has under the Criminal Justice Act 1988, s. 72AA), but the Court must not make an assumption in either of the situations described in subs.(6). An assumption must not be made if "the assumption is shown to be incorrect." It seems clear from the wording of subs.(6)(a) that the burden of showing that the assumption is incorrect falls on the defendant, who must rebut the assumption by proving the contrary. The second exclusion applies if "there would be a serious risk of injustice" if the assumption were made. Subsection (6)(b) does not indicate where any burden of proof falls. In respect of this exception, it is submitted that it is a matter for the court to determine in the exercise of its discretion whether there is a serious risk of injustice. It will be noted that the statutory phrase is "a serious risk of injustice", rather than "a risk of serious injustice." If the court does not make one of the assumptions, it is required by subs.(7) to state its reasons.

The substance of the four assumptions is closely based on the earlier legislation. The first assumption is that any property transferred to the defendant within the period of six years ending on the day on which proceedings were started against the defendant was obtained by him as a result of his general criminal conduct. The second assumption, which in practice is the assumption most likely to be made, is that any property held by the defendant at any time after the date of conviction was obtained by him as a result of his general criminal conduct. The third assumption is that any expenditure incurred by the defendant within a period of six years ending with the date on which the proceedings were started against him was met from property obtained by him as a result of his general criminal conduct. The fourth assumption is that any property obtained or assumed to have been obtained by the defendant was free of any other interest in the property. (Where the defendant has been subject to an earlier confiscation order made under the "general criminal conduct" provisions or their equivalent, the relevant period begins on the day the previous calculation of benefit was made, if that order was made within the six year period).

The assumptions are to some extent alternatives to each other and in the circumstances are of a particular case one assumption may take priority over another. A typical example would be that of an offender found in possession of drugs. It would be open to the Court to apply the first assumption to the drugs, and assume that they were transferred to him as a result of his general criminal conduct. In this case the Court would be required to value the drugs in accordance with ss.79 and 80 and include that value in the calculation of his benefit. Alternatively, and more realistically, the Court might draw the inference from the facts that the defendant purchased the drugs for cash, and that the cash used for the purpose was obtained from "general criminal conduct." Accordingly it would qualify under subs.(4) as "expenditure" incurred during the relevant period. Applying this assumption will probably yield a very different calculation of benefit from that provided by the application of the first assumption.

11   Time for payment

(1) The amount ordered to be paid under a confiscation order must be paid on the making of the order; but this is subject to the following provisions of this section.

(2) If the defendant shows that he needs time to pay the amount ordered to be paid, the court making the confiscation order may make an order allowing payment to be made in a specified period.

(3) The specified period—
   (a) must start with the day on which the confiscation order is made, and
   (b) must not exceed six months.

(4) If within the specified period the defendant applies to the Crown Court for the period to be extended and the court believes there are exceptional circumstances, it may make an order extending the period.

(5) The extended period—
   (a) must start with the day on which the confiscation order is made, and
   (b) must not exceed 12 months.

(6) An order under subsection (4)—
   (a) may be made after the end of the specified period, but
   (b) must not be made after the end of the period of 12 months starting with the day on which the confiscation order is made.

(7) The court must not make an order under subsection (2) or (4) unless it gives—
   (a) the prosecutor, or
   (b) if the Director was appointed as the enforcement authority for the order under section 34, the Director,
   an opportunity to make representations.

DEFINITIONS
    "confiscation order": s. 88(6)

GENERAL NOTE
    This section authorises the Crown Court, when it makes a confiscation order, to allow time for payment of the order. Under previous legislation, confiscation orders were subject to the same provisions as applied to a fine imposed by the Crown Court (see the Drug Trafficking Act 1994, s.9(1) and the Criminal Justice Act 1988, s.75(1)). These provisions included the Powers of Criminal Courts (Sentencing) Act 2000 s.139(1), which conferred the power to allow time for payment and to allow for payment by instalments.
    This provision gives the Crown Court more restricted powers to allow time for payment and makes no provision for payment by instalments. Unless an order is made under the section, the amount ordered to be paid under a confiscation order must be paid immediately on the making of the order. If the defendant shows that he needs time to pay the order, the court may make an order allowing payment to be made within a specified period which must not exceed six months from the day on which the confiscation order is made.
    Subsection (4) provides for an extension of that period. If the defendant makes a further application to the Crown Court within the specified period and Court believes that there are "exceptional circumstances" it may make an order extending the period. The extended period must not extend beyond 12 months from the day on which the confiscation order was made.
    Although the second application must be made within the original six month specified period, the order extending the period may be made after the end of that period, but not after the end of the period of 12 months starting with the day on which the confiscation order was made.
    It is not open to the Crown Court to make an order allowing twelve months for payment on the defendant's initial application, even though the defendant shows that there are exceptional circumstances in which this would be appropriate. The defendant must make a further application within the six month period.
    It is important for a defendant to make an application for time to pay the order, if he is unable to pay the full amount of the order immediately, as interest is payable under s.12 if the confiscation order cannot paid when it is required to be paid.

12 Interest on unpaid sums

(1) If the amount required to be paid by a person under a confiscation order is not paid when it is required to be paid, he must pay interest on the amount for the period for which it remains unpaid.

(2) The rate of interest is the same rate as that for the time being specified in section 17 of the Judgments Act 1838 (c. 110) (interest on civil judgment debts).

(3) For the purposes of this section no amount is required to be paid under a confiscation order if—

    (a) an application has been made under section 11(4),
    (b) the application has not been determined by the court, and
    (c) the period of 12 months starting with the day on which the confiscation order was made has not ended.

(4) In applying this Part the amount of the interest must be treated as part of the amount to be paid under the confiscation order.

DEFINITIONS
    "confiscation order": s. 88(6)

GENERAL NOTE
    This section substantially reproduces the effect of the Drug Trafficking Act 1994, s.10, and the Criminal Justice Act 1988, s.75A (as inserted by the Proceeds of Crime Act 1995.) Interest becomes payable if the confiscation order is not paid when it is required to be paid. If no order is made under s.11(2) allowing time for payment of the order, interest will become payable if the confiscation order is not paid immediately. If an order is made under s.11(2), interest will become payable if the order is not paid by the end of the period specified in the order. If the defendant makes makes an application for an extension of the period, and that application is granted, interest will become payable if the order is not paid within the period specified in the order extending the original specified period. If such an application is made and has not been

determined by the court before the end of 12 months starting with the day on which the order was made, interest becomes payable at the end of the 12 month period, whether or not the Court has made an order extending the time to payment under s.11(4). Any unpaid interest is added to the amount of the confiscation order.

13   Effect of order on court's other powers

(1) If the court makes a confiscation order it must proceed as mentioned in subsections (2) and (4) in respect of the offence or offences concerned.

(2) The court must take account of the confiscation order before—
   (a) it imposes a fine on the defendant, or
   (b) it makes an order falling within subsection (3).

(3) These orders fall within this subsection—
   (a) an order involving payment by the defendant, other than an order under section 130 of the Sentencing Act (compensation orders);
   (b) an order under section 27 of the Misuse of Drugs Act 1971 (c. 38) (forfeiture orders);
   (c) an order under section 143 of the Sentencing Act (deprivation orders);
   (d) an order under section 23 of the Terrorism Act 2000 (c. 11) (forfeiture orders).

(4) Subject to subsection (2), the court must leave the confiscation order out of account in deciding the appropriate sentence for the defendant.

(5) Subsection (6) applies if—
   (a) the Crown Court makes both a confiscation order and an order for the payment of compensation under section 130 of the Sentencing Act against the same person in the same proceedings, and
   (b) the court believes he will not have sufficient means to satisfy both the orders in full.

(6) In such a case the court must direct that so much of the compensation as it specifies is to be paid out of any sums recovered under the confiscation order; and the amount it specifies must be the amount it believes will not be recoverable because of the insufficiency of the person's means.

DEFINITIONS
"confiscation order": s. 88(6)
"defendant": s. 88(3)
"offence or offences concerned": s. 88(1) and 6(9)
"sentencing Act": s. 88(5)

GENERAL NOTE
This section (similar in effect to the Drug Trafficking Act 1994, s.2(5) and the Criminal Justice Act 1988. s.72(5)) assumes that the Court will proceed to make a confiscation order before sentencing the defendant for the offence or offences concerned. In practice it is likely that in most cases the Court will exercise the power of postponement given by s.14 and sentence the defendant before making the confiscation order under s.15.

The effect of the section is to require the Crown Court when sentencing a defendant in respect of whom it has made a confiscation order to take account of the confiscation order before imposing a fine, making any order involving payment by the defendant other than a compensation order, or making the other orders of forfeiture or deprivation specified in the section. A court which has made a confiscation order may leave the confiscation order out of account in deciding whether to make a compensation order in favour of the victim of the offence and in deciding the amount of the order. It is open to the Crown Court to make a confiscation order and a compensation order in respect of the same offence, even though this means that the defendant will be required to pay twice the amount involved in the offence (see *Mitchell and Mitchell* (2001) 2 Cr.App.R.(S.) 29 (at 141), *Williams* (2001) 1 Cr.App.R.(S.) 140 (at 500), decided on the Criminal Justice Act 1988, s.72). If the defendant has the means to pay both the confiscation order and the compensation order, there is no objection to making both orders. If the defendant does not have the means to pay both orders, the Crown Court made direct under subs.(6) that the compensation order, or a specified part of it, may be paid out of any amount recovered under the confiscation order.

Subsection (4) repeats the principle stated in both of the earlier provisions; in deciding the appropriate sentence for the offence, where it is not a financial penalty, the confiscation order must be left out of account. The defendant cannot claim that his sentence should be mitigated because a confiscation order has been made.

Procedural matters

14 Postponement

(1) The court may—
 (a) proceed under section 6 before it sentences the defendant for the offence (or any of the offences) concerned, or
 (b) postpone proceedings under section 6 for a specified period.
(2) A period of postponement may be extended.
(3) A period of postponement (including one as extended) must not end after the permitted period ends.
(4) But subsection (3) does not apply if there are exceptional circumstances.
(5) The permitted period is the period of two years starting with the date of conviction.
(6) But if—
 (a) the defendant appeals against his conviction for the offence (or any of the offences) concerned, and
 (b) the period of three months (starting with the day when the appeal is determined or otherwise disposed of) ends after the period found under subsection (5),
the permitted period is that period of three months.
(7) A postponement or extension may be made—
 (a) on application by the defendant;
 (b) on application by the prosecutor or the Director (as the case may be);
 (c) by the court of its own motion.
(8) If—
 (a) proceedings are postponed for a period, and
 (b) an application to extend the period is made before it ends,
the application may be granted even after the period ends.
(9) The date of conviction is—
 (a) the date on which the defendant was convicted of the offence concerned, or
 (b) if there are two or more offences and the convictions were on different dates, the date of the latest.
(10) References to appealing include references to applying under section 111 of the Magistrates' Courts Act 1980 (c. 43) (statement of case).
(11) A confiscation order must not be quashed only on the ground that there was a defect or omission in the procedure connected with the application for or the granting of a postponement.
(12) But subsection (11) does not apply if before it made the confiscation order the court—
 (a) imposed a fine on the defendant;
 (b) made an order falling within section 13(3);
 (c) made an order under section 130 of the Sentencing Act (compensation orders).

DEFINITIONS
"confiscation order": s. 88(6)
"defendant": s. 88(3)
"sentencing Act": s. 88(5)

GENERAL NOTE

The powers to postpone confiscation proceedings given by the Drug Trafficking Act 1994, s.3, and the Criminal Justice Act 1988, s.72A (as inserted by the Criminal Justice Act 1993) have led to a large number of difficulties and generated a substantial case law of their own. This provision, which must be read in conjunction with s.15, is derived from those sections, although with substantial changes.

Both of the earlier sections were premised on the assumption that in the normal case the Crown Court would deal with the confiscation order before sentencing the defendant (see the Drug Trafficking Act 1994, s.2(2) and the Criminal Justice Act 1988, s.71(1)). The power to postpone confiscation proceedings was provided in effect as an afterthought. (Historically, the power to postpone was added to the earlier versions of the legislation by the Criminal Justice Act 1993; the original versions of the legislation required confiscation matters to be dealt with before sentence in every case.) Section 14 does not make any assumption that the court will deal with confiscation matters before sentence. Subsection (1) appears to be even-handed in this respect. The court is given the option to deal with confiscation matters under s.6 before it sentences the defendant, or to postpone confiscation proceedings for a specified period. The statutory assumption of the earlier legislation that confiscation would come first is clearly not part of this provision. However it is clear that the court must address the question of confiscation before sentencing the defendant and either deal with the matter under subs.(1)(a) or postpone confiscation proceedings under subs.(1)(b). The court may not sentence the defendant without making any reference to confiscation, and then deal with confiscation matters on a subsequent occasion.

A second change in the law is a substantial increase in the period for which confiscation proceedings may be postponed. Under the previous legislation the period of postponement was not permitted to exceed six months in the absence of "exceptional circumstances." Under this legislation the permitted period is two years starting with the date of conviction. If there are "exceptional circumstances" an even longer period of postponement may be specified (subs.(4)), but it will seldom be necessary to rely on this provision.

As under existing legislation, a postponement may be made on the application of the defendant or the prosecutor (or the Director of the Assets Recovery Agency) or by the court on its own motion. A period of postponement may be extended in the same manner. An application for a postponement made during an existing period of postponement may be granted after the period of postponement has ended. It is not clear whether the court acting on its own motion may extend a period of postponement, where no application has been made within an existing period of postponement, after that period has ended.

As under the earlier legislation, the permitted period is affected if the defendant appeals against his conviction. If the defendant appeals against his conviction and the period of three months starting with the day on which the appeal is determined would end after the end of the period of two years starting with the date of conviction, the permitted period is the period of three months beginning with the day on which the appeal is determined.

Two further important changes are made under the section. Section 14(1)(b) provides that the court may postpone "proceedings under s.6." This appears to mean that what is to be postponed is the commencement of confiscation proceedings. Under the earlier legislation it was held that what was to be postponed was the determination of the amount to be recovered in the defendant's case. In other words, the court on postponing the confiscation proceedings had to specify the period within which the process would be completed. It appears that under this provision, it is sufficient to specify a period within which confiscation proceedings will begin.

Subsections (11) and (12) were added at a late stage in the progress of the Bill through Parliament. Their effect is not certain. Subsection (11) provides that "a confiscation order must not be quashed only on the ground that there was a defect or omission in the procedure connected with the application for or the granting of a postponement." This will leave open a number of questions. If the Crown Court has proceeded to sentence a defendant without addressing in any way the question of confiscation, and then proceeds to initiate confiscation proceedings after the normal period for variation of sentence has elapsed, and without purporting to postpone the proceedings at all under s.14, is that "a defect or omission in the procedure connected with the application for or the granting of a postponement?" Suppose the Crown Court has made an error in ordering a postponement of the confiscation proceedings so that it does not appear to have jurisdiction to continue with confiscation proceedings. Can the Crown Court take advantage of subs.(11), and proceed regardless of the difficulty, confident in the knowledge that any confiscation order which it makes may not be quashed by the Court of Appeal Criminal Division, or must the Crown Court abandon confiscation proceedings on the ground that it has no jurisdiction to proceed?

Subsection (12) creates a curious exception to subs.(11). A confiscation order may be quashed on grounds related to the postponement if before making the confiscation order the court imposed a fine on the defendant or made one of the other orders mentioned in subs.(12). The justification for this exception appears to be the duty of the court not to make any of those orders when confiscation proceedings are postponed (see s.15(2)).

15 Effect of postponement

(1) If the court postpones proceedings under section 6 it may proceed to sentence the defendant for the offence (or any of the offences) concerned.

(2) In sentencing the defendant for the offence (or any of the offences) concerned in the postponement period the court must not—
   (a) impose a fine on him,
   (b) make an order falling within section 13(3), or
   (c) make an order for the payment of compensation under section 130 of the Sentencing Act.

(3) If the court sentences the defendant for the offence (or any of the offences) concerned in the postponement period, after that period ends it may vary the sentence by—
   (a) imposing a fine on him,
   (b) making an order falling within section 13(3), or
   (c) making an order for the payment of compensation under section 130 of the Sentencing Act.

(4) But the court may proceed under subsection (3) only within the period of 28 days which starts with the last day of the postponement period.

(5) For the purposes of—
   (a) section 18(2) of the Criminal Appeal Act 1968 (c. 19) (time limit for notice of appeal or of application for leave to appeal), and
   (b) paragraph 1 of Schedule 3 to the Criminal Justice Act 1988 (c. 33) (time limit for notice of application for leave to refer a case under section 36 of that Act),
   the sentence must be regarded as imposed or made on the day on which it is varied under subsection (3).

(6) If the court proceeds to sentence the defendant under subsection (1), section 6 has effect as if the defendant's particular criminal conduct included conduct which constitutes offences which the court has taken into consideration in deciding his sentence for the offence or offences concerned.

(7) The postponement period is the period for which proceedings under section 6 are postponed.

DEFINITIONS
   "criminal conduct": s. 76
   "defendant": s. 88(3)
   "offence or offences concerned": s. 88(1) and 6(9)
   "sentencing": s. 88(4)
   "sentencing Act": s. 88(5)

GENERAL NOTE
   This section largely reproduces the Drug Trafficking Act 1994, s.3(7) to (10), and the Criminal Justice Act 1988, s.72A (7) to (9A). It provides for the powers of the court on sentencing a defendant in respect of the offence where confiscation proceedings have been postponed under s.14. The court may sentence the defendant in the normal way but must not make any of the orders specified in subs.(2). (Under the Criminal Justice Act 1988 it was permissible for a court sentencing a defendant in respect of whom confiscation proceedings had been postponed to make a compensation order at the time of sentence; this is no longer the case. Under this legislation, any compensation order must be delayed until after confiscation matters have been dealt with.)
   Where the defendant has been sentenced and subsequently a confiscation order is made following a postponement, the sentence originally passed may be varied by the addition of one of the orders mentioned in subs.(3) within 28 days starting with the last day of the period of postponement. This does not necessarily mean the day on which the confiscation order is actually

made. If for instance the confiscation order is made before the last day of the postponement period, the period of 28 days starts on the last day of the period to which the order was originally postponed. Conversely, if the confiscation proceedings are postponed for a specified period under s.14, but the actual order is not made until some time after the end of the specified period, as the confiscation hearing itself takes several weeks, beginning on the last day of the specified, it appears that the period for variation ends 28 days after the last day of the postponement period, even though the confiscation order has not been made by that date.

Where a sentence is varied by the addition of one of the orders mentioned in subs.(3), the sentence concerned is to be regarded as having been imposed on the date of the variation, for the purpose of time limits relating to appeal. It is possible that a defendant in respect of whom confiscation proceedings have been postponed may have appealed against the sentence imposed for the offence long before the confiscation proceedings have been concluded. This provision appears to give the defendant a second right of appeal against the sentence as varied under subs.(3.)

16 Statement of information

(1) If the court is proceeding under section 6 in a case where section 6(3)(a) applies, the prosecutor or the Director (as the case may be) must give the court a statement of information within the period the court orders.

(2) If the court is proceeding under section 6 in a case where section 6(3)(b) applies and it orders the prosecutor to give it a statement of information, the prosecutor must give it such a statement within the period the court orders.

(3) If the prosecutor or the Director (as the case may be) believes the defendant has a criminal lifestyle the statement of information is a statement of matters the prosecutor or the Director believes are relevant in connection with deciding these issues—
  (a) whether the defendant has a criminal lifestyle;
  (b) whether he has benefited from his general criminal conduct;
  (c) his benefit from the conduct.

(4) A statement under subsection (3) must include information the prosecutor or Director believes is relevant—
  (a) in connection with the making by the court of a required assumption under section 10;
  (b) for the purpose of enabling the court to decide if the circumstances are such that it must not make such an assumption.

(5) If the prosecutor or the Director (as the case may be) does not believe the defendant has a criminal lifestyle the statement of information is a statement of matters the prosecutor or the Director believes are relevant in connection with deciding these issues—
  (a) whether the defendant has benefited from his particular criminal conduct;
  (b) his benefit from the conduct.

(6) If the prosecutor or the Director gives the court a statement of information—
  (a) he may at any time give the court a further statement of information;
  (b) he must give the court a further statement of information if it orders him to do so, and he must give it within the period the court orders.

(7) If the court makes an order under this section it may at any time vary it by making another one.

DEFINITIONS
  "benefited": s. 76
  "criminal lifestyle": s. 75
  "criminal conduct": s. 76
  "defendant": s. 88(3)

GENERAL NOTE

This section substantially reproduces the effect of the Drug Trafficking Act 1994, s.11, and the Criminal Justice Act 1988, s.73, (as substituted by the Proceeds of Crime Act 1995) in relation to what were known as "prosecutors statements. They will now be known as "statements of information". (The change in title appears to be due to the fact that they will be made in some cases by the Director of the Assets Recovery Agency, rather than the prosecutor.) The section introduces variations related to the "criminal lifestyle" provisions of s.6.

The effect of the section is that if the Crown Court is proceeding with a view to a confiscation order on the application of the prosecutor or the Director, the prosecutor or the Director must give the Crown Court a statement of information within a period specified by the Crown Court . If the Crown Court is proceeding with a view to confiscation on its own initiative, it may order the prosecutor (but not the Director) to give such a statement within the specified period.

Special provision is made for cases where the prosecutor or Director believes that the defendant has a "criminal lifestyle." In such a case, the statement of information must include matters which the prosecutor or Director believes are relevant in connection with deciding whether the defendant has a "criminal lifestyle," whether he has benefited from his general criminal conduct, and the benefit from the conduct. The statement made in this context must include information relevant to the making of the required assumptions. This will normally consist of information relating to the defendant's assets or his expenditure and receipts during the relevant six year period specified in s.10(8).

In cases where the prosecutor or Director does not believe that the defendant has a criminal lifestyle, the content of the statement of information is limited to information relating to whether the defendant has benefited from his "particular criminal conduct," (that is, the offences for which he is to be sentenced, including offences taken into consideration) and the amount of his benefit.

Subsection (6) provides for further statements of information to be given, and for the Court to direct a further statement to be given.

17   Defendant's response to statement of information

(1) If the prosecutor or the Director gives the court a statement of information and a copy is served on the defendant, the court may order the defendant—

    (a) to indicate (within the period it orders) the extent to which he accepts each allegation in the statement, and

    (b) so far as he does not accept such an allegation, to give particulars of any matters he proposes to rely on.

(2) If the defendant accepts to any extent an allegation in a statement of information the court may treat his acceptance as conclusive of the matters to which it relates for the purpose of deciding the issues referred to in section 16(3) or (5) (as the case may be).

(3) If the defendant fails in any respect to comply with an order under subsection (1) he may be treated for the purposes of subsection (2) as accepting every allegation in the statement of information apart from—

    (a) any allegation in respect of which he has complied with the requirement;

    (b) any allegation that he has benefited from his general or particular criminal conduct.

(4) For the purposes of this section an allegation may be accepted or particulars may be given in a manner ordered by the court.

(5) If the court makes an order under this section it may at any time vary it by making another one.

(6) No acceptance under this section that the defendant has benefited from conduct is admissible in evidence in proceedings for an offence.

DEFINITIONS

   "criminal conduct": s. 76

   "defendant": s. 88(3)

GENERAL NOTE

This section substantially reproduces the effect of the Drug Trafficking Act 1994, s.11(5) to (10), and the Criminal Justice Act 1988, s.173(2) to (5). It should be distinguished from s.18, which deals with the situation where the court orders the defendant to produce information himself.

The effect of the section is that where a statement of information has been given to the court and a copy served on the defendant, the Crown Court may order the defendant to indicate to what extent he accepts the allegations made in the statement, and in so far as he does not accept an allegation, "to give particulars of any matters he proposes to rely on." If the defendant accepts any allegation, the Crown Court may treat that acceptance as conclusive. If the defendant fails to comply with an order under subs.(1), he may be treated as accepting every allegation in the statement of information other than an allegation in respect of which he has complied with the requirement, or an allegation that he has benefited from his general or particular criminal conned. The allegations which the defendant may be treated as having accepted will normally be allegations relevant to the making of the required assumptions under s.10, such as an allegation relating to his assets, receipts or expenditure within the relevant period.

No acceptance of an allegation by the defendant, whether directly made under subs.(2) or deemed to have been made under subs.(3) is admissible in evidence in proceedings for an offence.

18   Provision of information by defendant

(1) This section applies if—
    (a) the court is proceeding under section 6 in a case where section 6(3)(a) applies, or
    (b) it is proceeding under section 6 in a case where section 6(3)(b) applies or it is considering whether to proceed.

(2) For the purpose of obtaining information to help it in carrying out its functions the court may at any time order the defendant to give it information specified in the order.

(3) An order under this section may require all or a specified part of the information to be given in a specified manner and before a specified date.

(4) If the defendant fails without reasonable excuse to comply with an order under this section the court may draw such inference as it believes is appropriate.

(5) Subsection (4) does not affect any power of the court to deal with the defendant in respect of a failure to comply with an order under this section.

(6) If the prosecutor or the Director (as the case may be) accepts to any extent an allegation made by the defendant—
    (a) in giving information required by an order under this section, or
    (b) in any other statement given to the court in relation to any matter relevant to deciding the available amount under section 9,
  the court may treat the acceptance as conclusive of the matters to which it relates.

(7) For the purposes of this section an allegation may be accepted in a manner ordered by the court.

(8) If the court makes an order under this section it may at any time vary it by making another one.

(9) No information given under this section which amounts to an admission by the defendant that he has benefited from criminal conduct is admissible in evidence in proceedings for an offence.

DEFINITIONS
  "benefited": s. 76
  "criminal conduct": s. 76
  "defendant": s. 88(3)

GENERAL NOTE

This section substantially reproduces the effect of the Drug Trafficking Act 1994, s.12 and the Criminal Justice Act 1988, s.73A (as inserted by the Proceeds of Crime Act 1995).

The section empowers the Crown Court, when proceeding with a view to a confiscation order, whether on the application of the prosecutor or the Director, or on its own initiative, or is considering whether to proceed on its own initiative, to order the defendant to give it the "information specified in the order". There is no restriction on the kind of information which may be specified. If the defendant fails "without reasonable excuse" to comply with an order, the court "may draw such inference as it believes is appropriate" from the failure. (This does not prevent the Crown Court from dealing with the defendant for failing to comply with the order under any other power, such as the power to adjudge him guilty of contempt.)

The new section differs from those under the earlier legislation by the addition of subs.(9), which was not found in either s.12 of the 1994 Act or s.73A of the 1988 Act, although an equivalent provision was found in s.11 of the 1994 Act). Subsection (9) provides that no information given by the defendant in response to an order under the section which amounts to an admission that he has benefited from criminal conduct is admissible in evidence in proceedings for an offence. The addition of this subsection may well affect the matters which may be put forward by the defendant as a "reasonable excuse" under subs.(4) for failing to comply with the court's order. Under the earlier legislation, a defendant providing information in response to an order under one or other of the relevant sections might well have argued that the information required to be disclosed would expose him to the risk of prosecution for other offences, and that that was a "reasonable excuse" for failing to comply with the order. The addition of subs.(9) means that the defendant is protected from prosecution on the basis of such information and may therefore not argue that the risk of further prosecution is a "reasonable excuse" for failing to comply with the order.

Reconsideration

19　No order made: reconsideration of case

(1) This section applies if—
　(a) the first condition in section 6 is satisfied but no court has proceeded under that section,
　(b) there is evidence which was not available to the prosecutor on the relevant date,
　(c) before the end of the period of six years starting with the date of conviction the prosecutor or the Director applies to the Crown Court to consider the evidence, and
　(d) after considering the evidence the court believes it is appropriate for it to proceed under section 6.

(2) If this section applies the court must proceed under section 6, and when it does so subsections (3) to (8) below apply.

(3) If the court has already sentenced the defendant for the offence (or any of the offences) concerned, section 6 has effect as if his particular criminal conduct included conduct which constitutes offences which the court has taken into consideration in deciding his sentence for the offence or offences concerned.

(4) Section 8(2) does not apply, and the rules applying instead are that the court must—
　(a) take account of conduct occurring before the relevant date;
　(b) take account of property obtained before that date;
　(c) take account of property obtained on or after that date if it was obtained as a result of or in connection with conduct occurring before that date.

(5) In section 10—
　(a) the first and second assumptions do not apply with regard to property first held by the defendant on or after the relevant date;
　(b) the third assumption does not apply with regard to expenditure incurred by him on or after that date;

    (c) the fourth assumption does not apply with regard to property obtained (or assumed to have been obtained) by him on or after that date.

(6) The recoverable amount for the purposes of section 6 is such amount as—

    (a) the court believes is just, but

    (b) does not exceed the amount found under section 7.

(7) In arriving at the just amount the court must have regard in particular to—

    (a) the amount found under section 7;

    (b) any fine imposed on the defendant in respect of the offence (or any of the offences) concerned;

    (c) any order which falls within section 13(3) and has been made against him in respect of the offence (or any of the offences) concerned and has not already been taken into account by the court in deciding what is the free property held by him for the purposes of section 9;

    (d) any order which has been made against him in respect of the offence (or any of the offences) concerned under section 130 of the Sentencing Act (compensation orders).

(8) If an order for the payment of compensation under section 130 of the Sentencing Act has been made against the defendant in respect of the offence or offences concerned, section 13(5) and (6) above do not apply.

(9) The relevant date is—

    (a) if the court made a decision not to proceed under section 6, the date of the decision;

    (b) if the court did not make such a decision, the date of conviction.

(10) The date of conviction is—

    (a) the date on which the defendant was convicted of the offence concerned, or

    (b) if there are two or more offences and the convictions were on different dates, the date of the latest.

DEFINITIONS

"criminal conduct": s.76

"defendant": s.88(3)

"Free property": s.82

"offence or offences concerned": s.88(1) and 6(9)

"property": s.84

"sentencing Act": s.88(5)

GENERAL NOTE

This section substantially reproduces the effect of the Drug Trafficking Act 1994, s.13, and the Criminal Justice Act 1988, s.74A (as inserted by the Proceeds of Crime Act 1995), but with important variations.

The section allows the question of confiscation to be the reopened within the period of six years starting with a date of conviction, where the court did not proceed under s.6 at the time of conviction and the prosecutor has evidence which was not available to him on the date when the court decided not to proceed with a view to confiscation, or the date of conviction, if the question of confiscation was not considered. The power to reopen proceedings is not lost (as it is under s.74A of the 1988 Act, but not under s.13 of the Drug Trafficking Act 1994) if the prosecutor applied to the Court to proceed under s.6.

The critical question in relation to an order under the section is whether the prosecutor has "evidence which was not available" on the date of conviction, or when the decision not to proceed under the Act was made. It does not appear that the whole of the evidence on which the prosecution seek to rely must not have been available; it seems to be sufficient if some evidence has come to light which has not previously available. If the application is made within the six year period by the prosecutor or the Director, the Court has a discretion whether to initiate confiscation proceedings. (It is not mandatory for the Court to initiate confiscation proceedings, as it is under s.6 in the case of an application made at the normal time.)

If the Court in its discretion decides to initiate confiscation proceedings, the normal procedure is followed with certain variations. The court may include in the calculation of the benefit derived from "particular criminal conduct" the benefit derived from offences which were taken into consideration when the defendant was sentenced. The court may take account of conduct occurring before the date of conviction (or the date on which it was decided not to proceed with a view to confiscation) and of property obtained before that date, but may not take account of property obtained after the that date unless it was obtained as a result of or in connection with conduct occurring before that date.

In a "criminal lifestyle" case, the required assumptions do not apply to property held or obtained, or to expenditure incurred, after the date of conviction (or the date on which it was decided not to proceed with a view to confiscation.)

The rules governing the calculation of the amount to be recovered differ from those which apply in the normal case. The recoverable amount is such amount as "the Court believes is just," so long as it does not exceed the defendant's benefit or the "available amount" found in accordance with s.7(2). The effect of this provision (subs.(6) is to give the court a greater measure of discretion than it would have in the normal procedure under s.6. In deciding what amount is "just" in these circumstances the court is required by subs.(7) to have regard to orders made for the payment of money in respect of the offences. If the court made a compensation order when sentencing the defendant, it may not make an order under s.13(6) directing that the compensation order should be paid out of the proceeds of the confiscation order.

The provisions of the Act relating to statements of information, and orders requiring the defendant to provide information, apply (see s.26).

20   No order made: reconsideration of benefit

(1) This section applies if the following two conditions are satisfied.

(2) The first condition is that in proceeding under section 6 the court has decided that—

    (a) the defendant has a criminal lifestyle but has not benefited from his general criminal conduct, or

    (b) the defendant does not have a criminal lifestyle and has not benefited from his particular criminal conduct.

(3) If the court proceeded under section 6 because the Director asked it to, the second condition is that—

    (a) the Director has evidence which was not available to him when the court decided that the defendant had not benefited from his general or particular criminal conduct,

    (b) before the end of the period of six years starting with the date of conviction the Director applies to the Crown Court to consider the evidence, and

    (c) after considering the evidence the court concludes that it would have decided that the defendant had benefited from his general or particular criminal conduct (as the case may be) if the evidence had been available to it.

(4) If the court proceeded under section 6 because the prosecutor asked it to or because it believed it was appropriate for it to do so, the second condition is that—

    (a) there is evidence which was not available to the prosecutor when the court decided that the defendant had not benefited from his general or particular criminal conduct,

    (b) before the end of the period of six years starting with the date of conviction the prosecutor or the Director applies to the Crown Court to consider the evidence, and

    (c) after considering the evidence the court concludes that it would have decided that the defendant had benefited from his general or particular criminal conduct (as the case may be) if the evidence had been available to it.

(5) If this section applies the court—

    (a) must make a fresh decision under section 6(4)(b) or (c) whether the defendant has benefited from his general or particular criminal conduct (as the case may be);

   (b) may make a confiscation order under that section.

  (6) Subsections (7) to (12) below apply if the court proceeds under section 6 in pursuance of this section.

  (7) If the court has already sentenced the defendant for the offence (or any of the offences) concerned, section 6 has effect as if his particular criminal conduct included conduct which constitutes offences which the court has taken into consideration in deciding his sentence for the offence or offences concerned.

  (8) Section 8(2) does not apply, and the rules applying instead are that the court must—

    (a) take account of conduct occurring before the date of the original decision that the defendant had not benefited from his general or particular criminal conduct;

    (b) take account of property obtained before that date;

    (c) take account of property obtained on or after that date if it was obtained as a result of or in connection with conduct occurring before that date.

  (9) In section 10—

    (a) the first and second assumptions do not apply with regard to property first held by the defendant on or after the date of the original decision that the defendant had not benefited from his general or particular criminal conduct;

    (b) the third assumption does not apply with regard to expenditure incurred by him on or after that date;

    (c) the fourth assumption does not apply with regard to property obtained (or assumed to have been obtained) by him on or after that date.

  (10) The recoverable amount for the purposes of section 6 is such amount as—

    (a) the court believes is just, but

    (b) does not exceed the amount found under section 7.

  (11) In arriving at the just amount the court must have regard in particular to—

    (a) the amount found under section 7;

    (b) any fine imposed on the defendant in respect of the offence (or any of the offences) concerned;

    (c) any order which falls within section 13(3) and has been made against him in respect of the offence (or any of the offences) concerned and has not already been taken into account by the court in deciding what is the free property held by him for the purposes of section 9;

    (d) any order which has been made against him in respect of the offence (or any of the offences) concerned under section 130 of the Sentencing Act (compensation orders).

  (12) If an order for the payment of compensation under section 130 of the Sentencing Act has been made against the defendant in respect of the offence or offences concerned, section 13(5) and (6) above do not apply.

  (13) The date of conviction is the date found by applying section 19(10).

DEFINITIONS
  "criminal lifestyle": s.75
  "defendant": s.88(3)
  "offence or offences concerned": s.88(1) and 6(9)
  "property": s.84
  "Sentencing Act": s.88(5)

GENERAL NOTE

This section substantially reduces the effect of the Drug Trafficking Act 1994, s.15, and the Criminal Justice Act 1988, s.74 B (as inserted by the Proceeds of Crime Act 1995.) The section empowers the Court to reconsider the question whether a defendant has benefited from criminal conduct, in a case where it has previously considered the issue and decided that he has not benefited. The section applies equally to the question whether the defendant has benefited from his "general criminal conduct" in a "criminal lifestyle" case or his "particular criminal conduct" in other cases.

If the original confiscation proceedings were initiated on the application of the Director of the Assets Recovery Agency, the power given by the section may be exercised only if the Director has evidence which was not available to him when the court decided that the defendant had not benefited from his criminal conduct, and the Director makes an application to the Court within the period of six years beginning on the date of conviction. Where such an application is made, the court must consider the evidence. It the Court concludes that it would have decided that the defendant had benefited from his criminal conduct it the new evidence had been available, it must make a fresh decision as to whether the defendant had benefited. If it decides that he did benefit, the Court may then, in its discretion (subs.(4)(b)), proceed with a view to a confiscation order. There is no obligation on the Court to proceed, as there is under s.6(3)(a).

If the original confiscation proceedings were begun on the application of the prosecutor, the application to reconsider the question of benefit may be made either by the prosecutor or the Director of the Assets Recovery Agency. (The converse does not apply; if the original application was made by the Director, the prosecutor may not seek to reopen the proceedings under this section.)

The section makes no provision for cases where the Court has proceeded to make the original determination of benefit on its own initiative under s.6(3)(b).

If the Court does redetermine the issue of the defendant's benefit, and decides to proceed with a view to a confiscation order, the normal rules for making confiscation orders are modified in the same way as they are where the Court proceeds under s.19 (above).

The provisions of the Act relating to prosecutor's statements, and orders requiring the defendant to provide information, apply (see s.26).

21   Order made: reconsideration of benefit

(1) This section applies if—
   (a) a court has made a confiscation order,
   (b) there is evidence which was not available to the prosecutor or the Director at the relevant time,
   (c) the prosecutor or the Director believes that if the court were to find the amount of the defendant's benefit in pursuance of this section it would exceed the relevant amount,
   (d) before the end of the period of six years starting with the date of conviction the prosecutor or the Director applies to the Crown Court to consider the evidence, and
   (e) after considering the evidence the court believes it is appropriate for it to proceed under this section.

(2) The court must make a new calculation of the defendant's benefit from the conduct concerned, and when it does so subsections (3) to (6) below apply.

(3) If a court has already sentenced the defendant for the offence (or any of the offences) concerned section 6 has effect as if his particular criminal conduct included conduct which constitutes offences which the court has taken into consideration in deciding his sentence for the offence or offences concerned.

(4) Section 8(2) does not apply, and the rules applying instead are that the court must—
   (a) take account of conduct occurring up to the time it decided the defendant's benefit for the purposes of the confiscation order;
   (b) take account of property obtained up to that time;
   (c) take account of property obtained after that time if it was obtained as a result of or in connection with conduct occurring before that time.

(5) In applying section 8(5) the confiscation order must be ignored.

(6) In section 10—

    (a) the first and second assumptions do not apply with regard to property first held by the defendant after the time the court decided his benefit for the purposes of the confiscation order;

    (b) the third assumption does not apply with regard to expenditure incurred by him after that time;

    (c) the fourth assumption does not apply with regard to property obtained (or assumed to have been obtained) by him after that time.

(7) If the amount found under the new calculation of the defendant's benefit exceeds the relevant amount the court—

    (a) must make a new calculation of the recoverable amount for the purposes of section 6, and

    (b) if it exceeds the amount required to be paid under the confiscation order, may vary the order by substituting for the amount required to be paid such amount as it believes is just.

(8) In applying subsection (7)(a) the court must—

    (a) take the new calculation of the defendant's benefit;

    (b) apply section 9 as if references to the time the confiscation order is made were to the time of the new calculation of the recoverable amount and as if references to the date of the confiscation order were to the date of that new calculation.

(9) In applying subsection (7)(b) the court must have regard in particular to—

    (a) any fine imposed on the defendant for the offence (or any of the offences) concerned;

    (b) any order which falls within section 13(3) and has been made against him in respect of the offence (or any of the offences) concerned and has not already been taken into account by the court in deciding what is the free property held by him for the purposes of section 9;

    (c) any order which has been made against him in respect of the offence (or any of the offences) concerned under section 130 of the Sentencing Act (compensation orders).

(10) But in applying subsection (7)(b) the court must not have regard to an order falling within subsection (9)(c) if a court has made a direction under section 13(6).

(11) In deciding under this section whether one amount exceeds another the court must take account of any change in the value of money.

(12) The relevant time is—

    (a) when the court calculated the defendant's benefit for the purposes of the confiscation order, if this section has not applied previously;

    (b) when the court last calculated the defendant's benefit in pursuance of this section, if this section has applied previously.

(13) The relevant amount is—

    (a) the amount found as the defendant's benefit for the purposes of the confiscation order, if this section has not applied previously;

    (b) the amount last found as the defendant's benefit in pursuance of this section, if this section has applied previously.

(14) The date of conviction is the date found by applying section 19(10).

DEFINITIONS

"benefited": s.76

"confiscation order": s.88(6)

"criminal conduct": s.76

"defendant": s.88(3)

"free property": s.82
"offence or offences concerned": s.88(1) and 6(9)
"property": s.84
"sentencing Act": s.88(5)

GENERAL NOTE

This section substantially reproduces the effect the Drug Trafficking Act 1994, s.15 and the Criminal Justice Act 1988 (c.33) ("the 1988 Act"), s.74 C (as inserted by the Proceeds of Crime Act 1995 (c.11) (the 1995 Act"). The section allows for the determination of the amount of the defendant's benefit from criminal conduct to be revised if further evidence becomes available which indicates that the original calculation of the amount of benefit was incorrect.

The power to reopen the determination of benefit arises where an application is made by the prosecutor or the Director of the Assets Recovery Agency, and there is evidence which was not available to the prosecutor or the Director at the time when the amount of the benefit was calculated. (The requirement of new evidence not available at the time of the original determination was not included in either s.15 of the 1995 Act or s.74C of the 1988 Act.)

If an application is made within a period of six years starting with the date of conviction, the Court must consider the evidence and if it considers it appropriate to do so, in the exercise of its discretion (subs.(1)(e)) may make a new calculation of the defendant's benefit from criminal conduct. If the Court does make a new determination of the benefit, and the benefit exceeds the amount of the benefit as previously calculated (whether at the time of the original calculation, or a subsequent recalculation under this section) the recoverable amount must be recalculated, and if it exceeds the amount required to be paid under the original order, the Court may (in its discretion) vary the order by substituting "such amount as it believes to be just." The Court is not bound to substitute an amount calculated by reference to the new assessment of the amount of the benefit.

In other respects the procedure for calculating the amount of benefit is modified in the same way as under ss.19 and 20. The "available amount" (the combined value of the defendant's "free property" and "tainted gifts") is recalculated at the time of the new determination of the amount of benefit (subs.(8)). Property which has come into the defendant's possession after the original confiscation order was made may be taken into account for this purpose. If the Court has previously made a compensation order with a direction that the proceeds of the earlier confiscation order should be applied to satisfy the compensation order, the compensation order must not be taken into account in determining the revised amount of the order (subs.(10)).

Repeated applications for the recalculation of benefit may be made, so long as they are all made within six years of the date of conviction (subss. (12) and (13)).

The provisions of the Act relating to statements of information, and orders requiring the defendant to provide information, apply (see s.26).

22 Order made: reconsideration of available amount

(1) This section applies if—
    (a) a court has made a confiscation order,
    (b) the amount required to be paid was the amount found under section 7(2), and
    (c) an applicant falling within subsection (2) applies to the Crown Court to make a new calculation of the available amount.

(2) These applicants fall within this subsection—
    (a) the prosecutor;
    (b) the Director;
    (c) a receiver appointed under section 50 or 52.

(3) In a case where this section applies the court must make the new calculation, and in doing so it must apply section 9 as if references to the time the confiscation order is made were to the time of the new calculation and as if references to the date of the confiscation order were to the date of the new calculation.

(4) If the amount found under the new calculation exceeds the relevant amount the court may vary the order by substituting for the amount required to be paid such amount as—
    (a) it believes is just, but
    (b) does not exceed the amount found as the defendant's benefit from the conduct concerned.

(5) In deciding what is just the court must have regard in particular to—

   (a) any fine imposed on the defendant for the offence (or any of the offences) concerned;

   (b) any order which falls within section 13(3) and has been made against him in respect of the offence (or any of the offences) concerned and has not already been taken into account by the court in deciding what is the free property held by him for the purposes of section 9;

   (c) any order which has been made against him in respect of the offence (or any of the offences) concerned under section 130 of the Sentencing Act (compensation orders).

(6) But in deciding what is just the court must not have regard to an order falling within subsection (5)(c) if a court has made a direction under section 13(6).

(7) In deciding under this section whether one amount exceeds another the court must take account of any change in the value of money.

(8) The relevant amount is—

   (a) the amount found as the available amount for the purposes of the confiscation order, if this section has not applied previously;

   (b) the amount last found as the available amount in pursuance of this section, if this section has applied previously.

(9) The amount found as the defendant's benefit from the conduct concerned is—

   (a) the amount so found when the confiscation order was made, or

   (b) if one or more new calculations of the defendant's benefit have been made under section 21 the amount found on the occasion of the last such calculation.

DEFINITIONS

   "confiscation order": s.88(6)
   "criminal conduct": s.76
   "defendant": s.88(3)
   "free property": s.82
   "property": s.84
   "sentencing Act": s.88(5)

GENERAL NOTE

This section is derived from the Drug Trafficking Act 1994 s.16. There is no corresponding provision in the Criminal Justice Act 1988.

The section provides for a case in which the court has made a confiscation order, and the amount of the order was based on the "available amount" calculated in accordance with s.9, rather than the amount of the defendant's benefit. If the prosecutor, the Director of the Assets Recovery Agency, or a receiver, apply to the Court to make a new calculation of the available amount, the court must make the new calculation, applying s.9 to the circumstances as they apply at the time of the new calculation. If the amount found to be the "available amount" under the new calculation exceeds the amount found to be the "available amount" at the time of the previous calculation, the Court may (in its discretion) vary the order by substituting an amount which it "believes is just" but which does not exceed the amount found to be the defendant's benefit from the conduct concerned.

The power under the section arises whenever the value of the defendant's "free property" increases. It may apply where assets have been concealed by a defendant at the time the original order was made, where the value of the defendant's assets increase with the passage of time or inflation, or where the defendant acquires new assets by whatever means. Unlike the other provisions allowing the questions relating to confiscation to be reconsidered, this section is not subject to any time limit and there is no requirement that the applicant should have evidence which was not available at the time the original calculation was made. The only protection for a defendant against what might be thought to be an oppressive application of the section is in the discretion of the Court under subs.(4). This subsections allows the Court a general discretion whether or not to vary the order, and in the determination of the amount required to be paid under the order as varied.

The procedure for determining the amount to be recovered is subject to the same modifications as apply under s.21.

23 Inadequacy of available amount: variation of order

(1) This section applies if—
  (a) a court has made a confiscation order, and
  (b) the defendant, or a receiver appointed under section 50 or 52, applies to the Crown Court to vary the order under this section.
(2) In such a case the court must calculate the available amount, and in doing so it must apply section 9 as if references to the time the confiscation order is made were to the time of the calculation and as if references to the date of the confiscation order were to the date of the calculation.
(3) If the court finds that the available amount (as so calculated) is inadequate for the payment of any amount remaining to be paid under the confiscation order it may vary the order by substituting for the amount required to be paid such smaller amount as the court believes is just.
(4) If a person has been adjudged bankrupt or his estate has been sequestrated, or if an order for the winding up of a company has been made, the court must take into account the extent to which realisable property held by that person or that company may be distributed among creditors.
(5) The court may disregard any inadequacy which it believes is attributable (wholly or partly) to anything done by the defendant for the purpose of preserving property held by the recipient of a tainted gift from any risk of realisation under this Part.
(6) In subsection (4) "company" means any company which may be wound up under the Insolvency Act 1986 (c. 45) or the Insolvency (Northern Ireland) Order 1989 (S.I. 1989/2405 (N.I. 19)).

DEFINITIONS
  "confiscation order": s.88(6)
  "defendant": s.88(3)
  "property": s.84
  "realisable property": s.83
  "tainted gift": s.77

GENERAL NOTE
This section provides for the variation of the amount of a confiscation order on the ground that the "available amount" is inadequate to pay the amount of the order. It is derived in principle from the Drug Trafficking Act 1994, ss.17 and the Criminal Justice Act 1988, s.83, but with substantial modifications. In particular, unlike the earlier legislation which required an application to be made to the High Court, all of the proceedings under this section take place in the Crown Court.

The power of the Crown Court under this section arises where a confiscation order has been made and an application is made either by the defendant or by a receiver appointed to enforce the order. If an application is made, the Crown Court must recalculate the "available amount " as at the time of the recalculation. If the Court finds that the "available amount" as recalculated is inadequate for the payment or of any amount remaining to be paid under the confiscation order, it may (in its discretion) vary the confiscation order by substituting such smaller amount as the Court "believes is just." The Court is not obliged to reduce the amount of the order; as in the other provisions allowing for a variation of confiscation orders, the Court has a double discretion, first, whether to vary the order at all, and second, in the determination of the amount of the varied order. The Court is specifically authorised to disregard any inadequacy which it believes to be attributable to anything done by the defendant for the purpose of preserving property held by the recipient of a "tainted gift" from the risk of realisation. If the defendant has disposed of property, whether or before or after the original confiscation order was made, with a view to preventing that property from being realised, the Court may disregard any resulting in adequacy.

In the case of bankruptcy or winding up, the court must take into account in assessing the "available amount" the extent to which the realisable property may be distributed among creditors.

24   Inadequacy of available amount: discharge of order

(1) This section applies if—
   (a) a court has made a confiscation order,
   (b) a justices' chief executive applies to the Crown Court for the discharge of the order, and
   (c) the amount remaining to be paid under the order is less than £1,000.
(2) In such a case the court must calculate the available amount, and in doing so it must apply section 9 as if references to the time the confiscation order is made were to the time of the calculation and as if references to the date of the confiscation order were to the date of the calculation.
(3) If the court—
   (a) finds that the available amount (as so calculated) is inadequate to meet the amount remaining to be paid, and
   (b) is satisfied that the inadequacy is due wholly to a specified reason or a combination of specified reasons,
   it may discharge the confiscation order.
(4) The specified reasons are—
   (a) in a case where any of the realisable property consists of money in a currency other than sterling, that fluctuations in currency exchange rates have occurred;
   (b) any reason specified by the Secretary of State by order.
(5) The Secretary of State may by order vary the amount for the time being specified in subsection (1)(c).

DEFINITIONS
   "confiscation order": s.88(6)
   "property": s.84
   "realisable property": s.83

GENERAL NOTE
   This section has a very limited application. It applies if the amount remaining to be paid under a confiscation order is less than £1,000, and a justices' chief executive (acting on behalf of a magistrates' court responsible for enforcing the order under s.35) applies to the Crown Court for the discharge of the order on the ground that the realisable property consists of money in a currency other than sterling and that fluctuations in currency exchange rates have occurred. If such an application made, the court must recalculate the "available amount" as at the time of the recalculation; if it finds that the available amount (as recalculated) is inadequate to meet the amount remaining to be paid and that the inadequacy is wholly due to fluctuations in currency exchange rates, the court may discharge the confiscation order.
   The section makes provision for additional reasons for discharge to be specified by the Secretary of State by order.

25   Small amount outstanding: discharge of order

(1) This section applies if—
   (a) a court has made a confiscation order,
   (b) a justices' chief executive applies to the Crown Court for the discharge of the order, and
   (c) the amount remaining to be paid under the order is £50 or less.
(2) In such a case the court may discharge the order.
(3) The Secretary of State may by order vary the amount for the time being specified in subsection (1)(c).

DEFINITIONS
 "confiscation order": s. 88(6).

GENERAL NOTE
 This section provides a convenient procedure whereby the Crown Court is empowered to discharge a confiscation order where the amount remaining to be paid is £50 or less. If a justice's chief executive (acting for a magistrates court which is enforcing the order under s.35) applies to the Crown Court in such a case, the court may discharge the order.

26   Information

(1) This section applies if—
   (a) the court proceeds under section 6 in pursuance of section 19 or 20, or
   (b) the prosecutor or the Director applies under section 21.
(2) In such a case—
   (a) the prosecutor or the Director (as the case may be) must give the court a statement of information within the period the court orders;
   (b) section 16 applies accordingly (with appropriate modifications where the prosecutor or the Director applies under section 21);
   (c) section 17 applies accordingly;
   (d) section 18 applies as it applies in the circumstances mentioned in section 18(1).

GENERAL NOTE
 This section makes further procedural provision in connection with proceedings under ss.19 (where no order has been made), 20 (where the Court has decided that the defendant did not benefit from the offence or offences concerned) and 21 (where it is alleged that the amount of the defendant's benefit has been miscalculated.) In any such case, the prosecutor or Director must give the Court a statement of information (as defined in s.16) within the period which the court specifies, and the provisions relating to the defendant's response to a statement of information apply. The power of the Court to order the defendant to provide information under s.18 is also applied as if the Court were proceeding under s.6 in the normal way.

Defendant absconds

27   Defendant convicted or committed

(1) This section applies if the following two conditions are satisfied.
(2) The first condition is that a defendant absconds after—
   (a) he is convicted of an offence or offences in proceedings before the Crown Court,
   (b) he is committed to the Crown Court for sentence in respect of an offence or offences under section 3, 4 or 6 of the Sentencing Act, or
   (c) he is committed to the Crown Court in respect of an offence or offences under section 70 below (committal with a view to a confiscation order being considered).
(3) The second condition is that—
   (a) the prosecutor or the Director applies to the Crown Court to proceed under this section, and
   (b) the court believes it is appropriate for it to do so.
(4) If this section applies the court must proceed under section 6 in the same way as it must proceed if the two conditions there mentioned are satisfied; but this is subject to subsection (5).
(5) If the court proceeds under section 6 as applied by this section, this Part has effect with these modifications—
   (a) any person the court believes is likely to be affected by an order under section 6 is entitled to appear before the court and make representations;

    (b) the court must not make an order under section 6 unless the pros-
ecutor or the Director (as the case may be) has taken reasonable
steps to contact the defendant;

    (c) section 6(9) applies as if the reference to subsection (2) were to
subsection (2) of this section;

    (d) sections 10, 16(4), 17 and 18 must be ignored;

    (e) sections 19, 20 and 21 must be ignored while the defendant is still
an absconder.

(6) Once the defendant ceases to be an absconder section 19 has effect as
if subsection (1)(a) read—

        "(a) at a time when the first condition in section 27 was satisfied
the court did not proceed under section 6,".

(7) If the court does not believe it is appropriate for it to proceed under
this section, once the defendant ceases to be an absconder section 19
has effect as if subsection (1)(b) read—

        "(b) there is evidence which was not available to the prosecutor
or the Director on the relevant date,".

Definitions
   "confiscation order": s. 88(6)
   "defendant": s. 88(3)
   "Sentencing Act": s. 88(5)

General Note
   This section provides for the case of a defendant who has been convicted by the Crown Court,
or committed to the Crown Court for sentence, and who has absconded after the time of conviction or committal. Such a person is not eligible for a confiscation order under s.6, by virtue of
subs.(8) of that section. If the prosecutor or the Director of the Assets Recovery Agency applies
to the Crown Court, and the Crown Court believes that it is appropriate to do so, the Crown
Court must proceed under s.6 as it would in normal circumstances but subject to the modifications made by subs.(4).

   The modifications are that any person other than the defendant who is likely to be affected by
an order under s.6 (such as the holder of property said to be a "tainted gift") is entitled to appear
before the Crown Court and make representations and the Court must not make an order unless
the prosecutor or the Director has taken reasonable steps to contact the defendant. Sections 10
(required assumptions), 16(4) (statement of information relating to required assumptions),
17(defendant's response to statement of information) and 18 (order to defendant to provide
information) must be ignored. The power to reconsider questions relating to confiscation under
ss.19, 20 and 21 do not apply while the defendant remains an absconder; if he ceases to be an
absconder, they apply with the modifications made by subss.(6) and (7).

28   Defendant neither convicted nor acquitted

(1) This section applies if the following two conditions are satisfied.

(2) The first condition is that—

    (a) proceedings for an offence or offences are started against a
defendant but are not concluded,

    (b) he absconds, and

    (c) the period of two years (starting with the day the court believes he
absconded) has ended.

(3) The second condition is that—

    (a) the prosecutor or the Director applies to the Crown Court to pro-
ceed under this section, and

    (b) the court believes it is appropriate for it to do so.

(4) If this section applies the court must proceed under section 6 in the
same way as it must proceed if the two conditions there mentioned are
satisfied; but this is subject to subsection (5).

(5) If the court proceeds under section 6 as applied by this section, this
Part has effect with these modifications—

    (a) any person the court believes is likely to be affected by an order under section 6 is entitled to appear before the court and make representations;

    (b) the court must not make an order under section 6 unless the prosecutor or the Director (as the case may be) has taken reasonable steps to contact the defendant;

    (c) section 6(9) applies as if the reference to subsection (2) were to subsection (2) of this section;

    (d) sections 10, 16(4) and 17 to 20 must be ignored;

    (e) section 21 must be ignored while the defendant is still an absconder.

(6) Once the defendant has ceased to be an absconder section 21 has effect as if references to the date of conviction were to—

    (a) the day when proceedings for the offence concerned were started against the defendant, or

    (b) if there are two or more offences and proceedings for them were started on different days, the earliest of those days.

(7) If—

    (a) the court makes an order under section 6 as applied by this section, and

    (b) the defendant is later convicted in proceedings before the Crown Court of the offence (or any of the offences) concerned,

section 6 does not apply so far as that conviction is concerned.

DEFINITIONS
"concluded": s. 85 (3) to (8)
"defendant": s. 88(3)
"started": s. 85

GENERAL NOTE
This section provides for the case of a defendant who absconds after proceedings for an offence or offences have been started but before he has been convicted. If the defendant is still an absconder after two years from the date on which he originally absconded (presumably this will in most cases be the date on which he failed to surrender to bail) the prosecutor of the Director may apply to the Crown Court. There is no time limit on such an application, one the initial two year period has expired.

If such an application is made, and the Court considers it appropriate to do so, the Court may proceed under section 9 as in the normal way, but subject to the modifications made by subs.(4). These are substantially the same as those made by s.27(5) in the case of a person absconding after conviction, although there are minor differences in the wording of the two subsections. The only difference appears to be that under s.27, ss.19, 20, and 21 must be ignored while the defendant remains an absconder, but may be applied when he ceases to be an absconder. Under s.28, ss.19 and 20 must be ignored, and but do not come into force when the defendant ceases to be an absconder. Section 21 (revision of amount of benefit) applies (as modified by subs.(6)) when the defendant ceases to be an absconder.

If a defendant against whom an order is made under this section is eventually convicted, the court may not make a confiscation order under s.6 on the basis of the conviction, but in such a case there would be power to apply for a revision of the amount of the defendant's benefit under s.21. If he is subsequently tried and acquitted, the order may be discharged on an application by the defendant (see s.30).

29   Variation of order

(1) This section applies if—

    (a) the court makes a confiscation order under section 6 as applied by section 28,

    (b) the defendant ceases to be an absconder,

    (c) he is convicted of an offence (or any of the offences) mentioned in section 28(2)(a),

    (d) he believes that the amount required to be paid was too large (taking the circumstances prevailing when the amount was found for the purposes of the order), and

    (e) before the end of the relevant period he applies to the Crown Court to consider the evidence on which his belief is based.

(2) If (after considering the evidence) the court concludes that the defendant's belief is well founded—

    (a) it must find the amount which should have been the amount required to be paid (taking the circumstances prevailing when the amount was found for the purposes of the order), and

    (b) it may vary the order by substituting for the amount required to be paid such amount as it believes is just.

(3) The relevant period is the period of 28 days starting with—

    (a) the date on which the defendant was convicted of the offence mentioned in section 28(2)(a), or

    (b) if there are two or more offences and the convictions were on different dates, the date of the latest.

(4) But in a case where section 28(2)(a) applies to more than one offence the court must not make an order under this section unless it is satisfied that there is no possibility of any further proceedings being taken or continued in relation to any such offence in respect of which the defendant has not been convicted.

DEFINITIONS
    "confiscation order": s. 88(6)
    "defendant": s. 88(3)

GENERAL NOTE
    This section provides for the variation of a confiscation order made under s.28 in respect of a defendant who has absconded before the criminal proceedings against him have been concluded (but not in the case of a confiscation order made under s.27 in respect of a defendant who absconded after he has been convicted). If the defendant ceases to be an absconder and is convicted of any of the offences in respect of which the criminal proceedings were in progress when he absconded, he may apply to the Crown Court within twenty eight days of his conviction if he believes that the amount of the order was too large. If the Court on consideration of the evidence finds that the defendant's belief is well founded, the Court must find the amount which should have been required to be paid and it may vary the confiscation order by substituting that amount.

30   Discharge of order

(1) Subsection (2) applies if—

    (a) the court makes a confiscation order under section 6 as applied by section 28,

    (b) the defendant is later tried for the offence or offences concerned and acquitted on all counts, and

    (c) he applies to the Crown Court to discharge the order.

(2) In such a case the court must discharge the order.

(3) Subsection (4) applies if—

    (a) the court makes a confiscation order under section 6 as applied by section 28,

    (b) the defendant ceases to be an absconder,

    (c) subsection (1)(b) does not apply, and

    (d) he applies to the Crown Court to discharge the order.

(4) In such a case the court may discharge the order if it finds that—

    (a) there has been undue delay in continuing the proceedings mentioned in section 28(2), or

    (b) the prosecutor does not intend to proceed with the prosecution.

(5) If the court discharges a confiscation order under this section it may make such a consequential or incidental order as it believes is appropriate.

DEFINITIONS
  "confiscation order": s. 88(6)
  "defendant": s. 88(3)

GENERAL NOTE
  This section makes further provision for the case of a defendant who has absconded before criminal proceedings against him have been completed, and against whom a confiscation order has been made under s.28. If such a defendant is later tried for the offence or offences concerned, and is acquitted on all counts, he may apply to the Crown Court to discharge the order, and the Crown Court must discharge the order.

  If such a defendant ceases to be an absconder, but he is not tried for the offences concerned, he may apply to the Crown Court to discharge the order. In this case the Crown Court may, in its discretion, discharge the order if it finds either that there has been undue delay in continuing the proceedings for the offences or that the prosecutor does not intend to proceed with the prosecution.

Appeals

31   Appeal by prosecutor or Director

(1) If the Crown Court makes a confiscation order the prosecutor or the Director may appeal to the Court of Appeal in respect of the order.

(2) If the Crown Court decides not to make a confiscation order the prosecutor or the Director may appeal to the Court of Appeal against the decision.

(3) Subsections (1) and (2) do not apply to an order or decision made by virtue of section 19, 20, 27 or 28.

DEFINITIONS
  "confiscation order": s. 88(6)

GENERAL NOTE
  This section provides for an appeal to the Court of Appeal from a decision of the Crown Court by the prosecutor or the Director of the Assets Recovery Agency. Either the prosecutor or the director may appeal if the Crown Court makes a confiscation order, presumably on the ground that the amount of the order is less than the prosecutor or Director contends that it should be, or against a decision of the Crown Court not to make a confiscation order at all. The provision for appeal applies only to a confiscation order made (or not made) in the normal way following conviction. It does not apply to confiscation orders made or revised under those sections which allowed confiscation matters to be reconsidered at a later stage.

  This provision is an alternative to the normal procedure of review by way of a reference by the Attorney General under the Criminal Justice Act 1988 s.36, which is available in respect of decisions relating to confiscation orders.

  An appeal under this section may be made only with leave of the Court of Appeal (see s.89) and is to the Court of Appeal, Criminal Division.

32   Court's powers on appeal

(1) On an appeal under section 31(1) the Court of Appeal may confirm, quash or vary the confiscation order.

(2) On an appeal under section 31(2) the Court of Appeal may confirm the decision, or if it believes the decision was wrong it may—
    (a) itself proceed under section 6 (ignoring subsections (1) to (3)), or
    (b) direct the Crown Court to proceed afresh under section 6.

(3) In proceeding afresh in pursuance of this section the Crown Court must comply with any directions the Court of Appeal may make.

(4) If a court makes or varies a confiscation order under this section or in pursuance of a direction under this section it must—
    (a) have regard to any fine imposed on the defendant in respect of the offence (or any of the offences) concerned;
    (b) have regard to any order which falls within section 13(3) and has been made against him in respect of the offence (or any of the

offences) concerned, unless the order has already been taken into account by a court in deciding what is the free property held by the defendant for the purposes of section 9.

(5) If the Court of Appeal proceeds under section 6 or the Crown Court proceeds afresh under that section in pursuance of a direction under this section subsections (6) to (10) apply.

(6) If a court has already sentenced the defendant for the offence (or any of the offences) concerned, section 6 has effect as if his particular criminal conduct included conduct which constitutes offences which the court has taken into consideration in deciding his sentence for the offence or offences concerned.

(7) If an order has been made against the defendant in respect of the offence (or any of the offences) concerned under section 130 of the Sentencing Act (compensation orders)—

   (a) the court must have regard to it, and

   (b) section 13(5) and (6) above do not apply.

(8) Section 8(2) does not apply, and the rules applying instead are that the court must—

   (a) take account of conduct occurring before the relevant date;

   (b) take account of property obtained before that date;

   (c) take account of property obtained on or after that date if it was obtained as a result of or in connection with conduct occurring before that date.

(9) In section 10—

   (a) the first and second assumptions do not apply with regard to property first held by the defendant on or after the relevant date;

   (b) the third assumption does not apply with regard to expenditure incurred by him on or after that date;

   (c) the fourth assumption does not apply with regard to property obtained (or assumed to have been obtained) by him on or after that date.

(10) Section 26 applies as it applies in the circumstances mentioned in subsection (1) of that section.

(11) The relevant date is the date on which the Crown Court decided not to make a confiscation order.

DEFINITIONS

  "confiscation order": s. 88(6)

  "criminal conduct": s. 76

  "defendant": s. 88(3)

  "offence or offences concerned": s. 88(1) and 6(9)

  "property": s.84

GENERAL NOTE

  This section makes further provision for appeals by the prosecutor or the Director under s.31. On such an appeal, the Court of Appeal, Criminal Division may confirm, quash or vary the confiscation order. The section does not specifically state that the Court may vary the confiscation order by substituting a greater amount than was stated in the order made by the Crown Court, but this is a clearly implicit in the legislation. The Criminal Appeal Act 1968 s.11(3) provides that "On an appeal against sentence the Court of Appeal ... shall so exercise their powers under this subsection that taking the case as a whole the appellant is not more severely dealt with on appeal than he was dealt with by the court below." The restriction in s.11(3) appears to be limited to the exercise of the powers given by that subsection, and does not appear to apply to the exercise of the different powers given by this section. To hold otherwise would clearly be to frustrate the whole object of s.31.

  If the Court Appeal considers that the decision of the Crown Court in relation to the confiscation order was wrong, it may itself proceed under s.6 or remit the matter to the Crown Court with the direction to the Crown Court to "to proceed afresh." In doing so, the Crown Court must comply with any directions made by the Court of Appeal.

A court making or varying a confiscation order, or "proceeding afresh," must have regard to any fine or other financial order made against the defendant, unless the order has already been taken into account in making the original order. The court must not take account of property obtained on or after the date on which the decision of the Crown Court was made, unless the property was obtained as a result of or in connection with conduct occurring before that date. The required assumptions do not apply with regard to property held or obtained after the date on which be original decision of the Crown Court not to make a confiscation order was made, or to expenditure incurred by him after that date.

There is a possible difficulty in the definition of the "relevant date" in subs.(11). The "relevant date" is important for the purposes of subss.(8) and (9). It is the date which marks the cut-off point for the taking into account of conduct or property or the application of the required assumptions. Subsection (11) states that the "relevant date is the date on which the Crown Court decided not to make a confiscation order." An appeal to which s.32 applies may be made by the prosecutor or the Director on the ground that the Crown Court wrongly decided not to make a confiscation order, or that the Crown Court has made a confiscation order for less than the proper amount. Subsection (11) does not appear to contemplate the case where the Crown Court has made a confiscation order, but it is contended that the amount is too low. It is submitted that the subsection must be interpreted as if it included a reference to a case where the confiscation order has been made for what is contended to be an inadequate amount. There would be no logic in applying different rules in respect of the treatment of conduct and property, and the application of the assumptions, in this case.

33   Appeal to House of Lords

(1) An appeal lies to the House of Lords from a decision of the Court of Appeal on an appeal under section 31.

(2) An appeal under this section lies at the instance of—
  (a) the defendant or the prosecutor (if the prosecutor appealed under section 31);
  (b) the defendant or the Director (if the Director appealed under section 31).

(3) On an appeal from a decision of the Court of Appeal to confirm, vary or make a confiscation order the House of Lords may confirm, quash or vary the order.

(4) On an appeal from a decision of the Court of Appeal to confirm the decision of the Crown Court not to make a confiscation order or from a decision of the Court of Appeal to quash a confiscation order the House of Lords may—
  (a) confirm the decision, or
  (b) direct the Crown Court to proceed afresh under section 6 if it believes the decision was wrong.

(5) In proceeding afresh in pursuance of this section the Crown Court must comply with any directions the House of Lords may make.

(6) If a court varies a confiscation order under this section or makes a confiscation order in pursuance of a direction under this section it must—
  (a) have regard to any fine imposed on the defendant in respect of the offence (or any of the offences) concerned;
  (b) have regard to any order which falls within section 13(3) and has been made against him in respect of the offence (or any of the offences) concerned, unless the order has already been taken into account by a court in deciding what is the free property held by the defendant for the purposes of section 9.

(7) If the Crown Court proceeds afresh under section 6 in pursuance of a direction under this section subsections (8) to (12) apply.

(8) If a court has already sentenced the defendant for the offence (or any of the offences) concerned, section 6 has effect as if his particular criminal conduct included conduct which constitutes offences which the court has taken into consideration in deciding his sentence for the offence or offences concerned.

(9) If an order has been made against the defendant in respect of the offence (or any of the offences) concerned under section 130 of the Sentencing Act (compensation orders)—
  (a) the Crown Court must have regard to it, and
  (b) section 13(5) and (6) above do not apply.
(10) Section 8(2) does not apply, and the rules applying instead are that the Crown Court must—
  (a) take account of conduct occurring before the relevant date;
  (b) take account of property obtained before that date;
  (c) take account of property obtained on or after that date if it was obtained as a result of or in connection with conduct occurring before that date.
(11) In section 10—
  (a) the first and second assumptions do not apply with regard to property first held by the defendant on or after the relevant date;
  (b) the third assumption does not apply with regard to expenditure incurred by him on or after that date;
  (c) the fourth assumption does not apply with regard to property obtained (or assumed to have been obtained) by him on or after that date.
(12) Section 26 applies as it applies in the circumstances mentioned in subsection (1) of that section.
(13) The relevant date is—
  (a) in a case where the Crown Court made a confiscation order which was quashed by the Court of Appeal, the date on which the Crown Court made the order;
  (b) in any other case, the date on which the Crown Court decided not to make a confiscation order.

DEFINITIONS
  "confiscation order": s. 88(6)
  "criminal conduct": s. 76
  "defendant": s. 88(3)
  "free property": s. 82
  "offence or offences concerned": s. 88(1) and 6(9)
  "property": s.84
  "Sentencing Act": s. 88(5)

GENERAL NOTE
  This section provides for an appeal to the House of Lords from the decision of the Court of Appeal on an appeal by the prosecutor or the Director under s.31. The appeal may be brought by the defendant, or by the prosecutor if the prosecutor was the original appellant, or the Director if the Director was the original appellant. It is not open to the Director to appeal to the House of Lords in a case in which the prosecutor initiated the original appeal to the Court of Appeal, or vice versa.
  The statute does not provide, as in the case of any other appeal from the Court of Appeal Criminal Division to the House of Lords, that it is necessary for the Court of Appeal Criminal Division to grant a certificate that the case involves a point of law of general public importance (see Criminal Appeal Act 1968, s.33(2)), nor is there an express requirement to obtain the leave of the House of Lords for the appeal. The Criminal Appeal Act 1968, s.33 is expressly excluded (see s.90(1)), but the Secretary of State may by order make similar provisions (see s.90(2)).
  The powers of the House of Lords under this section are substantially similar to those of the Court of Appeal under s.32, but with some differences. If the House of Lords allows an appeal against a decision of the Court of Appeal to confirm the decision of the Crown Court not to make a confiscation order or from a decision of the Court of Appeal to quash a confiscation order, the House of Lords is empowered to confirm the decision or to direct the Crown Court to proceed afresh under s.6. There is no need in such a case (as there is in other cases) as for the case to be returned to the Court of Appeal. In a case where the appeal concerns the amount of the confiscation order, rather than the decision whether or not to make an order at all, the House of Lords may under subs.(3)"confirm, quash or vary the order." Unlike the Court of Appeal, it may not

itself proceed under s.6, and it may not, where what is an issue is the amount of the order as opposed to the decision whether or not to make an order at all, direct the Crown Court to "proceed afresh" under s.6.

Where the Crown Court proceeds afresh under a direction of the House of Lords, or any court (including the House of Lords) varies a confiscation order, the normal rules relating to the process of calculating the recoverable amount are modified in the same way as they are in relation to an appeal to the Court of Appeal, Criminal Division under s.31 (subss.(6) to (10).) There is a similar problem in the definition of the "relevant date" in subs.(13).

It is necessary to distinguish the powers and procedures arising on an appeal to the House of Lords under s.33 of this Act from those which would arise on an appeal to the House of Lords under the Criminal Appeal Act 1968, s.33. An appeal under s.33 of this Act can be made only as a consequence of an appeal by initiated by the prosecutor or the Director under s.31 of this Act. If the appeal to the Court of Appeal is initiated in this way, it seems that either the defendant or the prosecutor or the Director (as the case may be) may appeal to the House of Lords. If the original appeal was an appeal by the defendant under the Criminal Appeal Act 1968, s.10, or a reference by the Attorney General under the Criminal Justice Act 1988, s.36, the requirements of the 1968 Act apply. There must be a certificate that a point of law of general public importance is involved, and either the Court of Appeal or the House of Lords must give leave (see the Criminal Appeal Act 1968 s.33 and the Criminal Justice Act 1988 s.36(6)). In the case of an appeal under these provisions, or a further reference to the House of Lords following a reference by the Attorney General to the Court of Appeal, Criminal Division, if the House of Lords differs from the Court of Appeal, the House of Lords may remit the case to the Court of Appeal Criminal Division but not directly to the Crown Court (see the Criminal Appeal Act 1968, s.35(3) and the Criminal Justice Act 1988 s.36(5)).

Enforcement authority

34   **Enforcement authority**

(1) Subsection (2) applies if a court makes a confiscation order and any of the following paragraphs applies—
  (a) the court proceeded under section 6 after being asked to do so by the Director;
  (b) the court proceeded under section 6 by virtue of an application by the Director under section 19, 20, 27 or 28;
  (c) the court proceeded under section 6 as a result of an appeal by the Director under section 31(2) or 33;
  (d) before the court made the order the Director applied to the court to appoint him as the enforcement authority for the order.
(2) In any such case the court must appoint the Director as the enforcement authority for the order.

DEFINITIONS
"confiscation order": s. 88(6)

GENERAL NOTE
The section provides for the appointment of the Director of the Assets Recovery Agency as the enforcement authority in respect of confiscation orders made by the Crown Court or any court on an appeal from the Crown Court. If in any case the court has proceeded to make a confiscation order as a result of an application or appeal by the Director, or before the court made the confiscation order the Director has applied to the court to appoint him as the enforcement authority, the court must appoint the Director as the enforcement the authority for the order.

The section does not appear to authorise the Court to appoint the Director as the enforcement authority in any other case. It appears that if the Court has made the confiscation order on the application of the prosecutor, or has proceeded to make a confiscation order on its own initiative under s.6(3)(b), the Court may not appoint the Director as the enforcement authority, unless the Director applied to the court before the confiscation order was made. Once the order has been made in these circumstances, without an application by the Director to be appointed as the enforcement authority, there appears to be no power to appoint the Director even if he makes an application at a later time.

Enforcement as fines etc

35 Director not appointed as enforcement authority

(1) This section applies if a court—
  (a) makes a confiscation order, and
  (b) does not appoint the Director as the enforcement authority for the order.

(2) Sections 139(2) to (4) and (9) and 140(1) to (4) of the Sentencing Act (functions of court as to fines and enforcing fines) apply as if the amount ordered to be paid were a fine imposed on the defendant by the court making the confiscation order.

(3) In the application of Part 3 of the Magistrates' Courts Act 1980 (c. 43) to an amount payable under a confiscation order—
  (a) ignore section 75 of that Act (power to dispense with immediate payment);
  (b) such an amount is not a sum adjudged to be paid by a conviction for the purposes of section 81 (enforcement of fines imposed on young offenders) or a fine for the purposes of section 85 (remission of fines) of that Act;
  (c) in section 87 of that Act ignore subsection (3) (inquiry into means).

DEFINITIONS
  "confiscation order": s. 88(6)
  "defendant": s. 88(3)
  "Sentencing Act": s. 88(5)

GENERAL NOTE
  This section provides for cases where the Director is not appointed as the enforcement authority for a confiscation order under s.34. In such a case, the confiscation order is treated as if the amount ordered to be paid were a fine imposed on the defendant by the Court making the confiscation order. The provisions of the Powers of Criminal Courts (Sentencing) Act 2000 mentioned in subs.(2) apply in such a case. Under s.139(2), the Crown Court must fix a term of imprisonment to be served in default of the order, taking the terms from the table set out in s.139(4). The defendant may not be committed to prison immediately except as permitted by s.139(3). Section 139(9) applies the same provisions to fines imposed by the Court of Appeal or the House of Lords.
  Section 140(1) to (4) provides that fines imposed by the Crown Court are to be treated for the purpose of collection, enforcement and remission as having been imposed or forfeited by a magistrates court specified in an order made by the Crown Court, or by the magistrates court by which the offender was committed to the Crown Court or sent to the Crown Court for trial. Subsection (3) modifies the normal procedures for the enforcement of fines in the magistrates court in relation to confiscation orders. In particular, the power of the magistrates court to allow time for payment or allow further time for payment under the Magistrates' Courts Act 1980, s.75 does not apply, the power of the magistrates court to remit the fine under the Magistrates' Courts Act 1980, s.85 does not apply, and the Magistrates' Courts Act 1980 s.87(3) (which prohibits the initiation of civil proceedings before a means inquiry has been held) does not apply. The special provisions relating to offenders under 18 do not apply.

36 Director appointed as enforcement authority

(1) This section applies if a court—
  (a) makes a confiscation order, and
  (b) appoints the Director as the enforcement authority for the order.

(2) Section 139(2) to (4) and (9) of the Sentencing Act (functions of court as to fines) applies as if the amount ordered to be paid were a fine imposed on the defendant by the court making the confiscation order.

DEFINITIONS
  "confiscation order": s. 88(6)
  "defendant": s. 88(3)
  "Sentencing Act": s. 88(5)

General Note
This section makes provision for cases where the Court makes a confiscation order and appoints the Director of the Assets Recovery Agency as the enforcement authority. The section applies the Powers of Criminal Courts (Sentencing) Act 2000 139 (2), (3), and (4). These provisions require the Crown Court to impose a term of imprisonment or detention to be served in default of payment, provide that a person shall not be committed to prison in default forthwith other than in the circumstances indicated in subs.(3), and specify the table of terms from which the default term must be fixed. Subsection (9) applies the same provisions to orders made by the Court of Appeal or the House of Lords.

37　Director's application for enforcement

(1)　If the Director believes that the conditions set out in subsection (2) are satisfied he may make an ex parte application to the Crown Court for the issue of a summons against the defendant.

(2)　The conditions are that—
  (a)　a confiscation order has been made;
  (b)　the Director has been appointed as the enforcement authority for the order;
  (c)　because of the defendant's wilful refusal or culpable neglect the order is not satisfied;
  (d)　the order is not subject to appeal;
  (e)　the Director has done all that is practicable (apart from this section) to enforce the order.

(3)　If it appears to the Crown Court that the conditions are satisfied it may issue a summons ordering the defendant to appear before the court at the time and place specified in the summons.

(4)　If the defendant fails to appear before the Crown Court in pursuance of the summons the court may issue a warrant for his arrest.

(5)　If—
  (a)　the defendant appears before the Crown Court in pursuance of the summons or of a warrant issued under subsection (4), and
  (b)　the court is satisfied that the conditions set out in subsection (2) are satisfied,
it may issue a warrant committing the defendant to prison or detention for default in payment of the amount ordered to be paid by the confiscation order.

(6)　Subsection (7) applies if the amount remaining to be paid under the confiscation order when the warrant under subsection (5) is issued is less than the amount ordered to be paid.

(7)　In such a case the court must substitute for the term of imprisonment or detention fixed in respect of the order under section 139(2) of the Sentencing Act such term as bears to the original term the same proportion as the amount remaining to be paid bears to the amount ordered to be paid.

(8)　Subsections (9) and (10) apply if—
  (a)　the defendant has been committed to prison or detention in pursuance of a warrant issued under subsection (5), and
  (b)　a payment is made in respect of some or all of the amount remaining to be paid under the confiscation order.

(9)　If the payment is for the whole amount remaining to be paid the defendant must be released unless he is in custody for another reason.

(10)　If the payment is for less than that amount, the period of commitment is reduced so that it bears to the term fixed under section 139(2) of the Sentencing Act the same proportion as the amount remaining to be paid bears to the amount ordered to be paid.

Definitions
"confiscation order": s. 88(6)
"defendant": s. 88(3)
"Sentencing Act": s. 88(5)

GENERAL NOTE
This section makes provision for cases in which the defendant has failed to satisfy the confiscation order. If a confiscation order has been made, and the Director of the Assets Recovery Agency has been appointed as the enforcement authority, the Director may make an *ex parte* application to the Crown Court for the issue of a summons against the defendant. The confiscation order must not be subject to appeal (either by the defendant or by the prosecutor or Director under s.31), the Director must have done all that is practicable to enforce the order, and the failure to satisfy the order must be attributable to the defendant's "wilful refusal or culpable neglect." If it appears to the Crown Court that these conditions are satisfied, the Court may issue a summons to the defendant to appear; if the defendant fails to appear in pursuance of the summons, the Court may issue a warrant for his arrest. (There is no provision for the Crown Court to issue a warrant on the initial application of Director.)

If, when the defendant appears before the Crown Court, the Court is satisfied that the conditions set out in subs.(2) are satisfied, in particular that the Director has done all that is practicable to enforce the order and that the order is not satisfied because of the defendant's wilful refusal or culpable neglect, the Court may issue a warrant committing the defendant to prison or detention in default of payment.

If part of the amount ordered to be paid has been paid, the Court must reduce the default term to a term which bears the same proportion to the original default term (not the maximum default term fixed in the statutory table) as the amount remaining to be paid bears to the original amount ordered to be paid. If after the defendant has been committed to prison, payment is made in respect of some of the remaining amount, the period of detention or imprisonment is reduced proportionately. If the whole of the outstanding amount is paid, the defendant must be released unless he is in custody for some other reason.

38   Provisions about imprisonment or detention

(1) Subsection (2) applies if—

   (a) a warrant committing the defendant to prison or detention is issued for a default in payment of an amount ordered to be paid under a confiscation order in respect of an offence or offences, and

   (b) at the time the warrant is issued the defendant is liable to serve a term of custody in respect of the offence (or any of the offences).

(2) In such a case the term of imprisonment or of detention under section 108 of the Sentencing Act (detention of persons aged 18 to 20 for default) to be served in default of payment of the amount does not begin to run until after the term mentioned in subsection (1)(b) above.

(3) The reference in subsection (1)(b) to the term of custody the defendant is liable to serve in respect of the offence (or any of the offences) is a reference to the term of imprisonment, or detention in a young offender institution, which he is liable to serve in respect of the offence (or any of the offences).

(4) For the purposes of subsection (3) consecutive terms and terms which are wholly or partly concurrent must be treated as a single term and the following must be ignored—

   (a) any sentence suspended under section 118(1) of the Sentencing Act which has not taken effect at the time the warrant is issued;

   (b) in the case of a sentence of imprisonment passed with an order under section 47(1) of the Criminal Law Act 1977 (c. 45) (sentences of imprisonment partly served and partly suspended) any part of the sentence which the defendant has not at that time been required to serve in prison;

   (c) any term of imprisonment or detention fixed under section 139(2) of the Sentencing Act (term to be served in default of payment of fine etc) for which a warrant committing the defendant to prison or detention has not been issued at that time.

(5) If the defendant serves a term of imprisonment or detention in default of paying any amount due under a confiscation order, his serving that term does not prevent the confiscation order from continuing to have effect so far as any other method of enforcement is concerned.

DEFINITIONS
"confiscation order": s. 88(6)
"defendant": s. 88(3)
"Sentencing Act": s. 88(5)

GENERAL NOTE

This section makes further provision in connection with a term which the defendant is ordered to serve in default of payment of a confiscation order. It applies whether the warrant committing the defendant to prison is issued by the magistrates court under s.35 or the Crown Court under s.37.

Any default term does not begin to run until after of the defendant has served any other term of custody imposed in respect of the offence. It is not necessary for the Court to order that the default term will run consecutively to the other term. In the case of a defendant sentenced to a term of imprisonment for less than four years, he will normally cease to be "liable to serve a term of custody" at the expiration of half of the term of the sentence as pronounced by the court (Criminal Justice Act 1991 s.33). In the case of a defendant sentenced to a term of four years or more, whose liability to serve the sentence is dependent on the decision of the Parole Board, there is some uncertainty in the application of the section. Where the defendant is subject to terms of imprisonment which are consecutive or wholly or partly concurrent, the terms must be treated as a single term for the purpose of determining when the default term will begin. Suspended sentences which have not taken effect are ignored, as are partly suspended sentences imposed under the Criminal Law Act 1997 s.47(1), (which was repealed in the 1992.) Default terms in respect of which a warrant of commitment has not been issued are also ignored for this purpose.

This section ignores the amendments made to the Criminal Justice Act 1991 s.51(2) by the Crime and Disorder Act 1998. Under s.51(2) as so amended, consecutive terms and terms which are wholly or partly concurrent are treated as a single term only if the sentences were passed on the same occasion, or if they were passed on different occasions, and the person concerned was not released at anytime during the period between the passing of the first and the passing of the second sentence. The object of the amendments was to provide that where a defendant is released on licence from his sentence, and his licence is subsequently revoked under the Criminal Justice Act 1991 s.39 and he is returned to custody in respect of that sentence, any new sentence imposed while the defendant is the remainder of the licence period will not be treated as a single term including the original sentence. It appears that for the purpose of this section, that provision must be ignored.

A defendant who is committed to custody in default of payment of a confiscation order may have his term reduced under s.37 of this Act if any part payment is made while he is serving the default sentence. In other cases, a person serving a default sentence is liable to serve one half of the default term, if that term is a term of less than 12 month, or two-thirds if the term if the term is twelve months or more (see the Criminal Justice Act 1991 s.45). A person released from a default sentence is not subject to licence, irrespective of the length of the default term, and there is no provision for return to custody in the event of a conviction of a further offence. (A person committed to custody in default may be released on licence under the Criminal Justice Act 1991, s.36, on compassionate grounds, before he has served the required fraction of the term.)

Service of the default term does not extinguish the liability to pay the amount due under the confiscation order, and the confiscation order may be enforced by any other method of enforcement.

39   Reconsideration etc: variation of prison term

(1) Subsection (2) applies if—
    (a) a court varies a confiscation order under section 21, 22, 23, 29, 32 or 33,
    (b) the effect of the variation is to vary the maximum period applicable in relation to the order under section 139(4) of the Sentencing Act, and
    (c) the result is that that maximum period is less than the term of imprisonment or detention fixed in respect of the order under section 139(2) of the Sentencing Act.

(2) In such a case the court must fix a reduced term of imprisonment or detention in respect of the confiscation order under section 139(2) of the Sentencing Act in place of the term previously fixed.

(3) Subsection (4) applies if paragraphs (a) and (b) of subsection (1) apply but paragraph (c) does not.

(4) In such a case the court may amend the term of imprisonment or detention fixed in respect of the confiscation order under section 139(2) of the Sentencing Act.

(5) If the effect of section 12 is to increase the maximum period applicable in relation to a confiscation order under section 139(4) of the Sentencing Act, on the application of the appropriate person the Crown Court may amend the term of imprisonment or detention fixed in respect of the order under section 139(2) of that Act.

(6) The appropriate person is—

    (a) the Director, if he was appointed as the enforcement authority for the order under section 34;

    (b) the prosecutor, in any other case.

DEFINITIONS
  "confiscation order": s. 88(6)
  "Sentencing Act": s. 88(5)

GENERAL NOTE

This section provides for the variation of the default term if the amount of the confiscation order is varied after it has been made. It is not free from difficulty.

If the amount of the confiscation order is reduced, and the maximum period applicable to the revised amount of the order in the table of terms set out in the Powers of Criminal Courts (Sentencing) Act s.139(4) is different from the maximum term for the original amount, and less than the term of imprisonment actually fixed in respect of the original order, the court must fix a reduced term in place of the term originally fixed (subs.(2)). If the amount of the original order was £250,000, and the original default term was three years, and the amount of the order is reduced to £100,000, for which the maximum default term is two years, the court must reduce the default term in accordance with subs.(2).

If the amount of the order is reduced, but the default term in respect of the new term is within the same band of default terms as the original term, the court has no discretion to reduce the default term. Before the court may vary the default term under subs.(3), the amount of the confiscation order must have been varied (subs.(1)(a)) and "the effect of the variation is to vary the maximum period applicable in relation to the order" (subs.(1)(b)). Suppose the amount of the original order was £250,000 and the revised amount is £125,000. The default term was fixed at three years, which is the maximum default term for an amount exceeding £100,000 but not exceeding £250,000. The variation in the amount of the order has not affected the maximum default term and the power to vary the default term under subs.(3) does not arise.

If the amount of the order is increased under s.21 or 22, or following an appeal by the Director or prosecutor under s.32 or 33, the court may increase the default term, but again only if the result of the variation is that a new maximum default term applies. If on an application under s.21 or 22, the amount of the order is increased from £100,000 to £110,000, the relevant maximum default term under s.139(4) is increased from two years to three years; the requirements of subs.(3) are satisfied and the court may (in its discretion) increase the default term. If the original order was for £110,000, and the revised order is for £250,000, the maximum default term is the same in each case (three years), and the court may not increase the default term, even if it has fixed the default term (as it should have done) for the original order, towards the lower end of the bracket of two to three years, on basis of the amount of the order.

If the amount payable under a confiscation order is increased by the addition of unpaid interest under s.12, the Crown Court may amend the default term on the application of the Director or the prosecutor, but only if the maximum default term in respect of the new amount is greater than the maximum default term for the original amount.

Restraint orders

40   Conditions for exercise of powers

(1) The Crown Court may exercise the powers conferred by section 41 if any of the following conditions is satisfied.

(2) The first condition is that—
  (a) a criminal investigation has been started in England and Wales with regard to an offence, and
  (b) there is reasonable cause to believe that the alleged offender has benefited from his criminal conduct.
(3) The second condition is that—
  (a) proceedings for an offence have been started in England and Wales and not concluded, and
  (b) there is reasonable cause to believe that the defendant has benefited from his criminal conduct.
(4) The third condition is that—
  (a) an application by the prosecutor or the Director has been made under section 19, 20, 27 or 28 and not concluded, or the court believes that such an application is to be made, and
  (b) there is reasonable cause to believe that the defendant has benefited from his criminal conduct.
(5) The fourth condition is that—
  (a) an application by the prosecutor or the Director has been made under section 21 and not concluded, or the court believes that such an application is to be made, and
  (b) there is reasonable cause to believe that the court will decide under that section that the amount found under the new calculation of the defendant's benefit exceeds the relevant amount (as defined in that section).
(6) The fifth condition is that—
  (a) an application by the prosecutor or the Director has been made under section 22 and not concluded, or the court believes that such an application is to be made, and
  (b) there is reasonable cause to believe that the court will decide under that section that the amount found under the new calculation of the available amount exceeds the relevant amount (as defined in that section).
(7) The second condition is not satisfied if the court believes that—
  (a) there has been undue delay in continuing the proceedings, or
  (b) the prosecutor does not intend to proceed.
(8) If an application mentioned in the third, fourth or fifth condition has been made the condition is not satisfied if the court believes that—
  (a) there has been undue delay in continuing the application, or
  (b) the prosecutor or the Director (as the case may be) does not intend to proceed.
(9) If the first condition is satisfied—
  (a) references in this Part to the defendant are to the alleged offender;
  (b) references in this Part to the prosecutor are to the person the court believes is to have conduct of any proceedings for the offence;
  (c) section 77(9) has effect as if proceedings for the offence had been started against the defendant when the investigation was started.

DEFINITIONS
  "benefited": s. 76
  "criminal investigation": s. 88(2)
  "criminal conduct": s. 76
  "defendant": s. 88(3)
  "started": s. 85

GENERAL NOTE
  Sections 40 to 49 provide for restraint orders. Restraint orders are normally made before criminal proceedings are completed, in anticipation of a confiscation order. Section 40 lists five

different conditions under which the Crown Court may exercise the power to make it a restraint order.

The first two conditions relate to anticipated criminal proceedings. The first condition is that a criminal investigation has been started in England and Wales, and there is reasonable cause to believe that the alleged offender has benefited from his criminal conduct. The second condition is that proceedings for an offence had been started and not concluded, and there is reasonable cause to believe that the defendant has benefited from his criminal conduct. This condition is not satisfied if the court believes that there has been undue delay in continuing the proceedings, or that the prosecutor does not intend to proceed.

The third, fourth and fifth condition apply to cases where the prosecutor or the Director of the Assets Recovery Agency has made an application for a reconsideration of a decision relating to confiscation, or for a confiscation order against an absconder. If an application has been made under s.19,20,27 or 28 of the Act and has not been concluded, or the Court believes that such an application is to be made, and there is reasonable cause to believe that the defendant has benefited from his criminal conduct, the Court may make a restraint order. The fourth condition relates to an application under s.21 for a reconsideration of the amount of the defedant's benefit. If such an application has made, or the Court believes that such an application is to be made, and the Court believes there is reasonable cause to believe that it will decide that the amount of the defendant's is greater than the amount of the defendant's benefit as originally calculated, it may make a restraint order. The fifth condition makes similar provision in relation to an application under s.22 for a revision of the determination of the "available amount". None of these is satisfied if the Court believes there has been any undue delay in continuing the application, or the prosecutor or Director does not intend to proceed with the application.

41   Restraint orders

(1) If any condition set out in section 40 is satisfied the Crown Court may make an order (a restraint order) prohibiting any specified person from dealing with any realisable property held by him.

(2) A restraint order may provide that it applies—
   (a) to all realisable property held by the specified person whether or not the property is described in the order;
   (b) to realisable property transferred to the specified person after the order is made.

(3) A restraint order may be made subject to exceptions, and an exception may in particular—
   (a) make provision for reasonable living expenses and reasonable legal expenses;
   (b) make provision for the purpose of enabling any person to carry on any trade, business, profession or occupation;
   (c) be made subject to conditions.

(4) But an exception to a restraint order must not make provision for any legal expenses which—
   (a) relate to an offence which falls within subsection (5), and
   (b) are incurred by the defendant or by a recipient of a tainted gift.

(5) These offences fall within this subsection—
   (a) the offence mentioned in section 40(2) or (3), if the first or second condition (as the case may be) is satisfied;
   (b) the offence (or any of the offences) concerned, if the third, fourth or fifth condition is satisfied.

(6) Subsection (7) applies if—
   (a) a court makes a restraint order, and
   (b) the applicant for the order applies to the court to proceed under subsection (7) (whether as part of the application for the restraint order or at any time afterwards).

(7) The court may make such order as it believes is appropriate for the purpose of ensuring that the restraint order is effective.

(8) A restraint order does not affect property for the time being subject to a charge under any of these provisions—
   (a) section 9 of the Drug Trafficking Offences Act 1986 (c. 32);
   (b) section 78 of the Criminal Justice Act 1988 (c. 33);

(c) Article 14 of the Criminal Justice (Confiscation) (Northern Ireland) Order 1990 (S.I. 1990/2588 (N.I. 17));

(d) section 27 of the Drug Trafficking Act 1994 (c. 37);

(e) Article 32 of the Proceeds of Crime (Northern Ireland) Order 1996 (S.I. 1996/1299 (N.I. 9)).

(9) Dealing with property includes removing it from England and Wales.

DEFINITIONS
"defendant": s. 88(3)
"property": s.84
"realisable property": s. 83
"restraint order": s. 88(6), s. 41
"tainted gift": s. 77

GENERAL NOTE

This section provides for the content and effect of a restraint order. The order is made by the Crown Court (not, as under previous legislation, the High Court). The principal effect of a restraint order is to prohibit any person specified in the order from dealing with any "realisable property" held by him. The person so specified is not necessarily the defendant. The restraint order may apply generally to all realisable property held by the specified person, and to realisable property transferred to the specified person after the order has been made.

A restraint order may provide that certain expenditure is excepted from the effect of the order. It may in particular make provision for reasonable living expenses and for expenditure enabling the person specified to carry on his trade, business, profession or occupation. Provision may be made for reasonable legal expenses, but such provision must not include provision for expenses in connection with the offence which is the subject of an investigation which has not been completed or criminal proceedings which have not been concluded, or any offence in relation to which an application is made under the various provisions allowing for reconsideration of confiscation issues.

When a restraint order has been made, the person who has applied for the restraint order may apply to the Court to make any further order as court believes appropriate for the purpose of ensuring that the restraint order is effective. A restraint order does not affect property which is subject to a charge in relation to a confiscation order made under earlier legislation.

The powers given by this section must be exercised with regard to the matters listed in s.69.

42 Application, discharge and variation

(1) A restraint order—
　　(a) may be made only on an application by an applicant falling within subsection (2);
　　(b) may be made on an ex parte application to a judge in chambers.

(2) These applicants fall within this subsection—
　　(a) the prosecutor;
　　(b) the Director;
　　(c) an accredited financial investigator.

(3) An application to discharge or vary a restraint order or an order under section 41(7) may be made to the Crown Court by—
　　(a) the person who applied for the order;
　　(b) any person affected by the order.

(4) Subsections (5) to (7) apply to an application under subsection (3).

(5) The court—
　　(a) may discharge the order;
　　(b) may vary the order.

(6) If the condition in section 40 which was satisfied was that proceedings were started or an application was made, the court must discharge the order on the conclusion of the proceedings or of the application (as the case may be).

(7) If the condition in section 40 which was satisfied was that an investigation was started or an application was to be made, the court must discharge the order if within a reasonable time proceedings for the offence are not started or the application is not made (as the case may be).

DEFINITIONS
"restraint order": s. 88(6), s. 41

GENERAL NOTE
This section makes provision for various procedural questions in connection with restraint orders. An application for a restraint order may be made only by the prosecutor, the Director of the Assets Recovery Agency, or a financial investigator accredited by the Director under s.3. An application to make a restraint order may be made *ex parte* to a judge in chambers.

An application to discharge or vary a restraint order may be made by the person who applied for the order or any person affected by the order (such person may be the defendant or some other person specified in the order as the holder of the property concerned.) An application to vary or discharge a restraint order must be made to the Crown Court and presumably may not be made *ex parte*. On such an application, the Crown Court may discharge or vary the order. If the application for the restraint order was made on the basis that proceedings had started or that an application had been made, the court must discharge the order on the conclusion of the proceedings or application. It the restraint order was made on the basis that an investigation had started, or that an application was about to be made, the court must discharge the order if the proceedings have not started or the application has not been made within a reasonable time.

The powers given by this section must be exercised with regard to the matters listed in s.69.

43   Appeal to Court of Appeal

(1) If on an application for a restraint order the court decides not to make one, the person who applied for the order may appeal to the Court of Appeal against the decision.
(2) If an application is made under section 42(3) in relation to a restraint order or an order under section 41(7) the following persons may appeal to the Court of Appeal in respect of the Crown Court's decision on the application—
   (a) the person who applied for the order;
   (b) any person affected by the order.
(3) On an appeal under subsection (1) or (2) the Court of Appeal may—
   (a) confirm the decision, or
   (b) make such order as it believes is appropriate.

DEFINITIONS
"restraint order": s. 88(6), s. 41

GENERAL NOTE
This section provides for an appeal from the Crown Court to the Court of Appeal against a decision of the Crown Court not to make a restraint order. The person who applied for the order may appeal to the Court of Appeal, Criminal Division against the decision of the Crown Court, with leave of Court of Appeal, Criminal Division (see s.89). Where an application to discharge or vary a restraint order has been made, the person who applied for the order or any person affected by the order may appeal to the Court of Appeal from the Crown Court's decision. On such an appeal the Court of Appeal may confirm the decision of the Crown Court or make much order as it believes is appropriate.

The powers given by this section must be exercised with regard to the matters listed in s.69.

44   Appeal to House of Lords

(1) An appeal lies to the House of Lords from a decision of the Court of Appeal on an appeal under section 43.
(2) An appeal under this section lies at the instance of any person who was a party to the proceedings before the Court of Appeal.
(3) On an appeal under this section the House of Lords may—
   (a) confirm the decision of the Court of Appeal, or
   (b) make such order as it believes is appropriate.

GENERAL NOTE

This section makes provision for an appeal to the House of Lords from a decision of the Court of Appeal on an appeal against a decision of the Crown Court in connection with the making, variation or discharge of a restraint order. Any person who was a party to the proceedings before the Court of Appeal may appeal under this section. The House of Lords may confirm the decision of the Court of Appeal or make such order as it believes is appropriate.

The statute does not require either party to obtain a certificate from the Court of Appeal that the case involves a point of law of general public importance, or to obtain leave to appeal either from the Court of Appeal or the House of Lords, as it is in the case of an appeal against conviction or sentence under the Criminal Appeal Act 1968. The Criminal Appeal Act 1968, s.33 is excluded by s.90(1), but the Secretary of State is empowered by s.90(2) to make equivalent provision by order.

The powers given by this section must be exercised with regard to the matters listed in s.69.

45   Seizure

(1) If a restraint order is in force a constable or a customs officer may seize any realisable property to which it applies to prevent its removal from England and Wales.

(2) Property seized under subsection (1) must be dealt with in accordance with the directions of the court which made the order.

DEFINITIONS

"property": s.84
"realisable property": s. 83
"restraint order": s. 88(6), s. 41

GENERAL NOTE

This section enables a constable or customs officer to seize any realisable property to which a restraint order applies to prevent its removal from England and Wales.

The powers given by this section must be exercised with regard to the matters listed in s.69.

46   Hearsay evidence

(1) Evidence must not be excluded in restraint proceedings on the ground that it is hearsay (of whatever degree).

(2) Sections 2 to 4 of the Civil Evidence Act 1995 (c. 38) apply in relation to restraint proceedings as those sections apply in relation to civil proceedings.

(3) Restraint proceedings are proceedings—
  (a) for a restraint order;
  (b) for the discharge or variation of a restraint order;
  (c) on an appeal under section 43 or 44.

(4) Hearsay is a statement which is made otherwise than by a person while giving oral evidence in the proceedings and which is tendered as evidence of the matters stated.

(5) Nothing in this section affects the admissibility of evidence which is admissible apart from this section.

DEFINITIONS

"restraint order": s. 88(6), s. 41

GENERAL NOTE

This section provides that evidence must not be excluded in restraint proceedings (proceedings for a restraint order, for the discharge of a restraint order, or on appeal in connection with a restraint order) on the ground that it is hearsay. The Civil Evidence Act 1995, s.2 requires that a party proposing to adduce hearsay evidence shall give to the other party to the proceedings notice of that fact, and on request, such particulars of or relating to the evidence, as is reasonable and practicable in the circumstances for the purpose of enabling him to deal with any matters arising from its being hearsay. (This requirement may be excluded by agreement of the parties, and compliance with the duty to give notice may in any case be waived by the person to whom notice is required to be given.) Section 4 lists a number of matters which must or may be considered by a court in estimating the weight to be given to hearsay evidence in civil proceedings. Section 3 provides for Rules to be made in connection with the admission of hearsay evidence. The powers given by this section must be exercised with regard to the matters listed in s.69.

47   Supplementary

(1) The registration Acts—
   (a) apply in relation to restraint orders as they apply in relation to orders which affect land and are made by the court for the purpose of enforcing judgments or recognisances;
   (b) apply in relation to applications for restraint orders as they apply in relation to other pending land actions.
(2) The registration Acts are—
   (a) the Land Registration Act 1925 (c. 21);
   (b) the Land Charges Act 1972 (c. 61);
   (c) the Land Registration Act 2002 (c. 9).
(3) But no notice may be entered in the register of title under the Land Registration Act 2002 in respect of a restraint order.
(4) The person applying for a restraint order must be treated for the purposes of section 57 of the Land Registration Act 1925 (inhibitions) as a person interested in relation to any registered land to which—
   (a) the application relates, or
   (b) a restraint order made in pursuance of the application relates.

DEFINITIONS
   "benefited": s. 76
   "concluded": s. 85 (3) to (8)
   "confiscation order": s. 88(6)
   "criminal investigation": s. 88(2)
   "criminal lifestyle": s. 75
   "criminal conduct": s. 76
   "defendant": s. 88(3)
   "free property": s. 82
   "offence or offences concerned": s. 88(1) and 6(9)
   "property": s.84
   "realisable property": s. 83
   "restraint order": s. 88(6), s. 41
   "satisfied": s. 87
   "sentencing": s. 88(4)
   "Sentencing Act": s. 88(5)
   "started": s. 85
   "tainted gift": s. 77

Management receivers

48   Appointment

(1) Subsection (2) applies if—
   (a) the Crown Court makes a restraint order, and
   (b) the applicant for the restraint order applies to the court to proceed under subsection (2) (whether as part of the application for the restraint order or at any time afterwards).
(2) The Crown Court may by order appoint a receiver in respect of any realisable property to which the restraint order applies.

DEFINITIONS
   "property": s.84
   "realisable property": s. 83
   "restraint order": s. 88(6), s. 41

This section empowers the Crown Court to appoint a receiver in respect of any realisable property to which a restraint order made by the Court applies. The receiver may be appointed only on the application of the person who applied for the restraint order, whether at the time the restraint order was made or subsequently.

The powers given by this section must be exercised with regard to the matters listed in s.69.

49   Powers

(1) If the court appoints a receiver under section 48 it may act under this section on the application of the person who applied for the restraint order.

(2) The court may by order confer on the receiver the following powers in relation to any realisable property to which the restraint order applies—
  (a) power to take possession of the property;
  (b) power to manage or otherwise deal with the property;
  (c) power to start, carry on or defend any legal proceedings in respect of the property;
  (d) power to realise so much of the property as is necessary to meet the receiver's remuneration and expenses.

(3) The court may by order confer on the receiver power to enter any premises in England and Wales and to do any of the following—
  (a) search for or inspect anything authorised by the court;
  (b) make or obtain a copy, photograph or other record of anything so authorised;
  (c) remove anything which the receiver is required or authorised to take possession of in pursuance of an order of the court.

(4) The court may by order authorise the receiver to do any of the following for the purpose of the exercise of his functions—
  (a) hold property;
  (b) enter into contracts;
  (c) sue and be sued;
  (d) employ agents;
  (e) execute powers of attorney, deeds or other instruments;
  (f) take any other steps the court thinks appropriate.

(5) The court may order any person who has possession of realisable property to which the restraint order applies to give possession of it to the receiver.

(6) The court—
  (a) may order a person holding an interest in realisable property to which the restraint order applies to make to the receiver such payment as the court specifies in respect of a beneficial interest held by the defendant or the recipient of a tainted gift;
  (b) may (on the payment being made) by order transfer, grant or extinguish any interest in the property.

(7) Subsections (2), (5) and (6) do not apply to property for the time being subject to a charge under any of these provisions—
  (a) section 9 of the Drug Trafficking Offences Act 1986 (c. 32);
  (b) section 78 of the Criminal Justice Act 1988 (c. 33);
  (c) Article 14 of the Criminal Justice (Confiscation) (Northern Ireland) Order 1990 (S.I. 1990/2588 (N.I. 17));
  (d) section 27 of the Drug Trafficking Act 1994 (c. 37);
  (e) Article 32 of the Proceeds of Crime (Northern Ireland) Order 1996 (S.I. 1996/1299 (N.I. 9)).

(8) The court must not—
  (a) confer the power mentioned in subsection (2)(b) or (d) in respect of property, or

     (b) exercise the power conferred on it by subsection (6) in respect of
         property,

    unless it gives persons holding interests in the property a reasonable
    opportunity to make representations to it.

 (9) The court may order that a power conferred by an order under this
     section is subject to such conditions and exceptions as it specifies.

(10) Managing or otherwise dealing with property includes—

     (a) selling the property or any part of it or interest in it;

     (b) carrying on or arranging for another person to carry on any trade
         or business the assets of which are or are part of the property;

     (c) incurring capital expenditure in respect of the property.

DEFINITIONS
  "defendant": s. 88(3)
  "property": s.84
  "realisable property": s. 83
  "restraint order": s. 88(6), s. 41

GENERAL NOTE

  This section provides for the powers of a receiver appointed by the Crown Court under s.48 in
connection with a restraint order. The powers of the receiver in a particular case must be conferred on him specifically by the Crown Court. The powers which may be conferred on a receiver
are set out in subss.(2) to (4). . They include the power to take possession of, and manage or
otherwise deal with the property, to realise so much of the property as is necessary to meet to
receiver's remuneration and expenses, to make appropriate searches and inquiries in connection with the property and to conduct inquiries and searches in connection with the property.

  The court may also make orders against other persons, including the defendant or any other
person holding the property. The person concerned may be ordered to give the property to
which the restraint order applies to the receiver or to make a payment to the receiver in respect
of any beneficial interest held by the defendant in respect of the property. Property which is the
subject to a charge made under earlier confiscation legislation is excluded from all of these
provisions, other than those which authorise powers to make to searches and other inquiries
(subs.(3). The court must not confer on a receiver the power to manage or deal with property, or
to realise property, without giving any person interested in the property a reasonable opportunity to make representations to it. The same restriction applies to an order requiring a person to
make a payment to the receiver under subs.(6), but this provision does not apply to the power
conferred by subs.(4) to order a person in possession of property which is alleged to be realisable
property to give it to the receiver. It may be that a similar restriction would apply by virtue of
common law.

  The powers given by this section must be exercised with regard to the matters listed in s.69.

Enforcement receivers

50   Appointment

 (1) This section applies if—

     (a) a confiscation order is made,

     (b) it is not satisfied, and

     (c) it is not subject to appeal.

 (2) On the application of the prosecutor the Crown Court may by order
     appoint a receiver in respect of realisable property.

DEFINITIONS
  "confiscation order": s. 88(6)
  "property": s.84
  "realisable property": s. 83
  "satisfied": s. 87

GENERAL NOTE

  This section provides for the appointment of a receiver where the Crown Court has
made a confiscation order and the confiscation order and has not been satisfied, and the
Director of the Assets Recovery Agency has not been appointed under s.34 as the enforcement
authority for the order (see s.52). A receiver may not be appointed if the confiscation order

is "subject to appeal". (This restriction presumably applies to an appeal by the prosecutor or Director under s.31 as well as to an appeal by a defendant under the Criminal Appeal Act 1968 s.10). The receiver may be appointed on the application of the prosecutor.

It is not necessary for the court to delay the appointment of a receiver under this section until the period for allowed for payment by an order under s.11 has elapsed.

The powers given by this section must be exercised with regard to the matters listed in s.69.

51   Powers

(1) If the court appoints a receiver under section 50 it may act under this section on the application of the prosecutor.

(2) The court may by order confer on the receiver the following powers in relation to the realisable property—
  (a) power to take possession of the property;
  (b) power to manage or otherwise deal with the property;
  (c) power to realise the property, in such manner as the court may specify;
  (d) power to start, carry on or defend any legal proceedings in respect of the property.

(3) The court may by order confer on the receiver power to enter any premises in England and Wales and to do any of the following—
  (a) search for or inspect anything authorised by the court;
  (b) make or obtain a copy, photograph or other record of anything so authorised;
  (c) remove anything which the receiver is required or authorised to take possession of in pursuance of an order of the court.

(4) The court may by order authorise the receiver to do any of the following for the purpose of the exercise of his functions—
  (a) hold property;
  (b) enter into contracts;
  (c) sue and be sued;
  (d) employ agents;
  (e) execute powers of attorney, deeds or other instruments;
  (f) take any other steps the court thinks appropriate.

(5) The court may order any person who has possession of realisable property to give possession of it to the receiver.

(6) The court—
  (a) may order a person holding an interest in realisable property to make to the receiver such payment as the court specifies in respect of a beneficial interest held by the defendant or the recipient of a tainted gift;
  (b) may (on the payment being made) by order transfer, grant or extinguish any interest in the property.

(7) Subsections (2), (5) and (6) do not apply to property for the time being subject to a charge under any of these provisions—
  (a) section 9 of the Drug Trafficking Offences Act 1986 (c. 32);
  (b) section 78 of the Criminal Justice Act 1988 (c. 33);
  (c) Article 14 of the Criminal Justice (Confiscation) (Northern Ireland) Order 1990 (S.I. 1990/2588 (N.I. 17));
  (d) section 27 of the Drug Trafficking Act 1994 (c. 37);
  (e) Article 32 of the Proceeds of Crime (Northern Ireland) Order 1996 (S.I. 1996/1299 (N.I. 9)).

(8) The court must not—
  (a) confer the power mentioned in subsection (2)(b) or (c) in respect of property, or
  (b) exercise the power conferred on it by subsection (6) in respect of property,
  unless it gives persons holding interests in the property a reasonable opportunity to make representations to it.

(9) The court may order that a power conferred by an order under this section is subject to such conditions and exceptions as it specifies.

(10) Managing or otherwise dealing with property includes—
    (a) selling the property or any part of it or interest in it;
    (b) carrying on or arranging for another person to carry on any trade or business the assets of which are or are part of the property;
    (c) incurring capital expenditure in respect of the property.

DEFINITIONS
    "defendant": s. 88(3)
    "property": s.84
    "realisable property": s. 83
    "tainted gift": s. 77

GENERAL NOTE
    This section makes substantially similar provision in respect of receivers appointed to enforce confiscation orders as is made by s.49 in respect of receivers appointed in connection with restraint orders. (There is no provision under this section for the receiver to be empowered to realise property to meet his remuneration and expenses; compare s.49(2)(c) and (d) with s.51(2) (c) and (d).) The powers to be exercised by the receiver must be conferred specifically by the Crown Court in each particular case. Where the receiver is to be empowered to manage or deal with property thought to be realisable property, any person holding an interest in the property must be given a reasonable opportunity to make representations to the Crown Court. The same restriction replies to an order requiring a third person to make a payment to the receiver in respect of a beneficial interest held by the defendant for the recipient of a tainted gift, but not to an order to a person having possession of realisable of property to give possession of it to the receiver (subs.(8)).
    The powers given by this section must be exercised with regard to the matters listed in s.69.

Director's receivers

52   Appointment

(1) This section applies if—
    (a) a confiscation order is made, and
    (b) the Director is appointed as the enforcement authority for the order under section 34.

(2) But this section does not apply if—
    (a) the confiscation order was made by the Court of Appeal, and
    (b) when the Crown Court comes to proceed under this section the confiscation order has been satisfied.

(3) If this section applies the Crown Court must make an order for the appointment of a receiver in respect of realisable property.

(4) An order under subsection (3)—
    (a) must confer power on the Director to nominate the person who is to be the receiver, and
    (b) takes effect when the Director nominates that person.

(5) The Director must not nominate a person under subsection (4) unless at the time he does so the confiscation order—
    (a) is not satisfied, and
    (b) is not subject to appeal.

(6) A person nominated to be the receiver under subsection (4) may be—
    (a) a member of the staff of the Agency;
    (b) a person providing services under arrangements made by the Director.

(7) If this section applies section 50 does not apply.

DEFINITIONS
    "confiscation order": s. 88(6)
    "property": s.84
    "realisable property": s. 83
    "satisfied": s. 87

GENERAL NOTE
This section applies where a confiscation order has been made by the Crown Court, and the Director of the Assets Recovery Agency has been appointed as the enforcement authority in respect of the order under s.34. (The section does not apply if the confiscation order has been made by the Court of Appeal (presumably, on an appeal under s.32) and the order has been satisfied when the question of appointment of a receiver arises.) In a case to which s.52 applies, the Crown Court must make an order appointing a receiver (in the case where the Director is not appointed as the enforcing authority, the appointment or of a receiver to enforce the order is at the discretion of the Crown Court (s.15(2)).)

An order under this section must confer on the Director power to nominate the receiver; the Director must not nominate a person unless at the time he does so the confiscation order is not satisfied and is not "subject to appeal." (Presumably this restriction applies to appeals by the Director under s.31 as it does to appeals by the defendant under the Criminal Appeal Act 1968 s.10.)

The powers given by this section must be exercised with regard to the matters listed in s.69.

53   Powers

(1) If the court makes an order for the appointment of a receiver under section 52 it may act under this section on the application of the Director.

(2) The court may by order confer on the receiver the following powers in relation to the realisable property—
    (a) power to take possession of the property;
    (b) power to manage or otherwise deal with the property;
    (c) power to realise the property, in such manner as the court may specify;
    (d) power to start, carry on or defend any legal proceedings in respect of the property.

(3) The court may by order confer on the receiver power to enter any premises in England and Wales and to do any of the following—
    (a) search for or inspect anything authorised by the court;
    (b) make or obtain a copy, photograph or other record of anything so authorised;
    (c) remove anything which the receiver is required or authorised to take possession of in pursuance of an order of the court.

(4) The court may by order authorise the receiver to do any of the following for the purpose of the exercise of his functions—
    (a) hold property;
    (b) enter into contracts;
    (c) sue and be sued;
    (d) employ agents;
    (e) execute powers of attorney, deeds or other instruments;
    (f) take any other steps the court thinks appropriate.

(5) The court may order any person who has possession of realisable property to give possession of it to the receiver.

(6) The court—
    (a) may order a person holding an interest in realisable property to make to the receiver such payment as the court specifies in respect of a beneficial interest held by the defendant or the recipient of a tainted gift;
    (b) may (on the payment being made) by order transfer, grant or extinguish any interest in the property.

(7) Subsections (2), (5) and (6) do not apply to property for the time being subject to a charge under any of these provisions—
    (a) section 9 of the Drug Trafficking Offences Act 1986 (c. 32);
    (b) section 78 of the Criminal Justice Act 1988 (c. 33);
    (c) Article 14 of the Criminal Justice (Confiscation) (Northern Ireland) Order 1990 (S.I. 1990/2588 (N.I. 17));

(d) section 27 of the Drug Trafficking Act 1994 (c. 37);

(e) Article 32 of the Proceeds of Crime (Northern Ireland) Order 1996 (S.I. 1996/1299 (N.I. 9)).

(8) The court must not—

(a) confer the power mentioned in subsection (2)(b) or (c) in respect of property, or

(b) exercise the power conferred on it by subsection (6) in respect of property,

unless it gives persons holding interests in the property a reasonable opportunity to make representations to it.

(9) The court may order that a power conferred by an order under this section is subject to such conditions and exceptions as it specifies.

(10) Managing or otherwise dealing with property includes—

(a) selling the property or any part of it or interest in it;

(b) carrying on or arranging for another person to carry on any trade or business the assets of which are or are part of the property;

(c) incurring capital expenditure in respect of the property.

DEFINITIONS

"defendant": s. 88(3)

"property": s.84

"realisable property": s. 83

"tainted gift": s. 77

GENERAL NOTE

This section makes provision for the Crown Court to confer powers on a receiver nominated by the Director of the Assets Recovery Agency to enforce the confiscation order. It is identical to s.51, dealing with the power of the Crown Court to confer powers on a receiver appointed to enforce a confiscation order where the Director is not appointed as the enforcement authority. Although the appointment of a receiver is mandatory where the Director has been appointed as the enforcement authority and applies to the Crown Court for the appointment of the receiver, the question of which powers (among those identified in this section) are to be conferred on the receiver is within the discretion of the Crown Court.

The powers given by this section must be exercised with regard to the matters listed in s.69.

Application of sums

54   Enforcement receivers

(1) This section applies to sums which are in the hands of a receiver appointed under section 50 if they are—

(a) the proceeds of the realisation of property under section 51;

(b) sums (other than those mentioned in paragraph (a)) in which the defendant holds an interest.

(2) The sums must be applied as follows—

(a) first, they must be applied in payment of such expenses incurred by a person acting as an insolvency practitioner as are payable under this subsection by virtue of section 432;

(b) second, they must be applied in making any payments directed by the Crown Court;

(c) third, they must be applied on the defendant's behalf towards satisfaction of the confiscation order.

(3) If the amount payable under the confiscation order has been fully paid and any sums remain in the receiver's hands he must distribute them—

(a) among such persons who held (or hold) interests in the property concerned as the Crown Court directs, and

(b) in such proportions as it directs.

(4) Before making a direction under subsection (3) the court must give persons who held (or hold) interests in the property concerned a reasonable opportunity to make representations to it.

(5) For the purposes of subsections (3) and (4) the property concerned is—

    (a) the property represented by the proceeds mentioned in subsection (1)(a);

    (b) the sums mentioned in subsection (1)(b).

(6) The receiver applies sums as mentioned in subsection (2)(c) by paying them to the appropriate justices' chief executive on account of the amount payable under the order.

(7) The appropriate justices' chief executive is the one for the magistrates' court responsible for enforcing the confiscation order as if the amount ordered to be paid were a fine.

DEFINITIONS
"confiscation order": s. 88(6)
"defendant": s. 88(3)
"property": s.84

GENERAL NOTE
This section provides for the disposal of the proceeds of the realisation of property by a receiver appointed to enforce a confiscation order, or to any other sums held by the receiver in which to defendant holds an interest. It applies only to a receiver appointed under s.50 (cases where the Director is not appointed as the enforcement authority). The first priority is the payment of expenses incurred by an insolvency practitioner in relation to property which is subject to orders made under this or other confiscation legislation, by virtue of s.432. Second, the sums must be applied in making any payments directed by the Crown Court, other than a direction in respect of the payment of compensation under s.13(6), which is goverrned by s.55. Third, the sums must be applied towards the satisfaction of confiscation order. Sums applied to the satisfaction of the confiscation order must be paid to the appropriate Justices' Chief Executive (see s.35). Any surplus funds left over must be distributed as the Crown Court directs in accordance with subss.(3) and (4).

55   Sums received by justices' chief executive

(1) This section applies if a justices' chief executive receives sums on account of the amount payable under a confiscation order (whether the sums are received under section 54 or otherwise).

(2) The chief executive's receipt of the sums reduces the amount payable under the order, but he must apply the sums received as follows.

(3) First he must apply them in payment of such expenses incurred by a person acting as an insolvency practitioner as—

    (a) are payable under this subsection by virtue of section 432, but

    (b) are not already paid under section 54(2)(a).

(4) If the justices' chief executive received the sums under section 54 he must next apply them—

    (a) first, in payment of the remuneration and expenses of a receiver appointed under section 48, to the extent that they have not been met by virtue of the exercise by that receiver of a power conferred under section 49(2)(d);

    (b) second, in payment of the remuneration and expenses of the receiver appointed under section 50.

(5) If a direction was made under section 13(6) for an amount of compensation to be paid out of sums recovered under the confiscation order, the justices' chief executive must next apply the sums in payment of that amount.

(6) If any amount remains after the justices' chief executive makes any payments required by the preceding provisions of this section, the

amount must be treated for the purposes of section 60 of the Justices of the Peace Act 1997 (c. 25) (application of fines etc) as if it were a fine imposed by a magistrates' court.

(7) Subsection (4) does not apply if the receiver is a member of the staff of the Crown Prosecution Service or of the Commissioners of Customs and Excise; and it is immaterial whether he is a permanent or temporary member or he is on secondment from elsewhere.

DEFINITIONS
"confiscation order": s. 88(6)

GENERAL NOTE
This section provides for the disposal of sums of money received by a Justices' Chief Executive on account of a confiscation order. It covers payments made by a receiver under s.54, or payments made directly by a defendant.

If there are any payments due to an insolvency practitioner by virtue of s.432 of the Act, which have not already been paid, they must first be paid. If the sums have been received from a receiver, the next priority is the expenses of the receiver appointed in connection with a restraint order, which have not already been met. The next priority (also restricted to sums received from a receiver under s.54) is the payment of the remuneration and expenses of the receiver appointed to enforce a confiscation order. (The expenses of either class of receiver cannot be met out of money paid direct to the Justices' Chief Executive by or on behalf of the defendant). Next comes the satisfaction of a direction under s.13(6) that the sums recovered under the confiscation order be applied to the satisfaction of a compensation order. Any remaining amount is treated as a payment received in satisfaction of the confiscation order.

Any sum received by the Justices' Chief Executive reduces the amount payable under the confiscation order (and thus the term to be served in default, is the order is not fully satisfied) however the sum is applied under this section (subs.(2)).

56   Director's receivers

(1) This section applies to sums which are in the hands of a receiver appointed under section 52 if they are—
    (a) the proceeds of the realisation of property under section 53;
    (b) sums (other than those mentioned in paragraph (a)) in which the defendant holds an interest.

(2) The sums must be applied as follows—
    (a) first, they must be applied in payment of such expenses incurred by a person acting as an insolvency practitioner as are payable under this subsection by virtue of section 432;
    (b) second, they must be applied in making any payments directed by the Crown Court;
    (c) third, they must be applied on the defendant's behalf towards satisfaction of the confiscation order by being paid to the Director on account of the amount payable under it.

(3) If the amount payable under the confiscation order has been fully paid and any sums remain in the receiver's hands he must distribute them—
    (a) among such persons who held (or hold) interests in the property concerned as the Crown Court directs, and
    (b) in such proportions as it directs.

(4) Before making a direction under subsection (3) the court must give persons who held (or hold) interests in the property concerned a reasonable opportunity to make representations to it.

(5) For the purposes of subsections (3) and (4) the property concerned is—
    (a) the property represented by the proceeds mentioned in subsection (1)(a);
    (b) the sums mentioned in subsection (1)(b).

Definitions
  "confiscation order": s. 88(6)
  "defendant": s. 88(3)
  "property": s.84

General Note
    This section makes provision for the disposal of the money held by a receiver appointed under s.52, in a case where the Director of the Assets Recovery Agency has been appointed as the enforcement authority in respect of the confiscation order. The section corresponds with s.54. The sums in question are those held by the receiver as the proceeds of the realisation of property, and any other sums in which the defendant holds an interest.
    The order of priority of payments under subs.(2) is the same as in the case of an order under s.54. If any sums remain after the confiscation order has been satisfied and other payments have been met, they are to be distributed as the Crown Court directs, after giving persons who held or hold interests in the property concerned a reasonable opportunity to make representations. Sums to be applied to the satisfaction of the confiscation order must be paid to the Director.

57   Sums received by Director

(1) This section applies if the Director receives sums on account of the amount payable under a confiscation order (whether the sums are received under section 56 or otherwise).

(2) The Director's receipt of the sums reduces the amount payable under the order, but he must apply the sums received as follows.

(3) First he must apply them in payment of such expenses incurred by a person acting as an insolvency practitioner as—
   (a) are payable under this subsection by virtue of section 432, but
   (b) are not already paid under section 56(2)(a).

(4) If the Director received the sums under section 56 he must next apply them—
   (a) first, in payment of the remuneration and expenses of a receiver appointed under section 48, to the extent that they have not been met by virtue of the exercise by that receiver of a power conferred under section 49(2)(d);
   (b) second, in payment of the remuneration and expenses of the receiver appointed under section 52.

(5) If a direction was made under section 13(6) for an amount of compensation to be paid out of sums recovered under the confiscation order, the Director must next apply the sums in payment of that amount.

(6) Subsection (4) does not apply if the receiver is a member of the staff of the Agency or a person providing services under arrangements made by the Director.

Definitions
  "confiscation order": s. 88(6)

General Note
    This section, which corresponds to s.55, provides for the disposal of sums received by the Director of the Assets Recovery Agency, whether from a receiver appointed under s.54 or otherwise. The full amount received by the Director reduces the amount payable under the confiscation order, and therefore the term which the defendant is liable to serve in default, if any part of the confiscation order is left unsatisfied.
    The order of priority of the application of the money is the same as in the case of the receipt of money by a Justices' Chief Executive under s.55, except that monies received by the Director may not be applied to cover the remuneration and expenses of a receiver who is a member of staff of the Assets Recovery Agency, or who is providing services under arrangements made by the Director under s.1(6)(b).

Restrictions

58   Restraint orders

(1) Subsections (2) to (4) apply if a court makes a restraint order.

(2) No distress may be levied against any realisable property to which the order applies except with the leave of the Crown Court and subject to any terms the Crown Court may impose.

(3) If the order applies to a tenancy of any premises, no landlord or other person to whom rent is payable may exercise a right within subsection (4) except with the leave of the Crown Court and subject to any terms the Crown Court may impose.

(4) A right is within this subsection if it is a right of forfeiture by peaceable re-entry in relation to the premises in respect of any failure by the tenant to comply with any term or condition of the tenancy.

(5) If a court in which proceedings are pending in respect of any property is satisfied that a restraint order has been applied for or made in respect of the property, the court may either stay the proceedings or allow them to continue on any terms it thinks fit.

(6) Before exercising any power conferred by subsection (5), the court must give an opportunity to be heard to—

  (a) the applicant for the restraint order, and

  (b) any receiver appointed in respect of the property under section 48, 50 or 52.

DEFINITIONS
  "property": s.84
  "realisable property": s. 83
  "restraint order": s. 88(6), s. 41

GENERAL NOTE
  This section places restrictions on the rights of third parties in respect of property which is the subject of a restraint order. A third party may not levy distress against any realisable property subject to a restraint order except with leave of the Crown Court. In a case where a restraint order relates to the tenancy of any premises, no one to whom rent is payable may exercise the right of peaceable re-entry in respect of the premises in respect of failure to comply with the terms of the tenancy by the tenant, except with leave of the Crown Court. Where proceedings in respect of property subject to a restraint order are pending, the court before which the proceedings are pending made in its discretion stay the proceedings or allow them to continue. Before exercising this power, the court must give the applicant for the restraint order or any receiver appointed in respect of the property an opportunity to be heard.
  The powers given by this section must be exercised with regard to the matters listed in s.69.

59   Enforcement receivers

(1) Subsections (2) to (4) apply if a court makes an order under section 50 appointing a receiver in respect of any realisable property.

(2) No distress may be levied against the property except with the leave of the Crown Court and subject to any terms the Crown Court may impose.

(3) If the receiver is appointed in respect of a tenancy of any premises, no landlord or other person to whom rent is payable may exercise a right within subsection (4) except with the leave of the Crown Court and subject to any terms the Crown Court may impose.

(4) A right is within this subsection if it is a right of forfeiture by peaceable re-entry in relation to the premises in respect of any failure by the tenant to comply with any term or condition of the tenancy.

(5) If a court in which proceedings are pending in respect of any property

is satisfied that an order under section 50 appointing a receiver in respect of the property has been applied for or made, the court may either stay the proceedings or allow them to continue on any terms it thinks fit.

(6) Before exercising any power conferred by subsection (5), the court must give an opportunity to be heard to—
(a) the prosecutor, and
(b) the receiver (if the order under section 50 has been made).

DEFINITIONS
  "property": s.84
  "realisable property": s. 83

GENERAL NOTE
  This section makes provision restricting the rights of third parties in respect of realisable property, where the receiver has been appointed to enforce a confiscation order under s.50 (Director of the Assets Recovery Agency not appointed as enforcement authority). The restrictions are substantially similar to those which apply under s.58 where a restraint order is in force. It seems that they apply to property in respect of which the Crown Court has empowered the receiver to act under 51.
  The powers given by this section must be exercised with regard to the matters listed in s.69.

60   Director's receivers

(1) Subsections (2) to (4) apply if—
(a) the Crown Court has made an order under section 52 for the appointment of a receiver in respect of any realisable property, and
(b) the order has taken effect.
(2) No distress may be levied against the property except with the leave of the Crown Court and subject to any terms the Crown Court may impose.
(3) If the order is for the appointment of a receiver in respect of a tenancy of any premises, no landlord or other person to whom rent is payable may exercise a right within subsection (4) except with the leave of the Crown Court and subject to any terms the Crown Court may impose.
(4) A right is within this subsection if it is a right of forfeiture by peaceable re-entry in relation to the premises in respect of any failure by the tenant to comply with any term or condition of the tenancy.
(5) If a court (whether the Crown Court or any other court) in which proceedings are pending in respect of any property is satisfied that an order under section 52 for the appointment of a receiver in respect of the property has taken effect, the court may either stay the proceedings or allow them to continue on any terms it thinks fit.
(6) Before exercising any power conferred by subsection (5), the court must give an opportunity to be heard to—
(a) the Director, and
(b) the receiver.

DEFINITIONS
  "property": s.84

GENERAL NOTE
  This section makes provision in terms similar to s.59 for the case of a receiver appointed under s.52 on the application of the Director of the Assets Recovery Agency in respect of a confiscation order for which the Director has been appointed as the enforcement authority. It is substantially the same as s.59, except in respect of the persons to whom an opportunity to be heard must be given before the court exercises the power conferred by subs.(4). (See subs.(6) of each section).
  The powers given by this section must be exercised with regard to the matters listed in s.69.

Receivers: further provisions

61   Protection

If a receiver appointed under section 48, 50 or 52—
(a) takes action in relation to property which is not realisable property,
(b) would be entitled to take the action if it were realisable property, and
(c) believes on reasonable grounds that he is entitled to take the action,

he is not liable to any person in respect of any loss or damage resulting from the action, except so far as the loss or damage is caused by his negligence.

DEFINITIONS
"property": s.84
"realisable property": s. 83

GENERAL NOTE
This section protects a receiver appointed under s.48 (in respect of a restraint order), s.50 (in respect of a confiscation order where the Director is not appointed as the enforcement authority), or s.52 (in respect of a confiscation order where the Director is appointed as the enforcement authority). The receiver is protected from liability in respect of loss or damage resulting from any action taken by him in respect of property which is not realisable property, if he would be entitled to take the action if the property were realisable property, and the receiver did believe on reasonable grounds that he was entitled take the action which he took. The exception does not apply if the loss or damage is caused by the receiver's negligence.

Section 72 of the Act makes provision for the payment of compensation where there is "serious default" by members of services or agencies other than the Assets Recovery Agency.

62   Further applications

(1) This section applies to a receiver appointed under section 48, 50 or 52.
(2) The receiver may apply to the Crown Court for an order giving directions as to the exercise of his powers.
(3) The following persons may apply to the Crown Court—
    (a) any person affected by action taken by the receiver;
    (b) any person who may be affected by action the receiver proposes to take.
(4) On an application under this section the court may make such order as it believes is appropriate.

GENERAL NOTE
This section authorises a receiver to apply to the Crown Court to give directions as to the exercise of his powers. It applies to a receiver appointed under s.48 (in respect of a restraint order), s.50 (in respect of a confiscation order where the Director is not appointed as the enforcement authority), or s.52 (in respect of a confiscation order where the Director is appointed as the enforcement authority). A person affected by action taken by the receiver, or likely to be affected by action which the receiver proposes to take, may also make an application to the Crown Court.

On such an application, the court may make such order as it believes to be appropriate.

The powers given by this section must be exercised with regard to the matters listed in s.69.

63   Discharge and variation

(1) The following persons may apply to the Crown Court to vary or discharge an order made under any of sections 48 to 53—

(a) the receiver;
(b) the person who applied for the order or (if the order was made under section 52 or 53) the Director;
(c) any person affected by the order.

(2) On an application under this section the court—
(a) may discharge the order;
(b) may vary the order.

(3) But in the case of an order under section 48 or 49—
(a) if the condition in section 40 which was satisfied was that proceedings were started or an application was made, the court must discharge the order on the conclusion of the proceedings or of the application (as the case may be);
(b) if the condition which was satisfied was that an investigation was started or an application was to be made, the court must discharge the order if within a reasonable time proceedings for the offence are not started or the application is not made (as the case may be).

DEFINITIONS
"started": s. 85

GENERAL NOTE
This section provides for the variation or discharge by the Crown Court of orders appointing receivers, or authorising receivers to act in connection with realisable property. It applies to receivers appointed under s.48 (in respect of a restraint order), s.50 (in respect of a confiscation order where the Director is not appointed as the enforcement authority), or s.52 (in respect of a confiscation order where the Director is appointed as the enforcement authority).

Orders appointing the receiver, or authorising the receiver to act with respect to realisable property, may be varied or discharged on the application of the receiver, the person who applied for the order or the Director of the Assets Recovery Agency, or any person affected by the order.

If a receiver has been appointed in connection with a restraint order made in connection with criminal proceedings or an application under ss.19, 20, 27, or 28, the court must discharge the orders appointing the receiver and authorising the receiver to act on the conclusion of the criminal proceedings or the application. If the restraint order has been made on the ground that a criminal investigation has been started, or an application under ss.19, 20, 27, or 28 is about to be made, the court must discharge the order appointing the receiver and authorising him to act if within a reasonable time proceedings for the offence have not been started or the application under ss.19, 20, 27, or 28 has not been made. The section does not appear to require an application on the part of one of the persons mentioned in subs.(1) before orders may be discharged in these cases.

The powers given by this section must be exercised with regard to the matters listed in s.69.

64   Management receivers: discharge

(1) This section applies if—
(a) a receiver stands appointed under section 48 in respect of realisable property (the management receiver), and
(b) the court appoints a receiver under section 50 or makes an order for the appointment of a receiver under section 52.

(2) The court must order the management receiver to transfer to the other receiver all property held by the management receiver by virtue of the powers conferred on him by section 49.

(3) But in a case where the court makes an order under section 52 its order under subsection (2) above does not take effect until the order under section 52 takes effect.

(4) Subsection (2) does not apply to property which the management receiver holds by virtue of the exercise by him of his power under section 49(2)(d).

(5) If the management receiver complies with an order under subsection (2) he is discharged—
    (a) from his appointment under section 48;
    (b) from any obligation under this Act arising from his appointment.
(6) If this section applies the court may make such a consequential or incidental order as it believes is appropriate.

DEFINITIONS
"property": s.84
"realisable property": s. 83

GENERAL NOTE
This section provides for the case where a receiver has been appointed in connection with a restraint order. If the Crown Court makes a confiscation order and a receiver is appointed under s.50 or the Court authorises the appointment of a receiver by the Director of the Assets Recovery Agency, the Crown Court must order the receiver appointed in connection with the restraint order to transfer to the receiver appointed in connection with the confiscation order all property held by the first receiver by virtue of the exercise of his powers. An order must be made under this section even though the receiver appointed to enforce the confiscation order is the same person as the receiver appointed in connection with the restraint order. Where the Court has ordered the appointment of a receiver to be nominated by the Director of the Assets Recovery Agency, an order made by the Court under this section does not take effect until the receiver has been a nominated (see s.52(4)).

An order for the transfer of property does not apply to property held by the receiver in connection with the payment of his remuneration or expenses under s.49(2)(d). Once the original receiver has complied with the order, he is discharged from his appointment and any obligations arising from the appointment.

The powers given by this section must be exercised with regard to the matters listed in s.69.

65   Appeal to Court of Appeal

(1) If on an application for an order under any of sections 48 to 51 or section 53 the court decides not to make one, the person who applied for the order may appeal to the Court of Appeal against the decision.
(2) If the court makes an order under any of sections 48 to 51 or section 53, the following persons may appeal to the Court of Appeal in respect of the court's decision—
    (a) the person who applied for the order;
    (b) any person affected by the order.
(3) If on an application for an order under section 62 the court decides not to make one, the person who applied for the order may appeal to the Court of Appeal against the decision.
(4) If the court makes an order under section 62, the following persons may appeal to the Court of Appeal in respect of the court's decision—
    (a) the person who applied for the order;
    (b) any person affected by the order;
    (c) the receiver.
(5) The following persons may appeal to the Court of Appeal against a decision of the court on an application under section 63—
    (a) the person who applied for the order in respect of which the application was made or (if the order was made under section 52 or 53) the Director;
    (b) any person affected by the court's decision;
    (c) the receiver.
(6) On an appeal under this section the Court of Appeal may—
    (a) confirm the decision, or
    (b) make such order as it believes is appropriate.

GENERAL NOTE
This section provides for rights of the appeal in connection with orders for the appointment of receivers in connection with restraint orders or confiscation orders, and orders authorising

receivers so appointed to act with respect to realisable property. There is no right of appeal against an order made under s.52, which is mandatory.

Where an order has been made by the Crown Court , the person who has applied for an order or any person affected by the order may appeal to the Court of Appeal. Where the Crown Court has decided not to make an order, only the person who has applied for the order may appeal.

Provision is also made for appeals against decisions of the Crown Court made in relation to directions to be given to receivers under s.62, and decisions relating to the discharge and variation of orders under s.63.

Any appeal requires leave of the Court of Appeal (see s.89(1)). On an appeal under this section, the Court of Appeal may confirm the decision of the Crown Court, or make such order "as it believes is appropriate."

The powers given by this section must be exercised with regard to the matters listed in s.69.

66   Appeal to House of Lords

(1) An appeal lies to the House of Lords from a decision of the Court of Appeal on an appeal under section 65.
(2) An appeal under this section lies at the instance of any person who was a party to the proceedings before the Court of Appeal.
(3) On an appeal under this section the House of Lords may—
    (a) confirm the decision of the Court of Appeal, or
    (b) make such order as it believes is appropriate.

GENERAL NOTE

This section provides for an appeal to the House of Lords from a decision of the Court of Appeal on appeal under s.65. Any person who was a party to be proceedings before the Court of Appeal may appeal to the House of Lords. On such an appeal, the House of Lords may confirm the decision of the Court of Appeal or make such order as it believes is appropriate.

Section 66 does not require that the Court of Appeal should certify that the case involves a point of law or a general public importance, or that leave of the Court of Appeal or the House of Lords should be obtained (see s.90(1)), but the Secretary of State is empowered by s.90(2) to make an order containing provisions corresponding to those of the Criminal Appeal Act 1968, subject to any special modifications. Unless such an order is made, there appears to be an absolute right of appeal.

The powers given by this section must be exercised with regard to the matters listed in s.69.

Seized money

67   Seized money

(1) This section applies to money which—
    (a) is held by a person, and
    (b) is held in an account maintained by him with a bank or a building society.
(2) This section also applies to money which is held by a person and which—
    (a) has been seized by a constable under section 19 of the Police and Criminal Evidence Act 1984 (c. 60) (general power of seizure etc), and
    (b) is held in an account maintained by a police force with a bank or a building society.
(3) This section also applies to money which is held by a person and which—
    (a) has been seized by a customs officer under section 19 of the 1984 Act as applied by order made under section 114(2) of that Act, and
    (b) is held in an account maintained by the Commissioners of Customs and Excise with a bank or a building society.
(4) This section applies if the following conditions are satisfied—
    (a) a restraint order has effect in relation to money to which this section applies;

(b) a confiscation order is made against the person by whom the money is held;

(c) the Director has not been appointed as the enforcement authority for the confiscation order;

(d) a receiver has not been appointed under section 50 in relation to the money;

(e) any period allowed under section 11 for payment of the amount ordered to be paid under the confiscation order has ended.

(5) In such a case a magistrates' court may order the bank or building society to pay the money to the justices' chief executive for the court on account of the amount payable under the confiscation order.

(6) If a bank or building society fails to comply with an order under subsection (5)—

(a) the magistrates' court may order it to pay an amount not exceeding £5,000, and

(b) for the purposes of the Magistrates' Courts Act 1980 (c. 43) the sum is to be treated as adjudged to be paid by a conviction of the court.

(7) In order to take account of changes in the value of money the Secretary of State may by order substitute another sum for the sum for the time being specified in subsection (6)(a).

(8) For the purposes of this section—

(a) a bank is a deposit-taking business within the meaning of the Banking Act 1987 (c. 22);

(b) "building society" has the same meaning as in the Building Societies Act 1986 (c. 53).

DEFINITIONS
"confiscation order": s. 88(6)
"restraint order": s. 88(6), s. 41

GENERAL NOTE

This section applies to money held by a person in an account maintained with a bank or building society, and to money which has been seized by a constable or by a Customs officer under the Police and Criminal Evidence Act 1984 s.19 (which authorises the seizure of property from a person who has been arrested) and which is held in an account maintained by a police force or the Commissioners of Customs and Excise at a bank or building society. If all of the conditions specified in subs.(4) are satisfied, the magistrates court may order the bank or building society to pay the money to the Justices' Chief Executive for the magistrates court on account of the amount payable under the confiscation order. The first condition for making such an order is that a restraint order has effect in relation to the money concerned, and accordingly by virtue of s.40(2) the money must be "realisable property."

The powers given by this section must be exercised with regard to the matters listed in s.69.

Financial investigators

68   Applications and appeals

(1) Subsections (2) and (3) apply to—

(a) an application under section 41, 42, 48, 49 or 63;

(b) an appeal under section 43, 44, 65 or 66.

(2) An accredited financial investigator must not make such an application or bring such an appeal unless he falls within subsection (3).

(3) An accredited financial investigator falls within this subsection if he is one of the following or is authorised for the purposes of this section by one of the following—

(a) a police officer who is not below the rank of superintendent,

(b) a customs officer who is not below such grade as is designated by the Commissioners of Customs and Excise as equivalent to that rank,

(c) an accredited financial investigator who falls within a description specified in an order made for the purposes of this paragraph by the Secretary of State under section 453.

(4) If such an application is made or appeal brought by an accredited financial investigator any subsequent step in the application or appeal or any further application or appeal relating to the same matter may be taken, made or brought by a different accredited financial investigator who falls within subsection (3).

(5) If—

(a) an application for a restraint order is made by an accredited financial investigator, and

(b) a court is required under section 58(6) to give the applicant for the order an opportunity to be heard,

the court may give the opportunity to a different accredited financial investigator who falls within subsection (3).

DEFINITIONS
"restraint order": s. 88(6), s. 41

GENERAL NOTE

This section provides for the role "accredited financial investigators" in connection with applications for restraint orders, applications for the variation and discharge of restraint orders, the appointment of receivers in connection with restraint orders, the grant of powers to receivers in connection with restraint orders, applications for the discharge or variation of orders made in connection with restraint orders, or appeals in connection with such orders. The section provides that an accredited financial investigator must not make such an application or bring such an appeal unless he is one of those investigators specified in subs.(3). The section further provides that one accredited financial investigator within the scope of subs.(3) may be substituted for another at different stages of the relevant proceedings.

An accredited financial investigator is a person who has been accredited by the Director of the Assets Recovery Agency under s.3.

Exercise of powers

69 Powers of court and receiver

(1) This section applies to—

(a) the powers conferred on a court by sections 41 to 60 and sections 62 to 67;

(b) the powers of a receiver appointed under section 48, 50 or 52.

(2) The powers—

(a) must be exercised with a view to the value for the time being of realisable property being made available (by the property's realisation) for satisfying any confiscation order that has been or may be made against the defendant;

(b) must be exercised, in a case where a confiscation order has not been made, with a view to securing that there is no diminution in the value of realisable property;

(c) must be exercised without taking account of any obligation of the defendant or a recipient of a tainted gift if the obligation conflicts with the object of satisfying any confiscation order that has been or may be made against the defendant;

(d) may be exercised in respect of a debt owed by the Crown.

(3) Subsection (2) has effect subject to the following rules—

    (a) the powers must be exercised with a view to allowing a person other than the defendant or a recipient of a tainted gift to retain or recover the value of any interest held by him;

    (b) in the case of realisable property held by a recipient of a tainted gift, the powers must be exercised with a view to realising no more than the value for the time being of the gift;

    (c) in a case where a confiscation order has not been made against the defendant, property must not be sold if the court so orders under subsection (4).

(4) If on an application by the defendant, or by the recipient of a tainted gift, the court decides that property cannot be replaced it may order that it must not be sold.

(5) An order under subsection (4) may be revoked or varied.

DEFINITIONS

    "confiscation order": s. 88(6)

    "defendant": s. 88(3)

    "property": s.84

    "realisable property": s. 83

    "tainted gift": s. 77

GENERAL NOTE

This section establishes a number of general considerations which the court must take into account when exercising its various powers in relation to restraint orders and the enforcement of confiscation orders, and which receivers must take into account in the exercise of their functions.

The powers concerned must be exercised with a view to making available the value of the realisable property for satisfying any confiscation order that has been made or may be made against the defendant. In a case where a confiscation order has not been made, the various powers must be exercised with a view to securing that there is no diminution in the value of the realisable property. An obligation of the defendant or the recipient of a tainted gift must not be taken into account if the obligation conflicts with the object of satisfying a confiscation order that has been made or will be made. The duty to exercise the relevant powers with these objects in view is subject to the restrictions imposed by subs.(3). In particular, where a confiscation order has not yet been made, the defendant or the recipient of a tainted gift may apply to the Crown Court for an order that property held by a receiver must not be sold; if the court decides that the property cannot be replaced, it may order that the property must not be sold.

Committal

70   **Committal by magistrates' court**

(1) This section applies if—

    (a) a defendant is convicted of an offence by a magistrates' court, and

    (b) the prosecutor asks the court to commit the defendant to the Crown Court with a view to a confiscation order being considered under section 6.

(2) In such a case the magistrates' court—

    (a) must commit the defendant to the Crown Court in respect of the offence, and

    (b) may commit him to the Crown Court in respect of any other offence falling within subsection (3).

(3) An offence falls within this subsection if—

    (a) the defendant has been convicted of it by the magistrates' court or any other court, and

    (b) the magistrates' court has power to deal with him in respect of it.

(4) If a committal is made under this section in respect of an offence or offences—

    (a) section 6 applies accordingly, and

    (b) the committal operates as a committal of the defendant to be dealt with by the Crown Court in accordance with section 71.

(5) If a committal is made under this section in respect of an offence for which (apart from this section) the magistrates' court could have committed the defendant for sentence under section 3(2) of the Sentencing Act (offences triable either way) the court must state whether it would have done so.

(6) A committal under this section may be in custody or on bail.

DEFINITIONS

    "confiscation order": s. 88(6)
    "defendant": s. 88(3)
    "Sentencing Act": s. 88(5)

GENERAL NOTE

The Powers of Criminal Courts (Sentencing) Act 2000, s.3 empowers a magistrates' court to commit to the Crown Court for sentence a person who has been convicted summarily of an either way offence, in respect of whom the magistrates' court considers that its powers of punishment are inadequate. If the court considers that "greater punishment should be inflicted for the offence than the court has power to impose", the magistrates' court may commit the offender to the Crown Court, and the Crown Court may sentence the offender in any way in which it could deal with him if he had just been convicted before the Crown Court of the offence on indictment. There is no doubt that this provision authorises the magistrates' court to commit a defendant to the Crown Court for sentence on the ground that the case is one in which a confiscation order would be appropriate (a magistrates' court has no power under this Act to make any confiscation order.)

Section 70, which supplements the Powers of Criminal Courts (Sentencing) Act 2000, s.3, appears to have two distinct purposes. In respect of cases where the magistrates' court would be entitled, in its discretion, to commit a defendant for sentence under the Powers of Criminal Courts (Sentencing) Act 2000 s.3, this section imposes a mandatory obligation on the magistrates court to commit the defendant if the prosecutor asks the magistrates' court to commit the defendant with a view to a confiscation order being considered.

The second object of the section is to provide for the committal for sentence of defendants who have been convicted of summary offences and who are not eligible for committal for sentence except under the Powers of Criminal Courts (Sentencing) Act 2000 s.6, which applies only to a defendant committed under some other provision in connection with a different offence. Unlike the Powers of Criminal Courts (Sentencing) Act 2000 s.3, this provision applies to a defendant who has been convicted by a magistrates' court of "an offence." There is nothing in the section to restrict this expression to either way offences. Where the magistrates' court commits a defendant under this section in respect of an offence or offences, it may commit him in respect of other offences of which he has been convicted and in respect of which the magistrates' court has power to deal with the defendant, whether or not any question of confiscation arises in respect of that offence.

If the case is one in which the magistrates court would have had power to commit the defendant for sentence under the Powers of Criminal Courts (Sentencing) Act, s.3 (2), the magistrates' court must state whether it would have committed the defendant under that provision. Failure to make this statement will affect the powers of the Crown Court to deal with the defendant.

71   Sentencing by Crown Court

(1) If a defendant is committed to the Crown Court under section 70 in respect of an offence or offences, this section applies (whether or not the court proceeds under section 6).

(2) In the case of an offence in respect of which the magistrates' court has stated under section 70(5) that it would have committed the defendant for sentence, the Crown Court—

    (a) must inquire into the circumstances of the case, and

    (b) may deal with the defendant in any way in which it could deal with him if he had just been convicted of the offence on indictment before it.

(3) In the case of any other offence the Crown Court—

    (a) must inquire into the circumstances of the case, and

    (b) may deal with the defendant in any way in which the magistrates' court could deal with him if it had just convicted him of the offence.

DEFINITIONS

"defendant": s. 88(3)

GENERAL NOTE

This section provides the powers of the Crown Court to deal with an offender who has been committed by a magistrates court under s.70. The Crown Court must proceed under s.6 if an application is made by the prosecutor or the Director of the Assets Recovery Agency. If no such application is made, the Crown Court may proceed under the section if it considers it appropriate to do so.

If the magistrates court has stated in accordance with s.70 (5) that it would have committed the defendant for sentence under the Powers of Criminal Courts (Sentencing) Act 2000 s.3, the Crown Court must inquire into the circumstances of the case and may deal with the defendant in any way in which it could deal with him if he had just been convicted of the offence on indictment. The powers of the Crown Court in respect of sentence are not restricted in any way to those of the magistrates' court in this situation.

If the magistrates' court has not made a statement under s.70(5) in respect of an either way offence, or the offence is not an either way offence, the Crown Court, having inquired into the circumstances of the case, may deal with the defendant in any way in which the magistrates' court could deal with him if it had just convicted him of the offence. The Crown Court must observe all the restrictions on the powers of magistrates' courts, both in respect of the sentence which may be imposed for the individual offence, and the aggregate of consecutive sentences which may be imposed in respect of a number of offences under the Magistrates' Courts Act 1980, s.133.

Compensation

72 Serious default

(1) If the following three conditions are satisfied the Crown Court may order the payment of such compensation as it believes is just.

(2) The first condition is satisfied if a criminal investigation has been started with regard to an offence and proceedings are not started for the offence.

(3) The first condition is also satisfied if proceedings for an offence are started against a person and—

    (a) they do not result in his conviction for the offence, or

    (b) he is convicted of the offence but the conviction is quashed or he is pardoned in respect of it.

(4) If subsection (2) applies the second condition is that—

    (a) in the criminal investigation there has been a serious default by a person mentioned in subsection (9), and

    (b) the investigation would not have continued if the default had not occurred.

(5) If subsection (3) applies the second condition is that—

    (a) in the criminal investigation with regard to the offence or in its prosecution there has been a serious default by a person who is mentioned in subsection (9), and

    (b) the proceedings would not have been started or continued if the default had not occurred.

(6) The third condition is that an application is made under this section by a person who held realisable property and has suffered loss in consequence of anything done in relation to it by or in pursuance of an order under this Part.

(7) The offence referred to in subsection (2) may be one of a number of offences with regard to which the investigation is started.

(8) The offence referred to in subsection (3) may be one of a number of offences for which the proceedings are started.

(9) Compensation under this section is payable to the applicant and—

    (a) if the person in default was or was acting as a member of a police force, the compensation is payable out of the police fund from which the expenses of that force are met;

    (b) if the person in default was a member of the Crown Prosecution Service or was acting on its behalf, the compensation is payable by the Director of Public Prosecutions;

    (c) if the person in default was a member of the Serious Fraud Office, the compensation is payable by the Director of that Office;

    (d) if the person in default was a customs officer, the compensation is payable by the Commissioners of Customs and Excise;

    (e) if the person in default was an officer of the Commissioners of Inland Revenue, the compensation is payable by those Commissioners.

DEFINITIONS

  "property": s.84
  "realisable property": s. 83
  "started": s. 85

GENERAL NOTE

This section provides for the Crown Court to order the payment of compensation in cases where there has been "serious default" in the conduct of proceedings to which the restraint order or confiscation order is related.

Before any question of compensation can arise, three conditions, (which are expressed in the alternative) must be satisfied. The first condition is satisfied if a criminal investigation has been started in relation to an offence and proceedings are not started for the offence; alternatively, the first condition is satisfied if proceedings for an offence are started against a defendant but they do not result in his conviction, or his conviction is quashed or he is pardoned for the offence.

The second condition is that there has been a serious default by one of the persons mentioned in subs.(9) and that the criminal investigation would not have continued if the default had not occurred or the proceedings would not have been started or continued if the default had not occurred.

The third condition, which applies in any of these cases, is that the person who held realisable property (who may include the defendant) has suffered loss in consequence of anything done in relation to the realisable property as a result of an order made under the Act in connection with confiscation.

The concept of "serious default" is not elaborated in the Act. Compensation may not be ordered under this section against a person who is employed by or acting on behalf of the Assets Recovery Agency.

The Act provides no right of appeal in connection with decisions of the Crown Court made under this section.

73   Order varied or discharged

(1) This section applies if—

    (a) the court varies a confiscation order under section 29 or discharges one under section 30, and

    (b) an application is made to the Crown Court by a person who held realisable property and has suffered loss as a result of the making of the order.

(2) The court may order the payment of such compensation as it believes is just.

(3) Compensation under this section is payable—
    (a) to the applicant;
    (b) by the Lord Chancellor.

DEFINITIONS
    "confiscation order": s. 88(6)
    "property": s.84

GENERAL NOTE

This section applies to a confiscation order made under s.28 in respect of a defendant who has absconded after proceedings against him have been started but before they have been concluded. If in such a case the defendant is convicted of an offence and the Crown Court on application under s.29 reduces the amount of the confiscation order that has been made against the defendant, the Crown Court may order the payment of compensation, at its discretion, to any person who held realisable property and who has suffered loss as a result of the making of the order. Similarly if such a defendant has been tried for the offences and has been acquitted, and the Crown Court has accordingly discharged the confiscation order under s.30(2), the Crown Court on application may order the payment of compensation to any person who held realisable property and who has suffered loss as a result of the making of the order. Such persons may include the defendant. The amount of compensation in either case is "such compensation as it believes is just." It is not necessary in this case to show that there has been any default or negligence on the part of the prosecution or other agencies concerned with the order. The Act provides no right of appeal in connection with an order made under this section.

Enforcement abroad

74   **Enforcement abroad**

(1) This section applies if—
    (a) any of the conditions in section 40 is satisfied,
    (b) the prosecutor or the Director believes that realisable property is situated in a country or territory outside the United Kingdom (the receiving country), and
    (c) the prosecutor or the Director (as the case may be) sends a request for assistance to the Secretary of State with a view to it being forwarded under this section.

(2) In a case where no confiscation order has been made, a request for assistance is a request to the government of the receiving country to secure that any person is prohibited from dealing with realisable property.

(3) In a case where a confiscation order has been made and has not been satisfied, discharged or quashed, a request for assistance is a request to the government of the receiving country to secure that—
    (a) any person is prohibited from dealing with realisable property;
    (b) realisable property is realised and the proceeds are applied in accordance with the law of the receiving country.

(4) No request for assistance may be made for the purposes of this section in a case where a confiscation order has been made and has been satisfied, discharged or quashed.

(5) If the Secretary of State believes it is appropriate to do so he may forward the request for assistance to the government of the receiving country.

(6) If property is realised in pursuance of a request under subsection (3) the amount ordered to be paid under the confiscation order must be taken to be reduced by an amount equal to the proceeds of realisation.

(7) A certificate purporting to be issued by or on behalf of the requested government is admissible as evidence of the facts it states if it states—
    (a) that property has been realised in pursuance of a request under subsection (3),

(b) the date of realisation, and

(c) the proceeds of realisation.

(8) If the proceeds of realisation made in pursuance of a request under subsection (3) are expressed in a currency other than sterling, they must be taken to be the sterling equivalent calculated in accordance with the rate of exchange prevailing at the end of the day of realisation.

DEFINITIONS

"confiscation order": s. 88(6)

"property": s.84

"realisable property": s. 83

GENERAL NOTE

This section provides machinery designed to secure the enforcement in other jurisdictions of restraint orders made under s.40. The section applies if any of the conditions for making a restraint order under s.40 is satisfied (whether or not a restraint order has actually been made) and the prosecutor or the Director of the Assets Recovery Agency believes that realisable property is situated in a jurisdiction outside the United Kingdom.

In this situation, the prosecutor or Director may ask the Secretary of State to forward a request for assistance to the country concerned. If no confiscation order has yet been made, such a request is a request to the government of the overseas country to secure that any person is prohibited from dealing with a realisable property. If a confiscation order has been made and is still effective, a request is a request to secure that any person is prohibited from dealing with realisable property, and that the property is realised and the proceeds are applied in accordance with the law of the foreign jurisdiction. No request may be made where the confiscation order concerned has been satisfied, discharged or quashed.

The Secretary of State has a discretion whether or not to forward a request for assistance to the government of the country concerned. If property is realised in pursuance of a request under this section, the amount ordered to be paid under the confiscation order must be taken to be reduced by an amount equal to the proceeds of realisation, whether or not those proceeds are transmitted to the United Kingdom and applied directly to the satisfaction of the confiscation order. A certificate from the government of the overseas country is admissible as evidence of that the property has been realised, the date of realisation and the proceeds of realisation.

Interpretation

75   Criminal lifestyle

(1) A defendant has a criminal lifestyle if (and only if) the following condition is satisfied.

(2) The condition is that the offence (or any of the offences) concerned satisfies any of these tests—

(a) it is specified in Schedule 2;

(b) it constitutes conduct forming part of a course of criminal activity;

(c) it is an offence committed over a period of at least six months and the defendant has benefited from the conduct which constitutes the offence.

(3) Conduct forms part of a course of criminal activity if the defendant has benefited from the conduct and—

(a) in the proceedings in which he was convicted he was convicted of three or more other offences, each of three or more of them constituting conduct from which he has benefited, or

(b) in the period of six years ending with the day when those proceedings were started (or, if there is more than one such day, the earliest day) he was convicted on at least two separate occasions of an offence constituting conduct from which he has benefited.

(4) But an offence does not satisfy the test in subsection (2)(b) or (c) unless the defendant obtains relevant benefit of not less than £5000.

(5) Relevant benefit for the purposes of subsection (2)(b) is—

(a) benefit from conduct which constitutes the offence;

(b) benefit from any other conduct which forms part of the course of criminal activity and which constitutes an offence of which the defendant has been convicted;

(c) benefit from conduct which constitutes an offence which has been or will be taken into consideration by the court in sentencing the defendant for an offence mentioned in paragraph (a) or (b).

(6) Relevant benefit for the purposes of subsection (2)(c) is—

(a) benefit from conduct which constitutes the offence;

(b) benefit from conduct which constitutes an offence which has been or will be taken into consideration by the court in sentencing the defendant for the offence mentioned in paragraph (a).

(7) The Secretary of State may by order amend Schedule 2.

(8) The Secretary of State may by order vary the amount for the time being specified in subsection (4).

DEFINITIONS

"defendant": s. 88(3)

"started": s. 85

GENERAL NOTE

This section provides a definition of the concept of "criminal lifestyle" for the purposes of s.6(4). If the defendant is found to have a "criminal life style" the benefit which is to form the basis of the confiscation order is the benefit arising from his "general criminal conduct" rather than his "particular criminal conduct" , and the Crown Court in determining whether he has benefited and in deciding the amount of his benefit must make the assumptions set out in s.10.

The section provides three conditions, one of which must be satisfied before the defendant can be considered to have a "criminal lifestyle." The first condition is that he is convicted of one of the offences listed in Sched.2 of the Act. This schedule lists a considerable number of offences, including among others the most common offences under the Misuse of Drugs Act 1971 involving the production or supply of controlled drugs, corresponding offences under the Customs and Excise Management Act 1979 in relation to the importation or exportation of controlled drugs, money laundering offences under this Act (but not under the provisions of the earlier legislation), facilitating illegal entry contrary to the Immigration Act 1971, counterfeiting, certain offences involving infringement of copyrights, a number of offences relating to the control of prostitutes, and blackmail.

The second condition is that the offence or any of the offences of which the defendant is convicted "constitutes conduct forming part of a course of criminal activity." This term is elaborated in subs.(3). Conduct forms part of a course of criminal activity in two cases only.

The first limb of the definition of "course of criminal activity" is that the defendant has been convicted in the same proceedings of three or more offences in addition to be principal offence and each of the additional offences amounted to conduct from which he has benefited. To qualify under this definition, the defendant must have been convicted in the same proceedings of at least four offences from which he can be shown to have benefited, and the "relevant benefit" must be at least £5,000. In determining the "relevant benefit" arising out of a "course of criminal activity" where the defendant has been convicted of four or more offences on the same occasion, the court must take into account benefit arising from the conduct which constitutes the primary offence, benefit from any other offence which forms part of the course of criminal activity and which constitutes an offence of which the defendant has been convicted, and benefit from conduct which constitutes an offence which has been taken or will be taken into consideration by the court in sentencing the defendant for the principal offence or the additional offences.

An offence which is taken into consideration does not count as one of the additional three offences for the purpose of determining whether the defendant's conduct "forms part of a course of criminal activity" under subs.(3)(a), but the benefit arising from such offences can be taken into account in assessing the relevant benefit. In practice, this means that an indictment charging a defendant with offences in relation to which confiscation may be sought on the basis of a "course of criminal activity" (such as a persistent house burglar) should include at least four separate counts in the indictment, to satisfy the requirements of subs.(3)(a). Provided there are at least four counts in the indictment and that it can be shown that the defendant has benefited from each of those offences, benefit from any other offences taken into consideration can be considered for the purpose of determining the "relevant benefit".

The alternative limb of the definition of a "course of criminal activity" is that the defendant has been convicted on at least two separate occasions during the period of six years ending with a day when the proceedings for the present offence were started and that he has benefited from the offences in respect of which he was convicted on both of those occasions. The " relevant benefit" must amount to at least £5,000.

In determining the "relevant benefit" arising out of a "course of criminal activity" where the defendant has been convicted on two or more previous occasions, the court must take into account benefit arising from the conduct which constitutes the latest offence, benefit from any other offence which forms part of the course of criminal activity and which constitutes an offence of which the defendant has been convicted, (that is, the offences of which he was convicted on the two previous occasions and any other offences of which he was convicted during the relevant period) and benefit from conduct which constitutes an offence which has been taken or will be taken into consideration by the court in sentencing the defendant for the latest offence or any of the earlier offences.

The third condition for establishing "criminal lifestyle" is that the offence has been committed over a period of at least six months, that the defendant has benefited from the conduct which constitutes the offence, and that the amount of this benefit is not less than £5,000. This condition would be satisfied in the case of the defendant convicted of conspiring to defraud over a period of at least six months, provided the benefit reached the appropriate level. Where this condition is satisfied, the "relevant benefit" is the benefit arising from the conduct which constitutes the continuing offence, and the benefit from any other conduct which constitutes an offence which has been or will be taken into consideration in sentencing defendant for the principal offence.

76   Conduct and benefit

(1) Criminal conduct is conduct which—
  (a) constitutes an offence in England and Wales, or
  (b) would constitute such an offence if it occurred in England and Wales.
(2) General criminal conduct of the defendant is all his criminal conduct, and it is immaterial—
  (a) whether conduct occurred before or after the passing of this Act;
  (b) whether property constituting a benefit from conduct was obtained before or after the passing of this Act.
(3) Particular criminal conduct of the defendant is all his criminal conduct which falls within the following paragraphs—
  (a) conduct which constitutes the offence or offences concerned;
  (b) conduct which constitutes offences of which he was convicted in the same proceedings as those in which he was convicted of the offence or offences concerned;
  (c) conduct which constitutes offences which the court will be taking into consideration in deciding his sentence for the offence or offences concerned.
(4) A person benefits from conduct if he obtains property as a result of or in connection with the conduct.
(5) If a person obtains a pecuniary advantage as a result of or in connection with conduct, he is to be taken to obtain as a result of or in connection with the conduct a sum of money equal to the value of the pecuniary advantage.
(6) References to property or a pecuniary advantage obtained in connection with conduct include references to property or a pecuniary advantage obtained both in that connection and some other.
(7) If a person benefits from conduct his benefit is the value of the property obtained.

DEFINITIONS
  "defendant": s. 88(3)
  "offence or offences concerned": s. 88(1) and 6(9)
  "property": s.84

GENERAL NOTE
  This section provides definitions of the expressions "criminal conduct", "general criminal conduct", "particular criminal conduct" and "benefits." "Criminal conduct" is any conduct which constitutes an offence in England and Wales, or would constitute such an offence if it occurred in England and Wales. "General criminal conduct" is all of the defendant's criminal

conduct whether it occurred before or after the passing of the Act, or whether the property constituting the benefit from the conduct concerned was obtained before after the passing of the Act. One important aspect of this definition is that a court assessing the benefit derived in a "criminal lifestyle" case from the defendant's "general criminal conduct" must take into account all of the criminal conduct of the defendant wherever it took place, whether in England and Wales or elsewhere. In a "criminal lifestyle" case, the court is entitled to include in the assessment of benefit the benefit arising from offences committed abroad.

The definition of " particular criminal conduct" includes the conduct which constitutes the offence or offences of which the defendant has been convicted, the conduct which constitutes the offences of which he was convicted in the same proceedings, and conduct which constitutes offences which will be taken into consideration in deciding the sentence for those offences. This definition clearly excludes conduct constituting offences which are represented by sample or specimen counts, but which are not specifically taken into consideration in sentencing and the defendant.

The definition of "benefits" effectively restates the definition of "benefits" in the Criminal Justice Act 1988, s.71(4) and (5), with minor differences in the language. It is unfortunate that the expression "pecuniary advantage" was retained in this definition, in view of the difficulties to which the expression has given rise in cases arising under the earlier legislation (see in particular *Dimsey and Allan* [2000] 1 Cr.App.R.(S.) 497 and *Smith* [2002] 2 Cr.App.R.(S.) 37 (at 144)).

Subsection (6) restates the enigmatic provision of the Criminal Justice Act 1988, s.102 (5) and the Drug Trafficking Act 1994, s.63(2). The meaning of the expression "both in that connection and some other" in the context of the 1988 Act was considered by the Court of Appeal in *Attorney General's Reference No. 25 of 2001 (Frank Adam Moran)* [2002] 1 Cr.App.R.(S.) 95 (at 413), where the Court had to "confess to having some difficulty with that subsection."

77   Tainted gifts

(1) Subsections (2) and (3) apply if—
    (a) no court has made a decision as to whether the defendant has a criminal lifestyle, or
    (b) a court has decided that the defendant has a criminal lifestyle.

(2) A gift is tainted if it was made by the defendant at any time after the relevant day.

(3) A gift is also tainted if it was made by the defendant at any time and was of property—
    (a) which was obtained by the defendant as a result of or in connection with his general criminal conduct, or
    (b) which (in whole or part and whether directly or indirectly) represented in the defendant's hands property obtained by him as a result of or in connection with his general criminal conduct.

(4) Subsection (5) applies if a court has decided that the defendant does not have a criminal lifestyle.

(5) A gift is tainted if it was made by the defendant at any time after—
    (a) the date on which the offence concerned was committed, or
    (b) if his particular criminal conduct consists of two or more offences and they were committed on different dates, the date of the earliest.

(6) For the purposes of subsection (5) an offence which is a continuing offence is committed on the first occasion when it is committed.

(7) For the purposes of subsection (5) the defendant's particular criminal conduct includes any conduct which constitutes offences which the court has taken into consideration in deciding his sentence for the offence or offences concerned.

(8) A gift may be a tainted gift whether it was made before or after the passing of this Act.

(9) The relevant day is the first day of the period of six years ending with—
    (a) the day when proceedings for the offence concerned were started against the defendant, or
    (b) if there are two or more offences and proceedings for them were started on different days, the earliest of those days.

DEFINITIONS
"defendant": s. 88(3)
"offence or offences concerned": s. 88(1) and 6(9)
"property": s.84
"started": s. 85

GENERAL NOTE
This section provides a definition of the expression "tainted gift" which is relevant to determining the "available amount" in accordance with s.9, for the purpose of determining the "recoverable amount" under s.7 . What amounts to a "tainted gift" depends on whether and the court is proceeding on the basis that the defendant has a "criminal lifestyle" or not.

If the court has decided that the defendant has a "criminal lifestyle," or if no decision on the matter has yet been made, a gift is "tainted" if it was made by the defendant at any time within the period of six years ending on the day when the proceedings for the offence concerned were started. If the gift was made outside that period, it is "tainted" if it was a gift of property which was obtained by the defendant "as a result of or in connection with" his "general criminal conduct" or directly or indirectly represented in his hands property of obtained by him as a result of or in connection with his general criminal conduct.

If a court is not proceeding under the "criminal lifestyle" provisions, a gift is "tainted" if it was made by the defendant at any time after the date on which the offence (or the earliest of the offences) which constitutes his "particular criminal conduct" was committed. If the offence was a continuing offence, the offence is treated as having been committed on the first occasion when it was committed. Offences which are taken into consideration for the purpose of sentence are relevant for this purpose (subs.(7)). If any offences taken into consideration were committed on dates earlier than the date of the offence of which the defendant has been convicted, the relevant date for determining whether a gift is a "tainted" is the date on which the first of the offences taken into consideration was committed.

78   Gifts and their recipients

(1) If the defendant transfers property to another person for a consideration whose value is significantly less than the value of the property at the time of the transfer, he is to be treated as making a gift.

(2) If subsection (1) applies the property given is to be treated as such share in the property transferred as is represented by the fraction—

    (a) whose numerator is the difference between the two values mentioned in subsection (1), and

    (b) whose denominator is the value of the property at the time of the transfer.

(3) References to a recipient of a tainted gift are to a person to whom the defendant has made the gift.

DEFINITIONS
"defendant": s. 88(3)
"property": s.84

GENERAL NOTE
The effect of this provision is to extend the definition of "gift" beyond a simple gift for which no consideration is provided to include any transfer of property for a consideration of significantly less value than the value of the property transferred at the time of the transfer. Where there is a transfer of property for a consideration of less value than the value of the property, the "gift" is that share of the property determined in accordance with the formula in subs.(2). Some will prefer the language of the earlier legislation (the Drug Trafficking Act 1994, s.8(2)(b), which provided in such a case that the defendant should be treated as if he had "made a gift of such a share in the property as bears to the whole property the same proportion as the difference between the values referred to in para.(a) above bears to the value of the consideration provided by the defendant."

To apply the formula in subs.(2), the court should subtract value of the consideration from the value of the property at the time of the transfer, and divide the figure produced by the subtraction by value of the property at the time of the transfer, expressing the division as a fraction. The fraction should then be multiplied by the value of the property at the time of the transfer to produce the value of the gift at the time of the transfer. If the defendant has transferred a house then worth £100,000 for a consideration of £25,000, subtracting the consideration from the value produces a figure of £75,000; expressing the division of this figure by the value of the house produces the fraction 3/4, which represents the portion of the house which is treated as a gift. Multiplying the value of the house by this fraction results in the conclusion that the value of the gift at the time it was made was £75,000. This figure must then be adjusted in accordance with s.81 to determine the value to be attributed to the gift for the purposes of determining the "available amount". Alternatively, under s.81(2) the Court may take 3/4 of the value of the house at the time the confiscation order is made for that purpose.

79   Value: the basic rule

(1) This section applies for the purpose of deciding the value at any time of property then held by a person.

(2) Its value is the market value of the property at that time.

(3) But if at that time another person holds an interest in the property its value, in relation to the person mentioned in subsection (1), is the market value of his interest at that time, ignoring any charging order under a provision listed in subsection (4).

(4) The provisions are—
 (a) section 9 of the Drug Trafficking Offences Act 1986 (c. 32);
 (b) section 78 of the Criminal Justice Act 1988 (c. 33);
 (c) Article 14 of the Criminal Justice (Confiscation) (Northern Ireland) Order 1990 (S.I. 1990/2588 (N.I. 17));
 (d) section 27 of the Drug Trafficking Act 1994 (c. 37);
 (e) Article 32 of the Proceeds of Crime (Northern Ireland) Order 1996 (S.I. 1996/1299 (N.I. 9)).

(5) This section has effect subject to sections 80 and 81.

DEFINITIONS
  "property": s.84

GENERAL NOTE
  This section provides a basic rule for the determination of the value of property held by any person. The value of the property is its market value at the time in question, less the market value of any interest held by another person in the property at that time. The effect of any charging order made under the provisions of the earlier confiscation legislation listed in subs.(4) is disregarded.

80   Value of property obtained from conduct

(1) This section applies for the purpose of deciding the value of property obtained by a person as a result of or in connection with his criminal conduct; and the material time is the time the court makes its decision.

(2) The value of the property at the material time is the greater of the following—
 (a) the value of the property (at the time the person obtained it) adjusted to take account of later changes in the value of money;
 (b) the value (at the material time) of the property found under subsection (3).

(3) The property found under this subsection is as follows—
 (a) if the person holds the property obtained, the property found under this subsection is that property;
 (b) if he holds no part of the property obtained, the property found under this subsection is any property which directly or indirectly represents it in his hands;
 (c) if he holds part of the property obtained, the property found under this subsection is that part and any property which directly or indirectly represents the other part in his hands.

(4) The references in subsection (2)(a) and (b) to the value are to the value found in accordance with section 79.

DEFINITIONS
"property": s.84

GENERAL NOTE

This section applies where the Crown Court is required to determine the value of property obtained by a person as a result of or in connection with his criminal conduct. It will be relevant principally to the case where a court is required to make an assumption under s.10 of the Act in a "criminal lifestyle" case. It will also be relevant to the determination of the defendant's benefit from "particular criminal conduct" in a case where the criminal lifestyle provisions do not apply, but the offence concerned was committed at a significantly earlier date.

In such a case, there are two methods of calculating the figure, and the Crown Court must adopt the method which will produce the larger amount. One method is to determine the value of the property at the time the person obtained it, and adjust that figure to take account of later changes in the value of money. The alternative procedure applies only where the person concerned still holds the property obtained or holds other property which directly or indirectly represents the original property in his hands. In this case, the value of the property is the value at the material time, normally when the confiscation order is made.

If the defendant has received cash as a result of or in connection with his criminal conduct, the normal procedure will be to take the value of the received cash as the basis of the determination of the value and make any adjustment which is appropriate to take account of later changes in the value of money. If the defendant has received shares as a result of or in connection with his criminal conduct, it is open to the court to value the shares at the time they were obtained, adjust that figure to take account of later changes in the value of money and adopt that as the value of the property obtained. In such a case, the value of the property may be taken to have increased, notwithstanding that the defendant still holds the shares so obtained and that they have lost value in the intervening period.

If a defendant has obtained real property, such as a house, as a result of or in connection with criminal conduct, and still holds that property, the value of the property is the value of the house at the time the confiscation order is made, notwithstanding that this figure represents a large increase over the value of the house at the time it was obtained, and that the figure represents a greater increase than would be produced by adjusting the original value of the property to take account of changes in the value of money during the intervening period. The same would apply where the original house has been sold and the proceeds applied to the purchase of another house.

There is some uncertainty where the defendant obtains cash as a result of or in connection with his criminal conduct, and uses the cash to purchase property in one form or another, and the value of the property so purchased increases to a figure which is greater than the figure which would be calculated by adjusting the value of the cash obtained to allow for subsequent changes in the value of money. It is submitted that in this case the proper procedure is for the court to take the value of the money obtained and adjust it to take account of later changes in the value of money, rather than take the value of the property according to the valuation current at the time of the confiscation order. The property itself has not been obtained "as a result of or in connection with" the defendant's criminal conduct. The contrary argument is that in such a case, if it can be shown that the property concerned "directly or indirectly represents" the money a originally obtained as a result of criminal conduct, the current value of the property may be taken by virtue of subs.(3)(d). For this reasoning to apply, it would be necessary to show that the money originally obtained was used to purchase the property, and that the property was not purchased from the defendant's general pool of funds, to which the money obtained by criminal conduct was added.

81   Value of tainted gifts

(1) The value at any time (the material time) of a tainted gift is the greater of the following—

    (a) the value (at the time of the gift) of the property given, adjusted to take account of later changes in the value of money;

    (b) the value (at the material time) of the property found under subsection (2).

(2) The property found under this subsection is as follows—

    (a) if the recipient holds the property given, the property found under this subsection is that property;

    (b) if the recipient holds no part of the property given, the property found under this subsection is any property which directly or indirectly represents it in his hands;

    (c) if the recipient holds part of the property given, the property found under this subsection is that part and any property which directly or indirectly represents the other part in his hands.

  (3) The references in subsection (1)(a) and (b) to the value are to the value found in accordance with section 79.

<small>DEFINITIONS</small>
  "property": s.84

<small>GENERAL NOTE</small>
  The section makes provision for determining the value of a "tainted gift" as defined in s.77. The section substantially repeats the provisions of s.80 with minor modifications. The value of the tainted gift may be determined by taking the value of the property at the time it was given and adjusting that figure to take account of later changes in the value of money. Alternatively, if the recipient of the tainted gift still holds the property, the court may take the current value of the property as the value of the tainted gift. If the recipient holds property which directly or indirectly represents the original tainted gift in his hands, the court make take the current value of that property as the value of the tainted gift. The court is obliged to adopt whichever formula produces the greater figure.

82   Free property

Property is free unless an order is in force in respect of it under any of these provisions—

    (a) section 27 of the Misuse of Drugs Act 1971 (c. 38) (forfeiture orders);

    (b) Article 11 of the Criminal Justice (Northern Ireland) Order 1994 (S.I. 1994/2795 (N.I. 15)) (deprivation orders);

    (c) Part 2 of the Proceeds of Crime (Scotland) Act 1995 (c. 43) (forfeiture of property used in crime);

    (d) section 143 of the Sentencing Act (deprivation orders);

    (e) section 23 or 111 of the Terrorism Act 2000 (c. 11) (forfeiture orders);

    (f) section 246, 266, 295(2) or 298(2) of this Act.

<small>DEFINITIONS</small>
  "property": s.84
  "Sentencing Act": s. 88(5)

<small>GENERAL NOTE</small>
  This section provides a definition of "free property," which is relevant primarily for the purpose of determining the "available amount" under s.9. All property is free unless it is subject to one of the orders mentioned the section. The value of free property is determined in accordance with s.79, and if any other person holds an interest in the property, the value of that interest must be deducted from the value of the property concerned to the defendant.

83   Realisable property

Realisable property is—

    (a) any free property held by the defendant;

    (b) any free property held by the recipient of a tainted gift.

<small>DEFINITIONS</small>
  "defendant": s. 88(3)
  "free property": s. 82
  "property": s.84

<small>GENERAL NOTE</small>
  This section provides a definition of "realisable property." "Realisable property" is any "free property" (as defined in s.82) held by the defendant and any "free property" held by the

recipient of a "tainted gift". Free property held by either the defendant or the recipient of a tainted gift may be realisable whether or not it has any connection with the offence or the tainted gift. If a person has obtained cash as a result of or in connection with a crime, spent that cash and then has received further cash lawfully, for example as compensation for a personal injury, the cash so received is "realisable property". Similarly, if the person has received cash as a tainted gift and spent it, but subsequently receives property lawfully by way of a legacy, the property received by way of the legacy is "realisable property" in the hands of that person.

84   Property: general provisions

(1) Property is all property wherever situated and includes—
   (a) money;
   (b) all forms of real or personal property;
   (c) things in action and other intangible or incorporeal property.
(2) The following rules apply in relation to property—
   (a) property is held by a person if he holds an interest in it;
   (b) property is obtained by a person if he obtains an interest in it;
   (c) property is transferred by one person to another if the first one transfers or grants an interest in it to the second;
   (d) references to property held by a person include references to property vested in his trustee in bankruptcy, permanent or interim trustee (within the meaning of the Bankruptcy (Scotland) Act 1985 (c. 66)) or liquidator;
   (e) references to an interest held by a person beneficially in property include references to an interest which would be held by him beneficially if the property were not so vested;
   (f) references to an interest, in relation to land in England and Wales or Northern Ireland, are to any legal estate or equitable interest or power;
   (g) references to an interest, in relation to land in Scotland, are to any estate, interest, servitude or other heritable right in or over land, including a heritable security;
   (h) references to an interest, in relation to property other than land, include references to a right (including a right to possession).

GENERAL NOTE
   This section provides a general definition of property for the purposes of the Act.

85   Proceedings

(1) Proceedings for an offence are started—
   (a) when a justice of the peace issues a summons or warrant under section 1 of the Magistrates' Courts Act 1980 (c. 43) in respect of the offence;
   (b) when a person is charged with the offence after being taken into custody without a warrant;
   (c) when a bill of indictment is preferred under section 2 of the Administration of Justice (Miscellaneous Provisions) Act 1933 (c. 36) in a case falling within subsection (2)(b) of that section (preferment by Court of Appeal or High Court judge).
(2) If more than one time is found under subsection (1) in relation to proceedings they are started at the earliest of them.
(3) If the defendant is acquitted on all counts in proceedings for an offence, the proceedings are concluded when he is acquitted.
(4) If the defendant is convicted in proceedings for an offence and the conviction is quashed or the defendant is pardoned before a confiscation order is made, the proceedings are concluded when the conviction is quashed or the defendant is pardoned.

(5) If a confiscation order is made against the defendant in proceedings for an offence (whether the order is made by the Crown Court or the Court of Appeal) the proceedings are concluded—
  (a) when the order is satisfied or discharged, or
  (b) when the order is quashed and there is no further possibility of an appeal against the decision to quash the order.
(6) If the defendant is convicted in proceedings for an offence but the Crown Court decides not to make a confiscation order against him, the following rules apply—
  (a) if an application for leave to appeal under section 31(2) is refused, the proceedings are concluded when the decision to refuse is made;
  (b) if the time for applying for leave to appeal under section 31(2) expires without an application being made, the proceedings are concluded when the time expires;
  (c) if on appeal under section 31(2) the Court of Appeal confirms the Crown Court's decision, and an application for leave to appeal under section 33 is refused, the proceedings are concluded when the decision to refuse is made;
  (d) if on appeal under section 31(2) the Court of Appeal confirms the Crown Court's decision, and the time for applying for leave to appeal under section 33 expires without an application being made, the proceedings are concluded when the time expires;
  (e) if on appeal under section 31(2) the Court of Appeal confirms the Crown Court's decision, and on appeal under section 33 the House of Lords confirms the Court of Appeal's decision, the proceedings are concluded when the House of Lords confirms the decision;
  (f) if on appeal under section 31(2) the Court of Appeal directs the Crown Court to reconsider the case, and on reconsideration the Crown Court decides not to make a confiscation order against the defendant, the proceedings are concluded when the Crown Court makes that decision;
  (g) if on appeal under section 33 the House of Lords directs the Crown Court to reconsider the case, and on reconsideration the Crown Court decides not to make a confiscation order against the defendant, the proceedings are concluded when the Crown Court makes that decision.
(7) In applying subsection (6) any power to extend the time for making an application for leave to appeal must be ignored.
(8) In applying subsection (6) the fact that a court may decide on a later occasion to make a confiscation order against the defendant must be ignored.

DEFINITIONS
  "confiscation order": s. 88(6)
  "defendant": s. 88(3)

GENERAL NOTE
  This section provides definitions of the time at which proceedings for an offence or started and the time at which proceedings are concluded.
  Determining the time at which proceedings are started is relevant particularly to the application of the required assumptions under s.10, some of which relate to transactions taking place within the period of six years ending on the day when proceedings for the offence concerned were started.
  Determining the date on which proceedings are concluded is important in relation to various powers to discharge restraint orders, in particular under s.63, and the power to make a confiscation order against an absconder under s.28.

86   Applications

(1) An application under section 19, 20, 27 or 28 is concluded—

(a) in a case where the court decides not to make a confiscation order against the defendant, when it makes the decision;

(b) in a case where a confiscation order is made against him as a result of the application, when the order is satisfied or discharged, or when the order is quashed and there is no further possibility of an appeal against the decision to quash the order;

(c) in a case where the application is withdrawn, when the person who made the application notifies the withdrawal to the court to which the application was made.

(2) An application under section 21 or 22 is concluded—

(a) in a case where the court decides not to vary the confiscation order concerned, when it makes the decision;

(b) in a case where the court varies the confiscation order as a result of the application, when the order is satisfied or discharged, or when the order is quashed and there is no further possibility of an appeal against the decision to quash the order;

(c) in a case where the application is withdrawn, when the person who made the application notifies the withdrawal to the court to which the application was made.

DEFINITIONS
"confiscation order": s. 88(6)
"defendant": s. 88(3)

GENERAL NOTE
This section provides definitions of the time at which an application under ss.19 (reconsideration of the decision to consider confiscation), 20 (reconsideration of the amount of benefit), 27(defendant absconding after conviction) or 28 (defendant absconding after the proceedings have started and before the proceedings have been concluded) may be made. The definition is significant for the purposes of the making restraint orders in connection with such applications (s.40(4)) and 40(5)) and the discharge and variation of such restraint orders under s.63(3)(a).

87   Confiscation orders

(1) A confiscation order is satisfied when no amount is due under it.

(2) A confiscation order is subject to appeal until there is no further possibility of an appeal on which the order could be varied or quashed; and for this purpose any power to grant leave to appeal out of time must be ignored.

DEFINITIONS
"confiscation order": s. 88(6)

GENERAL NOTE
This section provides definitions of the point at which a confiscation order is "satisfied" and when a confiscation order is "subject to appeal".
The definition of "satisfied" is important for the purposes of ss.37, 50, 52, 74 and 85.
The definition of "subject to appeal" is important for the purposes of ss.37, 50 and 52.

88   Other interpretative provisions

(1) A reference to the offence (or offences) concerned must be construed in accordance with section 6(9).

(2) A criminal investigation is an investigation which police officers or other persons have a duty to conduct with a view to it being ascertained whether a person should be charged with an offence.

(3) A defendant is a person against whom proceedings for an offence have been started (whether or not he has been convicted).

(4) A reference to sentencing the defendant for an offence includes a reference to dealing with him otherwise in respect of the offence.

(5) The Sentencing Act is the Powers of Criminal Courts (Sentencing) Act 2000 (c. 6).

(6) The following paragraphs apply to references to orders—

   (a) a confiscation order is an order under section 6;

   (b) a restraint order is an order under section 41.

(7) Sections 75 to 87 and this section apply for the purposes of this Part.

DEFINITIONS
  "started": s. 85

General

89   Procedure on appeal to the Court of Appeal

(1) An appeal to the Court of Appeal under this Part lies only with the leave of that Court.

(2) Subject to rules of court made under section 53(1) of the Supreme Court Act 1981 (c. 54) (distribution of business between civil and criminal divisions) the criminal division of the Court of Appeal is the division—

   (a) to which an appeal to that Court under this Part is to lie, and

   (b) which is to exercise that Court's jurisdiction under this Part.

(3) In relation to appeals to the Court of Appeal under this Part, the Secretary of State may make an order containing provision corresponding to any provision in the Criminal Appeal Act 1968 (c. 19) (subject to any specified modifications).

GENERAL NOTE
  This section provides for appeals to the Court of Appeal under Part II of the Act. The appeals to which the section applies are those under ss.31 (appeal by prosecutor or Director against refusal of Crown Court to make confiscation order, or against amount of confiscation order), 43 (refusal to make restraint order) and 65 (appeal against decision of Crown Court relating to restraint orders). The effect of this section is that any appeal under these sections lies only with leave of the Court of Appeal, and that in general any such appeal lies to the Court of Appeal Criminal Division.

  The Secretary of State is empowered to make orders containing provisions corresponding to those in the Criminal Appeal Act 1968, subject to specified modifications.

90   Procedure on appeal to the House of Lords

(1) Section 33(3) of the Criminal Appeal Act 1968 (limitation on appeal from criminal division of the Court of Appeal) does not prevent an appeal to the House of Lords under this Part.

(2) In relation to appeals to the House of Lords under this Part, the Secretary of State may make an order containing provision corresponding to any provision in the Criminal Appeal Act 1968 (subject to any specified modifications).

GENERAL NOTE
  This section applies to appeals from the Court of Appeal, Criminal Division to the House of Lords under ss.33 (appeal by prosecutor or Director against a refusal of the Crown Court to make a confiscation order, or against the amount of a confiscation order, or an) 44 (refusal to make restraint order, or an appeal by a defendant against the decision of the Court of Appeal, Criminal Division on such an appeal) and 66 (appeal against order relating to restraint orders). The express exclusion of the Criminal Appeal Act 1968, s.33(3) from such appeals means that it is not necessary for an intending appellant to the House of Lords to secure a certificate that a point of law of general public importance is involved in the decision of the Court of Appeal, Criminal Division, which ought to be considered by the House of Lords, or the leave of the Court of Appeal or the House of Lords.

  The Secretary of State is empowered by subs.(2) to introduce such restrictions by order.

91   **Crown Court Rules**

In relation to—
(a) proceedings under this Part, or
(b) receivers appointed under this Part,
Crown Court Rules may make provision corresponding to provision
in Civil Procedure Rules.

PART 3

CONFISCATION: SCOTLAND

INTRODUCTION TO PART 3

So far as Scots law is concerned, this Act recasts and, to some extent, consolidates the law on proceeds of crime and will substantially replace the Proceeds of Crime (Scotland) Act 1995 and existing money laundering legislation. The UK Government has justified the recasting of the law by identifying at least 5 "deficiencies" in the existing legal regime (See the Second Reading speech of the Minister for Police, Courts and Drugs (Mr John Denham), *Hansard,* H.C., October 30, 2001, col.759), viz:

- The separate treatment of drug trafficking and other criminal activity makes the legislation ineffective when (as often) it is impossible to distinguish between the proceeds of drug trafficking and those of other criminal activities;
- The investigative powers were inadequate to trace assets;
- Restraint orders were not available at an early enough stage to permit assets to be "frozen" in time;
- The confiscation system was unduly complex; and
- Confiscation orders were poorly enforced.

The explanation which the Government gave of these deficiencies proceeded entirely on the basis of English law and there is room for argument about how far they applied to Scotland. In Scotland, where orders have been made under reference to assessments of the value of clearly identified and restrained property, recovery has been very much higher as a percentage of the value of orders made than has been the case elsewhere in the UK. Again, restraint has been available rather earlier in Scotland than in England. However, other deficiencies (such as the problems associated with treating drug proceeds and other proceeds separately) undeniably did apply to existing Scots law.

The reasons why the Scottish Executive was content to allow the matter to be dealt with in Westminster were explained by the Minister for Justice in the Sewell Motion debate as follows (*Scottish Parliament Official Report,* October 24, 2001, Col. 3250): "Legislation dealing with drug trafficking, money laundering and taxation is reserved, while other criminal and civil matters are within the legislative competence of this Parliament. A key principle of the bill is to put drug trafficking and other crimes on to an all-crimes basis. The principle applies to confiscation, civil recovery, money laundering and other provisions in the bill. It is the Executive's view that to attempt to legislate at Westminster for the reserved matters in the bill and at the same time to legislate in the Scottish Parliament for devolved matters would be highly complex and might lead to loopholes and inconsistencies between the two systems. Comprehensive UK legislation will therefore prove more effective and avoid the risk of inadvertent safe havens on either side of the border".

In general, it may be said that the attack on the financial aspects of crime has two aspects. First, substantial efforts are directed to identifying the proceeds of crime as the criminal attempts to launder them through the financial system and making that system an unfriendly environment for the criminal; and secondly, since it would be unrealistic to think that it would be possible to stop all proceeds from getting into the system, it is necessary to overcome commercial or legal confidentiality in order to trace the funds, to provide a restraint mechanism under which the property of the suspect can be frozen; and to provide a mechanism for confiscating the proceeds of a suspect who has been convicted of a proceeds-generating crime. As regards Scotland, the Act sets out to advance that strategy by

- Re-wording and re-enacting the Money Laundering offences;
- Extending and re-enacting the powers of investigation;
- Revising and re-enacting the Restraint Order mechanism;
- Providing for 4 distinct ways of taking the benefit out of crime, 2 of which are, at least in theory, new:
  - Seizure of cash;
  - Criminal confiscation;
  - Civil confiscation;
  - Taxation.

Part 3 of the Act, with which we are about to deal, addresses confiscation and restraint. In annotating this Part, and indeed in annotating the other parts of the Act which apply to Scotland, use is made of the Explanatory Notes prepared by the Home Office. At the time of writing (shortly after Royal Assent), the most up-to-date version of those Explanatory Notes referred to the Bill as it entered the House of Lords on February 28, 2002.

Confiscation orders

92　　Making of order

(1)　The court must act under this section where the following three conditions are satisfied.

(2)　The first condition is that an accused falls within either of the following paragraphs—

   (a)　he is convicted of an offence or offences, whether in solemn or summary proceedings, or

   (b)　in the case of summary proceedings in respect of an offence (without proceeding to conviction) an order is made discharging him absolutely.

(3)　The second condition is that the prosecutor asks the court to act under this section.

(4)　The third condition is that the court decides to order some disposal in respect of the accused; and an absolute discharge is a disposal for the purpose of this subsection.

(5)　If the court acts under this section it must proceed as follows—

   (a)　it must decide whether the accused has a criminal lifestyle;

   (b)　if it decides that he has a criminal lifestyle it must decide whether he has benefited from his general criminal conduct;

   (c)　if it decides that he does not have a criminal lifestyle it must decide whether he has benefited from his particular criminal conduct.

(6)　If the court decides under subsection (5)(b) or (c) that the accused has benefited from the conduct referred to—

   (a)　it must decide the recoverable amount, and

   (b)　it must make an order (a confiscation order) requiring him to pay that amount.

(7)　But the court must treat the duty in subsection (6) as a power if it believes that any victim of the conduct has at any time started or intends to start proceedings against the accused in respect of loss, injury or damage sustained in connection with the conduct.

(8)　Before making an order under this section the court must take into account any representations made to it by any person whom the court thinks is likely to be affected by the order.

(9)　The standard of proof required to decide any question arising under subsection (5) or (6) is the balance of probabilities.

(10)　The first condition is not satisfied if the accused is unlawfully at large (but section 111 may apply).

(11)　For the purposes of any appeal or review, an order under this section is a sentence.

(12)　References in this Part to the offence (or offences) concerned are to the offence (or offences) mentioned in subsection (2).

(13)　In this section and sections 93 to 118 "the court" means the High Court of Justiciary or the sheriff.

DEFINITIONS
  "court": s.92(13)
  "criminal lifestyle": s.142
  "general criminal conduct": s.143(2)
  "particular criminal conduct": s.143(3)
  "recoverable amount": s.93(1)

GENERAL NOTE

Section 92 sets out the basic confiscation order mechanism for Scotland and the rest of Part 3 may be seen as elaborating what is provided for in this section. Some have argued from time to time that confiscation is an unreasonable response which somehow breaches civil liberties (see the summary of opposition to the policy given by Ethan A Nadelmann, *Unlaundering Dirty Money Abroad: US Foreign Policy and Financial Secrecy Jurisdictions,* 18 Inter American Law Review 33, 38 (1986). For substantive criticism, see: B Fisse and D Fraser, *Some Antipodean Scepticisms about Forfeiture, Confiscation of Proceeds of Crime and Money Laundering Offences* ,44 Alabama Law Review 737 (1993); C Sallon and D Bedingfield, *Drugs, Money and the Law* (1993) Crim LR 165; Eric L Jensen and Jurg Gerber, *The Civil Forfeiture of Assets and the War on Drugs: Expanding Criminal Sanctions While Reducing Due Process Protections* 42 Crime and Delinquency 421 (1996)). That being so, it is worth noting the approach of the European Court of Human Rights in *Raimondo v. Italy* (1994) 18 EHRR 237, in which it was made clear that the Strasbourg Court was and is supportive of confiscation as a means of dealing with crime which generates proceeds. This is hardly surprising. ECHR is a Council of Europe Treaty and the Court is an organ of the Council of Europe. The Council of Europe has also been the forum in which the Convention on Laundering, Search, Seizure and Confiscation of the Proceeds from Crime 1990 was agreed and in which other important work on the subject has been carried on. The Convention sought to have confiscation applied to a wide range of predicate offences (that is, offences from which benefit is derived) and it is hardly likely that the European Court of Human Rights would undermine that intention. If nothing else, the agreement of the Convention represents a clear indication of the intention of the member States of the Council of Europe, all of which are Party to ECHR.

Paragraph 154 of the Explanatory Notes states that s.92 "makes it clear that the Bill contains two different confiscation regimes, only one of which may be applied in any particular case. One enables the confiscation of an accused's benefit from "general criminal conduct", the other the confiscation of an accused's benefit from "particular criminal conduct". General criminal conduct means any criminal conduct of the accused whenever the criminal conduct occurred .... Particular criminal conduct means the offences of which the accused has been convicted in the current proceedings to which the confiscation proceedings relate ... General criminal conduct includes particular criminal conduct."

Subs. (1)

The court must act. This mandatory approach applies the English law model to Scotland and contrasts with the discretionary approach set out in s.1 of the Proceeds of Crime (Scotland) Act 1995 ("the Scottish 1995 Act"). The change followed pressure from Government back-benchers in the House of Commons which seems to have overlooked what the commentator on *R v. Bragason* (1988) Crim LR 778 called "...the absurdity of making the Act mandatory in every case where the offender is convicted of a drug trafficking offence, even where it is obvious from the start that the offender has no realisable assets". However, as a result of subs.(3), and by contrast with the position elsewhere in the UK (see ss.6(3) and 158(3)), the Scottish court cannot act under this section unless the prosecutor asks it to do so.

Where the following three conditions are satisfied. For the conditions, see subss.(2), (3) and (4).

Subs. (2)

He is convicted of an offence or offences. The Scottish 1995 Act's restriction of the confiscation mechanism to offences prosecuted under solemn procedure and to summary offences carrying a potential penalty in excess of level 5 is abandoned. Confiscation is now available for *all* offences prosecuted in either the High Court or the sheriff court.

Subs. (3)

The Scottish Law Commission reported on proceeds of crime in their *Report on Confiscation and Forfeiture* (SLC Report No 147) and took the view that the initiative should lie with the prosecutor and that to give the court a discretion to consider confiscation *ex proprio motu* (as s.6(3) gives the English courts) would be to oblige the court to consider the matter pointlessly. They went on to say "(i)t is to be expected that a Scottish public prosecutor, who is required to act in the public interest and subject to the supervision of the Lord Advocate, would exercise his discretion only after careful consideration of all the relevant circumstances" (SLC Report para 6.3). Although the Report led to the Scottish 1995 Act, which is replaced by the present Act, the analysis it contains remains useful in a number of respects.

Subs. (5)

This subsection and the next are the procedural heart of the scheme of the Act as regards Scotland. Between them, they set out a step-by-step approach which the court must follow. The steps are as follows:

1. The court must consider whether the accused has a criminal lifestyle. That concept is elaborated in s.142, to which reference should be made. In brief, it arises if the offence

- is a money laundering offence
- is a drug trafficking offence
- is an offence involving trafficking in people or arms
- is an offence of directing terrorism
- is an offence of counterfeiting or against intellectual property
- is an offence of living on the earnings of prostitution or running a brothel; or
- is an offence of blackmail or extortion.

By s.142(3), the Scottish Ministers may amend this list. However, the accused also has a criminal lifestyle, by s.142, if the offence

- is part of a course of criminal activity (broadly speaking, he has been convicted of 3 or more offences in the one set of proceedings or has been convicted on at least two occasions in 6 years – but only offences from which he has benefited count); or
- is an offence committed over a period of at least six months.

In either of these cases, there must have been benefit of at least £5000.

2. If the court decides that the accused has a criminal lifestyle, it must decide whether he has benefited from his general criminal conduct. The concept of benefit is elaborated by s.94, which is complex. For present purposes only, the meaning may be said to be that the accused has obtained property as a result of or in connection with the conduct. The court's decision will be based on the statement of information which the prosecutor produces in terms of s.101 and the procedure which follows on that. "Criminal conduct", in terms of s.143, is conduct which constitutes an offence in Scotland or which would constitute an offence if it had occurred in Scotland (irrespective of whether it constitutes an offence where it was carried out). "*General* criminal conduct, again in terms of s.143, is all of the accused's criminal conduct, whether or not it occurred before the passing of the Act and whether or not benefit obtained from it was obtained before the passing of the Act.

3. Alternatively, if the court decides that the accused does not have a criminal lifestyle, it must nevertheless consider whether he has benefited from his particular criminal conduct – that is, the particular offence with which the court is dealing or other offences of which he was convicted in the same proceedings (as to which, see s.143(3)). The requirement to consider particular criminal conduct even where there is no criminal lifestyle indicates that the Act in fact contains two different confiscation regimes, only one of which may be applied in any particular case. One enables the confiscation of an accused's benefit from "general criminal conduct", the other the confiscation of an accused's benefit from "particular criminal conduct". General criminal conduct includes particular criminal conduct.

Subs. (6)

The fourth and fifth steps are set out in subs.(6). They are:

4. If the accused has benefited, either from general criminal conduct or from particular criminal conduct, the court must decide the "recoverable amount". That concept is explained in s93.

5. Having decided the recoverable amount, the court must make a confiscation order "requiring him to pay that amount". The words "requiring him to pay that amount" indicate that the nature of the confiscation order remains unchanged. A confiscation order is an order requiring the accused to pay money and does not directly confiscate anything. It is at the enforcement stage that the property of the accused may be directly attacked (as to which, see ss130-133). Note that the court must require "him" to pay the amount specified. *R v. Porter* (1990) 1 WLR 1260 makes it clear that joint and several confiscation orders are not appropriate.

Subs. (7)

There is a clear risk that the making and enforcement of a confiscation order might prejudice the victim of the accused's conduct in that the wiping out or substantial reduction of the accused's estate might leave him without means to meet any civil decree. This subsection allows the court to limit the order made to what it considers "just" (in terms of s.93(3)(a)) where it becomes aware of a victim's intention to pursue civil action. See with this s.97(6) which provides for the relationship between confiscation orders and compensation orders.

Subs. (8)

This subsection gives statutory sanction to the procedure which was followed in *HM Advocate v. McSalley* 2000 SLT 1235, in which the wife of the convicted respondent entered the process by minute before the order was made to argue (unsuccessfully) that an order which could not be satisfied except by sale of the family home would be disproportionate and hence a breach of Art.8 and Protocol 1, Art.1, ECHR. It will also make it possible for the victim of the offence in question to draw to the attention of the court his or her intention to pursue compensation in the civil courts.

Subs. (9)

The effect of this is to depart from the reasoned conclusion reached by the Scottish Law Commission. The original confiscation legislation, in both Scotland and England, did not prescribe any standard of proof and accordingly, it became necessary in *R v. Dickens* (1990) 2 WLR 1384 for the Court of Appeal to determine what the standard was. The Court reasoned that the context of the legislation and the nature of the penalties which were likely to be imposed made it clear that the standard of proof required is the criminal standard, namely proof beyond reasonable doubt. This decision was to provoke a considerable debate and in due course the Criminal Justice Act 1993 ss.7 and 27 were to reverse *Dickens* and apply the civil standard of proof in English cases. The reasoning was essentially that confiscation is reparative rather than penal but the Scottish Law Commission found this unconvincing. The Commission noted (SLC Report para 2.17) that to deprive a person of property, the use of which he has been enjoying, albeit wrongly, as his own is to punish him. They also noted the observation of Sir Thomas Bingham, MR in *re Barretto* (1994) 2 WLR 149 at 155 that the confiscation provisions are "in a broad sense penal, inflicting the vengeance of society on those who have transgressed in this field". They concluded that confiscation cannot satisfactorily be characterised as either exclusively reparative or exclusively penal (SLC Report para 2.17) and, because they were not prepared to share the view that confiscation is merely reparative, they recommended that the standard of proof which should apply in Scotland is the criminal standard (SLC Report para 6.5). In *Welch v United Kingdom* (1995) 20 EHRR 247, the European Court of Human Rights also reached the conclusion that a confiscation order is a penalty. The application was under Art.7 and the Court held that concept of a penalty in Art.7 is an autonomous Convention concept. The wording of Art.7(1) indicates that the starting point for the assessment of the existence of a penalty is whether the measure is imposed following conviction for a criminal offence. Other factors that may be taken into account are the nature and purpose of the measure in question, its characterisation under national law, the procedures involved in the making and implementation of the measure and its severity. The Court noted that, before a confiscation order could be made in English law, the accused must have been convicted of a drug trafficking offence. It considered that this link is not diminished by the fact that, due to the operation of the statutory presumptions concerning the extent to which the accused has benefited from drug trafficking, the court order may affect proceeds which are not directly related to the facts underlying the criminal conviction. It considered that, although the provisions were designed to ensure that proceeds were not available for use in future drug trafficking and that crime does not pay, the legislation also pursues the aim of punishing the offender. The aims of prevention and reparation are consistent with a punitive purpose and may be seen as constituent elements of the very notion of punishment. The Court further considered that several aspects of the making of an order under the 1986 Act were in keeping with the idea of a penalty even though they were essential to the preventive scheme inherent in the 1986 Act. These included the sweeping statutory assumptions, the fact that the confiscation order is directed to proceeds and not restricted to actual enrichment or profit, the discretion which the trial judge had in fixing the order to take account of the degree of culpability of the accused (not a feature of the present Act) and the possibility of imprisonment in default of payment. The Court considered that these elements, considered together, provide a strong indication of *inter alia* a regime of punishment. Looking behind appearances at the reality of the situation, whatever the characterisation of the measure of confiscation, the Court said that the fact remained that the applicant faced more far reaching detriment as a result of the order than that to which he was exposed at the time of the commission of the offences of which he was convicted. This reasoning was followed by the European Commission of Human Rights in *Taylor v. United Kingdom* Application No 31209/96; (1998) EHRLR 90.

Of course, none of this leads to the conclusion that subs.(9) involves any breach of the Convention rights; because ECHR does not prescribe any standard of proof even for conviction. What it does is to indicate that the confiscation order procedure, and subs.(9) in particular, represent a departure from the usual practice, in matters of sentencing, of ignoring anything asserted by the Crown which is disputed by the accused and not proved to the criminal standard (see generally *Galloway v. Adair* 1947 JC 7; *Burn v. Smith* 1978 JC 17 and *Dickens* (*supra*))

Subs. (11)

Subsection (11) avoids the contentious issue of whether confiscation is a penalty by equiparating confiscation with a sentence for the purposes of appeal, and hence making the usual avenues of appeal against sentence available, but offering no general principle.

93 Recoverable amount

(1) The recoverable amount for the purposes of section 92 is an amount equal to the accused's benefit from the conduct concerned.

(2) But if the accused shows that the available amount is less than that benefit the recoverable amount is—

   (a) the available amount, or

   (b) a nominal amount, if the available amount is nil.

(3) But if section 92(7) applies the recoverable amount is such amount as—

   (a) the court believes is just, but

   (b) does not exceed the amount found under subsection (1) or (2) (as the case may be).

(4) In calculating the accused's benefit from the conduct concerned for the purposes of subsection (1), any property in respect of which—

   (a) a recovery order is in force under section 266, or

   (b) a forfeiture order is in force under section 298(2),

  must be ignored.

(5) If the court decides the available amount, it must include in the confiscation order a statement of its findings as to the matters relevant for deciding that amount.

DEFINITIONS
"Available amount": s.95

GENERAL NOTE
According to para. 157 of the Explanatory Notes, this section provides for a method of calculating the amount recoverable under a confiscation order which is "much the same as in the existing confiscation statutes" (a curious analysis since the distinction between general criminal conduct and particular criminal conduct is entirely new). The Notes go on to say that "The amount is the amount of the accused's benefit from either his general criminal conduct or his particular criminal conduct (as the case may be), unless the amount available for confiscation is considered by the court and found to be less than the benefit in question, in which case the order must be made in that lesser amount. The amount available for confiscation is described as the available amount (equivalent to the term "the amount that might be realised" in the current legislation) and the amount which may be ordered to be confiscated as the recoverable amount (equivalent to "the amount to be recovered" in the current legislation). Subsection (2) is to the effect that the burden is on the accused to show that the available amount is less than the benefit and to show the extent of the available amount".

Subs. (1)
In terms of s.92(6), where the court decides that the accused has benefited from either general or particular criminal conduct, it must decide the recoverable amount and make a confiscation order in that amount. Subsection (1) of this section is the starting point for determining the recoverable amount. That amount will be an amount equal to the accused's benefit from the conduct concerned. In determining that amount (on a balance of probabilities – s.92(9)) in a case in which it decides that the accused has a criminal lifestyle, the court must apply the assumptions set out in s.96 unless the accused shows the assumption to be incorrect or to make such an assumption would create a serious risk of injustice. The effect of this, and the imposition on the accused by subs.(2) of the *onus* of showing that the amount available to satisfy a confiscation order is less than his benefit, is to allow the prosecutor to establish the possession or expenditure upon which the assumptions operate and then to leave it to the accused to do almost everything else. If he fails, an order will be made to the full extent of the benefit (see *R v. Ilsemann* (1990) 12 Cr App R (s) 398, *R v. Comiskey* (1991) 93 Cr App R 227 and *R v. Barwick* (2001) 1 Cr App R (S) 129). In practice, the prosecution has, in Scotland, tended to include in the information it places before the court information about what assets the accused actually *has* (and, hence, about what the 1995 Act called "realisable property") (see, for example, *HM Advocate v. McLean* 1993 SCCR 917). Whether that practice will survive the entry into force of the present Act, except to the extent necessary to found the s.96 assumptions as to property held by the accused, remains to be seen.

Subs. (2)

The purpose of the requirement to make an order at a nominal amount if the available amount is nil is to permit the court, at a later date, to operate ss.104 to 109, which permit variation of the order. This is not intended to operate exclusively (perhaps not even primarily) to the advantage of the accused. The Scottish Law Commission pointed out that, in view of the difficulties which face prosecutors in ascertaining the value of the benefit from crime and the value of the accused's realisable property, it is necessary to make provision for the situation in which a confiscation order has been made but it then appears that one or other of the relevant amounts is greater than was taken into account when the order was made (SLC Report para 7.1).

Subs. (4)

Recovery order. A recovery order is an order made in terms of the civil recovery provisions of the Act. Since civil recovery should only come into play if criminal confiscation cannot be pursued, the situation contemplated must be one in which the accused has been investigated twice and only on the second occasion has it been possible to convict him and proceed to criminal confiscation.

Forfeiture order A forfeiture order is the final stage in the procedure for seizure of cash which is believed to represent recoverable property or to be intended for use in unlawful conduct.

Subs. (5)

Paragraph 157 of the Explanatory Notes explains that "Where the court considers the available amount at the accused's request, subs.(4) requires it to include a statement of its calculations in the confiscation order. This is intended to assist enforcement by alerting the enforcement authorities to the property available for confiscation".

94   Accused's benefit

(1) If the court is acting under section 92 this section applies for the purpose of—

    (a) deciding whether the accused has benefited from conduct, and

    (b) deciding his benefit from the conduct.

(2) The court must take account of—

    (a) conduct occurring up to the time it makes its decision;

    (b) property obtained up to that time.

(3) Subsection (4) applies if—

    (a) the conduct concerned is general criminal conduct,

    (b) a confiscation order mentioned in subsection (5) has at an earlier time been made against the accused, and

    (c) his benefit for the purposes of that order was benefit from his general criminal conduct.

(4) His benefit found at the time the last confiscation order mentioned in subsection (3)(c) was made against him must be taken for the purposes of this section to be his benefit from his general criminal conduct at that time.

(5) If the conduct concerned is general criminal conduct the court must deduct the aggregate of the following amounts—

    (a) the amount ordered to be paid under each confiscation order previously made against the accused;

    (b) the amount ordered to be paid under each confiscation order previously made against him under—

        (i) the Drug Trafficking Offences Act 1986 (c. 32);

        (ii) Part 1 of the Criminal Justice (Scotland) Act 1987 (c. 41);

        (iii) Part 6 of the Criminal Justice Act 1988 (c. 33);

        (iv) the Criminal Justice (Confiscation) (Northern Ireland) Order 1990 (S.I. 1990/2588 (N.I.17));

        (v) Part 1 of the Drug Trafficking Act 1994 (c. 37);

        (vi) Part 1 of the Proceeds of Crime (Scotland) Act 1995 (c. 43);

        (vii) the Proceeds of Crime (Northern Ireland) Order 1996 (S.I. 1996/ 1299 (N.I.9)); or

        (viii) Part 2 or 4 of this Act.

(6) But subsection (5) does not apply to an amount which has been taken into account for the purposes of a deduction under that subsection on any earlier occasion.

(7) The reference to general criminal conduct in the case of a confiscation order made under any of the provisions listed in subsection (5)(b) is a reference to conduct in respect of which a court is required or entitled to make one or more assumptions for the purpose of assessing a person's benefit from the conduct.

DEFINITIONS
"general criminal conduct": s.143(2)

GENERAL NOTE
As subs.(1) makes clear, this section directs the court in determining whether and to what extent the accused has benefited from conduct. The determination is relatively straightforward so far as benefit from particular criminal conduct is concerned. It is only necessary to note that, in terms of subs.(2), the cut off point as to both conduct and property obtained is the time the court makes its decision. Any argument that the court should, for example, ignore property obtained after service of the indictment or after conviction would be misconceived.

That principle applies also in the case of benefit from general criminal conduct (which is defined for these purposes according to whether the court was required or entitled to make assumptions – that would include conduct to which the Scottish 1995 Act was applicable). In that case, however, there are two additional considerations:

1. If the accused has previously been the subject of a confiscation order in respect of general criminal conduct, his benefit at the time of that order (or the last of those orders, if there has been more than one) must be taken to be his benefit from general criminal conduct at that time. This means that neither the accused nor the prosecutor will be able to revisit old ground.

2. The court must deduct from the benefit the amount ordered to be paid under previous confiscation orders.

95   Available amount

(1) For the purposes of deciding the recoverable amount, the available amount is the aggregate of—

    (a) the total of the values (at the time the confiscation order is made) of all the free property then held by the accused minus the total amount payable in pursuance of obligations which then have priority, and

    (b) the total of the values (at that time) of all tainted gifts.

(2) An obligation has priority if—

    (a) it is an obligation of the accused to pay an amount due in respect of a fine or other order of a court which was imposed or made on conviction for an offence and at any time before the confiscation order is made, or

    (b) it is an obligation of the accused to pay a sum which would be—

        (i) a preferred debt if the accused's estate were sequestrated on the date of the confiscation order, or

        (ii) a preferential debt if his winding up were ordered on that date.

(3) In subsection (2)—

       "preferred debt" has the meaning given by section 51(2) of the Bankruptcy (Scotland) Act 1985 (c. 66);

       "preferential debt" has the meaning given by section 386 of the Insolvency Act 1986 (c. 45).

DEFINITIONS
"recoverable amount": s.93
"tainted gift": s.144

GENERAL NOTE

Subs. (1)

Recoverable amount. This, it will be recalled, is an amount equal to the accused's benefit from the conduct concerned unless the accused shows that the available amount is less than the benefit – in which case the recoverable amount is the available amount (s.93). The effect of that approach is that it is the accused who has both an interest and an *onus* to establish the available amount.

The available amount is the aggregate of. . . . The subsection contemplates three values: that of the free property held by the accused at the time the confiscation order is made (call it "x"), the amount payable in terms of obligations having priority (call it "y") and the value of tainted gifts (call it "z"). The calculation which the court must be performed may be expressed as $(x - y) + z$. No doubt the accused will wish to play down the value of free property and of tainted gifts and play up the value of obligations having priority. If so, he will find that the legislation does not assist him greatly. By s.148, property is free unless it is the subject of a confiscation order, a forfeiture order or a deprivation order (deprivation orders apply in England and Northern Ireland). The expression "free property" does not, therefore, limit the application of the section to property which is unencumbered, as might have been thought. The value of property is, by s.145, its market value (no doubt District Valuers will be asked to advise). Obligations which have priority are limited to those which relate to the payment of fines (subs.(2)(a)), preferred debts and preferential debts (subs.(2)(b)). Tainted gifts are defined very widely by s.144, *qv*. In other words, the values to be added together are defined so as to catch the market value of everything the accused owns or has alienated during the relevant period and the amount which may be set off against the value of property held is defined narrowly.

Subs. (3)

Preferred debt. Section 51(2) of the Bankruptcy (Scotland) Act 1985 defines "preferred debt" by reference to Pt.I of Sched.3 to that Act. They are, in brief, debts to the Inland Revenue debts due to Customs and Excise Social Security contributions, contributions to occupational pension schemes and the like and remuneration of employees, etc. The Insolvency Act 1986, s.386 also defines "preferential debt" under reference to a schedule (in this case, Sched.6) which includes money owed to the Inland Revenue for income tax deducted at source; VAT, car tax, betting and gaming duties; social security and pension scheme contributions; and remuneration etc. of employees.

96   Assumptions to be made in case of criminal lifestyle

(1) Where the court decides under section 92 that the accused has a criminal lifestyle it must make the following four assumptions for the purpose of—

(a) deciding whether he has benefited from his general criminal conduct, and

(b) deciding his benefit from the conduct.

(2) The first assumption is that any property transferred to the accused at any time after the relevant day was obtained by him—

(a) as a result of his general criminal conduct, and

(b) at the earliest time he appears to have held it.

(3) The second assumption is that any property held by the accused at any time after the date of conviction was obtained by him—

(a) as a result of his general criminal conduct, and

(b) at the earliest time he appears to have held it.

(4) The third assumption is that any expenditure incurred by the accused at any time after the relevant day was met from property obtained by him as a result of his general criminal conduct.

(5) The fourth assumption is that, for the purpose of valuing any property obtained (or assumed to have been obtained) by the accused, he obtained it free of any other interests in it.

(6) But the court must not make any of those assumptions in relation to particular property or expenditure if—

(a) the assumption is shown to be incorrect, or

(b) there would be a serious risk of injustice if the assumption were made.

(7) If the court does not make one or more of those assumptions it must state its reasons.

(8) The relevant day is the first day of the period of six years ending with—

  (a) the day when proceedings for the offence concerned were instituted against the accused, or

  (b) if there are two or more offences and proceedings for them were instituted on different days, the earliest of those days.

(9) But if a confiscation order mentioned in section 94(3)(c) has been made against the accused at any time during the period mentioned in subsection (8)—

  (a) the relevant day is the day when the accused's benefit was calculated for the purposes of the last such confiscation order;

  (b) the second assumption does not apply to any property which was held by him on or before the relevant day.

(10) The date of conviction is—

  (a) the date on which the accused was convicted of the offence concerned, or

  (b) if there are two or more offences and the convictions are on different dates, the date of the latest.

DEFINITIONS

"criminal lifestyle": s.142

"general criminal conduct": s.143(2)

GENERAL NOTE

Subs. (1)

The court ... must make the following four assumptions. The requirement to make the assumptions is a further example of the discarding of an approach which had worked satisfactorily in Scotland in favour of the application of the law which had applied in England. Section 3 of the Proceeds of Crime (Scotland) Act 1995 provided that the court "may" make the assumptions and the Scottish courts showed no reluctance to do so except to the extent that any particular assumption was shown to be incorrect (see in particular Lord Coulsfield's analysis in *Donnelly v. HM Advocate* 1999 JC 276). In terms of subs (6) an assumption which is shown to be incorrect should still not be made.

In a number of cases, attempts have been made to attack the use of the assumptions on Convention rights grounds; but these have been universally unsuccessful. In *Elton v. United Kingdom* (Application No 32344/96, September 11, 1997) it was argued for the applicant that the making of a confiscation order against him breached Art.6(2) ECHR in that it was based on an assumption rather than on proof beyond reasonable doubt. We leave aside the fact that this proposition depended in part on the fallacy that ECHR prescribes any particular standard of proof. The European Commission of Human Rights noted the European Court of Human Rights' remark in *Welch v. United Kingdom* (1995) 20 EHRR 247 (para. 36) that "it does not call into question in any respect the powers of confiscation conferred on the courts as a weapon in the fight against the scourge of drug trafficking" and went on to deal with the matter on the basis of the ordinary ECHR jurisprudence about presumptions, in terms of which the critical question is the rebuttability of the presumption in question (see especially *Salabiaku v. France* (1993) 13 EHRR 379 and *Pham Hoang v. France* (1996) 16 EHRR 53). The application was held to be manifestly ill founded, and hence inadmissible, on the basis that the assumptions do not apply if they are shown to be incorrect.

The Privy Council in *McIntosh, Petitioner* 2001 SLT 304, considered this issue in a specifically Scottish context. The Board held that the assumptions do not offend against Art.6.2. In part, this was on the basis that Article 6.2 has no application after conviction. The Board also considered, however, what the position would have been if Article 6.2 had applied. Lord Bingham of Cornhill said that "In weighing the balance between the general interest of the community and the rights of the individual, it will be relevant to ask ... what public threat the provision is directed to address, what the prosecutor must prove to transfer the onus to the defendant and what difficulty the defendant may have in discharging the onus laid upon him. In some cases the acceptability of a reverse onus provision will turn not on consideration of the provision in the abstract but on its application in a particular case...The right to a fair trial, guaranteed by Art.6(1), will ensure that any reverse onus provision is fairly applied in the given case."

Later in *McIntosh*, Lord Hope of Craighead applied these principles to the assumptions at issue. He said that they "serve the legitimate aim in the public interest of combating that activity (drug trafficking). They do so in a way that is proportionate. They relate to matters that ought to be within the accused's knowledge, and they are rebuttable by him at a hearing before a judge on the balance of probabilities. In my opinion a fair balance is struck between the legitimate aim and the rights of the accused".

It is worth noting that in July 2001 the European Court of Human Rights came to the same conclusion on almost identical reasoning in *Phillips v. United Kingdom* EHRLR 2001, 3, 331-333. For completeness, see also the House of Lords arriving at the same conclusion in an English law context in *R v. Benjafield* (2002) 1 All E.R. 815, (2002) 2 Cr App R 3.

Subs. (6)

This subsection provides an exception to the requirement to make the assumptions in 2 situations.

The assumption is shown to be incorrect. The wording is the same as that in s3 of the Proceeds of Crime (Scotland) Act 1995 and in equivalent English legislation, in relation to which it was held in *HM Advocate v. McLean* 1993 SCCR 917, *R v. Dickens* (1990) 2 WLR 1384 and *Donnelly v. HM Advocate* 1999 JC 276 that (as Lord Coulsfield put it in *Donnelly*) "the wording of the provision clearly shows that what is required is evidence that the assumptions should not be made rather than that they should" and that the requirement is to prove that on a balance of probabilities. In *Donnelly*, it was held that the production by the accused of a probative writ (in that case, a disposition) will not necessarily be conclusive as to a price paid for property and that the court can look behind it for the true position. In *HM Advocate v. McSalley* 2000 SLT 1235, Lady Cosgrove rejected the argument that if the accused demonstrates that the assumptions are incorrect to any extent it means that they cannot be made at all. She considered that it is open to the court to adjust the figures and that the substitution of different figures does not in any way interfere with the making of the assumptions.

There would be a serious risk of injustice. This wording has not previously appeared in Scottish confiscation legislation but did appear in English legislation. In *R v. Dore* (1997) 2 Cr App R (S) 152 the point was made that the risk of injustice relates to the making of the assumption, not to the consequences of the making of an order (so that the fact that the accused will be deprived of his family home is not relevant. Note also that in *Danison v. United Kingdom* (Application no. 45042/98, 7 September 1999) the European Court of Human Rights, in dealing with a complaint that it would be unjust to confiscate the home of his wife and child where the applicant himself had obtained only minimal benefit from the fraud of which he had been convicted, said that the question of whether or not the applicant had benefited from his offence and the extent of or relevance of his wife's interest in the property (if any) fell within the appreciation of the domestic courts. The Court found no evidence of arbitrariness or other reason which would warrant an investigation by it of the order made by the domestic court in this case. It held the application to be manifestly ill founded and, hence, inadmissible.

97   Effect of order on court's other powers

(1) If the court decides to make a confiscation order it must act as mentioned in subsections (2) and (4) in respect of the offence or offences concerned.

(2) The court must take account of the confiscation order before—
    (a) it imposes a fine on the accused, or
    (b) it makes an order falling within subsection (3).

(3) These orders fall within this subsection—
    (a) an order involving payment by the accused, other than a compensation order under section 249 of the Procedure Act (compensation orders);
    (b) an order under section 27 of the Misuse of Drugs Act 1971 (c. 38) (forfeiture orders);
    (c) an order under Part 2 of the Proceeds of Crime (Scotland) Act 1995 (c. 43) (forfeiture orders);
    (d) an order under section 23 of the Terrorism Act 2000 (c. 11) (forfeiture orders).

(4) Subject to subsection (2), the court must leave the confiscation order out of account in deciding the appropriate sentence for the accused.

(5) Subsection (6) applies if—

   (a) a court makes both a confiscation order and a compensation
        order under section 249 of the Procedure Act against the same
        person in the same proceedings, and
   (b) the court believes he will not have sufficient means to satisfy both
        the orders in full.
 (6) In such a case the court must direct that so much of the compensation
      as it specifies is to be paid out of any sums recovered under the confis-
      cation order; and the amount it specifies must be the amount it
      believes will not be recoverable because of the insufficiency of the per-
      son's means.

GENERAL NOTE
   Section 97 deals with the interaction of the confiscation order with other powers of the court.
Its effect is to give the confiscation order priority over all other financial penalties except a
compensation order. As regards a compensation order, if it appears that the accused will not
have sufficient means to pay both that and the confiscation order, the court must direct that so
much of the compensation order as it specifies (presumably, the shortfall) is to be paid out of
what is recovered under the confiscation order. The other important aspect of the section is the
requirement, in subs.(4), that the court must leave the confiscation order out of account in deciding the appropriate sentence for the accused. This is clearly appropriate if confiscation orders
are reparative rather than penal but there is a more fundamental reason for this approach which
applies even if the doubts expressed above about that are justified (see s.92). The Scottish Law
Commission commented (SLC Report para. 5.2): "Although we consider a confiscation order to
be in some degree penal in character we do not think it would be appropriate for an order to be
the only sentence or other means of dealing with the offender to be ordered by the court. For the
court only to make a confiscation order would be to indicate to the public that an offence of the
kind concerned would be tolerated if the offender could be parted from his proceeds." Gane has
made a similar point, noting that it would be "invidious if those with substantial assets which
could be confiscated could thereby hope to avoid other penalties such as imprisonment" (C
Gane, Criminal Justice (Scotland) Act 1987, Current Law Statutes Annotated 1987 Vol 2, 41-9).

98   Disposal of family home

 (1) This section applies where a confiscation order has been made in
      relation to any person and the prosecutor has not satisfied the court
      that the person's interest in his family home has been acquired as a
      benefit from his criminal conduct.
 (2) Where this section applies, then, before the administrator disposes of
      any right or interest in the person's family home he shall—
      (a) obtain the relevant consent; or
      (b) where he is unable to do so, apply to the court for authority to
           carry out the disposal.
 (3) On an application being made to it under subsection (2)(b), the court,
      after having regard to all the circumstances of the case including—
      (a) the needs and financial resources of the spouse or former spouse
           of the person concerned;
      (b) the needs and financial resources of any child of the family;
      (c) the length of the period during which the family home has been
           used as a residence by any of the persons referred to in paragraph
           (a) or (b),
      may refuse to grant the application or may postpone the granting of
      the application for such period (not exceeding 12 months) as it may
      consider reasonable in the circumstances or may grant the application
      subject to such conditions as it may prescribe.
 (4) Subsection (3) shall apply—
      (a) to an action for division and sale of the family home of the person
           concerned; or
      (b) to an action for the purpose of obtaining vacant possession of that
           home,
      brought by the administrator as it applies to an application under sub-
      section (2)(b) and, for the purposes of this subsection, any reference in

subsection (3) to the granting of the application shall be construed as a reference to the granting of decree in the action.

(5) In this section—

"family home", in relation to any person (in this subsection referred to as "the relevant person") means any property in which the relevant person has or had (whether alone or in common with any other person) a right or interest, being property which is occupied as a residence by the relevant person and his or her spouse or by the relevant person's spouse or former spouse (in any case with or without a child of the family) or by the relevant person with a child of the family;

"child of the family" includes any child or grandchild of either the relevant person or his or her spouse or former spouse, and any person who has been treated by either the relevant person or his or her spouse or former spouse as if he or she were a child of the relevant person, spouse or former spouse, whatever the age of such a child, grandchild or person may be; and

"relevant consent" means in relation to the disposal of any right or interest in a family home—

(a) in a case where the family home is occupied by the spouse or former spouse of the relevant person, the consent of the spouse or, as the case may be, of the former spouse, whether or not the family home is also occupied by the relevant person;

(b) where paragraph (a) does not apply, in a case where the family home is occupied by the relevant person with a child of the family, the consent of the relevant person.

DEFINITIONS

"Family home": subs.(5)

GENERAL NOTE

The Scottish Law Commission noted that, although the nature of property would as a general rule be irrelevant to questions in relation to a confiscation order, concerns could arise in the situation in which an offender's family is living in a family home which had in fact been acquired lawfully. They noted that insolvency legislation imposes restrictions on the sale of a bankrupt's family home and noted English case law to the effect that compensation orders should not be made where their effect would be to require the sale of the family home. They considered that protections for the family home equivalent to those in the Bankruptcy (Scotland) Act 1985 would be appropriate (SLC Report paras 4.15-4.18). This section enacts such protections. Their essence is that where a confiscation order has been made the Crown is not entitled to dispose of any right or interest in the family home without either the consent of the family members involved or the consent of the court. The Government spokesman in the House of Lords stressed that "the power applies only to a legally acquired interest of the defendant and is exercisable only where the court is satisfied that the defendant's spouse or another specified relative has asserted a claim to occupancy" (Lord Rooker, *Hansard,* H.L. April 22, 2002 Col 52).

Subs. (1)

The prosecutor has not satisfied the court. The section applies unless the prosecutor satisfies the court that the accused's interest in his family home was acquired with the fruits of his crime. These words must be read subject to s.96(1) which applies the assumptions to deciding the accused's benefit from his conduct. Although persons having an interest in property have a right to be heard (in terms of s.92(8)), s.96 does not restrict the application of the assumptions to a question with the accused. Nor does s.96(6) limit the possibility of showing an assumption to be incorrect to the accused. It appears, then, that a person having an interest in the accused's family home will be able to be heard at the confiscation hearing and will be bound by the assumptions unless he or she can show that an assumption is incorrect.

The Act is silent as to the standard of proof.

Family home. This is defined in subs.(4). It is primarily any property in which the person to whom a confiscation order relates ("the relevant person") resides with his spouse or a child of the family (which expression is defined widely by subs.(4)). Property occupied by a former spouse is also covered. Mere cohabitees are not protected.

Subs. (2)

Where the section applies the administrator must first seek consent. If it cannot get consent he must apply to the court.

Administrator. See ss.128-138 and Sched.3 for the appointment, functions and powers etc of administrators.

The relevant consent. This is defined by subs.(4). Where a relevant person's spouse occupies the property it is that spouse's consent which must be sought. Where the relevant person occupies the property with his child, it is the relevant person's consent which must be sought.

Subs. (3)

This subsection defines the court's powers on an application for its authority to carry out the disposal of a family home and also (by subs.(4)) where the Crown brings an action for division and sale in respect of such a home or to obtain vacant possession. The subsection also sets out the criteria which the court must apply. Presumably, in considering such an application, the court will keep in mind *R v. Dore* (1997) 2 Cr App R (S) 152, in which it was held that that the fact that the accused will be deprived of his family home is not relevant to the question of injustice in making the order. There will be a case for those representing family members to base their arguments on the right under Article 8 ECHR to respect for the home and also the right under Protocol 1, Article 1 ECHR to the peaceful enjoyment of possessions. It should, however, be recalled that in *Danison v. United Kingdom* (Application no. 45042/98, September 7, 1999) the European Court of Human Rights declined to intervene in a confiscation order which required the sale of the family home, on the basis that the matter was one for the domestic courts and that it found no arbitrariness.

Procedural matters

99   Postponement

(1) The court may—
   (a) proceed under section 92 before it sentences the accused for the offence (or any of the offences concerned), or
   (b) postpone proceedings under section 92 for a specified period.
(2) A period of postponement may be extended.
(3) A period of postponement (including one as extended) must not end after the permitted period ends.
(4) But subsection (3) does not apply if there are exceptional circumstances or if the accused has failed to comply with an order under section 102(1).
(5) The permitted period is the period of two years starting with the date of conviction.
(6) But if—
   (a) the accused appeals against his conviction for the offence (or any of the offences) concerned, and
   (b) the period of three months (starting with the day when the appeal is determined or otherwise disposed of) ends after the period found under subsection (5),
   the permitted period is that period of three months.
(7) A postponement or extension may be made—
   (a) on application by the accused;
   (b) on application by the prosecutor;
   (c) by the court of its own motion.
(8) If—
   (a) proceedings are postponed for a period, and
   (b) an application to extend the period is made before it ends,
   the application may be granted even after the period ends.
(9) The date of conviction is—
   (a) the date on which the accused was convicted of the offence concerned, or

(b) if there are two or more offences and the convictions were on different dates, the date of the latest.

(10) A confiscation order must not be quashed only on the ground that there was a defect or omission in the procedure connected with the application for or the granting of a postponement.

(11) But subsection (10) does not apply if before it made the confiscation order the court has—

(a) imposed a fine on the accused;

(b) made an order falling within section 97(3);

(c) made an order under section 249 of the Procedure Act.

DEFINITIONS
"Permitted period": subs.(5)

GENERAL NOTE
Under s.10 of the Scottish 1995 Act, the court had power to postpone where it considered that it required further information. The restriction of postponement to that particular ground has disappeared from the law, leaving the court a general discretion (which will, for example, permit account to be taken of the unavailability of a judge through illness). One might expect the court to be guided in its exercise of this discretion by the principle stated in the English Court of Appeal case of *R v. Steele and Shevki* (2001) Cr App R (S) 178 that confiscation orders should form part of the ordinary sentencing process, tempered by the Court of Appeal's recognition that, for lack of information, this will often be impracticable. Notice should also be taken of *HM Advocate v. Donnelly* 1996 SCCR 904, in which the High Court upheld a judge's decision to postpone a confiscation hearing beyond the then limit of 6 months after conviction, on the basis that the limit has no application where any allegation of the prosecutor's statement is being challenged by the accused or the basis of the non-acceptance by the accused is being challenged by the prosecutor.

That having been said, the length of the postponement available has been increased (by subs (5)) from six months to two years (longer in exceptional circumstances, by subs (4)). Since the law of the European Convention on Human Rights does not regard the determination of a criminal charge as completed until penalty has been settled (see, for example, *V v. United Kingdom* (2000) 30 E.H.R.R. 121) and since that law regards confiscation orders as penalties (*Welch v. United Kingdom* (1995) 20 EHRR 247), it must be at least arguable that the Art.6.1 guarantee of a hearing within a reasonable time would be breached in a case in which a postponement exceeded two years without a powerful reason.

The two year period is modified by subs.(6) where the accused appeals against conviction. In that case, the court may postpone confiscation for two years from conviction or until three months after the determination or disposal of the appeal, whichever is longer. One obvious benefit will be to avoid the need for a confiscation hearing where the conviction for the predicate offence is in doubt. There is no point in holding a five-day inquiry into the complicated financial affairs of a convicted accused if there is any real chance that the High Court will overturn the conviction and render the whole exercise nugatory.

The importance which the Government attaches to the confiscation mechanism is illustrated by subs.(10) which excludes the quashing of a confiscation order only on the ground that there was a procedural flaw in relation to a postponement (unless the court has imposed a financial penalty of a sort contemplated by subs.(11)).

100   Effect of postponement

(1) If the court postpones proceedings under section 92 it may proceed to sentence the accused for the offence (or any of the offences) concerned.

(2) Subsection (1) is without prejudice to sections 201 and 202 of the Procedure Act.

(3) In sentencing the accused for the offence (or any of the offences) concerned in the postponement period the court must not—

(a) impose a fine on him,

(b) make an order falling within section 97(3), or

(c) make an order for the payment of compensation under section 249 of the Procedure Act.

(4) If the court sentences the accused for the offence (or any of the offences) concerned in the postponement period, after that period ends it may vary the sentence by—
   (a) imposing a fine on him,
   (b) making an order falling within section 97(3), or
   (c) making an order for the payment of compensation under section 249 of the Procedure Act.

(5) But the court may proceed under subsection (4) only within the period of 28 days which starts with the last day of the postponement period.

(6) Where the court postpones proceedings under section 92 following conviction on indictment, section 109(1) of the Procedure Act (intimation of intention to appeal against conviction or conviction and sentence) has effect as if the reference to the final determination of the proceedings were a reference to the relevant day.

(7) Despite subsection (6), the accused may appeal under section 106 of the Procedure Act against any confiscation order made, or any other sentence passed, after the end of the postponement period, in respect of the conviction.

(8) Where the court postpones proceedings under section 92 following conviction on complaint—
   (a) section 176(1) of the Procedure Act (stated case: manner and time of appeal) has effect in relation to an appeal under section 175(2)(a) or (d) as if the reference to the final determination of the proceedings were a reference to the relevant day, and
   (b) the draft stated case in such an appeal must be prepared and issued within 3 weeks of the relevant day.

(9) Despite subsection (8), the accused may appeal under section 175(2)(b), and the prosecutor may appeal under section 175(3)(b), of the Procedure Act against any confiscation order made, or any other sentence passed, after the end of the postponement period, in respect of the conviction.

(10) The relevant day is—
   (a) in the case of an appeal against conviction where the court has sentenced the accused under subsection (1), the day on which the postponement period commenced;
   (b) in any other case, the day on which sentence is passed in open court.

(11) The postponement period is the period for which proceedings under section 92 are postponed.

GENERAL NOTE

Subs. (1)
The Scottish Law Commission and their consultees thought that a confiscation order should not operate to reduce any sentence of imprisonment imposed in respect of the same offence and also that it would be unfair to keep the accused in ignorance of the length of such a sentence until after a postponed confiscation hearing (SLC Report para. 6.25-6.26).

Subs. (2)
The sections referred to deal with adjournment for sentence and deferred sentence respectively.

Subs. (3)
In view of the fact that the accused's financial position will be fundamentally altered by a confiscation order it would not make sense to impose any other financial penalty before determining the amount to be paid under a confiscation order.

Subs. (6)
The postponement of a confiscation order would delay the final determination of proceedings. This subsection seeks to avoid delaying appeals against conviction, having regard, for

example, to the needs of trial judges in relation to their Reports for the High Court. In *Smith v. HMA* 1983 SCCR 30 the Lord Justice-General (Emslie) called attention (in the context of an inadequately stated ground of appeal) to the Crown's need for an opportunity to consider its position and to the trial judge's need in his report to explain and deal with the alleged misdirection. Both of these considerations argue with equal force for ensuring that the taking of such an appeal is brought to the attention of the Crown and the trial judge as soon as possible after the events which are to be aired before the High Court. Accordingly, by subs (10), the "relevant day" for the purposes of appeal against conviction is the start of the period of postponement.

Subs. (7)

Since subs.(6) has to apply to appeals against both conviction and sentence, this saving provision is required to preserve the position where an accused appeals against conviction but has no basis to complain about sentence until a confiscation order is made which he wishes to have reviewed either alone or in combination with the rest of his sentence.

101 Statement of information

(1) When the court is proceeding under section 92 the prosecutor must, within such period as the court may order, give the court a statement of information.

(2) If the prosecutor believes the accused has a criminal lifestyle the statement of information is a statement of matters the prosecutor believes are relevant in connection with deciding these issues—
   (a) whether the accused has a criminal lifestyle;
   (b) whether he has benefited from his general criminal conduct;
   (c) his benefit from the conduct.

(3) A statement under subsection (2) must include information the prosecutor believes is relevant—
   (a) in connection with the making by the court of a required assumption under section 96;
   (b) for the purpose of enabling the court to decide if the circumstances are such that it must not make such an assumption.

(4) If the prosecutor does not believe the accused has a criminal lifestyle the statement of information is a statement of matters the prosecutor believes are relevant in connection with deciding these issues—
   (a) whether the accused has benefited from his particular criminal conduct;
   (b) his benefit from the conduct.

(5) If the prosecutor gives the court a statement of information—
   (a) he may at any time give the court a further statement of information;
   (b) he must give the court a further statement of information if it orders him to do so, and he must give it within the period the court orders.

(6) If the court makes an order under this section it may at any time vary it by making another one.

DEFINITIONS

"criminal lifestyle": s.142
"general criminal conduct": s.143(2)

GENERAL NOTE

Under s.9(1) of the Scottish 1995 Act, the prosecutor had a discretion whether or not to lodge a statement of matters relevant to confiscation, though in practice this was always done. The present provision makes the provision of a statement by the prosecutor mandatory. It will, however, be recalled that in Scotland (by contrast with other UK jurisdictions) it is for the prosecutor to initiate the confiscation order procedure (see s.92(3)). Accordingly, on one view, the prosecutor continues to have an effective choice. In another respect, however, the requirement may be regarded as wasteful. The clear intention of the legislation is to widen the confiscation net considerably and, especially where there is no basis for arguing that the accused has a criminal lifestyle, so that the inquiry is into the benefit of particular criminal conduct, it is conceivable that the evidence led at trial will contain all the information necessary for the court to consider and make an order.

The use, in this section, of the expression "if the prosecutor believes" (and its in negative form in subs.(4)), is distinctly odd. It is not normally for the prosecutor to form any view on what he does or does not believe. Presumably, what Parliament intended to refer to was the prosecutor's intention to argue, or not to argue, that the accused has a criminal lifestyle.

No statutory form is prescribed for prosecutor's statements, though subss.(2) to (4) indicate the matters which they must address. Those matters are the things about which the court is required to come to decisions before determining whether to impose an order and, if so, for how much. Prosecutor's statements have in the past been reminiscent of the pursuer's pleadings in a civil action, and the answers lodged by the defence have followed that example and recalled the form of the defender's answers in such a case. However, beyond the prosecutor's option of accepting some or all of the defence allegations and the possibility of a further statement of information (subs (5)), there is no provision for adjustment of either the statement or answers in relation to confiscation and the civil pleadings analogy should not, therefore, be pressed too far.

102   Accused's response to statement of information

(1) When the prosecutor gives the court a statement of information and the court is satisfied that he has served a copy on the accused, the court shall order the accused—

  (a) to indicate the extent to which he accepts each allegation in the statement, and

  (b) so far as he does not accept such an allegation, to give particulars of any matters he proposes to rely on,

  within the period it orders.

(2) Where by virtue of section 99 the court postpones proceedings under section 92, the period ordered by the court under subsection (1) shall be a period ending not less than six months before the end of the permitted period mentioned in section 99.

(3) If the accused accepts to any extent an allegation in a statement of information the court may treat his acceptance as conclusive of the matters to which it relates for the purpose of deciding the issues referred to in section 101(2) or (4) (as the case may be).

(4) If the accused fails in any respect to comply with an order under subsection (1) he may be treated for the purposes of subsection (3) as accepting every allegation in the statement of information apart from—

  (a) any allegation in respect of which he has complied with the requirement;

  (b) any allegation that he has benefited from his general or particular criminal conduct.

(5) Where—

  (a) an allegation in a statement of information is challenged by the accused, or

  (b) the matters referred to in subsection (1)(b) are challenged by the prosecutor,

  the court must consider the matters being challenged at a hearing.

(6) The judge presiding at the hearing may, if he is not the trial judge and he considers it in the interests of justice to do so, adjourn the hearing to a date when the trial judge is available.

(7) If the court makes an order under this section it may at any time vary it by making another one.

(8) No acceptance under this section that the accused has benefited from conduct is admissible in evidence in proceedings for an offence.

GENERAL NOTE

According to the Explanatory Notes (para. 167), "The statement of information procedure is designed to provide a quick and effective method of identifying the extent of the accused's benefit where there is agreement between the accused and the prosecutor, and of identifying areas of dispute where there is not". The procedure is probably not perceived in that way by accused persons and their legal representatives. Agreements between prosecution and defence are voluntary matters, with no sanction for choosing not to enter into them. They can be dealt with quite readily by joint minute. The present procedure imposes an obligation on the accused to respond to the prosecutor's allegations and requires him to show his hand with regard to matters which he disputes.

Subs. (1)

Indicate. This word appeared in both the Criminal Justice (Scotland) Act 1987 and the Scottish 1995 Act. Its precise meaning is unclear. However, it seems to be somewhat less demanding than the word "specify" would have been and, when used in combination with the words "the basis of such non-acceptance", it perhaps eases the burden on the defence in relation to the detail required of them in answering the prosecutor's statement.

To give particulars. This seems to rule out both bare denials and the use of the formula "not known and not admitted". It is arguable that on any point where the defence answers did not go beyond one of these responses they would be irrelevant. The effect of subs.(4) is that failure to comply adequately with the requirements of this subsection will be that the accused will be held as having accepted the Crown's allegations

Subs. (8)

Paragraph 169 of the Explanatory Notes states that "the exemption is intended to encourage accused persons to be more forthcoming by preventing the admissions made from being used in a future prosecution against them or anybody else. Accused persons might otherwise be reluctant to admit benefit from criminal conduct which has not been the subject of a prosecution".

103 Provision of information by accused

(1) For the purpose of obtaining information to help it in carrying out its functions under section 92 the court may at any time order the accused to give it information specified in the order.

(2) An order under this section may require all or a specified part of the information to be given in a specified manner and before a specified date.

(3) If the accused fails without reasonable excuse to comply with an order under this section the court may draw such inference as it thinks appropriate.

(4) Subsection (3) does not affect any power of the court to deal with the accused in respect of a failure to comply with an order under this section.

(5) If the prosecutor accepts to any extent an allegation made by the accused—

   (a) in giving information required by an order under this section, or

   (b) in any other statement given to the court in relation to any matter relevant to deciding the available amount under section 95,

   the court may treat the acceptance as conclusive of the matters to which it relates.

(6) For the purposes of this section an allegation may be accepted in a manner ordered by the court.

(7) If the court makes an order under this section it may at any time vary it by making another order.

(8) No information given under this section which amounts to an admission by the accused that he has benefited from criminal conduct is admissible in evidence in proceedings for an offence.

GENERAL NOTE

The power to require information from the accused is one which has been available in English law for some time. According to para.170 of the Explanatory Notes, the provision "reproduces, with minimal changes, that in the current legislation". This is presumably a reference to the

Proceeds of Crime (Scotland) Act 1995, which the present writer also annotated. He is unable to recall or to trace any such existing provision applicable in Scotland.

The Explanatory Notes suggest (para.170) that the court might use the provision where, for example, the accused has proposed to rely on certain matters in responding to the statement of information, and the court considers that it requires more information from the accused in deciding the point at issue. It is not clear how this accords with ss 94, 98 and 104, the effect of which should be that if the accused fails (or chooses not) to provide the court with sufficient information to decide the point at issue, he fails to discharge the onus upon him and the prosecutor succeeds.

Mitchell, Taylor and Talbot note that the proposition that the exercise of the power breaches the right to silence which may be derived from Art.6(2) ECHR was rejected in *Re E and Re H*, Transcript CO CJA/162/2000 and 184/2000 (unreported, May 24, 2001) (*Mitchell, Taylor and Talbot on Confiscation and the Proceeds of Crime*, 3rd edition, Sweet & Maxwell, 2002, para.5.059).

Reconsideration

104   No order made: reconsideration of case

(1) This section applies if—
   (a) the first condition in section 92 is satisfied but no court has proceeded under that section,
   (b) the prosecutor has evidence which was not available to him on the relevant date,
   (c) before the end of the period of six years starting with the date of conviction the prosecutor applies to the court to consider the evidence, and
   (d) after considering the evidence the court thinks it is appropriate for it to proceed under section 92.
(2) The court must proceed under section 92, and when it does so subsections (3) to (8) below apply.
(3) If the court has already sentenced the accused for the offence (or any of the offences) concerned section 92(4) does not apply.
(4) Section 94(2) does not apply, and the rules applying instead are that the court must take account of—
   (a) conduct occurring before the relevant date;
   (b) property obtained before that date;
   (c) property obtained on or after that date if it was obtained as a result of or in connection with conduct occurring before that date.
(5) In relation to the assumptions that the court must make under section 96—
   (a) the first and second assumptions do not apply with regard to property first held by the accused on or after the relevant date;
   (b) the third assumption does not apply with regard to expenditure incurred by him on or after that date;
   (c) the fourth assumption does not apply with regard to property obtained (or assumed to have been obtained) by him on or after that date.
(6) The recoverable amount for the purposes of section 92 is such amount as—
   (a) the court believes is just, but
   (b) does not exceed the amount found under section 93.
(7) In arriving at the just amount the court must have regard in particular to—
   (a) the amount found under section 93;
   (b) any fine imposed on the accused in respect of the offence (or any of the offences) concerned;
   (c) any order which falls within section 97(3) and has been made against him in respect of the offence (or any of the offences) concerned and has not already been taken into account by a court in

deciding what is the free property held by the accused for the purposes of section 95;

(d) any compensation order which has been made against him in respect of the offence (or any of the offences) concerned under section 249 of the Procedure Act.

(8) If an order for payment of compensation under section 249 of the Procedure Act has been made against the accused in respect of the offence or offences concerned, section 97(5) and (6) do not apply.

(9) The relevant date is—

(a) if the court made a decision not to proceed under section 92, the date of the decision;

(b) if the court did not make such a decision, the date of the conviction.

(10) The date of conviction is—

(a) the date on which the accused was convicted of the offence concerned, or

(b) if there are two or more offences and the convictions were on different dates, the date of the latest.

(11) In this section references to the court are to the court which had jurisdiction in respect of the offence or offences concerned to make a confiscation order.

DEFINITIONS
"relevant date": subs (9)

GENERAL NOTE
The Scottish Law Commission pointed out that, in view of the difficulties which face prosecutors in ascertaining the value of the benefit from crime and the value of the accused's property, it is necessary to make provision for situations which can arise (SLC Report para. 7.1). This and the following sections make provision for that sort of situation and do so in terms which do not depart substantially from existing law. Section 106 deals with the situation in which the accused is convicted, no confiscation hearing is held and no confiscation order is made on conviction but benefit is discovered later. One possibility (contemplated by subs (5)) is that the benefit from crime carried out before conviction is received after conviction.

Subs. (1)
The prosecutor has evidence which was not available to him. This makes it clear that there must be new matter; the section does not give the prosecutor a second bite at the cherry if he was dissatisfied with the outcome of the first hearing.

The prosecutor applies. Although after the making of the confiscation order, its enforcement will not be in the prosecutor's hands, it is nevertheless the prosecutor and not the enforcement administrator who has the right to make application under this section.

Subs. (2)
The court. By subs.(11) jurisdiction is given to "the court which had jurisdiction in respect of the offence or offences concerned to make a confiscation order".

Subs. (7)
Since the accused will have been sentenced on the basis that there was not to be a confiscation order, the court must take into account any financial penalty which was imposed and any order for forfeiture, both of which affect his realisable property and which may have in fact affected his benefit from the offence. The obligation is to "have regard . . . to", not necessarily to deduct. How such a financial penalty will affect a confiscation order under s.92 will depend on the particular circumstances of the case.

105 No order made: reconsideration of benefit

(1) This section applies if the following two conditions are satisfied.

(2) The first condition is that in proceeding under section 92 the court has decided that—

(a) the accused has a criminal lifestyle but has not benefited from his general criminal conduct, or

    (b) the accused does not have a criminal lifestyle and has not ben-
efited from his particular criminal conduct.

(3) The second condition is that—

    (a) the prosecutor has evidence which was not available to him when
the court decided that the accused had not benefited from his general or particular criminal conduct,

    (b) before the end of the period of six years starting with the date of
conviction the prosecutor applies to the court to consider the evidence, and

    (c) after considering the evidence the court concludes that it would
have decided that the accused had benefited from his general or
particular criminal conduct (as the case may be) if the evidence
had been available to it.

(4) If this section applies the court—

    (a) must make a fresh decision under section 92(5)(b) or (c) as to
whether the accused has benefited from his general or particular
criminal conduct (as the case may be);

    (b) may make a confiscation order under that section.

(5) Subsections (6) to (11) below apply if the court proceeds under section
92 in pursuance of this section.

(6) If the court has already sentenced the accused for the offence (or any
of the offences) concerned section 92(4) does not apply.

(7) Section 94(2) does not apply, and the rules applying instead are that
the court must take account of—

    (a) conduct occurring before the date of the original decision that the
accused had not benefited from his general or particular criminal
conduct;

    (b) property obtained before that date;

    (c) property obtained on or after that date if it was obtained as a
result of or in connection with conduct occurring before that date.

(8) In relation to the assumptions that the court must make under section
96—

    (a) the first and second assumptions do not apply with regard to
property first held by the accused on or after the date of the original decision that the accused had not benefited from his general
or particular criminal conduct;

    (b) the third assumption does not apply with regard to expenditure
incurred by him on or after that date;

    (c) the fourth assumption does not apply with regard to property
obtained (or assumed to have been obtained) by him on or after
that date.

(9) The recoverable amount for the purposes of section 92 is such amount
as—

    (a) the court believes is just, but

    (b) does not exceed the amount found under section 93.

(10) In arriving at the just amount the court must have regard in particular
to—

    (a) the amount found under section 93;

    (b) any fine imposed on the accused in respect of the offence (or any
of the offences) concerned;

    (c) any order which falls within section 97(3) and has been made
against him in respect of the offence (or any of the offences) concerned and has not already been taken into account by a court in
deciding what is the free property held by the accused for the purposes of section 95;

    (d) any compensation order which has been made against him in
respect of the offence (or any of the offences) concerned under
section 249 of the Procedure Act.

(11) If an order for the payment of compensation under section 249 of the Procedure Act has been made against the accused in respect of the offence or offences concerned, section 97(5) and (6) do not apply.

(12) The date of conviction is the date found by applying section 104(10).

(13) In this section references to the court are to the court which had jurisdiction in respect of the offence or offences concerned to make a confiscation order.

GENERAL NOTE
   Section 105 applies where a hearing was held, the court decided that the accused had a criminal lifestyle but had not benefited from his general criminal conduct or that he did not have a criminal lifestyle and had not benefited from his particular criminal conduct. The principle underlying ss.105 and 106 is that the prosecutor should only apply for a reconsideration where new evidence comes to light. It is not appropriate for the prosecutor to have evidence at the time of the original proceedings, not to apply for a confiscation order on that occasion but to apply for a reconsideration at a later date.

106   Order made: reconsideration of benefit

(1) This section applies if—
   (a) a court has made a confiscation order,
   (b) there is evidence which was not available to the prosecutor at the relevant time,
   (c) the prosecutor believes that if the court were to find the amount of the accused's benefit in pursuance of this section it would exceed the relevant amount,
   (d) before the end of the period of six years starting with the date of conviction the prosecutor applies to the court to consider the evidence, and
   (e) after considering the evidence the court thinks it is appropriate for it to proceed under this section.

(2) The court must make a new calculation of the accused's benefit from the conduct concerned, and when it does so subsections (3) to (5) below apply.

(3) Section 94(2) does not apply, and the rules applying instead are that the court must take account of—
   (a) conduct occurring up to the time it decided the accused's benefit for the purposes of the confiscation order;
   (b) property obtained up to that time;
   (c) property obtained after that time if it was obtained as a result of or in connection with conduct occurring before that time.

(4) In applying section 94(3) the confiscation order must be ignored.

(5) In relation to the assumptions that the court must make under section 96—
   (a) the first and second assumptions do not apply with regard to property first held by the accused after the time the court decided his benefit for the purposes of the confiscation order;
   (b) the third assumption does not apply with regard to expenditure incurred by him after that time;
   (c) the fourth assumption does not apply with regard to property obtained (or assumed to have been obtained) by him after that time.

(6) If the amount found under the new calculation of the accused's benefit exceeds the relevant amount the court—
   (a) must make a new calculation of the recoverable amount for the purposes of section 92, and
   (b) if it exceeds the amount required to be paid under the confiscation order, may vary the order by substituting for the amount required to be paid such amount as it believes just.

(7) In applying subsection (6)(a) the court must—
    (a) take the new calculation of the accused's benefit;
    (b) apply section 95 as if references to the time the confiscation order is made were to the time of the new calculation of the recoverable amount and as if references to the date of the confiscation order were to the date of that new calculation.

(8) In applying subsection (6)(b) the court must have regard in particular to—
    (a) any fine imposed on the accused for the offence (or any of the offences) concerned;
    (b) any order which falls within section 97(3) and has been made against him in respect of the offence (or any of the offences) concerned and has not already been taken into account by a court in deciding what is the free property held by the accused for the purposes of section 95;
    (c) any order which has been made against him in respect of the offence (or any of the offences) concerned under section 249 of the Procedure Act.

(9) But in applying subsection (6)(b) the court must not have regard to an order falling within subsection (8)(c) if a court has made a direction under section 97(6).

(10) In deciding under this section whether one amount exceeds another the court must take account of any change in the value of money.

(11) The relevant time is—
    (a) when the court calculated the accused's benefit for the purposes of the confiscation order, if this section has not applied previously;
    (b) when the court last calculated the accused's benefit in pursuance of this section, if this section has applied previously.

(12) The relevant amount is—
    (a) the amount found as the accused's benefit for the purposes of the confiscation order, if this section has not applied previously;
    (b) the amount last found as the accused's benefit in pursuance of this section, if this section has applied previously.

(13) The date of conviction is the date found by applying section 104(10).

GENERAL NOTE
Section 106 enables the amount payable under a confiscation order, once made, to be increased. Application must be made to the court in which the original hearings took place within six years of the original conviction. The procedure may be used to increase the amount payable under a confiscation order on one or more occasions.

107   Order made: reconsideration of available amount

(1) This section applies if—
    (a) a court has made a confiscation order,
    (b) the amount required to be paid was the amount found under section 93(2), and
    (c) the prosecutor applies to the court to make a new calculation of the available amount.

(2) In a case where this section applies the court must make the new calculation, and in doing so it must apply section 95 as if references to the time the confiscation order is made were to the time of the new calculation and as if references to the date of the confiscation order were to the date of the new calculation.

(3) If the amount found under the new calculation exceeds the relevant amount the court may vary the order by substituting for the amount required to be paid such amount as—
    (a) it thinks is just, but

     (b) does not exceed the amount found as the accused's benefit from the conduct concerned.

(4) In arriving at the just amount the court must have regard in particular to—

     (a) any fine imposed on the accused for the offence (or any of the offences) concerned;

     (b) any order which falls within section 97(3) and has been made against him in respect of the offence (or any of the offences) concerned and has not already been taken into account by a court in deciding what is the free property held by the accused for the purposes of section 95;

     (c) any order which has been made against him in respect of the offence (or any of the offences) concerned under section 249 of the Procedure Act.

(5) But in deciding what is just the court must not have regard to an order falling within subsection (4)(c) if a court has made a direction under section 97(6).

(6) In deciding under this section whether one amount exceeds another the court must take account of any change in the value of money.

(7) The relevant amount is—

     (a) the amount found as the available amount for the purposes of the confiscation order, if this section has not applied previously;

     (b) the amount last found as the available amount in pursuance of this section, if this section has applied previously.

(8) The amount found as the accused's benefit from the conduct concerned is—

     (a) the amount so found when the confiscation order was made, or

     (b) if one or more new calculations of the accused's benefit have been made under section 106 the amount found on the occasion of the last such calculation.

GENERAL NOTE

    Paragraph 172 of the Explanatory Notes states that this section applies where the court made a confiscation order for an amount lower than the accused's assessed benefit because there was insufficient realisable property to satisfy an order in the full amount. The prosecutor may apply to the court for the court to recalculate the available amount. Any number of applications may be made (see Lord Rooker, *Hansard,* H.L. April 22, 2002, Col. 77) and there is no limitation to the time when an application may be made (in contrast to ss.104 to 106). If the court calculates that the available amount has increased, it may vary the amount payable under the confiscation order but may not increase it beyond the defendant's assessed benefit.

Subs. (4)

    This subsection is additional to the existing legislation. It requires the court to have regard to any fine or order as set out in s.97(3) imposed on the accused following the original conviction (because these may affect the amount the accused is able to pay).

108   Inadequacy of available amount: variation of order

(1) This section applies if—

     (a) a court has made a confiscation order, and

     (b) the accused or the prosecutor applies to the court to vary the order under this section.

(2) In such a case the court must calculate the available amount and in doing so it must apply section 95 as if references to the time the confiscation order is made were to the time of the calculation and as if references to the date of the confiscation order were to the date of the calculation.

(3) If the court finds that the available amount (as so calculated) is inadequate to meet the amount remaining to be paid it may vary the order

by substituting for the amount required to be paid such smaller amount as the court believes is just.

(4) If a person's estate has been sequestrated or he has been adjudged bankrupt, or if an order for the winding up of a company has been made, the court must take into account the extent to which realisable property held by him or by the company may be distributed among creditors.

(5) The court may disregard any inadequacy which it thinks is attributable (wholly or partly) to anything done by the accused for the purpose of preserving property held by the recipient of a tainted gift from any risk of realisation under this Part.

(6) In subsection (4) "company" means any company which may be wound up under the Insolvency Act 1986 (c. 45) or the Insolvency (Northern Ireland) Order 1989 (S.I. 1989/2405 (N.I. 19)).

GENERAL NOTE

Another situation identified by the Scottish Law Commission as requiring provision is that in which the value of accused's property is inadequate to meet an outstanding balance on the confiscation order. Such a situation might arise if, for example, an asset was accidentally destroyed or damaged. In the case of an investment, an adverse market movement could have a similar effect. Since s.120 applies to the enforcement of confiscation orders the provisions which apply to fines, failure to meet a confiscation order can result in the imposition of the alternative sentence of imprisonment. If the accused's available property is truly reduced below the level required to pay the confiscation order he has a very real incentive to apply for a reduction.

109   Inadequacy of available amount: discharge of order

(1) This section applies if—
  (a) a court has made a confiscation order,
  (b) the prosecutor applies to the court to discharge the order under this section, and
  (c) the amount remaining to be paid under the order is less than £1,000.

(2) In such a case the court must calculate the available amount, and in doing so it must apply section 95 as if references to the time the confiscation order is made were to the time of the calculation and as if references to the date of the confiscation order were to the date of the calculation.

(3) If the court—
  (a) finds that the available amount (as so calculated) is inadequate to meet the amount remaining to be paid, and
  (b) is satisfied that the inadequacy is due wholly to a specified reason or a combination of specified reasons,
it may discharge the confiscation order.

(4) The specified reasons are—
  (a) in a case where any of the realisable property consists of money in a currency other than sterling, that fluctuations in currency exchange rates have occurred;
  (b) any reason specified by the Scottish Ministers.

(5) The Scottish Ministers may by order vary the amount for the time being specified in subsection (1)(c).

GENERAL NOTE

This section provides for writing off a confiscation order when the amount outstanding is less than £1,000 and the reason is a fluctuation in the value of foreign currency, or some other reason specified by the Scottish Ministers. The provision has its origins in representations made by (English) justices' chief executives about the difficulties caused when small, unenforceable orders remain on their books indefinitely (see Lord Rooker, *Hansard*, H.L. April 22, 2002, Col.78.

110   Information

(1) This section applies if—

    (a) the court proceeds under section 92 in pursuance of section 104 or 105, or

    (b) the prosecutor applies under section 106.

(2) In such a case—

    (a) the prosecutor must give the court a statement of information within such period as the court may specify;

    (b) section 101 applies accordingly (with appropriate modifications where the prosecutor applies under section 106);

    (c) sections 102 and 103 apply accordingly.

GENERAL NOTE

Section 110 makes it clear that the earlier provisions dealing with statements of information and the provision of information by the accused apply to reconsideration proceedings as they apply to confiscation proceedings immediately following a conviction.

Accused unlawfully at large

111   Conviction or other disposal of accused

(1) This section applies if an accused is unlawfully at large after—

    (a) he is convicted of an offence or offences, whether in solemn or summary proceedings, or

    (b) in the case of summary proceedings in respect of an offence (without proceeding to conviction) an order is made discharging him absolutely.

(2) If this section applies the court may, on the application of the prosecutor and if it believes it is appropriate for it to do so, proceed under section 92 in the same way as it must proceed if the conditions there mentioned are satisfied; but this is subject to subsection (3).

(3) If the court proceeds under section 92 as applied by this section, this Part has effect with these modifications—

    (a) any person the court believes is likely to be affected by an order under section 92 is entitled to appear before the court and make representations;

    (b) the court must not make an order under section 92 unless the prosecutor has taken reasonable steps to contact the accused;

    (c) section 92(12) applies as if the reference to subsection (2) were to subsection (1) of this section;

    (d) sections 96, 101(3), 102 and 103 do not apply;

    (e) sections 104, 105 and 106 do not apply while the accused is still unlawfully at large.

(4) Once the accused has ceased to be unlawfully at large, section 104 has effect as if subsection (1)(a) read—

        "(a) in a case where section 111 applies the court did not proceed under section 92,".

GENERAL NOTE

There is an obvious incentive for an accused person to try to avoid a confiscation order (and indeed any other sentence) by fleeing from justice after conviction (a disturbing number of convicted persons get bail pending deferred sentence or appeal and then fail to appear at the continued, or appeal, hearing). This section seeks to ensure that confiscation orders cannot be avoided by this means. It applies the s.92 procedure subject to certain necessary variations. There is a requirement that the prosecutor has "taken reasonable steps to contact the accused". The obvious such step is the issuing of the non-appearance warrant (which the court has no doubt granted) to the police for execution.

112   Accused neither convicted nor acquitted

(1) This section applies if—

    (a) proceedings for an offence or offences are instituted against an accused but are not concluded,

    (b) he is unlawfully at large, and

    (c) the period of two years (starting with the day the court believes he first became unlawfully at large) has ended.

(2) If this section applies the court may, on an application by the prosecutor and if it believes it is appropriate for it to do so, proceed under section 92 in the same way as it must proceed if the conditions there mentioned are satisfied; but this is subject to subsection (3).

(3) If the court proceeds under section 92 as applied by this section, this Part has effect with these modifications—

    (a) any person the court believes is likely to be affected by an order under section 92 is entitled to appear before the court and make representations;

    (b) the court must not make an order under section 92 unless the prosecutor has taken reasonable steps to contact the accused;

    (c) section 92(12) applies as if the reference to subsection (2) were to subsection (1) of this section;

    (d) sections 96, 101(3), 102, 103, 104 and 105 do not apply;

    (e) section 106 does not apply while the accused is still unlawfully at large.

(4) Once the accused has ceased to be unlawfully at large, section 106 has effect as if references to the date of conviction were to—

    (a) the day when proceedings for the offence were instituted against the accused, or

    (b) if there are two or more offences and proceedings for them were instituted on different days, the earliest of those days.

(5) If—

    (a) the court makes an order under section 92 as applied by this section, and

    (b) the accused is later convicted of the offence (or any of the offences) concerned,

section 92 does not apply so far as that conviction is concerned.

GENERAL NOTE

    Section 112 deals with the situation in which the accused does not wait to be convicted before he flees. The trap for the Scottish practitioner lies in the definition of the commencement of proceedings in s.151(1). For the most part, that definition is unexceptional but it does include, at s.151(1)(b), a reference to the accused being charged with the offence without being arrested. Since one of the other options is appearance on petition or service of an indictment or complaint, the reference to charging relates, presumably, to charging by the police – something which does not commence proceedings for any other purpose. However, a person charged by the police but not arrested is not unlawfully at large. He is fully entitled to be at liberty and to go where he chooses.

113   Variation of order

(1) This section applies if—

    (a) the court makes a confiscation order under section 92 as applied by section 112,

    (b) the accused ceases to be unlawfully at large,

    (c) he is convicted of an offence (or any of the offences) mentioned in section 112(1)(a),

    (d) he believes that the amount required to be paid was too large (taking the circumstances prevailing when the amount was found for the purposes of the order), and

    (e) before the end of the relevant period he applies to the court to consider the evidence on which his belief is based.

(2) If (after considering the evidence) the court concludes that the accused's belief is well founded—

     (a) it must find the amount which should have been the amount required to be paid (taking the circumstances prevailing when the amount was found for the purposes of the order), and

     (b) it may vary the order by substituting for the amount required to be paid such amount as it believes is just.

(3) The relevant period is the period of 28 days starting with—

     (a) the date on which the accused was convicted of the offence mentioned in section 112(1)(a), or

     (b) if there are two or more offences and the convictions were on different dates, the date of the latest.

(4) But in a case where section 112(1)(a) applies to more than one offence the court must not make an order under this section unless it is satisfied that there is no possibility of any further proceedings being taken or continued in relation to any such offence in respect of which the accused has not been convicted.

114   Discharge of order

(1) Subsection (2) applies if—

     (a) the court makes a confiscation order under section 92 as applied by section 112,

     (b) the accused is later tried for the offence or offences concerned and acquitted of the offence or offences, and

     (c) he applies to the court to discharge the order.

(2) In such a case the court must discharge the order.

(3) Subsection (4) applies if—

     (a) the court makes a confiscation order under section 92 as applied by section 112,

     (b) the accused ceases to be unlawfully at large,

     (c) subsection (1)(b) does not apply, and

     (d) he applies to the court to discharge the order.

(4) In such a case the court may discharge the order if it finds that—

     (a) there has been undue delay in continuing the proceedings mentioned in section 112(1), or

     (b) the prosecutor does not intend to proceed with the prosecution.

(5) If the court discharges a confiscation order under this section it may make such a consequential or incidental order as it thinks is appropriate.

Appeals

115   Appeal by prosecutor

(1) Section 108 of the Procedure Act (Lord Advocate's right of appeal in solemn proceedings) is amended as provided in subsections (2) to (4).

(2) In subsection (1), after paragraph (c) insert—

     "(ca) a decision under section 92 of the Proceeds of Crime Act 2002 not to make a confiscation order;".

(3) In subsection (2)(b)(ii), for the words "or (c)" substitute ", (c) or (ca)".

(4) After subsection (2) insert—

     "(3) For the purposes of subsection (2)(b)(i) above in its application to a confiscation order by virtue of section 92(11) of the Proceeds of Crime Act 2002, the reference to the disposal being unduly lenient is a reference to the amount required to be paid by the order being unduly low."

(5) Section 175 of the Procedure Act (right of appeal in summary proceedings) is amended as provided in subsections (6) to (8).

(6) In subsection (4), after paragraph (c) insert—

     "(ca) a decision under section 92 of the Proceeds of Crime Act 2002 not to make a confiscation order;".

(7) In subsection (4A)(b)(ii), for the words "or (c)" substitute ", (c) or (ca)".

(8) After subsection (4A) insert—

"(4B) For the purposes of subsection (4A)(b)(i) above in its application to a confiscation order by virtue of section 92(11) of the Proceeds of Crime Act 2002, the reference to the disposal being unduly lenient is a reference to the amount required to be paid by the order being unduly low."

GENERAL NOTE

This section gives the prosecutor a clear power to appeal against any decision of the court not to make a confiscation order and also against any confiscation order where it considers that the amount required to be paid is unduly low. Section 108 of the Criminal Procedure (Scotland) Act 1995 operates by listing the disposals against which the Lord Advocate may appeal and subs.(2) of the present section adds a decision not to make a confiscation order to that list. Subsection (4) makes it clear that the amount of a confiscation order is within the category of sentences which the Lord Advocate can appeal as being "unduly lenient" (an expression which is to be understood in a confiscation context as "unduly low"). The usual approach of the High Court is only to interfere if the sentence appealed by the Crown fell outside the range of sentences which the sentencing judge could reasonably have considered appropriate, rather than that the sentence was not the one which the Appeal Court would have selected (see *HM Advocate v. Bell* 1995 SCCR 244 and *HM Advocate v. Gordon* 1996 SCCR 274). That case law has, however, been developed in a context in which there is very little statutory guidance for the sentencing court as to the selection of the appropriate sentence within a very wide band. The confiscation procedure, on the other hand, is one in which, given a set of findings in fact about the accused's financial position, one should reach the amount of the order by a process of mathematics. It remains to be seen how, if at all, the case law on Crown appeals against sentence will be applied to confiscation.

Payment and enforcement

116   Time for payment

(1) The amount ordered to be paid under a confiscation order must be paid on the making of the order; but this is subject to the following provisions of this section.

(2) If the accused shows that he needs time to pay the amount ordered to be paid, the court making the confiscation order may make an order allowing payment to be made in a specified period.

(3) The specified period—

    (a) must start with the day on which the confiscation order is made, and

    (b) must not exceed six months.

(4) If within the specified period the accused applies to the sheriff court for the period to be extended and the court, after giving the prosecutor an opportunity of being heard, believes there are exceptional circumstances, it may make an order extending the period.

(5) The extended period—

    (a) must start with the day on which the confiscation order is made, and

    (b) must not exceed 12 months.

(6) An order under subsection (4)—

    (a) may be made after the end of the specified period, but

    (b) must not be made after the end of the period of twelve months starting with the day on which the confiscation order is made.

(7) The court must not make an order under subsection (2) or (4) unless it gives the prosecutor an opportunity to make representations.

GENERAL NOTE

The rule is that a confiscation order is to be paid immediately, unless the accused can demonstrate to the court that he needs more time to pay. If the court is satisfied that it is required, the court may allow up to six months time to pay, and up to a further six months on a later occasion if there are exceptional reasons justifying the extension. One might expect time to be required for payment in any case in which the accused's assets are in anything other than completely liquid form.

117   Interest on unpaid sums

(1) If the amount required to be paid by a person under a confiscation order is not paid when it is required to be paid (whether when the order is made or within a period specified under section 116), he must pay interest on the amount for the period for which it remains unpaid.

(2) The rate of interest is the rate payable under a decree of the Court of Session.

(3) For the purposes of this section no amount is required to be paid under a confiscation order if—
    (a) an application has been made under section 116(4),
    (b) the application has not been determined by the court, and
    (c) the period of 12 months starting with the day on which the confiscation order was made has not ended.

(4) In applying this Part the amount of the interest must be treated as part of the amount to be paid under the confiscation order.

GENERAL NOTE

This section makes it clear that the accused must pay interest on a confiscation order which is not paid in full by the time allowed. It should not, however, be thought that this gives the accused the option, subject to a penalty in interest, of deferring payment of a confiscation order indefinitely. Section 118 applies the fines enforcement provisions to confiscation orders and s.128 makes provision for the appointment of enforcement administrators.

118   Application of provisions about fine enforcement

(1) The provisions of the Procedure Act specified in subsection (2) apply, with the qualifications mentioned in that subsection, in relation to a confiscation order as if the amount ordered to be paid were a fine imposed on the accused by the court making the confiscation order.

(2) Those provisions are—
    (a) section 211(3) to (6);
    (b) section 214(4) to (6), but as if the references in subsection (4) to payment by instalments were omitted;
    (c) section 216, but as if subsection (1)—
        (i) gave the prosecutor an opportunity to be heard at any enquiry under that subsection; and
        (ii) applied whether the offender was in prison or not;
    (d) section 217;
    (e) section 218(2) and (3);
    (f) section 219, provided that—
        (i) where a court imposes a period of imprisonment in respect of both a fine and a confiscation order the amounts in respect of which the period is imposed must, for the purposes of subsection (2), be aggregated;
        (ii) before imposing a period of imprisonment by virtue of that section the court must require a report from any administrator appointed in relation to the confiscation order as to whether and how he is likely to exercise his powers and duties under this Part and must take that report into account; and the court may, pending such exercise, postpone any decision as to such imposition; and
        (iii) where an administrator has not been appointed in relation to the confiscation order, or where the accused does not ask under section 116 for time for payment of any confiscation

order imposed by the court, the prosecutor may apply to the court to postpone the imposition of any period of imprisonment for a period not exceeding 3 months to enable the prosecutor to apply to the court for the appointment of an administrator;

(g) section 220, but as if the reference in subsection (1) to payment of a sum by the person included a reference to payment of the sum in respect of the person by an administrator appointed in relation to the confiscation order;

(h) section 221, except where an administrator is appointed in relation to the confiscation order;

    (i) section 222, except that for the purposes of that section "confiscation order" in subsection (1) above must be construed as including such an order within the meaning of the Drug Trafficking Act 1994 (c. 37), the Criminal Justice (Confiscation) (Northern Ireland) Order 1990 (S.I. 1990/2588 (N.I. 17)), the Proceeds of Crime (Northern Ireland) Order 1996 (S.I. 1996/ 1299 (N.I. 9)) or of Part 2 or 4 of this Act;

(j) section 223;

(k) section 224.

(3) Where a court, by virtue of subsection (1), orders the amount ordered to be paid under a confiscation order to be recovered by civil diligence under section 221 of the Procedure Act, any arrestment executed by a prosecutor under subsection (3) of section 124 of this Act is to be treated as having been executed by the court as if that subsection authorised such execution.

(4) Subsection (5) applies where—

(a) a warrant for apprehension of the accused is issued for a default in payment of the amount ordered to be paid under a confiscation order in respect of an offence or offences, and

(b) at the time the warrant is issued the accused is liable to serve a period of imprisonment or detention (other than one of life imprisonment or detention for life) in respect of the offence (or any of the offences).

(5) In such a case any period of imprisonment or detention to which the accused is liable by virtue of section 219 of the Procedure Act runs from the expiry of the period of imprisonment or detention mentioned in subsection (4)(b).

GENERAL NOTE

By this section, confiscation orders are enforced as if they were fines, except that it is possible for administrators to be appointed who will realise assets. By subs.(4) any period of imprisonment imposed in default of payment is to run consecutively to the sentence imposed in respect of the offence of which the accused was convicted. To seek no time to pay and the imposition of the alternative is, therefore, not likely to be regarded as an attractive option.

Restraint orders etc

119 Conditions for exercise of powers

(1) The court may exercise the powers conferred by section 120 if any of the following conditions is satisfied.

(2) The first condition is that—

(a) a criminal investigation has been instituted in Scotland with regard to an offence, and

(b) there is reasonable cause to believe that the alleged offender has benefited from his criminal conduct.

(3) The second condition is that—

   (a) proceedings for an offence have been instituted in Scotland and not concluded, and

   (b) there is reasonable cause to believe that the accused has benefited from his criminal conduct.

(4) The third condition is that—

   (a) an application by the prosecutor has been made under section 104, 105, 111 or 112 and not concluded, or the court believes that such an application is to be made, and

   (b) there is reasonable cause to believe that the accused has benefited from his criminal conduct.

(5) The fourth condition is that—

   (a) an application by the prosecutor has been made under section 106 and not concluded, or the court believes that such an application is to be made, and

   (b) there is reasonable cause to believe that the court will decide under that section that the amount found under the new calculation of the accused's benefit exceeds the relevant amount (as defined in that section).

(6) The fifth condition is that—

   (a) an application by the prosecutor has been made under section 107 and not concluded, or the court believes that such an application is to be made, and

   (b) there is reasonable cause to believe that the court will decide under that section that the amount found under the new calculation of the available amount exceeds the relevant amount (as defined in that section).

(7) The second condition is not satisfied if the court believes that—

   (a) there has been undue delay in continuing the proceedings, or

   (b) the prosecutor does not intend to proceed.

(8) If an application mentioned in the third, fourth or fifth condition has been made the condition is not satisfied if the court believes that—

   (a) there has been undue delay in continuing the application, or

   (b) the prosecutor does not intend to proceed.

(9) If the first condition is satisfied—

   (a) references in this Part to the accused are to the alleged offender;

   (b) references in this Part to the prosecutor are to the person the court believes is to have conduct of any proceedings for the offence;

   (c) section 144(8) has effect as if proceedings for the offence had been instituted against the accused when the investigation was instituted.

(10) In this section, sections 120 to 140 and Schedule 3 "the court" means—

   (a) the Court of Session, where a trial diet or a diet fixed for the purposes of section 76 of the Procedure Act in proceedings for the offence or offences concerned is to be, is being or has been held in the High Court of Justiciary;

   (b) the sheriff exercising his civil jurisdiction, where a diet referred to in paragraph (a) is to be, is being or has been held in the sheriff court.

GENERAL NOTE

   Sections 119 to 127 re-enact the "restraint order" mechanism first created for Scotland by the Criminal Procedure (Scotland) Act 1987. A restraint order interdicts those affected by it from dealing with their property and allows the Crown to use inhibition and arrestment to "freeze" property more effectively. The intended effect was described by Otton J. in *Re M* (1992) 1 All ER 537 thus: "The property to which the Restraint Order applies is no longer to be considered a part of the defendant's estate. He holds only notional title to such properties. All dealings with such property are to be held in abeyance until such time as the defendant is acquitted or a Confiscation Order is made and satisfied".

Restraint orders were first introduced by the Drug Trafficking Offences Act 1986 and were based on English *Mareva* injunctions. The English case law on restraint orders assumes the developed jurisprudence which surrounds such injunctions in English law but much of that jurisprudence has no application in Scotland. In particular, it is doubtful whether the Scottish courts have the power at common law to make an order for disclosure of the nature and location of assets such as is frequently associated with *Mareva* injunctions (see *In re T* (1992) 1 WLR 949) and the legislation does not provide them with the statutory power to do so. It was held in *In re O* (1991) 2 WLR 475 that the power to make an order for disclosure was inherent in the English legislation but that depended on the specific terms of s.37 of the Supreme Court Act 1981. (Contrast the specific powers given to the Court of Session by s.259 in making an interim administration order in respect of civil recovery).

There are two obvious problems associated with restraint orders. The first is that some estates will include assets which require active management if they are to retain their value and to provide for this s.127 provides for the appointment of management administrators. The nearest analogous office is that of receiver. The more pressing problem, especially from the perspective of the third party affected in some way by a restraint order, is the serious hardship which will sometimes be caused by the absolute nature of the order. To meet this, the Act provides in s.123 for the variation and recall of restraint orders but, as will be seen from that section, the conditions for such action are stringent.

Section 119 itself sets out the conditions for the exercise of the restraint power.

Subs. (2)

The point at which a restraint order may be made is brought forward to any time after a criminal investigation has been instituted, as defined in s.154 ("an investigation which police officers or other persons have a duty to conduct with a view to it being ascertained whether a person should be charged with an offence"). According to para.175 of the Explanatory Notes, "the change is likely to be of particular assistance in cases where the investigative process involves questioning the suspect (as often occurs, for example, in fraud cases) and the suspect is, accordingly, alerted to the risk that the authorities may be thinking of applying for a restraint order".

Subs. (3)

Proceedings have been instituted. Section 151(1) defines the institution of proceedings for the purposes of the present Act. Again, it includes the charging of the accused with the offence without his being arrested, though since an investigation may found a restraint order the practical effect of this oddity is likely to be less than in relation to s.112.

And not been concluded. See s.151(3) to (5).

Subs. (10)

The court. Restraint orders are matters for the civil courts, since they affect property rights. By subs.(10) the Court of Session has jurisdiction where the High Court is the trial court and the sheriff has jurisdiction where the sheriff court is the trial court. The Act does not give guidance about the court in which restraint orders should be sought where there is merely an investigation; but the Court of Session has universal jurisdiction except to the extent that it is specifically excluded by statute and it presumably, therefore, has competence in these matters.

120   Restraint orders etc

(1) If any condition set out in section 119 is satisfied the court may make an order (a restraint order) interdicting any specified person from dealing with any realisable property held by him.

(2) A restraint order may provide that it applies—

    (a) to all realisable property held by the specified person whether or not the property is described in the order;

    (b) to realisable property transferred to the specified person after the order is made.

(3) A restraint order may be made subject to exceptions, and an exception may in particular—

    (a) make provision for reasonable living expenses and reasonable legal expenses;

    (b) make provision for the purpose of enabling any person to carry on any trade, business, profession or occupation;

    (c) be made subject to conditions.

(4) But an exception to a restraint order may not make provision for any legal expenses which—

    (a) relate to an offence which falls within subsection (5), and

    (b) are incurred by a person against whom proceedings for the offence have been instituted or by a recipient of a tainted gift.

(5) These offences fall within this subsection—

    (a) the offence mentioned in section 119(2) or (3), if the first or second condition (as the case may be) is satisfied;

    (b) the offence (or any of the offences) concerned, if the third, fourth or fifth condition is satisfied.

(6) The court may make such order as it believes is appropriate for the purpose of ensuring that the restraint order is effective.

(7) A restraint order does not affect property subject to a charge under—

    (a) section 9 of the Drug Trafficking Offences Act 1986 (c. 32),

    (b) Part 6 of the Criminal Justice Act 1988 (c. 33),

    (c) Article 14 of the Criminal Justice (Confiscation) (Northern Ireland) Order 1990 (S.I. 1990/2588 (N.I. 17)),

    (d) section 27 of the Drug Trafficking Act 1994 (c. 37), or

    (e) Article 32 of the Proceeds of Crime (Northern Ireland) Order 1996 (S.I. 1996/1299 (N.I. 9)).

(8) Dealing with property includes removing the property from Scotland.

DEFINITIONS

"Realisable property": s.149

GENERAL NOTE

Section 120 explains the nature and effect of a restraint order. According to para.186 of the Explanatory Notes, "It is an order interdicting a specific person from dealing with any realisable property held by him. Thus it may be made both against the accused or person under investigation, and any other person holding realisable property".

Subs. (2)

The ambit of the restraint order is deliberately very wide. It reaches not only what the prosecutor knows the accused to possess but also anything which is undiscovered at the time of the making of the order and anything which the accused subsequently receives.

Subs. (3)

Subsection (3) provides for exceptions to be made for reasonable living and legal expenses and for carrying on any trade, business, profession or occupation. English restraint orders typically make provision for an exception for the reasonable living expenses of defendants, in terms of the Rules of the Supreme Court, Ord.115, r.4(1). Scottish restraint orders have not, in the past, usually made such exception, not least because the accused has usually been a remand prisoner with his living expenses being met by the Scottish Prison Service. However, the extension of the ambit of confiscation orders means that restraint orders are likely to be used more widely than in relation to drug traffickers alone and it may be that there will be some cases in which accused persons are at liberty and wish to make such applications. It must be kept clearly in view that English cases on living expenses are decided against a background of the Rules of Court and the jurisprudence on *Mareva* injunctions and will not necessarily be directly applicable as statements of principle which ought to apply in Scotland. It is, however, worth noting that Mann LJ pointed out in *Re Peters* (1988) 3 All ER 46 that exceptions for living expenses must always be subject to the need to leave sufficient property to satisfy any eventual confiscation order. Since in the past Scottish confiscation orders have tended to exhaust the accused's realisable property, the scope for such exceptions may be limited.

Reasonable legal expenses. It was held in *In re P, In re W* (1990) TLR 299 that where a restraint order is subject to the legal expenses exception it is proper for the order to direct taxation of his legal costs after verdict.

Subs. (4)

This subsection prevents funds under restraint from being released for legal expenses to defend the criminal charges in respect of which the restraint order is made or for legal expenses relating to those charges which are incurred by a recipient of a tainted gift. According to para.186 of the Explanatory Notes, legal aid will continue to be available in those circumstances.

Subs. (6)

This is, on the face of it, an extremely wide power. It may be that it has in contemplation the sorts of order which may be made as ancillary to *Mareva* injunctions in English law (discussed in these annotations in the context of s119) – for example, to bring funds back into the jurisdiction but, as noted above, some at least of those ancillary orders have a separate and specific statutory foundation.

Subs. (8)

This is consistent with s.329(1)(e).

121   Application, recall and variation

(1) This section applies to a restraint order.

(2) An order may be made on an ex parte application by the prosecutor, which may be heard in chambers.

(3) The prosecutor must intimate an order to every person affected by it.

(4) Subsection (3) does not affect the time when the order becomes effective.

(5) The prosecutor and any other person affected by the order may apply to the court to recall an order or to vary it; and subsections (6) to (9) apply in such a case.

(6) If an application under subsection (5) in relation to an order has been made but not determined, realisable property to which the order applies must not be realised.

(7) The court may—
    (a) recall the order;
    (b) vary the order.

(8) In the case of a restraint order, if the condition in section 119 which was satisfied was that proceedings were instituted or an application was made, the court must recall the order on the conclusion of the proceedings or of the application (as the case may be).

(9) In the case of a restraint order, if the condition in section 119 which was satisfied was that an investigation was instituted or an application was to be made, the court must recall the order if within a reasonable time proceedings for the offence are not instituted or the application is not made (as the case may be).

GENERAL NOTE

An application for a restraint order can only be made by the prosecutor. By subs.(2) the procedure is *ex parte* and in chambers. Once the order is obtained, the prosecutor must notify every person affected by it but by subs.(4) that requirement does not affect the time when it becomes effective. A restraint order is intended to be a temporary measure, designed to maintain the *status quo* until the court is in a position to make an order in relation to confiscation or forfeiture. Some mechanism is needed for the recall of such an order once its purpose has been served. Moreover, since a restraint order can affect the property rights of third parties it is necessary to provide some means of adjusting the order so as to minimise hardship to the blameless whilst maintaining the effectiveness of the order in general. Subsection (7) therefore makes provision for variation and recall. Variation or recall is discretionary except where proceedings are concluded. The kind of judgment which the court will have to exercise appears from *Re Peters* (1988) 1 QB 871 in which a restraint order was varied to allow specific payments in relation to the defendant's son's education. In matrimonial proceedings he was ordered to pay his wife a lump sum of £25,000. The Order was varied to enable that payment to be made. The prosecutor appealed and it was held that it was permissible to vary the Order so as not to disrupt the son's education but that the anticipatory discharge of liabilities which would arise only after the outcome of the trial was known was contrary to the terms and underlying purpose of the legislation. Note also an unreported English High Court case, *Re D and D* (see TJ Millington, *Restraint and Confiscation* Orders 1996) in which Hutchison, J, said that "perhaps a court which is making a variation will think that he may have to content himself in the exigencies in which he finds himself with something loess than a Rolls Royce lifestyle until his guilt or innocence is established.

By subs.(8), the court must recall the order when the proceedings are concluded.

122   Appeals

(1) If on an application for a restraint order the court decides not to make one, the prosecutor may reclaim or appeal to the Court of Session against the decision.

(2) The prosecutor and any person affected by the order may reclaim or appeal to the Court of Session against the decision of the court on an application under section 121(5).

GENERAL NOTE

This section provides the prosecutor with a right of appeal against a court's decision not to make a restraint order, and the prosecutor or any person affected by the order a right of appeal against the court's decision to vary or recall an order (or not to vary or recall it). Note that the right of appeal is to the Court of Session (the Inner House, obviously) but that there is no equivalent to s.44 which provides for an appeal in England from the Court of Appeal to the House of Lords.

123   Inhibition of property affected by order

(1) On the application of the Lord Advocate, the Court of Session may, in relation to the property mentioned in subsection (2), grant warrant for inhibition against any person specified in a restraint order.

(2) That property is the heritable realisable property to which the restraint order applies (whether generally or such of it as is specified in the application).

(3) The warrant for inhibition—

    (a) has effect as if granted on the dependence of an action for debt by the Lord Advocate against the person and may be executed, recalled, loosed or restricted accordingly, and

    (b) has the effect of letters of inhibition and must forthwith be registered by the Lord Advocate in the Register of Inhibitions and Adjudications.

(4) Section 155 of the Titles to Land Consolidation (Scotland) Act 1868 (c. 101) (effective date of inhibition) applies in relation to an inhibition for which warrant is granted under subsection (1) as it applies to an inhibition by separate letters or contained in a summons.

(5) The execution of an inhibition under this section in respect of property does not prejudice the exercise of an administrator's powers under or for the purposes of this Part in respect of that property.

(6) An inhibition executed under this section ceases to have effect when, or in so far as, the restraint order ceases to apply in respect of the property in relation to which the warrant for inhibition was granted.

(7) If an inhibition ceases to have effect to any extent by virtue of subsection (6) the Lord Advocate must—

    (a) apply for the recall or, as the case may be, the restriction of the inhibition, and

    (b) ensure that the recall or restriction is reflected in the Register of Inhibitions and Adjudications.

GENERAL NOTE

This section makes inhibition available as an ancillary to a restraint order but only upon application to the Court of Session. There seems to be no reason why such application should not be made even where the restraint order itself is appropriately obtained in the sheriff court.

124   Arrestment of property affected by order

(1) On the application of the prosecutor the court may, in relation to moveable realisable property to which a restraint order applies (whether generally or such of it as is specified in the application), grant warrant for arrestment.

(2) Such a warrant for arrestment may be granted only if the property would be arrestable if the person entitled to it were a debtor.

(3) A warrant under subsection (1) has effect as if granted on the dependence of an action for debt at the instance of the prosecutor against the person and may be executed, recalled, loosed or restricted accordingly.

(4) The execution of an arrestment under this section in respect of property does not prejudice the exercise of an administrator's powers under or for the purposes of this Part in respect of that property.

(5) An arrestment executed under this section ceases to have effect when, or in so far as, the restraint order ceases to apply in respect of the property in relation to which the warrant for arrestment was granted.

(6) If an arrestment ceases to have effect to any extent by virtue of subsection (5) the prosecutor must apply to the court for an order recalling, or as the case may be, restricting the arrestment.

GENERAL NOTE
    This section makes arrestment available, as if on the dependence.

125   Management administrators

(1) If the court makes a restraint order it may at any time, on the application of the prosecutor—
    (a) appoint an administrator to take possession of any realisable property to which the order applies and (in accordance with the court's directions) to manage or otherwise deal with the property;
    (b) order a person who has possession of property in respect of which an administrator is appointed to give him possession of it.

(2) An appointment of an administrator may be made subject to conditions or exceptions.

(3) Where the court makes an order under subsection (1)(b), the clerk of court must notify the accused and any person subject to the order of the making of the order.

(4) Any dealing of the accused or any such person in relation to property to which the order applies is of no effect in a question with the administrator unless the accused or, as the case may be, that person had no knowledge of the administrator's appointment.

(5) The court—
    (a) may order a person holding an interest in realisable property to which the restraint order applies to make to the administrator such payment as the court specifies in respect of a beneficial interest held by the accused or the recipient of a tainted gift;
    (b) may (on the payment being made) by order transfer, grant or extinguish any interest in the property.

(6) The court must not—
    (a) confer the power mentioned in subsection (1) to manage or otherwise deal with the property, or
    (b) exercise the power conferred on it by subsection (5),
unless it gives persons holding interests in the property a reasonable opportunity to make representations to it.

(7) The court may order that a power conferred by an order under this section is subject to such conditions and exceptions as it specifies.

(8) Managing or otherwise dealing with property includes—
    (a) selling the property or any part of it or interest in it;
    (b) carrying on or arranging for another person to carry on any trade or business the assets of which are or are part of the property;
    (c) incurring capital expenditure in respect of the property.

(9) Subsections (1)(b) and (5) do not apply to property for the time being subject to a charge under—

(a) section (9) of the Drug Trafficking Offences Act 1986 (c. 32);
(b) section 78 of the Criminal Justice Act 1988 (c. 33);
(c) Article 14 of the Criminal Justice (Confiscation) (Northern Ireland) Order 1990 (S.I. 1990/2588 (N.I. 17));
(d) section 27 of the Drug Trafficking Act 1994 (c. 37);
(e) Article 32 of the Proceeds of Crime (Northern Ireland) Order 1996 (S.I. 1996/1299 (N.I. 9)).

GENERAL NOTE

As paras 190-191 of the Explanatory Notes put it, this section "follows the current legislation in enabling an administrator to be appointed by the court where a restraint order has been made. The role of an administrator is to manage property to maintain its value until a confiscation order is made. The current legislation enables "an administrator" to be appointed on the application of the prosecutor. In fact, administrators perform two different functions. They manage property pending conviction (and sometimes afterwards) and they dispose of property to satisfy the confiscation order. The current legislation does not distinguish between them explicitly. The (Act) now deals separately with the two different sorts of administrators and calls them management administrators and enforcement administrators.

126   Seizure

(1) If a restraint order is in force a constable or a customs officer may seize any realisable property to which it applies to prevent its removal from Scotland.
(2) Property seized under subsection (1) must be dealt with in accordance with the directions of the court which made the order.

127   Restraint orders: restriction on proceedings and remedies

(1) While a restraint order has effect, the court may sist any action, execution or any legal process in respect of the property to which the order applies.
(2) If a court (whether the Court of Session or any other court) in which proceedings are pending in respect of any property is satisfied that a restraint order has been made or applied for or made in respect of the property, the court may either sist the proceedings or allow them to continue on any terms it thinks fit.
(3) Before exercising any power conferred by subsection (2), the court must give an opportunity to be heard to—
(a) the applicant for the restraint order;
(b) any administrator appointed under section 125.

Realisation of property: general

128   Enforcement administrators

(1) This section applies if—
(a) a confiscation order is made,
(b) it is not satisfied, and
(c) it is not subject to appeal.
(2) In such a case the court may on the application of the prosecutor exercise the powers conferred on it by this section.
(3) The court may appoint an administrator in respect of realisable property.
(4) An appointment of an administrator may be made subject to conditions or exceptions.
(5) The court may confer the powers mentioned in subsection (6) on an administrator appointed under subsection (3) above.
(6) Those powers are—
(a) power to take possession of any realisable property;
(b) power to manage or otherwise deal with the property;

  (c) power to realise any realisable property, in such manner as the court may specify.

 (7) The court may order any person who has possession of realisable property to give possession of it to an administrator referred to in subsection (5).

 (8) The clerk of court must notify the accused and any person subject to an order under subsection (7) of the making of the order.

 (9) Any dealing of the accused or any such person in relation to property to which the order applies is of no effect in a question with the administrator unless the accused or, as the case may be, that person had no knowledge of the administrator's appointment.

 (10) The court—

  (a) may order a person holding an interest in realisable property to make to the administrator such payment as the court specifies in respect of a beneficial interest held by the accused or the recipient of a tainted gift;

  (b) may (on the payment being made) by order transfer, grant or extinguish any interest in the property.

 (11) The court must not—

  (a) confer the power mentioned in subsection (6)(b) or (c) in respect of property, or

  (b) exercise the power conferred on it by subsection (10) in respect of property,

unless it gives persons holding interests in the property a reasonable opportunity to make representations to it.

 (12) Managing or otherwise dealing with property includes—

  (a) selling the property or any part of it or interest in it;

  (b) carrying on or arranging for another person to carry on any trade or business the assets of which are or are part of the property;

  (c) incurring capital expenditure in respect of the property.

 (13) The court may order that a power conferred by an order under this section is subject to such conditions and exceptions as it specifies.

 (14) Subsection (6) does not apply to property for the time being subject to a charge under—

  (a) section 9 of the Drug Trafficking Offences Act 1986 (c. 32);

  (b) section 78 of the Criminal Justice Act 1988 (c. 33);

  (c) Article 14 of the Criminal Justice (Confiscation) (Northern Ireland) Order 1990 (S.I. 1990/2588 (N.I. 17));

  (d) section 27 of the Drug Trafficking Act 1994 (c. 37);

  (e) Article 32 of the Proceeds of Crime (Northern Ireland) Order 1996 (S.I. 1996/1299 (N.I. 9)).

129 Management administrators: discharge

 (1) This section applies if—

  (a) an administrator stands appointed under section 125 in respect of realisable property (the management administrator), and

  (b) the court appoints an administrator under section 128.

 (2) The court must order the management administrator to transfer to the other administrator all property held by him by virtue of the powers conferred on him by section 125.

 (3) If the management administrator complies with an order under subsection (2) he is discharged—

  (a) from his appointment under that section,

  (b) from any obligation under this Act arising from his appointment.

130 Application of sums by enforcement administrator

 (1) This section applies to sums which—

(a) are in the hands of an administrator appointed under section 128(3), and

(b) fall within subsection (2).

(2) These sums fall within this subsection—

    (a) the proceeds of the realisation of property under section 128(6)(c);

    (b) any sums (other than those mentioned in paragraph (a)) in which the accused holds an interest.

(3) The sums must be applied as follows—

    (a) first, they must be applied in payment of such expenses incurred by a person acting as an insolvency practitioner as are payable under this subsection by virtue of section 432;

    (b) second, they must be applied in making any payments as directed by the court;

    (c) third, they must be applied on the accused's behalf towards satisfaction of the confiscation order.

(4) If the amount payable under any confiscation order has been fully paid and any sums remain in the administrator's hands he must distribute them—

    (a) among such persons who held (or hold) interests in the property concerned as the court directs, and

    (b) in such proportions as it directs.

(5) Before making a direction under subsection (4) the court must give persons who held (or hold) interests in the property concerned a reasonable opportunity to make representations to it.

(6) For the purposes of subsections (4) and (5) the property concerned is—

    (a) the property represented by the proceeds mentioned in subsection (2)(a);

    (b) the sums mentioned in subsection (2)(b).

(7) The administrator applies sums as mentioned in subsection (3)(c) by paying them to the appropriate clerk of court on account of the amount payable under the order.

(8) The appropriate clerk of court is the sheriff clerk of the sheriff court responsible for enforcing the confiscation order under section 211 of the Procedure Act as applied by section 118(1) of this Act.

131   Sums received by clerk of court

(1) This section applies if a clerk of court receives sums on account of the amount payable under a confiscation order (whether the sums are received under section 130 or otherwise).

(2) The clerk of court's receipt of the sums reduces the amount payable under the order, but he must apply the sums received as follows.

(3) First he must apply them in payment of such expenses incurred by a person acting as an insolvency practitioner as—

    (a) are payable under this subsection by virtue of section 432, but

    (b) are not already paid under section 130(3)(a).

(4) If the Lord Advocate has reimbursed the administrator in respect of remuneration or expenses under section 133 the clerk of court must next apply the sums in reimbursing the Lord Advocate.

(5) If the clerk of court received the sums under section 130 he must next apply them in payment of the administrator's remuneration and expenses.

(6) If a direction was made under section 97(6) for an amount of compensation to be paid out of sums recovered under the confiscation order, the clerk of court must next apply the sums in payment of that amount.

(7) If any amount remains after the clerk of court makes any payments required by the preceding provisions of this section, the amount must be disposed of in accordance with section 211(5) or (6) of the Procedure Act as applied by section 118(1) of this Act.

Exercise of powers

132   Powers of court and administrator

(1) This section applies to—
   (a) the powers conferred on a court by sections 119 to 131, 134 to 136 and Schedule 3;
   (b) the powers of an administrator appointed under section 125 or 128(3).
(2) The powers—
   (a) must be exercised with a view to the value for the time being of realisable property being made available (by the property's realisation) for satisfying any confiscation order that has been or may be made against the accused;
   (b) must be exercised, in a case where a confiscation order has not been made, with a view to securing that there is no diminution in the value of realisable property or of the proceeds of realisation;
   (c) must be exercised without taking account of any obligation of the accused or a recipient of a tainted gift if the obligation conflicts with the object of satisfying any confiscation order that has been or may be made against the accused;
   (d) may be exercised in respect of a debt owed by the Crown.
(3) Subsection (2) has effect subject to the following rules—
   (a) the powers must be exercised with a view to allowing a person other than the accused or a recipient of a tainted gift to retain or recover the value of any interest held by him;
   (b) in the case of realisable property held by a recipient of a tainted gift, the powers must be exercised with a view to realising no more than the value for the time being of the gift;
   (c) in a case where a confiscation order has not been made against the accused, property must not be realised if the court so orders under subsection (4).
(4) If on an application by the accused or by the recipient of a tainted gift the court decides that property cannot be replaced it may order that it must not be sold.
(5) An order under subsection (4) may be revoked or varied.

GENERAL NOTE
   This section is described by the Explanatory Notes as "an overarching clause that lays down general principles relating to the exercise of their enforcement powers by the court and administrators. It largely re-enacts the current legislation in that it emphasises, for example, that the satisfaction of a confiscation order takes precedence over any other obligations of the accused or the recipient of a tainted gift from the accused". Note, however, that there is new material in those parts of the section which require the powers to be exercised with a view to maintaining the value of the amount available for confiscation. The intention is to permit administrators to dispose of depreciating assets (subject to the right, in subs. (4) to challenge the administrator's decision to dispose of a particular asset on the grounds that the asset in question is irreplaceable).

Administrators: general

133   Protection of administrators

(1) If an administrator appointed under section 125 or 128(3)—
   (a) takes action in relation to property which is not realisable property,

(b) would be entitled to take the action if it were realisable property, and

(c) believes on reasonable grounds that he is entitled to take the action,

he is not liable to any person in respect of any loss or damage resulting from the action, except so far as the loss or damage is caused by his negligence.

(2) Subsection (3) applies if an administrator incurs expenses in the exercise of his functions at a time when—

(a) a confiscation order has not been made, or

(b) a confiscation order has been made but the administrator has recovered no money.

(3) As soon as is practicable after they have been incurred the expenses must be reimbursed by the Lord Advocate.

(4) Subsection (5) applies if—

(a) an amount is due in respect of the administrator's remuneration and expenses, but

(b) nothing (or not enough) is available to be applied in payment of them under section 131(4).

(5) The remuneration and expenses must be paid (or must be paid to the extent of the shortfall) by the Lord Advocate.

134   Protection of persons affected

(1) This section applies where an administrator is appointed under section 125 or 128(3).

(2) The following persons may apply to the court—

(a) any person affected by action taken by the administrator;

(b) any person who may be affected by action the administrator proposes to take.

(3) On an application under this section the court may make such order as it thinks appropriate.

135   Recall and variation of order

(1) The prosecutor, an administrator and any other person affected by an order made under section 125 or 128 may apply to the court to vary or recall the order.

(2) On an application under this section the court—

(a) may vary the order;

(b) may recall the order.

(3) But in the case of an order under section 125—

(a) if the condition in section 119 which was satisfied was that proceedings were started or an application was made, the court must recall the order on the conclusion of the proceedings or of the application (as the case may be);

(b) if the condition which was satisfied was that an investigation was started or an application was to be made, the court must recall the order if within a reasonable time proceedings for the offence are not started or the application is not made (as the case may be).

136   Appeals

(1) If on an application for an order under section 125 or 128 the court decides not to make one, the prosecutor may appeal to the Court of Session against the decision.

(2) If the court makes an order under section 125 or 128 the following persons may appeal to the Court of Session in respect of the court's decision—

(a) the prosecutor;

(b) any person affected by the order.

(3) If on an application for an order under section 134 the court decides not to make one, the person who applied for the order may appeal to the Court of Session against the decision.

(4) If the court makes an order under section 134, the following persons may appeal to the Court of Session in respect of the court's decision—
  (a) the person who applied for the order;
  (b) any person affected by the order;
  (c) the administrator.

(5) The following persons may appeal to the Court of Session against a decision of the court on an application under section 135—
  (a) the person who applied for the order in respect of which the application was made;
  (b) any person affected by the court's decision;
  (c) the administrator.

(6) On an appeal under this section the Court of Session may—
  (a) confirm the decision, or
  (b) make such order as it believes is appropriate.

137   Administrators: further provision

Schedule 3, which makes further provision about administrators appointed under section 125 and 128(3), has effect.

138   Administrators: restriction on proceedings and remedies

(1) Where an administrator is appointed under section 128, the court may sist any action, execution or other legal process in respect of the property to which the order appointing the administrator relates.

(2) If a court (whether the Court of Session or any other court) in which proceedings are pending in respect of any property is satisfied that an application has been made for the appointment of an administrator or that an administrator has been appointed in relation to that property, the court may either sist the proceedings or allow them to continue on any terms it thinks fit.

(3) Before exercising any power conferred by subsection (2) the court must give an opportunity to be heard to—
  (a) the prosecutor;
  (b) if appointed, the administrator.

Compensation

139   Serious default

(1) If the following three conditions are satisfied the court may order the payment of such compensation as it thinks is just.

(2) The first condition is satisfied if a criminal investigation has been instituted with regard to an offence and proceedings are not instituted for the offence.

(3) The first condition is also satisfied if proceedings for an offence are instituted against a person and—
  (a) they do not result in his conviction for the offence, or
  (b) he is convicted of the offence but the conviction is quashed or he is pardoned in respect of it.

(4) If subsection (2) applies the second condition is that—
  (a) in the criminal investigation there has been a serious default by a person mentioned in subsection (9), and
  (b) the investigation would not have continued if the default had not occurred.

(5) If subsection (3) applies the second condition is that—

(a) in the criminal investigation with regard to the offence or in its prosecution there has been a serious default by a person mentioned in subsection (9), and

(b) the proceedings would not have been instituted or continued if the default had not occurred.

(6) The third condition is that an application is made under this section by a person who held realisable property and has suffered loss in consequence of anything done in relation to it by or in pursuance of an order under this Part.

(7) The offence referred to in subsection (2) may be one of a number of offences with regard to which the investigation is instituted.

(8) The offence referred to in subsection (3) may be one of a number of offences for which the proceedings are instituted.

(9) Compensation under this section is payable to the applicant and—

(a) if the person in default was a constable of a police force (within the meaning of the Police (Scotland) Act 1967 (c. 77)), the compensation is payable by the police authority or joint police board for the police area for which that force is maintained;

(b) if the person in default was a constable not falling within paragraph (a), the compensation is payable by the body under whose authority he acts;

(c) if the person in default was a procurator fiscal or was acting on behalf of the Lord Advocate, the compensation is payable by the Lord Advocate;

(d) if the person in default was a customs officer, the compensation is payable by the Commissioners of Customs and Excise;

(e) if the person in default was an officer of the Commissioners of Inland Revenue, the compensation is payable by those Commissioners.

(10) Nothing in this section affects any delictual liability in relation to a serious default.

GENERAL NOTE

The power to freeze the whole estate of the accused and of an alleged recipient of a tainted gift carries with it the potential to do enormous damage to those estates and to the estates of others which might be affected by some mischance. Accordingly Parliament has provided a means by which the civil court (see s.119(10)) may be asked to order compensation. The ability of the civil court to do so is, however, very limited.

By subs.(1), the power to order compensation is discretionary. By subss.(2) and (3), the payment of compensation, even to a third party, depends on the absence of institution of proceedings, the acquittal of the accused, the quashing of his conviction or the grant of a pardon. There is no comfort under the Act for one who has lost where the accused is convicted, though subs.(10) preserves the ordinary law of delict and a remedy might exist there. More generally, the section requires the applicant to satisfy what may prove to be a most difficult set of criteria. First, the applicant has to satisfy the court that there has been "serious default" on the part of a person involved in the investigation or prosecution of the offences. It is not clear what the effect of the word "serious" will be but it might well require more than mere negligence. The adjective is applied to the default and not to the loss. It might mean that recklessness must be proved or perhaps even malice.

The class of persons involved in the investigation whose default can give rise to compensation is limited to those mentioned in subs.(9) and these are essentially police officers, procurators fiscal, advocate deputes and customs officers.

It must further be proved that, but for the default, the proceedings would not have been instituted or continued. This makes it clear that the default must have been in relation to something quite fundamental to the prosecution and it also raises interesting questions of proof, having regard to the reluctance the courts have traditionally shown to ordering the discovery of prosecution papers (see eg *Friel, Petitioner* 1981 SLT 113). Presumably that reluctance will be reduced where such discovery is required in order to adjudicate on a claim that there has been default such as to bring the section into play.

140   Confiscation order varied or discharged

(1) This section applies if—

    (a) the court varies a confiscation order under section 113 or discharges one under section 114, and

    (b) an application is made to the court by a person who held realisable property and has suffered loss as a result of the making of the order.

(2) The court may order the payment to the applicant of such compensation as it believes is just.

(3) Compensation payable under this section is payable by the Lord Advocate.

GENERAL NOTE

Paragraph 208 of the Explanatory Notes points out that this section allows compensation to be payable where a person who absconded before trial and against whom a confiscation order was subsequently made secures a variation or discharge of the order. The provision is not limited to serious default (as in s.139) because it is considered that the court should be able to exercise a more flexible approach in circumstances where a confiscation order has been made without the accused having been tried.

Enforcement abroad

141   Enforcement abroad

(1) This section applies if—

    (a) any of the conditions in section 119 are satisfied,

    (b) the prosecutor believes that realisable property is situated in a country or territory outside the United Kingdom (the receiving country), and

    (c) the prosecutor sends a request for assistance to the Secretary of State with a view to it being forwarded under this section.

(2) In a case where no confiscation order has been made, a request for assistance is a request to the government of the receiving country to secure that any person is prohibited from dealing with realisable property.

(3) In a case where a confiscation order has been made and has not been satisfied, discharged or quashed, a request for assistance is a request to the government of the receiving country to secure that—

    (a) any person is prohibited from dealing with realisable property,

    (b) realisable property is realised and the proceeds are applied in accordance with the law of the receiving country.

(4) No request for assistance may be made for the purposes of this section in a case where a confiscation order has been made and has been satisfied, discharged or quashed.

(5) If the Secretary of State believes it is appropriate to do so he may forward the request for assistance to the government of the receiving country.

(6) If property is realised in pursuance of a request under subsection (3) the amount ordered to be paid under the confiscation order must be taken to be reduced by an amount equal to the proceeds of the realisation.

(7) A certificate purporting to be issued by or on behalf of the requested government is sufficient evidence of the facts it states if it states—

    (a) that the property has been realised in pursuance of a request under subsection (3),

    (b) the date of realisation, and

    (c) the proceeds of realisation.

(8) If the proceeds of realisation made in pursuance of a request under subsection (3) are expressed in a currency other than sterling, they

must be taken to be the sterling equivalent calculated in accordance with the rate of exchange prevailing at the end of the day of realisation.

Interpretation

142   Criminal lifestyle

(1) An accused has a criminal lifestyle if (and only if) the offence (or any of the offences) concerned satisfies any of these tests—
  (a) it is specified in Schedule 4;
  (b) it constitutes conduct forming part of a course of criminal activity;
  (c) it is an offence committed over a period of at least six months and the accused has benefited from the conduct which constitutes the offence.

(2) Conduct forms part of a course of criminal activity if the accused has benefited from the conduct and—
  (a) in the proceedings in which he was convicted he was convicted of three or more other offences, each of three or more of them constituting conduct from which he has benefited, or
  (b) in the period of six years ending with the day when those proceedings were instituted (or, if there is more than one such day, the earliest day) he was convicted on at least two separate occasions of an offence constituting conduct from which he has benefited.

(3) But an offence does not satisfy the test in subsection (1)(b) or (c) unless the accused obtains relevant benefit of not less than £5000.

(4) Relevant benefit for the purposes of subsection (1)(b) is—
  (a) benefit from conduct which constitutes the offence;
  (b) benefit from any other conduct which forms part of the course of criminal activity and which constitutes an offence of which the accused has been convicted.

(5) Relevant benefit for the purposes of subsection (1)(c) is benefit from conduct which constitutes the offence.

(6) The Scottish Ministers may by order amend Schedule 4.

(7) The Scottish Ministers may by order vary the amount for the time being specified in subsection (3).

GENERAL NOTE
  The meaning of "criminal lifestyle" is central to the type of confiscation procedure to be followed in terms of s.92. This section does not require explanation beyond its terms but it should be noted that, in terms of subs. (3) it is open to the Scottish Ministers to amend the list of offences in Schedule 4.

143   Conduct and benefit

(1) Criminal conduct is conduct which—
  (a) constitutes an offence in Scotland, or
  (b) would constitute such an offence if it had occurred in Scotland.

(2) General criminal conduct of the accused is all his criminal conduct, and it is immaterial—
  (a) whether conduct occurred before or after the passing of this Act;
  (b) whether property constituting a benefit from conduct was obtained before or after the passing of this Act.

(3) Particular criminal conduct of the accused is all his criminal conduct which falls within the following paragraphs—
  (a) conduct which constitutes the offence or offences concerned;
  (b) conduct which constitutes offences of which he was convicted in the same proceedings as those in which he was convicted of the offence or offences concerned.

(4) A person benefits from conduct if he obtains property as a result of or in connection with the conduct.

(5) If a person obtains a pecuniary advantage as a result of or in connection with conduct, he is to be taken to obtain as a result of or in connection with the conduct a sum of money equal to the value of the pecuniary advantage.

(6) References to property or a pecuniary advantage obtained in connection with conduct include references to property or a pecuniary advantage obtained both in that connection and in some other.

(7) If a person benefits from conduct his benefit is the value of the property obtained.

GENERAL NOTE

Paragraph 216 of the Explanatory Notes points out that this section "unites in one new provision two similar but not identical definitions in the legislation relating to drug trafficking and that relating to other offences". In subs.(1)(b), note that this is not a double criminality test. It is enough if the conduct is a crime in Scotland. It need not be a crime in the jurisdiction in which it was done.

144   Tainted gifts and their recipients

(1) Subsections (2) and (3) apply if—
   (a) no court has made a decision as to whether the accused has a criminal lifestyle, or
   (b) a court has decided that the accused has a criminal lifestyle.

(2) A gift is tainted if it was made by the accused at any time after the relevant day.

(3) A gift is also tainted if it was made by the accused at any time and was of property—
   (a) which was obtained by the accused as a result of or in connection with his general criminal conduct, or
   (b) which (in whole or part and whether directly or indirectly) represented in the accused's hands property obtained by him as a result of or in connection with his general criminal conduct.

(4) Subsection (5) applies if a court has decided that an accused does not have a criminal lifestyle.

(5) A gift is tainted if it was made by the accused at any time after—
   (a) the date on which the offence concerned was committed, or
   (b) if his particular criminal conduct consists of two or more offences and they were committed on different dates, the earliest of those dates.

(6) For the purposes of subsection (5) an offence which is a continuing offence is committed on the first occasion when it is committed.

(7) A gift may be a tainted gift whether it was made before or after the passing of this Act.

(8) The relevant day is the first day of the period of six years ending with—
   (a) the day when proceedings for the offence concerned were instituted against the accused, or
   (b) if there are two or more offences and proceedings for them were instituted on different days, the earliest of those days.

(9) If the accused transfers property to another person (whether directly or indirectly) for a consideration whose value is significantly less than the value of the property at the time of the transfer, he is to be treated as making a gift.

(10) If subsection (9) applies the property given is to be treated as such share in the property transferred as is represented by the fraction—
   (a) whose numerator is the difference between the two values mentioned in subsection (9), and
   (b) whose denominator is the value of the property at the time of the transfer.

(11) References to a recipient of a tainted gift are to a person to whom the accused has (whether directly or indirectly) made the gift.

GENERAL NOTE
  According to para. 217 of the Explanatory Notes, this section "reappraises and aligns the two different tainted gift schemes currently found in the drug and non-drug legislation. The new scheme provides that, where the court has decided that the accused has a criminal lifestyle, any gift from the accused to any person in the six years before the institution of proceedings is caught, together with any gift at any time out of the proceeds of crime. This definition would apply both at the confiscation hearing and for the purposes of enforcement. However, if the court decides that the accused does not have a criminal lifestyle, only gifts made after the commission of the offence are caught. Again, this would apply at the confiscation hearing and for the purposes of enforcement".

145   Value: the basic rule

(1) This section applies for the purpose of deciding the value at any time of property then held by a person.

(2) Its value is the market value of the property at that time.

(3) But if at that time another person holds an interest in the property its value, in relation to the person mentioned in subsection (1), is the market value of his interest at that time ignoring any charging order under a provision listed in subsection (4).

(4) The provisions are—
  (a) section 9 of the Drug Trafficking Offences Act 1986 (c. 32);
  (b) section 78 of the Criminal Justice Act 1988 (c. 33);
  (c) Article 14 of the Criminal Justice (Confiscation) (Northern Ireland) Order 1990 (S.I. 1990/2588 (N.I. 17));
  (d) section 27 of the Drug Trafficking Act 1994 (c. 37);
  (e) Article 32 of the Proceeds of Crime (Northern Ireland) Order 1996 (S.I. 1996/1299 (N.I. 9)).

(5) This section has effect subject to sections 146 and 147.

146   Value of property obtained from conduct

(1) This section applies for the purpose of deciding the value of property obtained by a person as a result of or in connection with his criminal conduct; and the material time is the time the court makes its decision.

(2) The value of the property at the material time is the greater of the following—
  (a) the value of the property (at the time the person obtained it) adjusted to take account of later changes in the value of money;
  (b) the value (at the material time) of the property found under subsection (3).

(3) The property found under this subsection is—
  (a) if the person holds the property obtained, that property;
  (b) if he holds no part of the property obtained, any property which directly or indirectly represents it in his hands;
  (c) if he holds part of the property obtained, that part and any property which directly or indirectly represents the other part in his hands.

(4) The references in subsection (2)(a) and (b) to the value are to the value found in accordance with section 145.

147   Value of tainted gifts

(1) The value at any time (the material time) of a tainted gift is the greater of the following—

    (a) the value (at the time of the gift) of the property given, adjusted to take account of later changes in the value of money;

    (b) the value (at the material time) of the property found under subsection (2).

(2) The property found under this subsection is—

    (a) if the recipient holds the property given, that property;

    (b) if the recipient holds no part of the property given, any property which directly or indirectly represents it in his hands;

    (c) if the recipient holds part of the property given, that part and any property which directly or indirectly represents the other part in his hands.

(3) The references in subsection (1)(a) and (b) to the value are to the value found in accordance with section 145.

148   Free property

Property is free unless an order is in force in respect of it under—

    (a) section 27 of the Misuse of Drugs Act 1971 (c. 38) (forfeiture orders),

    (b) Article 11 of the Criminal Justice (Northern Ireland) Order 1994 (S.I. 1994/2795 (N.I. 15)) (deprivation orders),

    (c) Part 2 of the Proceeds of Crime (Scotland) Act 1995 (c. 43) (forfeiture of property used in crime),

    (d) section 143 of the Powers of Criminal Courts (Sentencing) Act 2000 (c. 6) (deprivation orders),

    (e) section 23 or 111 of the Terrorism Act 2000 (c. 11) (forfeiture orders), or

    (f) section 246, 266, 295(2) or 298(2) of this Act.

149   Realisable property

Realisable property is—

    (a) any free property held by the accused;

    (b) any free property held by the recipient of a tainted gift.

150   Property: general provisions

(1) Property is all property wherever situated and includes—

    (a) money;

    (b) all forms of property whether heritable or moveable and whether corporeal or incorporeal.

(2) The following rules apply in relation to property—

    (a) property is held by a person if he holds an interest in it;

    (b) property is obtained by a person if he obtains an interest in it;

    (c) property is transferred by one person to another if the first one transfers or grants an interest in it to the second;

    (d) references to property held by a person include references to his property vested in his permanent or interim trustee (within the meaning of the Bankruptcy (Scotland) Act 1985 (c. 66)), trustee in bankruptcy or liquidator;

    (e) references to an interest held by a person beneficially in property include references to an interest which would be held by him beneficially if the property were not so vested;

    (f) references to an interest, in relation to land in England, Wales or Northern Ireland, are to any legal estate or equitable interest or power;

    (g) references to an interest, in relation to land in Scotland, are to any estate, interest, servitude or other heritable right in or over land, including a heritable security;

    (h) references to an interest, in relation to property other than land, include references to a right (including a right to possession).

151   Proceedings

(1) Proceedings for an offence are instituted against a person—
  (a) on his arrest without warrant;
  (b) when he is charged with the offence without being arrested;
  (c) when a warrant to arrest him is granted;
  (d) when a warrant to cite him is granted;
  (e) when he first appears on petition or when an indictment or complaint is served on him.

(2) If more than one time is found under subsection (1) in relation to proceedings they are instituted at the earliest of those times.

(3) Proceedings for an offence are concluded when—
  (a) the trial diet is deserted simpliciter,
  (b) the accused is acquitted or, under section 65 or 147 of the Procedure Act, discharged or liberated,
  (c) the court sentences the accused without making a confiscation order and without postponing a decision as regards making such an order,
  (d) the court decides, after such a postponement, not to make a confiscation order,
  (e) the accused's conviction is quashed, or
  (f) the accused is pardoned.

(4) If a confiscation order is made against the accused in proceedings for an offence, the proceedings are concluded—
  (a) when the order is satisfied or discharged, or
  (b) when the order is quashed and there is no further possibility of an appeal against the decision to quash the order.

(5) If—
  (a) the accused is convicted in proceedings for an offence but the court decides not to make a confiscation order against him, and
  (b) on appeal under section 108(1)(ca) or 175(4)(ca) of the Procedure Act, the High Court of Justiciary refuses the appeal,
  the proceedings are concluded on the determination of the appeal.

152   Applications

(1) An application under section 104, 105, 111 or 112 is concluded—
  (a) in a case where the court decides not to make a confiscation order against the accused, when it makes the decision;
  (b) in a case where a confiscation order is made against him as a result of the application, when the order is satisfied or discharged, or when the order is quashed and there is no further possibility of an appeal against the decision to quash the order;
  (c) in a case where the application is withdrawn, when the prosecutor notifies the withdrawal to the court to which the application was made.

(2) An application under section 106 or 107 is concluded—
  (a) in a case where the court decides not to vary the confiscation order concerned, when it makes the decision;
  (b) in a case where the court varies the confiscation order as a result of the application, when the order is satisfied or discharged, or when the order is quashed and there is no further possibility of an appeal against the decision to quash the order;
  (c) in a case where the application is withdrawn, when the prosecutor notifies the withdrawal to the court to which the application was made.

153   Satisfaction of confiscation orders

(1) A confiscation order is satisfied—

(a) when no amount is due under it;

(b) where the accused against whom it was made serves a term of imprisonment or detention in default of payment of the amount due under the order, on the completion of that term of imprisonment or detention.

(2) A confiscation order is subject to appeal until there is no further possibility of an appeal on which the order could be varied or quashed; and for this purpose any power to grant leave to appeal out of time must be ignored.

154   Other interpretative provisions

(1) In this Part—

"accused" means a person against whom proceedings for an offence have been instituted (whether or not he has been convicted);

"clerk of court" includes the sheriff clerk;

"confiscation order" means an order under section 92;

"conviction", in relation to an offence, includes a finding that the offence has been committed;

"court" must be construed in accordance with sections 92(13) and 119(10);

"criminal investigation" means an investigation which police officers or other persons have a duty to conduct with a view to it being ascertained whether a person should be charged with an offence;

"the Procedure Act" means the Criminal Procedure (Scotland) Act 1995 (c. 46);

"restraint order" means an order under section 120.

(2) A reference to the offence (or offences) concerned must be construed in accordance with section 92(12).

(3) A reference to sentencing the accused for an offence includes a reference to dealing with him otherwise in respect of the offence.

General

155   Rules of court

(1) Provision may be made by act of sederunt as to—

(a) giving notice or serving any document for the purposes of this Part;

(b) the accountant of court's functions under Schedule 3;

(c) the accounts to be kept by the administrator in relation to the exercise of his functions.

(2) Subsection (1) is without prejudice to section 32 of the Sheriff Courts (Scotland) Act 1971 (c. 58) or section 5 of the Court of Session Act 1988 (c. 36).

PART 4

CONFISCATION: NORTHERN IRELAND

INTRODUCTION TO PART 4

Sections 156 to 171 establish the procedure for obtaining confiscation orders in Northern Ireland which is essentially the same for England and Wales. It has evolved out of the Drug Trafficking Act 1994 and the Criminal Justice Act 1988 and their Northern Ireland equivalent in the Proceeds of Crime (Northern Ireland) Order 1996 (S.I. 1996/1299 (N.I. 9)). However, there are now significant differences.

Confiscation orders

156   Making of order

(1) The Crown Court must proceed under this section if the following two conditions are satisfied.

(2) The first condition is that a defendant falls within either of the following paragraphs—
   (a) he is convicted of an offence or offences in proceedings before the Crown Court;
   (b) he is committed to the Crown Court in respect of an offence or offences under section 218 below (committal with a view to a confiscation order being considered).

(3) The second condition is that—
   (a) the prosecutor or the Director asks the court to proceed under this section, or
   (b) the court believes it is appropriate for it to do so.

(4) The court must proceed as follows—
   (a) it must decide whether the defendant has a criminal lifestyle;
   (b) if it decides that he has a criminal lifestyle it must decide whether he has benefited from his general criminal conduct;
   (c) if it decides that he does not have a criminal lifestyle it must decide whether he has benefited from his particular criminal conduct.

(5) If the court decides under subsection (4)(b) or (c) that the defendant has benefited from the conduct referred to it must—
   (a) decide the recoverable amount, and
   (b) make an order (a confiscation order) requiring him to pay that amount.

(6) But the court must treat the duty in subsection (5) as a power if it believes that any victim of the conduct has at any time started or intends to start proceedings against the defendant in respect of loss, injury or damage sustained in connection with the conduct.

(7) The court must decide any question arising under subsection (4) or (5) on a balance of probabilities.

(8) The first condition is not satisfied if the defendant absconds (but section 177 may apply).

(9) References in this Part to the offence (or offences) concerned are to the offence (or offences) mentioned in subsection (2).

DEFINITIONS
   "benefited": s.224(4)
   "confiscation order": s.236(5)
   "criminal lifestyle": s.223
   "criminal conduct": s.224
   "defendant": s.236(3)
   "offence": s.236(1)

GENERAL NOTE
   Section 156 sets out the basic framework for making a confiscation order in the Crown Court. This is virtually identical to s.6 which is the provision for England and Wales.
   The main distinction from s.6 is that there is no power in Northern Ireland for magistrates' courts to commit for sentence to the Crown Court. Therefore, under this section the Crown Court may make a confiscation order in just two circumstances, either if a defendant is convicted before the Crown Court or the defendant has been convicted in the magistrates' court and committed under s.218 to the Crown Court with a view to a confiscation order being considered.
   If the defendant absconds after conviction, he does not qualify for an order under this section (see subs. (8)), but the court may proceed under s.177 instead. It is not clear how this subsection

applies in the case where the offender absconds after confiscation proceedings have begun but before they have been concluded. It may be that once confiscation proceedings have begun, they are not affected by a subsequent failure of the defendant to appear. The object of the provision appears to be to provide for a defendant who is not present at the beginning of the confiscation proceedings.

Provided the defendant falls within one of these paragraphs (and the vast majority of defendants appearing before the Crown Court will do so) the court *must* proceed with a view to a confiscation order if it is asked to do so either by the prosecutor or by the Director of the Assets Recovery Agency, or if the court believes "it is appropriate for it to do so". The mandatory aspect of this section is qualified by subs. (6) which in affect allows the Crown Court not to make the decisions required by subs. (5) if believes that any victim of the offence has initiated, or intends to initiate, civil proceedings against the defendant.

Where the Crown Court embarks on confiscation proceedings, it must first decide whether the defendant has a "criminal lifestyle" as defined by s.223. A person has a "criminal lifestyle" if either he is convicted of one of the offences specified in Sched. 5 of the Act, or the offence constitutes "conduct forming part of a course of criminal activity", or if the offence was committed over a period of at least six months and the defendant has benefited from the conduct. "Course of criminal activity" is further defined in s.223(3). Sched. 5 lists a large number of offences, including offences under the Misuse of Drugs Act 1971, offences under the Customs and Excise Management Act 1979 connected with drugs or firearms, facilitating illegal entry, various offences connected with prostitution, blackmail, counterfeiting and certain copyright offences.

If the court decides that the defendant has a "criminal lifestyle" it must decide whether he has benefited from his "general criminal conduct". "General criminal conduct" is defined by s.224(2) as "all his criminal conduct," and the definition provides that it is immaterial whether conduct occurred before or after the passing of this Act or whether property constituting a benefit from conduct was obtained "before or after the passing of this Act". In making this decision, the court must make any of the assumptions required by s.160 which apply, unless the assumption is "shown to be incorrect" or there would be a "serious risk of injustice" if the assumption were made. If the court decides that the defendant does have a criminal lifestyle and has benefited from his general criminal conduct, it must determine the "recoverable amount" for the purposes of subs. (5). This is done by taking the benefit from the general criminal conduct as the starting point for calculation, making any reduction required by s.157(2).

If the court decides that the defendant does not have a "criminal lifestyle", the Court must then decide whether the defendant has benefited from his "particular criminal conduct". "Particular criminal conduct" is defined in s.224(3) as "all his criminal conduct" which "constitutes the offence or offences concerned", or "constitutes the offences of which he was convicted in the same proceedings as those in which he was convicted of the offence or offences concerned", or "constitutes offences which the court will be taking into consideration in deciding his sentence for the offence or offences concerned". It is clear that this definition does not include uncharged offences which are represented by specimen or sample counts in an indictment, unless those offences are specifically listed and the court is asked to take them into consideration under the conventional procedure for doing so.

The benefit from the defendant's particular criminal conduct forms the basis of the calculation of the "recoverable amount" for the purposes of s.157. In determining whether the defendant has benefited from his "particular criminal conduct" the court may not make any of the assumptions mentioned in s.160, which apply only in "criminal lifestyle" cases, but the court may order the defendant under s.168 of the Act to give the court "information specified in the order". If the defendant fails to comply with such an order, the court may "draw such inference as it believes is appropriate" (s.168(4)).

Any question arising in connection with whether the defendant has a criminal life style or whether he has benefited from his general or particular criminal conduct must be decided on a "balance of probabilities" (subs. (7)).

157   Recoverable amount

   (1) The recoverable amount for the purposes of section 156 is an amount equal to the defendant's benefit from the conduct concerned.

   (2) But if the defendant shows that the available amount is less than that benefit the recoverable amount is—

      (a) the available amount, or

      (b) a nominal amount, if the available amount is nil.

   (3) But if section 156(6) applies the recoverable amount is such amount as—

   (a) the court believes is just, but

   (b) does not exceed the amount found under subsection (1) or (2) (as the case may be).

(4) In calculating the defendant's benefit from the conduct concerned for the purposes of subsection (1), any property in respect of which—

   (a) a recovery order is in force under section 266, or

   (b) a forfeiture order is in force under section 298(2),

   must be ignored.

(5) If the court decides the available amount, it must include in the confiscation order a statement of its findings as to the matters relevant for deciding that amount.

DEFINITIONS

"available amount": s.159
"confiscation order": s.236(5)
"criminal conduct": s.224
"defendant": s.236(3)
"free property": s.230
"property": s.232

GENERAL NOTE

This section substantially reproduces the effect of the art. 8(3) of the 1996 Order. The court must make an order for the amount which it has assessed to be the defendant's benefit, unless either it exercises the discretion given by s.156(6) in a case where it believes that a victim of the offence has started or intends to start civil proceedings against the defendant, or the defendant shows that the "available amount" is less than the benefit. "Available amount" is defined by s.159. It includes the total of the values of all "free property" held by the defendant at the time the confiscation order is made, and the total value of all "tainted gifts". ("Free property" is defined in s.230; "tainted gifts" in s.225.)

Where the court exercises the discretion given by s.156(6) in a case where a victim is believed to be instituting civil proceedings, the amount of the confiscation order is such amount "as the court believes is just," but the amount must not exceed the amount of the defendant's benefit. It appears to be permissible for the court to make an order equal to the full amount of the defendant's benefit, and to disregard the civil proceedings if it considers it appropriate to do so.

If the defendant shows that the "available amount" is less than his benefit, the amount of the confiscation order ("the recoverable amount") is either the "available amount" itself, or the nominal amount. If the defendant shows that he has no assets and there are no "tainted gifts", the court must nevertheless make an order in a nominal amount.

If the court decides the "available amount", it must include in the confiscation order a statement of its findings as to the matters relevant to deciding that amount. This statement will be of particular importance if an application is subsequently made under ss.172 or 173 for a reconsideration of the "available amount."

The court has no discretion in determining the amount of the confiscation order once it has determined the amount of the defendant's benefit and the "available amount". Discretion arises only in a case where s.156(6) applies (civil proceedings instituted by a victim). The discretion given by the 1996 Order art. 7(1) to disregard a "gift caught by this Order" is not reproduced in this Act.

Subsection (4) might more logically have been included in s.156. It requires that any property which is subject to a recovery order under s.266 ("civil recovery") or s.298(2) (cash forfeited by a magistrates' court on application) should be disregarded in calculating the defendant's benefit.

158   Defendant's benefit

(1) If the court is proceeding under section 156 this section applies for the purpose of—

   (a) deciding whether the defendant has benefited from conduct, and

   (b) deciding his benefit from the conduct.

(2) The court must—

   (a) take account of conduct occurring up to the time it makes its decision;

   (b) take account of property obtained up to that time.

(3) Subsection (4) applies if—

   (a) the conduct concerned is general criminal conduct,

   (b) a confiscation order mentioned in subsection (5) has at an earlier time been made against the defendant, and

   (c) his benefit for the purposes of that order was benefit from his general criminal conduct.

(4) His benefit found at the time the last confiscation order mentioned in subsection (3)(c) was made against him must be taken for the purposes of this section to be his benefit from his general criminal conduct at that time.

(5) If the conduct concerned is general criminal conduct the court must deduct the aggregate of the following amounts—

   (a) the amount ordered to be paid under each confiscation order previously made against the defendant;

   (b) the amount ordered to be paid under each confiscation order previously made against him under any of the provisions listed in subsection (7).

(6) But subsection (5) does not apply to an amount which has been taken into account for the purposes of a deduction under that subsection on any earlier occasion.

(7) These are the provisions—

   (a) the Drug Trafficking Offences Act 1986 (c. 32);

   (b) Part 1 of the Criminal Justice (Scotland) Act 1987 (c. 41);

   (c) Part 6 of the Criminal Justice Act 1988 (c. 33);

   (d) the Criminal Justice (Confiscation) (Northern Ireland) Order 1990 (S.I. 1990/2588 (N.I. 17));

   (e) Part 1 of the Drug Trafficking Act 1994 (c. 37);

   (f) Part 1 of the Proceeds of Crime (Scotland) Act 1995 (c. 43);

   (g) the Proceeds of Crime (Northern Ireland) Order 1996 (S.I. 1996/1299 (N.I. 9));

   (h) Part 2 or 3 of this Act.

(8) The reference to general criminal conduct in the case of a confiscation order made under any of the provisions listed in subsection (7) is a reference to conduct in respect of which a court is required or entitled to make one or more assumptions for the purpose of assessing a person's benefit from the conduct.

DEFINITIONS

"benefited": s.224
"conduct": subs.(3)
"confiscation order": s.236(5)
"criminal conduct": s.224
"general criminal conduct": subs.(8)
"defendant": s.236(3)
"property": s.232

GENERAL NOTE

This section deals with two separate aspects of the calculation of the defendant's benefit under s.156(5).

Subsections (1) and (2) apply whether the court is proceeding under the "criminal lifestyle" provisions or otherwise. Its effect is that the court must take account of any conduct occurring before the decision on the question of benefit is made, or any property obtained up to that time. If the defendant obtains property from his criminal conduct after he has been convicted but before the confiscation order is made, that property must be taken into account in determining the "recoverable amount".

Subsections (3) to (8) apply only where the court is proceeding under the "criminal lifestyle" provisions, and the defendant has been subject to an earlier confiscation order. If the previous order was made under the "criminal lifestyle" provisions of this Act, the amount assessed to be the benefit from his "general criminal conduct" on that occasion must be treated as his benefit from his "general criminal conduct" at that time. If the previous order was made under earlier legislation which permitted or required the court to make assumptions, the benefit assessed for the purposes of that order is to be treated for the purposes of this section as benefit arising from the defendant's "general criminal conduct" (subss. (7) and (8)).

It appears that this amount may be included in the calculation of the defendant's benefit from general criminal conduct for the purposes of the latest order. The court will presumably be required to calculate the defendant's benefit from general criminal conduct arising since the original order was made, and add the two figures together to produce the new figure.

The court must then deduct from that figure the amount ordered to be paid by any previous confiscation orders in respect of "general criminal conduct", either under this Act or any of the provisions mentioned in subs. (7). The effect of subs. (8) seems to be that a confiscation order made under earlier legislation, in which the concept of "general criminal conduct" was unknown, is to be treated as having been made in respect of "general criminal conduct" if the court was empowered or required to make assumptions for the purpose of determining the defendant's benefit.

Although subs. (7) includes the Criminal Justice (Confiscation)(Northern Ireland) Order 1990 (S.I. 1990/2588 (N.I. 17) in the list of provisions concerned, it should be remembered that a court had power to make the assumptions only in relation to drug trafficking offences under this Order.

The practical effect of this section appears to be that where a court is proceeding to make a confiscation order under the "criminal lifestyle" provisions in respect of an offender who was subject to a confiscation order for drug trafficking made on an earlier occasion under the 1990 Order, the Court must include the value of the defendant's proceeds of drug trafficking as assessed on that occasion under art. 6 of the Order in the calculation of the benefit from his "general criminal conduct" on the current occasion, but must deduct from the calculation any amount ordered to be paid under the earlier confiscation order. It appears this would be the same for a confiscation order made under or a confiscation order made under the 1996 Order. However, where the earlier confiscation order was made under the 1990 Order in relation to an offence other than a drug trafficking offence, it seems that the confiscation order must be ignored for both purposes, although it may affect the calculation of the "available amount" under s.157(2) by virtue of s.159(2)(a).

159 Available amount

(1) For the purposes of deciding the recoverable amount, the available amount is the aggregate of—
  (a) the total of the values (at the time the confiscation order is made) of all the free property then held by the defendant minus the total amount payable in pursuance of obligations which then have priority, and
  (b) the total of the values (at that time) of all tainted gifts.

(2) An obligation has priority if it is an obligation of the defendant—
  (a) to pay an amount due in respect of a fine or other order of a court which was imposed or made on conviction of an offence and at any time before the time the confiscation order is made, or
  (b) to pay a sum which would be included among the preferential debts if the defendant's bankruptcy had commenced on the date of the confiscation order or his winding up had been ordered on that date.

(3) "Preferential debts" has the meaning given by Article 346 of the Insolvency (Northern Ireland) Order 1989 (S.I. 1989/2405 (N.I. 19)).

DEFINITIONS
  "confiscation order": s.236(5)
  "defendant": s.236(3)
  "free property": s.230
  "property": s.232
  "tainted gift": s.225

GENERAL NOTE
  Section 159 elaborates the definition of "the available amount". The section substantially reproduces the effect of art. 5 of the 1996 Order. The "available amount" is the sum of two calculations.
  The first calculation is the total value at the time the confiscation order is made of all the "free property" held by the defendant, minus the total amount payable in pursuance of "obligations which then have priority". Obligations which have priority are defined in subs. (2). They are essentially obligations to pay orders made by criminal courts upon conviction such as fines,

compensation orders or earlier confiscation orders, which were made before the current confis-cation order was made, and obligations to pay any sum which would be included among the preferential debts of the defendant if he had been made bankrupt on the date on which the confiscation order was made. Other general debts of the defendant, whenever contracted, are not "obligations which then have priority". A debt which is secured on the defendant's property by way of mortgage is to be taken into account in determining the value of the property by virtue of s.227(3), so that the practical effect is much the same. Unsecured debts will not count for this purpose.

The second calculation is the value of all "tainted gifts" (as defined in s.225).

160   Assumptions to be made in case of criminal lifestyle

(1) If the court decides under section 156 that the defendant has a criminal lifestyle it must make the following four assumptions for the purpose of—

    (a) deciding whether he has benefited from his general criminal con-duct, and

    (b) deciding his benefit from the conduct.

(2) The first assumption is that any property transferred to the defendant at any time after the relevant day was obtained by him—

    (a) as a result of his general criminal conduct, and

    (b) at the earliest time he appears to have held it.

(3) The second assumption is that any property held by the defendant at any time after the date of conviction was obtained by him—

    (a) as a result of his general criminal conduct, and

    (b) at the earliest time he appears to have held it.

(4) The third assumption is that any expenditure incurred by the defend-ant at any time after the relevant day was met from property obtained by him as a result of his general criminal conduct.

(5) The fourth assumption is that, for the purpose of valuing any property obtained (or assumed to have been obtained) by the defendant, he obtained it free of any other interests in it.

(6) But the court must not make a required assumption in relation to par-ticular property or expenditure if—

    (a) the assumption is shown to be incorrect, or

    (b) there would be a serious risk of injustice if the assumption were made.

(7) If the court does not make one or more of the required assumptions it must state its reasons.

(8) The relevant day is the first day of the period of six years ending with—

    (a) the day when proceedings for the offence concerned were started against the defendant, or

    (b) if there are two or more offences and proceedings for them were started on different days, the earliest of those days.

(9) But if a confiscation order mentioned in section 158(3)(c) has been made against the defendant at any time during the period mentioned in subsection (8)—

    (a) the relevant day is the day when the defendant's benefit was cal-culated for the purposes of the last such confiscation order;

    (b) the second assumption does not apply to any property which was held by him on or before the relevant day.

(10) The date of conviction is—

    (a) the date on which the defendant was convicted of the offence con-cerned, or

    (b) if there are two or more offences and the convictions were on different dates, the date of the latest.

DEFINITIONS
"benefited": s.224
"confiscation order": s.236(5)

"criminal lifestyle": s.223
"criminal conduct": s.224
"defendant": s.236(3)
"proceedings are started": s.233
"property": s.232

GENERAL NOTE

Section 160 is derived from art. 9 of the 1996 Order. s.160 applies only where the court is proceeding under the "criminal life style" provisions of s.156(4).

Where the court has decided that the defendant has a "criminal lifestyle" it must make the four assumptions for the purpose of deciding whether he has benefited from his general criminal conduct, and the amount of his benefit. The Court has no discretion to decide whether or not to make an assumption (as it has under art. 9 of the 1996 Order), but the court must not make an assumption in either of the situations described in subs. (6). An assumption must not be made if "the assumption is shown to be incorrect". It seems clear from the wording of subs. (6)(a) that the burden of showing that the assumption is incorrect falls on the defendant, who must rebut the assumption by proving the contrary. The second exclusion applies if "there would be a serious risk of injustice if the assumption were made". Subsection (6)(b) does not indicate where any burden of proof falls. In respect of this exception, it is submitted that it is a matter for the court to determine in the exercise of its discretion whether there is a serious risk of injustice. It will be noted that the statutory phrase is "a serious risk of injustice", rather than "a risk of serious injustice". If the court does not make one of the assumptions, it is required by subs. (7) to state its reasons.

The substance of the four assumptions is closely based on the earlier legislation. The first assumption is that any property transferred to the defendant within the period of six years ending on the day on which proceedings were started against the defendant was obtained by him as a result of his general criminal conduct. The second assumption, which in practice is the assumption most likely to be made, is that any property held by the defendant at any time after the date of conviction was obtained by him as a result of his general criminal conduct. The third assumption is that any expenditure incurred by the defendant within a period of six years ending with the date on which the proceedings were started against him was met from property obtained by him as a result of his general criminal conduct. The fourth assumption is that any property obtained or assumed to have been obtained by the defendant was free of any other interest in the property. (Where the defendant has been subject to an earlier confiscation order made under the "general criminal conduct" provisions or their equivalent, the relevant period begins on the day the previous calculation of benefit was made, if that order was made within the six year period.)

The assumptions are to some extent alternatives to each other and in the circumstances of a particular case one assumption may take priority over another. A typical example would be that of an offender found in possession of drugs. It would be open to the Court to apply the first assumption to the drugs, and assume that they were transferred to him as a result of his general criminal conduct. In this case the Court would be required to value the drugs in accordance with ss.227 and 228 and include that value in the calculation of his benefit. Alternatively, and more realistically, the Court might draw the inference from the facts that the defendant purchased the drugs for cash, and that the cash used for the purpose was obtained from "general criminal conduct". Accordingly it would qualify under subs. (4) as "expenditure" incurred during the relevant period. Applying this assumption will probably yield a very different calculation of benefit from that provided by the application of the first assumption.

161   Time for payment

(1) The amount ordered to be paid under a confiscation order must be paid on the making of the order; but this is subject to the following provisions of this section.

(2) If the defendant shows that he needs time to pay the amount ordered to be paid, the court making the confiscation order may make an order allowing payment to be made in a specified period.

(3) The specified period—
    (a) must start with the day on which the confiscation order is made, and
    (b) must not exceed six months.

(4) If within the specified period the defendant applies to the Crown Court for the period to be extended and the court believes there are

exceptional circumstances, it may make an order extending the period.

(5) The extended period—

    (a) must start with the day on which the confiscation order is made, and

    (b) must not exceed 12 months.

(6) An order under subsection (4)—

    (a) may be made after the end of the specified period, but

    (b) must not be made after the end of the period of 12 months starting with the day on which the confiscation order is made.

(7) The court must not make an order under subsection (2) or (4) unless it gives—

    (a) the prosecutor, or

    (b) if the Director was appointed as the enforcement authority for the order under section 184, the Director,

an opportunity to make representations.

DEFINITIONS
"confiscation order": s.236(5)

GENERAL NOTE

This section authorises the Crown Court, when it makes a confiscation order, to allow time for payment of the order. Under previous legislation, confiscation orders were subject to the same provisions as applied to a fine imposed by the Crown Court (see the 1996 Order art. 13). This provision gives the Crown Court more restricted powers to allow time for payment and makes no provision for payment by instalments. Unless an order is made under the section, the amount ordered to be paid under a confiscation order must be paid immediately on the making of the order. If the defendant shows that he needs time to pay the order, the court may make an order allowing payment to be made within a specified period which must not exceed six months from the day on which the confiscation order is made.

Subsection (4) provides for an extension of that period. If the defendant makes a further application to the Crown Court within the specified period and Court believes that there are "exceptional circumstances" it may make an order extending the period. The extended period must not extend beyond 12 months from the day on which the confiscation order was made.

Although the second application must be made within the original six month specified period, the order extending the period may be made after the end of that period, but not after the end of the period of 12 months starting with the day on which the confiscation order was made.

It is not open to the Crown Court to make an order allowing 12 months for payment on the defendant's initial application even though the defendant shows that there are exceptional circumstances in which this would be appropriate. The defendant must make a further application within the six month period.

It is important for a defendant to make an application for time to pay the order, if he is unable to pay the full amount of the order immediately, as interest is payable under s. 12 if the confiscation order cannot paid when it is required to be paid.

162   Interest on unpaid sums

(1) If the amount required to be paid by a person under a confiscation order is not paid when it is required to be paid, he must pay interest on the amount for the period for which it remains unpaid.

(2) The rate of interest is the same rate as that for the time being applying to a money judgment of the High Court.

(3) For the purposes of this section no amount is required to be paid under a confiscation order if—

    (a) an application has been made under section 161(4),

    (b) the application has not been determined by the court, and

    (c) the period of 12 months starting with the day on which the confiscation order was made has not ended.

(4) In applying this Part the amount of the interest must be treated as part of the amount to be paid under the confiscation order.

DEFINITIONS
"confiscation order": s.236(5)

GENERAL NOTE

This section substantially reproduces the effect of the 1996 Order, art. 14. Interest becomes payable if the confiscation order is not paid when it is required to be paid. If no order is made under s.161(2) allowing time for payment of the order, interest will become payable if the confiscation order is not paid immediately. If an order is made under s.161(2), interest will become payable if the order is not paid by the end of the period specified in the order. If the defendant makes an application for an extension of the period, and that application is granted, interest will become payable if the order is not paid within the period specified in the order extending the original specified period. If such an application is made and has not been determined by the court before the end of 12 months starting with the day on which the order was made, interest becomes payable at the end of the 12 month period, whether or not the Court has made an order extending the time to payment under s. 161(4). Any unpaid interest is added to the amount of the confiscation order.

163   Effect of order on court's other powers

(1) If the court makes a confiscation order it must proceed as mentioned in subsections (2) and (4) in respect of the offence or offences concerned.

(2) The court must take account of the confiscation order before—
    (a) it imposes a fine on the defendant, or
    (b) it makes an order falling within subsection (3).

(3) These orders fall within this subsection—
    (a) an order involving payment by the defendant, other than an order under Article 14 of the Criminal Justice (Northern Ireland) Order 1994 (S.I. 1994/2795 (N.I. 15)) (compensation orders);
    (b) an order under section 27 of the Misuse of Drugs Act 1971 (c. 38) (forfeiture orders);
    (c) an order under Article 11 of the Criminal Justice (Northern Ireland) Order 1994 (S.I. 1994/2795 (N.I. 15)) (deprivation orders);
    (d) an order under section 23 or 111 of the Terrorism Act 2000 (c. 11) (forfeiture orders).

(4) Subject to subsection (2), the court must leave the confiscation order out of account in deciding the appropriate sentence for the defendant.

(5) Subsection (6) applies if—
    (a) a court makes both a confiscation order and an order for the payment of compensation under Article 14 of the Criminal Justice (Northern Ireland) Order 1994 (S.I. 1994/2795 (N.I. 15)) against the same person in the same proceedings, and
    (b) the court believes he will not have sufficient means to satisfy both the orders in full.

(6) In such a case the court must direct that so much of the compensation as it specifies is to be paid out of any sums recovered under the confiscation order; and the amount it specifies must be the amount it believes will not be recoverable because of the insufficiency of the person's means.

DEFINITIONS
"confiscation order": s.236(5)
"defendant": s.236(3)
"offence or offences concerned": ss.236(1) and 156(9)

GENERAL NOTE

This section assumes that the Court will proceed to make a confiscation order before sentencing the defendant for the offence or offences concerned. In practice it is likely that in most cases the Court will exercise the power of postponement given by s.164 and sentence the defendant before making the confiscation order under s.165.

The effect of the section is to require the Crown Court when sentencing a defendant in respect of whom it has made a confiscation order to take account of the confiscation order before imposing a fine, making any order involving payment by the defendant other than a compensation order, or making the other orders of forfeiture or deprivation specified in the section. A court which has made a confiscation order may leave the confiscation order out of account in deciding whether to make a compensation order in favour of the victim of the offence and in deciding the amount of the order. It is open to the Crown Court to make a confiscation order and a compensation order in respect of the same offence, even though this means that the defendant will be required to pay twice the amount involved in the offence (see *Mitchell and Mitchell* (2001) 2 Cr.App.R.(S.) 29 (at 141), *Williams* (2001) 1 Cr.App.R.(S.) 140 (at 500)), decided on the Criminal Justice Act 1988 s. 72). If the defendant has the means to pay both the confiscation order and the compensation order, there is no objection to making both orders. If the defendant does not have the means to pay both orders, the Crown Court made direct under subs. (6) that the compensation order, or a specified part of it, may be paid out of any amount recovered under the confiscation order.

Subsection (4) repeats the principle stated in the earlier provisions (the 1996 Order art. 12); in deciding the appropriate sentence for the offence, where it is not a financial penalty, the confiscation order must be left out of account. The defendant cannot claim that his sentence should be mitigated because a confiscation order has been made.

Procedural matters

164 Postponement

(1) The court may—
    (a) proceed under section 161 before it sentences the defendant for the offence (or any of the offences) concerned, or
    (b) postpone proceedings under section 161 for a specified period.

(2) A period of postponement may be extended.

(3) A period of postponement (including one as extended) must not end after the permitted period ends.

(4) But subsection (3) does not apply if there are exceptional circumstances.

(5) The permitted period is the period of two years starting with the date of conviction.

(6) But if—
    (a) the defendant appeals against his conviction for the offence (or any of the offences) concerned, and
    (b) the period of three months (starting with the day when the appeal is determined or otherwise disposed of) ends after the period found under subsection (5),
the permitted period is that period of three months.

(7) A postponement or extension may be made—
    (a) on application by the defendant;
    (b) on application by the prosecutor or the Director (as the case may be);
    (c) by the court of its own motion.

(8) If—
    (a) proceedings are postponed for a period, and
    (b) an application to extend the period is made before it ends,
the application may be granted even after the period ends.

(9) The date of conviction is—
    (a) the date on which the defendant was convicted of the offence concerned, or
    (b) if there are two or more offences and the convictions were on different dates, the date of the latest.

(10) References to appealing include references to applying under Article 146 of the Magistrates' Courts (Northern Ireland) Order 1981 (S.I. 1981/1675 (N.I. 26)) (statement of case).

(11) A confiscation order must not be quashed only on the ground that there was a defect or omission in the procedure connected with the application for or the granting of a postponement.

(12) But subsection (11) does not apply if before it made the confiscation order the court—
    (a) imposed a fine on the defendant;
    (b) made an order falling within section 163(3);
    (c) made an order under Article 14 of the Criminal Justice (Northern Ireland) Order 1994 (S.I. 1994/2795 (N.I. 15)) (compensation orders).

DEFINITIONS
    "confiscation order": s.236(5)
    "defendant": s.236(3)

GENERAL NOTE
    The powers to postpone confiscation proceedings given by the Drug Trafficking Act 1994, s. 3, and the Criminal Justice Act 1988, s.72A (as inserted by the Criminal Justice Act 1993) have led to a large number of difficulties and generated a substantial case law of their own. These are the equivalents of art.11 of the 1996 Order. The provisions of s.164, which must be read in conjunction with s.165, are derived from those sections in the earlier legislation, although with substantial changes.
    The earlier sections were premised on the assumption that in the normal case the Crown Court would deal with the confiscation order before sentencing the defendant. The power to postpone confiscation proceedings was provided in effect as an afterthought. Section 164 does not make any assumption that the court will deal with confiscation matters before sentence. Subsection (1) appears to be even-handed in this respect. The court is given the option to deal with confiscation matters under s. 156 before it sentences the defendant, or to postpone confiscation proceedings for a specified period. (There appears to be a typing error in the Act as it refers to proceeding under s.161 but should be s.156) The statutory assumption of the earlier legislation that confiscation would come first is clearly not part of this provision. However it is clear that the court must address the question of confiscation before sentencing the defendant and either deal with the matter under subs. (1)(a) or postpone confiscation proceedings under subs. (1)(b). The court may not sentence the defendant without making any reference to confiscation, and then deal with confiscation matters on a subsequent occasion.
    A second change in the law is a substantial increase in the period for which confiscation proceedings may be postponed. Under the previous legislation the period of postponement was not permitted to exceed three months under the 1996 Order in the absence of "exceptional circumstances". Under this legislation the permitted period is two years starting with the data of conviction. If there are "exceptional circumstances" an even longer period of postponement may be specified (subs. (4)), but it will seldom be necessary to rely on this provision.
    As under existing legislation, a postponement may be made on the application of the defendant or the prosecutor (or the Director of the Assets Recovery Agency) or by the court on its own motion. A period of postponement may be extended in the same manner. An application for a postponement made during an existing period of postponement may be granted after the period of postponement has ended. It is not clear whether the court acting on its own motion may extend a period of postponement, where no application has been made within an existing period of postponement, after that period has ended.
    As under the earlier legislation, the permitted period is affected if the defendant appeals against his conviction. If the defendant appeals against his conviction and the period of three months starting with the day on which the appeal is determined would end after the end of the period of two years starting with the date of conviction, the permitted period is the period of three months beginning with the day on which the appeal is determined.
    Two further important changes are made under the section. Section 164(1)(b) provides that the court may postpone "proceedings under s.156". This appears to mean that what is to be postponed is the commencement of confiscation proceedings. Under the earlier legislation it was held that what was to be postponed was the determination of the amount to be recovered in the defendant's case. In other words, the court on postponing the confiscation proceedings had to specify the period within which the process would be completed. It appears that under this provision, it is sufficient to specify a period within which confiscation proceedings will begin.
    Subsections (11) and (12) were added at a late stage in the progress of the Bill through Parliament. Their effect is not certain. Subsections (11) provides that "a confiscation order must not be quashed only on the ground that there was a defect or omission in the procedure connected with the application for or the granting of a postponement". This will leave open a number of questions. If the Crown Court has proceeded to sentence a defendant without addressing in any way the question of confiscation and then proceeds to initiate confiscation proceedings after the normal period for variation of sentence has lapsed, and without purporting to postpone the

proceedings at all under s.164, is that "a defect or omission in the procedure connected with the application for or the granting of a postponement"? Suppose the Crown Court has made an error in ordering a postponement of the confiscation proceedings so that it does not appear to have jurisdiction to continue with confiscation proceedings. Can the Crown Court take advantage of subs. (11), and proceed regardless of the difficulty, confident in the knowledge that any confiscation order which it makes may not be quashed by the Court of Appeal Criminal Division, or must the Crown Court abandon confiscation proceedings on the ground that it has no jurisdiction to proceed?

Subsection (12) creates a curious exception to subs. (11). A confiscation order may be quashed on grounds related to the postponement if before making the confiscation order the court imposed a fine on the defendant or made one of the other orders mentioned in subs. (12). The justification for this exception appears to be the duty of the court not to make any of those orders when confiscation proceedings are postponed (see s.165(2)).

165   Effect of postponement

(1) If the court postpones proceedings under section 156 it may proceed to sentence the defendant for the offence (or any of the offences) concerned.

(2) In sentencing the defendant for the offence (or any of the offences) concerned in the postponement period the court must not—
   (a) impose a fine on him,
   (b) make an order falling within section 163(3), or
   (c) make an order for the payment of compensation under Article 14 of the Criminal Justice (Northern Ireland) Order 1994 (S.I. 1994/ 2795 (N.I. 15)).

(3) If the court sentences the defendant for the offence (or any of the offences) concerned in the postponement period, after that period ends it may vary the sentence by—
   (a) imposing a fine on him,
   (b) making an order falling within section 163(3), or
   (c) making an order for the payment of compensation under Article 14 of the Criminal Justice (Northern Ireland) Order 1994.

(4) But the court may proceed under subsection (3) only within the period of 28 days which starts with the last day of the postponement period.

(5) For the purposes of—
   (a) section 16(1) of the Criminal Appeal (Northern Ireland) Act 1980 (c. 47) (time limit for notice of appeal or of application for leave to appeal), and
   (b) paragraph 1 of Schedule 3 to the Criminal Justice Act 1988 (c. 33) (time limit for notice of application for leave to refer a case under section 36 of that Act),
   the sentence must be regarded as imposed or made on the day on which it is varied under subsection (3).

(6) If the court proceeds to sentence the defendant under subsection (1), section 156 has effect as if the defendant's particular criminal conduct included conduct which constitutes offences which the court has taken into consideration in deciding his sentence for the offence or offences concerned.

(7) The postponement period is the period for which proceedings under section 156 are postponed.

DEFINITIONS
   "criminal conduct": s.224
   "defendant": s.236(3)
   "offence or offences concerned": ss.236(1) and156(9)
   "sentencing": s.236(4)

GENERAL NOTE
   This section largely reproduces the 1996 Order art. 11. It provides for the powers of the court on sentencing a defendant in respect of the offence where confiscation proceedings have been

postponed under s.164. The court may sentence the defendant in the normal way but must not make any of the orders specified in subs. (2). Under the new legislation any compensation order must be delayed until after confiscation matters have been dealt with.

Where the defendant has been sentenced and subsequently a confiscation order is made following a postponement, the sentence originally passed may be varied by the addition of one of the orders mentioned in subs. (3) within 28 days starting with the last day of the period of postponement. This does not necessarily mean the day on which the confiscation order is actually made. If for instance the confiscation order is made before the last day of the postponement period, the period of 28 days starts on the last day of the period to which the order was originally postponed. Conversely, if the confiscation proceedings are postponed for a specified period under s.164, but the actual order is not made until some time after the end of the specified period, as the confiscation hearing itself takes several weeks, beginning on the last day of the specified, it appears that the period for variation ends 28 days after the last day of the postponement period, even though the confiscation order has not been made by that date.

Where a sentence is varied by the addition of one of the orders mentioned in subs. (3), the sentence concerned is to be regarded as having been imposed on the date of the variation, for the purpose of time limits relating to appeal. It is possible that a defendant in respect of whom confiscation proceedings have been postponed may have appealed against the sentence imposed for the offence long before the confiscation proceedings have been concluded. This provision appears to give the defendant a second right of appeal against the sentence as varied under subs. (3).

166   Statement of information

(1) If the court is proceeding under section 156 in a case where section 156(3)(a) applies, the prosecutor or the Director (as the case may be) must give the court a statement of information within the period the court orders.

(2) If the court is proceeding under section 156 in a case where section 156(3)(b) applies and it orders the prosecutor to give it a statement of information, the prosecutor must give it such a statement within the period the court orders.

(3) If the prosecutor or the Director (as the case may be) believes the defendant has a criminal lifestyle the statement of information is a statement of matters the prosecutor or the Director believes are relevant in connection with deciding these issues—

   (a) whether the defendant has a criminal lifestyle;
   (b) whether he has benefited from his general criminal conduct;
   (c) his benefit from the conduct.

(4) A statement under subsection (3) must include information the prosecutor or Director believes is relevant—

   (a) in connection with the making by the court of a required assumption under section 160;
   (b) for the purpose of enabling the court to decide if the circumstances are such that it must not make such an assumption.

(5) If the prosecutor or the Director (as the case may be) does not believe the defendant has a criminal lifestyle the statement of information is a statement of matters the prosecutor or the Director believes are relevant in connection with deciding these issues—

   (a) whether the defendant has benefited from his particular criminal conduct;
   (b) his benefit from the conduct.

(6) If the prosecutor or the Director gives the court a statement of information—

   (a) he may at any time give the court a further statement of information;
   (b) he must give the court a further statement of information if it orders him to do so, and he must give it within the period the court orders.

(7) If the court makes an order under this section it may at any time vary it by making another one.

DEFINITIONS
"benefited": s.224
"criminal conduct": s.224
"criminal lifestyle": s.223
"defendant": s.236(3)

GENERAL NOTE
The 1996 Order arts. 15 and 16 are the existing provisions which deal with the provision of information by the prosecution and defence. Prosecutor's information will now be known as "statements of information". (The change in title appears to be due to the fact that they will be made in some cases by the Director of the Assets Recovery Agency, rather than the prosecutor.) The section introduces variations related to the "criminal lifestyle" provisions of s. 156.

The effect of the section is that if the Crown Court is proceeding with a view to a confiscation order on the application of the prosecutor or the Director, the prosecutor or the Director must give the Crown Court a statement of information within a period specified by the Crown Court. If the Crown Court is proceeding with a view to confiscation on its own initiative, it may order the prosecutor (but not the Director) to give such a statement within the specified period.

Special provision is made for cases where the prosecutor or Director believes that the defendant has a "criminal lifestyle". In such a case, the statement of information must include matters which the prosecutor or Director believes are relevant in connection with deciding whether the defendant has a "criminal lifestyle", whether he has benefited from his general criminal conduct, and the benefit from the conduct. The statement made in this context must include information relevant to the making of the required assumptions. This will normally consist of information relating to the defendant's assets or his expenditure and receipts during the relevant six year period specified in s.160(8).

In cases where the prosecutor or Director does not believe that the defendant has a criminal lifestyle, the content of the statement of information is limited to information relating to whether the defendant has benefited from his "particular criminal conduct", (that is, the offences for which he is to be sentenced, including offences taken into consideration) and the amount of his benefit.

Subsection (6) provides for further statements of information to be given, and for the court to direct a further statement to be given.

167 Defendant's response to statement of information

(1) If the prosecutor or the Director gives the court a statement of information and a copy is served on the defendant, the court may order the defendant—
    (a) to indicate (within the period it orders) the extent to which he accepts each allegation in the statement, and
    (b) so far as he does not accept such an allegation, to give particulars of any matters he proposes to rely on.

(2) If the defendant accepts to any extent an allegation in a statement of information the court may treat his acceptance as conclusive of the matters to which it relates for the purpose of deciding the issues referred to in section 166(3) or (5) (as the case may be).

(3) If the defendant fails in any respect to comply with an order under subsection (1) he may be treated for the purposes of subsection (2) as accepting every allegation in the statement of information apart from—
    (a) any allegation in respect of which he has complied with the requirement;
    (b) any allegation that he has benefited from his general or particular criminal conduct.

(4) For the purposes of this section an allegation may be accepted or particulars may be given in a manner ordered by the court.

(5) If the court makes an order under this section it may at any time vary it by making another one.

(6) No acceptance under this section that the defendant has benefited from conduct is admissible in evidence in proceedings for an offence.

DEFINITIONS

"criminal conduct": s.224
"defendant": s.236(3)

GENERAL NOTE

This section should be distinguished from s. 168, which deals with the situation where the court orders the defendant to produce information himself.

The effect of the section is that where a statement of information has been given to the court and a copy served on the defendant, the Crown Court may order the defendant to indicate to what extent he accepts the allegations made in the statement, and in so far as he does not accept an allegation, "to give particulars of any matters he proposes to rely on". If the defendant accepts any allegation, the Crown Court may treat that acceptance as conclusive. If the defendant fails to comply with an order under subs. (1), he may be treated as accepting every allegation in the statement of information other than an allegation in respect of which he has complied with the requirement, or an allegation that he has benefited from his general or particular criminal conned. The allegations which the defendant may be treated as having accepted will normally be allegations relevant to the making of the required assumption under s. 160, such as an allegation relating to his assets, receipts or expenditure within the relevant period.

No acceptance of an allegation by the defendant, whether directly made under subs. (2) or deemed to have been made under subs. (3) is admissible in evidence in proceedings for an offence.

168 Provision of information by defendant

(1) This section applies if—
  (a) the court is proceeding under section 156 in a case where section 156(3)(a) applies, or
  (b) it is proceeding under section 156 in a case where section 156(3)(b) applies or it is considering whether to proceed.

(2) For the purpose of obtaining information to help it in carrying out its functions the court may at any time order the defendant to give it information specified in the order.

(3) An order under this section may require all or a specified part of the information to be given in a specified manner and before a specified date.

(4) If the defendant fails without reasonable excuse to comply with an order under this section the court may draw such inference as it believes is appropriate.

(5) Subsection (4) does not affect any power of the court to deal with the defendant in respect of a failure to comply with an order under this section.

(6) If the prosecutor or the Director (as the case may be) accepts to any extent an allegation made by the defendant—
  (a) in giving information required by an order under this section, or
  (b) in any other statement given to the court in relation to any matter relevant to deciding the available amount under section 159,
  the court may treat the acceptance as conclusive of the matters to which it relates.

(7) For the purposes of this section an allegation may be accepted in a manner ordered by the court.

(8) If the court makes an order under this section it may at any time vary it by making another one.

(9) No information given under this section which amounts to an admission by the defendant that he has benefited from criminal conduct is admissible in evidence in proceedings for an offence.

DEFINITIONS
    "benefited": s.224
    "criminal conduct": s.224
    "defendant": s.236(3)

GENERAL NOTE
    This section empowers the Crown Court, when proceeding with a view to a confiscation order, whether on the application of the prosecutor or the Director, or on its own initiative, or is considering whether to proceed on its own initiative, to order the defendant to give it the "information specified in the order". There is no restriction on the kind of information which may be specified. If the defendant fails "without reasonable excuse" to comply with an order, the court "may draw such inference as it believes is appropriate" from the failure. (This does not prevent the Crown Court from dealing with the defendant for failing to comply with the order under any other power, such as the power to adjudge him guilty of contempt.)
    Subsection (9) repeats art. 9(6) of the 1990 Order but was not found in the 1996 Order. Subs. (9) provides that no information given by the defendant in response to an order under the section which amounts to an admission that he has benefited from criminal conduct is admissible in evidence in proceedings for an offence. This may well affect the matters which may be put forward by the defendant as a "reasonable excuse" under subs. (4) for failing to comply with the court's order. Subsection (9) means that the defendant is protected from prosecution on the basis of such information and may therefore not argue that the risk of further prosecution is a "reasonable excuse" for failing to comply with the order.

Reconsideration

169   No order made: reconsideration of case

(1) This section applies if—
    (a) the first condition in section 156 is satisfied but no court has proceeded under that section,
    (b) there is evidence which was not available to the prosecutor on the relevant date,
    (c) before the end of the period of six years starting with the date of conviction the prosecutor or the Director applies to the Crown Court to consider the evidence, and
    (d) after considering the evidence the court believes it is appropriate for it to proceed under section 156.

(2) If this section applies the court must proceed under section 156, and when it does so subsections (3) to (8) below apply.

(3) If the court has already sentenced the defendant for the offence (or any of the offences) concerned, section 156 has effect as if his particular criminal conduct included conduct which constitutes offences which the court has taken into consideration in deciding his sentence for the offence or offences concerned.

(4) Section 158(2) does not apply, and the rules applying instead are that the court must—
    (a) take account of conduct occurring before the relevant date;
    (b) take account of property obtained before that date;
    (c) take account of property obtained on or after that date if it was obtained as a result of or in connection with conduct occurring before that date.

(5) In section 160—
    (a) the first and second assumptions do not apply with regard to property first held by the defendant on or after the relevant date;
    (b) the third assumption does not apply with regard to expenditure incurred by him on or after that date;
    (c) the fourth assumption does not apply with regard to property obtained (or assumed to have been obtained) by him on or after that date.

(6) The recoverable amount for the purposes of section 156 is such amount as—

(a) the court believes is just, but

(b) does not exceed the amount found under section 157.

(7) In arriving at the just amount the court must have regard in particular to—

(a) the amount found under section 157;

(b) any fine imposed on the defendant in respect of the offence (or any of the offences) concerned;

(c) any order which falls within section 163(3) and has been made against him in respect of the offence (or any of the offences) concerned and has not already been taken into account by the court in deciding what is the free property held by him for the purposes of section 159;

(d) any order which has been made against him in respect of the offence (or any of the offences) concerned under Article 14 of the Criminal Justice (Northern Ireland) Order 1994 (S.I. 1994/2795 (N.I. 15)) (compensation orders).

(8) If an order for the payment of compensation under Article 14 of the Criminal Justice (Northern Ireland) Order 1994 has been made against the defendant in respect of the offence or offences concerned, section 163(5) and (6) above do not apply.

(9) The relevant date is—

(a) if the court made a decision not to proceed under section 156, the date of the decision;

(b) if the court did not make such a decision, the date of conviction.

(10) The date of conviction is—

(a) the date on which the defendant was convicted of the offence concerned, or

(b) if there are two or more offences and the convictions were on different dates, the date of the latest.

DEFINITIONS

"criminal conduct": s. 224

"defendant": s. 236(3)

"free property": s. 230

"offence or offences concerned": s. 236(1) and 156 (2) and (9)

"property": s. 232

GENERAL NOTE

This section allows the question of confiscation to be the reopened within the period of six years starting with a date of conviction, where the court did not proceed under s.156 at the time of conviction and the prosecutor has evidence which was not available to him on the date when the court decided not to proceed with a view to confiscation, or the date of conviction, if the question of confiscation was not considered. The power to reopen proceedings is not lost if the prosecutor applied to the Court to proceed under s.156.

The critical question in relation to an order under the section is whether the prosecutor has "evidence which was not available" on the date of conviction, or when the decision not to proceed under the Act was made. It does not appear that the whole of the evidence on which the prosecution seek to rely must not have been available; it seems to be sufficient if some evidence has come to light that has not previously available. If the application is made within the six-year period by the prosecutor or the Director, the Court has a discretion whether to initiate confiscation proceedings. (It is not mandatory for the Court to initiate confiscation proceedings, as it is under s.156 in the case of an application made at the normal time.)

If the Court in its discretion decides to initiate confiscation proceedings, the normal procedure is followed with certain variations. The court may include in the calculation of the benefit derived from "particular criminal conduct" the benefit derived from offences that were taken into consideration when the defendant was sentenced. The court may take account of conduct occurring before the date of conviction (or the date on which it was decided not to proceed with a view to confiscation) and of property obtained before that date, but may not take account of property obtained after that date unless it was obtained as a result of or in connection with conduct occurring before that date.

In a "criminal lifestyle" case, the required assumptions do not apply to property held or obtained, or to expenditure incurred, after the date of conviction (or the date on which it was decided not to proceed with a view to confiscation.)

The rules governing the calculation of the amount to be recovered differ from those that apply in the normal case. The recoverable amount is such amount as "the Court believes is just," so long as it does not exceed the defendant's benefit or the "available amount" found in accordance with s.157(2). The effect of this provision, in subs.(6), is to give the court a greater measure of discretion than it would have in the normal procedure under s.156. In deciding what amount is "just" in these circumstances the court is required by subs. (7) to have regard to orders made for the payment of money in respect of the offences. If the court made a compensation order when sentencing the defendant, it may not make an order under s.163(6) directing that the compensation order should be paid out of the proceeds of the confiscation order.

The provisions of the Act relating to statements of information, and orders requiring the defendant to provide information, apply (see s.176).

170   No order made: reconsideration of benefit

(1) This section applies if the following two conditions are satisfied.
(2) The first condition is that in proceeding under section 156 the court has decided that—
    (a) the defendant has a criminal lifestyle but has not benefited from his general criminal conduct, or
    (b) the defendant does not have a criminal lifestyle and has not benefited from his particular criminal conduct.
(3) If the court proceeded under section 156 because the Director asked it to, the second condition is that—
    (a) the Director has evidence which was not available to him when the court decided that the defendant had not benefited from his general or particular criminal conduct,
    (b) before the end of the period of six years starting with the date of conviction the Director applies to the Crown Court to consider the evidence, and
    (c) after considering the evidence the court concludes that it would have decided that the defendant had benefited from his general or particular criminal conduct (as the case may be) if the evidence had been available to it.
(4) If the court proceeded under section 156 because the prosecutor asked it to or because it believed it was appropriate for it to do so, the second condition is that—
    (a) there is evidence which was not available to the prosecutor when the court decided that the defendant had not benefited from his general or particular criminal conduct,
    (b) before the end of the period of six years starting with the date of conviction the prosecutor or the Director applies to the Crown Court to consider the evidence, and
    (c) after considering the evidence the court concludes that it would have decided that the defendant had benefited from his general or particular criminal conduct (as the case may be) if the evidence had been available to it.
(5) If this section applies the court—
    (a) must make a fresh decision under section 156(4)(b) or (c) whether the defendant has benefited from his general or particular criminal conduct (as the case may be);
    (b) may make a confiscation order under that section.
(6) Subsections (7) to (12) below apply if the court proceeds under section 156 in pursuance of this section.
(7) If the court has already sentenced the defendant for the offence (or any of the offences) concerned, section 156 has effect as if his particu-

lar criminal conduct included conduct which constitutes offences which the court has taken into consideration in deciding his sentence for the offence or offences concerned.

(8) Section 158(2) does not apply, and the rules applying instead are that the court must—

(a) take account of conduct occurring before the date of the original decision that the defendant had not benefited from his general or particular criminal conduct;

(b) take account of property obtained before that date;

(c) take account of property obtained on or after that date if it was obtained as a result of or in connection with conduct occurring before that date.

(9) In section 160—

(a) the first and second assumptions do not apply with regard to property first held by the defendant on or after the date of the original decision that the defendant had not benefited from his general or particular criminal conduct;

(b) the third assumption does not apply with regard to expenditure incurred by him on or after that date;

(c) the fourth assumption does not apply with regard to property obtained (or assumed to have been obtained) by him on or after that date.

(10) The recoverable amount for the purposes of section 156 is such amount as—

(a) the court believes is just, but

(b) does not exceed the amount found under section 157.

(11) In arriving at the just amount the court must have regard in particular to—

(a) the amount found under section 157;

(b) any fine imposed on the defendant in respect of the offence (or any of the offences) concerned;

(c) any order which falls within section 163(3) and has been made against him in respect of the offence (or any of the offences) concerned and has not already been taken into account by the court in deciding what is the free property held by him for the purposes of section 159;

(d) any order which has been made against him in respect of the offence (or any of the offences) concerned under Article 14 of the Criminal Justice (Northern Ireland) Order 1994 (S.I. 1994/2795 (N.I. 15)) (compensation orders).

(12) If an order for the payment of compensation under Article 14 of the Criminal Justice (Northern Ireland) Order 1994 has been made against the defendant in respect of the offence or offences concerned, section 163(5) and (6) above do not apply.

(13) The date of conviction is the date found by applying section 169(10).

DEFINITIONS

"criminal lifestyle": s. 223

"defendant": s. 236(3)

"offence or offences concerned": ss. 236(1) and 156 (2) and (9)

"property": s.232

GENERAL NOTE

This section empowers the Court to reconsider the question whether a defendant has benefited from criminal conduct, in a case where it has previously considered the issue and decided that he has not benefited. The section applies equally to the question of whether the defendant has benefited from his "general criminal conduct" in a "criminal lifestyle" case or his "particular criminal conduct" in other cases.

If the original confiscation proceedings were initiated on the application of the Director of the Assets Recovery Agency, the power given by the section may be exercised only if the Director has evidence which was not available to him when the court decided that the defendant had not benefited from his criminal conduct, and if the Director makes an application to the Court within the period of six years beginning on the date of conviction. Where such an application is made, the court must consider the evidence. If the Court concludes that it would have decided that the defendant had benefited from his criminal conduct if the new evidence had been available, it must make a fresh decision as to whether the defendant had benefited. If it decides that he did benefit, the Court may then, in its discretion (subs. (5)(b)) make a confiscation order. There is no obligation on the Court to proceed to make a confiscation order, as there is under s.156(3)(a).

If the original confiscation proceedings were begun on the application of the prosecutor, the application to reconsider the question of benefit may be made either by the prosecutor or the Director of the Assets Recovery Agency. (The converse does not apply; if the original application was made by the Director, the prosecutor may not seek to reopen the proceedings under this section.)

The section makes no provision for cases where the Court has proceeded to make the original determination of benefit on its own initiative under s.156(3)(b).

If the court does re-determine the issue of the defendant's benefit, and decides to proceed with a view to making a confiscation order, the normal rules for making confiscation orders are modified in the same way as they are where the Court proceeds under s.169 (above).

The provisions of the Act relating to prosecutor's statements, and orders requiring the defendant to provide information, apply (see s.176).

171   Order made: reconsideration of benefit

(1) This section applies if—
   (a) a court has made a confiscation order,
   (b) there is evidence which was not available to the prosecutor or the Director at the relevant time,
   (c) the prosecutor or the Director believes that if the court were to find the amount of the defendant's benefit in pursuance of this section it would exceed the relevant amount,
   (d) before the end of the period of six years starting with the date of conviction the prosecutor or the Director applies to the Crown Court to consider the evidence, and
   (e) after considering the evidence the court believes it is appropriate for it to proceed under this section.

(2) The court must make a new calculation of the defendant's benefit from the conduct concerned, and when it does so subsections (3) to (6) below apply.

(3) If a court has already sentenced the defendant for the offence (or any of the offences) concerned section 156 has effect as if his particular criminal conduct included conduct which constitutes offences which the court has taken into consideration in deciding his sentence for the offence or offences concerned.

(4) Section 158(2) does not apply, and the rules applying instead are that the court must—
   (a) take account of conduct occurring up to the time it decided the defendant's benefit for the purposes of the confiscation order;
   (b) take account of property obtained up to that time;
   (c) take account of property obtained after that time if it was obtained as a result of or in connection with conduct occurring before that time.

(5) In applying section 158(5) the confiscation order must be ignored.

(6) In section 160—
   (a) the first and second assumptions do not apply with regard to property first held by the defendant after the time the court decided his benefit for the purposes of the confiscation order;
   (b) the third assumption does not apply with regard to expenditure incurred by him after that time;

(c) the fourth assumption does not apply with regard to property obtained (or assumed to have been obtained) by him after that time.

(7) If the amount found under the new calculation of the defendant's benefit exceeds the relevant amount the court—

(a) must make a new calculation of the recoverable amount for the purposes of section 156, and

(b) if it exceeds the amount required to be paid under the confiscation order, may vary the order by substituting for the amount required to be paid such amount as it believes is just.

(8) In applying subsection (7)(a) the court must—

(a) take the new calculation of the defendant's benefit;

(b) apply section 159 as if references to the time the confiscation order is made were to the time of the new calculation of the recoverable amount and as if references to the date of the confiscation order were to the date of that new calculation.

(9) In applying subsection (7)(b) the court must have regard in particular to—

(a) any fine imposed on the defendant for the offence (or any of the offences) concerned;

(b) any order which falls within section 163(3) and has been made against him in respect of the offence (or any of the offences) concerned and has not already been taken into account by the court in deciding what is the free property held by him for the purposes of section 159;

(c) any order which has been made against him in respect of the offence (or any of the offences) concerned under Article 14 of the Criminal Justice (Northern Ireland) Order 1994 (S.I. 1994/2795 (N.I. 15)) (compensation orders).

(10) But in applying subsection (7)(b) the court must not have regard to an order falling within subsection (9)(c) if a court has made a direction under section 163(6).

(11) In deciding under this section whether one amount exceeds another the court must take account of any change in the value of money.

(12) The relevant time is—

(a) when the court calculated the defendant's benefit for the purposes of the confiscation order, if this section has not applied previously;

(b) when the court last calculated the defendant's benefit in pursuance of this section, if this section has applied previously.

(13) The relevant amount is—

(a) the amount found as the defendant's benefit for the purposes of the confiscation order, if this section has not applied previously;

(b) the amount last found as the defendant's benefit in pursuance of this section, if this section has applied previously.

(14) The date of conviction is the date found by applying section 169(10).

DEFINITIONS

"benefited": s. 224(4)

"confiscation order": s. 236(5) and 156

"criminal conduct": s. 224

"defendant": s. 236(3)

"free property": s. 230

"offence or offences concerned": s. 236(1) and 156(2) and (9)

"property": s.232

GENERAL NOTE

This section allows for the determination of the amount of the defendant's benefit from criminal conduct to be revised if further evidence becomes available which indicates that the original calculation of the amount of benefit was incorrect.

The power to reopen the determination of benefit arises where an application is made by the prosecutor or the Director of the Assets Recovery Agency, and there is evidence that was not available to the prosecutor or the Director at the time when the amount of the benefit was calculated.

If an application is made within a period of six years starting with the date of conviction, the Court must consider the evidence and if it considers it appropriate to do so, in the exercise of its discretion (subs.(1)(e)) it may make a new calculation of the defendant's benefit from criminal conduct. If the Court does make a new determination of the benefit, and the benefit exceeds the amount of the benefit as previously calculated (whether at the time of the original calculation, or a subsequent recalculation under this section) the recoverable amount must be recalculated, and if it exceeds the amount required to be paid under the original order, the Court may (in its discretion) vary the order by substituting "such amount as it believes to be just." The Court is not bound to substitute an amount calculated by reference to the new assessment of the amount of the benefit.

In other respects the procedure for calculating the amount of benefit is modified in the same way as under ss 169 and 170. The "available amount" (the combined value of the defendant's "free property" and "tainted gifts") is recalculated at the time of the new determination of the amount of benefit (subs.(8). Property that has come into the defendant's possession after the original confiscation order was made may be taken into account for this purpose. If the Court has previously made a compensation order with a direction that the proceeds of the earlier confiscation order should be applied to satisfy the compensation order, the compensation order must not be taken into account in determining the revised amount of the order (subs.(10)).

Repeated applications for the recalculation of benefit may be made, so long as they are all made within six years of the date of conviction (subss (12) and (13)).

The provisions of the Act relating to statements of information, and orders requiring the defendant to provide information, apply (see s.176).

172   Order made: reconsideration of available amount

(1) This section applies if—
    (a) a court has made a confiscation order,
    (b) the amount required to be paid was the amount found under section 157(2), and
    (c) an applicant falling within subsection (2) applies to the Crown Court to make a new calculation of the available amount.

(2) These applicants fall within this subsection—
    (a) the prosecutor;
    (b) the Director;
    (c) a receiver appointed under section 198 or 200.

(3) In a case where this section applies the court must make the new calculation, and in doing so it must apply section 159 as if references to the time the confiscation order is made were to the time of the new calculation and as if references to the date of the confiscation order were to the date of the new calculation.

(4) If the amount found under the new calculation exceeds the relevant amount the court may vary the order by substituting for the amount required to be paid such amount as—
    (a) it believes is just, but
    (b) does not exceed the amount found as the defendant's benefit from the conduct concerned.

(5) In deciding what is just the court must have regard in particular to—
    (a) any fine imposed on the defendant for the offence (or any of the offences) concerned;
    (b) any order which falls within section 163(3) and has been made against him in respect of the offence (or any of the offences) concerned and has not already been taken into account by the court

in deciding what is the free property held by him for the purposes of section 159;

(c) any order which has been made against him in respect of the offence (or any of the offences) concerned under Article 14 of the Criminal Justice (Northern Ireland) Order 1994 (S.I. 1994/2795 (N.I. 15)) (compensation orders).

(6) But in deciding what is just the court must not have regard to an order falling within subsection (5)(c) if a court has made a direction under section 163(6).

(7) In deciding under this section whether one amount exceeds another the court must take account of any change in the value of money.

(8) The relevant amount is—

(a) the amount found as the available amount for the purposes of the confiscation order, if this section has not applied previously;

(b) the amount last found as the available amount in pursuance of this section, if this section has applied previously.

(9) The amount found as the defendant's benefit from the conduct concerned is—

(a) the amount so found when the confiscation order was made, or

(b) if one or more new calculations of the defendant's benefit have been made under section 171 the amount found on the occasion of the last such calculation.

DEFINITIONS

"confiscation order": s. 236(5) and 156
"criminal conduct": s. 224
"defendant": s. 236(3))
"free property": s. 230
"property": s.232

GENERAL NOTE

This section provides for a case in which the court has made a confiscation order, and the amount of the order was based on the "available amount" calculated in accordance with s.159, rather than the amount of the defendant's benefit. If the prosecutor, the Director of the Assets Recovery Agency, or a receiver, applies to the Court to make a new calculation of the available amount, the court must make the new calculation, applying s.159 to the circumstances as they apply at the time of the new calculation. If the amount found to be the "available amount" under the new calculation exceeds the amount found to be the "available amount" at the time of the previous calculation, the court may (in its discretion) vary the order by substituting an amount which it "believes is just" but which does not exceed the amount found to be the defendant's benefit from the conduct concerned.

The power under the section arises whenever the value of the defendant's "free property" increases. It may apply where assets have been concealed by a defendant at the time the original order was made, where the value of the defendant's assets increase with the passage of time or inflation, or where the defendant acquires new assets by whatever means. Unlike the other provisions allowing the questions relating to confiscation to be reconsidered, this section is not subject to any time limit and there is no requirement that the applicant should have evidence that was not available at the time the original calculation was made. The only protection for a defendant against what might be thought to be an oppressive application of the section is in the discretion of the Court under subs.(4). This subsection allows the Court a general discretion as to whether or not to vary the order, and in the determination of the amount required to be paid under the order as varied.

The procedure for determining the amount to be recovered is subject to the same modifications as apply under s.171.

173   Inadequacy of available amount: variation of order

(1) This section applies if—

(a) a court has made a confiscation order, and

    (b) the defendant, or a receiver appointed under section 198 or 200, applies to the Crown Court to vary the order under this section.

(2) In such a case the court must calculate the available amount, and in doing so it must apply section 159 as if references to the time the confiscation order is made were to the time of the calculation and as if references to the date of the confiscation order were to the date of the calculation.

(3) If the court finds that the available amount (as so calculated) is inadequate for the payment of any amount remaining to be paid under the confiscation order it may vary the order by substituting for the amount required to be paid such smaller amount as the court believes is just.

(4) If a person has been adjudged bankrupt or his estate has been sequestrated, or if an order for the winding up of a company has been made, the court must take into account the extent to which realisable property held by that person or that company may be distributed among creditors.

(5) The court may disregard any inadequacy which it believes is attributable (wholly or partly) to anything done by the defendant for the purpose of preserving property held by the recipient of a tainted gift from any risk of realisation under this Part.

(6) In subsection (4) "company" means any company which may be wound up under the Insolvency (Northern Ireland) Order 1989 (S.I. 1989/2405 (N.I. 19)) or the Insolvency Act 1986 (c. 45).

DEFINITIONS
    "confiscation order": s. 236(5) and 156
    "defendant": s. 236(3)
    "property": s.232
    "realisable property": s. 231
    "tainted gift": s. 225

GENERAL NOTE
    This section provides for the variation of the amount of a confiscation order on the ground that the "available amount" is inadequate to pay the amount of the order.

    The power of the Crown Court under this section arises where a confiscation order has been made and an application is made either by the defendant or by a receiver appointed to enforce the order. If an application is made, the Crown Court must recalculate the "available amount " as at the time of the recalculation. If the Court finds that the "available amount" as recalculated is inadequate for the payment or of any amount remaining to be paid under the confiscation order, it may (in its discretion) vary the confiscation order by substituting such smaller amount as the Court "believes is just." The Court is not obliged to reduce the amount of the order; as in the other provisions allowing for a variation of confiscation orders, the Court has a double discretion": first, whether to vary the order at all, and second, in the determination of the amount of the varied order. The Court is specifically authorised to disregard any inadequacy that it believes to be attributable to anything done by the defendant for the purpose of preserving property held by the recipient of a "tainted gift" from the risk of realisation. If the defendant has disposed of property, whether before or after the original confiscation order was made, with a view to preventing that property from being realised, the Court may disregard any resulting inadequacy.

    In the case of bankruptcy or winding up, the court must take into account in assessing the "available amount" the extent to which the realisable property may be distributed among creditors.

174   Inadequacy of available amount: discharge of order

(1) This section applies if—
    (a) a court has made a confiscation order,
    (b) the prosecutor applies to the Crown Court for the discharge of the order, and
    (c) the amount remaining to be paid under the order is less than £1,000.

(2) In such a case the court must calculate the available amount, and in doing so it must apply section 159 as if references to the time the confiscation order is made were to the time of the calculation and as if references to the date of the confiscation order were to the date of the calculation.

(3) If the court—

    (a) finds that the available amount (as so calculated) is inadequate to meet the amount remaining to be paid, and

    (b) is satisfied that the inadequacy is due wholly to a specified reason or a combination of specified reasons,

it may discharge the confiscation order.

(4) The specified reasons are—

    (a) in a case where any of the realisable property consists of money in a currency other than sterling, that fluctuations in currency exchange rates have occurred;

    (b) any reason specified by the Secretary of State by order.

(5) The Secretary of State may by order vary the amount for the time being specified in subsection (1)(c).

DEFINITIONS

    "confiscation order": s. 236(5) and 156
    "property": s.232
    "realisable property": s. 231

GENERAL NOTE

    This section has a very limited application. It applies if the amount remaining to be paid under a confiscation order is less than £1,000, and a prosecutor applies to the Crown Court for the discharge of the order on the ground that the realisable property consists of money in a currency other than sterling and that fluctuations in currency exchange rates have occurred. If such an application is made, the court must recalculate the "available amount" as at the time of the recalculation; if it finds that the available amount (as recalculated) is inadequate to meet the amount remaining to be paid and that the inadequacy is wholly due to fluctuations in currency exchange rates, the court may discharge the confiscation order.

    The section makes provision for additional reasons for discharge to be specified by the Secretary of State by order.

175   Small amount outstanding: discharge of order

(1) This section applies if—

    (a) a court has made a confiscation order,

    (b) a chief clerk applies to the Crown Court for the discharge of the order, and

    (c) the amount remaining to be paid under the order is £50 or less.

(2) In such a case the court may discharge the order.

(3) The Secretary of State may by order vary the amount for the time being specified in subsection (1)(c).

DEFINITIONS

    "confiscation order": ss 236(5) and 156

GENERAL NOTE

    This section provides a convenient procedure whereby the Crown Court is empowered to discharge a confiscation order where the amount remaining to be paid is £50 or less. If a chief clerk applies to the Crown Court in such a case, the court may discharge the order.

176   Information

(1) This section applies if—

    (a) the court proceeds under section 156 in pursuance of section 169 or 170, or

    (b) the prosecutor or the Director applies under section 171.

(2) In such a case—

   (a) the prosecutor or the Director (as the case may be) must give the court a statement of information within the period the court orders;

   (b) section 166 applies accordingly (with appropriate modifications where the prosecutor or the Director applies under section 171);

   (c) section 167 applies accordingly;

   (d) section 168 applies as it applies in the circumstances mentioned in section 168(1).

GENERAL NOTE

This section makes further procedural provision in connection with proceedings under ss 169 (where no order has been made), 170 (where the Court has decided that the defendant did not benefit from the offence or offences concerned) and 171 (where it is alleged that the amount of the defendant's benefit has been miscalculated.) In any such case, the prosecutor or director must give the Court a statement of information (as defined in s.166) within the period that the court specifies, and the provisions relating to the defendant's response to a statement of information apply. The power of the Court to order the defendant to provide information under s.168 is also applied as if the Court were proceeding under s.156 in the normal way.

Defendant absconds

177 Defendant convicted or committed

(1) This section applies if the following two conditions are satisfied.

(2) The first condition is that a defendant absconds after—

   (a) he is convicted of an offence or offences in proceedings before the Crown Court, or

   (b) he is committed to the Crown Court in respect of an offence or offences under section 218 below (committal with a view to a confiscation order being considered).

(3) The second condition is that—

   (a) the prosecutor or the Director applies to the Crown Court to proceed under this section, and

   (b) the court believes it is appropriate for it to do so.

(4) If this section applies the court must proceed under section 156 in the same way as it must proceed if the two conditions there mentioned are satisfied; but this is subject to subsection (5).

(5) If the court proceeds under section 156 as applied by this section, this Part has effect with these modifications—

   (a) any person the court believes is likely to be affected by an order under section 156 is entitled to appear before the court and make representations;

   (b) the court must not make an order under section 156 unless the prosecutor or the Director (as the case may be) has taken reasonable steps to contact the defendant;

   (c) section 156(9) applies as if the reference to subsection (2) were to subsection (2) of this section;

   (d) sections 160, 166(4), 167 and 168 must be ignored;

   (e) sections 169, 170 and 171 must be ignored while the defendant is still an absconder.

(6) Once the defendant has ceased to be an absconder section 169 has effect as if subsection (1)(a) read—

      "(a) at a time when the first condition in section 177 was satisfied the court did not proceed under section 156,".

(7) If the court does not believe it is appropriate for it to proceed under this section, once the defendant ceases to be an absconder section 169 has effect as if subsection (1)(b) read—

"(b) there is evidence which was not available to the prosecutor or the Director on the relevant date,".

DEFINITIONS
   "confiscation order": s. 236(5)
   "defendant": s. 236(3)

GENERAL NOTE
   This section provides for the case of a defendant who has been convicted by the Crown Court, or committed to the Crown Court for sentence, and who has absconded after the time of conviction or committal. Such a person is not eligible for a confiscation order under s.156, by virtue of subs.(8) of that section. If the prosecutor or the Director of the Assets Recovery Agency applies to the Crown Court, and the Crown Court believes that it is appropriate to do so, the Crown Court must proceed under s.156 as it would in normal circumstances but subject to the modifications made by subs.(5).
   The modifications are that any person other than the defendant who is likely to be affected by an order under s.156 (such as the holder of property said to be a "tainted gift") is entitled to appear before the Crown Court and make representations and the Court must not make an order unless the prosecutor or the Director has taken reasonable steps to contact the defendant. Sections 160 (required assumptions), 166(4) (statement of information relating to required assumptions), 167 (defendant's response to statement of information) and 168 (order to defendant to provide information) must be ignored. The power to reconsider questions relating to confiscation under ss.169, 170, 171 do not apply while the defendant remains an absconder; if he ceases to be an absconder, they apply with the modifications made by subss.(6) and (7).

178   Defendant neither convicted nor acquitted

(1) This section applies if the following two conditions are satisfied.
(2) The first condition is that—
   (a) proceedings for an offence or offences are started against a defendant but are not concluded,
   (b) he absconds, and
   (c) the period of two years (starting with the day the court believes he absconded) has ended.
(3) The second condition is that—
   (a) the prosecutor or the Director applies to the Crown Court to proceed under this section, and
   (b) the court believes it is appropriate for it to do so.
(4) If this section applies the court must proceed under section 156 in the same way as it must proceed if the two conditions there mentioned are satisfied; but this is subject to subsection (5).
(5) If the court proceeds under section 156 as applied by this section, this Part has effect with these modifications—
   (a) any person the court believes is likely to be affected by an order under section 156 is entitled to appear before the court and make representations;
   (b) the court must not make an order under section 156 unless the prosecutor or the Director (as the case may be) has taken reasonable steps to contact the defendant;
   (c) section 156(9) applies as if the reference to subsection (2) were to subsection (2) of this section;
   (d) sections 160, 166(4) and 167 to 170 must be ignored;
   (e) section 171 must be ignored while the defendant is still an absconder.
(6) Once the defendant has ceased to be an absconder section 171 has effect as if references to the date of conviction were to—
   (a) the day when proceedings for the offence concerned were started against the defendant, or
   (b) if there are two or more offences and proceedings for them were started on different days, the earliest of those days.

(7) If—
    (a) the court makes an order under section 156 as applied by this section, and
    (b) the defendant is later convicted in proceedings before the Crown Court of the offence (or any of the offences) concerned,
section 156 does not apply so far as that conviction is concerned.

DEFINITIONS
  "concluded": s.233(3) to (8)
  "defendant": s.236(3)
  "started": s.233

GENERAL NOTE
This section provides for the case of a defendant who absconds after proceedings for an offence or offences have been started but before he has been convicted. If the defendant is still an absconder after two years from the date on which he originally absconded (presumably this will in most cases be the date on which he failed to surrender to bail) the prosecutor of the Director may apply to the Crown Court. There is no time limit on such an application, once the initial two year period has expired.

If such an application is made, and the Court considers it appropriate to do so, the Court may proceed under section as in the normal way, but subject to the modifications made by subs.(5). These are substantially the same as those made by s.177(5) in the case of a person absconding after conviction, although there are minor differences in the wording of the two subsections. The only difference appears to be that under s.177, ss.169, 170, 171 must be ignored while the defendant remains an absconder, but may be applied when he ceases to be an absconder. Under s.178, ss.169 and 170 must be ignored, and but do not come into force when the defendant ceases to be an absconder. Section 171 (revision of amount of benefit) applies (as modified by subs.(6)) when the defendant ceases to be an absconder.

If a defendant against whom an order is made under this section is eventually convicted, the court may not make a confiscation order under s.156 on the basis of the conviction, but in such a case there would be power to apply for a revision of the amount of the defendant's benefit under s.171. If he is subsequently tried and acquitted, the order may be discharged on an application by the defendant (see s.180).

179   Variation of order

(1) This section applies if—
    (a) the court makes a confiscation order under section 156 as applied by section 178,
    (b) the defendant ceases to be an absconder,
    (c) he is convicted of an offence (or any of the offences) mentioned in section 178(2)(a),
    (d) he believes that the amount required to be paid was too large (taking the circumstances prevailing when the amount was found for the purposes of the order), and
    (e) before the end of the relevant period he applies to the Crown Court to consider the evidence on which his belief is based.
(2) If (after considering the evidence) the court concludes that the defendant's belief is well founded—
    (a) it must find the amount which should have been the amount required to be paid (taking the circumstances prevailing when the amount was found for the purposes of the order), and
    (b) it may vary the order by substituting for the amount required to be paid such amount as it believes is just.
(3) The relevant period is the period of 28 days starting with—
    (a) the date on which the defendant was convicted of the offence mentioned in section 178(2)(a), or
    (b) if there are two or more offences and the convictions were on different dates, the date of the latest.
(4) But in a case where section 178(2)(a) applies to more than one offence the court must not make an order under this section unless it is satis-

fied that there is no possibility of any further proceedings being taken or continued in relation to any such offence in respect of which the defendant has not been convicted.

DEFINITIONS
"confiscation order": s. 236(5)
"defendant": s.236(3)

GENERAL NOTE
This section provides for the variation of a confiscation order made under s.178 in respect of a defendant who has absconded before the criminal proceedings against him have been concluded (but not in the case of a confiscation order made under s.177 in respect of a defendant who absconded after he has been convicted). If the defendant ceases to be an absconder and is convicted of any of the offences in respect of which the criminal proceedings were in progress when he absconded, he may apply to the Crown Court within twenty eight days of his conviction if he believes that the amount of the order was too large. If the Court on consideration of the evidence finds that the defendant's belief is well founded, the Court must find the amount which should have been required to be paid and it may vary the confiscation order by substituting that amount.

180   Discharge of order

(1) Subsection (2) applies if—
  (a) the court makes a confiscation order under section 156 as applied by section 178,
  (b) the defendant is later tried for the offence or offences concerned and acquitted on all counts, and
  (c) he applies to the Crown Court to discharge the order.
(2) In such a case the court must discharge the order.
(3) Subsection (4) applies if—
  (a) the court makes a confiscation order under section 156 as applied by section 178,
  (b) the defendant ceases to be an absconder,
  (c) subsection (1)(b) does not apply, and
  (d) he applies to the Crown Court to discharge the order.
(4) In such a case the court may discharge the order if it finds that—
  (a) there has been undue delay in continuing the proceedings mentioned in section 178(2), or
  (b) the prosecutor does not intend to proceed with the prosecution.
(5) If the court discharges a confiscation order under this section it may make such a consequential or incidental order as it believes is appropriate.

DEFINITIONS
"confiscation order": s. 236(5)
"defendant": s. 236(3)

GENERAL NOTE
This section makes further provision for the case of a defendant who has absconded before criminal proceedings against him have been completed, and against whom a confiscation order has been made under s.178.

If such a defendant is later tried for the offence or offences concerned, and is acquitted on all counts, he may apply to the Crown Court to discharge the order, and the Crown Court must discharge the order.

If such a defendant ceases to be an absconder, but he is not tried for the offences concerned, he may apply to the Crown Court to discharge the order. In this case the Crown Court may, in its discretion, discharge the order if it finds either that there has been undue delay in continuing the proceedings for the offences or that the prosecutor does not intend to proceed with the prosecution.

Appeals

181   Appeal by prosecutor or Director

(1) If the Crown Court makes a confiscation order the prosecutor or the Director may appeal to the Court of Appeal in respect of the order.

(2) If the Crown Court decides not to make a confiscation order the prosecutor or the Director may appeal to the Court of Appeal against the decision.

(3) Subsections (1) and (2) do not apply to an order or decision made by virtue of section 169, 170, 177 or 178.

GENERAL NOTE

This section provides for an appeal to the Court of Appeal from a decision of the Crown Court by the prosecutor or the Director of the Assets Recovery Agency. Either the prosecutor or the director may appeal if the Crown Court makes a confiscation order, presumably on the ground that the amount of the order is less than the prosecutor or Director contends that it should be, or against a decision of the Crown Court not to make a confiscation order at all. The provision for appeal applies only to a confiscation order made (or not made) in the normal way following conviction. It does not apply to confiscation orders made or revised under those sections which allowed confiscation matters to be reconsidered at a later stage.

An appeal under this section may be made only with leave of the Court of Appeal (see s.237).

The Secretary of State may make an order corresponding to any provision in the Criminal Appeal (Northern Ireland) Act 1980 (see s.237(2)).

182   Court's powers on appeal

(1) On an appeal under section 181(1) the Court of Appeal may confirm, quash or vary the confiscation order.

(2) On an appeal under section 181(2) the Court of Appeal may confirm the decision, or if it believes the decision was wrong it may—

  (a) itself proceed under section 156 (ignoring subsections (1) to (3)), or

  (b) direct the Crown Court to proceed afresh under section 156.

(3) In proceeding afresh in pursuance of this section the Crown Court must comply with any directions the Court of Appeal may make.

(4) If a court makes or varies a confiscation order under this section or in pursuance of a direction under this section it must—

  (a) have regard to any fine imposed on the defendant in respect of the offence (or any of the offences) concerned;

  (b) have regard to any order which falls within section 163(3) and has been made against him in respect of the offence (or any of the offences) concerned, unless the order has already been taken into account by a court in deciding what is the free property held by the defendant for the purposes of section 159.

(5) If the Court of Appeal proceeds under section 156 or the Crown Court proceeds afresh under that section in pursuance of a direction under this section subsections (6) to (10) apply.

(6) If a court has already sentenced the defendant for the offence (or any of the offences) concerned, section 156 has effect as if his particular criminal conduct included conduct which constitutes offences which the court has taken into consideration in deciding his sentence for the offence or offences concerned.

(7) If an order has been made against the defendant in respect of the offence (or any of the offences) concerned under Article 14 of the

Criminal Justice (Northern Ireland) Order 1994 (S.I. 1994/2795 (N.I. 15)) (compensation orders)—
  (a) the court must have regard to it, and
  (b) section 163(5) and (6) above do not apply.
(8) Section 158(2) does not apply, and the rules applying instead are that the court must—
  (a) take account of conduct occurring before the relevant date;
  (b) take account of property obtained before that date;
  (c) take account of property obtained on or after that date if it was obtained as a result of or in connection with conduct occurring before that date.
(9) In section 160—
  (a) the first and second assumptions do not apply with regard to property first held by the defendant on or after the relevant date;
  (b) the third assumption does not apply with regard to expenditure incurred by him on or after that date;
  (c) the fourth assumption does not apply with regard to property obtained (or assumed to have been obtained) by him on or after that date.
(10) Section 176 applies as it applies in the circumstances mentioned in subsection (1) of that section.
(11) The relevant date is the date on which the Crown Court decided not to make a confiscation order.

DEFINITIONS
  "confiscation order": s.236(5)
  "criminal conduct": s.224
  "defendant": s.236(3)
  "offence or offences concerned": ss.236(1) and 15 6(9)
  "property": s.232

GENERAL NOTE
  This section makes a further provision for appeals of by the prosecutor or the Director under s.181. On such an appeal, the Court of Appeal may confirm quash or vary the confiscation order. The section does not specifically state that the court may vary the confiscation order by substituting a greater amount than was stated in the order made by the Crown Court, but this is a clearly implicit in the legislation.
  If the court appeal considers that the decision of the Crown Court in relation to the confiscation order was wrong, it may itself proceed under s. 156 or remit the matter to the Crown Court with the direction to the Crown Court to "to proceed afresh". In doing so, the Crown Court must comply with any corrections made by the Court of Appeal.
  A court making or varying a confiscation order, or "proceeding afresh" must have regard to any fine or other financial order made against the defendant, unless the order has already been taken into account in making the original order. The court must not take account of property obtained on or after the date on which the decision of the Crown Court was made, unless the property was obtained as a result of or in connection with the conduct occurring before that date. The required assumptions do not apply with regard to property held or obtained after the date on which the original decision of the Crown Court not to make a confiscation order was made, or to expenditure incurred by him after that date.
  There is a possible difficulty in the definition of the "relevant date" in subs. (11). The "relevant date" is important for the purposes of subss. (8) and (9). It is the date which marks the cut-off point for the taking into account of conduct or property or the application of the required assumptions. Subs. (11) states that the "relevant date is the date on which the Crown Court decided not to make a confiscation order". An appeal to which s. 182 applies may be made by the prosecutor or the Director on the ground that the Crown Court wrongly decided not to make a confiscation order, or that the Crown Court has made a confiscation order for less than the proper amount. Subsection (11) does not appear to contemplate the case where the Crown Court has made a confiscation order, but it is contended that the amount is too low. It is submitted that the subsection must be interpreted as if it included a reference to a case where the confiscation order has been made for what is contended to be an inadequate amount. There would be no logic in applying different rules in respect of the treatment of conduct and property, and the application of the assumptions, in this case.

183 Appeal to House of Lords

(1) An appeal lies to the House of Lords from a decision of the Court of Appeal on an appeal under section 181.

(2) An appeal under this section lies at the instance of—

  (a) the defendant or the prosecutor (if the prosecutor appealed under section 181);

  (b) the defendant or the Director (if the Director appealed under section 181).

(3) On an appeal from a decision of the Court of Appeal to confirm, vary or make a confiscation order the House of Lords may confirm, quash or vary the order.

(4) On an appeal from a decision of the Court of Appeal to confirm the decision of the Crown Court not to make a confiscation order or from a decision of the Court of Appeal to quash a confiscation order the House of Lords may—

  (a) confirm the decision, or

  (b) direct the Crown Court to proceed afresh under section 156 if it believes the decision was wrong.

(5) In proceeding afresh in pursuance of this section the Crown Court must comply with any directions the House of Lords may make.

(6) If a court varies a confiscation order under this section or makes a confiscation order in pursuance of a direction under this section it must—

  (a) have regard to any fine imposed on the defendant in respect of the offence (or any of the offences) concerned;

  (b) have regard to any order which falls within section 163(3) and has been made against him in respect of the offence (or any of the offences) concerned, unless the order has already been taken into account by a court in deciding what is the free property held by the defendant for the purposes of section 159.

(7) If the Crown Court proceeds afresh under section 156 in pursuance of a direction under this section subsections (8) to (12) apply.

(8) If a court has already sentenced the defendant for the offence (or any of the offences) concerned, section 156 has effect as if his particular criminal conduct included conduct which constitutes offences which the court has taken into consideration in deciding his sentence for the offence or offences concerned.

(9) If an order has been made against the defendant in respect of the offence (or any of the offences) concerned under Article 14 of the Criminal Justice (Northern Ireland) Order 1994 (S.I. 1994/2795 (N.I. 15)) (compensation orders)—

  (a) the Crown Court must have regard to it, and

  (b) section 163(5) and (6) above do not apply.

(10) Section 158(2) does not apply, and the rules applying instead are that the Crown Court must—

  (a) take account of conduct occurring before the relevant date;

  (b) take account of property obtained before that date;

  (c) take account of property obtained on or after that date if it was obtained as a result of or in connection with conduct occurring before that date.

(11) In section 160—

  (a) the first and second assumptions do not apply with regard to property first held by the defendant on or after the relevant date;

  (b) the third assumption does not apply with regard to expenditure incurred by him on or after that date;

    (c) the fourth assumption does not apply with regard to property obtained (or assumed to have been obtained) by him on or after that date.

(12) Section 176 applies as it applies in the circumstances mentioned in subsection (1) of that section.

(13) The relevant date is—

    (a) in a case where the Crown Court made a confiscation order which was quashed by the Court of Appeal, the date on which the Crown Court made the order;

    (b) in any other case, the date on which the Crown Court decided not to make a confiscation order.

DEFINITIONS

"confiscation order": s.236(5)
"criminal conduct": s.224
"defendant": s.236(3)
"free property": s.230
"offence or offences concerned": ss.236(1) and 156(9)
"property": s.232

GENERAL NOTE

This section provides for an appeal to the House of Lords from the decision of the Court of Appeal on an appeal by the prosecutor or the Director under s. 181. The appeal may be brought by the defendant or by the prosecutor if the prosecutor was the original appellant, or the Director if the Director was the original appellant. It is not open to the Director to appeal to the House of Lords in a case in which the prosecutor initiated the original appeal to the Court of Appeal, or vice versa.

The statute does not provide that it is necessary for the Court of Appeal to certify that the case involves a point of law of general public importance, nor is there an express requirement to obtain the leave of the House of Lords for the appeal. The Secretary of State may by order make similar provisions corresponding to any provision in the Criminal Appeal (Northern Ireland) Act 1980 (see s.238).

The powers of the House of Lords under this section are substantially similar to those of the Court of Appeal under s. 182, but with some differences. If the House of Lords allows an appeal against a decision of the Court of Appeal to confirm the decision of the Crown Court not to make a confiscation order or from a decision of the Court of Appeal to quash a confiscation order, the House of Lords is empowered to confirm the decision or to direct the Crown Court to proceed afresh under s. 156. There is no need in such a case (as there is in other cases) for the case to be returned to the Court of Appeal. In a case where the appeal concerns the amount of the confiscation order, rather than the decision whether or not to make an order at all, the House of Lords may under subs. (3) "confirm, quash or vary the order". Unlike the Court of Appeal, it may not itself proceed under s.6, and it may not, where what is an issue is the amount of the order as opposed to the decision whether or not to make an order at all, direct the Crown Court to "proceed afresh" under s. 156.

Where the Crown Court proceeds afresh under a direction of the House of Lords, or any court (including the House of Lords) varies a confiscation order, the normal rules relating to the process of calculating the recoverable amount are modified in the same way as they are in relation to an appeal to the Court of Appeal under s.181(6) to (10)). There is a similar problem in the definition of the "relevant date" in subs. (13).

An appeal under s. 183 of this Act can be made only as a consequence of an appeal by initiated by the prosecutor or the Director under s. 181 of this Act. If the appeal to the Court of Appeal is initiated in this way, it seems that either the defendant or the prosecutor or the Director (as the case may be) may appeal to the House of Lords. This section would have no affect if the original appeal was an appeal by the defendant under the Criminal Appeal Act (Northern Ireland) Act 1988.

Enforcement authority

184   **Enforcement authority**

(1) Subsection (2) applies if a court makes a confiscation order and any of the following paragraphs applies—

   (a) the court proceeded under section 156 after being asked to do so
       by the Director;
   (b) the court proceeded under section 156 by virtue of an application
       by the Director under section 169, 170, 177 or 178;
   (c) the court proceeded under section 156 as a result of an appeal by
       the Director under section 181(2) or 183;
   (d) before the court made the order the Director applied to the court
       to appoint him as the enforcement authority for the order.
 (2) In any such case the court must appoint the Director as the enforce-
     ment authority for the order.

DEFINITIONS
   "confiscation order": s. 236(5)

GENERAL NOTE
   The section provides for the appointment of the Director of the Assets Recovery Agency as
the enforcement authority in respect of confiscation orders made by the Crown Court or any
court on an appeal from the Crown Court. If in any case the court has proceeded to make a
confiscation order as a result of an application or appeal by the director, or before the court
made the confiscation order the Director has applied to the court to appoint him as the enforcement authority, the court must appoint the Director as the enforcement the authority for the
order.
   The section does not appear to authorise the Court to appoint the Director as the enforcement
authority in any other case. It appears that if the Court has made the confiscation order on the
application of the prosecutor, or has proceeded to make a confiscation order on its own initiative
under s.156(3)(b), the Court may not appoint the Director as the enforcement authority, unless
the Director applied to the court before the confiscation order was made. Once the order has
been made in these circumstances, without an application by the Director to be appointed as the
enforcement authority, there appears to be no power to appoint the Director even if he makes an
application at a later time.

Enforcement as fines etc

185   Enforcement as fines etc

 (1) This section applies if a court makes a confiscation order.
 (2) Section 35(1)(c), (2), (4) and (5) of the Criminal Justice Act (Northern
     Ireland) 1945 (c. 15) (functions of court as to fines) apply as if the
     amount ordered to be paid were a fine imposed on the defendant by
     the Crown Court.
 (3) An amount payable under a confiscation order is not a fine, costs, dam-
     ages or compensation for the purposes of Article 35 of the Criminal
     Justice (Northern Ireland) Order 1998 (S.I. 1998/1504 (N.I. 9)) (par-
     ent or guardian to pay fine etc. instead of child).

GENERAL NOTE
   This section makes clear that whenever the court makes a confiscation order the order will be
enforced as if it were a fine of the Crown Court in accordance with the cited legislation.

186   Director's application for enforcement

 (1) If the Director believes that the conditions set out in subsection (2) are
     satisfied he may make an ex parte application to the Crown Court for
     the issue of a summons against the defendant.
 (2) The conditions are that—
     (a) a confiscation order has been made;
     (b) the Director has been appointed as the enforcement authority for
         the order;
     (c) the order is not satisfied;
     (d) the order is not subject to appeal;
     (e) the Director has done all that is practicable (apart from this sec-
         tion) to enforce the order.

(3) If it appears to the Crown Court that the conditions are satisfied it may issue a summons ordering the defendant to appear before the court at the time and place specified in the summons.

(4) If the defendant fails to appear before the Crown Court in pursuance of the summons the court may issue a warrant for his arrest.

(5) If—

    (a) the defendant appears before the Crown Court in pursuance of the summons or of a warrant issued under subsection (4), and

    (b) the court is satisfied that the conditions set out in subsection (2) are satisfied,

it may issue a warrant committing the defendant to prison or to detention under section 5 of the Treatment of Offenders Act (Northern Ireland) 1968 (c. 29 (N.I.)) for default in payment of the amount ordered to be paid by the confiscation order.

(6) Subsection (7) applies if the amount remaining to be paid under the confiscation order when the warrant under subsection (5) is issued is less than the amount ordered to be paid.

(7) In such a case the court must substitute for the term of imprisonment or detention fixed in respect of the order under section 35(1) of the Criminal Justice Act (Northern Ireland) 1945 (c. 15 (N.I.)) such term as bears to the original term the same proportion as the amount remaining to be paid bears to the amount ordered to be paid.

DEFINITIONS

"confiscation order": s.236(5)

"defendant": s. 236(3)

GENERAL NOTE

This section makes provision for cases in which the defendant has failed to satisfy the confiscation order. If a confiscation order has been made, and the Director of the Assets Recovery Agency has been appointed as the enforcement authority, the Director may make an application without notice to the Crown Court for the issue of a summons against the defendant. The confiscation order must not be subject to appeal (either by the defendant or by the prosecutor or Director under s.181), the Director must have done all that is practicable to enforce the order and there are other conditions that if it appears to the Crown Court are satisfied, the Court may issue a summons to the defendant to appear; if the defendant fails to appear in pursuance of the summons, the Court may issue a warrant for his arrest. (There is no provision for the Crown Court to issue a warrant on the initial application of Director.) It should be noted that the equivalent section in Pt. 2 (s.37) contains a condition that the failure to satisfy the order must be attributable to the defendant's "wilful refusal or culpable neglect", so the test is harder to satisfy.

If, when the defendant appears before the Crown Court, the Court is satisfied that the conditions set out in subs.(2) are satisfied, in particular that the Director has done all that is practicable to enforce the order and that the order is not satisfied because of the defendant's wilful refusal or culpable neglect, the Court may issue a warrant under s.5 of the Treatment of Offenders Act (Northern Ireland) 1968 committing the defendant to prison or detention in default of payment.

If part of the amount ordered to be paid has been paid, the Court must reduce the default term to a term which bears the same proportion to the original default term (not the maximum default term fixed in the statutory table) the same proportion as the amount remaining to be paid bears to the original amount ordered to be paid. If after the defendant has been committed to prison, payment is made in respect of some of the remaining amount, the period of detention or imprisonment is reduced proportionately. If the whole of the outstanding amount is paid, the defendant must be released unless he is in custody for some other reason.

187 Provisions about imprisonment or detention

(1) Subsection (2) applies if—

    (a) a warrant committing the defendant to prison or detention is issued for a default in payment of an amount ordered to be paid under a confiscation order in respect of an offence or offences, and

(b) at the time the warrant is issued the defendant is liable to serve a term of custody in respect of the offence (or any of the offences).

(2) In such a case the term of imprisonment or of detention to be served in default of payment of the amount does not begin to run until after the term mentioned in subsection (1)(b) above.

(3) The reference in subsection (1)(b) to the term of custody the defendant is liable to serve in respect of the offence (or any of the offences) is a reference to the term of imprisonment, or detention under section 5 of the Treatment of Offenders Act (Northern Ireland) 1968 (c. 29 (N.I.)), which he is liable to serve in respect of the offence (or any of the offences).

(4) For the purposes of subsection (3) consecutive terms and terms which are wholly or partly concurrent must be treated as a single term and the following must be ignored—

(a) any sentence of imprisonment or order for detention suspended under section 18 of the Treatment of Offenders Act (Northern Ireland) 1968 which has not taken effect at the time the warrant is issued;

(b) any term of imprisonment or detention fixed under section 35(1)(c) of the Criminal Justice Act (Northern Ireland) 1945 (c. 15 (N.I.)) (term to be served in default of payment of fine etc) for which a warrant committing the defendant to prison or detention has not been issued at that time.

(5) If the defendant serves a term of imprisonment or detention in default of paying any amount due under a confiscation order, his serving that term does not prevent the confiscation order from continuing to have effect so far as any other method of enforcement is concerned.

DEFINITIONS
"confiscation order": s.236(5)
"defendant": s.236(3)

GENERAL NOTE

This section makes further provision in connection with a term which the defendant is ordered to serve in default of payment of a confiscation order. It applies whether the warrant committing the defendant to present is issued by the magistrates' court under or the Crown Court.

Any default term does not begin to run until after of the defendant has served any other term of custody imposed in respect of the offence. It is not necessary for the Court to order that the default term will run consecutively to the other term. In the case of a defendant sentenced to a term of imprisonment for less than four years, he will normally cease to be "liable to serve a term of custody" at the expiration of half of the term of the sentence as pronounced by the court (Criminal Justice Act 1991 s. 33). In the case of a defendant sentenced to a term of four years or more, whose liability to serve the sentence is dependent on the decision of the Parole Board, there is some uncertainty in the application of the section. Where the defendant is subject to terms of imprisonment which are consecutive or wholly or partly concurrent, the terms must be treated as a single term for the purpose of determining when the default term will begin. Suspended sentences which have not taken effect are ignored, as are partly suspended sentences imposed under the Criminal Law Act 1997 s. 47(1), (which was repealed in the 1992.) Default terms in respect of which a warrant of commitment has not been issued are also ignored for this purpose.

This section ignores the amendments made to the Criminal Justice Act 1991 s. 51(2) by the Crime and Disorder Act 1998. Under s. 51(2) as so amended, consecutive terms and terms which are wholly or partly concurrent are treated as a single term only if the sentences were passed on the same occasion, or if they were passed on different occasions, and the person concerned was not released at anytime during the period between the passing of the first and the passing of the second sentence. The object of the amendments was to provide that where a defendant is released on licence from his sentence, and his licence is subsequently revoked under the Criminal Justice Act 1991 s. 39 and he is returned to custody in respect of that sentence, any new sentence imposed while the defendant is the remainder of the licence period will not be treated as a single term including the original sentence. It appears that for the purpose of this action, that provision must be ignored.

Part 2 contains a reference to sentences which are partly served and partly suspended which does not appear in this section of Pt. 4. Also Pt. 2 contains reference to Young Offenders Institutions which Pt.4 does not.

A defendant who is committed to custody in default of payment of a confiscation order may have his term reduced under s. 186 of this Act if any part payment is made while he is serving the default sentence. In other cases, a person serving a default sentence is liable to serve one half of the default term, if that term is a term of less than 12 month, or two-thirds if the term if the term is twelve months or more (see the Criminal Justice Act 1991 s. 45). A person released from a default sentence is not subject to licence, irrespective of the length of the default term, and there is no provision for return to custody in the event of a conviction of a further offence. (A person so committed to custody in default may be released on licence under the Criminal Justice Act 1991, s.36, on compassionate grounds, before he has served the required fraction of the term.)

Service of the default term does not extinguish the liability to pay the amount due under the confiscation order, and the confiscation order may be enforced by any other method of enforcement.

188　Reconsideration etc: variation of prison term

(1) Subsection (2) applies if—
    (a) a court varies a confiscation order under section 171, 172, 173, 179, 182 or 183,
    (b) the effect of the variation is to vary the maximum period applicable in relation to the order under section 35(2) of the Criminal Justice Act (Northern Ireland) 1945 (c. 15 (N.I.)), and
    (c) the result is that that maximum period is less than the term of imprisonment or detention fixed in respect of the order under section 35(1)(c) of that Act.

(2) In such a case the court must fix a reduced term of imprisonment or detention in respect of the confiscation order under section 35(1)(c) of that Act in place of the term previously fixed.

(3) Subsection (4) applies if paragraphs (a) and (b) of subsection (1) apply but paragraph (c) does not.

(4) In such a case the court may amend the term of imprisonment or detention fixed in respect of the confiscation order under section 35(1)(c) of that Act.

(5) If the effect of section 162 is to increase the maximum period applicable in relation to a confiscation order under section 35(2) of that Act, on the application of the appropriate person the Crown Court may amend the term of imprisonment or detention fixed in respect of the order under section 35(1)(c) of that Act.

(6) The appropriate person is—
    (a) the Director, if he was appointed as the enforcement authority for the order under section 184;
    (b) the prosecutor, in any other case.

DEFINITIONS
"confiscation order": s.236(5)

GENERAL NOTE

This section provides for the variation of the default term if the amount of the confiscation order is varied after it has been made. It is not free from difficulty.

If the amount of the confiscation order is reduced, and the maximum period applicable to the revised amount of the order in the table of terms set out in the Powers of Criminal Courts (Sentencing) Act s. 139(4) is different from the maximum term for the original amount, and less than the term of imprisonment actually fixed in respect of the original order, the court must fix a reduced term in place of the term originally fixed (subs. (2)). If the amount of the original order was £250,000, and the original default term was three years, and the amount of the order is reduced to £100,000, for which the maximum default term is two years, the court must reduce the default term in accordance with subs.(2).

If the amount of the order is reduced, but the default term in respect of the new term is within the same band of default terms as the original term, the court has no discretion to reduce the default term. Before the court may vary the default term under subs.(3), the amount of the confiscation order must have been varied (subs.(1)(a)) and "the effect of the variation is to vary the maximum period applicable in relation to the order" (subs.(1)(b)). Suppose the amount of the original order was £250,000 and the revised amount is £125,000. The default term was fixed at three years, which is the maximum default term for an amount exceeding £100,000 but not exceeding £250,000. The variation in the amount of the order has not affected the maximum default term and the power to vary the default term under subs. (3) does not arise.

If the amount of the order is increased under ss.171 or 172, or following an appeal by the Director or prosecutor under ss.182 or 183, the court may increase the default term, but again only if the result of the variation is that a new maximum default term applies. If on an application under ss. 171 or 172, the amount of the order is increased from £100,000 to £110,000, the relevant maximum default term under s.220 is increased from two years to three years; the requirements of subs.(3) are satisfied and the court may (in its discretion) increase the default term. If the original order was for £110,000, and the revised order is for £250,000, the maximum default term is the same in each case (three years), and the court may not increase the default term, even if it has fixed the default term (as it should have done) for the original order, towards the lower end of the bracket of two to three years, on basis of the amount of the order.

If the amount payable under a confiscation order is increased by the addition of unpaid interest under s.162, the Crown Court may amend the default term on the application of the Director or the prosecutor, but only if the maximum default term in respect of the new amount is greater than the maximum default term for the original amount.

Restraint orders

189   Conditions for exercise of powers

(1) The High Court may exercise the powers conferred by section 190 if any of the following conditions is satisfied.

(2) The first condition is that—

    (a) a criminal investigation has been started in Northern Ireland with regard to an offence, and

    (b) there is reasonable cause to believe that the alleged offender has benefited from his criminal conduct.

(3) The second condition is that—

    (a) proceedings for an offence have been started in Northern Ireland and not concluded,

    (b) there is reasonable cause to believe that the defendant has benefited from his criminal conduct.

(4) The third condition is that—

    (a) an application by the prosecutor or the Director has been made under section 169, 170, 177 or 178 and not concluded, or the court believes that such an application is to be made, and

    (b) there is reasonable cause to believe that the defendant has benefited from his criminal conduct.

(5) The fourth condition is that—

    (a) an application by the prosecutor or the Director has been made under section 171 and not concluded, or the court believes that such an application is to be made, and

    (b) there is reasonable cause to believe that the court will decide under that section that the amount found under the new calculation of the defendant's benefit exceeds the relevant amount (as defined in that section).

(6) The fifth condition is that—

    (a) an application by the prosecutor or the Director has been made under section 172 and not concluded, or the court believes that such an application is to be made, and

    (b) there is reasonable cause to believe that the court will decide under that section that the amount found under the new calculation of the available amount exceeds the relevant amount (as defined in that section).

(7) The second condition is not satisfied if the court believes that—

    (a) there has been undue delay in continuing the proceedings, or

(b) the prosecutor does not intend to proceed.

(8) If an application mentioned in the third, fourth or fifth condition has been made the condition is not satisfied if the court believes that—

    (a) there has been undue delay in continuing the application, or

    (b) the prosecutor or the Director (as the case may be) does not intend to proceed.

(9) If the first condition is satisfied—

    (a) references in this Part to the defendant are to the alleged offender;

    (b) references in this Part to the prosecutor are to the person the court believes is to have conduct of any proceedings for the offence;

    (c) section 225(9) has effect as if proceedings for the offence had been started against the defendant when the investigation was started.

DEFINITIONS

"benefited": s. 224
"criminal investigation": s. 236(2)
"criminal conduct": s. 224
"defendant": s. 236(3)
"started": s. 233

GENERAL NOTE

Sections 189 to 195 provide for restraint orders. Restraint orders are normally made before criminal proceedings are completed, in anticipation of a confiscation order. Section 189 lists five different conditions under which the High Court may exercise the power to make a restraint order.

The first two conditions relate to anticipated criminal proceedings. The first condition is that a criminal investigation has been started in Northern Ireland, and there is reasonable cause to believe that the alleged offender has benefited from his criminal conduct. The second condition is that proceedings for an offence have been started and not concluded, and there is reasonable cause to believe that the defendant has benefited from his criminal conduct. This condition is not satisfied if the court believes that there has been undue delay in continuing, or that the prosecutor does not intend to proceed.

The third, fourth and fifth conditions apply to cases where the prosecutor or the Director of the Assets Recovery Agency has made an application for a reconsideration of a decision relating to confiscation, or for a confiscation order against an absconder. If an application has been made under ss.169, 170, 177 or 178 of the Act and has not been concluded, or the Court believes that such an application is to be made, and there is reasonable cause to believe that the defendant has benefited from his criminal conduct, the Court may make a restraint order. The fourth condition relates to an application under s.171 for a reconsideration of the amount of the defendant's benefit. If such an application has been made, or the Court believes that such an application is to be made, and the Court believes there is reasonable cause to believe that it will decide that the amount of the defendant's is greater than the amount of the defendant's benefit as originally calculated, it may make a restraint order. The fifth condition makes similar provision in relation to an application under s.172 for a revision of the determination of the "available amount". None of these is satisfied if the Court believes there has been any undue delay in continuing the application, or the prosecutor or Director does not intend to proceed with the application

It should be noted that in ss. 189,190 and 191 the High Court has the jurisdiction to deal with restraint orders. In the equivalent sections in Pts. 2, 40, 41 and 42, the jurisdiction of the High Court has been transferred to the Crown Court.

190   Restraint orders

(1) If any condition set out in section 189 is satisfied the High Court may make an order (a restraint order) prohibiting any specified person from dealing with any realisable property held by him.

(2) A restraint order may provide that it applies—

    (a) to all realisable property held by the specified person whether or not the property is described in the order;

     (b) to realisable property transferred to the specified person after the order is made.

  (3) A restraint order may be made subject to exceptions, and an exception may in particular—

     (a) make provision for reasonable living expenses and reasonable legal expenses;

     (b) make provision for the purpose of enabling any person to carry on any trade, business, profession or occupation;

     (c) be made subject to conditions.

  (4) But an exception to a restraint order may not make provision for any legal expenses which—

     (a) relate to an offence which falls within subsection (5), and

     (b) are incurred by the defendant or by a recipient of a tainted gift.

  (5) These offences fall within this subsection—

     (a) the offence mentioned in section 189(2) or (3), if the first or second condition (as the case may be) is satisfied;

     (b) the offence (or any of the offences) concerned, if the third, fourth or fifth condition is satisfied.

  (6) Subsection (7) applies if—

     (a) the court makes a restraint order, and

     (b) the applicant for the order applies to the court to proceed under subsection (7) (whether as part of the application for the restraint order or at any time afterwards).

  (7) The court may make such order as it believes is appropriate for the purpose of ensuring that the restraint order is effective.

  (8) A restraint order does not affect property for the time being subject to a charge under any of these provisions—

     (a) section 9 of the Drug Trafficking Offences Act 1986 (c. 32);

     (b) section 78 of the Criminal Justice Act 1988 (c. 33);

     (c) Article 14 of the Criminal Justice (Confiscation) (Northern Ireland) Order 1990 (S.I. 1990/2588 (N.I. 17));

     (d) section 27 of the Drug Trafficking Act 1994 (c. 37);

     (e) Article 32 of the Proceeds of Crime (Northern Ireland) Order 1996 (S.I. 1996/1299 (N.I. 9)).

  (9) Dealing with property includes removing it from Northern Ireland.

<small>DEFINITIONS</small>

"defendant": s. 236(3)
"property": s.232
"realisable property": s. 231
"restraint order": s. 236(5), s. 190
"tainted gift": s. 225

<small>GENERAL NOTE</small>

This section provides for the content and effect of a restraint order. The principal effect of a restraint order is to prohibit any person specified in the order from dealing with any "realisable property" held by him. The person so specified is not necessarily the defendant. The restraint order may apply generally to all realisable property held by the specified person, and to realisable property transferred to the specified person after the order has been made.

A restraint order may provide that certain expenditure is excepted from the effect of the order. It may in particular make provision for reasonable living expenses and for expenditure enabling the person specified to carry on his trade, business, profession or occupation. Provision may be made for reasonable legal expenses, but such provision must not include provision for expenses in connection with the offence which is the subject of an investigation which has not been completed or criminal proceedings which have not been concluded, or any offence in relation to which an application is made under the various provisions allowing for reconsideration of confiscation issues.

When a restraint order has been made, the person who has applied for the restraint order may apply to the Court to make any further order as court believes appropriate for the purpose of ensuring that the restraint order is effective. A restraint order does not affect property which is subject to a charge in relation to a confiscation order made under earlier legislation.

The powers given by this section must be exercised with regard to the matters listed in s.217.

191   Application, discharge and variation

(1) A restraint order—
    (a) may be made only on an application by an applicant falling within subsection (2);
    (b) may be made on an ex parte application to a judge in chambers.

(2) These applicants fall within this subsection—
    (a) the prosecutor;
    (b) the Director;
    (c) an accredited financial investigator.

(3) An application to discharge or vary a restraint order or an order under section 190(7) may be made to the High Court by—
    (a) the person who applied for the order;
    (b) any person affected by the order.

(4) Subsections (5) to (7) apply to an application under subsection (3).

(5) The court—
    (a) may discharge the order;
    (b) may vary the order.

(6) If the condition in section 189 which was satisfied was that proceedings were started or an application was made, the court must discharge the order on the conclusion of the proceedings or of the application (as the case may be).

(7) If the condition in section 189 which was satisfied was that an investigation was started or an application was to be made, the court must discharge the order if within a reasonable time proceedings for the offence are not started or the application is not made (as the case may be).

Definitions
    "restraint order": s.236(5), s. 190

General Note
    This section makes provision for various procedural questions in connection with restraint orders. An application for a restraint order may be made only by the prosecutor, the Director of the Assets Recovery Agency, or a financial investigator accredited by the Director under s.3. An application to make a restraint order may be made without notice to a judge in chambers.

    An application to discharge or vary a restraint order may be made by the person who applied for the order or any person affected by the order (such person may be the defendant or some other person specified in the order as the holder of the property concerned.) An application to vary or discharge a restraint order must be made to the High Court. On such an application, the High Court may discharge or vary the order. The Act does not provide that the prosecutor may apply for a variation without notice but presumably the Court Rules will do so as for such applications under the present legislation. If the application for the restraint order was made on the basis that proceedings had started or that an application had been made, the court must discharge the order on the conclusion of the proceedings or application. If the restraint order was made on the basis that an investigation had started, or that an application was about to be made, the court must discharge the order if the proceedings have not started or the application has not been made within a reasonable time.

    The powers given by this section must be exercised with regard to the matters listed in s. 217.

192   Appeal to Court of Appeal

(1) If on an application for a restraint order the court decides not to make one, the person who applied for the order may appeal to the Court of Appeal against the decision.

(2) If an application is made under section 191(3) in relation to a restraint order or an order under section 190(7) the following persons may appeal to the Court of Appeal in respect of the High Court's decision on the application—
   (a) the person who applied for the order;
   (b) any person affected by the order.
(3) On an appeal under subsection (1) or (2) the Court of Appeal may—
   (a) confirm the decision, or
   (b) make such order as it believes is appropriate.

DEFINITIONS
   "restraint order": s. 236(5), s. 190

GENERAL NOTE
   This section provides for an appeal from the High Court to the Court of Appeal against a decision of the High Court not to make a restraint order. The person who applied for the order may appeal to the Court of Appeal, against the decision of the High Court, with leave of Court of Appeal (see s. 237). Where an application to discharge or vary a restraint order has been made, the person who applied for the order or any person affected by the order may appeal to the Court of Appeal from the High Court's decision. On such an appeal the Court of Appeal may confirm the decision of the High Court or make such order as it believes is appropriate.
   The powers given by this section must be exercised with regard to the matters listed in s. 217.

193   Appeal to House of Lords

(1) An appeal lies to the House of Lords from a decision of the Court of Appeal on an appeal under section 192.
(2) An appeal under this section lies at the instance of any person who was a party to the proceedings before the Court of Appeal.
(3) On an appeal under this section the House of Lords may—
   (a) confirm the decision of the Court of Appeal, or
   (b) make such order as it believes is appropriate.

GENERAL NOTE
   This section makes provision for an appeal to the House of Lords from a decision of the Court of Appeal on an appeal against a decision of the High Court in connection with the making, variation or discharge of a restraint order. Any person who was a party to the proceedings before the Court of Appeal may appeal under this section. The House of Lords may confirm the decision of the Court of Appeal or make such order as it believes is appropriate.
   The statute does not require either party to obtain a certificate from the Court of Appeal that the case involves a point of law of general public importance, or to obtain leave to appeal either from the Court of Appeal or the House of Lords. See s.238 dealing with procedure on appeal to House of Lords – the Secretary of State is empowered to make an order containing provision which is equivalent to provision in The Criminal Appeal (Northern Ireland) Act 1980.
   The powers given by this section must be exercised with regard to the matters listed in s. 217.

194   Seizure

(1) If a restraint order is in force a constable or a customs officer may seize any realisable property to which it applies to prevent its removal from Northern Ireland.
(2) Property seized under subsection (1) must be dealt with in accordance with the directions of the court which made the order.

DEFINITIONS
   "property": s.232
   "realisable property": s.231
   "restraint order": s. 236(5), s.190

GENERAL NOTE
   This section enables a constable or customs officer to seize any realisable property to which a restraint order applies to prevent its removal from Northern Ireland.

The powers given by this section must be exercised with regard to the matters listed in s. 217 It should be noted that Pt. 2 contains s. 46 which deals with hearsay evidence and there is no equivalent section in Pt. 4.

195 Supplementary

(1) The person applying for a restraint order must be treated for the purposes of section 66 of the Land Registration Act (Northern Ireland) 1970 (c. 18 (N.I.)) (cautions) as a person interested in relation to any registered land to which—
    (a) the application relates, or
    (b) a restraint order made in pursuance of the application relates.

(2) Upon being served with a copy of a restraint order, the Registrar shall, in respect of any registered land to which a restraint order or an application for a restraint order relates, make an entry inhibiting any dealing with the land without the consent of the High Court.

(3) Subsections (2) and (4) of section 67 of the Land Registration Act (Northern Ireland) 1970 (inhibitions) shall apply to an entry made under subsection (2) as they apply to an entry made on the application of any person interested in the registered land under subsection (1) of that section.

(4) Where a restraint order has been protected by an entry registered under the Land Registration Act (Northern Ireland) 1970 or the Registration of Deeds Acts, an order discharging the restraint order may require that the entry be vacated.

(5) In this section—
    "Registrar" and "entry" have the same meanings as in the Land Registration Act (Northern Ireland) 1970; and
    "Registration of Deeds Acts" has the meaning given by section 46(2) of the Interpretation Act (Northern Ireland) 1954 (c. 33 (N.I.)).

DEFINITIONS
"benefited": s. 224
"concluded": s. 233 (3) to (8)
"confiscation order": s. 236(5)
"criminal investigation": s. 236(2)
"criminal lifestyle": s. 223
"criminal conduct": s. 224
"defendant": s. 236(3)
"free property": s. 230
"offence or offences concerned": s. 236(1) and 156(9)
"property": s. 232
"realisable property": s. 231
"restraint order": s. 236(5), s. 190
"satisfied": s. 235
"sentencing": s. 236(4)
"started": s. 233
"tainted gift": s. 225

Management receivers

196 Appointment

(1) Subsection (2) applies if—
    (a) the High Court makes a restraint order, and
    (b) the applicant for the restraint order applies to the court to proceed under subsection (2) (whether as part of the application for the restraint order or at any time afterwards).

(2) The High Court may by order appoint a receiver in respect of any realisable property to which the restraint order applies.

DEFINITIONS
  "property": s.232
  "realisable property": s.231
  "restraint order": s. 206

GENERAL NOTE
  This section empowers the High Court to appoint a receiver in respect of any realisable property to which a restraint order made by the Court applies. The receiver may be appointed only on the application of the person who applied for the restraint order, whether at the time the restraint order was made or subsequently.
  The powers given by this section must be exercised with regard to the matters listed in s.217.

197   Powers

(1) If the court appoints a receiver under section 196 it may act under this section on the application of the person who applied for the restraint order.

(2) The court may by order confer on the receiver the following powers in relation to any realisable property to which the restraint order applies—
  (a) power to take possession of the property;
  (b) power to manage or otherwise deal with the property;
  (c) power to start, carry on or defend any legal proceedings in respect of the property;
  (d) power to realise so much of the property as is necessary to meet the receiver's remuneration and expenses.

(3) The court may by order confer on the receiver power to enter any premises in Northern Ireland and to do any of the following—
  (a) search for or inspect anything authorised by the court;
  (b) make or obtain a copy, photograph or other record of anything so authorised;
  (c) remove anything which the receiver is required or authorised to take possession of in pursuance of an order of the court.

(4) The court may by order authorise the receiver to do any of the following for the purpose of the exercise of his functions—
  (a) hold property;
  (b) enter into contracts;
  (c) sue and be sued;
  (d) employ agents;
  (e) execute powers of attorney, deeds or other instruments;
  (f) take any other steps the court thinks appropriate.

(5) The court may order any person who has possession of realisable property to which the restraint order applies to give possession of it to the receiver.

(6) The court—
  (a) may order a person holding an interest in realisable property to which the restraint order applies to make to the receiver such payment as the court specifies in respect of a beneficial interest held by the defendant or the recipient of a tainted gift;
  (b) may (on the payment being made) by order transfer, grant or extinguish any interest in the property.

(7) Subsections (2), (5) and (6) do not apply to property for the time being subject to a charge under any of these provisions—
  (a) section 9 of the Drug Trafficking Offences Act 1986 (c. 32);
  (b) section 78 of the Criminal Justice Act 1988 (c. 33);
  (c) Article 14 of the Criminal Justice (Confiscation) (Northern Ireland) Order 1990 (S.I. 1990/2588 (N.I. 17));
  (d) section 27 of the Drug Trafficking Act 1994 (c. 37);
  (e) Article 32 of the Proceeds of Crime (Northern Ireland) Order 1996 (S.I. 1996/1299 (N.I. 9)).

(8) The court must not—
- (a) confer the power mentioned in subsection (2)(b) or (d) in respect of property, or
- (b) exercise the power conferred on it by subsection (6) in respect of property,

unless it gives persons holding interests in the property a reasonable opportunity to make representations to it.

(9) The court may order that a power conferred by an order under this section is subject to such conditions and exceptions as it specifies.

(10) Managing or otherwise dealing with property includes—
- (a) selling the property or any part of it or interest in it;
- (b) carrying on or arranging for another person to carry on any trade or business the assets of which are or are part of the property;
- (c) incurring capital expenditure in respect of the property.

DEFINITIONS
"defendant": s. 236(3)
"property": s.232
"realisable property": s. 231
"restraint order": s. 236(5), s. 206

GENERAL NOTE

This section provides for the powers of a receiver appointed by the High Court under s. 197 in connection with a restraint order. The powers of the receiver in a particular case must be conferred on him specifically by the High Court. The powers which may be conferred on a receiver are set out in subss. (2) to (4). They include the power to take possession of, and manage or otherwise deal with the property, to realise so much of the property as is necessary to meet to receiver's remuneration and expenses, to make appropriate searches and inquiries in connection with the property and to conduct inquiries and searches in connection with the property.

The court may also make orders against other persons, including the defendant or any other person holding the property. The person concerned may be ordered to give the property to which the restraint order applies to the receiver or to make a payment to the receiver in respect of any beneficial interest held by the defendant in respect of the property. Property which is the subject to a charge made under earlier confiscation legislation is excluded from all of these provisions, other than those which authorise powers to make to searches and other inquiries (subs. (3)). The court must not confer on a receiver the power to manage or deal with property, or to realise property, without giving any person interested in the property a reasonable opportunity to make representations to it. The same restriction applies to an order requiring a person to make a payment to the receiver under subs. (6), but this provision does not apply to the power conferred by subs. (5) to order a person in possession of property which is alleged to be realisable property to give it to the receiver. It may be that a similar restriction would apply by virtue of common law.

The powers given by this section must be exercised with regard to the matters listed in s. 217.

Enforcement receivers

198 Appointment

(1) This section applies if—
- (a) a confiscation order is made,
- (b) it is not satisfied, and
- (c) it is not subject to appeal.

(2) On the application of the prosecutor the Crown Court may by order appoint a receiver in respect of realisable property.

DEFINITIONS
"confiscation order": s. 236(5)
"property": s.232

"realisable property": s. 231
"satisfied": s. 235(1)

GENERAL NOTE
This section provides for the appointment of a receiver where the Crown Court has made a confiscation order and the confiscation order and has not been satisfied, and the Director of the Assets Recovery Agency has not been appointed under s. 184 as the enforcement authority for the order (see 200). A receiver may not be appointed if the confiscation order is "subject to appeal". (This restriction presumably applies to an appeal by the prosecutor or Director under s. 181 as well as to an appeal by a defendant under the Criminal Appeal (Northern Ireland) Act 1980. The receiver may be appointed on the application of the prosecutor.

It is not necessary for the court to delay the appointment of a receiver under this section until the period for allowed for payment by an order under s. 161 has elapsed.

The powers given by this section must be exercised with regard to the matters listed in s. 217.

199   Powers

(1) If the court appoints a receiver under section 198 it may act under this section on the application of the prosecutor.

(2) The court may by order confer on the receiver the following powers in relation to the realisable property—
    (a) power to take possession of the property;
    (b) power to manage or otherwise deal with the property;
    (c) power to realise the property, in such manner as the court may specify;
    (d) power to start, carry on or defend any legal proceedings in respect of the property.

(3) The court may by order confer on the receiver power to enter any premises in Northern Ireland and to do any of the following—
    (a) search for or inspect anything authorised by the court;
    (b) make or obtain a copy, photograph or other record of anything so authorised;
    (c) remove anything which the receiver is required or authorised to take possession of in pursuance of an order of the court.

(4) The court may by order authorise the receiver to do any of the following for the purpose of the exercise of his functions—
    (a) hold property;
    (b) enter into contracts;
    (c) sue and be sued;
    (d) employ agents;
    (e) execute powers of attorney, deeds or other instruments;
    (f) take any other steps the court thinks appropriate.

(5) The court may order any person who has possession of realisable property to give possession of it to the receiver.

(6) The court—
    (a) may order a person holding an interest in realisable property to make to the receiver such payment as the court specifies in respect of a beneficial interest held by the defendant or the recipient of a tainted gift;
    (b) may (on the payment being made) by order transfer, grant or extinguish any interest in the property.

(7) Subsections (2), (5) and (6) do not apply to property for the time being subject to a charge under any of these provisions—
    (a) section 9 of the Drug Trafficking Offences Act 1986 (c. 32);
    (b) section 78 of the Criminal Justice Act 1988 (c. 33);
    (c) Article 14 of the Criminal Justice (Confiscation) (Northern Ireland) Order 1990 (S.I. 1990/2588 (N.I. 17));
    (d) section 27 of the Drug Trafficking Act 1994 (c. 37);
    (e) Article 32 of the Proceeds of Crime (Northern Ireland) Order 1996 (S.I. 1996/1299 (N.I. 9)).

(8) The court must not—
    (a) confer the power mentioned in subsection (2)(b) or (c) in respect of property, or
    (b) exercise the power conferred on it by subsection (6) in respect of property,
unless it gives persons holding interests in the property a reasonable opportunity to make representations to it.
(9) The court may order that a power conferred by an order under this section is subject to such conditions and exceptions as it specifies.
(10) Managing or otherwise dealing with property includes—
    (a) selling the property or any part of it or interest in it;
    (b) carrying on or arranging for another person to carry on any trade or business the assets of which are or are part of the property;
    (c) incurring capital expenditure in respect of the property.

DEFINITIONS
"defendant": s. 236(3)
"property": s.232
"realisable property": s. 231
"tainted gift": s. 225

GENERAL NOTE
This section makes substantially similar provision in respect of receivers appointed to enforce confiscation orders as is made by s. 197 in respect of receivers appointed in connection with restraint orders. (There is no provision under this section for the receiver to be empowered to realise property to meet his remuneration and expenses; compare s. 197(2)(c) and (d) with s. 199(2)(c) and (d).) The powers to be exercised by the receiver must be conferred specifically by the Crown Court in each particular case. Where the receiver is to be empowered to manage or deal with property thought to be realisable property, any person holding an interest in the property must be given a reasonable opportunity to make representations to the Crown Court. The same restriction replies to an order requiring a third person to make a payment to the receiver in respect of a beneficial interest held by the defendant for the recipient of a tainted gift, but not to an order to a person having possession of realised of property to give possession of it to the receiver (subs. (8)).
The powers given by this section must be exercised with regard to the matters listed in s. 217.

Director's receivers

200   Appointment

(1) This section applies if—
    (a) a confiscation order is made, and
    (b) the Director is appointed as the enforcement authority for the order under section 184.
(2) But this section does not apply if—
    (a) the confiscation order was made by the Court of Appeal, and
    (b) when the Crown Court comes to proceed under this section the confiscation order has been satisfied.
(3) If this section applies the Crown Court must make an order for the appointment of a receiver in respect of realisable property.
(4) An order under subsection (3)—
    (a) must confer power on the Director to nominate the person who is to be the receiver, and
    (b) takes effect when the Director nominates that person.
(5) The Director must not nominate a person under subsection (4) unless at the time he does so the confiscation order—
    (a) is not satisfied, and
    (b) is not subject to appeal.
(6) A person nominated to be the receiver under subsection (4) may be—

    (a) a member of the staff of the Agency;
    (b) a person providing services under arrangements made by the Director.
(7) If this section applies section 198 does not apply.

DEFINITIONS
"confiscation order": s. 236(5)
"property": s. 232
"realisable property": s. 231
"satisfied": s. 235(1)

GENERAL NOTE

This section applies where a confiscation order has been made by the Crown Court, and the Director of the Assets Recovery Agency has been appointed as the enforcement authority in respect of the order under s. 184. (The section does not apply if the confiscation order has been made by the Court of Appeal (presumably, on an appeal under s. 182) and the order has been satisfied when the question of appointment of a receiver arises.) In a case to which s. 200 applies, the Crown Court must make an order appointing a receiver (in the case where the director is not appointed as the enforcing authority, the appointment or of a receiver to enforce the order is at the discretion of the Crown Court (s. 199(2)).

An order under this section must confer on the Director power to nominate the receiver; the Director must not nominate a person unless at the time he does so the confiscation order is not satisfied and is not "subject to appeal." (Presumably this restriction applies to appeals by the Director under s. 181 as it does to appeals by the defendant under the Criminal Appeal (Northern Ireland) Act 1980.

The powers given by this section must be exercised with regard to the matters listed in s. 217.

201 Powers

(1) If the court makes an order for the appointment of a receiver under section 200 it may act under this section on the application of the Director.
(2) The court may by order confer on the receiver the following powers in relation to the realisable property—
    (a) power to take possession of the property;
    (b) power to manage or otherwise deal with the property;
    (c) power to realise the property, in such manner as the court may specify;
    (d) power to start, carry on or defend any legal proceedings in respect of the property.
(3) The court may by order confer on the receiver power to enter any premises in Northern Ireland and to do any of the following—
    (a) search for or inspect anything authorised by the court;
    (b) make or obtain a copy, photograph or other record of anything so authorised;
    (c) remove anything which the receiver is required or authorised to take possession of in pursuance of an order of the court.
(4) The court may by order authorise the receiver to do any of the following for the purpose of the exercise of his functions—
    (a) hold property;
    (b) enter into contracts;
    (c) sue and be sued;
    (d) employ agents;
    (e) execute powers of attorney, deeds or other instruments;
    (f) take any other steps the court thinks appropriate.
(5) The court may order any person who has possession of realisable property to give possession of it to the receiver.
(6) The court—
    (a) may order a person holding an interest in realisable property to make to the receiver such payment as the court specifies in

respect of a beneficial interest held by the defendant or the recipient of a tainted gift;

    (b) may (on the payment being made) by order transfer, grant or extinguish any interest in the property.

(7) Subsections (2), (5) and (6) do not apply to property for the time being subject to a charge under any of these provisions—

    (a) section 9 of the Drug Trafficking Offences Act 1986 (c. 32);

    (b) section 78 of the Criminal Justice Act 1988 (c. 33);

    (c) Article 14 of the Criminal Justice (Confiscation) (Northern Ireland) Order 1990 (S.I. 1990/2588 (N.I. 17));

    (d) section 27 of the Drug Trafficking Act 1994 (c. 37);

    (e) Article 32 of the Proceeds of Crime (Northern Ireland) Order 1996 (S.I. 1996/1299 (N.I. 9)).

(8) The court must not—

    (a) confer the power mentioned in subsection (2)(b) or (c) in respect of property, or

    (b) exercise the power conferred on it by subsection (6) in respect of property,

unless it gives persons holding interests in the property a reasonable opportunity to make representations to it.

(9) The court may order that a power conferred by an order under this section is subject to such conditions and exceptions as it specifies.

(10) Managing or otherwise dealing with property includes—

    (a) selling the property or any part of it or interest in it;

    (b) carrying on or arranging for another person to carry on any trade or business the assets of which are or are part of the property;

    (c) incurring capital expenditure in respect of the property.

DEFINITIONS
"defendant": s. 236(3)
"property": s.232
"realisable property": s. 231
"tainted gift": s. 225

GENERAL NOTE
    This section makes provision for the Crown Court to confer powers on a receiver nominated by the Director of the Assets Recovery Agency to enforce the confiscation order. It is identical to s. 199, dealing with the power of the Crown Court to confer powers on a receiver appointed to enforce a confiscation order where the Director is not appointed as the enforcement authority. Although the appointment of a receiver is mandatory where the Director has been appointed as the enforcement authority and applies to the Crown Court for the appointment of the receiver, the question of which powers (among those identified in this section) are to be conferred on the receiver is within the discretion of the Crown Court.

    The powers given by this section must be exercised with regard to the matters listed in s. 217.

Application of sums

202   Enforcement receivers

(1) This section applies to sums which are in the hands of a receiver appointed under section 198 if they are—

    (a) the proceeds of the realisation of property under section 199;

    (b) sums (other than those mentioned in paragraph (a)) in which the defendant holds an interest.

(2) The sums must be applied as follows—

    (a) first, they must be applied in payment of such expenses incurred by a person acting as an insolvency practitioner as are payable under this subsection by virtue of section 432;

    (b) second, they must be applied in making any payments directed by the Crown Court;

    (c) third, they must be applied on the defendant's behalf towards satisfaction of the confiscation order.

(3) If the amount payable under the confiscation order has been fully paid and any sums remain in the receiver's hands he must distribute them—

    (a) among such persons who held (or hold) interests in the property concerned as the Crown Court directs, and

    (b) in such proportions as it directs.

(4) Before making a direction under subsection (3) the court must give persons who held (or hold) interests in the property concerned a reasonable opportunity to make representations to it.

(5) For the purposes of subsections (3) and (4) the property concerned is—

    (a) the property represented by the proceeds mentioned in subsection (1)(a);

    (b) the sums mentioned in subsection (1)(b).

(6) The receiver applies sums as mentioned in subsection (2)(c) by paying them to the appropriate chief clerk on account of the amount payable under the order.

(7) The appropriate chief clerk is the chief clerk of the court at the place where the confiscation order was made.

DEFINITIONS
"confiscation order": s. 236(5)
"defendant": s. 236(3)
"property": s. 232

GENERAL NOTE
This section provides for the disposal of the proceeds of the realisation of property by a receiver appointed to enforce a confiscation order, or to any other sums held by the receiver in which the defendant holds an interest. It applies only to a receiver appointed under s. 198 (cases where the Director is not appointed as the enforcement authority). The first priority is the payment of expenses incurred by an insolvency practitioner in relation to property which is subject to orders made under this or other confiscation legislation, by virtue of s. 432. Second, the sums must be applied in making any payments directed by the Crown Court, other than a direction in respect of the payment of compensation under s. 163(6), which is governed by s. 203. Third, the sums must be applied towards the satisfaction of confiscation order. Sums applied to the satisfaction of the confiscation order must be paid to the appropriate Justices' Chief Clerk (see s. 185). Any surplus funds left over must be distributed as the Crown Court directs in accordance with subss. (3) and (4).

203   Sums received by chief clerk

(1) This section applies if a chief clerk receives sums on account of the amount payable under a confiscation order (whether the sums are received under section 202 or otherwise).

(2) The chief clerk's receipt of the sums reduces the amount payable under the order, but he must apply the sums received as follows.

(3) First he must apply them in payment of such expenses incurred by a person acting as an insolvency practitioner as—

    (a) are payable under this subsection by virtue of section 432, but

    (b) are not already paid under section 202(2)(a).

(4) If the chief clerk received the sums under section 202 he must next apply them—

    (a) first, in payment of the remuneration and expenses of a receiver appointed under section 196, to the extent that they have not been met by virtue of the exercise by that receiver of a power conferred under section 197(2)(d);

    (b) second, in payment of the remuneration and expenses of the receiver appointed under section 198.

(5) If a direction was made under section 163(6) for an amount of compensation to be paid out of sums recovered under the confiscation

order, the chief clerk must next apply the sums in payment of that amount.

(6) If any amount remains after the chief clerk makes any payments required by the preceding provisions of this section, the amount must be treated for the purposes of section 20 of the Administration of Justice Act (Northern Ireland) 1954 (c. 9 (N.I.)) (application of fines) as if it were a fine.

(7) Subsection (4) does not apply if the receiver is a member of the staff of the Director of Public Prosecutions for Northern Ireland or of the Commissioners of Customs and Excise; and it is immaterial whether he is a permanent or temporary member or he is on secondment from elsewhere.

DEFINITIONS
"confiscation order": s. 236(5)

GENERAL NOTE
This section provides for the disposal of sums of money received by a Justices' Chief Clerk on account of a confiscation order. It covers payments made by a receiver under s. 202, or payments made directly by a defendant.

If there are any payments due to an insolvency practitioner by virtue of s. 432 of the Act, which have not already been paid, they must first be paid. If the sums have been received from a receiver, the next priority is the expenses of the receiver appointed in connection with a restraint order, which have not already been met. The next priority (also restricted to sums received from a receiver under s. 202) is the payment of the remuneration and expenses of the receiver appointed to enforce a confiscation order. (The expenses of either class of receiver cannot be met out of money paid direct to the Justice's Chief Clerk by or on behalf of the defendant). Next comes the satisfaction of a direction under s. 163(6) that the sums recovered under the confiscation order be applied to the satisfaction of a compensation order. Any remaining amount is treated as a payment received in satisfaction of the confiscation order.

Any sum received by the Justices' Chief Clerk reduces the amount payable under the confiscation order (and thus the term to be served in default if the order is not fully satisfied) however the sum is applied under this section (subs. (2)).

204   Director's receivers

(1) This section applies to sums which are in the hands of a receiver appointed under section 200 if they are—
    (a) the proceeds of the realisation of property under section 201;
    (b) sums (other than those mentioned in paragraph (a)) in which the defendant holds an interest.

(2) The sums must be applied as follows—
    (a) first, they must be applied in payment of such expenses incurred by a person acting as an insolvency practitioner as are payable under this subsection by virtue of section 432;
    (b) second, they must be applied in making any payments directed by the Crown Court;
    (c) third, they must be applied on the defendant's behalf towards satisfaction of the confiscation order by being paid to the Director on account of the amount payable under it.

(3) If the amount payable under the confiscation order has been fully paid and any sums remain in the receiver's hands he must distribute them—
    (a) among such persons who held (or hold) interests in the property concerned as the Crown Court directs, and
    (b) in such proportions as it directs.

(4) Before making a direction under subsection (3) the court must give persons who held (or hold) interests in the property concerned a reasonable opportunity to make representations to it.

(5) For the purposes of subsections (3) and (4) the property concerned is—

(a) the property represented by the proceeds mentioned in subsection (1)(a);

(b) the sums mentioned in subsection (1)(b).

DEFINITIONS

"confiscation order": s. 236(5)

"defendant": s. 236(3)

"property": s. 232

GENERAL NOTE

This section makes provision for the disposal of the money held by a receiver appointed under s.200, in a case where the Director of the Assets Recovery Agency has been appointed as the enforcement authority in respect of the confiscation order. The section corresponds with s. 202. The sums in question are those held by the receiver as the proceeds of the realisation of property, and any other sums in which the defendant holds an interest.

The order of priority of payments under subs. (2) is the same as in the case of an order under s. 202. If any sums remain after the confiscation order has been satisfied and other payments have been met, they are to be distributed as the Crown Court directs, after giving persons who held or hold interests in the property concerned a reasonable opportunity to make representations. Sums to be applied to the satisfaction of the confiscation order must be paid to be Director.

205 Sums received by Director

(1) This section applies if the Director receives sums on account of the amount payable under a confiscation order (whether the sums are received under section 204 or otherwise).

(2) The Director's receipt of the sums reduces the amount payable under the order, but he must apply the sums received as follows.

(3) First he must apply them in payment of such expenses incurred by a person acting as an insolvency practitioner as—

(a) are payable under this subsection by virtue of section 432, but

(b) are not already paid under section 204(2)(a).

(4) If the Director received the sums under section 204 he must next apply them—

(a) first, in payment of the remuneration and expenses of a receiver appointed under section 196, to the extent that they have not been met by virtue of the exercise by that receiver of a power conferred under section 197(2)(d);

(b) second, in payment of the remuneration and expenses of the receiver appointed under section 200.

(5) If a direction was made under section 163(6) for an amount of compensation to be paid out of sums recovered under the confiscation order, the Director must next apply the sums in payment of that amount.

(6) Subsection (4) does not apply if the receiver is a member of the staff of the Agency or a person providing services under arrangements made by the Director.

DEFINITIONS

"confiscation order": s. 236(5)

GENERAL NOTE

This section, which corresponds to s. 203, provides for the disposal of sums received by the Director of the Assets Recovery Agency, whether from a receiver appointed under s. 202 or otherwise,. The full amount received by the Director reduces the amount payable under the confiscation order, and therefore the term which the defendant is liable to serve in default, if any part of the confiscation order is left unsatisfied.

The order of priority of the application of the money is the same as in the case of the receipt of money by a Justices' Chief Clerk under s. 203, except that monies received by the Director may not be applied to cover the remuneration and expenses of a receiver who is a member of staff of the Assets Recovery Agency, or who is providing services under arrangements made by the Director under s. 1(6)(b).

Restrictions

206   Restraint orders

(1) Subsections (2) and (3) apply if a court makes a restraint order.

(2) If the order applies to a tenancy of any premises, no landlord or other person to whom rent is payable may exercise a right within subsection (3) except with the leave of the High Court and subject to any terms the High Court may impose.

(3) A right is within this subsection if it is a right of forfeiture by peaceable re-entry in relation to the premises in respect of any failure by the tenant to comply with any term or condition of the tenancy.

(4) If a court in which proceedings are pending in respect of any property is satisfied that a restraint order has been applied for or made in respect of the property, the court may either stay the proceedings or allow them to continue on any terms it thinks fit.

(5) Before exercising any power conferred by subsection (4), the court must give an opportunity to be heard to—

(a) the applicant for the restraint order, and

(b) any receiver appointed in respect of the property under section 196, 198 or 200.

DEFINITIONS
"property": s.232
"realisable property": s. 231
"restraint order": s. 236(5), s. 206

GENERAL NOTE

This section places restrictions on the rights of third parties in respect of property which is the subject of a restraint order. A third party may not levy distress against any realisable property subject to a restraint order except with leave of the High Court. In a case where a restraint order relates to the tenancy of any premises, no one to whom rent is payable may exercise the right of peaceable re-entry in respect of the premises in respect of failure to comply with the term of the tenancy by the tenant, except with leave of the High Court. Where proceedings in respect of property subject to a restraint order are pending, the court before which the proceedings are pending made in its discretion stay the proceedings or allow them to continue. Before exercising this power, the court must give the applicant for the restraint order or any receiver appointed in respect of the property an opportunity to be heard.

The powers given by this section must be exercised with regard to the matters listed in s. 217.

207   Enforcement receivers

(1) Subsections (2) and (3) apply if a court makes an order under section 198 appointing a receiver in respect of any realisable property.

(2) If the receiver is appointed in respect of a tenancy of any premises, no landlord or other person to whom rent is payable may exercise a right within subsection (3) except with the leave of the Crown Court and subject to any terms the Crown Court may impose.

(3) A right is within this subsection if it is a right of forfeiture by peaceable re-entry in relation to the premises in respect of any failure by the tenant to comply with any term or condition of the tenancy.

(4) If a court in which proceedings are pending in respect of any property is satisfied that an order under section 198 appointing a receiver in respect of the property has been applied for or made, the court may either stay the proceedings or allow them to continue on any terms it thinks fit.

(5) Before exercising any power conferred by subsection (4), the court must give an opportunity to be heard to—

(a) the prosecutor, and

(b) the receiver (if the order under section 198 has been made).

DEFINITIONS
"property": s.232
"realisable property": s. 231

GENERAL NOTE

This section makes provision restricting the rights of third parties in respect of realisable property, where the receiver has been appointed to enforce a confiscation order under s. 198 (Director of the Assets Recovery Agency not appointed as enforcement authority). The restrictions are substantially similar to those which apply under s. 206 where a restraint order is in force. It seems that they apply to property in respect of which the Crown Court has empowered the receiver to act under 199.

The powers given by this section must be exercised with regard to the matters listed in s. 217.

208   Director's receivers

(1) Subsections (2) and (3) apply if—
    (a) the Crown Court has made an order under section 200 for the appointment of a receiver in respect of any realisable property, and
    (b) the order has taken effect.

(2) If the order is for the appointment of a receiver in respect of a tenancy of any premises, no landlord or other person to whom rent is payable may exercise a right within subsection (3) except with the leave of the Crown Court and subject to any terms the Crown Court may impose.

(3) A right is within this subsection if it is a right of forfeiture by peaceable re-entry in relation to the premises in respect of any failure by the tenant to comply with any term or condition of the tenancy.

(4) If a court (whether the Crown Court or any other court) in which proceedings are pending in respect of any property is satisfied that an order under section 200 for the appointment of a receiver in respect of the property has taken effect, the court may either stay the proceedings or allow them to continue on any terms it thinks fit.

(5) Before exercising any power conferred by subsection (4), the court must give an opportunity to be heard to—
    (a) the Director, and
    (b) the receiver.

DEFINITIONS
"property": s.232

GENERAL NOTE

This section makes provision in terms similar to s. 207 for the case of a receiver appointed under s. 200 on the application of the Director of the Assets Recovery Agency in respect of a confiscation order for which the Director has been appointed as the enforcement authority. It is substantially the same as s. 207, except in respect of the persons to whom an opportunity to be heard must be given before the court exercises the power conferred by subs. (5).

The powers given by this section must be exercised with regard to the matters listed in s. 217.

Receivers: further provisions

209   Protection

If a receiver appointed under section 196, 198 or 200—
    (a) takes action in relation to property which is not realisable property,
    (b) would be entitled to take the action if it were realisable property, and

    (c) believes on reasonable grounds that he is entitled to take the action,

he is not liable to any person in respect of any loss or damage resulting from the action, except so far as the loss or damage is caused by his negligence.

DEFINITIONS
"property": s.232
"realisable property": s. 231

GENERAL NOTE
This section protects a receiver appointed under s. 196 (in respect of a restraint order), s. 198 (in respect of a confiscation order where the Director is not appointed as the enforcement authority), or s. 200 (in respect of a confiscation order where the Director is appointed as the enforcement authority). The receiver is protected from liability in respect of loss or damage resulting from any action taken by him in respect of property which is not realisable property, if he would be entitled to take the action if the property were realisable property, and the receiver did believe on reasonable grounds that he was entitled take the action which he took. The exception does not apply if the loss or damage is caused by the receiver's negligence.

    Section 220 of the Act makes provision for the payment of compensation where there is "serious default" by members of services or agencies other than the Assets Recovery Agency.

210   Further applications

(1) This section applies to a receiver appointed under section 196, 198 or 200.

(2) The receiver may apply—
    (a) to the High Court if he is appointed under section 196;
    (b) to the Crown Court if he is appointed under section 198 or 200,
for an order giving directions as to the exercise of his powers.

(3) The following persons may apply to the High Court if the receiver is appointed under section 196 or to the Crown Court if the receiver is appointed under section 198 or 200—
    (a) any person affected by action taken by the receiver;
    (b) any person who may be affected by action the receiver proposes to take.

(4) On an application under this section the court may make such order as it believes is appropriate.

GENERAL NOTE
This section authorises a receiver to apply to the court to give directions as to the exercise of his powers. It applies to a receiver appointed under s. 196 (in respect of a restraint order), s. 198 (in respect of a confiscation order where the Director is not appointed as the enforcement authority), or s. 200 (in respect of a confiscation order where the Director is appointed as the enforcement authority). A person affected by action taken by the receiver, or likely to be affected by action which the receiver proposes to take, may also make an application to the court.

    On such an application, the court may make such order as it believes to be appropriate.

    The powers given by this section must be exercised with regard to the matters listed in s. 217.

211   Discharge and variation

(1) The following persons may apply to the High Court to vary or discharge an order made under section 196 or 197 or to the Crown Court to vary or discharge an order made under any of sections 198 to 201—
    (a) the receiver;
    (b) the person who applied for the order or (if the order was made under section 200 or 201) the Director;
    (c) any person affected by the order.

(2) On an application under this section the court—
    (a) may discharge the order;
    (b) may vary the order.

(3) But in the case of an order under section 196 or 197—

    (a) if the condition in section 189 which was satisfied was that proceedings were started or an application was made, the court must discharge the order on the conclusion of the proceedings or of the application (as the case may be);

    (b) if the condition which was satisfied was that an investigation was started or an application was to be made, the court must discharge the order if within a reasonable time proceedings for the offence are not started or the application is not made (as the case may be).

DEFINITIONS
"started": s. 233

GENERAL NOTE

This section provides for the variation or discharge by the court of orders appointing receivers, or authorising receivers to act in connection with realisable property. It applies to receivers appointed under s. 196 (in respect of a restraint order), s. 198 (in respect of a confiscation order where the Director is not appointed as the enforcement authority), or s. 200 (in respect of a confiscation order where the Director is appointed as the enforcement authority).

Orders appointing the receiver, or authorising the receiver to act with respect to realisable property, may be varied or discharged on the application of the receiver, the person who applied for the order or the Director of the Assets Recovery Agency, or any person affected by the order.

If a receiver has been appointed in connection with a restraint order made in connection with criminal proceedings or an application under ss. 169, 170, 177, or 178, the court must discharge the orders appointing the receiver and authorising the receiver to act on the conclusion of the criminal proceedings or the application. If the restraint order has been made on the ground that a criminal investigation has been started, or an application under ss.169, 170, 177, or 178 is about to be made, the court must discharge the order appointing the receiver and authorising him to act if within a reasonable time proceedings for the offence have not been started or the application under ss.169, 170, 177, or 178 has not been made. The section does not appear to require an application on the part of one of the persons mentioned in subs. (1) before orders may be discharged in these cases.

The powers given by this section must be exercised with regard to the matters listed in s. 217.

212   Management receivers: discharge

(1) This section applies if—

    (a) a receiver stands appointed under section 196 in respect of realisable property (the management receiver), and

    (b) the court appoints a receiver under section 198 or makes an order for the appointment of a receiver under section 200.

(2) The court must order the management receiver to transfer to the other receiver all property held by the management receiver by virtue of the powers conferred on him by section 197.

(3) But in a case where the court makes an order under section 200 its order under subsection (2) above does not take effect until the order under section 200 takes effect.

(4) Subsection (2) does not apply to property which the management receiver holds by virtue of the exercise by him of his power under section 197(2)(d).

(5) If the management receiver complies with an order under subsection (2) he is discharged—

    (a) from his appointment under section 196;

    (b) from any obligation under this Act arising from his appointment.

(6) If this section applies the court may make such a consequential or incidental order as it believes is appropriate.

DEFINITIONS
"property": s.232
"realisable property": s. 231

GENERAL NOTE

This section provides for the case where a receiver has been appointed in connection with a restraint order. If the Crown Court makes a confiscation order and a receiver is appointed under s. 198 or the court authorises the appointment of a receiver by the Director of the Assets Recovery Agency, the Crown Court must order the receiver appointed in connection with the restraint order to transfer to the receiver appointed in connection with the confiscation order all property held by the first receiver by virtue of the exercise of his powers An order must be made under this section even though the receiver appointed to enforce the confiscation order is the same person as the receiver appointed in connection with the restraint order. Where the court has ordered the appointment of a receiver to be nominated by the Director of the Assets Recovery Agency, an order made by the court under this section does not take effect until the receiver has been a nominated (see s. 200(4)).

An order for the transfer of property does not apply to property held by the receiver in connection with the payment of his remuneration or expenses under s.197(2)(d). Once the original receiver has complied with the order, he is discharged from his appointment and any obligations arising from the appointment.

The powers given by this section must be exercised with regard to the matters listed in s. 217.

213   Appeal to Court of Appeal

(1) If on an application for an order under any of sections 196 to 199 or section 201 the court decides not to make one, the person who applied for the order may appeal to the Court of Appeal against the decision.

(2) If the court makes an order under any of sections 196 to 199 or section 201, the following persons may appeal to the Court of Appeal in respect of the court's decision—
   (a) the person who applied for the order;
   (b) any person affected by the order.

(3) If on an application for an order under section 210 the court decides not to make one, the person who applied for the order may appeal to the Court of Appeal against the decision.

(4) If the court makes an order under section 210, the following persons may appeal to the Court of Appeal in respect of the court's decision—
   (a) the person who applied for the order;
   (b) any person affected by the order;
   (c) the receiver.

(5) The following persons may appeal to the Court of Appeal against a decision of the court on an application under section 211—
   (a) the person who applied for the order in respect of which the application was made or (if the order was made under section 200 or 201) the Director;
   (b) any person affected by the court's decision;
   (c) the receiver.

(6) On an appeal under this section the Court of Appeal may—
   (a) confirm the decision, or
   (b) make such order as it believes if appropriate.

GENERAL NOTE

This section provides for rights of the appeal in connection with orders for the appointment of receivers in connection with restraint orders or confiscation orders, and orders or authorising receivers so appointed to act with respect to realisable property. There is no right of appeal against an order made under s. 200, which is mandatory.

Where an order has been made by the High Court or the Crown Court, the person who has applied for an order or any person affected by the order may appeal to the Court of Appeal. Where the High Court or the Crown Court has decided not to make an order, only the person who has applied for the order may appeal.

Provision is also made for appeals against decisions of the High Court or the Crown Court made in relation to directions to be given to receivers under s. 210, and decisions relating to the discharge and variation of orders under s. 211.

Any appeal requires leave of the Court of Appeal (see s. 237(1)). On an appeal under this section, the Court of Appeal may confirm the decision of the High Court or the Crown Court, or make such order "as it believes is appropriate."

The powers given by this section must be exercised with regard to the matters listed in s. 217.

214   Appeal to House of Lords

(1) An appeal lies to the House of Lords from a decision of the Court of Appeal on an appeal under section 213.

(2) An appeal under this section lies at the instance of any person who was a party to the proceedings before the Court of Appeal.

(3) On an appeal under this section the House of Lords may—
  (a) confirm the decision of the Court of Appeal, or
  (b) make such order as it believes is appropriate.

GENERAL NOTE

This section provides for an appeal to the House of Lords from a decision of the Court of Appeal on appeal under s. 213. Any person who was a party to be proceedings before the Court of Appeal may appeal to the House of Lords. On such an appeal, the House of Lords may confirm the decision of the Court of Appeal or make such order as it believes is appropriate.

Section 214 does not require that the Court of Appeal should certify that the case involves a point of law or a general public importance, or that leave of the Court of Appeal or the House of Lords should be obtained (see s. 238), but the Secretary of State is empowered by s. 238) to make an order containing provisions corresponding to those of the Criminal Appeal (Northern Ireland) Act 1980, subject to any special modifications. Unless such an order is made, there appears to be an absolute right of appeal.

The powers given by this section must be exercised with regard to the matters listed in s. 217.

Seized money

215   Seized money

(1) This section applies to money which—
  (a) is held by a person, and
  (b) is held in an account maintained by him with a bank or a building society.

(2) This section also applies to money which is held by a person and which—
  (a) has been seized by a constable under Article 21 of the Police and Criminal Evidence (Northern Ireland) Order 1989 (S.I. 1989/1341 (N.I. 12)) (general power of seizure etc), and
  (b) is held in an account maintained by a police force with a bank or a building society.

(3) This section also applies to money which is held by a person and which—
  (a) has been seized by a customs officer under Article 21 of the 1989 Order as applied by order made under Article 85(1) of that Order, and
  (b) is held in an account maintained by the Commissioners of Customs and Excise with a bank or a building society.

(4) This section applies if the following conditions are satisfied—
  (a) a restraint order has effect in relation to money to which this section applies;
  (b) a receiver has not been appointed under section 198 in relation to the money;
  (c) a confiscation order is made against the person by whom the money is held;
  (d) the Director has not been appointed as the enforcement authority for the confiscation order;
  (e) any period allowed under section 161 for payment of the amount ordered to be paid under the confiscation order has ended.

(5) In such a case on the application of the prosecutor a magistrates' court may order the bank or building society to pay the money to the appropriate chief clerk on account of the amount payable under the confiscation order.

(6) If a bank or building society fails to comply with an order under subsection (5)—
    (a) the magistrates' court may order it to pay an amount not exceeding £5,000, and
    (b) for the purposes of the Magistrates' Courts (Northern Ireland) Order 1981 (S.I. 1981/1675 (N.I. 26)) the sum is to be treated as adjudged to be paid by a conviction of the magistrates' court.

(7) In order to take account of changes in the value of money the Secretary of State may by order substitute another sum for the sum for the time being specified in subsection (6)(a).

(8) For the purposes of this section—
    (a) a bank is a deposit-taking business within the meaning of the Banking Act 1987 (c. 22);
    (b) "building society" has the same meaning as in the Building Societies Act 1986 (c. 53);
    (c) "appropriate chief clerk" has the same meaning as in section 202(7).

DEFINITIONS
"confiscation order": s. 236(5)
"restraint order": s. 236(5), s. 190

GENERAL NOTE
This section applies to money held by a person in an account maintained with a bank or building society, and to money which has been seized by a constable or by a Customs officer under the Police and Criminal Evidence (Northern Ireland) Order 1989 (S.I. 1989/1341 (N.I.12) art. 21 (which authorises the seizure of property from a person who has been arrested) and which is held in an account maintained by a police force or the Commissioners of Customs and Excise at a bank or building society. If all of the conditions specified in subs. (4) are satisfied, the magistrates court on the application of a prosecutor may order the bank or building society to pay the money to be justices' chief executive for the magistrates court on account of the amount payable under the confiscation order. The first condition for making such an order is that a restraint order has effect in relation to the money concerned, and accordingly by virtue of s. 189(2) the money must be "realisable property."

Subsection 5 refers to the "appropriate chief clerk" and subs.(8) refers to the definition found in s.202(7). The definition is concerned with the chief clerk at the court where the confiscation order was made. This is not the same as the equivalent section in Pt.2 because in Northern Ireland the confiscation orders are paid via the court where the order was made whereas in England and Wales a magistrates' court in the Petty Sessional Area is responsible for receiving payments in the same way as enforcing a fine of the Crown Court. Secondly it effectively distinguishes between administrative court clerks and legally trained court clerks.

The powers given by this section must be exercised with regard to the matters listed in s. 217.

Financial investigators

216   **Applications and appeals**

(1) This section applies to—
    (a) an application under section 190, 191, 196, 197 or 211;
    (b) an appeal under section 192, 193, 213 or 214.

(2) An accredited financial investigator must not make such an application or bring such an appeal unless he falls within subsection (3).

(3) An accredited financial investigator falls within this subsection if he is one of the following or is authorised for the purposes of this section by one of the following—
    (a) a police officer who is not below the rank of superintendent,
    (b) a customs officer who is not below such grade as is designated by the Commissioners of Customs and Excise as equivalent to that rank,

    (c) an accredited financial investigator who falls within a description specified in an order made for the purposes of this paragraph by the Secretary of State under section 453.

(4) If such an application is made or appeal brought by an accredited financial investigator any subsequent step in the application or appeal or any further application or appeal relating to the same matter may be taken, made or brought by a different accredited financial investigator who falls within subsection (3).

(5) If—

    (a) an application for a restraint order is made by an accredited financial investigator, and

    (b) a court is required under section 206(5) to give the applicant for the order an opportunity to be heard,

the court may give the opportunity to a different accredited financial investigator who falls within subsection (3).

DEFINITIONS
"restraint order": s. 236(5), s.190

GENERAL NOTE
This section provides for the role of "accredited financial investigators" in connection with applications for restraint orders, applications for the variation and discharge of restraint orders, the appointment of receivers in connection with restraint orders, the grant of powers to receivers in connection with restraint orders, applications for the discharge or variation of orders made in connection with restraint orders, or appeals in connection with such orders. The section provides that an accredited financial investigator must not make such an application or bring such an appeal unless he is one of those investigators specified in subs. (3). The section further provides that one accredited financial investigator within the scope of subs. (3) may be substituted for another at different stages of the relevant proceedings.

An accredited financial investigator is a person who has been accredited by the Director of the Assets Recovery Agency under s. 3.

Exercise of powers

217   Powers of court and receiver

(1) This section applies to—

    (a) the powers conferred on a court by sections 189 to 208 and sections 210 to 215;

    (b) the powers of a receiver appointed under section 196, 198 or 200.

(2) The powers—

    (a) must be exercised with a view to the value for the time being of realisable property being made available (by the property's realisation) for satisfying any confiscation order that has been or may be made against the defendant;

    (b) must be exercised, in a case where a confiscation order has not been made, with a view to securing that there is no diminution in the value of realisable property;

    (c) must be exercised without taking account of any obligation of the defendant or a recipient of a tainted gift if the obligation conflicts with the object of satisfying any confiscation order that has been or may be made against the defendant;

    (d) may be exercised in respect of a debt owed by the Crown.

(3) Subsection (2) has effect subject to the following rules—

    (a) the powers must be exercised with a view to allowing a person other than the defendant or a recipient of a tainted gift to retain or recover the value of any interest held by him;

    (b) in the case of realisable property held by a recipient of a tainted gift, the powers must be exercised with a view to realising no more than the value for the time being of the gift;

(c) in a case where a confiscation order has not been made against the defendant, property must not be realised if the court so orders under subsection (4).

(4) If on an application by the defendant, or by the recipient of a tainted gift, the court decides that property cannot be replaced it may order that it must not be sold.

(5) An order under subsection (4) may be revoked or varied.

DEFINITIONS
"confiscation order": s. 236(5)
"defendant": s. 236(3)
"property": s.232
"realisable property": s. 231
"tainted gift": s. 225

GENERAL NOTE
This establishes a number of general considerations which the court must take into account when exercising its various powers in relation to restraint orders and the enforcement of confiscation orders, and which receivers must take into account in the exercise of their functions.

The powers concerned must be exercised with a view to making available the value of the realisable property for satisfying any confiscation order that has been made or may be made against the defendant. In a case where a confiscation order has not been made, the various powers must be exercised with a view to securing that there is no diminution in the value of the realisable property. An obligation of the defendant or the recipient of a tainted gift must not be taken into account if the obligation conflicts with the object of satisfying a confiscation order that has been made or will be made. The duty to exercise the relevant powers with these objects in view is subject to the restrictions imposed by subs. (3). In particular, where a confiscation order has not yet been made, the defendant or the recipient of a tainted gift may apply to the Crown Court for an order that property held by a receiver must not be sold; if the court decides that the property cannot be replaced, it may order that the property must not be sold.

Committal

218 Committal by magistrates' court

(1) This section applies if—
(a) a defendant is convicted of an offence by a magistrates' court, and
(b) the prosecutor asks the court to commit the defendant to the Crown Court with a view to a confiscation order being considered under section 156.

(2) In such a case the magistrates' court—
(a) must commit the defendant to the Crown Court in respect of the offence, and
(b) may commit him to the Crown Court in respect of any other offence falling within subsection (3).

(3) An offence falls within this subsection if—
(a) the defendant has been convicted of it by the magistrates' court or any other court, and
(b) the magistrates' court has power to deal with him in respect of it.

(4) If a committal is made under this section in respect of an offence or offences—
(a) section 156 applies accordingly, and
(b) the committal operates as a committal of the defendant to be dealt with by the Crown Court in accordance with section 219.

(5) A committal under this section may be in custody or on bail.

DEFINITIONS
"confiscation order": s. 236(5)
"defendant": s. 236(3)

GENERAL NOTE
   This section imposes a mandatory obligation on the magistrates' court to commit the defendant if the prosecutor asks the magistrates' court to commit the defendant with a view to a confiscation order being considered.

219   Sentencing by Crown Court

   (1) If a defendant is committed to the Crown Court under section 218 in respect of an offence or offences, this section applies (whether or not the court proceeds under section 156).
   (2) The Crown Court—
      (a) must inquire into the circumstances of the case, and
      (b) may deal with the defendant in any way in which the magistrates' court could deal with him if it had just convicted him of the offence.

DEFINITIONS
   "defendant": s. 236(3)

GENERAL NOTE
   This section provides the powers of the Crown Court to deal with an offender who has been committed by a magistrate's court under s.218. The Crown Court *must* proceed under s.156 if an application is made by the prosecutor or the Director of the Assets Recovery Agency. If no such application is made, the Crown Court *may* proceed under the section if it considers it appropriate to do so.

Compensation

220   Serious default

   (1) If the following three conditions are satisfied the Crown Court may order the payment of such compensation as it believes is just.
   (2) The first condition is satisfied if a criminal investigation has been started with regard to an offence and proceedings are not started for the offence.
   (3) The first condition is also satisfied if proceedings for an offence are started against a person and—
      (a) they do not result in his conviction for the offence, or
      (b) he is convicted of the offence but the conviction is quashed or he is pardoned in respect of it.
   (4) If subsection (2) applies the second condition is that—
      (a) in the criminal investigation there has been a serious default by a person mentioned in subsection (9), and
      (b) the investigation would not have continued if the default had not occurred.
   (5) If subsection (3) applies the second condition is that—
      (a) in any criminal investigation with regard to the offence or in its prosecution there has been a serious default by a person who is mentioned in subsection (9), and
      (b) the proceedings would not have been started or continued if the default had not occurred.
   (6) The third condition is that an application is made under this section by a person who held realisable property and has suffered loss in consequence of anything done in relation to it by or in pursuance of an order under this Part.
   (7) The offence referred to in subsection (2) may be one of a number of offences with regard to which the investigation is started.
   (8) The offence referred to in subsection (3) may be one of a number of offences for which the proceedings are started.

(9) Compensation under this section is payable to the applicant and—

    (a) if the person in default was or was acting as a police officer within the meaning of the Police (Northern Ireland) Act 2000 (c. 32), the compensation is payable by the Chief Constable;

    (b) if the person in default was a member of the Director of Public Prosecutions for Northern Ireland or was acting on his behalf, the compensation is payable by the Director of Public Prosecutions for Northern Ireland;

    (c) if the person in default was a member of the Serious Fraud Office, the compensation is payable by the Director of that Office;

    (d) if the person in default was a customs officer, the compensation is payable by the Commissioners of Customs and Excise;

    (e) if the person in default was an officer of the Commissioners of Inland Revenue, the compensation is payable by those Commissioners.

DEFINITIONS

"property": s.232
"realisable property": s.231
"started": s.233

GENERAL NOTE

This section provides for the Crown Court to order the payment of compensation in cases where there has been "serious default" in the conduct of proceedings to which the restraint order or confiscation order is related.

Before any question of compensation can arise, three conditions, (which are expressed in the alternative) must be satisfied. The first condition is satisfied if a criminal investigation has been started in relation to an offence and proceedings are not started for the offence; alternatively, the first condition is satisfied if proceedings for an offence are started against a defendant but they do not result in his conviction, or his conviction is quashed or he is pardoned for the offence.

The second condition is that there has been a serious default by one of the persons mentioned in subs.(9) and that the criminal investigation would not have continued if the default had not occurred or the proceedings would not have been started or continued if the default had not occurred.

The third condition, which applies in any of these cases, is that the person who held realisable property (who may include the defendant) has suffered loss in consequence of anything done in relation to the realisable property as a result of an order made under the Act in connection with confiscation.

The concept of "serious default" is not elaborated in the Act. It would appear that compensation may not be ordered under this section against a person who is employed by or acting on behalf of the Assets Recovery Agency.

The Act provides no right of appeal in connection with decisions of the Crown Court made under this section.

221 Order varied or discharged

  (1) This section applies if—

    (a) the court varies a confiscation order under section 179 or discharges one under section 180, and

    (b) an application is made to the Crown Court by a person who held realisable property and has suffered loss as a result of the making of the order.

  (2) The court may order the payment of such compensation as it believes is just.

  (3) Compensation under this section is payable—

    (a) to the applicant;

    (b) by the Lord Chancellor.

DEFINITIONS

"confiscation order": s. 236(5)
"property": s.232

GENERAL NOTE
This section applies to a confiscation order made under s.178 in respect of a defendant who has absconded after proceedings against him have been started but before they have been concluded. If in such a case the defendant is convicted of an offence and the Crown Court on application under s.179 reduces the amount of the confiscation order that has been made against the defendant, the Crown Court may order the payment of compensation, at its discretion, to any person who held realisable property and who has suffered loss as a result of the making of the order. Similarly if such a defendant has been tried for the offences and has been acquitted, and the Crown Court has accordingly discharged the confiscation order under s.180(2), the Crown Court on application may order the payment of compensation to any person who held realisable property and who has suffered loss as a result of the making of the order. Such persons may include the defendant. The amount of compensation in either case is "such compensation as it believes is just". It is not necessary in this case to show that there has been any default or negligence on the part of the prosecution or other agencies concerned with the order. The Act provides no right of appeal in connection with an order made under this section.

Enforcement abroad

222 Enforcement abroad

(1) This section applies if—
    (a) any of the conditions in section 189 is satisfied,
    (b) the prosecutor or the Director believes that realisable property is situated in a country or territory outside the United Kingdom (the receiving country), and
    (c) the prosecutor or the Director (as the case may be) sends a request for assistance to the Secretary of State with a view to it being forwarded under this section.
(2) In a case where no confiscation order has been made, a request for assistance is a request to the government of the receiving country to secure that any person is prohibited from dealing with realisable property.
(3) In a case where a confiscation order has been made and has not been satisfied, discharged or quashed, a request for assistance is a request to the government of the receiving country to secure that—
    (a) any person is prohibited from dealing with realisable property;
    (b) realisable property is realised and the proceeds are applied in accordance with the law of the receiving country.
(4) No request for assistance may be made for the purposes of this section in a case where a confiscation order has been made and has been satisfied, discharged or quashed.
(5) If the Secretary of State believes it is appropriate to do so he may forward the request for assistance to the government of the receiving country.
(6) If property is realised in pursuance of a request under subsection (3) the amount ordered to be paid under the confiscation order must be taken to be reduced by an amount equal to the proceeds of realisation.
(7) A certificate purporting to be issued by or on behalf of the requested government is admissible as evidence of the facts it states if it states—
    (a) that property has been realised in pursuance of a request under subsection (3),
    (b) the date of realisation, and
    (c) the proceeds of realisation.
(8) If the proceeds of realisation made in pursuance of a request under subsection (3) are expressed in a currency other than sterling, they must be taken to be the sterling equivalent calculated in accordance with the rate of exchange prevailing at the end of the day of realisation.

DEFINITIONS
    "confiscation order": s. 236(5)
    "property": s.232
    "realisable property": s. 231

GENERAL NOTE

This section provides machinery designed to secure the enforcement in other jurisdictions of restraint orders made under s.189. The section applies if any of the conditions for making a restraint order under s.189 is satisfied (whether or not a restraint order has actually been made) and the prosecutor or the Director of the Assets Recovery Agency believes that realisable property is situated in a jurisdiction outside the United Kingdom.

In this situation, the prosecutor or Director may ask the Secretary of State to forward a request for assistance to the country concerned. If no confiscation order has yet been made, such a request is a request to the government of the overseas country to secure that any person is prohibited from dealing with a realisable property. If a confiscation order has been made and is still effective, a request is a request to secure that any person is prohibited from dealing with realisable property, and that the property is realised and the proceeds are applied in accordance with the law of the foreign jurisdiction. No request may be made where the confiscation order concerned has been satisfied, discharged or quashed.

The Secretary of State has a discretion whether or not to forward a request for assistance to the government of the country concerned. If property is realised in pursuance of a request under this section, the amount ordered to be paid under the confiscation order must be taken to be reduced by an amount equal to the proceeds of realisation, whether or not those proceeds are transmitted to the United Kingdom and applied directly to the satisfaction of the confiscation order. A certificate from the government of the overseas country is admissible as evidence of that the property has been realised, the date of realisation and the proceeds of realisation.

Interpretation

223   Criminal lifestyle

(1) A defendant has a criminal lifestyle if (and only if) the following condition is satisfied.

(2) The condition is that the offence (or any of the offences) concerned satisfies any of these tests—

   (a) it is specified in Schedule 5;

   (b) it constitutes conduct forming part of a course of criminal activity;

   (c) it is an offence committed over a period of at least six months and the defendant has benefited from the conduct which constitutes the offence.

(3) Conduct forms part of a course of criminal activity if the defendant has benefited from the conduct and—

   (a) in the proceedings in which he was convicted he was convicted of three or more other offences, each of three or more of them constituting conduct from which he has benefited, or

   (b) in the period of six years ending with the day when those proceedings were started (or, if there is more than one such day, the earliest day) he was convicted on at least two separate occasions of an offence constituting conduct from which he has benefited.

(4) But an offence does not satisfy the test in subsection (2)(b) or (c) unless the defendant obtains relevant benefit of not less than £5000.

(5) Relevant benefit for the purposes of subsection (2)(b) is—

   (a) benefit from conduct which constitutes the offence;

   (b) benefit from any other conduct which forms part of the course of criminal activity and which constitutes an offence of which the defendant has been convicted;

   (c) benefit from conduct which constitutes an offence which has been or will be taken into consideration by the court in sentencing the defendant for an offence mentioned in paragraph (a) or (b).

(6) Relevant benefit for the purposes of subsection (2)(c) is—

   (a) benefit from conduct which constitutes the offence;

   (b) benefit from conduct which constitutes an offence which has been or will be taken into consideration by the court in sentencing the defendant for the offence mentioned in paragraph (a).

(7) The Secretary of State may by order amend Schedule 5.

(8) The Secretary of State may by order vary the amount for the time being specified in subsection (4).

DEFINITIONS

"defendant": s.236(3)

"started": s. 233

GENERAL NOTE

This section provides a definition of the concept of "criminal lifestyle" for the purposes of s.156(4). If the defendant is found to have a "criminal life style" the benefit which is to form the basis of the confiscation order is the benefit arising from his "general criminal conduct" rather than his "particular criminal conduct", and the Crown Court in determining whether he has benefited and in deciding the amount of his benefit must make the assumptions set out in s.160.

Subsection (2) provides three conditions, only one of which must be satisfied before the defendant can be considered to have a "criminal lifestyle."

The first condition is that he is convicted of one of the offences listed in Sched. 5 of the Act. This schedule lists a considerable number of offences, including among others the most common offences under the Misuse of Drugs Act 1971 involving the production or supply of controlled drugs, corresponding offences under the Customs and Excise Management Act 1979 in relation to the importation or exportation of controlled drugs, money laundering offences under this Act (but not under the provisions of the earlier legislation), directing terrorism under the Terrorism Act 2000, facilitating illegal entry contrary to the Immigration Act 1971, arms trafficking under the Customs and Excise Management Act 1979, counterfeiting, certain offences involving infringement of copyrights, a number of offences relating to the control of prostitutes, and blackmail.

The second condition is that the offence or any of the offences of which the defendant is convicted "constitutes conduct forming part of a course of criminal activity". This term is elaborated in subs.(3) and there are two alternative limbs to the definition of what conduct forms part of a course of criminal activity.

The first limb is that the defendant has been convicted in the same proceedings of three or more offences in addition to the principal offence and each of the additional offences amounted to conduct from which he has benefited. To qualify under this definition, the defendant must have been convicted in the same proceedings of at least four offences from which he can be shown to have benefited and the "relevant benefit" must be at least £5,000. In determining the "relevant benefit" arising out of a "course of criminal activity" where the defendant has been convicted of four or more offences on the same occasion, the court must take into account benefit arising from the conduct which constitutes the primary offence, benefit from any other offence which forms part of the course of criminal activity and which constitutes an offence of which the defendant has been convicted, and benefit from conduct which constitutes an offence which has been taken or will be taken into consideration by the court in sentencing the defendant for the principal offence or the additional offences.

Thus, an offence which is taken into consideration does not count for the purpose of determining whether the defendant's conduct "forms part of a course of criminal activity" under subs.(3)(a), but the benefit arising from such offences can be taken into account in assessing the relevant benefit.

In practice, this means that an indictment charging a defendant with offences in relation to which confiscation may be sought on the basis of a "course of criminal activity" (such as a persistent house burglar) should include at least four separate counts in the indictment to satisfy the requirements of subs.(3)(a). Provided there are at least four counts on the indictment and it can be shown that the defendant has benefited from each of those offences, benefit from any other offences taken into consideration can be considered for the purpose of determining the "relevant benefit".

The alternative limb of the definition of a "course of criminal activity" is that the defendant has been convicted on at least two separate occasions during the period of six years ending with a day when the proceedings for the present offence were started and that he has benefited from the offences in respect of which he was convicted on both of those occasions. The "relevant benefit" must amount to at least £5,000. In determining the "relevant benefit" arising out of a "course of criminal activity" where the defendant has been convicted on two or more previous occasions, the court must take into account benefit arising from the conduct which constitutes the latest offence, benefit from any other offence which forms part of the course of criminal activity and which constitutes an offence on which the defendant has been convicted (that is, the offences of which he was convicted on the two previous occasions and any other offences of which he was convicted during the relevant period) and benefit from conduct which constitutes an offence which has been taken or will be taken into consideration by the court in sentencing the defendant for the latest offence or any of the earlier offences.

The third condition is that the offence has been committed over a period of at least six months, that the defendant has benefited from the conduct which constitutes the offence, and that the amount of this benefit is not less than £5,000. This condition would be satisfied in the case of the defendant convicted of conspiring to defraud over a period of at least six months, provided the benefit reached the appropriate level. Where this condition is satisfied, the "relevant benefit" is the benefit arising from the conduct which constitutes the continuing offence, and the benefit from any other conduct which constitutes an offence which has been or will be taken into consideration in sentencing defendant for the principal offence.

224   Conduct and benefit

(1) Criminal conduct is conduct which—
   (a) constitutes an offence in Northern Ireland, or
   (b) would constitute such an offence if it occurred in Northern Ireland.

(2) General criminal conduct of the defendant is all his criminal conduct, and it is immaterial—
   (a) whether conduct occurred before or after the passing of this Act;
   (b) whether property constituting a benefit from conduct was obtained before or after the passing of this Act.

(3) Particular criminal conduct of the defendant is all his criminal conduct which falls within the following paragraphs—
   (a) conduct which constitutes the offence or offences concerned;
   (b) conduct which constitutes offences of which he was convicted in the same proceedings as those in which he was convicted of the offence or offences concerned;
   (c) conduct which constitutes offences which the court will be taking into consideration in deciding his sentence for the offence or offences concerned.

(4) A person benefits from conduct if he obtains property as a result of or in connection with the conduct.

(5) If a person obtains a pecuniary advantage as a result of or in connection with conduct, he is to be taken to obtain as a result of or in connection with the conduct a sum of money equal to the value of the pecuniary advantage.

(6) References to property or a pecuniary advantage obtained in connection with conduct include references to property or a pecuniary advantage obtained both in that connection and some other.

(7) If a person benefits from conduct his benefit is the value of the property obtained.

DEFINITIONS
"defendant": s. 236(3)
"offence or offences concerned": s. 236(1) and 156(9)
"property": s. 232

GENERAL NOTE
This section provides definitions of the expressions "criminal conduct", "general criminal conduct", "particular criminal conduct" and "benefits". "Criminal conduct" is any conduct which constitutes an offence in Northern Ireland, or would constitute such an offence if it occurred in Northern Ireland. "General criminal conduct" is all of the defendant's criminal conduct whether it occurred before or after the passing of the Act, or whether the property constituting the benefit from the conduct concerned was obtained before after the passing of the Act. One important aspect of this definition is that a court assessing the benefit derived in a "criminal lifestyle" case from the defendant's "general criminal conduct" must take into account all of the criminal conduct of the defendant wherever it took place, whether in Northern Ireland or elsewhere. In a "criminal lifestyle" case, the court is entitled to include in the assessment of benefit the benefit arising from offences committed abroad.

The definition of " particular criminal conduct" includes the conduct which constitutes the offence or offences of which the defendant has been convicted, the conduct which constitutes the offences of which he was convicted in the same proceedings, and conduct which constitutes offences which will be taken into consideration in deciding the sentence for those offences. This definition clearly excludes conduct constituting offences which are represented by sample specimen counts, but which are not specifically taken into consideration in sentencing the defendant.

The definition of "benefits" effectively restates the definition of "benefits" in the Criminal Justice Act 1988, s.71(4) and (5), with minor differences in the language. It is unfortunate that the expression "pecuniary advantage" was retained in this definition, in view of the difficulties to which the expression has given rise in cases arising under the earlier legislation (see in particular *Dismay and Allan* (2000) 1 Cr.App.R.(S.) 497 and *Smith* (2002) 2 Cr.App.R.(S.) 37 (at 144)).

Subsection (6) restates the enigmatic provision of art.3(4) of the 1996 Order. The meaning of the expression "both in that connection and some other" in the context of the Criminal Justice Act 1988 (s.102(5)) was considered by the Court of Appeal in *Attorney General's Reference No. 25 of 2001 (Frank Adam Moran)* (2002) 1 Cr.App.R.(S.) 95 (at 413), where the Court had to "confess to having some difficulty with that subsection".

225   Tainted gifts

(1) Subsections (2) and (3) apply if—
  (a) no court has made a decision as to whether the defendant has a criminal lifestyle, or
  (b) a court has decided that the defendant has a criminal lifestyle.
(2) A gift is tainted if it was made by the defendant at any time after the relevant day.
(3) A gift is also tainted if it was made by the defendant at any time and was of property—
  (a) which was obtained by the defendant as a result of or in connection with his general criminal conduct, or
  (b) which (in whole or part and whether directly or indirectly) represented in the defendant's hands property obtained by him as a result of or in connection with his general criminal conduct.
(4) Subsection (5) applies if a court has decided that the defendant does not have a criminal lifestyle.
(5) A gift is tainted if it was made by the defendant at any time after—
  (a) the date on which the offence concerned was committed, or
  (b) if his particular criminal conduct consists of two or more offences and they were committed on different dates, the date of the earliest.
(6) For the purposes of subsection (5) an offence which is a continuing offence is committed on the first occasion when it is committed.
(7) For the purposes of subsection (5) the defendant's particular criminal conduct includes any conduct which constitutes offences which the court has taken into consideration in deciding his sentence for the offence or offences concerned.
(8) A gift may be a tainted gift whether it was made before or after the passing of this Act.
(9) The relevant day is the first day of the period of six years ending with—
  (a) the day when proceedings for the offence concerned were started against the defendant, or
  (b) if there are two or more offences and proceedings for them were started on different days, the earliest of those days.

DEFINITIONS
  "defendant": s.236(3)
  "offence or offences concerned": s.236(1) and 156(9)
  "property": s.232
  "started": s.222

GENERAL NOTE
  This section provides a definition of the expression "tainted gift" which is relevant to determining the "available amount" in accordance with s.156, for the purpose of determining the

"recoverable amount" under s.157. What amounts to a "tainted gift" depends on whether and the court is proceeding on the basis that the defendant has a "criminal lifestyle" or not.

If the court has decided that the defendant has a "criminal lifestyle," or if no decision on the matter has yet to be made, a gift is "tainted" if it was made by the defendant at any time within the period of six years ending on the day when the proceedings for the offence concerned were started. If the gift was made outside that period, it is "tainted" if it was a gift of property which was obtained by the defendant "as a result of or in connection with" his "general criminal conduct" or directly or indirectly represented in his hands property of obtained by him as a result of or in connection with his general criminal conduct.

If a court is not proceeding under the "criminal lifestyle" provisions, a gift is "tainted" if it was made by the defendant at any time after the date on which the offence (or the earliest of the offences) which constitutes his "particular criminal conduct" was committed. If the offence was a continuing offence, the offence is treated as having been committed on the first occasion when it was committed. Offences which are taken into consideration for the purpose of sentence are relevant for this purpose (subs.(7)). If any offences taken into consideration were committed on dates earlier than the date of the offence of which the defendant has been convicted, the relevant date for determining whether a gift is a "tainted" is the date on which the first of the offences taken into consideration was committed.

226   Gifts and their recipients

(1) If the defendant transfers property to another person for a consideration whose value is significantly less than the value of the property at the time of the transfer, he is to be treated as making a gift.

(2) If subsection (1) applies the property given is to be treated as such share in the property transferred as is represented by the fraction—
   (a) whose numerator is the difference between the two values mentioned in subsection (1), and
   (b) whose denominator is the value of the property at the time of the transfer.

(3) References to a recipient of a tainted gift are to a person to whom the defendant has made the gift.

DEFINITIONS
   "defendant": s.236(3)
   "property": s.232

GENERAL NOTE
The effect of this provision is to extend the definition of "gift" beyond a simple gift for which no consideration is provided to include any transfer of property for a consideration of significantly less value than the value of the property transferred at the time of the transfer. Where there is a transfer of property for a consideration of less value than the value of the property, the "gift" is that share of the property determined in accordance with the formula in subs.(2). Some will prefer the language of the earlier legislation (art.7(3)(b) of the 1996 Order), which provided in such a case that the defendant should be treated as if he had "made a gift of such a share in the property as bears to the whole property the same proportion as the difference between the values referred to in sub-paragraph (a) above bears to the value of the consideration provided by the defendant".

To apply the formula in subs. (2), the court should subtract value of the consideration from the value of the property at the time of the transfer, and divide the figure produced by the subtraction by value of the property at the time of the transfer, expressing the division as a fraction. The fraction should then be multiplied by the value of the property at the time of the transfer to produce the value of the gift at the time of the transfer. If the defendant has transferred a house then worth £100,000 for a consideration of £25,000, subtracting the consideration from the value produces a figure of £75,000; expressing the division of this figure by the value of the house produces the fraction 3/4, which represents the portion of the house which is treated as a gift. Multiplying the value of the house by this fraction results in the conclusion that the value of the gift at the time it was made was £75,000. This figure must then be adjusted in accordance with s.81 to determine the value to be attributed to the gift for the purposes of determining the "available amount". Alternatively, under s.229(2) the Court may take 3/4 of the value of the house at the time the confiscation order is made for that purpose.

227   Value: the basic rule

(1) This section applies for the purpose of deciding the value at any time of property then held by a person.

(2) Its value is the market value of the property at that time.

(3) But if at that time another person holds an interest in the property its value, in relation to the person mentioned in subsection (1), is the market value of his interest at that time, ignoring any charging order under a provision listed in subsection (4).

(4) The provisions are—

    (a) section 9 of the Drug Trafficking Offences Act 1986 (c. 32);

    (b) section 78 of the Criminal Justice Act 1988 (c. 33);

    (c) Article 14 of the Criminal Justice (Confiscation) (Northern Ireland) Order 1990 (S.I. 1990/2588 (N.I. 17));

    (d) section 27 of the Drug Trafficking Act 1994 (c. 37);

    (e) Article 32 of the Proceeds of Crime (Northern Ireland) Order 1996 (S.I. 1996/1299 (N.I. 9)).

(5) This section has effect subject to sections 228 and 229.

DEFINITIONS
  "property": s. 232

GENERAL NOTE
  This section provides a basic rule for the determination of the value of property held by any person. The value of the property is its market value at the time in question, less the market value of any interest held by another person in the property at that time. The effect of any charging order made under the provisions of the earlier confiscation legislation listed in subs.(4) is disregarded.

228   Value of property obtained from conduct

(1) This section applies for the purpose of deciding the value of property obtained by a person as a result of or in connection with his criminal conduct; and the material time is the time the court makes its decision.

(2) The value of the property at the material time is the greater of the following—

    (a) the value of the property (at the time the person obtained it) adjusted to take account of later changes in the value of money;

    (b) the value (at the material time) of the property found under subsection (3).

(3) The property found under this subsection is as follows—

    (a) if the person holds the property obtained, the property found under this subsection is that property;

    (b) if he holds no part of the property obtained, the property found under this subsection is any property which directly or indirectly represents it in his hands;

    (c) if he holds part of the property obtained, the property found under this subsection is that part and any property which directly or indirectly represents the other part in his hands.

(4) The references in subsection (2)(a) and (b) to the value are to the value found in accordance with section 227.

DEFINITIONS
  "property": s. 232

GENERAL NOTE
  This section applies where the Crown Court is required to determine the value of property obtained by a person as a result of or in connection with his criminal conduct. It will be relevant

principally to the case where a court is required to make an assumption under s.160 of the Act in a "criminal lifestyle" case. It will also be relevant to the determination of the defendant's benefit from "particular criminal conduct" in a case where the criminal lifestyle provisions do not apply, but the offence concerned was committed at a significantly earlier date.

In such a case, there are two methods of calculating the figure, and the Crown Court must adopt the method which will produce the larger amount. One method is to determine the value of the property at the time the person obtained it, and adjust that figure to take account of later changes in the value of money. The alternative procedure applies only where the person concerned still holds the property obtained or holds other property which directly or indirectly represents the original property in his hands. In this case, the value of the property is the value at the material time, normally when the confiscation order is made.

If the defendant has received cash as a result of or in connection with his criminal conduct, the normal procedure will be to take the value of the received cash as the basis of the determination of the value and make any adjustment that is appropriate to take account of later changes in the value of money. If the defendant has received shares as a result of or in connection with his criminal conduct, it is open to the court to value the shares at the time they were of obtained, adjust that figure to take account of later changes in the value of money and adopt that as the value of the property obtained. In such a case, the value of the property may be taken to have increased, notwithstanding that the defendant still holds the shares so obtained and that they have lost value in the intervening period.

If a defendant has obtained real property, such as a house, as a result of or in connection with criminal conduct, and still holds that property, the value of the property is the value of the house at the time the confiscation order is made, not withstanding that this figure represents a large increase over the value of the house at the time it was obtained, and that the figure represents a greater increase than would be produced by adjusting the original value of the property to take account of changes in the value of money owed during the intervening period. The same would apply where the original house has been sold and the proceeds applied to the purchase of another house.

There is some uncertainty where the defendant obtains cash as a result of or in connection with his criminal conduct, and uses the cash to purchase property in one form or another, and the value of the property so purchased increases to a figure which is greater than the figure which would be calculated by adjusting the value of the cash obtained to allow for subsequent changes in the value of money. It is submitted that in this case the proper procedure is for the court to take the value of the money obtained and adjust it to take account of later changes in the value of money, rather than take the value of the property according to the valuation current at the time of the confiscation order. The property itself has not been obtained "as a result of or in connection with" the defendant's criminal conduct. The contrary argument is that in such a case, if it can be shown that the property concerned "directly or indirectly represents" the money a originally obtained as a result of criminal conduct, the current value of the property may be taken by virtue of subs.(3)(d). For this reasoning to apply, it would be necessary to show that the money originally obtained was used to purchase the property, and that the property was not purchased from the defendant's general pool of funds, to which the money obtained by criminal conduct was added.

229   Value of tainted gifts

(1) The value at any time (the material time) of a tainted gift is the greater of the following—

    (a) the value (at the time of the gift) of the property given, adjusted to take account of later changes in the value of money;

    (b) the value (at the material time) of the property found under subsection (2).

(2) The property found under this subsection is as follows—

    (a) if the recipient holds the property given, the property found under this subsection is that property;

    (b) if the recipient holds no part of the property given, the property found under this subsection is any property which directly or indirectly represents it in his hands;

    (c) if the recipient holds part of the property given, the property found under this subsection is that part and any property which directly or indirectly represents the other part in his hands.

(3) The references in subsection (1)(a) and (b) to the value are to the value found in accordance with section 227.

DEFINITIONS
"property": s. 232

GENERAL NOTE

The section makes provision for determining the value of a "tainted gift" as defined in s.225. The section substantially repeats the provisions of s.228 with minor modifications. The value of the tainted gift may be determined by taking the value of the property at the time it was given and adjusting that figure to take account of later changes in the value of money. Alternatively, if the recipient of the tainted gift still holds the property, the court may take the current value of the property as the value of the tainted gift. If the recipient holds property which directly or indirectly represents the original tainted gift in his hands, the court make take the current value of that property as the value of the tainted gift. The court is obliged to adopt whichever formula produces the greater figure.

230   Free property

Property is free unless an order is in force in respect of it under any of these provisions—
  (a) section 27 of the Misuse of Drugs Act 1971 (c. 38) (forfeiture orders);
  (b) Article 11 of the Criminal Justice (Northern Ireland) Order 1994 (S.I. 1994/2795 (N.I. 15)) (deprivation orders);
  (c) Part 2 of the Proceeds of Crime (Scotland) Act 1995 (c. 43) (forfeiture of property used in crime);
  (d) section 143 of the Powers of Criminal Courts (Sentencing) Act 2000 (c. 6) (deprivation orders);
  (e) section 23 or 111 of the Terrorism Act 2000 (c. 11) (forfeiture orders);
  (f) section 246, 266, 295(2) or 298(2) of this Act.

DEFINITIONS
"property": s. 232

GENERAL NOTE

This section provides a definition of "free property," which is relevant primarily for the purpose of determining the "available amount" under s.159. All property is free unless it is subject to one of the orders mentioned the section. The value of free property is determined in accordance with s.227, and if any other person holds an interest in the property, the value of that interest must be deducted from the value of the property concerned to the defendant.

231   Realisable property

Realisable property is—
  (a) any free property held by the defendant;
  (b) any free property held by the recipient of a tainted gift.

DEFINITIONS
"defendant": s.236(3)
"free property": s.230
"property": s. 232

GENERAL NOTE

This section provides a definition of "realisable property". "Realisable property" is any "free property" (as defined in s.230) held by the defendant and any "free property" held by the recipient of a "tainted gift". Free property held by either the defendant or the recipient of a tainted gift may be realisable whether or not it has any connection with the offence or the tainted gift. If a person has obtained cash as a result of or in connection with a crime, spent that cash and then has received further cash lawfully, for example as compensation for a personal injury, the cash so received is "realisable property". Similarly, if the person has received cash as a tainted gift and spent it, but subsequently receives property lawfully by way of a legacy, the property received by way of the legacy is "realisable property" in the hands of that person.

232   Property: general provisions

(1) Property is all property wherever situated and includes—

(a) money;
(b) all forms of real or personal property;
(c) things in action and other intangible or incorporeal property.

(2) The following rules apply in relation to property—
    (a) property is held by a person if he holds an interest in it;
    (b) property is obtained by a person if he obtains an interest in it;
    (c) property is transferred by one person to another if the first one transfers or grants an interest in it to the second;
    (d) references to property held by a person include references to property vested in his trustee in bankruptcy, permanent or interim trustee (within the meaning of the Bankruptcy (Scotland) Act 1985 (c. 66)) or liquidator;
    (e) references to an interest held by a person beneficially in property include references to an interest which would be held by him beneficially if the property were not so vested;
    (f) references to an interest, in relation to land in Northern Ireland or England and Wales, are to any legal estate or equitable interest or power;
    (g) references to an interest, in relation to land in Scotland, are to any estate, interest, servitude or other heritable right in or over land, including a heritable security;
    (h) references to an interest, in relation to property other than land, include references to a right (including a right to possession).

GENERAL NOTE

This section provides a general definition of property for the purposes of the Act.

233 Proceedings

(1) Proceedings for an offence are started—
    (a) when a justice of the peace issues a summons or warrant under Article 20 of the Magistrates' Courts (Northern Ireland) Order 1981 (S.I. 1981/1675 (N.I. 26)) in respect of the offence;
    (b) when a person is charged with the offence after being taken into custody without a warrant;
    (c) when an indictment is preferred under section 2(2)(c), (e) or (f) of the Grand Jury (Abolition) Act (Northern Ireland) 1969 (c. 15 (N.I.)).

(2) If more than one time is found under subsection (1) in relation to proceedings they are started at the earliest of them.

(3) If the defendant is acquitted on all counts in proceedings for an offence, the proceedings are concluded when he is acquitted.

(4) If the defendant is convicted in proceedings for an offence and the conviction is quashed or the defendant is pardoned before a confiscation order is made, the proceedings are concluded when the conviction is quashed or the defendant is pardoned.

(5) If a confiscation order is made against the defendant in proceedings for an offence (whether the order is made by the Crown Court or the Court of Appeal) the proceedings are concluded—
    (a) when the order is satisfied or discharged, or
    (b) when the order is quashed and there is no further possibility of an appeal against the decision to quash the order.

(6) If the defendant is convicted in proceedings for an offence but the Crown Court decides not to make a confiscation order against him, the following rules apply—
    (a) if an application for leave to appeal under section 181(2) is refused, the proceedings are concluded when the decision to refuse is made;

(b) if the time for applying for leave to appeal under section 181(2) expires without an application being made, the proceedings are concluded when the time expires;

(c) if on an appeal under section 181(2) the Court of Appeal confirms the Crown Court's decision and an application for leave to appeal under section 183 is refused, the proceedings are concluded when the decision to refuse is made;

(d) if on appeal under section 181(2) the Court of Appeal confirms the Crown Court's decision, and the time for applying for leave to appeal under section 183 expires without an application being made, the proceedings are concluded when the time expires;

(e) if on appeal under section 181(2) the Court of Appeal confirms the Crown Court's decision, and on appeal under section 183 the House of Lords confirms the Court of Appeal's decision, the proceedings are concluded when the House of Lords confirms the decision;

(f) if on appeal under section 181(2) the Court of Appeal directs the Crown Court to reconsider the case, and on reconsideration the Crown Court decides not to make a confiscation order against the defendant, the proceedings are concluded when the Crown Court makes that decision;

(g) if on appeal under section 183 the House of Lords directs the Crown Court to reconsider the case, and on reconsideration the Crown Court decides not to make a confiscation order against the defendant, the proceedings are concluded when the Crown Court makes that decision.

(7) In applying subsection (6) any power to extend the time for making an application for leave to appeal must be ignored.

(8) In applying subsection (6) the fact that a court may decide on a later occasion to make a confiscation order against the defendant must be ignored.

DEFINITIONS
"confiscation order": s.236(5)
"defendant": s.236(3)

GENERAL NOTE
This section provides definitions of the time at which proceedings for an offence are started and the time at which proceedings are concluded.

Determining the time at which proceedings are started is relevant particularly to the application of the required assumptions under s.160, some of which relate to transactions taking place within the period of six years ending on the day when proceedings for the offence concerned were started.

Determining the date on which proceedings are concluded is important in relation to various powers to discharge restraint orders, in particular under s.211, and the power to make a confiscation order against an absconder under s.178.

234 Applications

(1) An application under section 169, 170, 177 or 178 is concluded—

(a) in a case where the court decides not to make a confiscation order against the defendant, when it makes the decision;

(b) in a case where a confiscation order is made against him as a result of the application, when the order is satisfied or discharged, or when the order is quashed and there is no further possibility of an appeal against the decision to quash the order;

(c) in a case where the application is withdrawn, when the person who made the application notifies the withdrawal to the court to which the application was made.

(2) An application under section 171 or 172 is concluded—

(a) in a case where the court decides not to vary the confiscation order concerned, when it makes the decision;

(b) in a case where the court varies the confiscation order as a result of the application, when the order is satisfied or discharged, or when the order is quashed and there is no further possibility of an appeal against the decision to quash the order;

(c) in a case where the application is withdrawn, when the person who made the application notifies the withdrawal to the court to which the application was made.

DEFINITIONS
"confiscation order": s.236(5)
"defendant": s.236(3)

GENERAL NOTE
This section provides definitions of the time at which an application under ss. 169 (reconsideration of the decision to consider confiscation), 170 (reconsideration of the amount of benefit), 177 (defendant absconding after conviction) or 178 (defendant absconding after the proceedings have started and before the proceedings have been concluded) may be made. The definition is significant for the purposes of the making restraint orders in connection with such applications (ss.189(4) and 189(5)) and the discharge and variation of such restraint orders under s. 211(3)(a).

235 Confiscation orders

(1) A confiscation order is satisfied when no amount is due under it.

(2) A confiscation order is subject to appeal until there is no further possibility of an appeal on which the order could be varied or quashed; and for this purpose any power to grant leave to appeal out of time must be ignored.

DEFINITIONS
"confiscation order": s. 236(5)

GENERAL NOTE
This section provides definitions of the point at which a confiscation order is "satisfied" and when a confiscation order is "subject to appeal".
The definition of "satisfied" is important for the purposes of ss.186, 198, 200, 222 and 233.
The definition of "subject to appeal" is important for the purposes of ss.186, 198 and 200.

236 Other interpretative provisions

(1) A reference to the offence (or offences) concerned must be construed in accordance with section 156(9).

(2) A criminal investigation is an investigation which police officers or other persons have a duty to conduct with a view to it being ascertained whether a person should be charged with an offence.

(3) A defendant is a person against whom proceedings for an offence have been started (whether or not he has been convicted).

(4) A reference to sentencing the defendant for an offence includes a reference to dealing with him otherwise in respect of the offence.

(5) The following paragraphs apply to references to orders—
    (a) a confiscation order is an order under section 156;
    (b) a restraint order is an order under section 190.

(6) Sections 223 to 235 and this section apply for the purposes of this Part.

DEFINITIONS
"started": s. 233

General

237 Procedure on appeal to the Court of Appeal

(1) An appeal to the Court of Appeal under this Part lies only with the leave of that Court.

(2) In relation to appeals to the Court of Appeal under this Part, the Secretary of State may make an order containing provision corresponding to any provision in the Criminal Appeal (Northern Ireland) Act 1980 (c. 47) (subject to any specified modifications).

GENERAL NOTE

This section provides for appeals to the Court of Appeal under Pt. IV of the Act. The appeals to which the section applies are those under ss. 181 (appeal by prosecutor or Director against refusal of Crown Court to make confiscation order, or against amount of confiscation order), 192 (refusal of the High Court to make restraint order) and 213 (appeal against decision of Crown Court relating to restraint orders). The effect of this section is that any appeal under these sections lies only with leave of the Court of Appeal.

The Secretary of State is empowered to make orders containing provisions corresponding to those in the Criminal Appeal (Northern Ireland) Act 1980, subject to specified modifications.

238　Procedure on appeal to the House of Lords

In relation to appeals to the House of Lords under this Part, the Secretary of State may make an order containing provision corresponding to any provision in the Criminal Appeal (Northern Ireland) Act 1980 (subject to any specified modifications).

GENERAL NOTE

This section applies to appeals from the Court of Appeal to the House of Lords under ss. 183 (appeal by prosecutor or Director against a refusal of the Crown Court to make a confiscation order, or against the amount of a confiscation order), or 193 (refusal of the High Court to make restraint order, or an appeal by a defendant against the decision of the Court of Appeal on such an appeal) and 214 (appeal against order relating to restraint orders).

The Secretary of State is empowered by this section to introduce provisions by order which correspond to provisions in the Criminal Appeal (Northern Ireland) Act 1980.

239　Crown Court Rules

In relation to—
(a) proceedings under this Part, or
(b) receivers appointed under this Part,
Crown Court Rules may make provision corresponding to provision in rules of court (within the meaning of section 120(1) of the Judicature (Northern Ireland) Act 1978 (c. 23)).

PART 5

CIVIL RECOVERY OF THE PROCEEDS ETC. OF UNLAWFUL CONDUCT

INTRODUCTION TO PART 5

Part 5 of the Act deals with two distinct schemes. The first (chapters 1 and 2) enables the "enforcement authority" (in England and Wales, that will be the Director of the Asset Recovery Agency) to make High Court applications for the civil recovery of property (other than just cash) that represents the proceeds of 'unlawful conduct'. The second scheme (chapters 1 and 3) empowers constables and customs officers to recover 'cash' of at least the minimum amount (say £10,000) by way of summary proceedings before a Magistrates' Court with a right of appeal by way of rehearing to the Crown Court (in England and Wales). "Cash" has a statutory definition (s.289(6)) and includes a wide range of monetary instruments.

Neither scheme is triggered by the conviction of any person. The Government is of the view that both schemes are manifestly civil in nature (including being civil proceedings for the purposes of the Human Rights Act 1998) and hence the reason why the two schemes appear together in Part 5 of the Act.

Applications for the civil recovery of property (other than just cash) are to be heard in the High Court because such cases might be complex involving many parties.

At first sight, it might seem illogical that 'cash', and other property not involving cash alone, should be the subject of two different procedures. The reasons for this were explained by the Attorney General in the House of Lords (*Hansard*, May 13 2002, Col.54-57) namely:
(i) existing cash detention/forfeiture proceedings take place in the Magistrates' Court;

(ii) the Magistrates are familiar with the concepts involved;

(iii) the current scheme has worked successfully;

(iv) arguments in the Magistrates' Court regarding cash tend to be narrower than those involving other types of property;

(v) the High Court would otherwise be unduly occupied by a potentially large number of inappropriate cases 'that would result in delays in listing cases and case costs would soar'; and

(vi) respondents have the protection of an appeal by way of rehearing to the Crown Court.

The recovery of cash in summary proceedings (chapter 3) is relatively quick and straightforward. The scheme represents a development of a process enacted initially under the Criminal Justice (International Cooperation) Act 1990, and then under Pt. II of the Drug Trafficking Act 1994. 'Terrorist cash' is dealt with under the Anti-Terrorism, Crime and Security Act 2001.

Cash forfeiture (chapter 3) embraces not only the civil recovery of cash that was obtained through unlawful conduct, but also cash "which is intended to be used in unlawful conduct" (see s.240(1)(b)) and ss. 289(1), (2); s.294(1), (2); s.298(2)) – i.e. cash as an instrument of unlawful conduct, including the proposed use of cash abroad if the conduct contemplated would be unlawful somewhere in the United Kingdom and in the State where the conduct was to be performed: see s.241(2). By contrast, civil recovery of property other than just cash (chapter 2) is limited to property "obtained through unlawful conduct", and does not extend to recovering property intended to be used as an instrument of crime, e.g. a boat, or a house intended to be used to produce amphetamine (see s.242, and s.241 for the definition of 'unlawful conduct'). It is not entirely clear why chapter 2 does not embrace the recovery of the intended instruments of crime, but one reason may be that there is uncertainty as to whether the civil recovery of such property would be ECHR/HRA 1998 compliant. A further reason may be a desire on the part of the Government to ensure that the priorities of law enforcement agencies, do not become skewed by a wide ranging application of powers, directed at cars, boats, homes or businesses (see para.5.10 of the P.I.U. Report, June 2000). As experience of Pt.5 increases, one suspects that the law will be extended to cover the instruments of crime whether cash or not.

Chapters 1 and 2

Variously styled 'civil forfeiture' (Home Office Working Group on Confiscation; Third Report, Novemeber 1998), 'asset recovery'; 'confiscation without conviction', and now 'civil recovery', the new powers are intended to provide an alternative method of tackling crime – particularly organised crime. The Government has made no secret of the fact that current asset recovery laws following conviction, have produced disappointing results: see para.4.2 of the HOWGC, 3rd Report 1998. Relatively few confiscation orders under the Drug Trafficking Act 1994 and Pt.VI of the Criminal Justice Act 1988 have been made 'against major criminals with substantial assets' (para.4.3, *ibid*). The Cabinet Office's Performance and Innovation Unit (see *Recovering the Proceeds of Crime*, June 2000) supported the introduction of 'civil forfeiture' on the grounds that it would take away from individuals property that 'was never legally owned by them' or which is intended for use in committing crime, and "open up a new route to tackling the assets of those currently beyond the reach of the law, by targeting the activities of organised crime heads who are remote from crimes committed to their order, yet who enjoy the benefits", and also to "allow the recovery of unlawful assets held in the United Kingdom, but derived from crime committed overseas" (para.5.2 of the P.I.U. Report). The Government wants to make the message clearer than ever that "crime does not pay" (see the speech of the Attorney General, *Hansard*, May 13 2002, H.L., col. 54).

Critics of civil recovery schemes tend to voice a mix of ideological and practical concerns, of which the most frequent are:

(i) that there will be cases where a recovery order will taint the reputation of a respondent almost as much as if a confiscation order was made against him, namely, where there is a finding that his unlawful conduct generated the recoverable property;

(ii) the civil process should not be used as a way of avoiding the rigours of due process in the criminal law;

(iii) if defects exist in the rules of evidence and procedure in the criminal law, that make it more difficult to prosecute offenders to conviction, then the solution is to change the rules of the criminal law;

(iv) major criminals will not 'stand around waiting for an interim receiving order to be served on them

(see Lord Lloyd of Berwick, *Hansard*, May 13 2002, H.L., cols. 65 to 69). The Government's response is that "the experience in Australia, in Italy, in Ireland ... and in the United States is that this process is an effective and important one; and indeed, that it does work" (per the Attorney General, *Hansard*, May 13 2002, H.L., col.74/75). Whether Pt. 5 'works' begs the question as to how success, or lack of it, is to be measured. The value of assets seized might be one indicator, but the rate of offending or the availability of illegal controlled drugs, might be better ones. Some commentators also voice concern about the extent to which a State should acquire assets in respect of the very acts it seeks to condemn: how should those assets be used or redistributed. The Performance and Innovation Unit was clearly alive to those concerns (see para. 5.10).

The effectiveness of civil recovery is linked to the extent to which other States adopt similar legislative regimes. Unlawfully acquired property that might be recovered by courts in one State, might be 'safely' held in another. Mutual recognition of foreign judgments in civil or criminal cases requires some harmonisation/approximation of laws. Accordingly, it is highly likely that other States will introduce stronger civil recovery laws.

Civil recovery laws in the USA are well developed, complex, and have existed for many years. In Ireland, the Proceeds of Crime Act 1996 empowers the High Court to restrain property that is or represents the proceeds of crime and which is in the possession or control of any person (s.2) and shall only be released if the claimant satisfies the court that the property should be released (s.3). Note that an interim order restraining the property, can only be made if the Court is *satisfied* (i.e. on a balance of probabilities) that the specified property is directly, or indirectly, the proceeds of crime. In New South Wales, a civil forfeiture regime exists by virtue of the Criminal Assets Recovery Act 1990 (CARA), but that Act is aimed at persons against whom it is proved (to the civil standard) that he/she committed a "serious offence" within the previous six years. All of that person's property is liable to forfeiture unless he/she proves it was lawfully acquired. The Proceeds of Crime Act (Aus) 1987 is conviction based. Australia is currently considering a federal/civil recovery regime along CARA lines: Proceeds of Crime Bill (Aus) 2002; and see *Restraining the Global Threat* C D Davey.

Although chapters 1 and 2 to Pt.5 of the Act more closely resemble the Irish scheme than Australian/USA legislation, it is best not to attempt to make direct comparisons. Part 5 is intended, by Government, to be one component in a joined-up strategic approach towards the confiscation of ill-gotten assets.

Part of the Government's case for the enactment of Pt.5, Chapters 1 and 2, is that "successful criminals acquire significant fortunes and act as bad role models for others, by demonstrating that crime can pay" (para. 3.5; P.I.U. Report June 2000). The Home Office estimated that some £440 million of criminal assets could be targeted by civil forfeiture across 400 individual cases. The press has identified some of those targets, but publicity has been less candid about the difficulties often encountered trying to bring such offenders to 'justice'. The target of one agency might be a valuable informer for another. Deciding whether to pursue civil recovery or to prosecute a 'target' will be the subject of detailed notes for guidance to ensure that priorities of law enforcement are not distorted, or that civil recovery becomes a 'soft option' – ironically for those most culpable and 'untouchable' in the criminal courts. In the House of Lords, the Attorney General (Lord Goldsmith) wanted to emphasise "the hierarchy" (*Hansard*, 13.5.02; col. 72). He said:

"First, I want to emphasise, therefore, the hierarchy. The prosecution of offences will remain the priority in all cases .... It is very important to note that the director will have no power to prosecute. The power to prosecute will be the power of the existing prosecution agencies in England and Scotland. It is clear from the hierarchy which has been identified that the prosecution of offences will remain the priority in all cases. That is not intended as a soft option. For example, it is made clear in the draft guidance that it would not be a proper exercise of the prosecutorial discretion—there are two tests for prosecution, the evidential and the public interest test—to say that in the public interest there is no need to prosecute because there is the alternative of civil recovery.

However, in what kinds of cases may civil recovery take place? One example would be where the law enforcement authority has carried out a criminal investigation and consulted the prosecuting authority and a decision not to institute criminal proceedings has been taken applying normal evidential and public interest criteria. I acknowledge that that would be such a case, but I emphasise that the decision not to prosecute would be taken without regard to whether civil recovery may be available.

But there are many other examples which do not even touch on the possibility that the respondent is actually himself or herself being accused of criminal conduct; where the person suspected of the unlawful conduct through which property was obtained is not available because that person is dead or abroad and there is no reasonable prospect of securing their extradition. That is even before any advice has been given to such people to leave the jurisdiction.

A related example would be if a person had been convicted of an offence abroad, for example, for drug-related crime, but had recoverable property in the United Kingdom. The important point is that law enforcement and prosecution authorities will ensure that the possibility of bringing criminal proceedings has been fully considered in every case."

Many of the concerns voiced about the application of civil recovery powers, are tied in with concerns about due-process, and protections that exist in criminal proceedings that might be lost if proceedings are civil in nature. The Government believe that Pt. 5 is HRA compliant. However, *Hansard* reveals that some senior figures in the House of Lords were not confident that all aspects of Pt.5 are ECHR compliant. For example, property obtained through unlawful conduct is "recoverable property" for the purposes of Pt.5 (s.304(1)) and s.316(3) reads that for the "purpose of deciding whether or not property was recoverable at any time (including times before commencement) it is to be assumed that (the Act) was in force at that and any other relevant time". This means that property is recoverable whether it was obtained before or after the Act came into force. If civil recovery is a 'penalty', for the purposes of Article 7 of the HRA 1998, then the argument runs that the 'penalty' imposed by way of a civil recovery order will be greater than the one applicable at the time the offence was committed: see the speeches of Lord Kingsland, and Lord Goodhart, *Hansard*, May 13 2002, H.L., col. 59; and Lord Berwick *ibid.*, col.65. However, the Government advanced a strong case in support of the view that Article 7 is not engaged (see Lord Goldsmith *Hansard*, May 13 2002, H.L., col.72). The civil recovery process focuses on the origin of property and not on the culpability of the person holding it. Secondly, civil recovery that involves a consideration of conduct that is criminal, is not new to the law of the United Kingdom. Civil claims based on allegations of fraud do not always result in a finding that the process is in fact criminal, or that the order made by the court constitutes a 'penalty' for the purposes of the Human Rights Act 1998. In any event, there will be many cases that relate to property acquired after the Act came into force. Again, there seems to be no violation of the HRA if a civil recovery action follows an unsuccessful prosecution provided the proceedings do not constitute an abuse of process, or they are not maliciously motivated. The Attorney General gave examples of cases that could be pursued by way of civil recovery, namely, prosecutions that collapsed due to witness intimidation or other procedural/evidential reasons (see *Hansard*, May 13 2002, H.L., col.77). There is no question of double jeopardy because the same property cannot be recovered twice: see *Hansard*, May 13 2002, H.L., col.79.

CHAPTER 1

INTRODUCTORY

240 General purpose of this Part

(1) This Part has effect for the purposes of—
    (a) enabling the enforcement authority to recover, in civil proceedings before the High Court or Court of Session, property which is, or represents, property obtained through unlawful conduct,
    (b) enabling cash which is, or represents, property obtained through unlawful conduct, or which is intended to be used in unlawful conduct, to be forfeited in civil proceedings before a magistrates' court or (in Scotland) the sheriff.
(2) The powers conferred by this Part are exercisable in relation to any property (including cash) whether or not any proceedings have been brought for an offence in connection with the property.

DEFINITIONS
"cash": s.316(1), s.289(6)
"enforcement authority": s.316(1)
"property": s.316(4), (5), (6), (7)
"property obtained through unlawful conduct": s.316(1), s.242
"unlawful conduct": s.316(1), s.242

GENERAL NOTE
This provision should be read in conjunction with ss.241, 242, and chapter 4 i.e. ss.304-310.

Subs. (1)
This subsection explains that Pt5 has two schemes. The first scheme enables the Director (in England and Wales) to recover in civil proceedings, property which is or represents property obtained through unlawful conduct. Thus, in England and Wales it is the Director of the Asset Recovery Agency who is the 'enforcement authority' (s.316(1)). "Property" means property of all types including 'money' (s.316(4)) irrespective as to whether it is situated in the United King-

dom or abroad. The property must have been "obtained through unlawful conduct" (see s.242 and s.241). It will be seen that by s.304(1) "property obtained through unlawful conduct" (s.242) is also prima facie "recoverable property". Thus, where a thief steals a valuable painting, the painting is "property obtained through unlawful conduct" (s.304) if he has it in his hands. The reason for enacting chapter 4 to Part 5 of the Act, is that frequently the original property will have passed through other hands before action is taken by the Director. Sections 304-310 explain the extent to which the Director can trace the original property, or the converted property, into the hands of others and perhaps to recover the property from them. By s.308(1), property is deemed no longer to be recoverable from a person who acquires it in good faith without notice of the defect.

The second scheme (s.240(1)(b)) is much simpler and enables ill-gotten cash to be recovered in the Magistrates' Court (in England and Wales) under provisions enacted in Chapter 3 to Part 5 of the Act (ss.289-303). Note that proceedings are initiated not by the Director, but (in England and Wales) either by the Commissioners of Customs and Excise, or by a constable. These provisions replace and expand a scheme originally enacted under the Criminal Justice (International Co-operation) Act 1990 and later under Part II of the Drug Trafficking Act 1994. Note that chapter 3 includes cash intended to be used for the commission of an unlawful act.

Subs. (2)

Civil proceedings for the recovery of property, or cash, may be brought irrespective as to whether criminal proceedings have been initiated in respect of the underlying conduct, or not. The same property cannot be recovered twice but where criminal proceedings fail, or have been abandoned, it is open to the relevant agency to continue with (or initiate) civil recovery proceedings.

The powers are exercisable under Pt.5 irrespective as to whether the property was "obtained through unlawful conduct" before the commencement of the 2002 Act, or not. For a discussion as to whether s.240 is HRA compliant: see *Hansard,* May 13 2002, H.L., col.65-75.

241   "Unlawful conduct"

(1) Conduct occurring in any part of the United Kingdom is unlawful conduct if it is unlawful under the criminal law of that part.

(2) Conduct which—
   (a) occurs in a country outside the United Kingdom and is unlawful under the criminal law of that country, and
   (b) if it occurred in a part of the United Kingdom, would be unlawful under the criminal law of that part,
   is also unlawful conduct.

(3) The court or sheriff must decide on a balance of probabilities whether it is proved—
   (a) that any matters alleged to constitute unlawful conduct have occurred, or
   (b) that any person intended to use any cash in unlawful conduct.

DEFINITIONS
  "country": s.316(1)
  "the court": s.316(1)
  "unlawful conduct": s.316(1)

GENERAL NOTE

Subs. (1)

Conduct that is contrary to the criminal law of any part of the United Kingdom is "unlawful conduct". This seems to mean that conduct that is unlawful, for example in Scotland but not in England, would nevertheless be "unlawful conduct".

Subss. (2) and (3)

This provision envisages a dual criminality test to the extent that conduct must be unlawful where the acts were performed, as well as being unlawful if committed somewhere within the United Kingdom (e.g. England, even if the conduct would not be unlawful in Scotland). It is for the court, on a balance of probabilities, to resolve issues arising under s.241.

242   **"Property obtained through unlawful conduct"**

(1) A person obtains property through unlawful conduct (whether his own conduct or another's) if he obtains property by or in return for the conduct.

(2) In deciding whether any property was obtained through unlawful conduct—

    (a) it is immaterial whether or not any money, goods or services were provided in order to put the person in question in a position to carry out the conduct,

    (b) it is not necessary to show that the conduct was of a particular kind if it is shown that the property was obtained through conduct of one of a number of kinds, each of which would have been unlawful conduct.

DEFINITION
"property":

GENERAL NOTE

Subs. (1)

Property will be obtained 'through unlawful conduct' if the respondent acquires it as a fruit of that conduct (e.g. stealing a painting) or 'in return for the conduct' (e.g. X was given cash to drive a lorry loaded with cannabis from Spain to the United Kingdom). It is immaterial that the person who obtained the property did not perform the 'unlawful conduct', (e.g. a painting obtained by X was stolen on his behalf). There is an argument for saying that the definition of property obtained through unlawful conduct is narrower than the definition of 'benefit' for the purposes of Part 2 of the Act. Thus s.76(4) states that a person 'benefits from conduct if he obtains property *as a result of or in connection with* the conduct' (emphasis added). The proceeds from the sale of a book that explained how the author committed a high-value armed robbery might be a benefit for the purposes of s.76(4), but arguably not "property obtained through unlawful conduct".

Subs. (2)

As the *Explanatory Notes* state, this subsection provides that it is not necessary to show that property was obtained through unlawful conduct of a particular kind. Property might have been acquired by committing many different types of offences, e.g., drug dealing, stealing radios, shoplifting, and selling counterfeit currency.

CHAPTER 2

CIVIL RECOVERY IN THE HIGH COURT OR COURT OF SESSION

Proceedings for recovery orders

243   **Proceedings for recovery orders in England and Wales or Northern Ireland**

(1) Proceedings for a recovery order may be taken by the enforcement authority in the High Court against any person who the authority thinks holds recoverable property.

(2) The enforcement authority must serve the claim form—

    (a) on the respondent, and

    (b) unless the court dispenses with service, on any other person who the authority thinks holds any associated property which the authority wishes to be subject to a recovery order,

wherever domiciled, resident or present.

(3) If any property which the enforcement authority wishes to be subject to a recovery order is not specified in the claim form it must be described in the form in general terms; and the form must state whether it is alleged to be recoverable property or associated property.

(4) The references above to the claim form include the particulars of claim, where they are served subsequently.

<small>DEFINITIONS</small>
"associated property": s.316(1), s.245
"enforcement authority": s.316(1)
"recovery order": s.316(1); s.266
"recoverable property": s.316(1); ss.304 to 310.
"respondent": s.316(1)
"the court": s.316(1)

<small>GENERAL NOTE</small>
This section should be read in conjunction with Pt. 5, Chapter 4 (ss.304-310), and s.245 (associated property).

The Director of the Asset Recovery Agency (the 'enforcement authority') may initiate civil recovery proceedings in the High Court against any person whom the Director "thinks" holds "recoverable property". In the House of Lords (*Hansard*, Committee Stage, May 13 2002, col. 97) Baroness Buscombe moved an amendment to leave out "thinks" and to insert "has reasonable grounds to believe". This was later withdrawn following representations by Lord Goldsmith that s.243(1) merely identifies the target of the proceedings but that the "reasonableness of the proceedings are safeguarded in an entirely different way", namely, that the court would scrutinise the application and strike out an unmeritorious claim (*Hansard*, col.98). He added:

"I hope that it will be accepted that the director will bring sensible claims and that the director and his staff will be intelligent. I know that the noble Baroness, by her forensic example, was not suggesting otherwise. That is another practical safeguard that will be in place."

Note that the Director may initiate proceedings in one of two ways. He may (and probably should endeavour to) commence proceedings by serving a Claim Form under s.243(2). This will always involve serving the form on at least the respondent. However, the Director may have reason to apply to the High Court for an "Interim Receiving Order" (s.246) - perhaps without notice, see s.246(3) - before serving a Claim Form, e.g. to freeze assets before they are disposed of.

Whichever route the Director takes, the object is ultimately to persuade the High Court to make a "recovery order" under s.266 in respect of "recoverable property".

"Recoverable property" is defined by s.304 to mean property obtained by a person "through unlawful conduct" i.e. "by or in return for (unlawful conduct as defined by s.241)": see s.242.

Property may remain 'recoverable property' even if it passes into the hands of another e.g. a money launderer (consider s.304(2)) but it will not be recoverable if one of the exceptions apply (e.g. a person who bought the property in good faith without notice of the unlawful conduct, see s.308).

Frequently, 'recoverable property' will be mixed with the legitimate interests of third parties. For example, freehold land might be purchased through unlawful conduct, but an innocent third party might have bought a tenancy unaware of the history of the landlord. In this situation, the proprietary interest of the third party is "associated property" (defined by s.245) - the value of which is not "recoverable property'. Nevertheless, the Director might wish to apply to the Court for orders as to the disposal or use of the property under a 'recovery order', whilst endeavouring to safeguard the interests of the person holding 'associated property'. Accordingly, the Director, if he wishes to pursue civil recovery under Pt. 5 Chapter 2, must serve a Claim Form (a) on the Respondent and (b) on any other person who is thought to hold associated property. In (b), the court might be persuaded to dispense with service.

If the Director commences proceedings by way of a Claim Form, he should (if possible) specify the property in question, failing which the property may be specified in general terms, and the form should particularise whether the property is 'recoverable' or 'associated' property.

244   Proceedings for recovery orders in Scotland

(1) Proceedings for a recovery order may be taken by the enforcement authority in the Court of Session against any person who the authority thinks holds recoverable property.
(2) The enforcement authority must serve the application—
  (a) on the respondent, and
  (b) unless the court dispenses with service, on any other person who the authority thinks holds any associated property which the authority wishes to be subject to a recovery order,
  wherever domiciled, resident or present.

(3) If any property which the enforcement authority wishes to be subject to a recovery order is not specified in the application it must be described in the application in general terms; and the application must state whether it is alleged to be recoverable property or associated property.

DEFINITIONS
"Associated property": s.245.
"Enforcement authority": The Scottish Ministers (see s.316(1))
"Recoverable property": s.304
"Recovery order": s.266

GENERAL NOTE

As s.240 explains, this Part of the Act has effect for the purpose of enabling the "enforcement authority" – the Scottish Ministers – to "recover" in civil proceedings before the Court of Session property which is, or which represents, property obtained through unlawful conduct. By s.241(1), conduct occurring in any part of the UK is unlawful conduct if it is unlawful under the criminal law of that part. By s.241(2), conduct outside the UK is also unlawful conduct if it is unlawful under the criminal law where it occurred *and* would have been unlawful under the criminal law of a part of the UK. By contrast with other provisions in this Act (for example, the definition of criminal conduct for money laundering purposes in s.340), this *is* a double criminality requirement. Property is obtained through unlawful conduct, in terms of s.242, if it is obtained by or in return for the conduct.

Subs. (1)

Proceedings for a recovery order. This is a new remedy and the Act does not by any means provide a comprehensive procedural code for such actions. One awaits an Act of Sederunt. Note, however, that in terms of s.266 a recovery order (a) vests the property in the trustee for civil recovery (as to his functions, see s.267) and (b) must be made if the court is satisfied that any property is recoverable.

Enforcement authority. Section 316 identifies the Scottish Ministers as the enforcement authority as regards Scotland. In practice, it is understood that the responsibilities will be discharged by and under the supervision of the Lord Advocate.

Against any person who the authority thinks holds recoverable property. Recoverable property is property obtained through unlawful conduct (see s.304(1)). Notwithstanding the apparently wide scope of the present section, ss.304 to 310 actually impose strict limits on the extent to which property may be "followed" or "traced" and provide rules about what is to happen if the property has been mixed with other property. Those rules are not precisely the same as the Scots common law rules as to the commixtion or confusion of moveable property.

245   "Associated property"

(1) "Associated property" means property of any of the following descriptions (including property held by the respondent) which is not itself the recoverable property—
  (a) any interest in the recoverable property,
  (b) any other interest in the property in which the recoverable property subsists,
  (c) if the recoverable property is a tenancy in common, the tenancy of the other tenant,
  (d) if (in Scotland) the recoverable property is owned in common, the interest of the other owner,
  (e) if the recoverable property is part of a larger property, but not a separate part, the remainder of that property.

(2) References to property being associated with recoverable property are to be read accordingly.

(3) No property is to be treated as associated with recoverable property consisting of rights under a pension scheme (within the meaning of sections 273 to 275).

DEFINITIONS
"associated property": s.316(1), s.245
"interest": s.316(1)

"property": s.316(1)
"recoverable property": s.316(1)
"respondent": s.316(1)

GENERAL NOTE
Frequently, 'recoverable property' will be mixed with the legitimate interests of third parties. For example, freehold land might be purchased through unlawful conduct, but an innocent third party might have bought a tenancy unaware of the history of the landlord. In this situation, the proprietary interest of the third party is "associated property" (defined by s.245) - the value of which is not "recoverable property". Examples of s.245(1)(a) to (e) appear in the *Explanatory Notes* but all instances distinguish between the interest that is tainted (and thus recoverable property) and the interest that was innocently acquired (but which is associated with the recoverable part of the property). The practical relevance of property being treated as 'associated property' is that the Director may take action in respect of the entirety of the property although ultimately, the value of 'associated property' is not recoverable and some way will have to be found to reflect that fact e.g. payment equal to the value of the 'associated property'.

Subs. (3)
Without express statutory provision, the position of innocent parties who have rights under a pension scheme might be very uncertain in cases where a respondent has an interest in a pension fund that is 'recoverable property' for the purposes of the Act. This subsection ensures that related interests of persons other than the respondent are not treated as 'associated property'.

Interim receiving orders (England and Wales and Northern Ireland)

246 Application for interim receiving order

(1) Where the enforcement authority may take proceedings for a recovery order in the High Court, the authority may apply to the court for an interim receiving order (whether before or after starting the proceedings).

(2) An interim receiving order is an order for—
  (a) the detention, custody or preservation of property, and
  (b) the appointment of an interim receiver.

(3) An application for an interim receiving order may be made without notice if the circumstances are such that notice of the application would prejudice any right of the enforcement authority to obtain a recovery order in respect of any property.

(4) The court may make an interim receiving order on the application if it is satisfied that the conditions in subsections (5) and, where applicable, (6) are met.

(5) The first condition is that there is a good arguable case—
  (a) that the property to which the application for the order relates is or includes recoverable property, and
  (b) that, if any of it is not recoverable property, it is associated property.

(6) The second condition is that, if—
  (a) the property to which the application for the order relates includes property alleged to be associated property, and
  (b) the enforcement authority has not established the identity of the person who holds it,
  the authority has taken all reasonable steps to do so.

(7) In its application for an interim receiving order, the enforcement authority must nominate a suitably qualified person for appointment as interim receiver, but the nominee may not be a member of the staff of the Agency.

(8) The extent of the power to make an interim receiving order is not limited by sections 247 to 255.

DEFINITIONS
"associated property": s.316, s.245
"claim form": s.243(2), s.243(4)

"enforcement authority": s.316,
"the Court": s.316
"interim receiving order": s.316, s.246(2)
"recovery order": s.316, s.266

GENERAL NOTE

The Director is the "enforcement authority" in England and Wales for the purpose of this Part of the Act. He may apply for an interim receiving order before, or after, serving a Claim Form (see s.243) on the respondent and on other persons who hold 'associated property'. Particulars of Claim may be served subsequent to service of the Form (s.243(4)). It will be seen that the Director may initiate proceedings in two ways: either by serving a Claim Form under s.243 (which seems to be the standard way), or by applying for an 'interim receiving order' under s.246. Experience may show that the latter route is most often used by the Director. An application may be made 'without notice' (s.246(3)) if the Director considers that he must act swiftly to avoid recoverable property being moved out of the jurisdiction, or concealed.

The procedure for making an 'interim receiving order' under the Act builds on the long experience of the High Court in respect of applications for restraint orders under earlier confiscation laws (notably under the Drug Trafficking Offences Act 1986, the Drug Trafficking Act 1994, and Part VI of the Criminal Justice Act 1988), and in respect of applications for *Mareva* injunctions.

The primary purpose of an 'interim receiving order' is to freeze 'recoverable property' – that is to say property which is 'obtained through unlawful conduct' (see ss.304 to 310, chap.4; and s.242). However, in practice it will usually be the case that 'recoverable property' is not free of interests held by third parties. For example, the respondent holds the freehold interest in a house but he has let out rooms to third parties. In such a case, the tenancies are examples of 'associated property', and at some stage the court may be asked to make orders that enable the Director to recover the value of the 'recoverable property' whilst preserving (if possible) the value of the 'associated property' of third parties. Accordingly, as a protective measure, an 'interim receiving order' will freeze both 'recoverable property' and 'associated property'. Given the hardship that such orders may cause, the High Court must be satisfied that the conditions in subs.(4) and, if necessary subs.(6) are satisfied. The latter subsection concerns those who hold 'associated property': the Director must take all reasonable steps to identify those who hold such property before applying for an interim receiving order. Concern was expressed by some of their Lordships in Committee (*Hansard*, May 13 2002, col.100) that the legislation does not have enough safeguards in place in respect of 'associated property' – that the definition is too wide and thus includes property that it should not: see the speech of Lord Goodhart. There seems to have been common ground that an interim order ought not to be made, or that there should be no order to sell associated property in cases where "the recoverable property on its own can be efficiently and effectively realised without recourse to the associated property" (Lord Goodhart, *Hansard*, 13.5.2002, col.101). However, in practice, cases tend to be more complex and involve linked interests. The Attorney General stated (Lord Goldsmith):

"Let me make clear what I have in mind. First, we would not expect proceedings to be brought in respect of non-recoverable property unless the enforcement authority considered it proportionate to do so, taking into account all the circumstances, including how best to satisfy any right it has to recover the recoverable property.

There is no purpose in the enforcement authority proceeding unnecessarily in relation to associated property.

But if the enforcement authority makes an application—we are now considering the receiving order stage—it will be for the court to decide in accordance with its discretion what property is to be covered by the order ... it does not end there, because (s.254(2) formerly clause 260(2)) explicitly provides that:

"The court may vary an interim receiving order so as to exclude from the property to which the order applies any property which is ... associated property if the court thinks that the satisfaction of any right of the enforcement authority to recover the property obtained through unlawful conduct will not be prejudiced".

I suggest that that entirely meets the noble Lord's point, in the sense that the court can on an application made to vary ... the order so as to exclude property if, in the court's view, it will not prejudice the right to recovery."

When applying for an 'interim receiving order', the Director must nominate a person to act as 'interim receiver'. This must not be a member of the Asset Recovery Agency (s.246(7)). Accordingly, the Director will nominate a receiver in private practice. Under earlier confiscation laws, applications for a receiver, or management receiver, were made only after the Applicant secured the agreement of a receiver to act as such. This makes sound practical sense. If the High Court makes orders freezing assets, the agency will wish to act expeditiously. By the time the parties attend Court on the hearing of the application for an interim receiving order, a nominated receiver will have entered into correspondence with the Director, and reached agreement, as to the receiver's function, responsibilities, and remuneration. In this connection, the reader should note the powers of the receiver under Sched.6 to the Act, and to read ss.247 to 255. It will be seen, that by s.246(8), the High Court retains its inherent jurisdiction to make a wide range of orders with respect to the appointment of an interim receiver. Note that by s.252, an interim receiving order must ("subject to any exclusions") prohibit any person whose property the order applies, from dealing with the property.

247 Functions of interim receiver

(1) An interim receiving order may authorise or require the interim receiver—

  (a) to exercise any of the powers mentioned in Schedule 6,

  (b) to take any other steps the court thinks appropriate,

for the purpose of securing the detention, custody or preservation of the property to which the order applies or of taking any steps under subsection (2).

(2) An interim receiving order must require the interim receiver to take any steps which the court thinks necessary to establish—

  (a) whether or not the property to which the order applies is recoverable property or associated property,

  (b) whether or not any other property is recoverable property (in relation to the same unlawful conduct) and, if it is, who holds it.

(3) If—

  (a) the interim receiver deals with any property which is not property to which the order applies, and

  (b) at the time he deals with the property he believes on reasonable grounds that he is entitled to do so in pursuance of the order,

the interim receiver is not liable to any person in respect of any loss or damage resulting from his dealing with the property except so far as the loss or damage is caused by his negligence.

DEFINITIONS

"interim receiving order": s.316(1), s.246(2)

"property": s.316(4)

"recoverable property": s.316, ss.304 to 310

GENERAL NOTE

The interim receiver must focus on matters set out in s.247(2), namely, whether property that is the subject of the order is 'recoverable property', and whether there is more recoverable property in existence, and if so, to ascertain who holds it. He/she must act with the object of 'securing the detention, custody or preservation of the property to which the order applies'. The phrase 'preservation of the property' may in practice be synonymous with 'preserving the *value* of the property'. By virtue of para.5 to Sched.6 to the Act, an interim receiver has the power to manage property and to sell assets 'before their value diminishes'.

It follows that the interim receiver is not merely required to manage recoverable property, but has an investigative role too. It is important to note that by virtue of Pt.8 of the Act, the Director has power to carry out a 'civil recovery investigation' (see s.341(2)) which means that he may ascertain whether property is recoverable, who holds it, the whereabouts of that property, and the extent of that property. Significantly, s.341(3) states that an investigation ceases in cases where "an interim receiving order applies to the property in question" (s.341(3)(b)). In other words, before the Director successfully applies for an interim receiving order, the Director may investigate matters relating to recoverable property but thereafter, the Director loses those powers and the interim receiver takes over those tasks under the supervision of the Court.

With the above in mind, it will be seen from Sched.6 to the Act that an interim receiver has wide powers including the power to 'obtain information', and (controversially perhaps) 'to require a person to answer any question' subject to the protections in Sched. 6, para.2, and to 'manage any property' (Sched.6, para.5).

The power to compel a person to answer questions under Sched.6, para.2, is far reaching. A person must answer questions unless a court makes orders regarding matters subject to legal professional privilege (see para.4). Rules restricting the disclosure of information will not spare the interviewee from answering questions (see para.2(2)). Answers may not used against him in criminal proceedings (para.2(3)) unless the interviewee is prosecuted for perjury, or where in other criminal proceedings he gives evidence inconsistent with his answer to the receiver (para.2(4), (5)). There is no right against self-incrimination under Sched.6 para.2, in respect of civil proceedings.

Managing property includes selling, or disposing of assets 'which are perishable or which ought to be disposed of before their value diminishes' (para.5(2)(a)). Thus, a receiver may sell perishable goods or goods that significantly depreciate in value over time e.g. cars, electrical goods such as high value computers. Problems are likely to be encountered where property is jointly owned but the receiver wishes to dispose of property in order to maintain its value. In such a case, a third party who holds 'associated property' may apply to the court under s.251 for directions as to the exercise of the interim receiver's functions and/or make application under s.254 for an exclusion of property on the grounds that his interest/share is not recoverable. However, it will be seen that although the court does have power to exclude non-recoverable property this is subject to court being satisfied that the right of the Director to recover 'recoverable property' will not be prejudiced: s.254(2).

The receiver also has power to carry on a business (para.5(2)(b)). This often leads to conflicts and tensions between the receiver and the person who ordinarily owns/manages the business.

One of the issues that is not directly dealt with by the Act is who shoulders the burden of paying the receiver's costs. Under previous confiscation legislation, the respondent could be ordered to pay the receiver's costs: *Hughes v. AMCE* [2002] EWCA Civ. 734. Under the Act, the assumption appears to be that it is for the Director to remunerate the receiver.

An interim receiver may require any person to bring property or documents relating to property back into the jurisdiction of the Court (s.250).

248   Registration

(1) The registration Acts—
   (a) apply in relation to interim receiving orders as they apply in relation to orders which affect land and are made by the court for the purpose of enforcing judgements or recognisances,
   (b) apply in relation to applications for interim receiving orders as they apply in relation to other pending land actions.
(2) The registration Acts are—
   (a) the Land Registration Act 1925 (c. 21),
   (b) the Land Charges Act 1972 (c. 61), and
   (c) the Land Registration Act 2002 (c. 9).
(3) But no notice may be entered in the register of title under the Land Registration Act 2002 in respect of an interim receiving order.
(4) A person applying for an interim receiving order must be treated for the purposes of section 57 of the Land Registration Act 1925 (inhibitions) as a person interested in relation to any registered land to which—
   (a) the application relates, or
   (b) an interim receiving order made in pursuance of the application relates.

DEFINITIONS
   "interim receiving orders": s.316, s.246(2)
   "the court": s.316

GENERAL NOTE
   This section was inserted by way of a House of Lords amendment to the Bill in Committee (*Hansard*, May 13 2002, col.105). Its purpose is simply to ensure that orders are registered as pending land actions.

249   Registration (Northern Ireland)

(1) A person applying for an interim receiving order must be treated for the purposes of section 66 of the Land Registration Act (Northern Ireland) 1970 (c. 18 (N.I.)) (cautions) as a person interested in relation to any registered land to which—
   (a) the application relates, or

  (b) an interim receiving order made in pursuance of the application relates.

(2) Upon being served with a copy of an interim receiving order, the Registrar must, in respect of any registered land to which an interim receiving order or an application for an interim receiving order relates, make an entry inhibiting any dealing with the land without the consent of the High Court.

(3) Subsections (2) and (4) of section 67 of the Land Registration Act (Northern Ireland) 1970 (inhibitions) apply to an entry made under subsection (2) as they apply to an entry made on the application of any person interested in the registered land under subsection (1) of that section.

(4) Where an interim receiving order has been protected by an entry registered under the Land Registration Act (Northern Ireland) 1970 or the Registration of Deeds Acts, an order setting aside the interim receiving order may require that entry to be vacated.

(5) In this section—

    "Registrar" and "entry" have the same meanings as in the Land Registration Act (Northern Ireland) 1970, and

    "Registration of Deeds Acts" has the meaning given by section 46(2) of the Interpretation Act (Northern Ireland) 1954 (c. 33 (N.I.)).

250 Duties of respondent etc.

(1) An interim receiving order may require any person to whose property the order applies—

  (a) to bring the property to a place (in England and Wales or, as the case may be, Northern Ireland) specified by the interim receiver or place it in the custody of the interim receiver (if, in either case, he is able to do so),

  (b) to do anything he is reasonably required to do by the interim receiver for the preservation of the property.

(2) An interim receiving order may require any person to whose property the order applies to bring any documents relating to the property which are in his possession or control to a place (in England and Wales or, as the case may be, Northern Ireland) specified by the interim receiver or to place them in the custody of the interim receiver.

    "Document" means anything in which information of any description is recorded.

DEFINITIONS
  "document": s.250(2)
  "interim receiving order": s.316, s.246(2)
  "property": s.316(4)

GENERAL NOTE
  See the General Note to s.247 above.

251 Supervision of interim receiver and variation of order

(1) The interim receiver, any party to the proceedings and any person affected by any action taken by the interim receiver, or who may be affected by any action proposed to be taken by him, may at any time apply to the court for directions as to the exercise of the interim receiver's functions.

(2) Before giving any directions under subsection (1), the court must (as well as giving the parties to the proceedings an opportunity to be heard) give such an opportunity to the interim receiver and to any person who may be interested in the application.

(3) The court may at any time vary or set aside an interim receiving order.
(4) Before exercising any power under this Chapter to vary or set aside an interim receiving order, the court must (as well as giving the parties to the proceedings an opportunity to be heard) give such an opportunity to the interim receiver and to any person who may be affected by the court's decision.

DEFINITIONS
  "the Court": s.316
  "interim receiving order": s.316, s.246(2)

GENERAL NOTE
  See General Note to s.247 above.

252   Restrictions on dealing etc. with property

(1) An interim receiving order must, subject to any exclusions made in accordance with this section, prohibit any person to whose property the order applies from dealing with the property.
(2) Exclusions may be made when the interim receiving order is made or on an application to vary the order.
(3) An exclusion may, in particular, make provision for the purpose of enabling any person—
    (a) to meet his reasonable living expenses, or
    (b) to carry on any trade, business, profession or occupation,
    and may be made subject to conditions.
(4) But an exclusion may not be made for the purpose of enabling any person to meet any legal expenses in respect of proceedings under this Part.
(5) If the excluded property is not specified in the order it must be described in the order in general terms.
(6) The power to make exclusions must be exercised with a view to ensuring, so far as practicable, that the satisfaction of any right of the enforcement authority to recover the property obtained through unlawful conduct is not unduly prejudiced.

DEFINITIONS
  "interim receiving order": s.316, s.246(2)
  "property": s.316(4)
  "property obtained through unlawful conduct": s.316, s.242

GENERAL NOTE
    This section should be read in conjunction with s.246 above. The purpose of an interim receiving order is to freeze both 'recoverable property' and 'associated property', and therefore it makes obvious sense for the court to prohibit any person who holds an interest in the property from dealing with it. This is subject to exclusions ordered by the court pursuant to s.252(2)-(5). Typical exclusions relate to assets released to meet 'reasonable living expenses', or 'to carry on any trade, business, profession or occupation'. The court has to strike a balance between the right of the Director to recovery the proceeds of crime, and protecting the interests of persons who hold an interest in the relevant property. At this stage the court has not made an express finding that the property was obtained through unlawful conduct – this is an interlocutory stage. However, it should be noted that the persons affected by an interim receiving order are not just the respondent in respect of his 'recoverable property' but third parties who hold 'associated property' that is not excluded from the order.
    This section was the subject of detailed debate in the House of Lords (*Hansard*, May 13, 2002, col.108) and the subject of amendments that were either not moved or withdrawn (e.g. Amendment No.216). The thrust of the amendments was that third parties should be placed under less restriction than the respondent in respect of their own property. The Government's position, in short, is that the court has a wide discretion to make exclusions in respect of expenditure reasonably incurred.

There will be difficult issues as to what are 'reasonable living expenses' – presumably, regard must be had to the lifestyle of the person seeking the exclusion before the interim order was made.

By s.252(4), an exclusion may not be made for the purpose of enabling a person to meet legal expenses in respect of proceedings under Pt. 5. This seems to envisage that exclusions may be made to fund legal costs in respect of proceedings other than under Pt.5. The issue of releasing funds for legal expenses was explained in some detail by the Attorney General in the House of Lords (*Hansard*, May 13 2002, col.112):

"Funding will be made available to respondents and third parties in civil recovery proceedings. In order to be granted public funding, they will need to satisfy a means test and a merits test. Parties to civil recovery proceedings will need to meet the standard means test, but the standard merits test will be relaxed to the extent necessary to ensure that everyone has access to legal funding who needs it and who qualifies financially. So there should not be a problem because the legal costs should be met either out of assets which are not subject to the receiving order or through legal aid with the adjustment to the merits test to which I have referred . . . .If the director loses the case, the court will be able to order him to pay the respondent's legal costs. That will be towards the end of the process but it is still a very important procedure. Compensation is also payable under provisions in the Bill . . . "

Under previous confiscation legislation, monies released to pay for legal costs could and sometimes did, bite heavily into the pool of restrained funds. The High Court has been able to oversee the level of fees claimed or paid to lawyers in respect of confiscation cases, but the new scheme is intended to minimise legal costs (if public funds are involved) but a party will still be able to privately instruct a lawyer out of unfrozen assets (whether held by the party concerned or by family and friends). This might expose the Government to the complaint that those with access to a wide circle of wealth will be more likely to secure the more talented lawyers on a privately funded basis.

Subs. (5)

The purpose of this subsection was explained by the Attorney General (*Hansard*, May 13, 2002, col.114):

" 'General' does not mean uncertainty. It simply means that the order need not be turned into an unwieldy list, as might otherwise be thought to be the position . . . .Therefore, a generic description can be given. Of course it will need to be sufficiently certain and precise. However, it might, for example, allow for the release of a sum of money without having to specify which notes or coins that should entail. That must be sensible. That is the reason for the inclusion of the subsection."

253   Restriction on proceedings and remedies

(1) While an interim receiving order has effect—
    (a) the court may stay any action, execution or other legal process in respect of the property to which the order applies,
    (b) no distress may be levied against the property to which the order applies except with the leave of the court and subject to any terms the court may impose.

(2) If a court (whether the High Court or any other court) in which proceedings are pending in respect of any property is satisfied that an interim receiving order has been applied for or made in respect of the property, the court may either stay the proceedings or allow them to continue on any terms it thinks fit.

(3) If the interim receiving order applies to a tenancy of any premises, no landlord or other person to whom rent is payable may exercise any right of forfeiture by peaceable re-entry in relation to the premises in respect of any failure by the tenant to comply with any term or condition of the tenancy, except with the leave of the court and subject to any terms the court may impose.

(4) Before exercising any power conferred by this section, the court must (as well as giving the parties to any of the proceedings in question an opportunity to be heard) give such an opportunity to the interim receiver (if appointed) and any person who may be affected by the court's decision.

DEFINITIONS
"interim receiving order": s.316, s.246(2)
"property": s.316(4)
"the Court": s.316

GENERAL NOTE
At the time an interim receiving order is made, there may be collateral legal proceedings in existence or taken in respect of the property. This has been problematic in previous confiscation legislation where, for example, the wife of a respondent charged with a criminal offence, is pursuing a divorce and seeks property orders in respect of restrained assets. The issue is whether the Court must preserve assets for the purpose of satisfying a confiscation order even if that might defeat orders that would otherwise be made in favour of a third party. The effect of s.253 is to give the High Court, and a court in which collateral proceeds exist, discretion to stay or to allow collateral proceedings to continue: and see *HMCE v. MCA* [2002] EWCA Civ. 1039. What is not entirely clear is what should happen in the event that courts conflict as to whether proceedings should be stayed or continued.

254 Exclusion of property which is not recoverable etc.

(1) If the court decides that any property to which an interim receiving order applies is neither recoverable property nor associated property, it must vary the order so as to exclude it.

(2) The court may vary an interim receiving order so as to exclude from the property to which the order applies any property which is alleged to be associated property if the court thinks that the satisfaction of any right of the enforcement authority to recover the property obtained through unlawful conduct will not be prejudiced.

(3) The court may exclude any property within subsection (2) on any terms or conditions, applying while the interim receiving order has effect, which the court thinks necessary or expedient.

DEFINITIONS
"associated property": s.316(1), s.245
"enforcement authority": s.316
"interim receiving order": s.316, s.246(2)
"property": s.316(4)
"the Court": s.316

GENERAL NOTE
See the General Note to ss.246 and 247.

255 Reporting

(1) An interim receiving order must require the interim receiver to inform the enforcement authority and the court as soon as reasonably practicable if he thinks that—
   (a) any property to which the order applies by virtue of a claim that it is recoverable property is not recoverable property,
   (b) any property to which the order applies by virtue of a claim that it is associated property is not associated property,
   (c) any property to which the order does not apply is recoverable property (in relation to the same unlawful conduct) or associated property, or
   (d) any property to which the order applies is held by a person who is different from the person it is claimed holds it,
   or if he thinks that there has been any other material change of circumstances.

(2) An interim receiving order must require the interim receiver—
   (a) to report his findings to the court,
   (b) to serve copies of his report on the enforcement authority and on any person who holds any property to which the order applies or who may otherwise be affected by the report.

D<small>EFINITIONS</small>
  "associated property": s.316(1), s.245
  "recoverable property": s.316(1); ss.304 to 310.
  "the Court": s.316
  "unlawful conduct": s.316(1), s.241

G<small>ENERAL</small> N<small>OTE</small>
  Read this section in conjunction with s.247, and s.341. By virtue of Part 8 of the Act, the Director has power to carry out a 'civil recovery investigation' (see s.341(2)), which means that he may ascertain whether property is recoverable, who holds it, the whereabouts of that property, and the extent of that property. Significantly, s.341(3) states that an investigation ceases in cases where "an interim receiving order applies to the property in question" (s.341(3)(b)). In other words, before the Director successfully applies for an interim receiving order, the Director may investigate matters relating to recoverable property but thereafter, the Director loses those powers and the interim receiver takes over those tasks under the supervision of the Court. Section 255 is therefore part of that supervisory process.

Interim administration orders (Scotland)

256   Application for interim administration order

(1) Where the enforcement authority may take proceedings for a recovery order in the Court of Session, the authority may apply to the court for an interim administration order (whether before or after starting the proceedings).

(2) An interim administration order is an order for—
  (a) the detention, custody or preservation of property, and
  (b) the appointment of an interim administrator.

(3) An application for an interim administration order may be made without notice if the circumstances are such that notice of the application would prejudice any right of the enforcement authority to obtain a recovery order in respect of any property.

(4) The court may make an interim administration order on the application if it is satisfied that the conditions in subsections (5) and, where applicable, (6) are met.

(5) The first condition is that there is a probabilis causa litigandi—
  (a) that the property to which the application for the order relates is or includes recoverable property, and
  (b) that, if any of it is not recoverable property, it is associated property.

(6) The second condition is that, if—
  (a) the property to which the application for the order relates includes property alleged to be associated property, and
  (b) the enforcement authority has not established the identity of the person who holds it,
  the authority has taken all reasonable steps to do so.

(7) In its application for an interim administration order, the enforcement authority must nominate a suitably qualified person for appointment as interim administrator, but the nominee may not be a member of the staff of the Scottish Administration.

(8) The extent of the power to make an interim administration order is not limited by sections 257 to 264.

G<small>ENERAL</small> N<small>OTE</small>

Subs. (1)
  Where the enforcement authority may take proceedings. See s.244.
  The authority may apply. Note that the conditions in subss (5) and(6) require to be met. The application may be made before the proceedings for a recovery order are commenced.

Subs. (2)

An interim administration order may be thought of as the equivalent of a restraint order (as to which, see ss.119 to 127) with a management administrator; but only as its equivalent – the two are not the same. In particular, note the investigative duty imposed on an interim administrator by s.257(2).

Subs. (3).

If the circumstances are such that notice … would prejudice any right … to obtain a recovery order. By s.244(3) the property in respect of which an order is sought must be specified or at least described in general terms. There is an obvious risk that alerting the respondent would allow him a chance to divest himself of or conceal the property.

Subs. (7)

Paragraph 323 of the Explanatory Notes explains that "The interim administrator on appointment becomes an officer of the court and his functions (set out in (s.257)) require him to act to secure the detention, custody or preservation of the property pending resolution of its fate.

257 Functions of interim administrator

(1) An interim administration order may authorise or require the interim administrator—
    (a) to exercise any of the powers mentioned in Schedule 6,
    (b) to take any other steps the court thinks appropriate,
for the purpose of securing the detention, custody or preservation of the property to which the order applies or of taking any steps under subsection (2).

(2) An interim administration order must require the interim administrator to take any steps which the court thinks necessary to establish—
    (a) whether or not the property to which the order applies is recoverable property or associated property,
    (b) whether or not any other property is recoverable property (in relation to the same unlawful conduct) and, if it is, who holds it.

(3) If—
    (a) the interim administrator deals with any property which is not property to which the order applies, and
    (b) at the time he deals with the property he believes on reasonable grounds that he is entitled to do so in pursuance of the order,
the interim administrator is not liable to any person in respect of any loss or damage resulting from his dealing with the property except so far as the loss or damage is caused by his negligence.

GENERAL NOTE

The Government's intentions as regards this section are well explained in paras 324 to 328 of the Explanatory Notes:

"The detailed functions of an interim administrator will be conferred by the court's order itself. The court's discretion to confer whatever powers it considers appropriate to the circumstances of an individual case are at large, provided always they are for the purpose set out at subss.(1) and (2). Up until the interim administration order, or the raising of proceedings (whichever comes first), the Scottish Ministers have access to the civil investigation powers set out in Pt. 8. Thereafter, they cease to have access to these powers and the duty of taking whatever further steps are needed to establish the facts about the property is placed upon the interim administrator acting under the Court's direction. Sched.6, which is introduced by subs.(1)(a), makes explicit mention of some of the more significant powers that the court may choose to confer on an interim administrator … Although the court has a wide discretion over the powers and functions which may be conferred on an interim administrator, there are some duties under which he must always be placed. Subsection (2) sets these out. He will always be required to take the necessary steps to establish:
- whether in his view the property is to any extent recoverable or associated property, and
- whether there is any other property which is recoverable in relation to the same unlawful conduct.

Subsection (3) provides legal protection for the interim administrator if he mistakenly, but honestly and reasonably, deals with property which is not the property specified in the order. He will have immunity from any legal claims in respect of loss or damage caused by such dealing, unless it can be shown that it was caused by his negligence".

Particular note should be taken of the investigative duty imposed on the administrator by subs. (2). The fruits of that investigation are likely to be of considerable significance in any Proof in connection with the application for a recovery order.

258   Inhibition of property affected by order

(1) On the application of the enforcement authority, the Court of Session may, in relation to the property mentioned in subsection (2), grant warrant for inhibition against any person specified in an interim administration order.

(2) That property is heritable property situated in Scotland to which the interim administration order applies (whether generally or such of it as is specified in the application).

(3) The warrant for inhibition—

(a) has effect as if granted on the dependence of an action for debt by the enforcement authority against the person and may be executed, recalled, loosed or restricted accordingly, and

(b) has the effect of letters of inhibition and must forthwith be registered by the enforcement authority in the register of inhibitions and adjudications.

(4) Section 155 of the Titles to Land Consolidation (Scotland) Act 1868 (c. 101) (effective date of inhibition) applies in relation to an inhibition for which warrant is granted under subsection (1) as it applies to an inhibition by separate letters or contained in a summons.

(5) The execution of an inhibition under this section in respect of property does not prejudice the exercise of an interim administrator's powers under or for the purposes of this Part in respect of that property.

(6) An inhibition executed under this section ceases to have effect when, or in so far as, the interim administration order ceases to apply in respect of the property in relation to which the warrant for inhibition was granted.

(7) If an inhibition ceases to have effect to any extent by virtue of subsection (6) the enforcement authority must—

(a) apply for the recall or, as the case may be, the restriction of the inhibition, and

(b) ensure that the recall or restriction is reflected in the register of inhibitions and adjudications.

GENERAL NOTE

This section empowers the court to grant warrant for inhibition, as if on the dependence of an action for debt. The wording "against any person specified in an interim administration order", combined with subs. (2), suggests that inhibition will be available even before the institution of proceedings for a recovery order.

259   Duties of respondent etc.

(1) An interim administration order may require any person to whose property the order applies—

(a) to bring the property to a place (in Scotland) specified by the interim administrator or place it in the custody of the interim administrator (if, in either case, he is able to do so),

(b) to do anything he is reasonably required to do by the interim administrator for the preservation of the property.

(2) An interim administration order may require any person to whose property the order applies to bring any documents relating to the property which are in his possession or control to a place (in Scotland) specified by the interim administrator or to place them in the custody of the interim administrator.

"Document" means anything in which information of any description is recorded.

GENERAL NOTE
Given the duty of investigation which is laid on the interim administrator by s.257, it is entirely conceivable that he will discover property which was not known to exist when the interim administration order was obtained. It is not clear whether the property affected by subs.(1)(a) of the present section must be specified in the interim administration order or whether it will me enough that it is described in general terms. If the former, it is to be noted that s.260 makes provision for the variation of the order.

260   Supervision of interim administrator and variation of order

(1) The interim administrator, any party to the proceedings and any person affected by any action taken by the interim administrator, or who may be affected by any action proposed to be taken by him, may at any time apply to the court for directions as to the exercise of the interim administrator's functions.

(2) Before giving any directions under subsection (1), the court must (as well as giving the parties to the proceedings an opportunity to be heard) give such an opportunity to the interim administrator and to any person who may be interested in the application.

(3) The court may at any time vary or recall an interim administration order.

(4) Before exercising any power under this Chapter to vary or set aside an interim administration order, the court must (as well as giving the parties to the proceedings an opportunity to be heard) give such an opportunity to the interim administrator and to any person who may be affected by the court's decision.

GENERAL NOTE
This section does two distinct things. First, it makes it possible to apply to the court for directions as to the exercise of the interim administrator's functions; and, second, it empowers the court to vary or recall an interim administration order. The two are not necessarily related. The section does not say who may apply for variation or recall. One can see readily enough that the interim administrator might require to do so in connection with requiring the repatriation of property in terms of s.259; and equally readily that the respondent might require to do so in order to secure exclusions of the sort contemplated by s.261.

261   Restrictions on dealing etc. with property

(1) An interim administration order must, subject to any exclusions made in accordance with this section, prohibit any person to whose property the order applies from dealing with the property.

(2) Exclusions may be made when the interim administration order is made or on an application to vary the order.

(3) An exclusion may, in particular, make provision for the purpose of enabling any person—
   (a) to meet his reasonable living expenses, or
   (b) to carry on any trade, business, profession or occupation,
   and may be made subject to conditions.

(4) But an exclusion may not be made for the purpose of enabling any person to meet any legal expenses in respect of proceedings under this Part.

(5) If the excluded property is not specified in the order it must be described in the order in general terms.

(6) The power to make exclusions must be exercised with a view to ensuring, so far as practicable, that the satisfaction of any right of the enforcement authority to recover the property obtained through unlawful conduct is not unduly prejudiced.

GENERAL NOTE
Compare with this section the provisions of s.121. It is not yet clear whether the case law on the variation of restraint orders in connection with criminal confiscation (for example, to permit living expenses to be met) will apply to exclusions under this section.

262   Restriction on proceedings and remedies

(1) While an interim administration order has effect, the court may sist any action, execution or other legal process in respect of the property to which the order applies.

(2) If a court (whether the Court of Session or any other court) in which proceedings are pending in respect of any property is satisfied that an interim administration order has been applied for or made in respect of the property, the court may either sist the proceedings or allow them to continue on any terms it thinks fit.

(3) Before exercising any power conferred by this section, the court must (as well as giving the parties to any of the proceedings in question an opportunity to be heard) give such an opportunity to the interim administrator (if appointed) and any person who may be affected by the court's decision.

GENERAL NOTE
The need to preserve property for recovery carries with it an obvious need to bring about a pause in any legal proceedings relating to that property and this section makes it possible for courts to sist such proceedings.

263   Exclusion of property which is not recoverable etc.

(1) If the court decides that any property to which an interim administration order applies is neither recoverable property nor associated property, it must vary the order so as to exclude it.

(2) The court may vary an interim administration order so as to exclude from the property to which the order applies any property which is alleged to be associated property if the court thinks that the satisfaction of any right of the enforcement authority to recover the property obtained through unlawful conduct will not be prejudiced.

(3) The court may exclude any property within subsection (2) on any terms or conditions, applying while the interim administration order has effect, which the court thinks necessary or expedient.

GENERAL NOTE

Subs. (1)
This subsection leaves the court no discretion and that is clearly right and proper where the court has decided that the property in question is neither recoverable property nor associated property. Paragraph 335 of the Explanatory Notes contemplates that such a decision may be based on an application by a person who may be affected by the court's order or a report by an interim administrator. One can imagine that the latter possibility would present the court with fewer difficulties than the former.

Subs. (2)
Associated property, in terms of s.245, is property which is not itself the recoverable property but is, in one of five specified ways, related to it. Often the interest in that property will be that of a person other than the respondent in the proceedings for a recovery order and in some cases (for example, where there is a standard security securing a loan made *bona fide* in relation to heritable property) it will be possible to separate it off. In such cases, the Court may (the power is discretionary) exclude the associated property. No doubt each case will have to be looked at on its own facts.

264   Reporting

(1) An interim administration order must require the interim administrator to inform the enforcement authority and the court as soon as reasonably practicable if he thinks that—
    (a) any property to which the order applies by virtue of a claim that it is recoverable property is not recoverable property,
    (b) any property to which the order applies by virtue of a claim that it is associated property is not associated property,
    (c) any property to which the order does not apply is recoverable property (in relation to the same unlawful conduct) or associated property, or
    (d) any property to which the order applies is held by a person who is different from the person it is claimed holds it,
    or if he thinks that there has been any other material change of circumstances.

(2) An interim administration order must require the interim administrator—
    (a) to report his findings to the court,
    (b) to serve copies of his report on the enforcement authority and on any person who holds any property to which the order applies or who may otherwise be affected by the report.

GENERAL NOTE
    Note that para. 337 of the Explanatory Notes states that the interim administrator's report "may comprise a comprehensive account of the nature and origins of, and interests in, the property in question. It will be capable of being used as a basis to establish agreed facts and to identify disputed matters that will fall to be resolved at the final hearing".

265   Arrestment of property affected by interim administration order

(1) On the application of the enforcement authority or the interim administrator the Court of Session may, in relation to moveable recoverable property to which an interim administration order applies (whether generally or such of it as is specified in the application), grant warrant for arrestment.

(2) An application by the enforcement authority under subsection (1) may be made at the same time as the application for the interim administration order or at any time thereafter.

(3) Such a warrant for arrestment may be granted only if the property would be arrestable if the person entitled to it were a debtor.

(4) A warrant under subsection (1) has effect as if granted on the dependence of an action for debt at the instance of the enforcement authority or, as the case may be, the interim administrator against the person and may be executed, recalled, loosed or restricted accordingly.

(5) The execution of an arrestment under this section in respect of property does not prejudice the exercise of an interim administrator's powers under or for the purposes of this Part in respect of that property.

(6) An arrestment executed under this section ceases to have effect when, or in so far as, the interim administration order ceases to apply in respect of the property in relation to which the warrant for arrestment was granted.

(7) If an arrestment ceases to have effect to any extent by virtue of subsection (6) the enforcement authority or, as the case may be, the interim administrator must apply to the Court of Session for an order recalling or, as the case may be, restricting the arrestment.

GENERAL NOTE
This section empowers the court to grant warrant for arrestment in relation to moveable recoverable property, as if on the dependence of an action for debt.

Vesting and realisation of recoverable property

266 Recovery orders

(1) If in proceedings under this Chapter the court is satisfied that any property is recoverable, the court must make a recovery order.
(2) The recovery order must vest the recoverable property in the trustee for civil recovery.
(3) But the court may not make in a recovery order—
   (a) any provision in respect of any recoverable property if each of the conditions in subsection (4) or (as the case may be) (5) is met and it would not be just and equitable to do so, or
   (b) any provision which is incompatible with any of the Convention rights (within the meaning of the Human Rights Act 1998 (c. 42)).
(4) In relation to a court in England and Wales or Northern Ireland, the conditions referred to in subsection (3)(a) are that—
   (a) the respondent obtained the recoverable property in good faith,
   (b) he took steps after obtaining the property which he would not have taken if he had not obtained it or he took steps before obtaining the property which he would not have taken if he had not believed he was going to obtain it,
   (c) when he took the steps, he had no notice that the property was recoverable,
   (d) if a recovery order were made in respect of the property, it would, by reason of the steps, be detrimental to him.
(5) In relation to a court in Scotland, the conditions referred to in subsection (3)(a) are that—
   (a) the respondent obtained the recoverable property in good faith,
   (b) he took steps after obtaining the property which he would not have taken if he had not obtained it or he took steps before obtaining the property which he would not have taken if he had not believed he was going to obtain it,
   (c) when he took the steps, he had no reasonable grounds for believing that the property was recoverable,
   (d) if a recovery order were made in respect of the property, it would, by reason of the steps, be detrimental to him.
(6) In deciding whether it would be just and equitable to make the provision in the recovery order where the conditions in subsection (4) or (as the case may be) (5) are met, the court must have regard to—
   (a) the degree of detriment that would be suffered by the respondent if the provision were made,
   (b) the enforcement authority's interest in receiving the realised proceeds of the recoverable property.
(7) A recovery order may sever any property.
(8) A recovery order may impose conditions as to the manner in which the trustee for civil recovery may deal with any property vested by the order for the purpose of realising it.
(9) This section is subject to sections 270 to 278.

DEFINITIONS
"associated property": s.316(1), s.245
"property": s.316(4)

"recoverable property": s.316(1); ss.304 to 310.
"the Court": s.316
"trustee for civil recovery": s.267(1)

GENERAL NOTE
   This section should be read in conjunction with ss.241, 242 (property obtained through unlawful conduct), ss.304-310 (recoverable property), s.316 (interpretation), s.276 (consent orders), s.278 (limit on the recovery of property), and ss.281-282 (victims of theft and other exemptions).
   The statute provides that as a general rule, all property obtained through unlawful conduct is 'recoverable property'. 'Unlawful conduct' is defined by s.241 and the property must have been obtained by a person in the circumstances described in s.242 (contrast with the definition of 'benefit' for the purposes of Pt.2: see s.76(4)).
   If the court is satisfied that property is recoverable, it *must* make a 'recovery order'. The effect of that order is to vest the property in the 'trustee for civil recovery' (see s.266(2), s.267 and sch.7). However, although many cases will be contested, s.276 empowers the Court to order that proceedings for a recovery order be stayed on terms agreed by the parties for the disposal of the proceedings, if each person (whose property is the subject of proceedings) is both a party to the proceedings and to the agreement. The court has wide discretion to make appropriate orders as part of a consent order: s.276(2)(b). It follows that consent orders can only be made with the approval of the court and subject to the court examining the terms of the proposed order. This is to ensure that consent orders are fair and appropriate.
   The making of a recovery order will be relatively straightforward if all that has to be recovered is "original property" (see s.305(1)) obtained from unlawful conduct (e.g. a stolen painting found in the hands of the thief).
   Frequently, original property will have been passed on to another (e.g. the handler of stolen goods). In such cases, the original property may be followed into his hands by virtue of s.304(3), because it was obtained by the handler, on disposal of it by the thief. Similarly, by virtue of s.304(3)(b) it may be followed down a line of handlers because each obtained it "on disposal by ... a person into whose hands it may ... be followed." What is therefore being followed is the 'original property'.
   However, the thief might swap a valuable stolen painting for a car. By s.305(2), the car "represents the original property" and the car may be followed in the same way as the original painting (s.305(3)). Furthermore, the car also becomes 'recoverable property' (s.305(1)). If the car is then swapped for a boat, s.305 repeats the process, so that the painting, the car and the boat, become traceable and 'recoverable property'. Where recoverable property is mixed with other property, the proportion of the mixed property "which is attributable to the recoverable property represents the property obtained through unlawful conduct" (s.306(2)). That takes one back to s.305(1), and a similar approach applies to accruing profits (s.307).
   Thus in each of the above cases, the property is recoverable. However, there are general exceptions set out in s.308. If any of those exceptions apply, the property ceases to be 'recoverable property'. For example, property purchased in good faith without notice of its illicit origin, ceases to be recoverable: s.308(1).
   Complex cases are likely to involve a network of transactions that lead to many items of property. Each line of transactions, starts with an item of 'original property'. Branches may emerge from that line that reveal the existence of other items of property that represent the original property ("representative property" – see s.305(2)). The Director is not permitted to recover all of this property but to recover either the original property (if it still exists and if he can recover it), or so much of the representative property as equates to the value of the original property: see s.278. Section 278 enacts rules relating to situations in which a recovery order may be made and sets limits on the Director's ability to recover items of property.
   Section 266 provides further safeguards so that a court may not make provision in a recovery order that would violate the HRA 1998 or the ECHR (s.266(3)). Again, a court may not make provision in an order if it would not be equitable to do so in the circumstances specified in s.266(4): for example, a person obtained recoverable property in good faith (a car) and he used it in good faith (e.g. he modified the engine and put on alloy wheels) and a recovery order would be detrimental to him: see s.266(4). By s.281, a person who claims that an item of property belongs to him, may apply for a declaration to that effect. If the application is successful, the property is not recoverable. Such a person must show that he was deprived of that property by unlawful conduct: s.281(3)(a).
   A 'recovery order' may sever any property: s.266(7). Note that 'recoverable property' is to be distinguished from 'associated property' (see s.245, and see the annotations in respect of that section). In practice, property will often include recoverable property held by the respondent and linked interests ('associated property') held by third parties. The object of s.266(7) – read in conjunction with ss.271 and 272 – is that the court is given power to make orders that enable the

trustee for civil recovery to realise property obtained through unlawful conduct whilst preserving the value of the interest of a third party.

267 Functions of the trustee for civil recovery

(1) The trustee for civil recovery is a person appointed by the court to give effect to a recovery order.
(2) The enforcement authority must nominate a suitably qualified person for appointment as the trustee.
(3) The functions of the trustee are—
    (a) to secure the detention, custody or preservation of any property vested in him by the recovery order,
    (b) in the case of property other than money, to realise the value of the property for the benefit of the enforcement authority, and
    (c) to perform any other functions conferred on him by virtue of this Chapter.
(4) In performing his functions, the trustee acts on behalf of the enforcement authority and must comply with any directions given by the authority.
(5) The trustee is to realise the value of property vested in him by the recovery order, so far as practicable, in the manner best calculated to maximise the amount payable to the enforcement authority.
(6) The trustee has the powers mentioned in Schedule 7.
(7) References in this section to a recovery order include an order under section 276 and references to property vested in the trustee by a recovery order include property vested in him in pursuance of an order under section 276.

DEFINITIONS
"enforcement authority": s.316
"property": s.316(4)
"recovery order": s.316(1), s.266
"trustee for civil recovery": s.267(1)

GENERAL NOTE
This section should be read in conjunction with Sched.7. The trustee's aim is to realise property in a manner best calculated to maximise the amount payable to the Director of ARA (see s.267(5)). To this end, the Act gives the trustee the powers set out in Sched.7 and he acts on behalf of the Director of ARA. Therefore, the trustee must comply with the directions of the Director: s.267(4).

268 Recording of recovery order (Scotland)

(1) The clerk of the court must immediately after the making of a recovery order which relates to heritable property situated in Scotland send a certified copy of it to the keeper of the register of inhibitions and adjudications for recording in that register.
(2) Recording under subsection (1) is to have the effect, as from the date of the recovery order, of an inhibition at the instance of the trustee for civil recovery against the person in whom the heritable property was vest prior to that date.

269 Rights of pre-emption, etc.

(1) A recovery order is to have effect in relation to any property despite any provision (of whatever nature) which would otherwise prevent, penalise or restrict the vesting of the property.
(2) A right of pre-emption, right of irritancy, right of return or other similar right does not operate or become exercisable as a result of the vesting of any property under a recovery order.
A right of return means any right under a provision for the return or reversion of property in specified circumstances.

(3) Where property is vested under a recovery order, any such right is to have effect as if the person in whom the property is vested were the same person in law as the person who held the property and as if no transfer of the property had taken place.

(4) References to rights in subsections (2) and (3) do not include any rights in respect of which the recovery order was made.

(5) This section applies in relation to the creation of interests, or the doing of anything else, by a recovery order as it applies in relation to the vesting of property.

DEFINITIONS
"property": s.316(4)
"recovery order": s.316(1), s.266

GENERAL NOTE
The section is explained by the Government in the Explanatory Notes to this Act. In summary, the effect of the section is that a recovery order will override provisions that would otherwise prevent, or limit, the vesting of property in the trustee. The example given is that of person who has a "right-to-buy" option on property. That right will not be immediately exercisable so as to prevent the property vesting in the trustee, but it will become exercisable as soon as the trustee decides to sell the property.

270   Associated and joint property

(1) Sections 271 and 272 apply if the court makes a recovery order in respect of any recoverable property in a case within subsection (2) or (3).

(2) A case is within this subsection if—
   (a) the property to which the proceedings relate includes property which is associated with the recoverable property and is specified or described in the claim form or (in Scotland) application, and
   (b) if the associated property is not the respondent's property, the claim form or application has been served on the person whose property it is or the court has dispensed with service.

(3) A case is within this subsection if—
   (a) the recoverable property belongs to joint tenants, and
   (b) one of the tenants is an excepted joint owner.

(4) An excepted joint owner is a person who obtained the property in circumstances in which it would not be recoverable as against him; and references to the excepted joint owner's share of the recoverable property are to so much of the recoverable property as would have been his if the joint tenancy had been severed.

(5) Subsections (3) and (4) do not extend to Scotland.

DEFINITIONS
"associated property": s. 316(1), s. 245
"claim form": s.243
"recoverable property": s.316(1); ss.304 to 310.

GENERAL NOTE
See annotations in respect of s.266. This section should be read in conjunction with ss.245, 266, 271 and 272.

A recover order may affect property that has mixed interests, that is to say, the respondent holds an interest that is 'recoverable property' but there are other linked interests held by innocent third parties (associated property), or where property is held by two or more persons as if they were one (i.e. jointly). It would obviously be unjust if the court could recover property (or its value) that should remain with a third party. Without express provision, joint tenants create potential legal difficulties under the Act because joint tenants are treated as a single owner of property. For example, the respondent and his wife might be joint tenants of property that was acquired by each drawing from their own resources to meet the purchase price. It is the respondent's contribution that ought to be recoverable. Subsections (3) and (4) are intended to ensure that in such a case the third party is an "excepted joint owner" against whom property is not recoverable.

The associated property might relate to a house in which the freehold is held by the respondent but third parties hold tenancies in the same property. The trustee could insist that the property be vested in him so that he might sell the property. This could produce harsh results on the third parties. Section 271 permit agreements to be reached so that the tenants might combine to buy the freehold and make a payment to the trustee for civil recovery in lieu of the recoverable property. Other provisions in s.271 enable agreement to be reached as to payment to be made to third parties who have suffered loss as a result of an interim receiving order. Where it is not possible to reach agreement on the disposal of the property, which is the subject of a recovery order, s.272 is engaged. This enables the property to vest in the trustee for civil recovery but he may then make payments to third parties in lieu of their interests. There is also scope for a court to order that a third party should enjoy a right e.g. to live in a house for life. The court must take into account the interests of third parties, but to balance against such interests, the interest of the Director to recover the proceeds of unlawful conduct.

271   Agreements about associated and joint property

(1) Where—
    (a) this section applies, and
    (b) the enforcement authority (on the one hand) and the person who holds the associated property or who is the excepted joint owner (on the other) agree,
the recovery order may, instead of vesting the recoverable property in the trustee for civil recovery, require the person who holds the associated property or who is the excepted joint owner to make a payment to the trustee.

(2) A recovery order which makes any requirement under subsection (1) may, so far as required for giving effect to the agreement, include provision for vesting, creating or extinguishing any interest in property.

(3) The amount of the payment is to be the amount which the enforcement authority and that person agree represents—
    (a) in a case within section 270(2), the value of the recoverable property,
    (b) in a case within section 270(3), the value of the recoverable property less the value of the excepted joint owner's share.

(4) But if—
    (a) an interim receiving order or interim administration order applied at any time to the associated property or joint tenancy, and
    (b) the enforcement authority agrees that the person has suffered loss as a result of the interim receiving order or interim administration order,
the amount of the payment may be reduced by any amount the enforcement authority and that person agree is reasonable, having regard to that loss and to any other relevant circumstances.

(5) If there is more than one such item of associated property or excepted joint owner, the total amount to be paid to the trustee, and the part of that amount which is to be provided by each person who holds any such associated property or who is an excepted joint owner, is to be agreed between both (or all) of them and the enforcement authority.

(6) A recovery order which makes any requirement under subsection (1) must make provision for any recoverable property to cease to be recoverable.

<small>DEFINITIONS</small>
  "associated property": s. 316(1), s.245
  "enforcement authority": s.316
  "interim receiving order": s.316, s.246(2)
  "recoverable property": s.316(1); ss.304 to 310.

GENERAL NOTE
See the General Note to s.270.

272   Associated and joint property: default of agreement

(1) Where this section applies, the court may make the following provision if—
   (a) there is no agreement under section 271, and
   (b) the court thinks it just and equitable to do so.

(2) The recovery order may provide—
   (a) for the associated property to vest in the trustee for civil recovery
        or (as the case may be) for the excepted joint owner's interest to
        be extinguished, or
   (b) in the case of an excepted joint owner, for the severance of his
        interest.

(3) A recovery order making any provision by virtue of subsection (2)(a)
may provide—
   (a) for the trustee to pay an amount to the person who holds the
        associated property or who is an excepted joint owner, or
   (b) for the creation of interests in favour of that person, or the impo-
        sition of liabilities or conditions, in relation to the property vested
        in the trustee,
or for both.

(4) In making any provision in a recovery order by virtue of subsection (2)
or (3), the court must have regard to—
   (a) the rights of any person who holds the associated property or who
        is an excepted joint owner and the value to him of that property
        or, as the case may be, of his share (including any value which
        cannot be assessed in terms of money),
   (b) the enforcement authority's interest in receiving the realised pro-
        ceeds of the recoverable property.

(5) If—
   (a) an interim receiving order or interim administration order
        applied at any time to the associated property or joint tenancy,
        and
   (b) the court is satisfied that the person who holds the associated
        property or who is an excepted joint owner has suffered loss as a
        result of the interim receiving order or interim administration
        order,
a recovery order making any provision by virtue of subsection (2) or
(3) may require the enforcement authority to pay compensation to
that person.

(6) The amount of compensation to be paid under subsection (5) is the
amount the court thinks reasonable, having regard to the person's loss
and to any other relevant circumstances.

DEFINITIONS
   "associated property": s. 316(1), s.245
   "excepted joint owner": s.270(4)
   "recovery order": s.316(1), s.266

GENERAL NOTE
See the General Note to s.270.

273   Payments in respect of rights under pension schemes

(1) This section applies to recoverable property consisting of rights under
a pension scheme.

(2) A recovery order in respect of the property must, instead of vesting the property in the trustee for civil recovery, require the trustees or managers of the pension scheme—

   (a) to pay to the trustee for civil recovery within a prescribed period the amount determined by the trustees or managers to be equal to the value of the rights, and

   (b) to give effect to any other provision made by virtue of this section and the two following sections in respect of the scheme.

This subsection is subject to sections 276 to 278.

(3) A recovery order made by virtue of subsection (2) overrides the provisions of the pension scheme to the extent that they conflict with the provisions of the order.

(4) A recovery order made by virtue of subsection (2) may provide for the recovery by the trustees or managers of the scheme (whether by deduction from any amount which they are required to pay to the trustee for civil recovery or otherwise) of costs incurred by them in—

   (a) complying with the recovery order, or

   (b) providing information, before the order was made, to the enforcement authority, interim receiver or interim administrator.

(5) None of the following provisions applies to a court making a recovery order by virtue of subsection (2)—

   (a) any provision of section 159 of the Pension Schemes Act 1993 (c. 48), section 155 of the Pension Schemes (Northern Ireland) Act 1993 (c. 49), section 91 of the Pensions Act 1995 (c. 26) or Article 89 of the Pensions (Northern Ireland) Order 1995 (S.I. 1995/3213 (N.I. 22)) (which prevent assignment and the making of orders that restrain a person from receiving anything which he is prevented from assigning),

   (b) any provision of any enactment (whenever passed or made) corresponding to any of the provisions mentioned in paragraph (a),

   (c) any provision of the pension scheme in question corresponding to any of those provisions.

DEFINITIONS
"associated property": s. 316(1), s.245
"enforcement authority": s.316
"pension scheme": s.275(4)
"property": s.316(4)
"recovery order": s.316(1), s.266
"trustee for civil recovery": s.267(1)
"trustees or managers": s.275(5)

GENERAL NOTE

Rights in pension funds create special problems if those rights represent 'recoverable property' because such rights cannot be vested in the trustee for civil recovery and dealt with separately. Accordingly, by s.273(2)(a) the trustees or managers of the pension scheme must "pay to the trustee for civil recovery" an amount equal to the value of the rights held by the respondent. There already exist methods for valuing pension rights of individual beneficiaries under a pension scheme. Section 275(1) enables the Secretary of State to make Regulations regarding the method by which the value of pension rights may be calculated and verified.

If terms of the pension are in conflict with an order of the court, then the latter prevails: see s.273(3). Where the trustees of the pension fund incur costs either in complying with the recovery order or when supplying information, those costs may be recoverable under s.273(4). Costs may be repaid out of the sums paid to the trustee for civil recovery, or in some other way: s.273(4). The trustees will be required to make adjustments to the pension scheme to ensure that the respondent's benefit from the pension is reduced – perhaps to nil: see s.274.

The obligations on trustees to meet the requirements of the Act can be resolved by agreement under the terms of a consent order which meets with the approval of the court: s.277.

274   Consequential adjustment of liabilities under pension schemes

(1) A recovery order made by virtue of section 273(2) must require the trustees or managers of the pension scheme to make such reduction in the liabilities of the scheme as they think necessary in consequence of the payment made in pursuance of that subsection.

(2) Accordingly, the order must require the trustees or managers to provide for the liabilities of the pension scheme in respect of the respondent's recoverable property to which section 273 applies to cease.

(3) So far as the trustees or managers are required by the recovery order to provide for the liabilities of the pension scheme in respect of the respondent's recoverable property to which section 273 applies to cease, their powers include (in particular) power to reduce the amount of—

(a) any benefit or future benefit to which the respondent is or may be entitled under the scheme,

(b) any future benefit to which any other person may be entitled under the scheme in respect of that property.

DEFINITIONS
"pension scheme": s.275(4)
"recoverable property": ss.304 to 310
"the respondent": s.316(1)
"trustees or managers": s.275(5)

GENERAL NOTE
See the General Note to s.273 above.

275   Pension schemes: supplementary

(1) Regulations may make provision as to the exercise by trustees or managers of their powers under sections 273 and 274, including provision about the calculation and verification of the value at any time of rights or liabilities.

(2) The power conferred by subsection (1) includes power to provide for any values to be calculated or verified—

(a) in a manner which, in the particular case, is approved by a prescribed person, or

(b) in accordance with guidance from time to time prepared by a prescribed person.

(3) Regulations means regulations made by the Secretary of State after consultation with the Scottish Ministers; and prescribed means prescribed by regulations.

(4) A pension scheme means an occupational pension scheme or a personal pension scheme; and those expressions have the same meaning as in the Pension Schemes Act 1993 (c. 48) or, in relation to Northern Ireland, the Pension Schemes (Northern Ireland) Act 1993 (c. 49).

(5) In relation to an occupational pension scheme or a personal pension scheme, the trustees or managers means—

(a) in the case of a scheme established under a trust, the trustees,

(b) in any other case, the managers.

(6) References to a pension scheme include—

(a) a retirement annuity contract (within the meaning of Part 3 of the Welfare Reform and Pensions Act 1999 (c. 30) or, in relation to Northern Ireland, Part 4 of the Welfare Reform and Pensions (Northern Ireland) Order 1999),

(b) an annuity or insurance policy purchased, or transferred, for the purpose of giving effect to rights under an occupational pension scheme or a personal pension scheme,

    (c) an annuity purchased, or entered into, for the purpose of discharging any liability in respect of a pension credit under section 29(1)(b) of the Welfare Reform and Pensions Act 1999 (c. 30) or, in relation to Northern Ireland, Article 26(1)(b) of the Welfare Reform and Pensions (Northern Ireland) Order 1999.

(7) References to the trustees or managers—

    (a) in relation to a retirement annuity contract or other annuity, are to the provider of the annuity,

    (b) in relation to an insurance policy, are to the insurer.

(8) Subsections (3) to (7) have effect for the purposes of this group of sections (that is, sections 273 and 274 and this section).

DEFINITIONS
"trustees or managers": s.275(5)
"pension scheme": s.275(4)

GENERAL NOTE
See the General Note to s.273 above

276   Consent orders

(1) The court may make an order staying (in Scotland, sisting) any proceedings for a recovery order on terms agreed by the parties for the disposal of the proceedings if each person to whose property the proceedings, or the agreement, relates is a party both to the proceedings and the agreement.

(2) An order under subsection (1) may, as well as staying (or sisting) the proceedings on terms—

    (a) make provision for any property which may be recoverable property to cease to be recoverable,

    (b) make any further provision which the court thinks appropriate.

(3) Section 280 applies to property vested in the trustee for civil recovery, or money paid to him, in pursuance of the agreement as it applies to property vested in him by a recovery order or money paid under section 271.

DEFINITIONS
"recoverable property": ss.304 to 310
"recovery order": s.316(1), s.266
"property": s.316(4)
"the Court": s.316
"trustee for civil recovery": s.267(1)

GENERAL NOTE
Although many cases will be contested, s.276 empowers the Court to order that proceedings for a recovery order be stayed on terms agreed by the parties for the disposal of the proceedings, if each person (whose property is the subject to the proposed order) is both a party to the proceedings and to the agreement. The court has wide discretion to make appropriate orders as part of a consent order: s.276(2)(b). It follows that consent orders can only be made with the approval of the court and subject to the court examining the terms of the proposed order. This is to ensure that consent orders are fair and appropriate.

277   Consent orders: pensions

(1) This section applies where recoverable property to which proceedings under this Chapter relate includes rights under a pension scheme.

(2) An order made under section 276—

    (a) may not stay (in Scotland, sist) the proceedings on terms that the rights are vested in any other person, but

    (b) may include provision imposing the following requirement, if the trustees or managers of the scheme are parties to the agreement by virtue of which the order is made.

(3) The requirement is that the trustees or managers of the pension scheme—

    (a) make a payment in accordance with the agreement, and

    (b) give effect to any other provision made by virtue of this section in respect of the scheme.

(4) The trustees or managers of the pension scheme have power to enter into an agreement in respect of the proceedings on any terms on which an order made under section 276 may stay (in Scotland, sist) the proceedings.

(5) The following provisions apply in respect of an order under section 276, so far as it includes the requirement mentioned in subsection (3).

(6) The order overrides the provisions of the pension scheme to the extent that they conflict with the requirement.

(7) The order may provide for the recovery by the trustees or managers of the scheme (whether by deduction from any amount which they are required to pay in pursuance of the agreement or otherwise) of costs incurred by them in—

    (a) complying with the order, or

    (b) providing information, before the order was made, to the enforcement authority, interim receiver or interim administrator.

(8) Sections 273(5) and 274 (read with section 275) apply as if the requirement were included in an order made by virtue of section 273(2).

(9) Section 275(4) to (7) has effect for the purposes of this section.

DEFINITIONS

  "pension scheme": s.275(4)

  "recoverable property": ss.304 to 310

  "trustees or managers": s.275(5)

GENERAL NOTE

  This section should be read in conjunction with s.276. The obligations on trustees to meet the requirements of the Act can be resolved by agreement under the terms of a consent order which meets with the approval of the court: s.277. Note that the court will supervise the making of a consent order. Section 276 does not envisage that the parties will be able to agree terms out of court and then expect the Court to make the order merely on the say-so of the parties. The task of the court is to ensure that a consent order is fair and appropriate.

278   Limit on recovery

(1) This section applies if the enforcement authority seeks a recovery order—

    (a) in respect of both property which is or represents property obtained through unlawful conduct and related property, or

    (b) in respect of property which is or represents property obtained through unlawful conduct where such an order, or an order under section 276, has previously been made in respect of related property.

(2) For the purposes of this section—

    (a) the original property means the property obtained through unlawful conduct,

    (b) the original property, and any items of property which represent the original property, are to be treated as related to each other.

(3) The court is not to make a recovery order if it thinks that the enforcement authority's right to recover the original property has been satisfied by a previous recovery order or order under section 276.

(4) Subject to subsection (3), the court may act under subsection (5) if it thinks that—

    (a) a recovery order may be made in respect of two or more related items of recoverable property, but

    (b) the making of a recovery order in respect of both or all of them is not required in order to satisfy the enforcement authority's right to recover the original property.

(5) The court may in order to satisfy that right to the extent required make a recovery order in respect of—

    (a) only some of the related items of property, or

    (b) only a part of any of the related items of property,

or both.

(6) Where the court may make a recovery order in respect of any property, this section does not prevent the recovery of any profits which have accrued in respect of the property.

(7) If—

    (a) an order is made under section 298 for the forfeiture of recoverable property, and

    (b) the enforcement authority subsequently seeks a recovery order in respect of related property,

the order under section 298 is to be treated for the purposes of this section as if it were a recovery order obtained by the enforcement authority in respect of the forfeited property.

(8) If—

    (a) in pursuance of a judgment in civil proceedings (whether in the United Kingdom or elsewhere), the claimant has obtained property from the defendant ("the judgment property"),

    (b) the claim was based on the defendant's having obtained the judgment property or related property through unlawful conduct, and

    (c) the enforcement authority subsequently seeks a recovery order in respect of property which is related to the judgment property,

the judgment is to be treated for the purposes of this section as if it were a recovery order obtained by the enforcement authority in respect of the judgment property.

    In relation to Scotland, "claimant" and "defendant" are to be read as "pursuer" and "defender".

(9) If—

    (a) property has been taken into account in deciding the amount of a person's benefit from criminal conduct for the purpose of making a confiscation order, and

    (b) the enforcement authority subsequently seeks a recovery order in respect of related property,

the confiscation order is to be treated for the purposes of this section as if it were a recovery order obtained by the enforcement authority in respect of the property referred to in paragraph (a).

(10) In subsection (9), a confiscation order means—

    (a) an order under section 6, 92 or 156, or

    (b) an order under a corresponding provision of an enactment mentioned in section 8(7)(a) to (g),

and, in relation to an order mentioned in paragraph (b), the reference to the amount of a person's benefit from criminal conduct is to be read as a reference to the corresponding amount under the enactment in question.

DEFINITIONS

"associated property": s. 316(1), s.245
"enforcement authority": s.316
"original property": s.278(2)(a) and see s.305(1)
"property": s.316(4)
"property obtained through unlawful conduct": s.316(1), s.242
"property which represent the original property": s.305(2)
"recoverable property": ss.304 to 310
"related property": s.278(2)(b)

"the Court": s.316
"unlawful conduct": s.316(1), s.242

GENERAL NOTE

This section should be read in conjunction with s.279 (supplementary provisions), ss.241, 242 (property obtained through unlawful conduct), ss.304-310 (recoverable property), s.316 (interpretation), s.266 (recovery orders), and s.276 (consent orders).

The 2002 Act provides that as a general rule, all property obtained through unlawful conduct is 'recoverable property'. If the court is satisfied that property is recoverable, it *must* make a 'recovery order'. The effect of that order is to vest the property in the 'trustee for civil recovery' (see s.266(2), s.267 and sch.7). The making of a recovery order will be relatively straightforward if all that has to be recovered is "original property" (see s.305(1) and s.278(2)(a)) obtained from unlawful conduct (e.g. a stolen painting found in the hands of the thief).

Frequently, original property will have been passed to another. In such cases, the original property may be followed down the line of transactions (see s.304(3)) so that what is being followed remains the 'original property'. Property acquired in exchange for the original property, represents the original property ("representative property"). Representative property is itself traceable (s.305) and it is recoverable (s.305(1)). Where recoverable property is mixed with other property, the proportion of the mixed property "which is attributable to the recoverable property represents the property obtained through unlawful conduct" (s.306(2)) and becomes recoverable. A similar approach applies to accruing profits (s.307).

Complex cases are likely to involve a network of transactions that lead to many items of property of which some will be 'original property', and others representative property. The Director is not permitted to recover all of this property but to recover either the original property (if it still exists and if he can), or so much of the representative property as equates to the value of the original property. Section 278 enacts rules identifying situations in which a recovery order may be made and sets limits on the Director's ability to recover items of property

Subss. (1), (2)

Both s.278(2)(a) and s.305(1) describe property obtained through unlawful conduct as "original property".

Section 278 also refers to "related property" (see subs.(2)(b)). Original property and property that represents the original property are to be treated as "related to each other": s.278(2)(b). At first sight this might be thought to mean that 'related property' could be 'original property', or property that represents the original property, or both. However, the draftsman probably intended merely to draw a distinction between 'original property', and property that represents original property, in which case it might have been preferable for the section to say as much, or for the section to use the expression "representative property" rather than "related property": see s.279 that does speak of "representative property".

Subss. (3), (7), (8), (9) and (10)

These provisions are of similar effect. A court shall not make a recovery order if the original order (or its value) has been satisfied by way of a previous recovery order, or by way of a consent order (under s.276). Similarly, a court must not make a recovery order in respect of cash that has already been forfeited by summary process under s.298 (subs.(7)), or where property is the subject of the judgment of another court (subs.(8)), or where property is to realised under a confiscation order in criminal proceedings (subss.(9) and (10)).

Subss. (4), (5) and (6)

The court may recover one, two, or more, items of 'related property' but only to the extent necessary to recover the value of the 'original property'. Accordingly, the court is given wide power to make a recovery order in respect of some or all of the related items (see subs.(4)(a)) or only part or parts of the related items of property (subs.(4)(b)). The court can thus pick-and-mix, but only in a manner that is appropriate and fair.

Accrued profits may also be recovered (subs.(6)).

279   Section 278: supplementary

(1) Subsections (2) and (3) give examples of the satisfaction of the enforcement authority's right to recover the original property.

(2) If—

    (a) there is a disposal, other than a part disposal, of the original property, and

(b) other property (the representative property) is obtained in its place,

the enforcement authority's right to recover the original property is satisfied by the making of a recovery order in respect of either the original property or the representative property.

(3) If—

(a) there is a part disposal of the original property, and

(b) other property (the representative property) is obtained in place of the property disposed of,

the enforcement authority's right to recover the original property is satisfied by the making of a recovery order in respect of the remainder of the original property together with either the representative property or the property disposed of.

(4) In this section—

(a) a part disposal means a disposal to which section 314(1) applies,

(b) the original property has the same meaning as in section 278.

DEFINITIONS
"enforcement authority": s.316
"original property": s.278(2)(a) and see s.305(1)
"recovery order": s.316(1), s.266
"representative property": s.279(2)(b)

GENERAL NOTE
See the General Note to s.278 above.

280 Applying realised proceeds

(1) This section applies to—

(a) sums which represent the realised proceeds of property which was vested in the trustee for civil recovery by a recovery order or which he obtained in pursuance of a recovery order,

(b) sums vested in the trustee by a recovery order or obtained by him in pursuance of a recovery order.

(2) The trustee is to make out of the sums—

(a) first, any payment required to be made by him by virtue of section 272,

(b) second, any payment of expenses incurred by a person acting as an insolvency practitioner which are payable under this subsection by virtue of section 432(10),

and any sum which remains is to be paid to the enforcement authority.

DEFINITIONS
"enforcement authority": s.316
"recovery order": s.316(1), s.266
"trustee for civil recovery": s.267(1)

GENERAL NOTE
Section 280 regulates how monies obtained by the trustee in civil recovery shall be applied by the trustee. The monies might come to him as a result of a sale of property transferred to him for that purpose, or paid under the terms of an agreement or consent order, or by way of an amount equal to the value of the respondent's right in a pension scheme.

Exemptions etc.

281 Victims of theft, etc

(1) In proceedings for a recovery order, a person who claims that any property alleged to be recoverable property, or any part of the property, belongs to him may apply for a declaration under this section.

(2) If the applicant appears to the court to meet the following condition, the court may make a declaration to that effect.

(3) The condition is that—
    (a) the person was deprived of the property he claims, or of property which it represents, by unlawful conduct,
    (b) the property he was deprived of was not recoverable property immediately before he was deprived of it, and
    (c) the property he claims belongs to him.

(4) Property to which a declaration under this section applies is not recoverable property.

DEFINITIONS
"property": s.316(4)
"recovery order": s.316(1), s.266
"unlawful conduct": s.316(1), s.242

GENERAL NOTE
A person who claims that an item of property belongs to him, may apply for a declaration to that effect, and if the application is successful the property is not recoverable. Such a person must show that he was deprived of that property by unlawful conduct: s.281(3)(a). According to the Government's Explanatory Notes this need not be the unlawful conduct relied on by the Director. The example is given of a drug trafficker who steals money to buy further supplies of a controlled drug. Although the Director may seek a recovery order on the grounds of the respondent's unlawful drug trafficking, the victim of the theft may seek a declaration on the basis that he was deprived of the property by unlawful conduct of a different sort - namely theft.

It is perhaps a moot point whether a person who initially lost property in the street, but which was then found and retained by the respondent, would succeed in obtaining a declaration on the basis that he was deprived of the property by unlawful conduct.

282   Other exemptions

(1) Proceedings for a recovery order may not be taken against any person in circumstances of a prescribed description; and the circumstances may relate to the person himself or to the property or to any other matter.

    In this subsection, prescribed means prescribed by an order made by the Secretary of State after consultation with the Scottish Ministers.

(2) Proceedings for a recovery order may not be taken in respect of cash found at any place in the United Kingdom unless the proceedings are also taken in respect of property other than cash which is property of the same person.

(3) Proceedings for a recovery order may not be taken against the Financial Services Authority in respect of any recoverable property held by the authority.

(4) Proceedings for a recovery order may not be taken in respect of any property which is subject to any of the following charges—
    (a) a collateral security charge, within the meaning of the Financial Markets and Insolvency (Settlement Finality) Regulations 1999 (S.I. 1999/2979),
    (b) a market charge, within the meaning of Part 7 of the Companies Act 1989 (c. 40),
    (c) a money market charge, within the meaning of the Financial Markets and Insolvency (Money Market) Regulations 1995 (S.I. 1995/2049),
    (d) a system charge, within the meaning of the Financial Markets and Insolvency Regulations 1996 (S.I. 1996/1469) or the Financial Markets and Insolvency Regulations (Northern Ireland) 1996 (S.R. 1996/252).

(5) Proceedings for a recovery order may not be taken against any person in respect of any recoverable property which he holds by reason of his acting, or having acted, as an insolvency practitioner.

Acting as an insolvency practitioner has the same meaning as in section 433.

DEFINITIONS
"insolvency practitioner": s.433
"prescribed": s.282(1)
"recovery order": s.316(1), s.266
"property": s.316(4)

GENERAL NOTE
This section contains a number of important exceptions

Subs. (1)
The Secretary of State will be able to make Orders (subject to the approval of both Houses of Parliament) to exempt a person, or class of persons, or property, from proceedings for civil recovery.

Subs. (2)
An important exception exists in relation to cash. The House of Lords debated in Committee (*Hansard*, May 13, 2002, col.56) whether it was appropriate to pursue the civil recovery of cash in summary proceedings under Pt. 5, chap.3, rather than by way of proceedings in the High Court for a recovery order (Chap.2). The reason for maintaining a simplified method of recovery where only cash is involved was explained by the Attorney General (*Hansard*, May 13, 2002, col.56):

"(s.282(2)) establishes that civil recovery proceedings may be taken only if they involve property other than cash that is held by the same person. Proceedings involving cash alone—in effect, where cash is identified and seized by the police or Customs and Excise in the circumstances that are provided for in Chapter 3—are to be brought under the cash forfeiture proceedings.

(Subsection (2)) is intended to avoid confusion about which scheme applies to cash that is found within the United Kingdom that is alleged to be recoverable property ... Chapter 3 has been designed specifically for cash alone. It has provisions in relation to the continued detention of cash—for example ... in relation to placing the moneys in an interest-bearing account. Those features are specific to cash and do not appear in Chapter 2.

Those features reflect the fact that we have established procedures for dealing with cash that is found by law enforcement officers that are effective, as they have previously proved to be, and which can have quick results ... .The civil process will be applied to more complex cases, which do not involve cash alone."

Accordingly, where a respondent is in possession of both cash and other property that is said to be 'recoverable property', it would be open to the Director to include cash in the amount to be recovered under a recovery order (Pt.5, chap.2).

Subss (3), (4), and (5)
These provisions provide immunity in respect of persons and property specified in the relevant provision.

Miscellaneous

283   Compensation

(1) If, in the case of any property to which an interim receiving order or interim administration order has at any time applied, the court does not in the course of the proceedings decide that the property is recoverable property or associated property, the person whose property it is may make an application to the court for compensation.
(2) Subsection (1) does not apply if the court—
   (a) has made a declaration in respect of the property by virtue of section 281, or
   (b) makes an order under section 276.
(3) If the court has made a decision by reason of which no recovery order could be made in respect of the property, the application for compensation must be made within the period of three months beginning—
   (a) in relation to a decision of the High Court in England and Wales, with the date of the decision or, if any application is made for leave to appeal, with the date on which the application is with-

drawn or refused or (if the application is granted) on which any proceedings on appeal are finally concluded,

(b) in relation to a decision of the Court of Session or of the High Court in Northern Ireland, with the date of the decision or, if there is an appeal against the decision, with the date on which any proceedings on appeal are finally concluded.

(4) If, in England and Wales or Northern Ireland, the proceedings in respect of the property have been discontinued, the application for compensation must be made within the period of three months beginning with the discontinuance.

(5) If the court is satisfied that the applicant has suffered loss as a result of the interim receiving order or interim administration order, it may require the enforcement authority to pay compensation to him.

(6) If, but for section 269(2), any right mentioned there would have operated in favour of, or become exercisable by, any person, he may make an application to the court for compensation.

(7) The application for compensation under subsection (6) must be made within the period of three months beginning with the vesting referred to in section 269(2).

(8) If the court is satisfied that, in consequence of the operation of section 269, the right in question cannot subsequently operate in favour of the applicant or (as the case may be) become exercisable by him, it may require the enforcement authority to pay compensation to him.

(9) The amount of compensation to be paid under this section is the amount the court thinks reasonable, having regard to the loss suffered and any other relevant circumstances.

DEFINITIONS
   "associated property": s. 316(1), s.245
   "enforcement authority": s.316
   "interim receiving order": s.316, s.246(2)
   "property": s.316(4)
   "recovery order": s.316(1), s.266
   "recoverable property": ss.304 to 310

GENERAL NOTE
   The House of Lords in Committee (*Hansard*, May 13, 2002, col.118) debated what is now s.283 extensively. Concern was expressed that the section did not go far enough to protect (in compensation) innocent third parties who suffer loss or damage as a result of the Director obtaining an interim receiving order. Section 283 provides compensation only to persons who hold property, which is the subject of the interim receiving order. Lord Kingsland said (*Hansard*, May 13, 2002, col.118):
   "... in the standard freezing order, it is usual to give an undertaking to pay the costs of any third party who has suffered loss if the court decides that the third party should be compensated for that loss. That is a standard undertaking extracted from an applicant for a freezing order in a civil court.
   An interim receiving order or an interim administration order is a more drastic remedy than a freezing order. We believe that, at the very least, there should be a similar provision for compensation as regards innocent third parties who have suffered loss as a result of an interim receiving order or an interim administration order.
   I emphasise that the right to compensation should not be automatic. Innocent third parties may suffer loss as a result of interim receiving orders or interim administration orders; but not all of them should be entitled to compensation regardless of the circumstances. They may be the authors of their own misfortune, and it would be wrong to impose an unlimited liability on an enforcement authority carrying out a public duty regardless of the circumstances. Compensation should be payable only where the court thinks fit."
   A third party who might suffer loss, is the unsecured creditor who enters into a contractual relationship with the respondent only to find that the State might acquire all the property that is recoverable (e.g. a builder who constructed a kitchen extension to a house that is recoverable property). The Government's position was, and remains, firmly against widening the scope of compensation to include such parties:

"It is appropriate to distinguish between different categories of people who may, in theory, be affected by an order that is made. The position of a respondent is covered by the Bill as it stands and a secured creditor will be protected because associated property will be protected like any other associated property .... The Bill also recognises the third category, which is the prior claims of preferential debts. They receive priority over civil recovery. Those categories are dealt with.

The remaining issue is that of unsecured creditors. The proposal behind the amendment is that unsecured creditors also should take priority over the settlement of the recovery order. The Government's view is that they should not ....

We note that the director will seek to recover the proceeds of unlawful conduct to prevent and to disrupt organised crime. The director will be acting on behalf of the state in cases where there may be no identifiable victim. The underlying principle is that the person in possession of the proceeds of unlawful conduct should not be able to retain that wealth on the basis that it never properly belonged to him. The unsecured lender inevitably exposes him or herself to a wide range of risks. ... The fact that the borrower may be subject to a recovery order is but one of those risks to which an unsecured lender puts himself. The borrower or the recipient of goods or services may turn out to be insolvent; he may die without leaving an adequate estate; or he may simply default.

The ....making of the recovery order does not absolve the respondent of the obligation to pay his debts. They remain payable out of other property. It will probably be relatively unusual to have a case where the civil recovery results in insolvency of the respondent. The fact that the unsecured lender may lose out is simply a consequence of the fact that he has provided services on credit to someone who turns out not to be sufficiently solvent.

The second point is that this amendment (to extend compensation to include unsecured creditors) would have an adverse effect in practical terms on the operation of an effective civil recovery system; it would simply invite claims from bogus creditors who, in reality, were associates of the respondent. We are entirely unpersuaded by suggestions previously made in relation to Part 2 that it would be easy to differentiate bogus compensation claims from legitimate claims. For practical reasons, therefore, and also for reasons of principle, the amendment is opposed."

284   Payment of interim administrator or trustee (Scotland)

Any fees or expenses incurred by an interim administrator, or a trustee for civil recovery appointed by the Court of Session, in the exercise of his functions are to be reimbursed by the Scottish Ministers as soon as is practicable after they have been incurred.

285   Effect on diligence of recovery order (Scotland)

(1) An arrestment or poinding of any recoverable property executed on or after the appointment of the trustee for civil recovery is ineffectual in a question with the trustee.

(2) Any recoverable property so arrested or poinded, or (if the property has been sold) the proceeds of sale, must be handed over to the trustee for civil recovery.

(3) A poinding of the ground in respect of recoverable property on or after such an appointment is ineffectual in a question with the trustee for civil recovery except for the interest mentioned in subsection (4).

(4) That interest is—
   (a) interest on the debt of a secured creditor for the current half yearly term, and
   (b) arrears of interest on that debt for one year immediately before the commencement of that term.

(5) On and after such appointment no other person may raise or insist in an adjudication against recoverable property or be confirmed as an executor-creditor on that property.

(6) An inhibition on recoverable property shall cease to have effect in relation to any heritable property comprised in the recoverable property on such appointment.

(7) The provisions of this section apply in relation to—
   (a) an action of maills and duties, and
   (b) an action for sequestration of rent,
as they apply in relation to an arrestment or poinding.

286   Scope of powers (Scotland)

(1) Orders under this Chapter may be made by the Court of Session in respect of a person wherever domiciled, resident or present.

(2) Such an order may be made by the Court of Session in respect of moveable property wherever situated.

(3) But such an order in respect of a person's moveable property may not be made by the Court of Session where—

   (a) the person is not domiciled, resident or present in Scotland, and

   (b) the property is not situated in Scotland,

unless the unlawful conduct took place in Scotland.

287   Financial threshold

(1) At any time when an order specifying an amount for the purposes of this section has effect, the enforcement authority may not start proceedings for a recovery order unless the authority reasonably believes that the aggregate value of the recoverable property which the authority wishes to be subject to a recovery order is not less than the specified amount.

(2) The power to make an order under subsection (1) is exercisable by the Secretary of State after consultation with the Scottish Ministers.

(3) If the authority applies for an interim receiving order or interim administration order before starting the proceedings, subsection (1) applies to the application instead of to the start of the proceedings.

(4) This section does not affect the continuation of proceedings for a recovery order which have been properly started or the making or continuing effect of an interim receiving order or interim administration order which has been properly applied for.

288   Limitation

(1) After section 27 of the Limitation Act 1980 (c. 58) there is inserted—

"27A Actions for recovery of property obtained through unlawful conduct etc.

(1) None of the time limits given in the preceding provisions of this Act applies to any proceedings under Chapter 2 of Part 5 of the Proceeds of Crime Act 2002 (civil recovery of proceeds of unlawful conduct).

(2) Proceedings under that Chapter for a recovery order in respect of any recoverable property shall not be brought after the expiration of the period of twelve years from the date on which the Director's cause of action accrued.

(3) Proceedings under that Chapter are brought when—

   (a) a claim form is issued, or

   (b) an application is made for an interim receiving order,

whichever is the earlier.

(4) The Director's cause of action accrues in respect of any recoverable property—

   (a) in the case of proceedings for a recovery order in respect of property obtained through unlawful conduct, when the property is so obtained,

   (b) in the case of proceedings for a recovery order in respect of any other recoverable property, when the property obtained through unlawful conduct which it represents is so obtained.

(5) If—

    (a) a person would (but for the preceding provisions of this Act) have a cause of action in respect of the conversion of a chattel, and

    (b) proceedings are started under that Chapter for a recovery order in respect of the chattel,

section 3(2) of this Act does not prevent his asserting on an application under section 281 of that Act that the property belongs to him, or the court making a declaration in his favour under that section.

(6) If the court makes such a declaration, his title to the chattel is to be treated as not having been extinguished by section 3(2) of this Act.

(7) Expressions used in this section and Part 5 of that Act have the same meaning in this section as in that Part."

(2) After section 19A of the Prescription and Limitation (Scotland) Act 1973 (c. 52) there is inserted—

"19B Actions for recovery of property obtained through unlawful conduct etc.

(1) None of the time limits given in the preceding provisions of this Act applies to any proceedings under Chapter 2 of Part 5 of the Proceeds of Crime Act 2002 (civil recovery of proceeds of unlawful conduct).

(2) Proceedings under that Chapter for a recovery order in respect of any recoverable property shall not be commenced after the expiration of the period of twelve years from the date on which the Scottish Ministers' right of action accrued.

(3) Proceedings under that Chapter are commenced when—

    (a) the proceedings are served, or

    (b) an application is made for an interim administration order,

whichever is the earlier.

(4) The Scottish Ministers' right of action accrues in respect of any recoverable property—

    (a) in the case of proceedings for a recovery order in respect of property obtained through unlawful conduct, when the property is so obtained,

    (b) in the case of proceedings for a recovery order in respect of any other recoverable property, when the property obtained through unlawful conduct which it represents is so obtained.

(5) Expressions used in this section and Part 5 of that Act have the same meaning in this section as in that Part."

(3) After Article 72 of the Limitation (Northern Ireland) Order 1989 (SI 1989/1339 (N.I. 11)) there is inserted—

"72A Actions for recovery of property obtained through unlawful conduct etc.

(1) None of the time limits fixed by Parts II and III applies to any proceedings under Chapter 2 of Part 5 of the Proceeds of Crime Act 2002 (civil recovery of proceeds of unlawful conduct).

(2) Proceedings under that Chapter for a recovery order in respect of any recoverable property shall not be brought after the expiration of the period of twelve years from the date on which the Director's cause of action accrued.

(3) Proceedings under that Chapter are brought when—

(a) a claim form is issued, or

(b) an application is made for an interim receiving order,

whichever is the earlier.

(4) The Director's cause of action accrues in respect of any recoverable property—

(a) in the case of proceedings for a recovery order in respect of property obtained through unlawful conduct, when the property is so obtained,

(b) in the case of proceedings for a recovery order in respect of any other recoverable property, when the property obtained through unlawful conduct which it represents is so obtained.

(5) If—

(a) a person would (but for a time limit fixed by this Order) have a cause of action in respect of the conversion of a chattel, and

(b) proceedings are started under that Chapter for a recovery order in respect of the chattel,

Article 17(2) does not prevent his asserting on an application under section 281 of that Act that the property belongs to him, or the court making a declaration in his favour under that section.

(6) If the court makes such a declaration, his title to the chattel is to be treated as not having been extinguished by Article 17(2).

(7) Expressions used in this Article and Part 5 of that Act have the same meaning in this Article as in that Part."

CHAPTER 3

RECOVERY OF CASH IN SUMMARY PROCEEDINGS

INTRODUCTION TO CHAPTER 3

Section 289 empowers constables and officers of customs and excise to search for cash that was obtained through unlawful conduct (i.e. 'recoverable property') but the powers are subject to a raft of statutory safeguards to prevent unwarranted and unnecessarily intrusive searches being carried out by officers. Accountability is woven into chapter 3. Accordingly, in the ordinary way, an officer must not carry out a search without prior approval of a justice of the peace (in England and Wales) or of a senior officer (e.g. a police officer of at least the rank of inspector). The one exception is when it is impracticable for the officer to seek prior approval for a search because, for example, the officer has reasonable grounds to suspect that cash is about to be disposed of: the officer must act quickly.

In cases where an officer performs a search on his/her own initiative (or even with the prior authority of a senior officer), and the searching officer *either* fails to seize cash that is recoverable property, *or* he is duty-bound to return the cash within 48 hours after seizing it, that officer must submit a written report to a person approved by the Secretary of State (s.290(6)). The report must include particulars as to why it was not practicable to obtain the approval of a justice of the peace (s.290(7)(b)). It follows that no report need be completed if the searching officer obtains prior approval from a justice of the peace. The thinking of the legislature appears to be that it can be assumed that a court is impartial and will only give prior approval for a search after carefully examining the merits of the application. The role of the 'appointed person' is to monitor the circumstances and manner in which the powers conferred by s.289 have been exercised, and to make recommendations to Government: see s.291. The Secretary of State must draw up a Code of Practice in connection with powers exercisable under s.289 (see ss.292 and 293). The Government clearly wishes to avoid criticisms of the sort that have been levelled in respect of stop-and-search powers. Data and statistics provided by the 'appointed person', regarding the use of powers under s.289, should be invaluable to researchers and commentators on the criminal justice process.

The powers vested in constables and customs officers to seize cash, to investigate its origins and/or intended use, and if necessary to apply for its forfeiture before a Magistrates' Court, are a development of well-established rules under previous legislation (namely, the Criminal Justice (International Cooperation) Act 1990, and the Pt. II of the Drug Trafficking Act 1994).

Whilst many of the statutory provisions in chapter 3 will therefore echo earlier legislation, a number of significant changes to the law should be noted. Under earlier legislation, it was only possible to forfeit cash that directly or indirectly represented any person's proceeds of drug trafficking, or was intended by any person for use in drug trafficking. Chapter 3 applies to cash that represents the proceeds of any form of 'unlawful conduct' or intended to be used for such conduct. Note the extended meaning of 'unlawful conduct': see s.241. Secondly, earlier legislation concerned cash that was being imported into, or exported from, the United Kingdom including cash "being brought to any place in the United Kingdom for the purpose of being exported" (Drug Trafficking Act 1994, s.48(1)). Now it is immaterial that the cash was not intended for import/export. Thirdly, the definition of 'cash' under the 2002 Act is much extended (s.289(6),(7)) and includes postal orders, banker's drafts, bearer bonds and bearer shares, and any kind of monetary instrument. Fourthly, Pt. II of the Drug Trafficking Act 1994 did not give officers a power to search for cash, but chapter 3 to Pt.5 of the 2002 Act does do so.

There is no doubt that proceedings under chapter 3 to Pt.5 of the Act are civil in nature and therefore the civil standard of proof applies throughout. This was the position under Part II of the Drug Trafficking Act 1994: see *Best* (May 23, 1995, Unreported, D.C.); *Butt v. HM Customs and Excise*, and see *Daura v. HM Customs and Excise* (Unreported, 2002, Admin. Crt.). The rules of evidence are those applicable in civil proceedings and thus the Civil Evidence Act 1995 applies. Legal aid, on a criminal legal aid certificate, is not available for the purpose of opposing an application for the detention of cash or for the purposes of applying for the cash to be released: see *Crawley Justices, Ex p. Ohakwe* (1994) Crim. L.R. 936.

Searches

289   Searches

(1) If a customs officer or constable who is lawfully on any premises has reasonable grounds for suspecting that there is on the premises cash—
  (a) which is recoverable property or is intended by any person for use in unlawful conduct, and
  (b) the amount of which is not less than the minimum amount,
  he may search for the cash there.

(2) If a customs officer or constable has reasonable grounds for suspecting that a person (the suspect) is carrying cash—
  (a) which is recoverable property or is intended by any person for use in unlawful conduct, and
  (b) the amount of which is not less than the minimum amount,
  he may exercise the following powers.

(3) The officer or constable may, so far as he thinks it necessary or expedient, require the suspect—
  (a) to permit a search of any article he has with him,
  (b) to permit a search of his person.

(4) An officer or constable exercising powers by virtue of subsection (3)(b) may detain the suspect for so long as is necessary for their exercise.

(5) The powers conferred by this section—
  (a) are exercisable only so far as reasonably required for the purpose of finding cash,
  (b) are exercisable by a customs officer only if he has reasonable grounds for suspecting that the unlawful conduct in question relates to an assigned matter (within the meaning of the Customs and Excise Management Act 1979 (c. 2)).

(6) Cash means—
  (a) notes and coins in any currency,
  (b) postal orders,
  (c) cheques of any kind, including travellers' cheques,
  (d) bankers' drafts,
  (e) bearer bonds and bearer shares,
  found at any place in the United Kingdom.

(7) Cash also includes any kind of monetary instrument which is found at any place in the United Kingdom, if the instrument is specified by the Secretary of State by an order made after consultation with the Scottish Ministers.

(8) This section does not require a person to submit to an intimate search or strip search (within the meaning of section 164 of the Customs and Excise Management Act 1979 (c. 2)).

DEFINITIONS
"cash": s.316(1), s.289(6),(7)
"recoverable property": ss.304 to 310
"the minimum amount": s.303
"unlawful conduct": s.316(1), s.242

GENERAL NOTE

Subs. (1)
The officer must be lawfully on premises – for example, by way of a search warrant. He may be lawfully on private premises if he is exercising his powers under the Police and Criminal Evidence Act 1984, or under the Customs and Excise Management Act 1979, or where he has been invited to be present on private property. The officer must have reasonable grounds to suspect that the cash is "on the premises" and is either 'recoverable' property' as defined by ss.304 to 310 (that it is or represents property obtained through unlawful conduct), or that the cash is intended for use in unlawful conduct by any person. The amount of cash must be for the 'minimum amount' (s.303) – a figure specified by the Secretary of State, and which will probably be initially set at £10,000.

Subss (2), (3), (4) and (5)
Read these subsections in conjunction with ss.290 to 293 inclusive. Powers exercisable under subs.(2) can only be directed against the person suspected of carrying 'cash'. If the officer holds the requisite grounds for suspicion concerning the cash, he may require the suspect to permit a search of his person (other than an intimate or strip search: see s.289(8)), or to permit a search of any article he has with him e.g. a suitcase or a car (s.289(3)(a)). If the suspect declines to cooperate voluntarily, the officer may detain the suspect for so long as is necessary for that purpose: s.289(4). What is not clear is whether an officer has power to search a person who is concealing a high value monetary instrument in an intimate place. The answer, by virtue of s.289(8) seems to be 'no', and chapter 3 makes no provision for a power of arrest to carry out an intimate search.

290 Prior approval

(1) The powers conferred by section 289 may be exercised only with the appropriate approval unless, in the circumstances, it is not practicable to obtain that approval before exercising the power.

(2) The appropriate approval means the approval of a judicial officer or (if that is not practicable in any case) the approval of a senior officer.

(3) A judicial officer means—
  (a) in relation to England and Wales and Northern Ireland, a justice of the peace,
  (b) in relation to Scotland, the sheriff.

(4) A senior officer means—
  (a) in relation to the exercise of the power by a customs officer, a customs officer of a rank designated by the Commissioners of Customs and Excise as equivalent to that of a senior police officer,
  (b) in relation to the exercise of the power by a constable, a senior police officer.

(5) A senior police officer means a police officer of at least the rank of inspector.

(6) If the powers are exercised without the approval of a judicial officer in a case where—
  (a) no cash is seized by virtue of section 294, or
  (b) any cash so seized is not detained for more than 48 hours,
  the customs officer or constable who exercised the powers must give a written report to the appointed person.

(7) The report must give particulars of the circumstances which led him to believe that—
  (a) the powers were exercisable, and
  (b) it was not practicable to obtain the approval of a judicial officer.
(8) In this section and section 291, the appointed person means—
  (a) in relation to England and Wales and Northern Ireland, a person appointed by the Secretary of State,
  (b) in relation to Scotland, a person appointed by the Scottish Ministers.
(9) The appointed person must not be a person employed under or for the purposes of a government department or of the Scottish Administration; and the terms and conditions of his appointment, including any remuneration or expenses to be paid to him, are to be determined by the person appointing him.

DEFINITIONS
  "appointed person": s.290(8)
  "appropriate approval": s.290(2)
  "cash": s.316(1), s.289(6)
  "judicial officer": s.290(3)
  "senior officer": s.290(4)
  "senior police officer": s.290(5)

GENERAL NOTE
  In cases where an officer performs a search on his/her own initiative (or with the prior authority of a senior officer), and the searching officer *either* fails to seize cash that is recoverable property, *or* he is duty-bound to return the cash within 48 hours after seizing it, that officer must submit a written report to a person approved by the Secretary of State (s.290(6)). The report must include particulars as to why it was not practicable to obtain the approval of a justice of the peace (s.290(7)(b)). It follows that no report need be completed if the searching officer obtains prior approval from a justice of the peace. The thinking of the legislature appears to be that it can be assumed that a court is impartial and will only give prior approval for a search after carefully examining the merits of the application. The role of the 'appointed person' is to monitor the circumstances and manner in which the powers conferred by s.289 have been exercised, and to make recommendations to Government: see s.291.

291 Report on exercise of powers

(1) As soon as possible after the end of each financial year, the appointed person must prepare a report for that year.
    "Financial year" means—
      (a) the period beginning with the day on which this section comes into force and ending with the next 31 March (which is the first financial year), and
      (b) each subsequent period of twelve months beginning with 1 April.
(2) The report must give his opinion as to the circumstances and manner in which the powers conferred by section 289 are being exercised in cases where the customs officer or constable who exercised them is required to give a report under section 290(6).
(3) In the report, he may make any recommendations he considers appropriate.
(4) He must send a copy of his report to the Secretary of State or, as the case may be, the Scottish Ministers, who must arrange for it to be published.
(5) The Secretary of State must lay a copy of any report he receives under this section before Parliament; and the Scottish Ministers must lay a copy of any report they receive under this section before the Scottish Parliament.

DEFINITIONS
  "appointed person": s.290(8)
  "financial year": s.291(1)

GENERAL NOTE
  Read this section in conjunction with ss.289 and 290.

292   Code of practice

(1) The Secretary of State must make a code of practice in connection with the exercise by customs officers and (in relation to England and Wales and Northern Ireland) constables of the powers conferred by virtue of section 289.

(2) Where he proposes to issue a code of practice he must—
  (a) publish a draft,
  (b) consider any representations made to him about the draft by the Scottish Ministers or any other person,
  (c) if he thinks it appropriate, modify the draft in the light of any such representations.

(3) He must lay a draft of the code before Parliament.

(4) When he has laid a draft of the code before Parliament he may bring it into operation by order.

(5) He may revise the whole or any part of the code issued by him and issue the code as revised; and subsections (2) to (4) apply to such a revised code as they apply to the original code.

(6) A failure by a customs officer or constable to comply with a provision of the code does not of itself make him liable to criminal or civil proceedings.

(7) The code is admissible in evidence in criminal or civil proceedings and is to be taken into account by a court or tribunal in any case in which it appears to the court or tribunal to be relevant.

GENERAL NOTE
  This section must be read in conjunction with ss.289 to 291 inclusive. The Secretary of State must draw up a Code of Conduct and lay a copy of the draft before Parliament. A failure by an officer to comply with the Code does not of itself make him liable to criminal or civil proceedings (s.292(6)) and neither will a breach of the Code necessarily result in evidence, obtained by the officer purporting to exercise his statutory powers under chapter 3, being excluded or proceedings being stayed. However, the code is admissible in criminal and civil proceedings and must be taken into account in any case in which it appears to the court to be relevant: s.292(7).

293   Code of practice (Scotland)

(1) The Scottish Ministers must make a code of practice in connection with the exercise by constables in relation to Scotland of the powers conferred by virtue of section 289.

(2) Where they propose to issue a code of practice they must—
  (a) publish a draft,
  (b) consider any representations made to them about the draft,
  (c) if they think it appropriate, modify the draft in the light of any such representations.

(3) They must lay a draft of the code before the Scottish Parliament.

(4) When they have laid a draft of the code before the Scottish Parliament they may bring it into operation by order.

(5) They may revise the whole or any part of the code issued by them and issue the code as revised; and subsections (2) to (4) apply to such a revised code as they apply to the original code.

(6) A failure by a constable to comply with a provision of the code does not of itself make him liable to criminal or civil proceedings.

(7) The code is admissible in evidence in criminal or civil proceedings and is to be taken into account by a court or tribunal in any case in which it appears to the court or tribunal to be relevant.

Seizure and detention

294 Seizure of cash

(1) A customs officer or constable may seize any cash if he has reasonable grounds for suspecting that it is—
    (a) recoverable property, or
    (b) intended by any person for use in unlawful conduct.
(2) A customs officer or constable may also seize cash part of which he has reasonable grounds for suspecting to be—
    (a) recoverable property, or
    (b) intended by any person for use in unlawful conduct,
    if it is not reasonably practicable to seize only that part.
(3) This section does not authorise the seizure of an amount of cash if it or, as the case may be, the part to which his suspicion relates, is less than the minimum amount.

DEFINITIONS
"cash": s.316(1), s.289(6)
"the minimum amount": s.303
"part": s.316(1)
"recoverable property": ss.304 to 310
"unlawful conduct": s.316(1), s.242

GENERAL NOTE
The basis for seizing cash is wider under the 2002 Act than it was under Pt. II of the Drug Trafficking Act 1994. Now, the officer may seize cash if he has reasonable grounds for suspecting that it is either "recoverable property" or "intended . . . for use in unlawful conduct" (s.294(1)), and he may seize cash even if his suspicion relates to 'part' of it (s.294(2)) – but that part must be worth at least the 'minimum amount' (see s.294(3)). The latter provision may only be exercised if it is not reasonably practicable to seize the relevant 'part' – for example, the officer finds a wealth of monetary instruments of which 'part' is suspected to be used in unlawful conduct, but only by careful and time consuming examination of the remainder, would it be practicable to seize the relevant 'part'.

The officer must have reasonable grounds for this suspicion. Each case will be decided on its own facts. The officer would be entitled to take into account a number of features including, for example, whether the cash was concealed; explanations offered by persons who have an interest in the cash; the circumstances in which the cash was being handled (see *Bassick and Osbourne*, March 22, 1993, Unreported, D.C.); the amount of cash that was being transported; whether traces of a controlled drug were detected on part or all of the cash (see *Thomas*, January 20, 1995, Unreported, D.C.). It is not necessary for the officer to suspect that the person carrying the cash has himself been engaged in unlawful conduct or that he intended to use the cash for that purpose: see *Thomas*.

295 Detention of seized cash

(1) While the customs officer or constable continues to have reasonable grounds for his suspicion, cash seized under section 294 may be detained initially for a period of 48 hours.
(2) The period for which the cash or any part of it may be detained may be extended by an order made by a magistrates' court or (in Scotland) the sheriff; but the order may not authorise the detention of any of the cash—
    (a) beyond the end of the period of three months beginning with the date of the order,

(b) in the case of any further order under this section, beyond the end of the period of two years beginning with the date of the first order.

(3) A justice of the peace may also exercise the power of a magistrates' court to make the first order under subsection (2) extending the period.

(4) An application for an order under subsection (2)—
   (a) in relation to England and Wales and Northern Ireland, may be made by the Commissioners of Customs and Excise or a constable,
   (b) in relation to Scotland, may be made by the Scottish Ministers in connection with their functions under section 298 or by a procurator fiscal,

and the court, sheriff or justice may make the order if satisfied, in relation to any cash to be further detained, that either of the following conditions is met.

(5) The first condition is that there are reasonable grounds for suspecting that the cash is recoverable property and that either—
   (a) its continued detention is justified while its derivation is further investigated or consideration is given to bringing (in the United Kingdom or elsewhere) proceedings against any person for an offence with which the cash is connected, or
   (b) proceedings against any person for an offence with which the cash is connected have been started and have not been concluded.

(6) The second condition is that there are reasonable grounds for suspecting that the cash is intended to be used in unlawful conduct and that either—
   (a) its continued detention is justified while its intended use is further investigated or consideration is given to bringing (in the United Kingdom or elsewhere) proceedings against any person for an offence with which the cash is connected, or
   (b) proceedings against any person for an offence with which the cash is connected have been started and have not been concluded.

(7) An application for an order under subsection (2) may also be made in respect of any cash seized under section 294(2), and the court, sheriff or justice may make the order if satisfied that—
   (a) the condition in subsection (5) or (6) is met in respect of part of the cash, and
   (b) it is not reasonably practicable to detain only that part.

(8) An order under subsection (2) must provide for notice to be given to persons affected by it.

DEFINITIONS
  "cash": s.316(1), s.289(6)
  "part": s.316(1)
  "recoverable property": ss.304 to 310
  "unlawful conduct": s.316(1), s.242

GENERAL NOTE
  This section re-enacts much of what was contained in s.42(2) and (3) of the Drug Trafficking Act 1994.
  An order for the detention of cash cannot endure longer than three months (s.295(2)), but further orders can be made by the court provided the total period of detention does not exceed two years from the date of the first order (s.295(2), formerly s.42(3) of the Drug Trafficking Act 1994).
  It should be noted that these powers may be exercised even if no criminal proceedings have been instituted (or even contemplated) against any person for a drug trafficking offence in connection with cash seized. Where criminal proceedings are instituted, or where application is made to forfeit the money on the basis that it represents the proceeds of unlawful conduct, or

intended to be used for that purpose, the cash is not to be released until the relevant proceedings have been concluded: see s.295(5)(b) and s.296(6)(b).

The fact that there as been a defect in the process by which the application was made, for example, an inappropriate form was used, will probably not render the detention of cash unlawful: see *Luton JJ Ex p. Abecasis* (2000) 164 JP 265.

296 Interest

(1) If cash is detained under section 295 for more than 48 hours, it is at the first opportunity to be paid into an interest-bearing account and held there; and the interest accruing on it is to be added to it on its forfeiture or release.

(2) In the case of cash detained under section 295 which was seized under section 294(2), the customs officer or constable must, on paying it into the account, release the part of the cash to which the suspicion does not relate.

(3) Subsection (1) does not apply if the cash or, as the case may be, the part to which the suspicion relates is required as evidence of an offence or evidence in proceedings under this Chapter.

DEFINITIONS
  "cash": s.316(1), s.289(6)
  "part": s.316(1)

GENERAL NOTE
  This makes provision for cash detained for longer than 48 hours being put in an interest bearing account (payable to the Crown if forfeited or to the person entitled to possession if released). The Divisional Court has emphasised that it was important that similar provisions enacted under Pt. II to the Drug Trafficking Act 1994 were complied with strictly: *Uxbridge Magistrates' Court, Ex p. Henry* (1994) Crim. L.R. 581, applied in *Walsh v. Commissioners of Customs and Excise* (June 12, 2001).

297 Release of detained cash

(1) This section applies while any cash is detained under section 295.

(2) A magistrates' court or (in Scotland) the sheriff may direct the release of the whole or any part of the cash if the following condition is met.

(3) The condition is that the court or sheriff is satisfied, on an application by the person from whom the cash was seized, that the conditions in section 295 for the detention of the cash are no longer met in relation to the cash to be released.

(4) A customs officer, constable or (in Scotland) procurator fiscal may, after notifying the magistrates' court, sheriff or justice under whose order cash is being detained, release the whole or any part of it if satisfied that the detention of the cash to be released is no longer justified.

DEFINITIONS
  "cash": s.316(1), s.289(6)
  "part": s.316(1)

GENERAL NOTE
  A party who seeks the release of cash, seized under s.294, has two possible routes. First, he may attempt to persuade a customs officer (or a police officer) to release the cash. The officer can only do so if he is satisfied that its detention is no longer justified and he informs the court that he proposes to release the money. However, the usual route for the release of cash will be by way of an application to the Magistrates' Court (or to the Sheriff in Scotland) under s.297. The applicant must be the person from whom the cash was seized: this restriction exists to prevent the court from becoming immersed in a dispute between the person from whom the cash was seized, and the person claiming to be the rightful owner of the cash. There is separate statutory provision under s.301 of the Act for victims and other owners of cash to make an application to the court for the release of the cash, or part of it.

  The applicant must establish that the conditions justifying the detention of the cash no longer exist: in this regard, note the decision of the court in respect of Part II of the Drug Trafficking Act

1994: see *Customs and Excise Commissioners v. Shah* (1999) 163 JP 759. It is perhaps arguable that the wording of s.295 and s.297 might lead to a different result.

Forfeiture

298   **Forfeiture**

(1) While cash is detained under section 295, an application for the forfeiture of the whole or any part of it may be made—
   (a) to a magistrates' court by the Commissioners of Customs and Excise or a constable,
   (b) (in Scotland) to the sheriff by the Scottish Ministers.

(2) The court or sheriff may order the forfeiture of the cash or any part of it if satisfied that the cash or part—
   (a) is recoverable property, or
   (b) is intended by any person for use in unlawful conduct.

(3) But in the case of recoverable property which belongs to joint tenants, one of whom is an excepted joint owner, the order may not apply to so much of it as the court thinks is attributable to the excepted joint owner's share.

(4) Where an application for the forfeiture of any cash is made under this section, the cash is to be detained (and may not be released under any power conferred by this Chapter) until any proceedings in pursuance of the application (including any proceedings on appeal) are concluded.

DEFINITIONS
    "cash": s.316(1), s.289(6)
    "excepted joint owner": s.316(1)
    "part": s.316(1)
    "recoverable property": ss.304 to 310
    "share": s.316(1)
    "unlawful conduct": s.316(1), s.242

GENERAL NOTE
    Note that it is not necessary to establish that the person from whom the cash was seized, obtained the cash through unlawful conduct or that he/she intended that the cash should be used in unlawful conduct: consider *Thomas* (January 20, 1995, unreported, DC); and see *Pruijsen v. HMCE* (October 18, 1999).
    The court is entitled to look at all the surrounding circumstances including explanations given by those who, for example, intended to use the cash or carried it; the circumstances in which the cash was transported; the lack or presence of traces of a controlled drug on the cash (see *Thomas*, and *Bassick* March 22, 1993, Unreported, D.C.).
    The fact that the person in possession of the cash has been acquitted of criminal charges in respect of the unlawful conduct alleged, does not necessarily prevent the circumstances giving rise to those charges being adduced in evidence in forfeiture proceedings: *HMCE v. Thorp* (November 28, 1996).
    Subsection (3) is necessary by reason of the nature of a joint ownership/tenancy. Such tenancies create potential legal difficulties under the Act because joint tenants are treated as a single owner of property. For example, the respondent and his wife might be joint tenants of property that was acquired by each drawing from their own resources. It is the respondent's contribution that is intended to be recoverable under Pt.5. When 'cash' is involved that is held jointly, similar problems might arise without express statutory provision. Subsection (3) is intended to ensure that in such a case the third party is an "excepted joint owner" against whom his share of the cash is not recoverable under chap.3.

299   **Appeal against forfeiture**

(1) Any party to proceedings in which an order is made under section 298 for the forfeiture of cash who is aggrieved by the order may appeal—
   (a) in relation to England and Wales, to the Crown Court,
   (b) in relation to Scotland, to the Court of Session,

(c) in relation to Northern Ireland, to a county court.
(2) An appeal under subsection (1) must be made within the period of 30 days beginning with the date on which the order is made.
(3) The appeal is to be by way of a rehearing.
(4) The court hearing the appeal may make any order it thinks appropriate.
(5) If the court upholds the appeal, it may order the release of the cash.

DEFINITIONS
"cash": s.316(1), s.289(6)

GENERAL NOTE
This section broadly corresponds to s.44 of the Drug Trafficking Act 1994. Note that the time limit is 30 days, beginning on the day the forfeiture order is made. Appeal is to the Crown Court and it is an appeal by way of a rehearing. There is no power to extend the period for an appeal: *West London JJ Ex p. Lamai* (July 6, 2000). Unlike s.44(4) of the Drug Trafficking Act 1994 there is no provision for the release of forfeited cash to meet reasonable legal expenses: and see *Commissioners of C & E v. Harris* (January 29, 1999).

300   Application of forfeited cash

(1) Cash forfeited under this Chapter, and any accrued interest on it—
  (a) if forfeited by a magistrates' court in England and Wales or Northern Ireland, is to be paid into the Consolidated Fund,
  (b) if forfeited by the sheriff, is to be paid into the Scottish Consolidated Fund.
(2) But it is not to be paid in—
  (a) before the end of the period within which an appeal under section 299 may be made, or
  (b) if a person appeals under that section, before the appeal is determined or otherwise disposed of.

DEFINITIONS
"cash": s.316(1), s.289(6)

Supplementary

301   Victims and other owners

(1) A person who claims that any cash detained under this Chapter, or any part of it, belongs to him may apply to a magistrates' court or (in Scotland) the sheriff for the cash or part to be released to him.
(2) The application may be made in the course of proceedings under section 295 or 298 or at any other time.
(3) If it appears to the court or sheriff concerned that—
  (a) the applicant was deprived of the cash to which the application relates, or of property which it represents, by unlawful conduct,
  (b) the property he was deprived of was not, immediately before he was deprived of it, recoverable property, and
  (c) that cash belongs to him,
  the court or sheriff may order the cash to which the application relates to be released to the applicant.
(4) If—
  (a) the applicant is not the person from whom the cash to which the application relates was seized,
  (b) it appears to the court or sheriff that that cash belongs to the applicant,

    (c) the court or sheriff is satisfied that the conditions in section 295 for the detention of that cash are no longer met or, if an application has been made under section 298, the court or sheriff decides not to make an order under that section in relation to that cash, and

    (d) no objection to the making of an order under this subsection has been made by the person from whom that cash was seized,

the court or sheriff may order the cash to which the application relates to be released to the applicant or to the person from whom it was seized.

DEFINITIONS
"cash": s.316(1), s.289(6)
"recoverable property": ss.304 to 310
"unlawful conduct": s.316(1), s.242

GENERAL NOTE
Under s.297, the applicant must be the person from whom the cash was seized: this restriction exists to prevent the court from becoming immersed in a dispute between the person from whom the cash was seized, and the person claiming to be the rightful owner of the cash. There is separate statutory provision under s.301 of the Act for victims and other owners of cash to make an application to the court for the release of the cash, or part of it.

302   Compensation

  (1) If no forfeiture order is made in respect of any cash detained under this Chapter, the person to whom the cash belongs or from whom it was seized may make an application to the magistrates' court or (in Scotland) the sheriff for compensation.

  (2) If, for any period beginning with the first opportunity to place the cash in an interest-bearing account after the initial detention of the cash for 48 hours, the cash was not held in an interest-bearing account while detained, the court or sheriff may order an amount of compensation to be paid to the applicant.

  (3) The amount of compensation to be paid under subsection (2) is the amount the court or sheriff thinks would have been earned in interest in the period in question if the cash had been held in an interest-bearing account.

  (4) If the court or sheriff is satisfied that, taking account of any interest to be paid under section 296 or any amount to be paid under subsection (2), the applicant has suffered loss as a result of the detention of the cash and that the circumstances are exceptional, the court or sheriff may order compensation (or additional compensation) to be paid to him.

  (5) The amount of compensation to be paid under subsection (4) is the amount the court or sheriff thinks reasonable, having regard to the loss suffered and any other relevant circumstances.

  (6) If the cash was seized by a customs officer, the compensation is to be paid by the Commissioners of Customs and Excise.

  (7) If the cash was seized by a constable, the compensation is to be paid as follows—

    (a) in the case of a constable of a police force in England and Wales, it is to be paid out of the police fund from which the expenses of the police force are met,

    (b) in the case of a constable of a police force in Scotland, it is to be paid by the police authority or joint police board for the police area for which that force is maintained,

    (c) in the case of a police officer within the meaning of the Police (Northern Ireland) Act 2000 (c. 32), it is to be paid out of money provided by the Chief Constable.

(8) If a forfeiture order is made in respect only of a part of any cash detained under this Chapter, this section has effect in relation to the other part.

303 "The minimum amount"

(1) In this Chapter, the minimum amount is the amount in sterling specified in an order made by the Secretary of State after consultation with the Scottish Ministers.

(2) For that purpose the amount of any cash held in a currency other than sterling must be taken to be its sterling equivalent, calculated in accordance with the prevailing rate of exchange.

CHAPTER 4

GENERAL

Recoverable property

304 Property obtained through unlawful conduct

(1) Property obtained through unlawful conduct is recoverable property.

(2) But if property obtained through unlawful conduct has been disposed of (since it was so obtained), it is recoverable property only if it is held by a person into whose hands it may be followed.

(3) Recoverable property obtained through unlawful conduct may be followed into the hands of a person obtaining it on a disposal by—
   (a) the person who through the conduct obtained the property, or
   (b) a person into whose hands it may (by virtue of this subsection) be followed.

DEFINITIONS
   "property": s.316(4), (5), (6), (7)
   "property obtained through unlawful conduct": s.316(1), s.242
   "recoverable property": ss.304 to 310
   "unlawful conduct": s.316(1), s.242

GENERAL NOTE
   Sections 304 to 310 inclusive should be read together. The making of a recovery order will be relatively straightforward if all that has to be recovered is "original property" (see s.305(1)) obtained from unlawful conduct (e.g. a stolen painting found in the hands of the thief).
   Frequently, original property will have been passed on to another (e.g. the handler of stolen goods). In such cases, the original property may be followed into his hands by virtue of s.304(3), because it was obtained by the handler, on disposal of it by the thief. Similarly, by virtue of s.304(3)(b) it may be followed down a line of handlers because each obtained it "on disposal by ... a person into whose hands it may ... be followed." What is therefore being followed is the 'original property'.

305 Tracing property, etc.

(1) Where property obtained through unlawful conduct ("the original property") is or has been recoverable, property which represents the original property is also recoverable property.

(2) If a person enters into a transaction by which—
   (a) he disposes of recoverable property, whether the original property or property which (by virtue of this Chapter) represents the original property, and
   (b) he obtains other property in place of it,
   the other property represents the original property.

(3) If a person disposes of recoverable property which represents the original property, the property may be followed into the hands of the

person who obtains it (and it continues to represent the original property).

GENERAL NOTE
A thief might swap a valuable stolen painting for a car. By s.305(2), the car "represents the original property" and the car may be followed in the same way as the original painting (s.305(3)). Furthermore, the car also becomes 'recoverable property' (s.305(1)). If the car is then swapped for a boat, s.305 repeats the process, so that the painting, the car and the boat, become traceable and 'recoverable property'.

306   Mixing property

(1) Subsection (2) applies if a person's recoverable property is mixed with other property (whether his property or another's).
(2) The portion of the mixed property which is attributable to the recoverable property represents the property obtained through unlawful conduct.
(3) Recoverable property is mixed with other property if (for example) it is used—
   (a) to increase funds held in a bank account,
   (b) in part payment for the acquisition of an asset,
   (c) for the restoration or improvement of land,
   (d) by a person holding a leasehold interest in the property to acquire the freehold.

GENERAL NOTE
Where recoverable property is mixed with other property, the proportion of the mixed property "which is attributable to the recoverable property represents the property obtained through unlawful conduct" (s.306(2)). That takes one back to s.305(1), and a similar approach applies to accruing profits (s.307).

307   Recoverable property: accruing profits

(1) This section applies where a person who has recoverable property obtains further property consisting of profits accruing in respect of the recoverable property.
(2) The further property is to be treated as representing the property obtained through unlawful conduct.

"recoverable property": ss.304 to 310
"unlawful conduct": s.316(1), s.242

<small>GENERAL NOTE</small>
See the General Note to ss.304 to 306 inclusive.

308   General exceptions

(1) If—

   (a) a person disposes of recoverable property, and

   (b) the person who obtains it on the disposal does so in good faith, for value and without notice that it was recoverable property,

the property may not be followed into that person's hands and, accordingly, it ceases to be recoverable.

(2) If recoverable property is vested, forfeited or otherwise disposed of in pursuance of powers conferred by virtue of this Part, it ceases to be recoverable.

(3) If—

   (a) in pursuance of a judgment in civil proceedings (whether in the United Kingdom or elsewhere), the defendant makes a payment to the claimant or the claimant otherwise obtains property from the defendant,

   (b) the claimant's claim is based on the defendant's unlawful conduct, and

   (c) apart from this subsection, the sum received, or the property obtained, by the claimant would be recoverable property,

the property ceases to be recoverable.

In relation to Scotland, "claimant" and "defendant" are to be read as "pursuer" and "defender".

(4) If—

   (a) a payment is made to a person in pursuance of a compensation order under Article 14 of the Criminal Justice (Northern Ireland) Order 1994 (S.I. 1994/2795 (N.I. 15)), section 249 of the Criminal Procedure (Scotland) Act 1995 (c. 46) or section 130 of the Powers of Criminal Courts (Sentencing) Act 2000 (c. 6), and

   (b) apart from this subsection, the sum received would be recoverable property,

the property ceases to be recoverable.

(5) If—

   (a) a payment is made to a person in pursuance of a restitution order under section 27 of the Theft Act (Northern Ireland) 1969 (c. 16 (N.I.)) or section 148(2) of the Powers of Criminal Courts (Sentencing) Act 2000 or a person otherwise obtains any property in pursuance of such an order, and

   (b) apart from this subsection, the sum received, or the property obtained, would be recoverable property,

the property ceases to be recoverable.

(6) If—

   (a) in pursuance of an order made by the court under section 382(3) or 383(5) of the Financial Services and Markets Act 2000 (c. 8) (restitution orders), an amount is paid to or distributed among any persons in accordance with the court's directions, and

   (b) apart from this subsection, the sum received by them would be recoverable property,

the property ceases to be recoverable.

(7) If—

   (a) in pursuance of a requirement of the Financial Services Authority under section 384(5) of the Financial Services and Markets Act 2000 (power of authority to require restitution), an amount is paid to or distributed among any persons, and

(b) apart from this subsection, the sum received by them would be recoverable property,

the property ceases to be recoverable.

(8) Property is not recoverable while a restraint order applies to it, that is—

   (a) an order under section 41, 120 or 190, or

   (b) an order under any corresponding provision of an enactment mentioned in section 8(7)(a) to (g).

(9) Property is not recoverable if it has been taken into account in deciding the amount of a person's benefit from criminal conduct for the purpose of making a confiscation order, that is—

   (a) an order under section 6, 92 or 156, or

   (b) an order under a corresponding provision of an enactment mentioned in section 8(7)(a) to (g),

and, in relation to an order mentioned in paragraph (b), the reference to the amount of a person's benefit from criminal conduct is to be read as a reference to the corresponding amount under the enactment in question.

(10) Where—

   (a) a person enters into a transaction to which section 305(2) applies, and

   (b) the disposal is one to which subsection (1) or (2) applies,

this section does not affect the recoverability (by virtue of section 305 (2)) of any property obtained on the transaction in place of the property disposed of.

DEFINITIONS
"property": s.316(4)
"property obtained through unlawful conduct": s.316(1), s.242
"property which represent the original property": s.305(2)
"recoverable property": ss.304 to 310
"unlawful conduct": s.316(1), s.242

GENERAL NOTE
Read this section in conjunction with ss.304 to 307 inclusive. General exceptions are set out in s.308. If any of those exceptions apply, the property ceases to be 'recoverable property'. For example, property purchased in good faith without notice of its illicit origin, ceases to be recoverable: s.308(1). It will be seen that the exceptions are specific and narrow in scope.

309   Other exemptions

(1) An order may provide that property is not recoverable or (as the case may be) associated property if—

   (a) it is prescribed property, or

   (b) it is disposed of in pursuance of a prescribed enactment or an enactment of a prescribed description.

(2) An order may provide that if property is disposed of in pursuance of a prescribed enactment or an enactment of a prescribed description, it is to be treated for the purposes of section 278 as if it had been disposed of in pursuance of a recovery order.

(3) An order under this section may be made so as to apply to property, or a disposal of property, only in prescribed circumstances; and the circumstances may relate to the property or disposal itself or to a person who holds or has held the property or to any other matter.

(4) In this section, an order means an order made by the Secretary of State after consultation with the Scottish Ministers, and prescribed means prescribed by the order.

310   Granting interests

(1) If a person grants an interest in his recoverable property, the question whether the interest is also recoverable is to be determined in the same manner as it is on any other disposal of recoverable property.

(2) Accordingly, on his granting an interest in the property ("the property in question")—

    (a) where the property in question is property obtained through unlawful conduct, the interest is also to be treated as obtained through that conduct,

    (b) where the property in question represents in his hands property obtained through unlawful conduct, the interest is also to be treated as representing in his hands the property so obtained.

Insolvency

311   Insolvency

(1) Proceedings for a recovery order may not be taken or continued in respect of property to which subsection (3) applies unless the appropriate court gives leave and the proceedings are taken or (as the case may be) continued in accordance with any terms imposed by that court.

(2) An application for an order for the further detention of any cash to which subsection (3) applies may not be made under section 295 unless the appropriate court gives leave.

(3) This subsection applies to recoverable property, or property associated with it, if—

    (a) it is an asset of a company being wound up in pursuance of a resolution for voluntary winding up,

    (b) it is an asset of a company and a voluntary arrangement under Part 1 of the 1986 Act, or Part 2 of the 1989 Order, has effect in relation to the company,

    (c) an order under section 2 of the 1985 Act, section 286 of the 1986 Act or Article 259 of the 1989 Order (appointment of interim trustee or interim receiver) has effect in relation to the property,

    (d) it is an asset comprised in the estate of an individual who has been adjudged bankrupt or, in relation to Scotland, of a person whose estate has been sequestrated,

    (e) it is an asset of an individual and a voluntary arrangement under Part 8 of the 1986 Act, or Part 8 of the 1989 Order, has effect in relation to him, or

    (f) in relation to Scotland, it is property comprised in the estate of a person who has granted a trust deed within the meaning of the 1985 Act.

(4) An application under this section, or under any provision of the 1986 Act or the 1989 Order, for leave to take proceedings for a recovery order may be made without notice to any person.

(5) Subsection (4) does not affect any requirement for notice of an application to be given to any person acting as an insolvency practitioner or to the official receiver (whether or not acting as an insolvency practitioner).

(6) References to the provisions of the 1986 Act in sections 420 and 421 of that Act, or to the provisions of the 1989 Order in Articles 364 or 365 of that Order, (insolvent partnerships and estates of deceased persons) include subsections (1) to (3) above.

(7) In this section—

    (a) the 1985 Act means the Bankruptcy (Scotland) Act 1985 (c. 66),

    (b) the 1986 Act means the Insolvency Act 1986 (c. 45),

    (c) the 1989 Order means the Insolvency (Northern Ireland) Order 1989 (S.I. 1989/2405 (N.I. 19)), and in subsection (8) "the applicable enactment" means whichever enactment mentioned in paragraphs (a) to (c) is relevant to the resolution, arrangement, order or trust deed mentioned in subsection (3).

(8) In this section—

    (a) an asset means any property within the meaning of the applicable enactment or, where the 1985 Act is the applicable enactment, any property comprised in an estate to which the 1985 Act applies,

    (b) the appropriate court means the court which, in relation to the resolution, arrangement, order or trust deed mentioned in subsection (3), is the court for the purposes of the applicable enactment or, in relation to Northern Ireland, the High Court,

    (c) acting as an insolvency practitioner has the same meaning as in section 433,

    (d) other expressions used in this section and in the applicable enactment have the same meaning as in that enactment.

Delegation of enforcement functions

312 Performance of functions of Scottish Ministers by constables in Scotland

(1) In Scotland, a constable engaged in temporary service with the Scottish Ministers in connection with their functions under this Part may perform functions, other than those specified in subsection (2), on behalf of the Scottish Ministers.

(2) The specified functions are the functions conferred on the Scottish Ministers by—

    (a) sections 244(1) and (2) and 256(1) and (7) (proceedings in the Court of Session),

    (b) section 267(2) (trustee for civil recovery),

    (c) sections 271(3) and (4) and 272(5) (agreements about associated and joint property),

    (d) section 275(3) (pension schemes),

    (e) section 282(1) (exemptions),

    (f) section 283(5) and (8) (compensation),

    (g) section 287(2) (financial threshold),

    (h) section 293(1) (code of practice),

    (i) section 298(1) (forfeiture),

    (j) section 303(1) (minimum amount).

313 Restriction on performance of Director's functions by police

(1) In spite of section 1(6), nothing which the Director is authorised or required to do for the purposes of this Part may be done by—

    (a) a member of a police force,

    (b) a member of the Police Service of Northern Ireland,

    (c) a person appointed as a police member of the National Criminal Intelligence Service under section 9(1)(b) of the Police Act 1997 (c. 50),

    (d) a person appointed as a police member of the National Crime Squad under section 55(1)(b) of that Act.

(2) In this section—

    (a) "member of a police force" has the same meaning as in the Police Act 1996 (c. 16) and includes a person who would be a member of a police force but for section 97(3) of that Act (police officers engaged on service outside their force),

    (b) "member of the Police Service of Northern Ireland" includes a person who would be a member of the Police Service of Northern Ireland but for section 27(3) of the Police (Northern Ireland) Act 1998 (c. 32) (members of that service engaged on other police service).

Interpretation

314   Obtaining and disposing of property

(1) References to a person disposing of his property include a reference—
  (a) to his disposing of a part of it, or
  (b) to his granting an interest in it,
  (or to both); and references to the property disposed of are to any property obtained on the disposal.

(2) A person who makes a payment to another is to be treated as making a disposal of his property to the other, whatever form the payment takes.

(3) Where a person's property passes to another under a will or intestacy or by operation of law, it is to be treated as disposed of by him to the other.

(4) A person is only to be treated as having obtained his property for value in a case where he gave unexecuted consideration if the consideration has become executed consideration.

315   Northern Ireland courts

In relation to the practice and procedure of courts in Northern Ireland, expressions used in this Part are to be read in accordance with rules of court.

316   General interpretation

(1) In this Part—
  "associated property" has the meaning given by section 245,
  "cash" has the meaning given by section 289(6) or (7),
  "constable", in relation to Northern Ireland, means a police officer within the meaning of the Police (Northern Ireland) Act 2000 (c. 32),
  "country" includes territory,
  "the court" (except in sections 253(2) and (3) and 262(2) and (3) and Chapter 3) means the High Court or (in relation to proceedings in Scotland) the Court of Session,
  "dealing" with property includes disposing of it, taking possession of it or removing it from the United Kingdom,
  "enforcement authority"—
      (a) in relation to England and Wales and Northern Ireland, means the Director,
      (b) in relation to Scotland, means the Scottish Ministers,
  "excepted joint owner" has the meaning given by section 270(4),
  "interest", in relation to land—
      (a) in the case of land in England and Wales or Northern Ireland, means any legal estate and any equitable interest or power,
      (b) in the case of land in Scotland, means any estate, interest, servitude or other heritable right in or over land, including a heritable security,
  "interest", in relation to property other than land, includes any right (including a right to possession of the property),
  "interim administration order" has the meaning given by section 256(2),
  "interim receiving order" has the meaning given by section 246(2),
  "the minimum amount" (in Chapter 3) has the meaning given by section 303,
  "part", in relation to property, includes a portion,
  "premises" has the same meaning as in the Police and Criminal Evidence Act 1984 (c. 60),

"property obtained through unlawful conduct" has the meaning given by section 242,

"recoverable property" is to be read in accordance with sections 304 to 310,

"recovery order" means an order made under section 266,

"respondent" means—

    (a) where proceedings are brought by the enforcement authority by virtue of Chapter 2, the person against whom the proceedings are brought,

    (b) where no such proceedings have been brought but the enforcement authority has applied for an interim receiving order or interim administration order, the person against whom he intends to bring such proceedings,

"share", in relation to an excepted joint owner, has the meaning given by section 270(4),

"unlawful conduct" has the meaning given by section 241,

"value" means market value.

(2) The following provisions apply for the purposes of this Part.

(3) For the purpose of deciding whether or not property was recoverable at any time (including times before commencement), it is to be assumed that this Part was in force at that and any other relevant time.

(4) Property is all property wherever situated and includes—

    (a) money,

    (b) all forms of property, real or personal, heritable or moveable,

    (c) things in action and other intangible or incorporeal property.

(5) Any reference to a person's property (whether expressed as a reference to the property he holds or otherwise) is to be read as follows.

(6) In relation to land, it is a reference to any interest which he holds in the land.

(7) In relation to property other than land, it is a reference—

    (a) to the property (if it belongs to him), or

    (b) to any other interest which he holds in the property.

(8) References to the satisfaction of the enforcement authority's right to recover property obtained through unlawful conduct are to be read in accordance with section 279.

(9) Proceedings against any person for an offence are concluded when—

    (a) the person is convicted or acquitted,

    (b) the prosecution is discontinued or, in Scotland, the trial diet is deserted simpliciter, or

    (c) the jury is discharged without a finding.

PART 6

REVENUE FUNCTIONS

INTRODUCTION TO PART 6

Part 6 of the Act (Revenue Functions) (ss.317 to 326 inclusive, and Sched.8) implements the proposals of the Performance and Innovation Unit of the Cabinet Office, made in their report published in June 2000, that the efficiency of asset recovery arrangements would be increased if the new Assets Recovery Agency ("ARA") were to be enabled to carry out tax functions in relation to criminal gains and criminal property. Note that it is only certain Inland Revenue functions which can be vested in the Director of the ARA: the Act does not extend to any functions (for example, in relation to VAT or customs duties) of the Commissioners of Customs and Excise. The Director has the initiative to decide whether or not to invoke the Revenue functions. He may do so if the appropriate "qualifying condition" is satisfied – that is, he has reasonable grounds to suspect that the income or gain of a person (or company) is taxable, or there has been or may be a charge to inheritance tax, and the income or gain has arisen as a result (whether wholly or partly or directly or indirectly) of any person's criminal conduct (as defined in s.326(1) to (3)), or the charge to inheritance tax relates to criminal property (as defined in s.326 (4) *et seq.*). There are separate provisions relating to the general Revenue functions (ss. 317 to 320) and to the Revenue inheritance tax functions (ss. 321 to 326). The Director invokes the Revenue functions by serving a notice on the Commissioners of Inland Revenue (the Board) (ss.317(2), 321(2), 322(2)). Service of such a notice vests the appropriate Revenue functions in the Director, but does not divest the Inland Revenue of them (ss.317(7), 321(6), 322(6)). It is thus intended that, among other things, routine work can continue to be carried out by the Inland Revenue, notwithstanding the fact that Revenue functions are also at the same time vested in the Director. The Director also has the initiative to decide to withdraw from the exercise of any Revenue functions. He may do so at any time by the service on the Board of a notice of withdrawal (s.317(4)(a), 321(4)(a), 322(4)(a)) and must do so if the qualifying condition ceases to be satisfied, that is, he ceases to have reasonable grounds to suspect that taxable income or gains arise from criminal conduct, or that there has been or may be a charge to inheritance tax in relation to criminal property. There is specific provision (s.324) requiring the Director in the exercise of Revenue functions to apply any interpretation of the law and any concessions (broadly defined in s.324(6)) published by the Inland Revenue and to take account of other material published by the Board (for example the "Inspectors' Manuals" – s.324(4)). Criminal conduct which can give rise to the invocation by the Director of the Revenue functions does not include conduct constituting an offence relating to a matter under the care and management of the Board (for example, direct tax fraud), and therefore the Inland Revenue's functions and responsibilities in relation to the investigation of direct tax fraud and the recovery of tax lost thereby are not affected by this Part of the Act.

General functions

317 Director's general Revenue functions

(1) For the purposes of this section the qualifying condition is that the Director has reasonable grounds to suspect that—
  (a) income arising or a gain accruing to a person in respect of a chargeable period is chargeable to income tax or is a chargeable gain (as the case may be) and arises or accrues as a result of the person's or another's criminal conduct (whether wholly or partly and whether directly or indirectly), or
  (b) a company is chargeable to corporation tax on its profits arising in respect of a chargeable period and the profits arise as a result of the company's or another person's criminal conduct (whether wholly or partly and whether directly or indirectly).

(2) If the qualifying condition is satisfied the Director may serve on the Commissioners of Inland Revenue (the Board) a notice which—
  (a) specifies the person or the company (as the case may be) and the period, and
  (b) states that the Director intends to carry out, in relation to the person or the company (as the case may be) and in respect of the period, such of the general Revenue functions as are specified in the notice.

(3) Service of a notice under subsection (2) vests in the Director, in relation to the person or the company (as the case may be) and in respect of the period, such of the general Revenue functions as are specified in the notice; but this is subject to section 318.

(4) The Director—
  (a) may at any time serve on the Board a notice of withdrawal of the notice under subsection (2);
  (b) must serve such a notice of withdrawal on the Board if the qualifying condition ceases to be satisfied.

(5) A notice under subsection (2) and a notice of withdrawal under subsection (4) may be in respect of one or more periods.

(6) Service of a notice under subsection (4) divests the Director of the functions concerned in relation to the person or the company (as the case may be) and in respect of the period or periods specified in the notice.

(7) The vesting of a function in the Director under this section does not divest the Board or an officer of the Board of the function.

(8) If—
    (a) apart from this section the Board's authorisation would be required for the exercise of a function, and
    (b) the function is vested in the Director under this section,
    the authorisation is not required in relation to the function as so vested.
(9) It is immaterial whether a chargeable period or any part of it falls before or after the passing of this Act.

<small>DEFINITIONS</small>
    "chargeable gain": s.326(12); s.15(2) Taxation of Chargeable Gains Act 1992 (c.12)
    "chargeable period": s.326(12); s.118 Taxes Management Act 1970 (c.9); s.288 Taxation of Chargeable Gains Act 1992; s.832(1) Income and Corporation Taxes Act 1988 (c.1)
    "criminal conduct": s.326(1) to (3)
    "general Revenue functions": s.323(1)
    "officer of the Board": s.326(11)
    "the Board": s.326(12); s.118 Taxes Management Act 1970
    "the Director": s.1(2)
    "the Taxes Acts": s.326(12); s.118 Taxes Management Act 1970; Sch1 Interpretation Act 1978 (c.30)

<small>GENERAL NOTE</small>
    This section deals with the Director's general Revenue functions (as opposed to his Revenue inheritance tax functions – see: ss.321, 322). The general Revenue functions are defined in s.323 (1) and are such of the functions vested in the Board (the Commissioners of Inland Revenue) or an officer of the Board as relate to:
    (a) income tax;
    (b) capital gains tax;
    (c) corporation tax;
    (d) national insurance contributions;
    (e) statutory sick pay;
    (f) statutory maternity pay;
    (g) statutory paternity pay;
    (h) statutory adoption pay; or
    (i) student loans.
    They do not include other Revenue functions, such as those relating to stamp duty. The scheme of the section is that once the Director has reasonable grounds to suspect that taxable income or profits have arisen or accrued as a result of any person's criminal conduct (*i.e.* that the qualifying condition is satisfied) he may serve on the Board a notice specifying the taxpayer and the period concerned, and stating that he intends to carry out in relation to the specified taxpayer and in respect of the specified period, such of the general Revenue functions as are specified in the notice. The service of such a notice vests the specified general Revenue functions in the Director (but does not divest the Board or an officer of the Board of them – s.317(7)) until the Director serves a notice of withdrawal on the Board – which he may do at any time, but must do if the qualifying condition ceases to be satisfied. A notice of withdrawal divests the Director of the functions concerned to the extent specified in the notice. The general Revenue functions can be exercised in respect of any chargeable period whether or not any part of it falls before the passing of the Act (s.317(9)).

Subs. (1)
    Subsection (1) sets out the qualifying condition as it applies (a) in relation to a person who is not a company, and (b) in relation to a company. It requires that the Director must have reasonable grounds to suspect that the person's or company's taxable income, profits or gains arise or accrue as a result of criminal conduct (defined in s.326(1) to (3)), whether wholly or partly, and whether directly or indirectly, and whether the criminal conduct is the conduct of the person or company concerned or any other person or company.

Subs. (2)
    Subsection (2) sets out the Director's power to serve a notice on the Board, which must specify both the person or the company concerned and also the chargeable period concerned – though the notice may cover more than one chargeable period (s.317(5)). The notice must also specify which of the general Revenue functions the Director intends to carry out.

Subs. (3)
    Subsection (3) vests in the Director the general Revenue functions indicated in the notice served under subs.(2) but subject to s.318 (Revenue functions regarding employment).

Subs. (4)

Subsection (4) entitles the Director to serve on the Board at any time a notice of withdrawal of a notice served under subs.(2) – in relation to one or more chargeable periods (s.317(5)), and obliges him to do so if the qualifying condition (see: subs.(1)) ceases to be satisfied.

Subs. (6)

Subsection (6) provides that the service of a notice of withdrawal under subs.(4) divests the Director of the general Revenue functions in respect of the chargeable period or periods specified in the notice.

Subs. (7)

Subsection (7) provides that the vesting of a Revenue function in the Director does not divest the Board or an officer of the Board of the function.

Subs. (8)

Subsection (8) excludes any requirement of the Taxes Acts that the Board's authorisation is needed for the exercise of any general Revenue function, in a case where that function is vested in the Director under this section.

318   Revenue functions regarding employment

(1) Subsection (2) applies if—
    (a) the Director serves a notice or notices under section 317(2) in relation to a company and in respect of a period or periods, and
    (b) the company is an employer.
(2) The general Revenue functions vested in the Director do not include functions relating to any requirement which—
    (a) is imposed on the company in its capacity as employer, and
    (b) relates to a year of assessment which does not fall wholly within the period or periods.
(3) Subsection (4) applies if—
    (a) the Director serves a notice or notices under section 317(2) in relation to an individual and in respect of a year or years of assessment, and
    (b) the individual is a self-employed earner.
(4) The general Revenue functions vested in the Director do not include functions relating to any liability to pay Class 2 contributions in respect of a period which does not fall wholly within the year or years of assessment.
(5) In this section in its application to Great Britain—
    (a) "self-employed earner" has the meaning given by section 2(1)(b) of the Social Security Contributions and Benefits Act 1992 (c. 4);
    (b) "Class 2 contributions" must be construed in accordance with section 1(2)(c) of that Act.
(6) In this section in its application to Northern Ireland—
    (a) "self-employed earner" has the meaning given by section 2(1)(b) of the Social Security Contributions and Benefits (Northern Ireland) Act 1992 (c. 7);
    (b) "Class 2 contributions" must be construed in accordance with section 1(2)(c) of that Act.

DEFINITIONS

"Class 2 contributions": subs. (5)(b); s. 1(2)(c), Social Security Contributions and Benefits Act 1992 (c.4), or, in relation to Northern Ireland, subs. (6)(b); s. 1(2)(c) Social Security Contributions and Benefits (Northern Ireland) Act 1992 (c.7)

"self-employed earner": subs. (5)(a); s.2(1)(b), Social Security Contributions and Benefits Act 1992,

or, in relation to Northern Ireland, subs. (6)(a); s.2(1)(b), Social Security Contributions and Benefits (Northern Ireland) Act 1992

GENERAL NOTE

This section excludes particular Revenue functions from being general Revenue functions in relation to which a notice can be served by the Director on the Board under s.317(2). The functions concerned are some (but not all) of those Revenue functions which relate to requirements imposed on a *company* in its capacity as employer – including the requirement to operate PAYE and deduct national insurance contributions in respect of its employees' emoluments – and some (but not all) of those Revenue functions which relate to a *self-employed individual's* liability to pay Class 2 national insurance contributions. The details are set out below. It is noteworthy that an *individual's* obligations as an employer, to operate PAYE in respect of his employees, etc., are not excluded by this section, and that the exclusion only operates in any case so far as the periods relevant to a company's obligation as employer, or an individual's liability to make Class 2 contributions, are not wholly within the period(s) specified in the notice served by the Director under s.317(2).

Subss.(1) and (2)

Subsections (1) and (2) exclude, in any case where a notice is served in relation to a *company* – see s. 317(2) and (1)(b) – which is an *employer*, those Revenue functions relating to any requirement imposed on the company in its capacity as an employer which "relate to a year of assessment which does not fall wholly within the period or periods" in respect of which the notice under s.317(2) is served – see subs. (2)(b). The Home Office Explanatory Notes accompanying the Bill explain that this provision is inserted to deal with the "mismatch" between accounting periods relevant to corporation tax, which will be the chargeable periods for a company specified in any notice served by the Director under s.317(2), and years of assessment, which are relevant to the company's obligations as employer to account for its employees' income tax (under PAYE), national insurance contributions and student loan repayments. The Director can only take over responsibility for the Revenue functions relevant to such responsibilities of a company in its capacity as employer where the relevant periods for those matters fall wholly within a period or periods for which the Director has served a notice under s.317(2).

Subss.(3) and (4)

Subsections (3) and (4) similarly exclude, in any case where a notice is served by the Director in relation to an *individual*, those Revenue functions relating to any liability of the individual to pay Class 2 national insurance contributions "in respect of a period which does not fall wholly within the year or years of assessment" in respect of which the notice under s.317(2) is served – see subs. (4). Class 2 contributions are flat-rate contributions payable weekly under s.11 Social Security Contributions and Benefits Act 1992 by "self-employed earners", defined as persons who are "gainfully employed in Great Britain (or Northern Ireland – see: the Northern Ireland legislation) otherwise than in employed earner's employment (whether or not [they are] also employed in such employment)" – see: s.2(1)(b) of the 1992 Act. The Director can only take over responsibility for the Revenue functions relevant to such liabilities of an individual where the relevant periods for those liabilities (the weeks concerned) fall wholly within a period or periods for which the Director has served a notice under s.317(2).

319   Source of income

(1) For the purpose of the exercise by the Director of any function vested in him by virtue of this Part it is immaterial that he cannot identify a source for any income.

(2) An assessment made by the Director under section 29 of the Taxes Management Act 1970 (c. 9) (assessment where loss of tax discovered) in respect of income charged to tax under Case 6 of Schedule D must not be reduced or quashed only because it does not specify (to any extent) the source of the income.

(3) If the Director serves on the Board a notice of withdrawal under section 317(4), any assessment made by him under section 29 of the Taxes Management Act 1970 is invalid to the extent that it does not specify a source for the income.

(4) Subsections (2) and (3) apply in respect of years of assessment whenever occurring.

GENERAL NOTE

It is a general rule of income tax that income is taxable only if a source of that income is identified. For example, income is taxable under Case I of Schedule D if a trade (not being a

Schedule A business – relating to the exploitation of UK land) is identified as the source of that income. Although most income is now self-assessed by taxpayers, there remains the Revenue function of assessing income to tax where for whatever reason it has not been self-assessed. This Revenue function will of course be central to the Director's concerns when he serves a notice under s.317(2). This section removes from the Director, in exercising any Revenue function, any obligation to identify a source for any income. This is necessary to the effective use of the Director's powers, because he will be acting on his reasonable suspicion and it is to be expected that the source of any income arising or accruing as a result of criminal conduct may be well concealed.

Subss.(1) and (2)
Subsections (1) and (2) make this provision and (by subs.(2)) it is specifically provided that an assessment made by the Director under s.29 Taxes Management Act 1970 (the power to assess to tax where any loss of tax is discovered) which charges income to tax under Case 6 of Schedule D (tax in respect of any annual profits or gains not falling under any other Case of Schedule D and not charged by virtue of Schedule A or E – see: s.18(1) Income and Corporation Taxes Act 1988) must not be reduced (presumably on appeal) or quashed (presumably on judicial review) only because it does not specify (to any extent) the source of the income.

Subs. (3)
However, by subs.(3) it is provided that if the assessing function reverts to the Inland Revenue by virtue of the service by the Director of a notice of withdrawal under s.317(4), an assessment made by the Director under s.29 of the 1970 Act becomes invalid to the extent that it does not specify a source for the income.

Subs. (4)
Subsection (4) makes clear that these rules apply, for whatever year of assessment an assessment is made, thus giving the provisions retrospective effect.

320 Appeals

(1) An appeal in respect of the exercise by the Director of general Revenue functions shall be to the Special Commissioners.

(2) The Presiding Special Commissioner may nominate one or more assessors to assist the Special Commissioners in any appeal to be heard by them in respect of the exercise by the Director of any of his Revenue functions.

(3) An assessor nominated under subsection (2)—
  (a) must have special knowledge and experience of the matter to which the appeal relates, and
  (b) must be selected from a panel of persons appointed for the purposes of this section by the Lord Chancellor after consultation with the Scottish Ministers.

(4) Regulations made under section 56B of the Taxes Management Act 1970 may include provision as to the manner in which an assessor nominated under subsection (2) is to assist the Special Commissioners.

(5) The remuneration of an assessor nominated under subsection (2) must be paid by the Lord Chancellor and must be at such rate as he decides.

DEFINITIONS
"the Presiding Special Commissioner": s.326(12); s.4(1) Taxes Management Act 1970
"the Special Commissioners": s.326(12); s.4(1) Taxes Management Act 1970

GENERAL NOTE

Subs. (1)
Subsection (1) provides that any appeal in respect of the exercise by the Director of the general Revenue functions must be to the Special Commissioners. In the normal case, where the functions are exercised by the Inland Revenue, there is often a possibility of appealing to General Commissioners (a more local appeal body) rather than the Special Commissioners. This

possibility is excluded by this section in a case where the Director has exercised the general Revenue functions.

Subs. (2)

Subsection (2) authorises the Presiding Special Commissioner (who nominates the panel of Special Commissioners to hear an appeal) to nominate one or more assessors to assist the Special Commissioners in an appeal against the exercise by the Director of a general Revenue function.

The assessor(s) concerned must have special knowledge and experience of the matter to which the appeal relates (which, it may be supposed, will often be technical, for example relating to insurance or other financial services) and must be drawn from a panel of assessors appointed for the purpose by the Lord Chancellor after consultation with the Scottish Ministers (subs.(3)).

The Lord Chancellor's power to make regulations about the practice and procedure to be followed in connection with tax appeals (under s.56B Taxes Management Act 1970) is extended (by subs.(4)) to include provision as to how an assessor is to assist the Special Commissioners.

Subs. (5)

Subsection (5) charges the Lord Chancellor with the responsibility of paying remuneration to assessors at such rate as he decides.

Inheritance tax functions

321   Director's functions: transfers of value

(1) For the purposes of this section the qualifying condition is that the Director has reasonable grounds to suspect that—
   (a) there has been a transfer of value within the meaning of the Inheritance Tax Act 1984 (c. 51), and
   (b) the value transferred by it is attributable (in whole or part) to criminal property.

(2) If the qualifying condition is satisfied the Director may serve on the Board a notice which—
   (a) specifies the transfer of value, and
   (b) states that the Director intends to carry out the Revenue inheritance tax functions in relation to the transfer.

(3) Service of a notice under subsection (2) vests in the Director the Revenue inheritance tax functions in relation to the transfer.

(4) The Director—
   (a) may at any time serve on the Board a notice of withdrawal of the notice under subsection (2);
   (b) must serve such a notice of withdrawal on the Board if the qualifying condition ceases to be satisfied.

(5) Service of a notice under subsection (4) divests the Director of the Revenue inheritance tax functions in relation to the transfer.

(6) The vesting of a function in the Director under this section does not divest the Board or an officer of the Board of the function.

(7) It is immaterial whether a transfer of value is suspected to have occurred before or after the passing of this Act.

DEFINITION

"criminal property"; s.326(4) to (10)
"the Board": s.326(12); s.118 Taxes Management Act 1970
"the Revenue inheritance tax functions"; s.323(2),(3)
"transfer of value": subs. (1)(a); s.3 Inheritance Tax Act 1984 (c. 51)
"value transferred" by a transfer of value: subs. (1); s.3(1) Inheritance Tax Act 1984

GENERAL NOTE

This section and the following section deal with the Director's Revenue inheritance tax functions, as opposed to his general Revenue functions. The Revenue inheritance tax functions (as generally defined in s.323(2) – but see the exceptions in s.323(3)) are "such functions vested in the Board [of Inland Revenue] or in an officer of the Board as relate to inheritance tax". As with the general Revenue functions, this section (and s.322) gives the Director the initiative to assume the Revenue inheritance tax functions in any case where he suspects that a transfer of value has been made where the value transferred is (in whole or in part) attributable to criminal property.

The basic scheme of inheritance tax is to charge tax on a "transfer of value", which is a disposition made by a person such that the value of his estate goes down (see: s.3(1) Inheritance Tax Act 1984). There is an important exception to this principle in the case of "settlements without interests in possession" (see Chap. III of Pt. III of the Inheritance Tax Act 1984), which are, broadly, settlements where no-one has the right to call for the income of the trust property (discretionary settlements). In the case of such settlements, inheritance tax is not charged by reference to a "transfer of value", but is instead charged by ten-yearly periodic charges on the value of the trust property, and by a charge when an event occurs which reduces the value of the trust property. Such settlements are dealt with in s.322.

For the normal case of a charge to inheritance tax, however, which includes a charge on a transfer of value made on death, and a charge on a transfer of value made when a discretionary settlement is made, this section makes provision for the Director to exercise the Revenue inheritance tax functions where he reasonably suspects that the value transferred by the transfer of value is attributable (in whole or in part) to criminal property – as defined in s.326(4) to (10).

Subs. (1)
Subsection (1) sets out the qualifying condition, which is that the Director has reasonable grounds to suspect that there has been a transfer of value and that the value transferred by it is attributable (in whole or in part) to criminal property.

Subs. (2)
Subsection (2) provides that where the qualifying condition is satisfied, the Director may serve on the Board (of Inland Revenue) a notice which specifies the transfer of value and states that the Director intends to carry out the Revenue inheritance tax functions in relation to the transfer.

Subs. (3)
By subs.(3) on the service of a notice under subs. (2) the Revenue inheritance tax functions become vested in the Director in relation to the transfer. This will usually mean that he, and not the Inland Revenue, will investigate the transfer and assess it to inheritance tax.

Subs. (4)
Subsection (4) entitles the Director to serve on the Board, at any time, a notice of withdrawal of a notice served under subs.(2), and he must do so if the qualifying condition ceases to be satisfied. This is a parallel provision to that of s.317(4) in relation to the general Revenue functions.

Subs. (5)
If a notice is served under subs.(4) subs.(5) divests the Director of the Revenue inheritance tax functions in relation to the transfer.

Subs. (6)
However, by subs.(6) it is expressly provided that the vesting of the Revenue inheritance tax functions in the Director does not divest the Inland Revenue of them.

Subs. (7)
By subs.(7) it is expressly provided that the section is to have retrospective effect, in that it can apply in relation to any transfer of value suspected to have occurred before or after the passing of the Act.

322   Director's functions: certain settlements

(1) For the purposes of this section the qualifying condition is that the Director has reasonable grounds to suspect that—
   (a) all or part of the property comprised in a settlement is relevant property for the purposes of Chapter 3 of Part 3 of the Inheritance Tax Act 1984 (settlements without interest in possession), and
   (b) the relevant property is (in whole or part) criminal property.
(2) If the qualifying condition is satisfied the Director may serve on the Board a notice which—

(a) specifies the settlement concerned,
(b) states that the Director intends to carry out the Revenue inheritance tax functions in relation to the settlement, and
(c) states the period for which he intends to carry them out.
(3) Service of a notice under subsection (2) vests in the Director the Revenue inheritance tax functions in relation to the settlement for the
period.
(4) The Director—
(a) may at any time serve on the Board a notice of withdrawal of the
notice under subsection (2);
(b) must serve such a notice of withdrawal on the Board if the qualifying condition ceases to be satisfied.
(5) Service of a notice under subsection (4) divests the Director of the
Revenue inheritance tax functions in relation to the settlement for the
period.
(6) The vesting of a function in the Director under this section does not
divest the Board or an officer of the Board of the function.
(7) It is immaterial whether the settlement is commenced or a charge to
tax arises or a period or any part of it falls before or after the passing of
this Act.

DEFINITIONS
"criminal property": s.326(4) to (10)
"relevant property": subs. (1)(a); s.58 Inheritance Tax Act 1984
"settlements without interest in possession": Chapter III, Part III, Inheritance Tax Act 1984
"the Board": s.326(12); s.118 Taxes Management Act 1970

GENERAL NOTE
This section deals with the Director's Revenue inheritance tax functions in cases where no
transfer of value is suspected. As stated in the General Note to the previous section (s.321), this
may occur where there is a settlement without an interest in possession within the meaning of
Chap.III of Pt.III of the Inheritance Tax Act 1984 - broadly, where there is a discretionary trust
in relation to which no-one is entitled to call for the trust income. Where a settlement holds
property in which there is no interest in possession, the property is referred to as "relevant
property" - see the definition in s.58 Inheritance Tax Act 1984, which is incorporated by subs.
(1)(a). It is important to note that any particular settlement can be *both* a settlement with an
interest in possession *and* a settlement without an interest in possession - for example where part
of the trust property is held on trust for a life-tenant (who is entitled to the income of that part
during his lifetime) and the other part of the trust property is held on discretionary trusts. In such
a case the "relevant property" (in which no interest in possession subsists) will be subject to
Chap.III of Pt. III of the Inheritance Tax Act 1984, while the other part of the settlement property will not.

Subs. (1)
Subsection (1) sets out the qualifying condition, which is that the Director has reasonable
grounds to suspect that all or part of the property comprised in a settlement is "relevant property" and that the relevant property is (in whole or in part) criminal property.

Subs. (2)
Subsection (2) provides that where the qualifying condition is satisfied, the Director may
serve on the Board (of Inland Revenue) a notice which specifies the settlement concerned and
states that the Director intends to carry out the Revenue inheritance tax functions in relation to
the settlement and, also, the period for which he intends to carry them out.

Subs. (2)
Subsection (3) provides that the service of a notice under subs.(2) vests in the Director the
Revenue inheritance tax functions in relation to the settlement for the period. This will usually
mean that he, and not the Inland Revenue, will investigate and assess the settlement to inheritance tax.

Subs. (4)
Subsection (4) entitles the Director to serve on the Board a notice of withdrawal of a notice
served under subs.(2), at any time, and he must do so if the qualifying condition ceases to be

satisfied. This is a parallel provision to that of s.317(4) in relation to the general Revenue functions (and to that of s.321(4) in relation to the Revenue inheritance tax functions in the case of a suspected transfer of value).

Subs. (5)

If a notice is served under subs.(4) subs.(5) divests the Director of the Revenue inheritance tax functions in relation to the transfer.

Subs. (6)

However, by subs.(6) it is expressly provided that the vesting of the Revenue inheritance tax functions in the Director does not divest the Inland Revenue of them.

Subs. (7)

By subs.(7) it is expressly provided that the section is to have retrospective effect, in that it can apply in relation to any settlement or charge to inheritance tax whether it arises before of after the passing of the Act, and the section can apply to a period whether it or any part of it falls before or after the passing of the Act.

General

323   Functions

(1) The general Revenue functions are such of the functions vested in the Board or in an officer of the Board as relate to any of the following matters—

    (a) income tax;

    (b) capital gains tax;

    (c) corporation tax;

    (d) national insurance contributions;

    (e) statutory sick pay;

    (f) statutory maternity pay;

    (g) statutory paternity pay;

    (h) statutory adoption pay;

    (i) student loans.

(2) The Revenue inheritance tax functions are such functions vested in the Board or in an officer of the Board as relate to inheritance tax.

(3) But the general Revenue functions and the Revenue inheritance tax functions do not include any of the following functions—

    (a) functions relating to the making of subordinate legislation (within the meaning given by section 21(1) of the Interpretation Act 1978 (c. 30));

    (b) the function of the prosecution of offences;

    (c) the function of authorising an officer for the purposes of section 20BA of the Taxes Management Act 1970 (c. 9) (orders for delivery of documents);

    (d) the function of giving information under that section;

    (e) the function of approving an officer's application for the purposes of section 20C of the Taxes Management Act 1970 (warrant to enter and search premises);

    (f) the function of applying under that section.

(4) For the purposes of this section in its application to Great Britain—

    (a) national insurance contributions are contributions payable under Part 1 of the Social Security Contributions and Benefits Act 1992 (c. 4);

    (b) "statutory sick pay" must be construed in accordance with section 151(1) of that Act;

    (c) "statutory maternity pay" must be construed in accordance with section 164(1) of that Act;

    (d) "statutory paternity pay" must be construed in accordance with section 171ZA of that Act;

    (e) "statutory adoption pay" must be construed in accordance with section 171ZL of that Act;

    (f) "student loans" must be construed in accordance with the Education (Student Loans) (Repayment) Regulations 2000 (S.I. 2000/944).

(5) For the purposes of this section in its application to Northern Ireland—

    (a) national insurance contributions are contributions payable under Part 1 of the Social Security Contributions and Benefits (Northern Ireland) Act 1992 (c. 7);

    (b) "statutory sick pay" must be construed in accordance with section 147(1) of that Act;

    (c) "statutory maternity pay" must be construed in accordance with section 160(1) of that Act;

    (d) "statutory paternity pay" must be construed in accordance with any Northern Ireland legislation which corresponds to Part 12ZA of the Social Security Contributions and Benefits Act 1992;

    (e) "statutory adoption pay" must be construed in accordance with any Northern Ireland legislation which corresponds to Part 12ZB of that Act;

    (f) "student loans" must be construed in accordance with the Education (Student Loans) (Repayment) Regulations (Northern Ireland) 2000 (S.R. 2000/121).

DEFINITIONS
    "the Board": s.326(1); s.118 Taxes Management Act 1970
    "officer of the Board": s.326(11)

In relation to the application of this section to Great Britain
    "national insurance contributions": subs. (4)(a); Part I, Social Security Contributions and Benefits Act 1992
    "statutory adoption pay": subs. (4)(e); s.171ZL Social Security Contributions and Benefits Act 1992
    "statutory maternity pay": subs. (4)(c); s.164(1) Social Security Contributions and Benefits Act 1992
    "statutory paternity pay": subs. (4)(d); s.171ZA Social Security Contributions and Benefits Act 1992
    "Statutory sick pay": subs. (4)(b); s.151(1) Social Security Contributions and Benefits Act 1992
    "student loans": subs. 4(f); Education (Student Loans) (Repayment) Regulations (S.I. 2000 No. 944)

In relation to the application of this section to Northern Ireland
    "national insurance contributions": subs. (5)(a); Part I, Social Security Contributions and Benefits (Northern Ireland) Act 1992
    "statutory adoption pay": subs. (5)(e); to be construed in accordance with any Northern Ireland legislation which corresponds to Part 12ZB of the Social Security Contributions and Benefits Act 1992
    "statutory maternity pay": subs. (5)(c); s.160(1) Social Security Contributions and Benefits (Northern Ireland) Act 1992
    "statutory paternity pay": subs. (5)(d); to be construed in accordance with any Northern Ireland legislation which corresponds to Part 12ZA of the Social Security Contributions and Benefits Act 1992
    "statutory sick pay": subs. (5)(b); s.147(1) Social Security Contributions and Benefits (Northern Ireland) Act 1992
    "student loans"; subs. (5)(f); Education (Student Loans) (Repayment) Regulations (Northern Ireland) (S.R 2000 No. 121)

GENERAL NOTE
    This section defines, by subs.(1), the general Revenue functions, and, by subs.(2), the Revenue inheritance tax functions, but subject, in both cases to the exceptions provided by subs.(3).

The *general Revenue functions* are such of the functions vested in the Inland Revenue (the Board or an officer of the Board) as relate to any of the following:

(a) income tax;
(b) capital gains tax;
(c) corporation tax;
(d) national insurance contributions;
(e) statutory sick pay;
(f) statutory maternity pay;
(g) statutory paternity pay;
(h) statutory adoption pay;
(i) student loans.

Note that there are other functions of the Inland Revenue not within this definition (or the definition of Revenue inheritance tax functions) - for example, their functions relating to stamp duty.

The *Revenue inheritance tax functions* are such functions vested in the Board or an officer of the Board as relate to inheritance tax.

The *exclusions* from the definitions of the general Revenue functions and the Revenue inheritance tax functions are provided by subs.(3).

They are:

(a) functions relating to the *making of subordinate legislation* within the meaning given by s.21(1) of the Interpretation Act 1978 (c.30), for example regulations;
(b) the function of the *prosecution* of offences;
(c) the function of *authorising an officer for the purposes of section 20BA of the Taxes Management Act 1970;*
(d) the function of *giving information under section 20BA of the Taxes Management Act 1970;*
(e) The function of *approving an officer's application for the purposes of section 20C of the Taxes Management Act 1970;*
(f) The function of *applying under section 20C of the Taxes Management Act 1970.*

As to subss.(3)(c) and (d), these relate to s.20BA of the Taxes Management Act 1970 which enacts a procedure for a court order requiring the delivery of documents to the Board for the purpose of investigating and/or prosecuting offences involving serious tax fraud. Under this procedure, the Board may authorise officers for the purposes of the section, who may give information on oath to a circuit judge in support of an application for such a court order. Both the function of authorising an officer for the purposes of the section and the function of giving information under the section are excepted from the Revenue functions which may be assumed by the Director under this Part of the Act.

As to subss.(3) (e) and (f), these relate to s.20C of the Taxes Management Act 1970 which enacts a procedure for the entry (if necessary, by force) on to premises with a warrant, for the purpose of seizing and removing any things found there which an officer of the Board exercising the powers conferred by the warrant has reasonable cause to believe may be required as evidence for the purposes of proceedings in relation to offences involving serious tax fraud. Under this procedure, the Board must approve an application for a warrant, and an officer of the Board must satisfy a circuit judge by information on oath that he is acting with the approval of the Board given in relation to the particular case and that there is reasonable ground for suspecting that an offence involving serious tax fraud is being, has been or is about to be committed, and that evidence of it is to be found on the premises specified in the information. Both the function of approving an officer's application for a warrant under s.20C and the function of applying to the judge for a warrant under that section are excluded from the Revenue functions which may be assumed by the Director under this Part of the Act.

324   Exercise of Revenue functions

(1) This section applies in relation to the exercise by the Director of—
   (a) general Revenue functions;
   (b) Revenue inheritance tax functions.
(2) Paragraph (b) of section 1(6) does not apply.
(3) The Director must apply—
   (a) any interpretation of the law which has been published by the Board;
   (b) any concession which has been published by the Board and which is available generally to any person falling within its terms.
(4) The Director must also take account of any material published by the Board which does not fall within subsection (3).

(5) The Director must provide the Board with such documents and information as they consider appropriate.

(6) "Concession" includes any practice, interpretation or other statement in the nature of a concession.

DEFINITIONS
"concession": subs. (6)
"the Board": s.326(12); s.118 Taxes Management Act 1970
"the general Revenue functions": s.323(1)
"the Revenue inheritance tax functions": s.323(2),(3)

GENERAL NOTE
The main effect of this section is to ensure that when the Director exercises any Revenue functions, he does so himself, or by a member of his staff and not any "outsourced" contractor, and in a manner consistent with the way in which they would otherwise be exercised by the Inland Revenue, that is to say, by applying interpretations of the law and general concessions, which have been published by the Board of Inland Revenue, and by taking account of other material published by the Board. The section also provides that the Director must provide the Board with any documents and information which the Board considers appropriate. This last provision is the only provision which provides that any information must be given by the Director to the Board relating to his exercise of any Revenue functions. The Board of Inland Revenue have no other statutory means of knowing how the Director is exercising the Revenue functions, let alone any statutory supervision or control of the exercise of those functions.

Subs. (1)
Subsection (1) states that the exercise by the Director of both the general Revenue functions and the Revenue inheritance tax functions are governed by the provisions of this section.

Subs. (2)
Subsection (2), by disapplying s.1(6)(b) of the Act to the exercise of the Revenue functions provides that they may only be carried out by the Director and/or member(s) of the staff of the Assets Recovery Agency, and not by any "outsourced" contractor.

Subs. (3)
Subsection (3) provides that the Director (and his staff) must apply any interpretations of the law published by the Inland Revenue and any generally applicable concessions (defined broadly in subs.(6)) published by the Inland Revenue, when exercising any of the Revenue functions.

Subs. (4)
Subsection (4) requires the Director (and his staff) to take account of other material published by the Inland Revenue when exercising the Revenue functions. This most obviously includes the published Inspector's Manuals.

Subs. (5)
Subsection (5) obliges the Director to provide to the Board of Inland Revenue and documents and information considered by the Board to be appropriate.

325   **Declarations**

(1) As soon as practicable after the appointment of a person as the Director he must make a declaration in the form set out in Schedule 8 before a member of the Board.

(2) Every member of the staff of the Agency who is authorised under section 1(6)(a) to carry out any of the functions of the Director under this Part must, as soon as practicable after being so authorised, make a declaration in the form set out in Schedule 8 before a person nominated by the Director for the purpose.

DEFINITIONS
"the Agency": s.1(1)
"the Board": s.326(12); s.118 Taxes Management Act 1970
"the Director: s.1(2)

GENERAL NOTE

This section makes provision for declarations to be made by the Director on his appointment, and by every member of the staff of the Assets Recovery Agency, who is authorised (under s.1(6)(a) of the Act) to carry out any of the Revenue functions vested in the Director under this Part. The forms of the two declarations are set out in Schedule 8 to the Act.

Subs. (1)

Subsection (1) covers the declaration to be made by a person on appointment as the Director. The declaration is to be made as soon as practicable after appointment before a member of the Board of Inland Revenue.

Subs. (2)

Subsection (2) covers the declaration to be made by every member of the staff of the Agency who is authorised to carry out any of the Revenue functions from time to time vested in the Director. The declaration is to be made as soon as practicable after authorisation before a person nominated by the Director for the purpose.

326   Interpretation

(1) Criminal conduct is conduct which—
  (a) constitutes an offence in any part of the United Kingdom, or
  (b) would constitute an offence in any part of the United Kingdom if it occurred there.
(2) But criminal conduct does not include conduct constituting an offence relating to a matter under the care and management of the Board.
(3) In applying subsection (1) it is immaterial whether conduct occurred before or after the passing of this Act.
(4) Property is criminal property if it constitutes a person's benefit from criminal conduct or it represents such a benefit (in whole or part and whether directly or indirectly); and it is immaterial—
  (a) who carried out the conduct;
  (b) who benefited from it.
(5) A person benefits from conduct if he obtains property as a result of or in connection with the conduct.
(6) If a person obtains a pecuniary advantage as a result of or in connection with conduct, he is to be taken to obtain as a result of or in connection with the conduct a sum of money equal to the value of the pecuniary advantage.
(7) References to property or a pecuniary advantage obtained in connection with conduct include references to property or a pecuniary advantage obtained in both that connection and some other.
(8) If a person benefits from conduct his benefit is the property obtained as a result of or in connection with the conduct.
(9) Property is all property wherever situated and includes—
  (a) money;
  (b) all forms of property, real or personal, heritable or moveable;
  (c) things in action and other intangible or incorporeal property.
(10) The following rules apply in relation to property—
  (a) property is obtained by a person if he obtains an interest in it;
  (b) references to an interest, in relation to land in England and Wales or Northern Ireland, are to any legal estate or equitable interest or power;
  (c) references to an interest, in relation to land in Scotland, are to any estate, interest, servitude or other heritable right in or over land, including a heritable security;
  (d) references to an interest, in relation to property other than land, include references to a right (including a right to possession).
(11) Any reference to an officer of the Board includes a reference to—

      (a) a collector of taxes;
      (b) an inspector of taxes.
(12) Expressions used in this Part and in the Taxes Acts have the same meaning as in the Taxes Acts (within the meaning given by section 118 of the Taxes Management Act 1970 (c. 9)).
(13) This section applies for the purposes of this Part.

DEFINITIONS
    "criminal conduct": subs.(1) to (3)
    "criminal property": subs.(4) to (1)
    "officer of the Board": subs.(11)
    "the Board": subs.(12); s.118 Taxes Management Act 1970

GENERAL NOTE
    This section is the interpretation section for the purposes of Pt. 6 of the Act (Revenue functions) – see: subs.(13). It contains definitions of "criminal conduct", "criminal property" and "officer of the Board", and also, by subs.(12), imports into Pt. 6 meanings given in the Taxes Acts for expressions used in Pt. 6. Section 118 Taxes Management Act 1970, read together with Sched.1 to the Interpretation Act 1978 (c.30), provides that the Taxes Acts are: all enactments relating to income tax, the enactments relating to the taxation of income and chargeable gains of companies and of company distributions (principally the Income and Corporation Taxes Act 1988), the Taxation of Chargeable Gains Act 1992 and all other enactments relating to capital gains tax and the Development Land Tax Act 1976 and any other enactment relating to development land tax (although this last reference to enactments relating to development land tax is otiose following the abolition of that tax).
    "Criminal conduct" is defined by subs.(1) as conduct which constitutes an offence in any part of the UK or would constitute any offence in any part of the UK if it occurred there. There is thus effectively no territorial limitation to criminal conduct for the purpose of this Part. There is an exception provided by subs.(2) to the effect that criminal conduct does not include conduct constituting an offence relating to a matter under the care and management of the Board of Inland Revenue – thus offences of direct tax fraud (though not, for example, VAT fraud) are excluded, and the Inland Revenue's position as investigator and prosecutor of such offences is not affected by this Part. Subsection (3) introduces retrospective effect to the definition of criminal conduct by providing that it is immaterial in applying the definition whether conduct occurred before or after the passing of the Act.
    "Criminal property" is defined by subs.(4) as property constituting a person's benefit from criminal conduct and property representing such a benefit, and it is expressly provided that it is immaterial who carried out the conduct and who benefited from it. Thus "criminal property" can be property held by persons other than those who have committed criminal conduct.
    Subsection (5) provides that a person benefits from conduct if he obtains property as a result of or in connection with the conduct. Some causation linking the conduct with the obtaining of the property is therefore necessary to establish that the property constitutes (or represents) a person's benefit from criminal conduct.
    It is provided by subs.(6) that the obtaining of a pecuniary advantage as a result of or in connection with conduct is to be treated for the purposes of the definition of criminal property as the obtaining of a sum of money equal to the value of the pecuniary advantage.
    Subsection (7) provides in effect that property or a pecuniary advantage obtained in connection with both criminal conduct and in some other connection is to be treated as obtained in connection with criminal conduct, thus removing a possible defence where a person alleges that property or a pecuniary advantage was obtained not only in connection with criminal conduct, but also in some innocent connection.
    Subsection (8) provides that if a person benefits from conduct, his benefit is the property obtained as a result of or in connection with the conduct.
    Subsections (9) and (10) contain rules defining "property" and how property is "obtained" for these purposes. "Property" includes money, all forms of property, real or personal, heritable or moveable, things in action and other intangible or incorporeal property. Property is "obtained" by a person if he obtains an interest in it, and an "interest" is defined both in relation to land and in relation to property other than land. In relation to land in England and Wales or Northern Ireland, an "interest" includes any legal estate or equitable interest or power (subs.(10)(b)). In relation to land in Scotland, an "interest" includes any estate, interest, servitude or other heritable right in or over land, including a heritable security. Subsection (10)(d) provides that in relation to property other than land, "interest" includes any right (including a right to possession).

Subsection (11) provides that an officer of the Board includes a collector of taxes and an inspector of taxes.

PART 7

MONEY LAUNDERING

INTRODUCTION TO PART 7

The expression "money laundering" has been said (DA Chaikin, *Money Laundering: An Investigatory Perspective* (1991) 2 Criminal Law Forum 467, 468, quoting a comment by the US delegation at a meeting of the Working Committee on the Development of Financial Investigative Techniques, ICPO-Interpol, Paris, April 10, 1985) to derive from mafia ownership of laundromats in the United States during prohibition. The profits of bootlegging, gambling and prostitution were intermixed with the legitimate takings from these businesses and the illicit income attributed to the legitimate activities. This activity was, however, double edged. It was for tax evasion rather than murder and mayhem that Al Capone was eventually imprisoned.

The problem for the successful organised criminal is that there comes a point at which the "profits" of a laundry-or any other cash intensive business-become too good to be true. Other businesses must be sought and devices created for laundering what may be very large amounts of money. The need is partly-but only partly-met by the exploitation of "underground" banking systems which were not developed for criminal purposes but which, by their secret and unregulated character, are ideally suited for money laundering. However, the legitimate financial system is so well established and so pervasive that it becomes very difficult for the launderer to avoid it, especially if he wishes to have the use of the money and for it to appear to be legitimate. He must therefore find a way to place his proceeds of crime in the financial system.

This *placement* stage is the first stage in the classic analysis of laundering schemes (See, for example, W Gilmore, *Dirty Money*, Council of Europe Press, 1995, p37) and it is followed by *layering*. This is the stage at which the proceeds are moved through the system so as to disguise the audit trail. Layering will frequently involve changes in the form of the asset, on the basis that whereas transfers of money from one bank account to another can be followed with relative ease, the purchase and resale of high value corporeal movables is a good deal harder to follow, especially if cross border transactions are involved. Indeed 80 per cent of all laundering schemes in a Canadian study had an international dimension (ME Beare and S Schneider, *Tracing of Illicit Funds: Money Laundering in Canada*, Ministry of the Solicitor General of Canada, 1990, p.xxiii and the Financial Action Task Force ("FATF"), established by the G-7 Summit in Paris in July 1989 "to assess the results of the cooperation already undertaken to prevent the utilisation of the banking system and financial institutions for the purpose of money laundering, and to consider additional preventative measures in this field, including the adaptation of the statutory and regulatory systems to enhance multilateral legal assistance" has said that "the stage of drugs cash movements between countries is crucial in the detection of money laundering." (Recommendations, reproduced in *Money Laundering* Hume Papers on Public Policy, Vol 1 No 2, Summer 1993, ed MacQueen p28).

The final stage in laundering is *integration*, where the proceeds are returned to the direct control of the criminal, having acquired an apparently legitimate source.

The money laundering operation is most likely to be vulnerable at the placement stage because it is at that stage that the explanation for the funds will be thinnest, unsupported by the body of circumstantial evidence which will accrue during layering. If money laundering can be detected at that stage, not only will the attempt to make the funds in question appear legitimate be nipped in the bud but the predicate offence itself (that is, the offence which generates the proceeds) may be detected and prosecuted, in which case there will be an opportunity to secure the confiscation of the benefit which the offender has derived from his crimes. In common with other countries, with European law and with the relevant treaties, UK law primarily targets the placement stage (though several legislative provisions also apply to the layering process).

The Act contains three substantive money laundering offences, one offence of failing to disclose suspicion and one offence of "tipping off". The Explanatory Notes suggest (para 465 *et seq*) that these provisions "simplify" the existing offences. That is, no doubt, true, as far as it goes. In several respects, however, they also make them even less forgiving than those existing offences. In the key provision (s.330) for example, the requirement used to be to make a disclosure as soon as reasonably practicable. The element of reasonableness has been removed and the obligation now is to disclose as soon as practicable. That is, arguably, significantly more demanding and allows less time to think.

For all of the substantive offences, the Bill provides for a penalty of up to 14 years' prison. The English courts have been imposing significant sentences for money laundering offences, justifying that by reference to the Court of Appeal's approval, in *R v. Greenwood* (1995) 16 Cr App R (S) 614 (approved in *R v. Simpson* (1998) 2 Cr App R (S) 111 (CA Crim Div)) of the remark of a sentencing judge that launderers "are nearly as bad", but not quite as bad, as those who actually do the dealing.

Offences

327 **Concealing etc**

(1) A person commits an offence if he—
   (a) conceals criminal property;
   (b) disguises criminal property;
   (c) converts criminal property;
   (d) transfers criminal property;
   (e) removes criminal property from England and Wales or from Scotland or from Northern Ireland.

(2) But a person does not commit such an offence if—
   (a) he makes an authorised disclosure under section 338 and (if the disclosure is made before he does the act mentioned in subsection (1)) he has the appropriate consent;
   (b) he intended to make such a disclosure but had a reasonable excuse for not doing so;
   (c) the act he does is done in carrying out a function he has relating to the enforcement of any provision of this Act or of any other enactment relating to criminal conduct or benefit from criminal conduct.

(3) Concealing or disguising criminal property includes concealing or disguising its nature, source, location, disposition, movement or ownership or any rights with respect to it.

DEFINITIONS
"Authorised disclosure": s338

GENERAL NOTE

Subs. (1)
Conceals ... disguises Note the definition in subs (3). The concepts involved in subs (1) are subject to a degree of overlap and it will not always be easy, or necessary, to determine, for example, where concealment ends and disguise begins.
Criminal property. See s.340(3).
Removes criminal property from. Hitherto, the law prohibited removal of property from "the jurisdiction" without explaining whether, by "jurisdiction", it meant the UK as a whole or simply one of its constituent jurisdictions. This subsection makes it clear that it is not necessary to move the property out of the UK in order to commit the offence. It is enough to move property out of one of the UK's constituent jurisdictions. So criminal property which takes the form of a credit balance with a bank in Edinburgh cannot be moved to a bank in London without committing the offence, even if no other steps are taken to conceal or disguise it. There is, however, some comfort for the innocent who is used as an intermediary in such a transaction (for example, a banker) in that before a person can be guilty of the offence he must, in terms of the definition of criminal property in s.340, know or suspect that it constitutes or represents a benefit from criminal conduct. A banker (or anyone else working in the regulated sector) who has such knowledge or forms such a suspicion is required, by s.330, to make a disclosure to the authorities. Failure to do so is an offence. We shall discuss that offence below; but for the purposes of s.327, it is worth noting that, by subs (2), the making of a disclosure will prevent the person concerned being guilty of a s.327 offence.

Subs. (2)
It is an important objective of UK anti-money laundering law to encourage the making of disclosures which will contribute to intelligence about money laundering and organized crime. Accordingly, even from the earliest examples of money laundering offences, the making of a

disclosure has been a defence to what would otherwise constitute crime. As to authorized disclosures, see s.338.

Subs. (3)

This wording is derived directly from Art.3(1)(b)(ii) of the UN Convention Against Illicit Traffic in Narcotic Drugs and Psychotropic Substances 1988.

328   Arrangements

(1) A person commits an offence if he enters into or becomes concerned in an arrangement which he knows or suspects facilitates (by whatever means) the acquisition, retention, use or control of criminal property by or on behalf of another person.

(2) But a person does not commit such an offence if—

   (a) he makes an authorised disclosure under section 338 and (if the disclosure is made before he does the act mentioned in subsection (1)) he has the appropriate consent;

   (b) he intended to make such a disclosure but had a reasonable excuse for not doing so;

   (c) the act he does is done in carrying out a function he has relating to the enforcement of any provision of this Act or of any other enactment relating to criminal conduct or benefit from criminal conduct.

DEFINITIONS

"Authorised disclosure": s.338

GENERAL NOTE

This section is derived from s.50 of the Drug Trafficking Act 1994, s.38 of the Criminal Law (Consolidation) (Scotland) Act 1995 and s.93A of the Criminal Justice Act 1988. Section 50 of the 1994 Act was considered by the Court of Appeal in *R v. Tarsemwal Lal Sabharwal* (2001) 2 Cr. App. R. (S.) 81 and it was held that it is not necessary to identify the particular offence from which the proceeds are derived. That case was an application for leave to appeal against conviction and sentence, the applicant having been convicted of conspiracy to facilitate the retention of the proceeds of drug trafficking. He had been concerned in exchanging a sum in excess of £50 million into Dutch guilders. Such conduct had been held, in *R v. Macmaster* (1999) 1 Cr App R 402, to be capable of constituting the facilitation of retention. Rose LJ had said that the words "retention or control" "...are apt to cover facilitation, by conversion of the sterling, without reference to what the reason or purpose for that conversion was. As it seems to us, what the guilders which came into the appellant's hands were to be used for was immaterial. It is to be noted that there is no reference in the section to the purpose for which, as distinct from the means by which, the facilitation takes place. The offence is committed if, the other conditions of the section being satisfied, retention or control is facilitated. In our judgment, the conversion of sterling, which was admittedly the proceeds of drug trafficking, into guilders, was, provided the jury found the necessary ingredients, capable of being an offence contrary to s.50(1)(a)." In *Sabharwal*, Hunt, J, giving the Opinion of the Court, said that "...the prosecution submitted that the evil which is aimed at under these sections and similar sections dealing with criminal conduct is to ensure that people who do assist in the laundering of money obtained from drug trafficking of any kind should be punished. In seeking to convict under such a count as this, it is sufficient to show that the money is the proceeds of drug trafficking in general, not that it comes from any individual offence, or indeed group of offences, or identifies one particular individual or group of individuals. *We accept that that is right.* If, of course, known offences can be identified, then all well and good. If known offenders can be identified, all well and good. In some cases that will be possible...But if the prosecution cannot, they are perfectly entitled to proceed as this prosecution did"(emphasis added). It is also worth noting that the sentence imposed in the *Sabharwal* case was one of 12 years' imprisonment. The Court of Appeal held that this was an entirely appropriate sentence for the extent of the transactions to which the applicant was party.

As to authorised disclosures, see what was said in relation to s.327(2) and, with it, s.338.

329   Acquisition, use and possession

(1) A person commits an offence if he—

    (a) acquires criminal property;
    (b) uses criminal property;
    (c) has possession of criminal property.
  (2) But a person does not commit such an offence if—
    (a) he makes an authorised disclosure under section 338 and (if the disclosure is made before he does the act mentioned in subsection (1)) he has the appropriate consent;
    (b) he intended to make such a disclosure but had a reasonable excuse for not doing so;
    (c) he acquired or used or had possession of the property for adequate consideration;
    (d) the act he does is done in carrying out a function he has relating to the enforcement of any provision of this Act or of any other enactment relating to criminal conduct or benefit from criminal conduct.
  (3) For the purposes of this section—
    (a) a person acquires property for inadequate consideration if the value of the consideration is significantly less than the value of the property;
    (b) a person uses or has possession of property for inadequate consideration if the value of the consideration is significantly less than the value of the use or possession;
    (c) the provision by a person of goods or services which he knows or suspects may help another to carry out criminal conduct is not consideration.

DEFINITIONS
"Authorised disclosure": s.338

GENERAL NOTE
This offence consists in acquiring, using or having possession of criminal property. It is essential (and probably something of a relief) to recall that, by s.340, property is only criminal property if the alleged offender knows or suspects that it constitutes benefit from criminal conduct. *Bona fide* possession of property which turns out to be criminal property is not an offence in terms of s.329. It is, by subs.(2)(c) a defence to a charge of committing an offence under this section that the person charged acquired or used the property or had possession of it for adequate consideration. The heart of the offence is, accordingly, acquisition of the property either without consideration or for inadequate consideration. The word "consideration" is a familiar one (though more so in English Law than in Scots Law) and there is no reason to suppose that the word here has anything other than its ordinary meaning of "any act of the plaintiff from which the defendant derives a benefit or advantage, or any labour, detriment, or inconvenience, sustained by the plaintiff, provided such act is performed, or such inconvenience suffered, by the plaintiff with the consent, either express or implied, of the defendant" (*Laythoarp v. Bryant* 5 LJCP 220). Note, however, that the adequacy or otherwise of the consideration falls to be judged according to the criteria set out in subs.(3).

330   Failure to disclose: regulated sector

  (1) A person commits an offence if each of the following three conditions is satisfied.
  (2) The first condition is that he—
    (a) knows or suspects, or
    (b) has reasonable grounds for knowing or suspecting,
  that another person is engaged in money laundering.
  (3) The second condition is that the information or other matter—
    (a) on which his knowledge or suspicion is based, or
    (b) which gives reasonable grounds for such knowledge or suspicion,
  came to him in the course of a business in the regulated sector.
  (4) The third condition is that he does not make the required disclosure as soon as is practicable after the information or other matter comes to him.

(5) The required disclosure is a disclosure of the information or other matter—
   (a) to a nominated officer or a person authorised for the purposes of this Part by the Director General of the National Criminal Intelligence Service;
   (b) in the form and manner (if any) prescribed for the purposes of this subsection by order under section 339.

(6) But a person does not commit an offence under this section if—
   (a) he has a reasonable excuse for not disclosing the information or other matter;
   (b) he is a professional legal adviser and the information or other matter came to him in privileged circumstances;
   (c) subsection (7) applies to him.

(7) This subsection applies to a person if—
   (a) he does not know or suspect that another person is engaged in money laundering, and
   (b) he has not been provided by his employer with such training as is specified by the Secretary of State by order for the purposes of this section.

(8) In deciding whether a person committed an offence under this section the court must consider whether he followed any relevant guidance which was at the time concerned—
   (a) issued by a supervisory authority or any other appropriate body,
   (b) approved by the Treasury, and
   (c) published in a manner it approved as appropriate in its opinion to bring the guidance to the attention of persons likely to be affected by it.

(9) A disclosure to a nominated officer is a disclosure which—
   (a) is made to a person nominated by the alleged offender's employer to receive disclosures under this section, and
   (b) is made in the course of the alleged offender's employment and in accordance with the procedure established by the employer for the purpose.

(10) Information or other matter comes to a professional legal adviser in privileged circumstances if it is communicated or given to him—
   (a) by (or by a representative of) a client of his in connection with the giving by the adviser of legal advice to the client,
   (b) by (or by a representative of) a person seeking legal advice from the adviser, or
   (c) by a person in connection with legal proceedings or contemplated legal proceedings.

(11) But subsection (10) does not apply to information or other matter which is communicated or given with the intention of furthering a criminal purpose.

(12) Schedule 9 has effect for the purpose of determining what is—
   (a) a business in the regulated sector;
   (b) a supervisory authority.

(13) An appropriate body is any body which regulates or is representative of any trade, profession, business or employment carried on by the alleged offender.

GENERAL NOTE

This is arguably the most important of the money laundering provisions. The section forms the cornerstone of UK anti-money laundering strategy and also implements Articles 6 and 7 of the Directive on prevention of the use of the financial system for the purpose of money laundering (Council Directive 91/308/EEC OJ/L166/77). Article 6 places a duty on EC member states to ensure that credit and financial institutions and their directors and employees co-operate fully with the authorities by informing them, at their own initiative, of any fact which might be an indication of money laundering and providing, on request, all necessary information.

Article 7 requires institutions to refrain from carrying out suspect transactions until they have made such disclosure. The other provisions of this Act dealing with money laundering fall short of the requirements of these Articles in that, while they protect a person who chooses to make a disclosure, they do not require the making of a report; nor do they catch employees who are not personally involved in the relevant transaction but who become aware of laundering activity.

Subs. (1)
A person commits an offence if ... By s.334(2), the penalty is, on indictment, up to five years' imprisonment or a fine or both, and, on summary conviction, up to six months' imprisonment or a fine not exceeding the statutory maximum or both.

Subs. (2)
The first condition is ... This, the first of the three conditions required by subs.(1), breaks down into 3 distinct possibilities. It will be satisfied if the accused:
- knows that another person is engaged in money laundering; or
- suspects that another person is engaged in money laundering; or
- has reasonable grounds for knowing or suspecting that another person is engaged in money laundering.

There are, accordingly, both subjective and objective possibilities. Subjectively, the accused may himself know or suspect that a person is engaged in money laundering. But even if he does not, he may objectively have reasonable grounds for such knowledge or suspicion.

Knows. Mitchell, Taylor and Talbot, writing about the predecessor English offence have suggested that, as to the meaning of "knowing", an analogy may be drawn with the law on possession of stolen property. (*Mitchell, Taylor and Talbot on Confiscation and the Proceeds of Crime*, 3rd edition, Sweet & Maxwell, 2002, para 9.021). There is clearly some force in that suggestion and it would mean that "knowing" would include not only direct information but also circumstances which to persons of ordinary understanding and situated such as the accused was must have led to the conclusion that the other person was engaged in money laundering (see generally, Theft Act 1968 s.22; *R v. Hall (Edward)* (1985) Crim L.R. 377 and, for Scots law, *Alison* i, 330).

Suspects. Mitchell, Taylor and Talbot have also suggested (para 9.022) that suspicion may be constituted by an inkling or fleeting thought that property might be the proceeds of crime. This depends, however, on a dictionary definition and it is not clear that Parliament intended or intends something quite as slender to constitute grounds for convicting a person working in a financial institution of an offence which carries a potential five year sentence. The courts have not construed the expression and might not now require to do so, because from the point of view of proof, unless the accused has articulated his knowledge or suspicion to some other person, one might expect the Crown to concentrate on reasonable grounds for suspicion, which avoids the need to prove the state of mind of the accused and also avoids the need to determine exactly what constitutes "suspicion".

Reasonable grounds for knowing or suspecting. It seems likely that the enquiry should be into the information which the accused possessed at the time of the failure to disclose.

That another person is engaged in money laundering. The expression "money laundering" is defined by s.340(11). Essentially, it is an act which constitutes an offence under ss.327, 328 or 329, an attempt or conspiracy thereat or accession thereto. It is also an act which would constitute such an offence if done in the United Kingdom. The most obvious and significant change which this definition and s.330 in combination introduce is that previously the obligation to report applied only to suspicion of drug trafficking and to certain aspects of the law on terrorism. Now applies to all forms of criminal conduct.

Subs. (3)
The second condition is that the information ... *came to him in the course of a business in the regulated sector.* Subsection (12) tells us that the regulated sector is defined by a list in Sched.9, which is in turn derived from the list of "relevant financial business" in para.4 of the Money Laundering Regulations 1993 (SI 1993 No 1933). For solicitors affected by that list (as many will be) there is limited comfort in the fact that s.330(6)(b) contains an exemption for information which comes to a professional legal adviser in privileged circumstances – though such circumstances are defined somewhat restrictively.

Subs. (4)
The third condition is that he does not make the required disclosure. As to what constitutes the required disclosure, see subs.(5).

As soon as is practicable. The requirement to disclose "as soon as practicable" represents a more unforgiving approach than the earlier legislation which only demanded the making of a disclosure as soon as reasonably practicable. The element of reasonableness has been removed.

Subs. (5)

The required disclosure. The definition of this expression represents a development on the earlier requirement, which was to make a disclosure to a constable or customs officer. Now, the disclosure must be to "a nominated officer or a person authorised ... by the Director General of the National Criminal Intelligence Service"("NCIS").

Nominated officer See subs.(9)

National Criminal Intelligence Service ("NCIS"). The NCIS web site (http://www.ncis.co.uk) explains that "NCIS works on behalf of all the United Kingdom's law enforcement agencies. It provides a range of intelligence products and services to aid the fight against serious and organised crime. NCIS specialises in four business areas: the provision of strategic intelligence overviews for national targeting of organised criminality; the supply of operational intelligence on the most difficult and dangerous criminal organisations; the supply of specialist coordinating functions and facilities for UK law enforcement; the publication of intelligence 'know-how' products for law enforcement." The NCIS Economic Crime Branch describes itself as the UK's Financial Intelligence Unit and its most important function is said (again on the NCIS web site) to be "to analyse the suspicious transaction reports ("STRs") it receives from the financial sector and disseminate these to law enforcement". The expression "suspicious transaction report" is, however, misleading in the United Kingdom context. In some other jurisdictions – notably the USA – the focus is indeed on transactions. It is very important, however, to grasp that in terms of s.330 what is to be disclosed is information which either causes the person to know or suspect money laundering or gives reasonable grounds to know or suspect money laundering. In other words, the focus is on the activity, not on the transaction. No doubt the transaction will often constitute the information which is the basis for the suspicion or grounds for suspicion; but not always and there is a risk that thinking in terms of suspicious transaction reporting will mislead some into not reporting things which should be reported.

In the form and manner (if any) prescribed. See s.339. At the time of writing, no form has been prescribed but there is a disclosure form template at http://www.ncis.co.uk/disclosure.asp and (for security reasons) this must be returned by post or fax to the Economic Crime Unit, National Criminal Intelligence Service, PO Box 8000, London SE11 5EN, Fax: 020 7238 8286.

Subs. (6)

Reasonable excuse This defence has existed in earlier anti money laundering legislation but does not seem to have been considered by the courts - or not in any detail. There was a recent article in the *Times* (David Corker, "Money laundering: a cautionary tale", *Times* Law pages, July 23, 2002, 4) which described the conviction of, and imposition of a six month prison sentence on, a solicitor who, having formed a suspicion did not report it because he had taken advice on his obligations and that advice turned out to be wrong. One might have thought that, if anything could amount to reasonable excuse, that could (the article was, however, arguing a quasi-political point and it is not clear that the account of the facts which it gave was sufficiently objective to provide a proper foundation for analysis). Note, however, subs.(8), which requires the court to take into account any guidance issued by a supervisory authority.

Privileged circumstances (See subs.(10)).

Subs. (7)

Such an employer would be committing an offence in terms of Reg.5 of the Money Laundering Regulations 1993

Subs. (8)

Supervisory authority. See subs.(12) and Sched.9 to determine what is a supervisory authority

Other appropriate body. See subs.(13). The leading guidance is that issued by the Joint Money Laundering Steering Group on behalf of a number of trade associations in the financial services industry. It has been approved by the Treasury and can be found at http:// www.jmlsg.org.uk.

Subs. (9)

Nominated officer. The reference is to the person required by Reg.14 of the Money Laundering Regulations 1993 as part of the internal reporting procedures required by Regs 5 and 14. Note that, in terms of ss.335 and 336, that officer commits offences if, in circumstances analogous to those applicable to all Regulated Sector workers in terms of s.334, he fails to make a disclosure to NCIS.

Subs. (10)

In *R v. Special Commissioner, Ex p Morgan Grenfell and Co Ltd* (2002) STC 786; (2002) UKHL 21, Lord Hoffman noted (at paras 7 and 8 of his speech) that legal professional privilege "is a fundamental human right long established in the common law. It is a necessary corollary of the right of any person to obtain skilled advice about the law. Such advice cannot be effectively obtained unless the client is able to put all the facts before the adviser without fear that they may afterwards be disclosed and used to his prejudice. The cases establishing this principle are collected in the speech of Lord Taylor of Gosforth CJ in *R v. Derby Magistrates Court, Ex p. B* (1996) AC 487. It has been held by the European Court of Human Rights to be part of the right of privacy guaranteed by article 8 of the Convention (*Campbell v. United Kingdom* (1992) 15 EHRR 137; *Foxley v. United Kingdom* (2000) 31 EHRR 637) and held by the European Court of Justice to be a part of Community law: *A M & S Europe Ltd v. Commission of the European Communities* (Case 155/79) (1983) QB 878 ... the courts will ordinarily construe general words in a statute, although literally capable of having some startling or unreasonable consequence, such as overriding fundamental human rights, as not having been intended to do so. An intention to override such rights must be expressly stated or appear by necessary implication".

In considering this area it is important to keep in mind the distinction which Lord Denning and Lord Diplock both drew in *Parry-Jones v. Law Society* (1969) 1 Ch 1, between legal professional privilege and confidentiality. As Lord Denning put it (at 6), "We all know that, as between solicitor and client, there are two privileges. The first is the privilege relating to legal proceedings, commonly called legal professional privilege. A solicitor must not produce or disclose in any legal proceedings any of the communications between himself and his client without the client's consent. The second privilege arises out of the confidence subsisting between solicitor and client similar to the confidence which applies between doctor and patient, banker and customer, accountant and client, and the like. The law implies a term into the contract whereby a professional man is to keep his client's affairs secret and not to disclose them to anyone without just cause...This particularly applies in the relationship of solicitor and client. The solicitor is not to disclose his client's affairs to anyone at all except under the most special and exceptional circumstances. Lord Diplock put it thus (at 9): "strictly speaking, privilege refers to a right to withhold from a court, or a tribunal exercising judicial functions, material which would otherwise be admissible in evidence. What we are concerned with here is the contractual duty of confidence, generally implied though sometimes expressed, between a solicitor and client. Such a duty exists not only between solicitor and client, but, for example, between banker and customer, doctor and patient and accountant and client. Such a duty of confidence is subject to, and overridden by, the duty of any party to that contract to comply with the law of the land. If it is the duty of such a party to a contract, whether at common law or under statute, to disclose in defined circumstances confidential information, then he must do so, and any express contract to the contrary would be illegal and void."

It seems clear that, in the present section, it is the narrower concept of legal professional privilege which is in issue and not the wider one of confidentiality. It is suggested that it therefore relates to legal work, narrowly defined, and is not intended to apply to in relation to other types of business conducted by solicitors, such as financial services work and advice or (in Scotland at least) the purchase and sale of houses and arrangement of finance for that purpose. In *R v. Inner London Crown Court Ex p. Bains and Bains* (1988) QB 579, the Divisional Court held that the records of conveyancing are not covered, though related correspondence might be. Note the clear exclusion from the exception, in subs.(11), of anything communicated with the intention of furthering a criminal purpose (including, of course, money laundering). This gives statutory form to the outcome of *R v. Central Criminal Court Ex p. Francis and Francis* (1989) AC 346, in which the House of Lords held, in relation to a production order, that items otherwise subject to privilege are not so subject if held with the intention (not necessarily on the part of the holder) of furthering a criminal purpose.

331   Failure to disclose: nominated officers in the regulated sector

(1) A person nominated to receive disclosures under section 330 commits an offence if the conditions in subsections (2) to (4) are satisfied.

(2) The first condition is that he—
   (a) knows or suspects, or
   (b) has reasonable grounds for knowing or suspecting,
   that another person is engaged in money laundering.

(3) The second condition is that the information or other matter—
   (a) on which his knowledge or suspicion is based, or
   (b) which gives reasonable grounds for such knowledge or suspicion,
   came to him in consequence of a disclosure made under section 330.

(4) The third condition is that he does not make the required disclosure as soon as is practicable after the information or other matter comes to him.

(5) The required disclosure is a disclosure of the information or other matter—

    (a) to a person authorised for the purposes of this Part by the Director General of the National Criminal Intelligence Service;

    (b) in the form and manner (if any) prescribed for the purposes of this subsection by order under section 339.

(6) But a person does not commit an offence under this section if he has a reasonable excuse for not disclosing the information or other matter.

(7) In deciding whether a person committed an offence under this section the court must consider whether he followed any relevant guidance which was at the time concerned—

    (a) issued by a supervisory authority or any other appropriate body,

    (b) approved by the Treasury, and

    (c) published in a manner it approved as appropriate in its opinion to bring the guidance to the attention of persons likely to be affected by it.

(8) Schedule 9 has effect for the purpose of determining what is a supervisory authority.

(9) An appropriate body is a body which regulates or is representative of a trade, profession, business or employment.

GENERAL NOTE

This section deals with the position of the nominated officer referred to in s.330(5) and applies to him or her a regime which is effectively the same as that set out in s.330.

332   Failure to disclose: other nominated officers

(1) A person nominated to receive disclosures under section 337 or 338 commits an offence if the conditions in subsections (2) to (4) are satisfied.

(2) The first condition is that he knows or suspects that another person is engaged in money laundering.

(3) The second condition is that the information or other matter on which his knowledge or suspicion is based came to him in consequence of a disclosure made under section 337 or 338.

(4) The third condition is that he does not make the required disclosure as soon as is practicable after the information or other matter comes to him.

(5) The required disclosure is a disclosure of the information or other matter—

    (a) to a person authorised for the purposes of this Part by the Director General of the National Criminal Intelligence Service;

    (b) in the form and manner (if any) prescribed for the purposes of this subsection by order under section 339.

(6) But a person does not commit an offence under this section if he has a reasonable excuse for not disclosing the information or other matter.

333   Tipping off

(1) A person commits an offence if—

    (a) he knows or suspects that a disclosure falling within section 337 or 338 has been made, and

    (b) he makes a disclosure which is likely to prejudice any investigation which might be conducted following the disclosure referred to in paragraph (a).

(2) But a person does not commit an offence under subsection (1) if—

    (a) he did not know or suspect that the disclosure was likely to be prejudicial as mentioned in subsection (1);

    (b) the disclosure is made in carrying out a function he has relating to the enforcement of any provision of this Act or of any other enactment relating to criminal conduct or benefit from criminal conduct;

    (c) he is a professional legal adviser and the disclosure falls within subsection (3).

(3) A disclosure falls within this subsection if it is a disclosure—

    (a) to (or to a representative of) a client of the professional legal adviser in connection with the giving by the adviser of legal advice to the client, or

    (b) to any person in connection with legal proceedings or contemplated legal proceedings.

(4) But a disclosure does not fall within subsection (3) if it is made with the intention of furthering a criminal purpose.

GENERAL NOTE

Part of the point of the requirements to report suspicion is that the authorities should be able to investigate the activities of the suspected person without it becoming known to him that he is suspected. In order to preserve the integrity of such investigations, Art.8 of the Directive provides that: "Credit and financial institutions and their directors and employees shall not disclose to the customer concerned nor to other third persons that information has been transmitted to the authorities in accordance with Arts 6 and 7 or that a money laundering investigation is being carried out." The Act contains provisions designed to prevent the suspect from being tipped off. The present provision is concerned with knowledge or suspicion of the making of a disclosure, rather than of the existence of an investigation, for the obvious reason that the making of the disclosure has to be protected but that the information in the disclosure might not of itself be sufficient to trigger an investigation.

Subs. (1)

A person Notwithstanding the terms of the Directive, the offence created by this subsection is not restricted to credit and financial institutions. Nor does it apply solely to those working in the regulated sector. Instead, it applies to anyone at all who, having the requisite *mens rea*, does anything at all which is likely to prejudice the investigation, even if that investigation is at a very early stage.

Knows or suspects that a disclosure ... has been made. Note that it is not sufficient for this offence that the accused has reasonable grounds for knowledge or suspicion. The Crown must prove that he actually knew or suspected.

334   Penalties

(1) A person guilty of an offence under section 327, 328 or 329 is liable—

    (a) on summary conviction, to imprisonment for a term not exceeding six months or to a fine not exceeding the statutory maximum or to both, or

    (b) on conviction on indictment, to imprisonment for a term not exceeding 14 years or to a fine or to both.

(2) A person guilty of an offence under section 330, 331, 332 or 333 is liable—

    (a) on summary conviction, to imprisonment for a term not exceeding six months or to a fine not exceeding the statutory maximum or to both, or

    (b) on conviction on indictment, to imprisonment for a term not exceeding five years or to a fine or to both.

Consent

335   Appropriate consent

(1) The appropriate consent is—

    (a) the consent of a nominated officer to do a prohibited act if an authorised disclosure is made to the nominated officer;

    (b) the consent of a constable to do a prohibited act if an authorised disclosure is made to a constable;

    (c) the consent of a customs officer to do a prohibited act if an authorised disclosure is made to a customs officer.

(2) A person must be treated as having the appropriate consent if—

    (a) he makes an authorised disclosure to a constable or a customs officer, and

    (b) the condition in subsection (3) or the condition in subsection (4) is satisfied.

(3) The condition is that before the end of the notice period he does not receive notice from a constable or customs officer that consent to the doing of the act is refused.

(4) The condition is that—

    (a) before the end of the notice period he receives notice from a constable or customs officer that consent to the doing of the act is refused, and

    (b) the moratorium period has expired.

(5) The notice period is the period of seven working days starting with the first working day after the person makes the disclosure.

(6) The moratorium period is the period of 31 days starting with the day on which the person receives notice that consent to the doing of the act is refused.

(7) A working day is a day other than a Saturday, a Sunday, Christmas Day, Good Friday or a day which is a bank holiday under the Banking and Financial Dealings Act 1971 (c. 80) in the part of the United Kingdom in which the person is when he makes the disclosure.

(8) References to a prohibited act are to an act mentioned in section 327(1), 328(1) or 329(1) (as the case may be).

(9) A nominated officer is a person nominated to receive disclosures under section 338.

(10) Subsections (1) to (4) apply for the purposes of this Part.

336   Nominated officer: consent

(1) A nominated officer must not give the appropriate consent to the doing of a prohibited act unless the condition in subsection (2), the condition in subsection (3) or the condition in subsection (4) is satisfied.

(2) The condition is that—

    (a) he makes a disclosure that property is criminal property to a person authorised for the purposes of this Part by the Director General of the National Criminal Intelligence Service, and

    (b) such a person gives consent to the doing of the act.

(3) The condition is that—

    (a) he makes a disclosure that property is criminal property to a person authorised for the purposes of this Part by the Director General of the National Criminal Intelligence Service, and

    (b) before the end of the notice period he does not receive notice from such a person that consent to the doing of the act is refused.

(4) The condition is that—

    (a) he makes a disclosure that property is criminal property to a person authorised for the purposes of this Part by the Director General of the National Criminal Intelligence Service,

    (b) before the end of the notice period he receives notice from such a person that consent to the doing of the act is refused, and

    (c) the moratorium period has expired.

(5) A person who is a nominated officer commits an offence if—

    (a) he gives consent to a prohibited act in circumstances where none of the conditions in subsections (2), (3) and (4) is satisfied, and

    (b) he knows or suspects that the act is a prohibited act.

  (6) A person guilty of such an offence is liable—

    (a) on summary conviction, to imprisonment for a term not exceeding six months or to a fine not exceeding the statutory maximum or to both, or

    (b) on conviction on indictment, to imprisonment for a term not exceeding five years or to a fine or to both.

  (7) The notice period is the period of seven working days starting with the first working day after the nominated officer makes the disclosure.

  (8) The moratorium period is the period of 31 days starting with the day on which the nominated officer is given notice that consent to the doing of the act is refused.

  (9) A working day is a day other than a Saturday, a Sunday, Christmas Day, Good Friday or a day which is a bank holiday under the Banking and Financial Dealings Act 1971 (c. 80) in the part of the United Kingdom in which the nominated officer is when he gives the appropriate consent.

  (10) References to a prohibited act are to an act mentioned in section 327(1), 328(1) or 329(1) (as the case may be).

  (11) A nominated officer is a person nominated to receive disclosures under section 338.

Disclosures

337 Protected disclosures

  (1) A disclosure which satisfies the following three conditions is not to be taken to breach any restriction on the disclosure of information (however imposed).

  (2) The first condition is that the information or other matter disclosed came to the person making the disclosure (the discloser) in the course of his trade, profession, business or employment.

  (3) The second condition is that the information or other matter—

    (a) causes the discloser to know or suspect, or

    (b) gives him reasonable grounds for knowing or suspecting,

    that another person is engaged in money laundering.

  (4) The third condition is that the disclosure is made to a constable, a customs officer or a nominated officer as soon as is practicable after the information or other matter comes to the discloser.

  (5) A disclosure to a nominated officer is a disclosure which—

    (a) is made to a person nominated by the discloser's employer to receive disclosures under this section, and

    (b) is made in the course of the discloser's employment and in accordance with the procedure established by the employer for the purpose.

GENERAL NOTE

  Article 9 of the Directive requires States to provide immunity from civil suit for disclosures in good faith of information to the enforcement authorities and this section provides that immunity. Note that, although the obligation to make a disclosure applies only to information received in the course of a business in the regulated sector, the immunity is provided for disclosures by any person. This is consistent with fact that ss.327, 328 and 329 recognise the making of a disclosure as a defence to the offences which those sections create. According to para. 477 of the Explanatory Notes, "the protection extends not just to the regulated sector which is required to make disclosures in order to avoid committing an offence under (s.330) but also to those carrying out any trade, profession, business or employment, even if this is not in the regulated sector, who voluntarily make disclosures about money laundering to the police. This includes those exercising a profession in a voluntary capacity such as accountants or solicitors giving free advice. It does *not*, however, mean that they become subject to the failure to disclose offence at (s.330)".

By contrast with s.330, the disclosures protected by this section may be made to constables or customs officers and not merely to NCIS (and nominated officers). It remains the case, however, that to qualify as a protected disclosure, the disclosure must be made "as soon as practicable" and not merely as soon as reasonably practicable.

338   Authorised disclosures

(1) For the purposes of this Part a disclosure is authorised if—
   - (a) it is a disclosure to a constable, a customs officer or a nominated officer by the alleged offender that property is criminal property,
   - (b) it is made in the form and manner (if any) prescribed for the purposes of this subsection by order under section 339, and
   - (c) the first or second condition set out below is satisfied.
(2) The first condition is that the disclosure is made before the alleged offender does the prohibited act.
(3) The second condition is that—
   - (a) the disclosure is made after the alleged offender does the prohibited act,
   - (b) there is a good reason for his failure to make the disclosure before he did the act, and
   - (c) the disclosure is made on his own initiative and as soon as it is practicable for him to make it.
(4) An authorised disclosure is not to be taken to breach any restriction on the disclosure of information (however imposed).
(5) A disclosure to a nominated officer is a disclosure which—
   - (a) is made to a person nominated by the alleged offender's employer to receive authorised disclosures, and
   - (b) is made in the course of the alleged offender's employment and in accordance with the procedure established by the employer for the purpose.
(6) References to the prohibited act are to an act mentioned in section 327(1), 328(1) or 329(1) (as the case may be).

GENERAL NOTE

Paragraphs 479 and 480 of the Explanatory Notes explain that this section "sets out the circumstances in which a disclosure will be 'authorised' for the purposes of affording a defence to the principal money laundering offences in (ss.327 to 329). Where a disclosure is 'authorised' for these purposes, then it is not to be taken to breach any rule which would otherwise restrict that disclosure. This is necessary because, in the course of their business, those working inside or outside the regulated sector may need to complete a transaction that they know or suspect could constitute one of the three principal money laundering offences. This clause gives them the means of obtaining the authorisation necessary to complete the transaction, if the disclosure is made before a transaction is completed; or provides a defence against the failure to disclose offence if the disclosure is made as soon as possible after the transaction has taken place and there was a good reason not to make it before".

339   Form and manner of disclosures

(1) The Secretary of State may by order prescribe the form and manner in which a disclosure under section 330, 331, 332 or 338 must be made.
(2) An order under this section may also provide that the form may include a request to the discloser to provide additional information specified in the form.
(3) The additional information must be information which is necessary to enable the person to whom the disclosure is made to decide whether to start a money laundering investigation.
(4) A disclosure made in pursuance of a request under subsection (2) is not to be taken to breach any restriction on the disclosure of information (however imposed).

(5) The discloser is the person making a disclosure mentioned in subsection (1).
(6) Money laundering investigation must be construed in accordance with section 341(4).
(7) Subsection (2) does not apply to a disclosure made to a nominated officer.

GENERAL NOTE
   At the time of writing, no form has been prescribed but there is a disclosure form template at http://www.ncis.co.uk/disclosure.asp and (for security reasons) this must be returned by post or fax to the Economic Crime Unit, National Criminal Intelligence Service, PO Box 8000, London SE11 5EN, Fax: 020 7238 8286.

Interpretation

340   Interpretation
   (1) This section applies for the purposes of this Part.
   (2) Criminal conduct is conduct which—
      (a) constitutes an offence in any part of the United Kingdom, or
      (b) would constitute an offence in any part of the United Kingdom if it occurred there.
   (3) Property is criminal property if—
      (a) it constitutes a person's benefit from criminal conduct or it represents such a benefit (in whole or part and whether directly or indirectly), and
      (b) the alleged offender knows or suspects that it constitutes or represents such a benefit.
   (4) It is immaterial—
      (a) who carried out the conduct;
      (b) who benefited from it;
      (c) whether the conduct occurred before or after the passing of this Act.
   (5) A person benefits from conduct if he obtains property as a result of or in connection with the conduct.
   (6) If a person obtains a pecuniary advantage as a result of or in connection with conduct, he is to be taken to obtain as a result of or in connection with the conduct a sum of money equal to the value of the pecuniary advantage.
   (7) References to property or a pecuniary advantage obtained in connection with conduct include references to property or a pecuniary advantage obtained in both that connection and some other.
   (8) If a person benefits from conduct his benefit is the property obtained as a result of or in connection with the conduct.
   (9) Property is all property wherever situated and includes—
      (a) money;
      (b) all forms of property, real or personal, heritable or moveable;
      (c) things in action and other intangible or incorporeal property.
   (10) The following rules apply in relation to property—
      (a) property is obtained by a person if he obtains an interest in it;
      (b) references to an interest, in relation to land in England and Wales or Northern Ireland, are to any legal estate or equitable interest or power;
      (c) references to an interest, in relation to land in Scotland, are to any estate, interest, servitude or other heritable right in or over land, including a heritable security;
      (d) references to an interest, in relation to property other than land, include references to a right (including a right to possession).
   (11) Money laundering is an act which—

    (a) constitutes an offence under section 327, 328 or 329,
    (b) constitutes an attempt, conspiracy or incitement to commit an offence specified in paragraph (a),
    (c) constitutes aiding, abetting, counselling or procuring the commission of an offence specified in paragraph (a), or
    (d) would constitute an offence specified in paragraph (a), (b) or (c) if done in the United Kingdom.
(12) For the purposes of a disclosure to a nominated officer—
    (a) references to a person's employer include any body, association or organisation (including a voluntary organisation) in connection with whose activities the person exercises a function (whether or not for gain or reward), and
    (b) references to employment must be construed accordingly.
(13) References to a constable include references to a person authorised for the purposes of this Part by the Director General of the National Criminal Intelligence Service.

GENERAL NOTE

Subs. (1)
Note the limited application of these definitions. Some of them (for example, "criminal conduct") are used with slightly different meanings elsewhere in the Act .

Subs. (2)
Note that this is not a double criminality requirement. It is enough if the conduct would constitute an offence in any part of the UK. It does not have to constitute an offence in the jurisdiction in which it was done. Also, contrast ss.76, 143 and 224, which, for confiscation purposes, limit extraterritorial criminal conduct to conduct which would be an offence in the particular *part* of the UK in which they respectively apply.

Subs. (3)
The element of knowledge or suspicion is critical to the protection of the innocent employee in the financial services or banking industry who unwittingly handles a transaction which would otherwise expose him or her to liability in terms of ss.327 to 329.

Subs. (11)
Paragraph (d) conceals a complexity, in that aiding and abetting is governed in English law by statute but in Scots law by common law principles. The two are not necessarily the same. It is not yet clear whether s.340(11)(d) is to be construed as relating to the part of the United Kingdom in which the prosecution is being conducted or as relating to "any part of" the United Kingdom (contrast the wording of subs.(2) of this section). What *is* clear is that the crime need not have occurred in the UK, so long as the conduct would have been criminal in the UK if it had occurred here. It is *not* necessary to establish that it was criminal in the jurisdiction in which it took place. This is not a double criminality requirement.

PART 8

INVESTIGATIONS

INTRODUCTION TO PART 8
Many of the powers in Pt. 8 are based on ones that already exist in respect of drug trafficking and terrorist investigations. It is their extension for the purposes of tracing proceeds of crime and the investigation of money laundering which is new and some are of particular interest. The customer information order requires financial institutions to identify any account held by somebody under investigation. The account monitoring order requires financial institutions to supply information about transactions on an account over a specified period. Under a power similar to that enjoyed by the Director of the Serious Fraud Office, the disclosure order allows the Director of the ARA to compel a person to answer questions, provide information or produce documents. In addition, civilian financial investigators of law enforcement authorities may exercise some investigation powers, provided that they have been accredited by the Agency.
For criminal investigations in general, powers are available under s.9, Sched.1 of the Police and Criminal Evidence Act 1984. For terrorist offences, see ss.38 and 39, Terrorism Act 2000.

The relationship between such criminal investigations and those directed at the proceeds of crime was discussed in *R* v. *Southwark Crown Court Ex p. Bowles* (1998) AC 641 in deciding on the correct application of s.93H of the Drug Trafficking Act 1994, the model for the production order in this Part. It was held that an application for a production order must be directed towards assisting the recovery of proceeds of crime. However, where it is also the purpose of the application to support an investigation into the commission of a crime, the judge has to ask which is the dominant purpose. If the dominant purpose is to investigate the proceeds, the application should be granted even if it incidentally supports a crime investigation. Furthermore, if evidence of crime is then obtained, the fact that it was obtained under the production order is not a reason for excluding it under s.78, Police and Criminal Evidence Act 1984. This general approach can be taken to apply to the other investigation powers in this Part: with the exception of the money laundering investigation, which specifically deals with the matter, the powers available cannot be used to investigate the commission of criminal offences, only the proceeds of crime. The other notable comparison between the powers in this Part and those in Sch.1 of the Police and Criminal Evidence Act 1984 is that the latter involve an *inter partes* procedure which is not required under this Act.

[handwritten: Dominant purpose = RU SH CC exp Bowles]

CHAPTER 1

INTRODUCTION

341   Investigations

(1) For the purposes of this Part a confiscation investigation is an investigation into—

(a) whether a person has benefited from his criminal conduct, or

(b) the extent or whereabouts of his benefit from his criminal conduct.

(2) For the purposes of this Part a civil recovery investigation is an investigation into—

(a) whether property is recoverable property or associated property,

(b) who holds the property, or

(c) its extent or whereabouts.

(3) But an investigation is not a civil recovery investigation if—

(a) proceedings for a recovery order have been started in respect of the property in question,

(b) an interim receiving order applies to the property in question,

(c) an interim administration order applies to the property in question, or

(d) the property in question is detained under section 295.

(4) For the purposes of this Part a money laundering investigation is an investigation into whether a person has committed a money laundering offence.

DEFINITIONS
   "associated property": s.245; s.414(2)
   "criminal conduct": s.413; s.416(9)
   "interim administration order": s.256(2); s.316(1); subss.(7) and (9)
   "interim receiving order": s.246(2); s.316(1); s.416(7) and (9)
   "property": s.414; s.416(9)
   "recoverable property": ss.304-310; s.316(1); s.414(2); s.416(9)
   "recovery order": s.266; s.316(1); s.416(7) and (9)

GENERAL NOTE
   Three types of investigation to which Pt. 8 applies – confiscation, civil recovery and money laundering – are defined in this section. The civil recovery investigation is defined so as to exclude investigations that may be conducted in connection with recovery order proceedings, interim receiving or administration orders, or the detention of seized cash.

342   Offences of prejudicing investigation

(1) This section applies if a person knows or suspects that an appropriate officer or (in Scotland) a proper person is acting (or proposing to act)

in connection with a confiscation investigation, a civil recovery investigation or a money laundering investigation which is being or is about to be conducted.

(2) The person commits an offence if—

  (a) he makes a disclosure which is likely to prejudice the investigation, or

  (b) he falsifies, conceals, destroys or otherwise disposes of, or causes or permits the falsification, concealment, destruction or disposal of, documents which are relevant to the investigation.

(3) A person does not commit an offence under subsection (2)(a) if—

  (a) he does not know or suspect that the disclosure is likely to prejudice the investigation,

  (b) the disclosure is made in the exercise of a function under this Act or any other enactment relating to criminal conduct or benefit from criminal conduct or in compliance with a requirement imposed under or by virtue of this Act, or

  (c) he is a professional legal adviser and the disclosure falls within subsection (4).

(4) A disclosure falls within this subsection if it is a disclosure—

  (a) to (or to a representative of) a client of the professional legal adviser in connection with the giving by the adviser of legal advice to the client, or

  (b) to any person in connection with legal proceedings or contemplated legal proceedings.

(5) But a disclosure does not fall within subsection (4) if it is made with the intention of furthering a criminal purpose.

(6) A person does not commit an offence under subsection (2)(b) if—

  (a) he does not know or suspect that the documents are relevant to the investigation, or

  (b) he does not intend to conceal any facts disclosed by the documents from any appropriate officer or (in Scotland) proper person carrying out the investigation.

(7) A person guilty of an offence under subsection (2) is liable—

  (a) on summary conviction, to imprisonment for a term not exceeding six months or to a fine not exceeding the statutory maximum or to both, or

  (b) on conviction on indictment, to imprisonment for a term not exceeding five years or to a fine or to both.

(8) For the purposes of this section—

  (a) "appropriate officer" must be construed in accordance with section 378;

  (b) "proper person" must be construed in accordance with section 412.

DEFINITIONS

"appropriate officer": subs.(8)(a); s.378; s.416(2) and (9)
"civil recovery investigation": s.341(2) and (3); s.416(1) and (9)
"confiscation investigation": s.341(1); s.416(1) and (9)
"document": s.379; s.416(2) and (9)
"money laundering investigation": s.341(4); s.416(1) and (9)

GENERAL NOTE

To commit this offence, directed at prejudicial disclosures or "tampering" with evidence, the defendant must know or suspect that a relevant investigation is being or about to be conducted. There are separate defences for each limb. In relation to prejudicial disclosure, there will not be an offence if: the defendant does not know or suspect that the disclosure is likely to prejudice the investigation; if there is a statutory requirement to disclose; or if a professional legal adviser is involved. By subs.(4) in respect of the latter, however, the adviser must have disclosed the information to a client in connection with giving legal advice to that client, or to any person in connection with actual or contemplated legal proceedings. But such disclosures will not qualify if they were made with the intention of furthering a criminal purpose (subs.(5). In relation to tampering, there will not be an offence if the defendant does not know or suspect that the documents are relevant to the investigation or does not intend to conceal the facts from the appropriate investigating officer.

CHAPTER 2

ENGLAND AND WALES AND NORTHERN IRELAND

Judges and courts

343   Judges

(1) In this Chapter references to a judge in relation to an application must be construed in accordance with this section.
(2) In relation to an application for the purposes of a confiscation investigation or a money laundering investigation a judge is—
  (a) in England and Wales, a judge entitled to exercise the jurisdiction of the Crown Court;
  (b) in Northern Ireland, a Crown Court judge.
(3) In relation to an application for the purposes of a civil recovery investigation a judge is a judge of the High Court.

DEFINITIONS
  "civil recovery investigation": s.341(2) and (3); s.416(1) and (9)
  "confiscation investigation": s.341(1); s.416(1) and (9)
  "money laundering investigation": s.341(4); s.416(1) and (9)

GENERAL NOTE
  In England and Wales, applications in respect of confiscation and money laundering investigations must be made to a judge entitled to exercise the jurisdiction of the Crown Court, namely, Circuit judges, Recorders and High Court judges. For the purposes of civil recovery investigations, the appropriate judge is a High Court judge.

344   Courts

In this Chapter references to the court are to—
  (a) the Crown Court, in relation to an order for the purposes of a confiscation investigation or a money laundering investigation;
  (b) the High Court, in relation to an order for the purposes of a civil recovery investigation.

DEFINITIONS
  "civil recovery investigation": s.341(2) and (3); s.416(1) and (9)
  "confiscation investigation": s.341(1); s.416(1) and (9)
  "money laundering investigation": s.341(4); s.416(1) and (9)

GENERAL NOTE
  There are supplementary provisions in ss.351, 362, 369 and 375, which remedy the absence, in the Crown Court, of the High Court's normal powers in respect of variation and discharge of orders and the power to initiate contempt of court proceedings for failure to comply with an order.

Production orders

345   Production orders

(1) A judge may, on an application made to him by an appropriate officer, make a production order if he is satisfied that each of the requirements for the making of the order is fulfilled.
(2) The application for a production order must state that—
  (a) a person specified in the application is subject to a confiscation investigation or a money laundering investigation, or

  (b) property specified in the application is subject to a civil recovery investigation.

(3) The application must also state that—
  (a) the order is sought for the purposes of the investigation;
  (b) the order is sought in relation to material, or material of a description, specified in the application;
  (c) a person specified in the application appears to be in possession or control of the material.

(4) A production order is an order either—
  (a) requiring the person the application for the order specifies as appearing to be in possession or control of material to produce it to an appropriate officer for him to take away, or
  (b) requiring that person to give an appropriate officer access to the material,
within the period stated in the order.

(5) The period stated in a production order must be a period of seven days beginning with the day on which the order is made, unless it appears to the judge by whom the order is made that a longer or shorter period would be appropriate in the particular circumstances.

DEFINITIONS
 "appropriate officer": subs.(8)(a); s.378; s.416(2) and (9)
 "civil recovery investigation": s.341(2) and (3); s.416(1) and (9)
 "confiscation investigation": s.341(1); s.416(1) and (9)
 "judge": s.343
 "money laundering investigation": s.341(4); s.416(1) and (9)

GENERAL NOTE
 The power to make a production order is available for confiscation, money laundering and civil recovery investigations. It is modelled on, but broadens the extent of, the similar powers in s.93H of the Criminal Justice Act 1988, s.55 of the Drug Trafficking Act 1994 and Art.50 of the Proceeds of Crime (Northern Ireland) Order 1996.

346 Requirements for making of production order

(1) These are the requirements for the making of a production order.

(2) There must be reasonable grounds for suspecting that—
  (a) in the case of a confiscation investigation, the person the application for the order specifies as being subject to the investigation has benefited from his criminal conduct;
  (b) in the case of a civil recovery investigation, the property the application for the order specifies as being subject to the investigation is recoverable property or associated property;
  (c) in the case of a money laundering investigation, the person the application for the order specifies as being subject to the investigation has committed a money laundering offence.

(3) There must be reasonable grounds for believing that the person the application specifies as appearing to be in possession or control of the material so specified is in possession or control of it.

(4) There must be reasonable grounds for believing that the material is likely to be of substantial value (whether or not by itself) to the investigation for the purposes of which the order is sought.

(5) There must be reasonable grounds for believing that it is in the public interest for the material to be produced or for access to it to be given, having regard to—
  (a) the benefit likely to accrue to the investigation if the material is obtained;
  (b) the circumstances under which the person the application specifies as appearing to be in possession or control of the material holds it.

"associated property": s.245; s.414(2)
"civil recovery investigation": s.341(2) and (3); s.416(1) and (9)
"confiscation investigation": s.341(1); s.416(1) and (9)
"criminal conduct": s.413; s.416(9)
"money laundering investigation": s.341(4); s.416(1) and (9)
"money laundering offence": s.415; s.416(9)
"production order": s.345(4); s.416(2) and (9)
"property": s.414; s.416(9)
"recoverable property": ss.304-310; s.316(1); s.414(2); s.416(9)

GENERAL NOTE
Under each of s.93H(4)(c) of the Criminal Justice Act 1988, s.55(4)(c) of the Drug Trafficking Act 1994 and Art.50(5) of the Proceeds of Crime (Northern Ireland) Order 1996, there was a public interest test to be satisfied before an order could be issued, as an important safeguard. This section originally did not contain such a provision because the Government took the view that sufficient protection was provided by the general application of the Human Rights Act 1998. The expectation was that the judge, obliged to act in a way that is compatible with the European Convention on Human Rights, will be required to balance the interference with Convention rights (here especially the right to privacy in Art.8) with the benefit to be gained from making an order. That balancing process requires the benefit to be necessary and proportionate, even though, under this section, there must be reasonable grounds for believing that the material will deliver "substantial" value to the investigation. Notwithstanding this human rights protection, the House of Lords insisted that a public interest test was still necessary and it was accepted by the Commons in the closing stages of the Bill's passage through Parliament.

Generally, the requirement of reasonable belief imposes a stricter test than reasonable suspicion and implies that there are objective grounds for thinking that a state of affairs exists.

347 Order to grant entry

(1) This section applies if a judge makes a production order requiring a person to give an appropriate officer access to material on any premises.

(2) The judge may, on an application made to him by an appropriate officer and specifying the premises, make an order to grant entry in relation to the premises.

(3) An order to grant entry is an order requiring any person who appears to an appropriate officer to be entitled to grant entry to the premises to allow him to enter the premises to obtain access to the material.

DEFINITIONS
"appropriate officer": subs.(8)(a); s.378; s.416(2) and (9)
"judge": s.343
"premises": s.379
"production order": s.345(4); s.416

GENERAL NOTE
This power replaces but reflects similar provisions in s.93H of the Criminal Justice Act 1988, s.55 of the Drug Trafficking Act 1994 and Art.50 of the Proceeds of Crime (Northern Ireland) Order 1996. There is no requirement that the application must be made at a separate time from the application for the production order itself.

348 Further provisions

(1) A production order does not require a person to produce, or give access to, privileged material.

(2) Privileged material is any material which the person would be entitled to refuse to produce on grounds of legal professional privilege in proceedings in the High Court.

(3) A production order does not require a person to produce, or give access to, excluded material.

(4) A production order has effect in spite of any restriction on the disclosure of information (however imposed).

(5) An appropriate officer may take copies of any material which is produced, or to which access is given, in compliance with a production order.

(6) Material produced in compliance with a production order may be retained for so long as it is necessary to retain it (as opposed to copies of it) in connection with the investigation for the purposes of which the order was made.

(7) But if an appropriate officer has reasonable grounds for believing that—

    (a) the material may need to be produced for the purposes of any legal proceedings, and

    (b) it might otherwise be unavailable for those purposes,

it may be retained until the proceedings are concluded.

DEFINITIONS

"appropriate officer": subs.(8)(a); s.378; s.416(2) and (9)

"excluded material": s.379

"production order": s.345(4); s.416(2) and (9)

GENERAL NOTE

In subss.(1) and (2), privileged material is defined in terms of High Court proceedings, thereby invoking the greater protection provided in civil proceedings. In criminal proceedings, inadvertent or accidental waiver of privilege, or improper revealing of privileged information, may nevertheless result in disclosure being compelled, under the rule in *Calcraft* v. *Guest* (1998) 1 QB 759.

The effect of subss.(1)-(3) is that special procedure material (under s.14, Police and Criminal Evidence Act 1984) can be covered by a production order.

Subsection (4) makes it clear that a production order cannot be resisted by claims of confidentiality, data protection or other statutory protection.

349   Computer information

(1) This section applies if any of the material specified in an application for a production order consists of information contained in a computer.

(2) If the order is an order requiring a person to produce the material to an appropriate officer for him to take away, it has effect as an order to produce the material in a form in which it can be taken away by him and in which it is visible and legible.

(3) If the order is an order requiring a person to give an appropriate officer access to the material, it has effect as an order to give him access to the material in a form in which it is visible and legible.

DEFINITIONS

"appropriate officer": subs.(8)(a); s.378; s.416(2) and (9)

"production order": s.345(4); s.416(3) and (9)

GENERAL NOTE

This section reflects similar but shorter provisions in s.93H of the Criminal Justice Act 1988, s.55 of the Drug Trafficking Act 1994 and Art.50 of the Proceeds of Crime (Northern Ireland) Order 1996. A production order does not provide for digital material to be taken away. The data on computer hard drives or any portable media, such as floppy disks or CD-ROMs, must be rendered intelligible on the premises. The section does not envisage a situation where the data might be hidden from the investigators within the computer: the existence of the material must be known before the production order is obtained. If there is any possibility that computerised information will be moved or destroyed, the authorities can be anticipated to apply for a search and seizure warrant, under ss.352 and 353, which could authorise removal of the computer and other physical media. As to whether the section authorises the production of networked computer material, see the note to s.352, below.

350 Government departments

(1) A production order may be made in relation to material in the possession or control of an authorised government department.

(2) An order so made may require any officer of the department (whether named in the order or not) who may for the time being be in possession or control of the material to comply with it.

(3) An order containing such a requirement must be served as if the proceedings were civil proceedings against the department.

(4) If an order contains such a requirement—

   (a) the person on whom it is served must take all reasonable steps to bring it to the attention of the officer concerned;

   (b) any other officer of the department who is in receipt of the order must also take all reasonable steps to bring it to the attention of the officer concerned.

(5) If the order is not brought to the attention of the officer concerned within the period stated in the order (in pursuance of section 345(4)) the person on whom it is served must report the reasons for the failure to—

   (a) a judge entitled to exercise the jurisdiction of the Crown Court or (in Northern Ireland) a Crown Court judge, in the case of an order made for the purposes of a confiscation investigation or a money laundering investigation;

   (b) a High Court judge, in the case of an order made for the purposes of a civil recovery investigation.

(6) An authorised government department is a government department, or a Northern Ireland department, which is an authorised department for the purposes of the Crown Proceedings Act 1947 (c. 44).

Definition
"production order": s.345(4); s.416(2) and (9)

General Note
This section is similar to s.93J(11) of the Criminal Justice Act 1988, s.59(11) of the Drug Trafficking Act 1994 and Art.54(11) of the Proceeds of Crime (Northern Ireland) Order 1996. For the purposes of this section, and to reflect the effect of devolution in Northern Ireland, Northern Ireland departments are treated as government departments.

351 Supplementary

(1) An application for a production order or an order to grant entry may be made ex parte to a judge in chambers.

(2) Rules of court may make provision as to the practice and procedure to be followed in connection with proceedings relating to production orders and orders to grant entry.

(3) An application to discharge or vary a production order or an order to grant entry may be made to the court by—

   (a) the person who applied for the order;

   (b) any person affected by the order.

(4) The court—

   (a) may discharge the order;

   (b) may vary the order.

(5) If an accredited financial investigator, a constable or a customs officer applies for a production order or an order to grant entry, an application to discharge or vary the order need not be by the same accredited financial investigator, constable or customs officer.

(6) References to a person who applied for a production order or an order to grant entry must be construed accordingly.

(7) Production orders and orders to grant entry have effect as if they were orders of the court.

(8) Subsections (2) to (7) do not apply to orders made in England and Wales for the purposes of a civil recovery investigation.

DEFINITIONS
"accredited financial investigator": s.453
"civil recovery investigation": s.341(2) and (3); s.416(1) and (9)
"the court": s.344
"customs officer": s.454
"judge": s.343
"order to grant entry": s.347(3); s.416(2) and (9)
"production order": s.345(4); s.416(2) and (9)

GENERAL NOTE

Subs. (7)
Production orders and orders to grant entry have effect as if they were orders of the Crown Court (or the High Court in Northern Ireland). The consequence is to enable proceedings for contempt of court to be issued if the orders are not complied with.

Subs. (8)
These supplementary provisions relate to orders made by the Crown Court, which does not have inherent power, and therefore requires authority, to discharge or vary or to institute proceedings for contempt of court. They are not needed for the High Court in England and Wales, which already has such power. But they are needed for the High Court in Northern Ireland, which does not.

Search and seizure warrants

352   Search and seizure warrants

(1) A judge may, on an application made to him by an appropriate officer, issue a search and seizure warrant if he is satisfied that either of the requirements for the issuing of the warrant is fulfilled.

(2) The application for a search and seizure warrant must state that—
  (a) a person specified in the application is subject to a confiscation investigation or a money laundering investigation, or
  (b) property specified in the application is subject to a civil recovery investigation.

(3) The application must also state—
  (a) that the warrant is sought for the purposes of the investigation;
  (b) that the warrant is sought in relation to the premises specified in the application;
  (c) that the warrant is sought in relation to material specified in the application, or that there are reasonable grounds for believing that there is material falling within section 353(6), (7) or (8) on the premises.

(4) A search and seizure warrant is a warrant authorising an appropriate person—
  (a) to enter and search the premises specified in the application for the warrant, and
  (b) to seize and retain any material found there which is likely to be of substantial value (whether or not by itself) to the investigation for the purposes of which the application is made.

(5) An appropriate person is—
  (a) a constable or a customs officer, if the warrant is sought for the purposes of a confiscation investigation or a money laundering investigation;
  (b) a named member of the staff of the Agency, if the warrant is sought for the purposes of a civil recovery investigation.

(6) The requirements for the issue of a search and seizure warrant are—
  (a) that a production order made in relation to material has not been complied with and there are reasonable grounds for believing

that the material is on the premises specified in the application for the warrant, or

    (b) that section 353 is satisfied in relation to the warrant.

DEFINITIONS

  "Agency": s.1(1)
  "appropriate officer": subs.(8)(a); s.378; s.416(2) and (9)
  "civil recovery investigation": s.341(2) and (3); s.416(1) and (9)
  "confiscation investigation": s.341(1); s.416(1) and (9)
  "the court": s.344
  "customs officer": s.454
  "judge": s.343
  "money laundering investigation": s.341(4); s.416(1) and (9)
  "money laundering offence": s.415; s.416(9)
  "premises": s.379
  "production order": s.345(4); s.416(2) and (9)

GENERAL NOTE

These powers are derived from s.93I of the Criminal Justice Act 1988, s.56 of the Drug Trafficking Act 1994 and Art.51 of the Proceeds of Crime (Northern Ireland) Order 1996. There are two bases for the warrant: either where a production order has been made and not complied with, and there are reasonable grounds to believe that the material specified in the warrant is on the premises; or that the requirements of s.353 are met. Note the distinction between the appropriate officer, who may apply for the warrant, and the "appropriate person", in subss.(4) and (5), who may execute the warrant. The category of appropriate persons who may do so is limited for confiscation or money laundering investigations. But for civil recovery investigations, a named member of staff of the ARA, who is not an appropriate officer under s.378(7), is specified.

353   Requirements where production order not available

  (1) This section is satisfied in relation to a search and seizure warrant if—
      (a) subsection (2) applies, and
      (b) either the first or the second set of conditions is complied with.
  (2) This subsection applies if there are reasonable grounds for suspecting that—
      (a) in the case of a confiscation investigation, the person specified in the application for the warrant has benefited from his criminal conduct;
      (b) in the case of a civil recovery investigation, the property specified in the application for the warrant is recoverable property or associated property;
      (c) in the case of a money laundering investigation, the person specified in the application for the warrant has committed a money laundering offence.
  (3) The first set of conditions is that there are reasonable grounds for believing that—
      (a) any material on the premises specified in the application for the warrant is likely to be of substantial value (whether or not by itself) to the investigation for the purposes of which the warrant is sought,
      (b) it is in the public interest for the material to be obtained, having regard to the benefit likely to accrue to the investigation if the material is obtained, and
      (c) it would not be appropriate to make a production order for any one or more of the reasons in subsection (4).
  (4) The reasons are—
      (a) that it is not practicable to communicate with any person against whom the production order could be made;
      (b) that it is not practicable to communicate with any person who would be required to comply with an order to grant entry to the premises;

(c) that the investigation might be seriously prejudiced unless an appropriate person is able to secure immediate access to the material.

(5) The second set of conditions is that—

   (a) there are reasonable grounds for believing that there is material on the premises specified in the application for the warrant and that the material falls within subsection (6), (7) or (8),

   (b) there are reasonable grounds for believing that it is in the public interest for the material to be obtained, having regard to the benefit likely to accrue to the investigation if the material is obtained, and

   (c) any one or more of the requirements in subsection (9) is met.

(6) In the case of a confiscation investigation, material falls within this subsection if it cannot be identified at the time of the application but it—

   (a) relates to the person specified in the application, the question whether he has benefited from his criminal conduct or any question as to the extent or whereabouts of his benefit from his criminal conduct, and

   (b) is likely to be of substantial value (whether or not by itself) to the investigation for the purposes of which the warrant is sought.

(7) In the case of a civil recovery investigation, material falls within this subsection if it cannot be identified at the time of the application but it—

   (a) relates to the property specified in the application, the question whether it is recoverable property or associated property, the question as to who holds any such property, any question as to whether the person who appears to hold any such property holds other property which is recoverable property, or any question as to the extent or whereabouts of any property mentioned in this paragraph, and

   (b) is likely to be of substantial value (whether or not by itself) to the investigation for the purposes of which the warrant is sought.

(8) In the case of a money laundering investigation, material falls within this subsection if it cannot be identified at the time of the application but it—

   (a) relates to the person specified in the application or the question whether he has committed a money laundering offence, and

   (b) is likely to be of substantial value (whether or not by itself) to the investigation for the purposes of which the warrant is sought.

(9) The requirements are—

   (a) that it is not practicable to communicate with any person entitled to grant entry to the premises;

   (b) that entry to the premises will not be granted unless a warrant is produced;

   (c) that the investigation might be seriously prejudiced unless an appropriate person arriving at the premises is able to secure immediate entry to them.

(10) An appropriate person is—

   (a) a constable or a customs officer, if the warrant is sought for the purposes of a confiscation investigation or a money laundering investigation;

   (b) a member of the staff of the Agency, if the warrant is sought for the purposes of a civil recovery investigation.

DEFINITIONS

  "associated property": s.245; s.414(2)

  "civil recovery investigation": s.341(2) and (3); s.416(1) and (9)

"criminal conduct": s.413; s.416(9)
"confiscation investigation": s.341(1); s.416(1) and (9)
"customs officer": s.454
"judge": s.343
"money laundering investigation": s.341(4); s.416(1) and (9)
"premises": s.379
"production order": s.345(4); s.416(2) and (9)
"property": s.414; s.416(9)
"recoverable property": ss.304-310; s.316(1); s.414(2); s.416(9)
"search and seizure warrant": s.352(4); s.416(2) and (9)

GENERAL NOTE

These powers may be invoked where a production order cannot be made for a series of reasons. Two alternative sets of conditions are required to be satisfied in addition to the reasonable suspicion in subs.(2). Essentially, these are that: either communication with a view to securing a production order must be impossible or seriously prejudicial to the investigation; or the material must not be capable of being sufficiently described to justify a production order and immediate access is necessary and will not otherwise be granted.

Under s.93I of the Criminal Justice Act 1988, s.56 of the Drug Trafficking Act 1994 and Art.51 of the Proceeds of Crime (Northern Ireland) Order 1996 there was a public interest test to be satisfied before an order could be issued, as an important safeguard. It only was inserted into this section in the closing stages of the Bill's passage: see the note to s.346, above.

354   Further provisions: general

(1) A search and seizure warrant does not confer the right to seize privileged material.

(2) Privileged material is any material which a person would be entitled to refuse to produce on grounds of legal professional privilege in proceedings in the High Court.

(3) A search and seizure warrant does not confer the right to seize excluded material.

DEFINITIONS

"excluded material": s.379
"search and seizure warrant": s.352(4); s.416(2) and (9)

GENERAL NOTE

See the General Note to s.348, above.

355   Further provisions: confiscation and money laundering

(1) This section applies to—
    (a) search and seizure warrants sought for the purposes of a confiscation investigation or a money laundering investigation, and
    (b) powers of seizure under them.

(2) In relation to such warrants and powers, the Secretary of State may make an order which applies the provisions to which subsections (3) and (4) apply subject to any specified modifications.

(3) This subsection applies to the following provisions of the Police and Criminal Evidence Act 1984 (c. 60)—
    (a) section 15 (search warrants—safeguards);
    (b) section 16 (execution of warrants);
    (c) section 21 (access and copying);
    (d) section 22 (retention).

(4) This subsection applies to the following provisions of the Police and Criminal Evidence (Northern Ireland) Order 1989 (S.I. 1989/1341 (N.I. 12))—
    (a) Article 17 (search warrants—safeguards);
    (b) Article 18 (execution of warrants);
    (c) Article 23 (access and copying);
    (d) Article 24 (retention).

GENERAL NOTE
  See the General Note to s.356, below.

356   Further provisions: civil recovery

(1) This section applies to search and seizure warrants sought for the purposes of civil recovery investigations.

(2) An application for a warrant may be made ex parte to a judge in chambers.

(3) A warrant may be issued subject to conditions.

(4) A warrant continues in force until the end of the period of one month starting with the day on which it is issued.

(5) A warrant authorises the person it names to require any information which is held in a computer and is accessible from the premises specified in the application for the warrant, and which the named person believes relates to any matter relevant to the investigation, to be produced in a form—

   (a) in which it can be taken away, and

   (b) in which it is visible and legible.

(6) If—

   (a) the Director gives written authority for members of staff of the Agency to accompany the person a warrant names when executing it, and

   (b) a warrant is issued,

the authorised members have the same powers under it as the person it names.

(7) A warrant may include provision authorising a person who is exercising powers under it to do other things which—

   (a) are specified in the warrant, and

   (b) need to be done in order to give effect to it.

(8) Copies may be taken of any material seized under a warrant.

(9) Material seized under a warrant may be retained for so long as it is necessary to retain it (as opposed to copies of it) in connection with the investigation for the purposes of which the warrant was issued.

(10) But if the Director has reasonable grounds for believing that—

   (a) the material may need to be produced for the purposes of any legal proceedings, and

   (b) it might otherwise be unavailable for those purposes,

it may be retained until the proceedings are concluded.

GENERAL NOTE
  There appear to be some inconsistencies about the way that the Act treats computerised information. By subs.(5), the authorised person can require information to be produced from a remote computer on a network. The computer holding the information may be on an intranet or on the Internet. However, there is no comparable provision in s.355. Furthermore, the formu-

lation differs from that in s.349, which may suggest that the latter applies only to material in computers on the premises, although a literal reading is consistent with network access also.

The power in subs.(7) is required because the member of the ARA who executes the warrant does not have an automatic right to use reasonable force to do so.

Disclosure orders

357 Disclosure orders

(1) A judge may, on an application made to him by the Director, make a disclosure order if he is satisfied that each of the requirements for the making of the order is fulfilled.

(2) No application for a disclosure order may be made in relation to a money laundering investigation.

(3) The application for a disclosure order must state that—
    (a) a person specified in the application is subject to a confiscation investigation which is being carried out by the Director and the order is sought for the purposes of the investigation, or
    (b) property specified in the application is subject to a civil recovery investigation and the order is sought for the purposes of the investigation.

(4) A disclosure order is an order authorising the Director to give to any person the Director considers has relevant information notice in writing requiring him to do, with respect to any matter relevant to the investigation for the purposes of which the order is sought, any or all of the following—
    (a) answer questions, either at a time specified in the notice or at once, at a place so specified;
    (b) provide information specified in the notice, by a time and in a manner so specified;
    (c) produce documents, or documents of a description, specified in the notice, either at or by a time so specified or at once, and in a manner so specified.

(5) Relevant information is information (whether or not contained in a document) which the Director considers to be relevant to the investigation.

(6) A person is not bound to comply with a requirement imposed by a notice given under a disclosure order unless evidence of authority to give the notice is produced to him.

DEFINITIONS
    "civil recovery investigation": s.341(2) and (3); s.416(1) and (9)
    "confiscation investigation": s.341(1); s.416(1) and (9)
    "Director": s.1(2)
    "document": s.379; s.416(2) and (9)
    "judge": s.343
    "money laundering investigation": s.341(4); s.416(1) and (9)
    "property": s.414

GENERAL NOTE
    The disclosure order is available only to the Director and only in respect of confiscation and civil recovery investigations (he has no role in the investigation of money laundering offences). From the Director's point of view, it will have two advantages in making investigations more efficient. First, it provides him with continuing powers for the purposes of the investigation rather than having to apply for a series of production orders. Secondly, it will allow relevant individuals to be interviewed and explain the nature of the material. Information in bank or transaction reports can be very complex and can be difficult to interpret without the assistance of provider. The Director of the Serious Fraud Office has similar powers and they have also been used in Northern Ireland.

    The notice in writing includes notice given by electronic means: s.416(8) and (9).

358   Requirements for making of disclosure order

(1) These are the requirements for the making of a disclosure order.

(2) There must be reasonable grounds for suspecting that—
   (a) in the case of a confiscation investigation, the person specified in the application for the order has benefited from his criminal conduct;
   (b) in the case of a civil recovery investigation, the property specified in the application for the order is recoverable property or associated property.

(3) There must be reasonable grounds for believing that information which may be provided in compliance with a requirement imposed under the order is likely to be of substantial value (whether or not by itself) to the investigation for the purposes of which the order is sought.

(4) There must be reasonable grounds for believing that it is in the public interest for the information to be provided, having regard to the benefit likely to accrue to the investigation if the information is obtained.

DEFINITIONS
   "associated property": s.245; s.414(2)
   "civil recovery investigation": s.341(2) and (3); s.416(1) and (9)
   "confiscation investigation": s.341(1); s.416(1) and (9)
   "criminal conduct": s.413; s.416(9)
   "disclosure order": s.357(4); s.416(2) and (9)
   "recoverable property": ss.304-310; s.316(1); s.414(2); s.416(9)

GENERAL NOTE
   The Government recognised that disclosure orders involve extensive powers and will be intrusive. The expectation is that they will be used only where other powers will not be sufficient to obtain the material being pursued. When considering the application, the judge may be expected to consider whether an order would be a proportionate measure in terms of Art.6 of the European Convention on Human Rights. However, the public interest requirement was inserted into this section in the closing stages of the Bill's passage: see the note to s.346, above.

359   Offences

(1) A person commits an offence if without reasonable excuse he fails to comply with a requirement imposed on him under a disclosure order.

(2) A person guilty of an offence under subsection (1) is liable on summary conviction to—
   (a) imprisonment for a term not exceeding six months,
   (b) a fine not exceeding level 5 on the standard scale, or
   (c) both.

(3) A person commits an offence if, in purported compliance with a requirement imposed on him under a disclosure order, he—
   (a) makes a statement which he knows to be false or misleading in a material particular, or
   (b) recklessly makes a statement which is false or misleading in a material particular.

(4) A person guilty of an offence under subsection (3) is liable—
   (a) on summary conviction, to imprisonment for a term not exceeding six months or to a fine not exceeding the statutory maximum or to both, or
   (b) on conviction on indictment, to imprisonment for a term not exceeding two years or to a fine or to both.

DEFINITION
   "disclosure order": s.357(4); s.416(2) and (9)

360 Statements

(1) A statement made by a person in response to a requirement imposed on him under a disclosure order may not be used in evidence against him in criminal proceedings.

(2) But subsection (1) does not apply—

    (a) in the case of proceedings under Part 2 or 4,

    (b) on a prosecution for an offence under section 359(1) or (3),

    (c) on a prosecution for an offence under section 5 of the Perjury Act 1911 (c. 6) or Article 10 of the Perjury (Northern Ireland) Order 1979 (S.I. 1979/1714 (N.I. 19)) (false statements), or

    (d) on a prosecution for some other offence where, in giving evidence, the person makes a statement inconsistent with the statement mentioned in subsection (1).

(3) A statement may not be used by virtue of subsection (2)(d) against a person unless—

    (a) evidence relating to it is adduced, or

    (b) a question relating to it is asked,

by him or on his behalf in the proceedings arising out of the prosecution.

DEFINITION

"disclosure order": s.357(4); s.416(2) and (9)

GENERAL NOTE

Following *Saunders v. United Kingdom* (1997) 23 EHRR 313, various disclosure powers were amended to prevent a statement made under compulsion from being used to incriminate him. This was achieved under Sched.3 to the Youth Justice and Criminal Evidence Act 1999. Similar provision is made in this section.

361 Further provisions

(1) A disclosure order does not confer the right to require a person to answer any privileged question, provide any privileged information or produce any privileged document, except that a lawyer may be required to provide the name and address of a client of his.

(2) A privileged question is a question which the person would be entitled to refuse to answer on grounds of legal professional privilege in proceedings in the High Court.

(3) Privileged information is any information which the person would be entitled to refuse to provide on grounds of legal professional privilege in proceedings in the High Court.

(4) Privileged material is any material which the person would be entitled to refuse to produce on grounds of legal professional privilege in proceedings in the High Court.

(5) A disclosure order does not confer the right to require a person to produce excluded material.

(6) A disclosure order has effect in spite of any restriction on the disclosure of information (however imposed).

(7) The Director may take copies of any documents produced in compliance with a requirement to produce them which is imposed under a disclosure order.

(8) Documents so produced may be retained for so long as it is necessary to retain them (as opposed to a copy of them) in connection with the investigation for the purposes of which the order was made.

(9) But if the Director has reasonable grounds for believing that—

    (a) the documents may need to be produced for the purposes of any legal proceedings, and

(b) they might otherwise be unavailable for those purposes,

they may be retained until the proceedings are concluded.

DEFINITIONS
"document": s.379; s.416(2) and (9)
"Director": s.1(2)
"disclosure order": s.357(4); s.416(2) and (9)
"excluded material": s.379

GENERAL NOTE
See the General Note to s.348, above.

362 Supplementary

(1) An application for a disclosure order may be made ex parte to a judge in chambers.

(2) Rules of court may make provision as to the practice and procedure to be followed in connection with proceedings relating to disclosure orders.

(3) An application to discharge or vary a disclosure order may be made to the court by—
   (a) the Director;
   (b) any person affected by the order.

(4) The court—
   (a) may discharge the order;
   (b) may vary the order.

(5) Subsections (2) to (4) do not apply to orders made in England and Wales for the purposes of a civil recovery investigation.

DEFINITIONS
"civil recovery investigation": s.341(2) and (3); s.416(1) and (9)
"the court": s.344
"Director": s.1(2)
"disclosure order": s.357(4); s.416(2) and (9)
"judge": s.343

GENERAL NOTE
See the General Note to s.351, above. There is no contempt power, however, because s.359 makes non-compliance an offence.

Customer information orders

363 Customer information orders

(1) A judge may, on an application made to him by an appropriate officer, make a customer information order if he is satisfied that each of the requirements for the making of the order is fulfilled.

(2) The application for a customer information order must state that—
   (a) a person specified in the application is subject to a confiscation investigation or a money laundering investigation, or
   (b) property specified in the application is subject to a civil recovery investigation and a person specified in the application appears to hold the property.

(3) The application must also state that—
   (a) the order is sought for the purposes of the investigation;
   (b) the order is sought against the financial institution or financial institutions specified in the application.

(4) An application for a customer information order may specify—
   (a) all financial institutions,
   (b) a particular description, or particular descriptions, of financial institutions, or

    (c) a particular financial institution or particular financial institutions.

(5) A customer information order is an order that a financial institution covered by the application for the order must, on being required to do so by notice in writing given by an appropriate officer, provide any such customer information as it has relating to the person specified in the application.

(6) A financial institution which is required to provide information under a customer information order must provide the information to an appropriate officer in such manner, and at or by such time, as an appropriate officer requires.

(7) If a financial institution on which a requirement is imposed by a notice given under a customer information order requires the production of evidence of authority to give the notice, it is not bound to comply with the requirement unless evidence of the authority has been produced to it.

DEFINITIONS
    "appropriate officer": subs.(8)(a); s.378; s.416(2) and (9)
    "civil recovery investigation": s.341(2) and (3); s.416(1) and (9)
    "confiscation investigation": s.341(1); s.416(1) and (9)
    "document": s.379; s.416(2) and (9)
    "financial institution": s.416(4), (5) and Sched.9; s.416(9)
    "judge": s.343
    "money laundering investigation": s.341(4); s.416(1) and (9)
    "property": s.414; s.416(9)

GENERAL NOTE
    The customer information order provides new powers to require banks or other financial institutions to identify any account held by a person under investigation. It has already been used with apparent success in Northern Ireland to discover unknown bank accounts in connection with terrorist investigations. It is envisaged that it will be used at the early stages of investigation to discover which organisation or persons has dealings with the suspect. Thereafter, one or more production orders may be sought to obtain more specific information. Since this is another invasive power, which can also impose substantial costs on the institutions concerned, only a senior appropriate officer may apply for the order, under s.369(7).
    The notice in writing includes notice given by electronic means: s.416(8) and (9).

364   Meaning of customer information

(1) "Customer information", in relation to a person and a financial institution, is information whether the person holds, or has held, an account or accounts at the financial institution (whether solely or jointly with another) and (if so) information as to—
    (a) the matters specified in subsection (2) if the person is an individual;
    (b) the matters specified in subsection (3) if the person is a company or limited liability partnership or a similar body incorporated or otherwise established outside the United Kingdom.

(2) The matters referred to in subsection (1)(a) are—
    (a) the account number or numbers;
    (b) the person's full name;
    (c) his date of birth;
    (d) his most recent address and any previous addresses;
    (e) the date or dates on which he began to hold the account or accounts and, if he has ceased to hold the account or any of the accounts, the date or dates on which he did so;
    (f) such evidence of his identity as was obtained by the financial institution under or for the purposes of any legislation relating to money laundering;

   (g) the full name, date of birth and most recent address, and any previous addresses, of any person who holds, or has held, an account at the financial institution jointly with him;

   (h) the account number or numbers of any other account or accounts held at the financial institution to which he is a signatory and details of the person holding the other account or accounts.

(3) The matters referred to in subsection (1)(b) are—

   (a) the account number or numbers;

   (b) the person's full name;

   (c) a description of any business which the person carries on;

   (d) the country or territory in which it is incorporated or otherwise established and any number allocated to it under the Companies Act 1985 (c. 6) or the Companies (Northern Ireland) Order 1986 (S.I. 1986/1032 (N.I. 6)) or corresponding legislation of any country or territory outside the United Kingdom;

   (e) any number assigned to it for the purposes of value added tax in the United Kingdom;

   (f) its registered office, and any previous registered offices, under the Companies Act 1985 or the Companies (Northern Ireland) Order 1986 (S.I. 1986/1032 (N.I. 6)) or anything similar under corresponding legislation of any country or territory outside the United Kingdom;

   (g) its registered office, and any previous registered offices, under the Limited Liability Partnerships Act 2000 (c. 12) or anything similar under corresponding legislation of any country or territory outside Great Britain;

   (h) the date or dates on which it began to hold the account or accounts and, if it has ceased to hold the account or any of the accounts, the date or dates on which it did so;

   (i) such evidence of its identity as was obtained by the financial institution under or for the purposes of any legislation relating to money laundering;

   (j) the full name, date of birth and most recent address and any previous addresses of any person who is a signatory to the account or any of the accounts.

(4) The Secretary of State may by order provide for information of a description specified in the order—

   (a) to be customer information, or

   (b) no longer to be customer information.

(5) Money laundering is an act which—

   (a) constitutes an offence under section 327, 328 or 329 of this Act or section 18 of the Terrorism Act 2000 (c. 11), or

   (b) would constitute an offence specified in paragraph (a) if done in the United Kingdom.

DEFINITION
"financial institution": s.416(4), (5) and Sched.9; s.416(9)

GENERAL NOTE
   In subss.(2)(f) and (3)(i), the information is evidence of identity already obtained by the financial institution in compliance with the Money Laundering Regulations 1993 (S.I. 1993 No. 1933).

365 Requirements for making of customer information order

(1) These are the requirements for the making of a customer information order.

(2) In the case of a confiscation investigation, there must be reasonable grounds for suspecting that the person specified in the application for the order has benefited from his criminal conduct.

(3) In the case of a civil recovery investigation, there must be reasonable grounds for suspecting that—
  (a) the property specified in the application for the order is recoverable property or associated property;
  (b) the person specified in the application holds all or some of the property.

(4) In the case of a money laundering investigation, there must be reasonable grounds for suspecting that the person specified in the application for the order has committed a money laundering offence.

(5) In the case of any investigation, there must be reasonable grounds for believing that customer information which may be provided in compliance with the order is likely to be of substantial value (whether or not by itself) to the investigation for the purposes of which the order is sought.

(6) In the case of any investigation, there must be reasonable grounds for believing that it is in the public interest for the customer information to be provided, having regard to the benefit likely to accrue to the investigation if the information is obtained.

DEFINITIONS
"associated property": s.245; s.414(2)
"civil recovery investigation": s.341(2) and (3); s.416(1) and (9)
"confiscation investigation": s.341(1); s.416(1) and (9)
"criminal conduct": s.413; s.416(9)
"customer information": s.364; s.416(2) and (9)
"customer information order": s.363(5); s.416(2) and (9)
"financial institution": s.416(4), (5) and Sched.9; s.416(9)
"money laundering investigation": s.341(4); s.416(1) and (9)
"money laundering offence": s.415; s.416(9)
"property": s.414; s.416(9)
"recoverable property": ss.304-310; s.316(1); s.414(2); s.416(9)

GENERAL NOTE
When considering the application, the judge may be expected to consider whether an order would be a proportionate measure in terms of Art.6 of the European Convention on Human Rights. However, the public interest requirement, in subs.(6), was inserted into this section in the closing stages of the Bill's passage: see the General Note to s.346, above.

366   Offences

(1) A financial institution commits an offence if without reasonable excuse it fails to comply with a requirement imposed on it under a customer information order.

(2) A financial institution guilty of an offence under subsection (1) is liable on summary conviction to a fine not exceeding level 5 on the standard scale.

(3) A financial institution commits an offence if, in purported compliance with a customer information order, it—
  (a) makes a statement which it knows to be false or misleading in a material particular, or
  (b) recklessly makes a statement which is false or misleading in a material particular.

(4) A financial institution guilty of an offence under subsection (3) is liable—
  (a) on summary conviction, to a fine not exceeding the statutory maximum, or
  (b) on conviction on indictment, to a fine.

DEFINITIONS
"customer information order": s.363(5); s.416(2) and (9)
"financial institution": s.416(4), (5) and Sched.9; s.416(9)

367   Statements

(1) A statement made by a financial institution in response to a customer information order may not be used in evidence against it in criminal proceedings.

(2) But subsection (1) does not apply—
(a) in the case of proceedings under Part 2 or 4,
(b) on a prosecution for an offence under section 366(1) or (3), or
(c) on a prosecution for some other offence where, in giving evidence, the financial institution makes a statement inconsistent with the statement mentioned in subsection (1).

(3) A statement may not be used by virtue of subsection (2)(c) against a financial institution unless—
(a) evidence relating to it is adduced, or
(b) a question relating to it is asked,
by or on behalf of the financial institution in the proceedings arising out of the prosecution.

DEFINITIONS
"customer information order": s.363(5); s.416(2) and (9)
"financial institution": s.416(4), (5) and Sched.9; s.416(9)

GENERAL NOTE
See the General Note to s.360, above.

368   Disclosure of information

A customer information order has effect in spite of any restriction on the disclosure of information (however imposed).

DEFINITION
"customer information order": s.363(5); s.416(2) and (9)

GENERAL NOTE
A customer information cannot be resisted by claims of confidentiality, data protection or other statutory protection.

369   Supplementary

(1) An application for a customer information order may be made ex parte to a judge in chambers.

(2) Rules of court may make provision as to the practice and procedure to be followed in connection with proceedings relating to customer information orders.

(3) An application to discharge or vary a customer information order may be made to the court by—
(a) the person who applied for the order;
(b) any person affected by the order.

(4) The court—
(a) may discharge the order;
(b) may vary the order.

(5) If an accredited financial investigator, a constable or a customs officer applies for a customer information order, an application to discharge or vary the order need not be by the same accredited financial investigator, constable or customs officer.

(6) References to a person who applied for a customer information order must be construed accordingly.

(7) An accredited financial investigator, a constable or a customs officer may not make an application for a customer information order or an application to vary such an order unless he is a senior appropriate officer or he is authorised to do so by a senior appropriate officer.

(8) Subsections (2) to (6) do not apply to orders made in England and Wales for the purposes of a civil recovery investigation.

DEFINITIONS
"accredited financial investigator": s.453
"appropriate officer": subs.(8)(a); s.378; s.416(2) and (9)
"civil recovery investigation": s.341(2) and (3); s.416(1) and (9)
"the court": s.344
"customer information order": s.363(5); s.416(2) and (9)
"customs officer": s.454
"judge": s.343
"senior appropriate officer": s.378; s.416(2) and (9)

GENERAL NOTE
See the General Notes to s.351 and 355, above. As with s.355, there is no contempt power because, in this case, s.370 makes non-compliance an offence.

Account monitoring orders

370   **Account monitoring orders**

(1) A judge may, on an application made to him by an appropriate officer, make an account monitoring order if he is satisfied that each of the requirements for the making of the order is fulfilled.

(2) The application for an account monitoring order must state that—
   (a) a person specified in the application is subject to a confiscation investigation or a money laundering investigation, or
   (b) property specified in the application is subject to a civil recovery investigation and a person specified in the application appears to hold the property.

(3) The application must also state that—
   (a) the order is sought for the purposes of the investigation;
   (b) the order is sought against the financial institution specified in the application in relation to account information of the description so specified.

(4) Account information is information relating to an account or accounts held at the financial institution specified in the application by the person so specified (whether solely or jointly with another).

(5) The application for an account monitoring order may specify information relating to—
   (a) all accounts held by the person specified in the application for the order at the financial institution so specified,
   (b) a particular description, or particular descriptions, of accounts so held, or
   (c) a particular account, or particular accounts, so held.

(6) An account monitoring order is an order that the financial institution specified in the application for the order must, for the period stated in the order, provide account information of the description specified in the order to an appropriate officer in the manner, and at or by the time or times, stated in the order.

(7) The period stated in an account monitoring order must not exceed the period of 90 days beginning with the day on which the order is made.

DEFINITIONS
"appropriate officer": subs.(8)(a); s.378; s.416(2) and (9)
"civil recovery investigation": s.341(2) and (3); s.416(1) and (9)
"confiscation investigation": s.341(1); s.416(1) and (9)
"financial institution": s.416(4), (5) and Sched.9; s.416(9)
"judge": s.343
"money laundering investigation": s.341(4); s.416(1) and (9)
"property": s.414; s.416(9)

GENERAL NOTE
The account monitoring order requires a bank or other financial institution to provide information about transactions on a suspect account or accounts for a specified period of time. Similar provisions have also already been used to some effect in terrorist investigations and this section extends their use generally to proceeds of crime and money laundering investigations. Obtaining the order will avoid the need to secure a series of production orders to monitor the transactions being investigated. However, the order is limited to 90 days.

371 Requirements for making of account monitoring order

(1) These are the requirements for the making of an account monitoring order.

(2) In the case of a confiscation investigation, there must be reasonable grounds for suspecting that the person specified in the application for the order has benefited from his criminal conduct.

(3) In the case of a civil recovery investigation, there must be reasonable grounds for suspecting that—
  (a) the property specified in the application for the order is recoverable property or associated property;
  (b) the person specified in the application holds all or some of the property.

(4) In the case of a money laundering investigation, there must be reasonable grounds for suspecting that the person specified in the application for the order has committed a money laundering offence.

(5) In the case of any investigation, there must be reasonable grounds for believing that account information which may be provided in compliance with the order is likely to be of substantial value (whether or not by itself) to the investigation for the purposes of which the order is sought.

(6) In the case of any investigation, there must be reasonable grounds for believing that it is in the public interest for the account information to be provided, having regard to the benefit likely to accrue to the investigation if the information is obtained.

DEFINITIONS
"account information": s.370(4); s.416(2) and (9)
"account monitoring order": s.370(6); s.416(2) and (9)
"associated property": s.245; s.414(2)
"civil recovery investigation": s.341(2) and (3); s.416(1) and (9)
"confiscation investigation": s.341(1); s.416(1) and (9)
"criminal conduct": s.413; s.416(9)
"money laundering investigation": s.341(4); s.416(1) and (9)
"money laundering offence": s.415; s.416(9)
"property": s.414; s.416(9)
"recoverable property": ss.304-310; s.316(1); s.414(2); s.416(9)

GENERAL NOTE
In deciding whether to grant an account monitoring order, the judge will have to consider whether the continued monitoring is proportionate, in terms of Art.6 of the European Convention on Human Rights. However, the public interest requirement, in subs.(6), was inserted into this section in the closing stages of the Bill's passage: see the General Note to s.346, above.

372 Statements

(1) A statement made by a financial institution in response to an account monitoring order may not be used in evidence against it in criminal proceedings.

(2) But subsection (1) does not apply—
  (a) in the case of proceedings under Part 2 or 4,

(b) in the case of proceedings for contempt of court, or
(c) on a prosecution for an offence where, in giving evidence, the financial institution makes a statement inconsistent with the statement mentioned in subsection (1).
(3) A statement may not be used by virtue of subsection (2)(c) against a financial institution unless—
(a) evidence relating to it is adduced, or
(b) a question relating to it is asked,
by or on behalf of the financial institution in the proceedings arising out of the prosecution.

DEFINITIONS
"account monitoring order": s.370(6); s.416(2) and (9)
"financial institution": s.416(4), (5) and Sched.9; s.416(9)

GENERAL NOTE
See the General Note to s.360, above.

373 Applications

An application for an account monitoring order may be made ex parte to a judge in chambers.

DEFINITIONS
"account monitoring order": s.370(6); s.416(2) and (9)
"judge": s.343

GENERAL NOTE
A customer information cannot be resisted by claims of confidentiality, data protection or other statutory protection.

374 Disclosure of information

An account monitoring order has effect in spite of any restriction on the disclosure of information (however imposed).

DEFINITION
"account monitoring order": s.370(6); s.416(2) and (9)

375 Supplementary

(1) Rules of court may make provision as to the practice and procedure to be followed in connection with proceedings relating to account monitoring orders.
(2) An application to discharge or vary an account monitoring order may be made to the court by—
(a) the person who applied for the order;
(b) any person affected by the order.
(3) The court—
(a) may discharge the order;
(b) may vary the order.
(4) If an accredited financial investigator, a constable or a customs officer applies for an account monitoring order, an application to discharge or vary the order need not be by the same accredited financial investigator, constable or customs officer.
(5) References to a person who applied for an account monitoring order must be construed accordingly.
(6) Account monitoring orders have effect as if they were orders of the court.

(7) This section does not apply to orders made in England and Wales for the purposes of a civil recovery investigation.

GENERAL NOTE
See the General Note to s.351 above.

Evidence overseas

376   Evidence overseas

(1) This section applies if the Director is carrying out a confiscation investigation.
(2) A judge on the application of the Director or a person subject to the investigation may issue a letter of request if he thinks that there is evidence in a country or territory outside the United Kingdom—
   (a) that such a person has benefited from his criminal conduct, or
   (b) of the extent or whereabouts of that person's benefit from his criminal conduct.
(3) The Director may issue a letter of request if he thinks that there is evidence in a country or territory outside the United Kingdom—
   (a) that a person subject to the investigation has benefited from his criminal conduct, or
   (b) of the extent or whereabouts of that person's benefit from his criminal conduct.
(4) A letter of request is a letter requesting assistance in obtaining outside the United Kingdom such evidence as is specified in the letter for use in the investigation.
(5) The person issuing a letter of request must send it to the Secretary of State.
(6) If the Secretary of State believes it is appropriate to do so he may forward a letter received under subsection (5)—
   (a) to a court or tribunal which is specified in the letter and which exercises jurisdiction in the place where the evidence is to be obtained, or
   (b) to an authority recognised by the government of the country or territory concerned as the appropriate authority for receiving letters of request.
(7) But in a case of urgency the person issuing the letter of request may send it directly to the court or tribunal mentioned in subsection (6)(a).
(8) Evidence obtained in pursuance of a letter of request must not be used—
   (a) by any person other than the Director or a person subject to the investigation;
   (b) for any purpose other than that for which it is obtained.
(9) Subsection (8) does not apply if the authority mentioned in subsection (6)(b) consents to the use.
(10) Evidence includes documents and other articles.
(11) Rules of court may make provision as to the practice and procedure to be followed in connection with proceedings relating to the issue of letters of request by a judge under this section.

"confiscation investigation": s.341(1); s.416(1) and (9)
"criminal conduct": s.413; s.416(9)
"Director": s.1(2)
"document": s.379; s.416(2) and (9)
"judge": s.343

Code of practice

377   Code of practice

(1) The Secretary of State must prepare a code of practice as to the exercise by all of the following of functions they have under this Chapter—
 (a) the Director;
 (b) members of the staff of the Agency;
 (c) accredited financial investigators;
 (d) constables;
 (e) customs officers.

(2) After preparing a draft of the code the Secretary of State—
 (a) must publish the draft;
 (b) must consider any representations made to him about the draft;
 (c) may amend the draft accordingly.

(3) After the Secretary of State has proceeded under subsection (2) he must lay the code before Parliament.

(4) When he has done so the Secretary of State may bring the code into operation on such day as he may appoint by order.

(5) A person specified in subsection (1)(a) to (e) must comply with a code of practice which is in operation under this section in the exercise of any function he has under this Chapter.

(6) If such a person fails to comply with any provision of such a code of practice he is not by reason only of that failure liable in any criminal or civil proceedings.

(7) But the code of practice is admissible in evidence in such proceedings and a court may take account of any failure to comply with its provisions in determining any question in the proceedings.

(8) The Secretary of State may from time to time revise a code previously brought into operation under this section; and the preceding provisions of this section apply to a revised code as they apply to the code as first prepared.

(9) The following provisions do not apply to an appropriate officer in the exercise of any function he has under this Chapter—
 (a) section 67(9) of the Police and Criminal Evidence Act 1984 (c. 60) (application of codes of practice under that Act to persons other than police officers);
 (b) Article 66(8) of the Police and Criminal Evidence (Northern Ireland) Order 1989 (S.I. 1989/1341 (N.I. 12)) (which makes similar provision for Northern Ireland).

"accredited financial investigator": s.453
"Agency": s.1(1)
"appropriate officer": subs.(8)(a); s.378; s.416(2) and (9)
"civil recovery investigation": s.341(2) and (3); s.416(1) and (9)
"customs officer": s.454
"Director": s.1(2)

GENERAL NOTE
This provision is modelled on the para.8 of Sched.2 to the Proceeds of Crime (Northern Ireland) Order 1996 (S.I. 1996 No. 1299). Breach of a provision of the code will not render a person liable to proceedings but the code will be admissible as evidence.

Interpretation

378   Officers

(1) In relation to a confiscation investigation these are appropriate officers—
   (a) the Director;
   (b) an accredited financial investigator;
   (c) a constable;
   (d) a customs officer.

(2) In relation to a confiscation investigation these are senior appropriate officers—
   (a) the Director;
   (b) a police officer who is not below the rank of superintendent;
   (c) a customs officer who is not below such grade as is designated by the Commissioners of Customs and Excise as equivalent to that rank;
   (d) an accredited financial investigator who falls within a description specified in an order made for the purposes of this paragraph by the Secretary of State under section 453.

(3) In relation to a civil recovery investigation the Director (and only the Director) is—
   (a) an appropriate officer;
   (b) a senior appropriate officer.

(4) In relation to a money laundering investigation these are appropriate officers—
   (a) an accredited financial investigator;
   (b) a constable;
   (c) a customs officer.

(5) For the purposes of section 342, in relation to a money laundering investigation a person authorised for the purposes of money laundering investigations by the Director General of the National Criminal Intelligence Service is also an appropriate officer.

(6) In relation to a money laundering investigation these are senior appropriate officers—
   (a) a police officer who is not below the rank of superintendent;
   (b) a customs officer who is not below such grade as is designated by the Commissioners of Customs and Excise as equivalent to that rank;
   (c) an accredited financial investigator who falls within a description specified in an order made for the purposes of this paragraph by the Secretary of State under section 453.

(7) But a person is not an appropriate officer or a senior appropriate officer in relation to a money laundering investigation if he is—
   (a) a member of the staff of the Agency, or
   (b) a person providing services under arrangements made by the Director.

DEFINITIONS
   "accredited financial investigator": s.453
   "Agency": s.1(1)
   "confiscation investigation": s.341(1); s.416(1) and (9)
   "customs officer": s.454
   "Director": s.1(2)
   "money laundering investigation": s.341(4); s.416(1) and (9)

GENERAL NOTE
   The Director has an important personal role in instigating civil recovery investigations, by subs.(3). In addition, members of the Agency's staff and any accredited financial investigators employed by the Agency cannot invoke the money laundering investigation powers, by subs.(7).

379   Miscellaneous

"Document", "excluded material" and "premises" have the same meanings as in the Police and Criminal Evidence Act 1984 (c. 60) or (in relation to Northern Ireland) the Police and Criminal Evidence (Northern Ireland) Order 1989 (S.I. 1989/1341 (N.I. 12)).

CHAPTER 3

SCOTLAND

Production orders

380   Production orders

(1) The sheriff may, on an application made to him by the appropriate person, make a production order if he is satisfied that each of the requirements for the making of the order is fulfilled.

(2) In making a production order in relation to property subject to a civil recovery investigation, the sheriff shall act in the exercise of his civil jurisdiction.

(3) The application for a production order must state that—
   (a) a person specified in the application is subject to a confiscation investigation or a money laundering investigation, or
   (b) property specified in the application is subject to a civil recovery investigation.

(4) The application must also state that—
   (a) the order is sought for the purposes of the investigation;
   (b) the order is sought in relation to material, or material of a description, specified in the application;
   (c) a person specified in the application appears to be in possession or control of the material.

(5) A production order is an order either—
   (a) requiring the person the application for the order specifies as appearing to be in possession or control of material to produce it to a proper person for him to take away, or
   (b) requiring that person to give a proper person access to the material,
   within the period stated in the order.

(6) The period stated in a production order must be a period of seven days beginning with the day on which the order is made, unless it appears to the sheriff that a longer or shorter period would be appropriate in the particular circumstances.

DEFINITIONS
  "Appropriate person": s.412

GENERAL NOTE
  Section 380 replaces s.18 of the Proceeds of Crime (Scotland) Act 1995 and s.31 of the Criminal Law (Consolidation)(Scotland) Act 1995. It provides for the making of production orders and "production order" is defined as an order either requiring the person the application specifies as appearing to be in possession or control of material to produce it to a proper person for him to take away; or requiring that person to give a proper person access to that material, within the period stated in the order (The period is, by subs (6), usually seven days).
  Section 384 makes it clear that if (as is very likely) the information is contained in a computer, the production order has effect as an order to produce the material in a form which is visible and legible. Production orders are not the same as search warrants. They are better characterised as orders of court addressed to particular persons or categories of persons to do specific things. It is suggested, therefore, that the case law on search warrants is likely to be of limited assistance in relation to production orders.
  In *R v. Crown Court at Southwark Ex p. Customs and Excise Commissioners* (1989) 3 All ER 673, the Divisional Court in England held that there was nothing in the legislation to restrict the

making of such orders to cases being investigated by UK investigators. On the contrary, Watkins LJ said that one of the purposes of the legislation is to advance the international co-operation to which the UK is bound by the UN Single Convention on Narcotic Drugs 1961 (the case concerned a drug trafficking investigation). The Court held that the judge who had granted the order had exceeded his powers when he attached a condition preventing Customs and Excise from communicating the results of the execution of the order to foreign investigators without special leave of the Court.

Subs. (1)

The sheriff may. R v. Crown Court at Southwark Ex p. Customs and Excise Commissioners suggests that the court retains a discretion to refuse an order, even where the conditions are satisfied. It is, however, hard to see grounds on which such a refusal would be reasonable and no doubt the Crown would pursue the matter by Bill of Advocation.

On an application. Under the two sections which are replaced by the present provision (see the General Note above), procedure has been by way of petition, to which s.134 of the Criminal Procedure (Scotland) Act 1995 (incidental applications) applies (see Act of Adjournal (Criminal Procedure Rules) 1996 Rules 37.1 and 39.1). Note, however, that subs (2) has the effect of applying civil rules where the order is sought in connection with a civil recovery investigation. As to the content of the application under the present Act, see subss (3) and (4). Section 386(1) provides that an application for a production order may be made *ex parte* in chambers.

Appropriate person. The "appropriate person" is defined by s.412 as the procurator fiscal in relation to a confiscation investigation or a money laundering investigation and as the Scottish Ministers in relation to a civil recovery investigation.

If he is satisfied that each of the requirements for the making of the order is fulfilled. For the requirements, see s.381.

Subs. (4)

Note that, by subs (3), the order must be sought in connection with a confiscation or money laundering investigation or a civil recovery investigation. In *R v. Crown Court at Southwark ex p Bowles* (1988) 2 All ER 193 (HL) an accountant, who had been served with a production order in relation to clients who faced charges of dishonesty was advised by her solicitors that the police should have obtained a search warrant rather than a production order. There was an issue about how far the material sought was required for the investigation of benefit from crime and how far it was required to assist the substantive prosecution case. She sought judicial review to quash the production order. The case ultimately went to the House of Lords where it was held that the court, in considering an application for a production order which might also assist the substantive prosecution case, should apply the dominant purpose test. Lord Hutton said that the order should be granted if the true and dominant purpose is that for which the legislation provides the power (namely, in the present section, a confiscation, civil recovery or money laundering investigation) but refused if the true and dominant purpose is to carry out an investigation into the substantive (predicate) offence and bring a prosecution.

381   Requirements for making of production order

(1) These are the requirements for the making of a production order.

(2) There must be reasonable grounds for suspecting that—

    (a) in the case of a confiscation investigation, the person the application for the order specifies as being subject to the investigation has benefited from his criminal conduct;

    (b) in the case of a civil recovery investigation, the property the application for the order specifies as being subject to the investigation is recoverable property or associated property;

    (c) in the case of a money laundering investigation, the person the application for the order specifies as being subject to the investigation has committed a money laundering offence.

(3) There must be reasonable grounds for believing that the person the application specifies as appearing to be in possession or control of the material so specified is in possession or control of it.

(4) There must be reasonable grounds for believing that the material is likely to be of substantial value (whether or not by itself) to the investigation for the purposes of which the order is sought.

(5) There must be reasonable grounds for believing that it is in the public interest for the material to be produced or for access to it to be given, having regard to—

    (a) the benefit likely to accrue to the investigation if the material is obtained,

    (b) the circumstances under which the person the application specifies as appearing to be in possession or control of the material holds it.

GENERAL NOTE

Paragraph 518 of the Explanatory Notes states that "The Human Rights Act 1998 requires a judge not to act in a way which is incompatible with Convention rights. So, for example, an appropriate person will have to satisfy the sheriff that any infringement of, for example, a suspect's right to privacy under Art.8(1) of the Convention is proportionate to the benefit to be gained from making an order".

Subs. (4)

This provision was derived from the Police and Criminal Evidence Act 1984, into which it was originally introduced in order to prevent "fishing expeditions" (see MDA Freeman, *Police and Criminal Evidence Act 1984* Current Law Statutes Annotated 1984 p60-34).

382   Order to grant entry

(1) This section applies if a sheriff makes a production order requiring a person to give a proper person access to material on any premises.

(2) The sheriff may, on an application made to him by the appropriate person and specifying the premises, make an order to grant entry in relation to the premises.

(3) An order to grant entry is an order requiring any person who appears to the appropriate person to be entitled to grant entry to the premises to allow a proper person to enter the premises to obtain access to the material.

383   Further provisions

(1) A production order does not require a person to produce, or give access to, any items subject to legal privilege.

(2) A production order has effect in spite of any restriction on the disclosure of information (however imposed).

(3) A proper person may take copies of any material which is produced, or to which access is given, in compliance with a production order.

(4) Material produced in compliance with a production order may be retained for so long as it is necessary to retain it (as opposed to copies of it) in connection with the investigation for the purposes of which the order was made.

(5) But if a proper person has reasonable grounds for believing that—

    (a) the material may need to be produced for the purposes of any legal proceedings, and

    (b) it might otherwise be unavailable for those purposes,

it may be retained until the proceedings are concluded.

GENERAL NOTE

Subs. (1)

This exemption has a long history and it is important to note that in *R v. Central Criminal Court ex p Francis and Francis* (1989) AC 346 the House of Lords held, in relation to such orders under DTOA, that items otherwise subject to privilege are not so subject if held with the intention (not necessarily on the part of the holder) of furthering a criminal purpose. Money laundering would be an obvious example of such a purpose. Note also the consideration of legal professional privilege generally under the heading of s.330, above.

384 Computer information

(1) This section applies if any of the material specified in an application for a production order consists of information contained in a computer.

(2) If the order is an order requiring a person to produce the material to a proper person for him to take away, it has effect as an order to produce the material in a form in which it can be taken away by him and in which it is visible and legible.

(3) If the order is an order requiring a person to give a proper person access to the material, it has effect as an order to give him access to the material in a form in which it is visible and legible.

385 Government departments

(1) A production order may be made in relation to material in the possession or control of an authorised government department.

(2) An order so made may require any officer of the department (whether named in the order or not) who may for the time being be in possession or control of the material to comply with it.

(3) If an order contains such a requirement—
    (a) the person on whom it is served must take all reasonable steps to bring it to the attention of the officer concerned;
    (b) any other officer of the department who is in receipt of the order must also take all reasonable steps to bring it to the attention of the officer concerned.

(4) If the order is not brought to the attention of the officer concerned within the period stated in the order (in pursuance of section 380(5)) the person on whom it is served must report the reasons for the failure to—
    (a) the sheriff in the case of an order made for the purposes of a confiscation investigation or a money laundering investigation;
    (b) the sheriff exercising a civil jurisdiction in the case of an order made for the purposes of a civil recovery investigation.

(5) In this section, "authorised government department" includes a government department which is an authorised department for the purposes of the Crown Proceedings Act 1947 (c. 44) and the Scottish Administration.

GENERAL NOTE

This section extends the scope of a production order to cover material held by an authorised government department and is similar to existing powers in s.20 of the Proceeds of Crime (Scotland) Act 1995 and s.35 of the of the Criminal Law (Consolidation) (Scotland) Act 1995. The provision is necessary to take account of the rule, most recently enunciated by the House of Lords in *Lord Advocate v Dumbarton District Council* 1990 SC (HL) 1 and applied in *Scottish Criminal Cases Review Commission, Petitioners*, 2001 SLT 1198 that the Crown is not bound by statutory provisions except by express words or necessary implication.

Subs. (5)

Note the inclusion of the Scottish Administration within the category of Government departments for these purposes.

386 Supplementary

(1) An application for a production order or an order to grant entry may be made ex parte to a sheriff in chambers.

(2) Provision may be made by rules of court as to the discharge and variation of production orders and orders to grant entry.

(3) Rules of court under subsection (2) relating to production orders and orders to grant entry—
  (a) made in a confiscation investigation or a money laundering investigation shall, without prejudice to section 305 of the Criminal Procedure (Scotland) Act 1995 (c. 46) be made by act of adjournal;
  (b) made in a civil recovery investigation shall, without prejudice to section 32 of the Sheriff Courts (Scotland) Act 1971 (c. 58) be made by act of sederunt.
(4) An application to discharge or vary a production order or an order to grant entry may be made to the sheriff by—
  (a) the person who applied for the order;
  (b) any person affected by the order.
(5) The sheriff may—
  (a) discharge the order;
  (b) vary the order.

Search warrants

387   Search warrants

(1) The sheriff may, on an application made to him by the appropriate person, issue a search warrant if he is satisfied that either of the requirements for the issuing of the warrant is fulfilled.
(2) In issuing a search warrant in relation to property subject to a civil recovery investigation, the sheriff shall act in the exercise of his civil jurisdiction.
(3) The application for a search warrant must state that—
  (a) a person specified in the application is subject to a confiscation investigation or a money laundering investigation, or
  (b) property specified in the application is subject to a civil recovery investigation.
(4) A search warrant is a warrant authorising a proper person—
  (a) to enter and search the premises specified in the application for the warrant, and
  (b) to seize and retain any material specified in the warrant which is found there and which is likely to be of substantial value (whether or not by itself) to the investigation for the purposes of which the application is made.
(5) The requirements for the issue of a search warrant are—
  (a) that a production order made in relation to material has not been complied with and there are reasonable grounds for believing that the material is on the premises specified in the application for the warrant, or
  (b) that section 388 is satisfied in relation to the warrant.
(6) An application for a search warrant may be made ex parte to a sheriff in chambers.

DEFINITIONS
  "Appropriate person": s.412

GENERAL NOTE
  The section provides a search warrant for the situation in which a production order has not been complied with (subs.(5)), in which it is not practicable to communicate with any person against whom a production order could be made (s.388(4)(a) and (b)) or that the investigation would be seriously prejudiced unless immediate access to the material could be secured (s.388 (4)(c). Paragraph 522 of the Explanatory Notes suggests that the impracticable to communicate criterion might be met for example, where the person who owns the material is abroad and that

the second set of conditions (subss.(5) to (9)) might be met where it is impossible to describe the material (for the purposes of a production order) and access will not be gained without a warrant (e.g. to the residence of the suspect).

The criteria for the granting of a search warrant are based on those for the grant of a production order. Note, however, that the general rule is that the procurator fiscal is always entitled, even in relation to a statutory offence, to seek a warrant at common law from the Sheriff unless statute specifically excludes that right in the particular circumstances (*McNeill, Complainer* 1984 SLT 157). The present Act does not exclude that right. In general, the Sheriff is, of course, perfectly entitled to refuse to grant a warrant if after considering in light of Article 8.2 ECHR the balance to be struck between the public interest in the detection of crime on the one hand and the interest of the citizen whose property it is intended to search on the other he or she is not satisfied that it would be proportionate or otherwise necessary or appropriate to grant the warrant. Such a refusal has been reported (Green's Criminal Law Bulletin, June 1993) where it was apparent that the true purpose of the search was not directly proof of the offence which had been reported to the police (indecent assault during a consultation with an aromatherapist) but an attempt to recover a list of other customers in the hope that interviewing them would discover other offences so as to enable the *Moorov* doctrine to be invoked.

By subs.(6) the application for a search warrant may be made *ex parte* in chambers, as is the invariable practice as regards other types of search warrant.

The search warrant lasts for one month (s.390(2)) and authorises the person executing it to require information held in a computer to be produced in a form which is visible and legible.

388   Requirements where production order not available

(1) This section is satisfied in relation to a search warrant if—
    (a) subsection (2) applies, and
    (b) either the first or the second set of conditions is complied with.
(2) This subsection applies if there are reasonable grounds for suspecting that—
    (a) in the case of a confiscation investigation, the person specified in the application for the warrant has benefited from his criminal conduct;
    (b) in the case of a civil recovery investigation, the property specified in the application for the warrant is recoverable property or associated property;
    (c) in the case of a money laundering investigation, the person specified in the application for the warrant has committed a money laundering offence.
(3) The first set of conditions is that there are reasonable grounds for believing that—
    (a) any material on the premises specified in the application for the warrant is likely to be of substantial value (whether or not by itself) to the investigation for the purposes of which the warrant is sought,
    (b) it is in the public interest for the material to be obtained, having regard to the benefit likely to accrue to the investigation if the material is obtained, and
    (c) it would not be appropriate to make a production order for any one or more of the reasons in subsection (4).
(4) The reasons are—
    (a) that it is not practicable to communicate with any person against whom the production order could be made;
    (b) that it is not practicable to communicate with any person who would be required to comply with an order to grant access to the material or to grant entry to the premises on which the material is situated;
    (c) that the investigation might be seriously prejudiced unless a proper person is able to secure immediate access to the material.
(5) The second set of conditions is that—

(a) there are reasonable grounds for believing that there is material on the premises specified in the application for the warrant and that the material falls within subsection (6), (7) or (8),

(b) there are reasonable grounds for believing that it is in the public interest for the material to be obtained, having regard to the benefit likely to accrue to the investigation if the material is obtained, and

(c) any one or more of the requirements in subsection (9) is met.

(6) In the case of a confiscation investigation, material falls within this subsection if it cannot be identified at the time of the application but it—

(a) relates to the person specified in the application, the question whether he has benefited from his criminal conduct or any question as to the extent or whereabouts of his benefit from his criminal conduct, and

(b) is likely to be of substantial value (whether or not by itself) to the investigation for the purposes of which the warrant is sought.

(7) In the case of a civil recovery investigation, material falls within this subsection if it cannot be identified at the time of the application but it—

(a) relates to the property specified in the application, the question whether it is recoverable property or associated property, the question as to who holds any such property, any question as to whether the person who appears to hold any such property holds other property which is recoverable property, or any question as to the extent or whereabouts of any property mentioned in this paragraph, and

(b) is likely to be of substantial value (whether or not by itself) to the investigation for the purposes of which the warrant is sought.

(8) In the case of a money laundering investigation, material falls within this subsection if it cannot be identified at the time of the application but it—

(a) relates to the person specified in the application or the question whether he has committed a money laundering offence, and

(b) is likely to be of substantial value (whether or not by itself) to the investigation for the purposes of which the warrant is sought.

(9) The requirements are—

(a) that it is not practicable to communicate with any person entitled to grant entry to the premises;

(b) that entry to the premises will not be granted unless a warrant is produced;

(c) that the investigation might be seriously prejudiced unless a proper person arriving at the premises is able to secure immediate entry to them.

389   Further provisions: general

A search warrant does not confer the right to seize any items subject to legal privilege.

390   Further provisions: confiscation, civil recovery and money laundering

(1) This section applies to search warrants sought for the purposes of confiscation investigations, civil recovery investigations or money laundering investigations.

(2) A warrant continues in force until the end of the period of one month starting with the day on which it is issued.

(3) A warrant authorises the person executing it to require any information which is held in a computer and is accessible from the premises specified in the application for the warrant, and which the proper per-

son believes relates to any matter relevant to the investigation, to be produced in a form—

   (a) in which it can be taken away, and

   (b) in which it is visible and legible.

(4) Copies may be taken of any material seized under a warrant.

(5) A warrant issued in relation to a civil recovery investigation may be issued subject to conditions.

(6) A warrant issued in relation to a civil recovery investigation may include provision authorising the person executing it to do other things which—

   (a) are specified in the warrant, and

   (b) need to be done in order to give effect to it.

(7) Material seized under a warrant issued in relation to a civil recovery investigation may be retained for so long as it is necessary to retain it (as opposed to copies of it) in connection with the investigation for the purposes of which the warrant was issued.

(8) But if the Scottish Ministers have reasonable grounds for believing that—

   (a) the material may need to be produced for the purposes of any legal proceedings, and

   (b) it might otherwise be unavailable for those purposes,

it may be retained until the proceedings are concluded.

Disclosure orders

391 Disclosure orders

(1) The High Court of Justiciary, on an application made to it by the Lord Advocate in relation to confiscation investigations, or the Court of Session, on an application made to it by the Scottish Ministers in relation to civil recovery investigations, may make a disclosure order if it is satisfied that each of the requirements for the making of the order is fulfilled.

(2) No application for a disclosure order may be made in relation to a money laundering investigation.

(3) The application for a disclosure order must state that—

   (a) a person specified in the application is subject to a confiscation investigation and the order is sought for the purposes of the investigation, or

   (b) property specified in the application is subject to a civil recovery investigation and the order is sought for the purposes of the investigation.

(4) A disclosure order is an order authorising the Lord Advocate or the Scottish Ministers to give to any person the Lord Advocate considers or the Scottish Ministers consider has relevant information, notice in writing requiring him to do, with respect to any matter relevant to the investigation for the purposes of which the order is sought, any or all of the following—

   (a) answer questions, either at a time specified in the notice or at once, at a place so specified;

   (b) provide information specified in the notice, by a time and in a manner so specified;

   (c) produce documents, or documents of a description, specified in the notice, either at or by a time so specified or at once, and in a manner so specified.

(5) Relevant information is information (whether or not contained in a document) which the Lord Advocate considers or the Scottish Ministers consider to be relevant to the investigation.

(6) A person is not bound to comply with a requirement imposed by a notice given under a disclosure order unless evidence of authority to give the notice is produced to him.

GENERAL NOTE

Disclosure orders are orders authorising the Lord Advocate or (in relation to a civil recovery investigation) the Scottish Ministers to give written notice requiring a person to answer questions, provide information or produce documents. They represent an application to proceeds of crime law of effectively the same powers which are provided for serious fraud investigations by ss.27 to 30 of the Criminal Law (Consolidation) (Scotland) Act 1995. That means that the orders are available for use against the accused as well as in relation to witnesses. Failure to comply is a summary offence in terms of s.393, carrying a potential penalty of six months' prison. Also in terms of s.393, making a false or misleading statement is an indictable offence, carrying a potential penalty of two years' imprisonment.

As might be expected, such orders are hedged about with a number of restrictions. The first of these is that they are only available on application to the High Court of Justiciary or (in the case of a civil recovery investigation) the Court of Session (subs (1)). The second is that they are not available for money laundering investigations (subs (2)). According to the Explanatory Notes (para. 525), "because of the necessarily invasive nature of such an order, it is not thought appropriate that such a power should be available for investigations into money laundering offences, although comparable powers exist in the Terrorism Act 2000 in relation to terrorist offences as well as terrorist funding".

The third restriction (if it can properly be called a restriction) is that certain requirements must be satisfied. These are set out in s.392.

Paragraph 527 of the Explanatory Notes suggests that "Because of their intrusive nature, it is not anticipated that disclosure orders will be sought unless other powers, such as production orders, have already been sought or would demonstrably not suffice to enable the required information to be obtained. Indeed, this would be one of the points the High Court or the Court of Session would be expected to consider as part of his consideration of the proportionality test which would apply by virtue of s.6 of the Human Rights Act 1998". This, of course, assumes that the grant and use of a disclosure order engages a Convention right, interference with which requires to be justified in terms of necessity in a democratic society. Although this will often be the case, it should not be assumed too readily that it always will. A disclosure order is simply a requirement to answer questions and produce information. The equivalent serious fraud powers are used to overcome obligations of confidentiality (for example, owed by banks to their customers) but (in Scotland) only very rarely in relation to the principal suspect. It is at least questionable whether Article 8 ECHR (for instance) has any application to the recovery of bank records and the obtaining of a statement from a bank manager where the bank has been used as an innocent intermediary in a money laundering scheme carried out through the medium of a shell company. A judge considering an application should, it is suggested, always consider first whether a Convention right is engaged and then whether what is proposed is an interference with it before considering whether necessity, including proportionality, is an issue.

392   Requirements for making of disclosure order

(1) These are the requirements for the making of a disclosure order.
(2) There must be reasonable grounds for suspecting that—
  (a) in the case of a confiscation investigation, the person specified in the application for the order has benefited from his criminal conduct;
  (b) in the case of a civil recovery investigation, the property specified in the application for the order is recoverable property or associated property.
(3) There must be reasonable grounds for believing that information which may be provided in compliance with a requirement imposed under the order is likely to be of substantial value (whether or not by itself) to the investigation for the purposes of which the order is sought.
(4) There must be reasonable grounds for believing that it is in the public interest for the information to be provided, having regard to the benefit likely to accrue to the investigation if the information is obtained.

GENERAL NOTE
Compare the conditions which apply to the obtaining of a production order in terms of s.381. Those s.381 conditions which are not relevant are omitted. Otherwise, the conditions are identical.

393   Offences

(1) A person commits an offence if without reasonable excuse he fails to comply with a requirement imposed on him under a disclosure order.

(2) A person guilty of an offence under subsection (1) is liable on summary conviction to—
   (a) imprisonment for a term not exceeding six months,
   (b) a fine not exceeding level 5 on the standard scale, or
   (c) both.

(3) A person commits an offence if, in purported compliance with a requirement imposed on him under a disclosure order, he—
   (a) makes a statement which he knows to be false or misleading in a material particular, or
   (b) recklessly makes a statement which is false or misleading in a material particular.

(4) A person guilty of an offence under subsection (3) is liable—
   (a) on summary conviction, to imprisonment for a term not exceeding six months or to a fine not exceeding the statutory maximum or to both, or
   (b) on conviction on indictment, to imprisonment for a term not exceeding two years or to a fine or to both.

394   Statements

(1) A statement made by a person in response to a requirement imposed on him under a disclosure order may not be used in evidence against him in criminal proceedings.

(2) But subsection (1) does not apply—
   (a) in the case of proceedings under Part 3,
   (b) on a prosecution for an offence under section 393(1) or (3),
   (c) on a prosecution for perjury, or
   (d) on a prosecution for some other offence where, in giving evidence, the person makes a statement inconsistent with the statement mentioned in subsection (1).

(3) A statement may not be used by virtue of subsection (2)(d) against a person unless—
   (a) evidence relating to it is adduced, or
   (b) a question relating to it is asked,
   by him or on his behalf in the proceedings arising out of the prosecution.

395   Further provisions

(1) A disclosure order does not confer the right to require a person to answer any question, provide any information or produce any document which he would be entitled to refuse to answer, provide or produce on grounds of legal privilege.

(2) A disclosure order has effect in spite of any restriction on the disclosure of information (however imposed).

(3) The Lord Advocate and the Scottish Ministers may take copies of any documents produced in compliance with a requirement to produce them which is imposed under a disclosure order.

(4) Documents so produced may be retained for so long as it is necessary to retain them (as opposed to a copy of them) in connection with the investigation for the purposes of which the order was made.

(5) But if the Lord Advocate has, or the Scottish Ministers have, reasonable grounds for believing that—
  (a) the documents may need to be produced for the purposes of any legal proceedings, and
  (b) they might otherwise be unavailable for those purposes,
they may be retained until the proceedings are concluded.

396 Supplementary

(1) An application for a disclosure order may be made ex parte to—
  (a) in the case of an order made in a confiscation investigation, a judge of the High Court of Justiciary;
  (b) in the case of an order made in a civil recovery investigation, a judge of the Court of Session,
in chambers.

(2) Provision may be made by rules of court as to the discharge and variation of disclosure orders.

(3) Rules of court under subsection (2) relating to disclosure orders—
  (a) made in a confiscation investigation shall, without prejudice to section 305 of the Criminal Procedure (Scotland) Act 1995 (c. 46) be made by act of adjournal;
  (b) made in a civil recovery investigation shall, without prejudice to section 5 of the Court of Session Act 1988 (c. 36), be made by act of sederunt.

(4) An application to discharge or vary a disclosure order may be made to a judge of the court which made the order by—
  (a) the Lord Advocate or the Scottish Ministers;
  (b) any person affected by the order.

(5) The court may—
  (a) discharge the order;
  (b) vary the order.

Customer information orders

397 Customer information orders

(1) The sheriff may, on an application made to him by the appropriate person, make a customer information order if he is satisfied that each of the requirements for the making of the order is fulfilled.

(2) In making a customer information order in relation to property subject to a civil recovery investigation the sheriff shall act in the exercise of his civil jurisdiction.

(3) The application for a customer information order must state that—
  (a) a person specified in the application is subject to a confiscation investigation or a money laundering investigation, or
  (b) property specified in the application is subject to a civil recovery investigation and a person specified in the application appears to hold the property.

(4) The application must also state that—
  (a) the order is sought for the purposes of the investigation;
  (b) the order is sought against the financial institution or financial institutions specified in the application.

(5) An application for a customer information order may specify—
  (a) all financial institutions,
  (b) a particular description, or particular descriptions, of financial institutions, or
  (c) a particular financial institution or particular financial institutions.

(6) A customer information order is an order that a financial institution covered by the application for the order must, on being required to do

so by notice in writing given by the appropriate person, provide any such customer information as it has relating to the person specified in the application.

(7) A financial institution which is required to provide information under a customer information order must provide the information to a proper person in such manner, and at or by such time, as that person requires.

(8) If a financial institution on which a requirement is imposed by a notice given under a customer information order requires the production of evidence of authority to give the notice, it is not bound to comply with the requirement unless evidence of the authority has been produced to it.

GENERAL NOTE

A customer information order is an order that a financial institution must, on being required to do so in writing given by the appropriate person, provide any customer information as it has about the person specified in the application. The Government's intention is that such an order would require all (or a targeted sample of) banks and other financial institutions to provide details of any accounts held by the person who is the subject of a confiscation or money laundering investigation. The order also applies to persons who appear to hold a property which is subject to a civil recovery investigation. Section 398 sets out the definition of "customer information" for individuals and for companies and partnerships. In the case of an individual that information is:

Customer information orders may be made by sheriffs on application by the appropriate person (again as defined in s.412). The requirements for the making of such an order are very similar to those applicable for other investigative tools under the Act

As with the disclosure order, there are offences connected with customer information orders and these are set out in s.400.

398 Meaning of customer information

(1) "Customer information", in relation to a person and a financial institution, is information whether the person holds, or has held, an account or accounts at the financial institution (whether solely or jointly with another) and (if so) information as to—

   (a) the matters specified in subsection (2) if the person is an individual;

   (b) the matters specified in subsection (3) if the person is a company or limited liability partnership or a similar body incorporated or otherwise established outside the United Kingdom.

(2) The matters referred to in subsection (1)(a) are—

   (a) the account number or numbers;

   (b) the person's full name;

   (c) his date of birth;

   (d) his most recent address and any previous addresses;

   (e) the date or dates on which he began to hold the account or accounts and, if he has ceased to hold the account or any of the accounts, the date or dates on which he did so;

   (f) such evidence of his identity as was obtained by the financial institution under or for the purposes of any legislation relating to money laundering;

   (g) the full name, date of birth and most recent address, and any previous addresses, of any person who holds, or has held, an account at the financial institution jointly with him;

   (h) the account number or numbers of any other account or accounts held at the financial institution to which he is a signatory and details of the person holding the other account or accounts.

(3) The matters referred to in subsection (1)(b) are—

   (a) the account number or numbers;

(b) the person's full name;
(c) a description of any business which the person carries on;
(d) the country or territory in which it is incorporated or otherwise established and any number allocated to it under the Companies Act 1985 (c. 6) or the Companies (Northern Ireland) Order 1986 (S.I. 1986/1032 (N.I. 6)) or corresponding legislation of any country or territory outside the United Kingdom;
(e) any number assigned to it for the purposes of value added tax in the United Kingdom;
(f) its registered office, and any previous registered offices, under the Companies Act 1985 or the Companies (Northern Ireland) Order 1986 (S.I. 1986/1032 (N.I. 6)) or anything similar under corresponding legislation of any country or territory outside the United Kingdom;
(g) its registered office, and any previous registered offices, under the Limited Liability Partnerships Act 2000 (c. 12) or anything similar under corresponding legislation of any country or territory outside Great Britain;
(h) the date or dates on which it began to hold the account or accounts and, if it has ceased to hold the account or any of the accounts, the date or dates on which it did so;
(i) such evidence of its identity as was obtained by the financial institution under or for the purposes of any legislation relating to money laundering;
(j) the full name, date of birth and most recent address and any previous addresses of any person who is a signatory to the account or any of the accounts.

(4) The Scottish Ministers may by order provide for information of a description specified in the order—
  (a) to be customer information, or
  (b) no longer to be customer information.

(5) Money laundering is an act which—
  (a) constitutes an offence under section 327, 328 or 329 of this Act or section 18 of the Terrorism Act 2000 (c. 11), or
  (b) would constitute an offence specified in paragraph (a) if done in the United Kingdom.

399   **Requirements for making of customer information order**

(1) These are the requirements for the making of a customer information order.

(2) In the case of a confiscation investigation, there must be reasonable grounds for suspecting that the person specified in the application for the order has benefited from his criminal conduct.

(3) In the case of a civil recovery investigation, there must be reasonable grounds for suspecting that—
  (a) the property specified in the application for the order is recoverable property or associated property;
  (b) the person specified in the application holds all or some of the property.

(4) In the case of a money laundering investigation, there must be reasonable grounds for suspecting that the person specified in the application for the order has committed a money laundering offence.

(5) In the case of any investigation, there must be reasonable grounds for believing that customer information which may be provided in compliance with the order is likely to be of substantial value (whether or not by itself) to the investigation for the purposes of which the order is sought.

(6) In the case of any investigation there must be reasonable grounds for believing that it is in the public interest for the customer information to be provided, having regard to the benefit likely to accrue to the investigation if the information is obtained.

400   Offences

(1) A financial institution commits an offence if without reasonable excuse it fails to comply with a requirement imposed on it under a customer information order.

(2) A financial institution guilty of an offence under subsection (1) is liable on summary conviction to a fine not exceeding level 5 on the standard scale.

(3) A financial institution commits an offence if, in purported compliance with a customer information order, it—

   (a) makes a statement which it knows to be false or misleading in a material particular, or

   (b) recklessly makes a statement which is false or misleading in a material particular.

(4) A financial institution guilty of an offence under subsection (3) is liable—

   (a) on summary conviction, to a fine not exceeding the statutory maximum, or

   (b) on conviction on indictment, to a fine.

GENERAL NOTE

As the sanctions are directed at non-compliant institutions rather than an individual they are solely financial. Financial institutions will, of course, scarcely notice these penalties; but the effect of any action the appropriate regulator might take as a result of a conviction will no doubt be a very substantial deterrent.

401   Statements

(1) A statement made by a financial institution in response to a customer information order may not be used in evidence against it in criminal proceedings.

(2) But subsection (1) does not apply—

   (a) in the case of proceedings under Part 3,

   (b) on a prosecution for an offence under section 400(1) or (3), or

   (c) on a prosecution for some other offence where, in giving evidence, the financial institution makes a statement inconsistent with the statement mentioned in subsection (1).

(3) A statement may not be used by virtue of subsection (2)(c) against a financial institution unless—

   (a) evidence relating to it is adduced, or

   (b) a question relating to it is asked,

by or on behalf of the financial institution in the proceedings arising out of the prosecution.

402   Further provisions

A customer information order has effect in spite of any restriction on the disclosure of information (however imposed).

403   Supplementary

(1) An application for a customer information order may be made ex parte to a sheriff in chambers.

(2) Provision may be made by rules of court as to the discharge and variation of customer information orders.

(3) Rules of court under subsection (2) relating to customer information orders—

    (a) made in a confiscation investigation or a money laundering investigation shall, without prejudice to section 305 of the Criminal Procedure (Scotland) Act 1995 (c. 46), be made by act of adjournal;

    (b) made in a civil recovery investigation shall, without prejudice to section 32 of the Sheriff Courts (Scotland) Act 1971 (c. 58), be made by act of sederunt.

(4) An application to discharge or vary a customer information order may be made to the sheriff by—

    (a) the person who applied for the order;

    (b) any person affected by the order.

(5) The sheriff may—

    (a) discharge the order;

    (b) vary the order.

Account monitoring orders

404   Account monitoring orders

(1) The sheriff may, on an application made to him by the appropriate person, make an account monitoring order if he is satisfied that each of the requirements for the making of the order is fulfilled.

(2) In making an account monitoring order in relation to property subject to a civil recovery investigation, the sheriff shall act in the exercise of his civil jurisdiction.

(3) The application for an account monitoring order must state that—

    (a) a person specified in the application is subject to a confiscation investigation or a money laundering investigation, or

    (b) property specified in the application is subject to a civil recovery investigation and a person specified in the application appears to hold the property.

(4) The application must also state that—

    (a) the order is sought for the purposes of the investigation;

    (b) the order is sought against the financial institution specified in the application in relation to account information of the description so specified.

(5) Account information is information relating to an account or accounts held at the financial institution specified in the application by the person so specified (whether solely or jointly with another).

(6) The application for an account monitoring order may specify information relating to—

    (a) all accounts held by the person specified in the application for the order at the financial institution so specified,

    (b) a particular description, or particular descriptions, of accounts so held, or

    (c) a particular account, or particular accounts, so held.

(7) An account monitoring order is an order that the financial institution specified in the application for the order must, for the period stated in the order, provide account information of the description specified in the order to the proper person in the manner, and at or by the time or times, stated in the order.

(8) The period stated in an account monitoring order must not exceed the period of 90 days beginning with the day on which the order is made.

GENERAL NOTE

    An account monitoring order is an order that a financial institution must provide information about an account (for example, details of all transactions passing through the account) during an ongoing period, not exceeding 90 days. The information would normally be provided in the form of a bank statement. The order may be made by a sheriff and the preconditions are similar to those for production orders. It is worth noting that s.408(4) contemplates the discharge or variation of account monitoring orders at the instance not only of the applicant for the order but also of any person affected by the order. This category clearly includes both the financial institution in question and the person whose account is subject to such action; but one question which has not yet been answered is how this possibility interacts with the tipping off offences.

405   Requirements for making of account monitoring order

(1) These are the requirements for the making of an account monitoring order.

(2) In the case of a confiscation investigation, there must be reasonable grounds for suspecting that the person specified in the application for the order has benefited from his criminal conduct.

(3) In the case of a civil recovery investigation, there must be reasonable grounds for suspecting that—
  (a) the property specified in the application for the order is recoverable property or associated property;
  (b) the person specified in the application holds all or some of the property.

(4) In the case of a money laundering investigation, there must be reasonable grounds for suspecting that the person specified in the application for the order has committed a money laundering offence.

(5) In the case of any investigation, there must be reasonable grounds for believing that account information which may be provided in compliance with the order is likely to be of substantial value (whether or not by itself) to the investigation for the purposes of which the order is sought.

(6) In the case of any investigation, there must be reasonable grounds for believing that it is in the public interest for the account information to be provided, having regard to the benefit likely to accrue to the investigation if the information is obtained.

406   Statements

(1) A statement made by a financial institution in response to an account monitoring order may not be used in evidence against it in criminal proceedings.

(2) But subsection (1) does not apply—
  (a) in the case of proceedings under Part 3;
  (b) in the case of proceedings for contempt of court, or
  (c) on a prosecution for an offence where, in giving evidence, the financial institution makes a statement inconsistent with the statement mentioned in subsection (1).

(3) A statement may not be used by virtue of subsection (2)(c) against a financial institution unless—
  (a) evidence relating to it is adduced, or
  (b) a question relating to it is asked,
  by or on behalf of the financial institution in the proceedings arising out of the prosecution.

407   Further provisions

An account monitoring order has effect in spite of any restriction on the disclosure of information (however imposed).

408   Supplementary

(1) An application for an account monitoring order may be made ex parte to a sheriff in chambers.

(2) Provision may be made by rules of court as to the discharge and variation of account monitoring orders.

(3) Rules of court under subsection (2) relating to account monitoring orders—

    (a) made in a confiscation investigation or a money laundering investigation shall, without prejudice to section 305 of the Criminal Procedure (Scotland) Act 1995 (c. 46), be made by act of adjournal;

    (b) made in a civil recovery investigation shall, without prejudice to section 32 of the Sheriff Courts (Scotland) Act 1971 (c. 58), be made by act of sederunt.

(4) An application to discharge or vary an account monitoring order may be made to the sheriff by—

    (a) the person who applied for the order;

    (b) any person affected by the order.

(5) The sheriff may—

    (a) discharge the order;

    (b) vary the order.

General

409   Jurisdiction of sheriff

(1) A sheriff may grant a production order, search warrant, customer information order or account monitoring order under this Act in relation to property situated in any area of Scotland notwithstanding that it is outside the area of that sheriff.

(2) Any such order or warrant may, without being backed or endorsed by another sheriff, be executed throughout Scotland in the same way as it may be executed within the sheriffdom of the sheriff who granted it.

(3) This section is without prejudice to any existing rule of law or to any other provision of this Act.

410   Code of practice

(1) The Scottish Ministers must prepare a code of practice as to the exercise by proper persons of functions they have under this Chapter.

(2) After preparing a draft of the code the Scottish Ministers—

    (a) must publish the draft;

    (b) must consider any representations made to them about the draft;

    (c) may amend the draft accordingly.

(3) After the Scottish Ministers have proceeded under subsection (2) they must lay the code before the Scottish Parliament.

(4) When they have done so, the Scottish Ministers may bring the code into operation on such day as they may appoint by order.

(5) A proper person must compy with a code of practice which is in operation under this section in the exercise of any function he has under this Chapter.

(6) If a proper person fails to comply with any provision of a code of practice issued under this section he is not by reason only of that failure liable in any criminal or civil proceedings.

(7) But the code of practice is admissible in evidence in such proceedings and a court may take account of any failure to comply with its provisions in determining any questions in the proceedings.

(8) The Scottish Ministers may from time to time revise a code previously brought into operation under this section; and the preceding provisions of this section apply to a revised code as they apply to the code as first prepared.

411　Performance of functions of Scottish Ministers by constables in Scotland

(1) In Scotland, a constable engaged in temporary service with the Scottish Ministers in connection with their functions under this Part may perform functions, other than those specified in subsection (2), on behalf of the Scottish Ministers.

(2) The specified functions are the functions conferred on the Scottish Ministers by—

(a) section 380(1) (production orders),
(b) section 382(2) (entry orders),
(c) section 386(4) (supplementary to production and entry orders),
(d) section 387(1) (search warrants),
(e) section 391(1) (disclosure orders),
(f) section 396(4) (supplementary to disclosure orders),
(g) section 397(1) (customer information orders),
(h) section 403(4) (supplementary to customer information orders),
(i) section 404(1) (account monitoring orders),
(j) section 408(4) (supplementary to account monitoring orders).

412　Interpretation

In this Chapter, unless the context otherwise requires—

"appropriate person" means—

(a) the procurator fiscal, in relation to a confiscation investigation or a money laundering investigation,
(b) the Scottish Ministers, in relation to a civil recovery investigation;

references to a "constable" include references to a customs and excise officer;

"legal privilege" means protection in legal proceedings from disclosure, by virtue of any rule of law relating to the confidentiality of communications; and "items subject to legal privilege" are—

(a) communications between a professional legal adviser and his client, or
(b) communications made in connection with or in contemplation of legal proceedings and for the purposes of those proceedings,

which would be so protected.

"premises" include any place and, in particular, include—

(a) any vehicle, vessel, aircraft or hovercraft;
(b) any offshore installation within the meaning of section 1 of the Mineral Workings (Offshore Installations) Act 1971 (c. 61) and any tent or movable structure;

"proper person" means—

(a) a constable, in relation to a confiscation investigation or a money laundering investigation;
(b) the Scottish Ministers or a person named by them, in relation to a civil recovery investigation.

CHAPTER 4

INTERPRETATION

413　Criminal conduct

(1) Criminal conduct is conduct which—

(a) constitutes an offence in any part of the United Kingdom, or
(b) would constitute an offence in any part of the United Kingdom if it occurred there.

(2) A person benefits from conduct if he obtains property or a pecuniary advantage as a result of or in connection with the conduct.

(3) References to property or a pecuniary advantage obtained in connection with conduct include references to property or a pecuniary advantage obtained in both that connection and some other.

(4) If a person benefits from conduct his benefit is the property or pecuniary advantage obtained as a result of or in connection with the conduct.

(5) It is immaterial—

    (a) whether conduct occurred before or after the passing of this Act, and

    (b) whether property or a pecuniary advantage constituting a benefit from conduct was obtained before or after the passing of this Act.

414   Property

(1) Property is all property wherever situated and includes—

    (a) money;

    (b) all forms of property, real or personal, heritable or moveable;

    (c) things in action and other intangible or incorporeal property.

(2) "Recoverable property" and "associated property" have the same meanings as in Part 5.

(3) The following rules apply in relation to property—

    (a) property is obtained by a person if he obtains an interest in it;

    (b) references to an interest, in relation to land in England and Wales or Northern Ireland, are to any legal estate or equitable interest or power;

    (c) references to an interest, in relation to land in Scotland, are to any estate, interest, servitude or other heritable right in or over land, including a heritable security;

    (d) references to an interest, in relation to property other than land, include references to a right (including a right to possession).

415   Money laundering offences

(1) An offence under section 327, 328 or 329 is a money laundering offence.

(2) Each of the following is a money laundering offence—

    (a) an attempt, conspiracy or incitement to commit an offence specified in subsection (1);

    (b) aiding, abetting, counselling or procuring the commission of an offence specified in subsection (1).

416   Other interpretative provisions

(1) These expressions are to be construed in accordance with these provisions of this Part—

    civil recovery investigation: section 341(2) and (3)

    confiscation investigation: section 341(1)

    money laundering investigation: section 341(4)

(2) In the application of this Part to England and Wales and Northern Ireland, these expressions are to be construed in accordance with these provisions of this Part—

    account information: section 370(4)

    account monitoring order: section 370(6)

    appropriate officer: section 378

    customer information: section 364

    customer information order: section 363(5)

    disclosure order: section 357(4)

    document: section 379

order to grant entry: section 347(3)
production order: section 345(4)
search and seizure warrant: section 352(4)
senior appropriate officer: section 378.

(3) In the application of this Part to Scotland, these expressions are to be construed in accordance with these provisions of this Part—
account information: section 404(5)
account monitoring order: section 404(7)
customer information: section 398
customer information order: section 397(6)
disclosure order: section 391(4)
production order: section 380(5)
proper person: section 412
search warrant: section 387(4).

(4) "Financial institution" means a person carrying on a business in the regulated sector.

(5) But a person who ceases to carry on a business in the regulated sector (whether by virtue of paragraph 5 of Schedule 9 or otherwise) is to continue to be treated as a financial institution for the purposes of any requirement under—
 (a) a customer information order, or
 (b) an account monitoring order,
to provide information which relates to a time when the person was a financial institution.

(6) References to a business in the regulated sector must be construed in accordance with Schedule 9.

(7) "Recovery order", "interim receiving order" and "interim administration order" have the same meanings as in Part 5.

(8) References to notice in writing include references to notice given by electronic means.

(9) This section and sections 413 to 415 apply for the purposes of this Part.

PART 9

INSOLVENCY ETC.

INTRODUCTION TO PART 9

This Part of the 2002 Act deals with the potential conflicts that can arise between the confiscatory mechanisms created by this Act and the inclusive nature of insolvency regimes which seek to encompass within the estate for the benefit of creditors all of the assets of the defendant debtor. This interface has caused difficulties in the past - see for example *Re M (Restraint Order)* [1992] 2 WLR 340 (a case involving interim orders made under s.252 Insolvency Act 1986 and receivers appointed to enforce restraint orders made under s. 8 of the Drug Trafficking Offence Act 1986). In this particular instance Otton J ruled that the criminal law procedures took priority over the protective regime made available to debtors in financial distress. For general discussion of the problems of interface and other matters see K. Rees, *Confiscating the Proceeds of Crime - The Effect on Legitimate Creditors and Bona Fide Third Parties* (1996) 12 IL & P 120.

Part 9 does not seek to radically change existing law: rather its seeks to consolidate and clarify how the eclectic rules found previously in the Criminal Justice Act 1988 (ss. 84-87) and Drug Trafficking Offences Act 1994 (ss. 32-35) will operate in the context of the regime introduced by the 2002 Act. These earlier statutory provisions are repealed by the 2002 Act.

It should be borne in mind that this problem of conflicts between competing legal regimes may not entirely be a matter of accident. It not unknown for a criminal facing confiscation proceedings to seek to frustrate the authorities by initiating bankruptcy in the hope that his assets will be claimed by friendly creditors rather than hostile prosecuting authorities. In this situation, the 2002 Act makes it clear that this opportunistic strategy will be unsuccessful.

Although the defendant in recovery proceedings will often be an individual who has been made bankrupt (or is about to enter into that status) it may on occasions be a company, in which case the interface with the complexities of corporate insolvency law will need to be addressed. Thus Part 9 contains provisions relating to companies undergoing both the winding up and receivership processes. There may also be an opportunity to disregard the apparent corporate ownership of property and by lifting the veil of separate personality to treat property as belonging to an individual. In connection with this issue see *Re H (Restraint Order: Realisable Property)* [1996] 2 BCLC 500.

Comparable provision is made by Part 9 for insolvency regimes operating in Scotland and Northern Ireland. Some more intelligent drafting could surely have resulted in reducing the number of sections in the 2002 by producing suitably worded composite provisions applicable throughout the UK. At things stand at present Pt. 9 is heavily burdened by what is arguably unnecessary repetition.

Part 9 was not the subject of a great deal of amendment or debate as it progressed through Parliament - for limited discussion see Official Report, November 27, 2001, cols 341-342 (Standing Committee B), Official Report, January 10, 2002, cols 906-907 (Standing Committee B); Official Report January 29, 2002, cols 1262-1274. Some amendments of a largely cosmetic nature were made to the rules on tainted gifts in the passage of the Bill through the House of Lords. The House of Lords did suggest a number of other technical amendments - see the List of Lords' Amendments ordered to be printed by the Commons on July 11, 2002. More significantly there was also an attempt by Their Lordships to introduce a statutory compensation right for genuine creditors affected by the use of confiscation against a debtor but the government defeated this amendment (see below)

When reading this Part of the Act reference should be made to Sched.11 (introduced by s. 456). In particular, note that confiscation orders are treated as akin to fines and therefore are not released by discharge from bankruptcy (Sched.11 para. 16(2). Also on discharge property which has been excluded from the estate by virtue of this Act may revert to the estate if the restraint order is discharged or a confiscation order is satisfied, or either type of order is quashed ; this is achieved by the insertion of new ss. 306A, 306B and 306C into the Insolvency Act 1986 by para. 16(3) of Sched. 11. Comparable provision is made for Scotland and Northern Ireland by paras 15 and 20 of Sched. 11 respectively. These provisions appear to have been an afterthought - see Official Report, 29 January 2002 col 1263. For discussion see Official Report, House of Commons, 5 February 2002 (Standing Committee B) cols 1408-1409.

The 2002 Act does also refer to the issue of insolvency on other occasions. For example, see s. 9 which excludes from the confiscation process funds needed to cover debts which would rank as preferential debts on bankruptcy). Again note s. 23 which deals with the variation of confiscation orders where the defendant has since become bankrupt. In addition s. 311 emphasises that where a defendant to civil recovery proceedings has become insolvent the leave of the court will be required before those recovery proceedings can be commenced or continued. A similar restriction is imposed by s. 311 on the continued detention of cash apparently belonging to a person who is subject to formal insolvency proceedings. Recovery proceedings under Part V may not be instituted against an insolvency practitioner in respect of property which he holds by virtue of his office (s. 282(5))

Finally, it should be noted that Pt. 9 merely addresses the position of creditors where the defendant with the criminal lifestyle has been formally declared insolvent. There may of course be difficult issues to address with regard to creditors of such a person where no formal insolvency procedure has yet commenced but where the consequence of confiscation may be to render the defendant insolvent. A restraint order may make provision for the payment of certain prior legitimate debts (s. 41(3)). Apart from this concession, the government refused to require compensation to be paid by the enforcement authority to genuine creditors of a person with a criminal lifestyle who lose out because of the invoking of recovery proceedings. This issue was the subject of much debate in the Commons - Official Report, House of Commons, Standing Committee B (Fifth and Sixth sittings, November 20, 2001) cols 168-194, where the government fought off the creation of such a compensation right. Nevertheless, the House of Lords included a formal compensation right through a late amendment of the Bill (see amendment No. 9 in the List of Lords Amendments ordered to be printed by the Commons on 11 July 2002 referring to clause 10 of the Bill amended on Report). On the Bill's return to the lower chamber The Commons rejected this and other related amendments - Official Report, House of Commons, Vol 389 cols 507-527 (18 July 2002). The reason given was that to introduce such a compensation scheme would be tantamount to levying a charge on the public exchequer. There was also no justification for preferring such creditors from other creditors of the defendant.

Bankruptcy in England and Wales

417   Modifications of the 1986 Act

(1) This section applies if a person is adjudged bankrupt in England and Wales.

(2) The following property is excluded from his estate for the purposes of Part 9 of the 1986 Act—

    (a) property for the time being subject to a restraint order which was made under section 41, 120 or 190 before the order adjudging him bankrupt;

    (b) any property in respect of which an order under section 50 or 52 is in force;

    (c) any property in respect of which an order under section 128(3) is in force;

    (d) any property in respect of which an order under section 198 or 200 is in force.

(3) Subsection (2)(a) applies to heritable property in Scotland only if the restraint order is recorded in the General Register of Sasines or registered in the Land Register of Scotland before the order adjudging the person bankrupt.

(4) If in the case of a debtor an interim receiver stands at any time appointed under section 286 of the 1986 Act and any property of the debtor is then subject to a restraint order made under section 41, 120 or 190 the powers conferred on the receiver by virtue of that Act do not apply to property then subject to the restraint order.

DEFINITIONS
"1986 Act" : s. 434(1)
"restraint order" : s. 41

GENERAL NOTE
The aim of the bankruptcy regime is to include within the estate as many assets as possible which should then be realised for the benefit of creditors. Where bankruptcy has not already commenced by the time confiscation proceedings are afoot the inclusive reach of bankruptcy law must take a back seat and give priority to the criminal confiscation procedures. Note here Schedule 11 with its provisions for the subsequent inclusion in the bankruptcy estate of assets not required for confiscation.

Subss (1) and (2)
On bankruptcy the estate cannot encompass property which is the subject of a restraint order or other specified order under this Act. Note for comparison Criminal Justice Act 1988 s. 84(1) and Drug Trafficking Act 1994 s. 32(1).

Subs. (3)
This makes special provision for heritable property in Scotland and requires the restraint order to be registered to be effective.

Subs. (4)
The powers of an interim receiver appointed in respect of a debtor under s. 286 of the Insolvency Act 1986 do not extend to property which is subject to a restraint order. The point here is that formally bankruptcy proceedings do not commence until the bankruptcy order is made (Insolvency Act 1986 s. 278). For statutory predecessors see Criminal Justice Act 1988 s. 84(5) and Drug Trafficking Act 1994 s. 32(4).

418   Restriction of powers

(1) If a person is adjudged bankrupt in England and Wales the powers referred to in subsection (2) must not be exercised in relation to the property referred to in subsection (3).

(2) These are the powers—

    (a) the powers conferred on a court by sections 41 to 67 and the powers of a receiver appointed under section 48, 50 or 52;

    (b) the powers conferred on a court by sections 120 to 136 and Schedule 3 and the powers of an administrator appointed under section 125 or 128(3);

    (c) the powers conferred on a court by sections 190 to 215 and the powers of a receiver appointed under section 196, 198 or 200.

(3) This is the property—
  (a) property which is for the time being comprised in the bankrupt's estate for the purposes of Part 9 of the 1986 Act;
  (b) property in respect of which his trustee in bankruptcy may (without leave of the court) serve a notice under section 307, 308 or 308A of the 1986 Act (after-acquired property, tools, tenancies etc);
  (c) property which is to be applied for the benefit of creditors of the bankrupt by virtue of a condition imposed under section 280(2)(c) of the 1986 Act;
  (d) in a case where a confiscation order has been made under section 6 or 156 of this Act, any sums remaining in the hands of a receiver appointed under section 50, 52, 198 or 200 of this Act after the amount required to be paid under the confiscation order has been fully paid;
  (e) in a case where a confiscation order has been made under section 92 of this Act, any sums remaining in the hands of an administrator appointed under section 128 of this Act after the amount required to be paid under the confiscation order has been fully paid.
(4) But nothing in the 1986 Act must be taken to restrict (or enable the restriction of) the powers referred to in subsection (2).
(5) In a case where a petition in bankruptcy was presented or a receiving order or adjudication in bankruptcy was made before 29 December 1986 (when the 1986 Act came into force) this section has effect with these modifications—
  (a) for the reference in subsection (3)(a) to the bankrupt's estate for the purposes of Part 9 of that Act substitute a reference to the property of the bankrupt for the purposes of the 1914 Act;
  (b) omit subsection (3)(b);
  (c) for the reference in subsection (3)(c) to section 280(2)(c) of the 1986 Act substitute a reference to section 26(2) of the 1914 Act;
  (d) for the reference in subsection (4) to the 1986 Act substitute a reference to the 1914 Act.

DEFINITIONS
  "powers" : subs. (2)
  "property" : subs. (3)
  "1986 Act" : s.434(1)
  "1914 Act" : s.434(1)

GENERAL NOTE
  This deals with the converse scenario where the person who is being subjected to confiscation proceedings has already been declared bankrupt. In this situation powers under the 2002 Act are restricted. Note s. 84(2) of the Criminal Justice Act 1988 and Drug Trafficking Act 1994 s. 32(2) for previous statutory provisions to the same effect.

Subss (1)-(3)
  If the defendant is already undergoing the bankruptcy process, property which forms part of the estate or which might be so included through the operation of bankruptcy provisions (e.g. after-acquired property) cannot be made subject to a restraint order or dealt with by a receiver/administrator as part of a confiscation process. This is justifiable because at this stage the bankrupt's property is in effect held on trust for his or her creditors. Surplus property left over after the confiscation process has been exhausted also falls to the estate and the State does not enjoy a windfall.

Subs. (4)
  This is a clarifying and saving provision offering protection for the exercise of powers under the 2002 Act from intrusion by provisions in the Insolvency Act 1986.

Subs. (5)
This deals with those few old bankruptcies which were initiated under the pre 1986 bankruptcy laws. There are few such bankruptcies in operation and the limited significance of this provision will further diminish with the passage of time.

419   Tainted gifts

(1) This section applies if a person who is adjudged bankrupt in England and Wales has made a tainted gift (whether directly or indirectly).

(2) No order may be made under section 339, 340 or 423 of the 1986 Act (avoidance of certain transactions) in respect of the making of the gift at any time when—

 (a) any property of the recipient of the tainted gift is subject to a restraint order under section 41, 120 or 190, or

 (b) there is in force in respect of such property an order under section 50, 52, 128(3), 198 or 200.

(3) Any order made under section 339, 340 or 423 of the 1986 Act after an order mentioned in subsection (2)(a) or (b) is discharged must take into account any realisation under Part 2, 3 or 4 of this Act of property held by the recipient of the tainted gift.

(4) A person makes a tainted gift for the purposes of this section if he makes a tainted gift within the meaning of Part 2, 3 or 4.

(5) In a case where a petition in bankruptcy was presented or a receiving order or adjudication in bankruptcy was made before 29 December 1986 (when the 1986 Act came into force) this section has effect with the substitution for a reference to section 339, 340 or 423 of the 1986 Act of a reference to section 27, 42 or 44 of the 1914 Act.

DEFINITIONS
"tainted gift" : subs (4) and s. 77
"1986 Act": s. 434(1)

GENERAL NOTE
This provision was remodelled during its passage through the House of Lords. This section deals with the problem of "tainted gifts" (defined referentially by subs. (5)) on bankruptcy where there is a restraint order dimension. It is a key policy of modern insolvency law that the estate should not be diminished by unjustified transfers at an undervalue or transfers designed to defeat creditors occurring just prior to the bankruptcy. Equally the 2002 Act sets in place a regime to recover tainted gifts (see for example s. 77). Section 419 seeks to address the interface between activation of a transactional avoidance process and the intervention of a confiscatory process in respect of tainted gifts by a criminal; generally the latter regime will take priority.
For similar provisions in earlier legislation see Criminal Justice Act 1988 s. 84(6) and Drug Trafficking Act 1994 s. 32(5).

Subss (1), (2) and (4)
Powers of transactional avoidance on bankruptcy pursuant to ss. 339, 340 and 423 of the Insolvency Act 1986 in respect of transactions at an undervalue, preferences and transactions defrauding creditors cannot be exercised in respect of property which constitutes a tainted gift within the meaning of this Act if criminal proceedings have begun and recovery orders have been imposed in respect of that property. The reference to s. 340 was a late inclusion in the Bill.

Subs. (3)
Any order made subsequently under ss. 339, 340 or 423 after an order under the 2002 Act has been discharged must take account of sums realised under that earlier order. Again the reference to s. 340 represents a late amendment.

Subs. (5)
Again this deals with bankruptcies initiated under the old law.

Sequestration in Scotland

420   Modifications of the 1985 Act

(1) This section applies if an award of sequestration is made in Scotland.

(2) The following property is excluded from the debtor's estate for the purposes of the 1985 Act—
  (a) property for the time being subject to a restraint order which was made under section 41, 120 or 190 before the award of sequestration;
  (b) any property in respect of which an order under section 50 or 52 is in force;
  (c) any property in respect of which an order under section 128(3) is in force;
  (d) any property in respect of which an order under section 198 or 200 is in force.

(3) Subsection (2)(a) applies to heritable property in Scotland only if the restraint order is recorded in the General Register of Sasines or registered in the Land Register of Scotland before the award of sequestration.

(4) It shall not be competent to submit a claim in relation to a confiscation order to the permanent trustee in accordance with section 48 of the 1985 Act; and the reference here to a confiscation order is to any confiscation order that has been or may be made against the debtor under Part 2, 3 or 4 of this Act.

(5) If at any time in the period before the award of sequestration is made an interim trustee stands appointed under section 2(5) of the 1985 Act and any property in the debtor's estate is at that time subject to a restraint order made under section 41, 120 or 190, the powers conferred on the trustee by virtue of that Act do not apply to property then subject to the restraint order.

Insolvency provisions - Scotland

The law in Scotland relating to the insolvency of non-company debtors other than limited liability partnerships differs from that in other parts of Great Britain, and accordingly separate provision is made for Scotland in this respect. The law relating to the insolvency of companies and limited liability partnerships is in many respects the same in Scotland as it is in England and Wales, and accordingly the winding up of companies in Scotland and in England and Wales is dealt with together, with separate references to distinctively Scottish provisions where appropriate, while the provisions relating to floating charges and limited liability partnerships apply equally to Scotland.

Definitions

"award of sequestration": s. 434(2): s.12(4) of the Bankruptcy (Scotland) Act 1985.
"confiscation order": subs. (4).
"the 1985 Act": s. 434(1)(c).

General Note

This section is based on para. 1(1) and (4) of Sched. 2 of the Proceeds of Crime (Scotland) Act 1995 and sets out the position where an award of sequestration is made in Scotland subsequent to the making of a restraint order in Scotland, England, Wales or Northern Ireland, an order for the appointment of an enforcement or Director's receiver in England, Wales or Northern Ireland or an order for the appointment of an enforcement administrator in Scotland. The basic rule is that property affected by such orders is excluded from the debtor's estate for the purposes of the sequestration; in other words, the orders made under this Act take precedence over a subsequent sequestration. The purpose of this section is "to prevent defendants from attempting to use the insolvency legislation to defeat the purpose of the confiscation legislation" (Explanatory Notes accompanying the Bill).

It should be noted, however, that as a result of consequential amendments to the Bankruptcy (Scotland) Act 1985 made by para. 15(4) of Sched. 11, where property has been excluded from a debtor's estate for the purposes of his or her sequestration by virtue of this section and the restraint order is subsequently discharged, there is a surplus in the hands of a receiver or administrator following satisfaction of a confiscation order or a confiscation order is discharged or quashed, the property or surplus as the case may be will then vest in the permanent trustee as part of the debtor's estate. These amendments, which add new ss. 31A, 31B and 31C to the

Bankruptcy (Scotland) Act 1985, were deemed necessary on the basis that such an outcome would not otherwise result.

It should also be noted that Sched. 11, para. 15(5) also adds a new subs. (3) to s. 55 of the Bankruptcy (Scotland) Act 1985 to clarify that the debtor's discharge does not release him or her from liability to pay a confiscation order.

Subs. (1)

Section 434(2) provides that an award of sequestration is made on the date of sequestration within the meaning of s. 12(4) of the Bankruptcy (Scotland) Act 1985. This provides that where the petition for sequestration is presented by the debtor, the date of sequestration is the date on which the award of sequestration is made, while where the petition for sequestration is presented by someone other than the debtor, the date of sequestration is the date on which the first warrant to cite the debtor was granted.

Subs. (2)

This subsection sets out the basic rule that property affected by a restraint order in Scotland, England, Wales or Northern Ireland, an order for the appointment of an enforcement or Director's receiver in England, Wales or Northern Ireland or an order for the appointment of an enforcement administrator in Scotland is excluded from the debtor's estate for the purposes of the sequestration.

Subs. (3)

This subsection qualifies the basic rule in relation to restraint orders by providing that heritable property affected by a restraint order made before the award of sequestration is only excluded from the debtor's estate where the restraint order was recorded in the Register of Sasines or Land Register (as appropriate) before the award of sequestration. Where the restraint order has not been so recorded, the heritable property affected by it will form part of the debtor's estate for the purposes of the sequestration. It will therefore be important to check whether a restraint order made before the award of sequestration has also been recorded in the appropriate Register before the award of sequestration when considering its effect on heritable property of the debtor.

Subs. (4)

This subsection prevents a claim for sums due under an existing or future confiscation order being made in the debtor's sequestration by making it incompetent to submit such a claim to the permanent trustee under s. 48 of the Bankruptcy (Scotland) Act 1985. The submission of a claim under that section is necessary for a creditor to establish his entitlement to vote at meetings (other than the statutory meeting) and to a dividend; preventing submission of a claim under that section therefore effectively prevents a creditor from being able to vote at meetings other than the statutory meeting or obtain a dividend. It should be noted, however, that for the purpose of voting at the statutory meeting, claims may be submitted to the interim trustee under s. 22 of the Bankruptcy (Scotland) Act 1985. Such claims are deemed to be re-submitted to the permanent trustee under s. 48(2) of the Bankruptcy (Scotland) Act 1985, but while any such deemed re-submission would appear to be prevented by this subsection, there seems to be nothing to stop a claim being submitted to the interim trustee for the purposes of voting at the statutory meeting. This seems somewhat anomalous.

Subs. (5)

Where the debtor consents or cause is shown (for example, where it is demonstrated that it is necessary to take immediate steps to preserve assets or there is danger that the debtor will destroy records or abscond), it is possible for the court to appoint an interim trustee before making an award of sequestration. This subsection provides for such a situation by providing that where such an interim trustee is appointed subsequent to the making of a restraint order in Scotland, England, Wales or Northern Ireland, the interim trustee may not exercise his powers in relation to the property affected by the restraint order.

421   Restriction of powers

   (1) If an award of sequestration is made in Scotland the powers referred to in subsection (2) must not be exercised in relation to the property referred to in subsection (3).

   (2) These are the powers—

      (a) the powers conferred on a court by sections 41 to 67 and the powers of a receiver appointed under section 48, 50 or 52;

  (b) the powers conferred on a court by sections 120 to 136 and Schedule 3 and the powers of an administrator appointed under section 125 or 128(3);
  (c) the powers conferred on a court by sections 190 to 215 and the powers of a receiver appointed under section 196, 198 or 200.

(3) This is the property—
  (a) property which is for the time being comprised in the whole estate of the debtor within the meaning of section 31(8) of the 1985 Act;
  (b) any income of the debtor which has been ordered under section 32(2) of that Act to be paid to the permanent trustee;
  (c) any estate which under section 31(10) or 32(6) of that Act vests in the permanent trustee;
  (d) in a case where a confiscation order has been made under section 6 or 156 of this Act, any sums remaining in the hands of a receiver appointed under section 50, 52, 198 or 200 of this Act after the amount required to be paid under the confiscation order has been fully paid;
  (e) in a case where a confiscation order has been made under section 92 of this Act, any sums remaining in the hands of an administrator appointed under section 128 of this Act after the amount required to be paid under the confiscation order has been fully paid.

(4) But nothing in the 1985 Act must be taken to restrict (or enable the restriction of) the powers referred to in subsection (2).

(5) In a case where (despite the coming into force of the 1985 Act) the 1913 Act applies to a sequestration, subsection (3) above has effect as if for paragraphs (a) to (c) there were substituted—
  "(a) property which is for the time being comprised in the whole property of the debtor which vests in the trustee under section 97 of the 1913 Act;
  (b) any income of the bankrupt which has been ordered under section 98(2) of that Act to be paid to the trustee;
  (c) any estate which under section 98(1) of that Act vests in the trustee."

(6) In a case where subsection (5) applies, subsection (4) has effect as if for the reference to the 1985 Act there were substituted a reference to the 1913 Act.

DEFINITIONS
  "award of sequestration": s. 434(2): s.12(4) of the Bankruptcy (Scotland) Act 1985.
  "the 1913 Act": s. 434(1)(a).
  "the 1985 Act": s. 434(1)(c).
  "whole estate of the debtor": subs. 3(a): s. 31(8) of the Bankruptcy (Scotland) Act 1985.
  "whole property of the debtor": subs. 5(a): s. 97 of the Bankruptcy (Scotland) Act 1913.

GENERAL NOTE
  This section is based on para. 1(2) of Sched. 2 of the Proceeds of Crime (Scotland) Act 1995 and sets out the circumstances in which an award of sequestration will take precedence over the provisions of this Act. Firstly, it provides that where there is an existing award of sequestration, no property which forms part of the sequestrated estate and no income which has been ordered to be paid to the trustee under the bankruptcy legislation may subsequently be made subject to a restraint order in Scotland, England, Wales or Northern Ireland or be affected by the appointment of any receiver in England, Wales or Northern Ireland or any administrator in Scotland. Secondly, it prevents a court from exercising its powers under this Act to distribute any sums remaining in the hands of any receiver or administrator following satisfaction of a confiscation order where an award of sequestration has been made in order to ensure that any such sums will fall into the sequestrated estate for distribution to the creditors in the sequestration rather than being distributed under the provisions of this Act. The section makes provision for seques-

trations awarded under the Bankruptcy (Scotland) Act 1913 as well as those awarded under the Bankruptcy (Scotland) Act 1985.

Subs. (1)

Section 434(2) provides that an award of sequestration is made on the date of sequestration within the meaning of s. 12(4) of the Bankruptcy (Scotland) Act 1985. This provides that where the petition for sequestration is presented by the debtor, the date of sequestration is the date on which the award of sequestration is made, while where the petition for sequestration is presented by someone other than the debtor, the date of sequestration is the date on which the first warrant to cite the debtor was granted.

Subss. (5) and (6)

Sequestrations awarded before 1 April 1986 continue to be regulated by the provisions of the Bankruptcy (Scotland) Act 1913. These subsections ensure that the provisions of this section apply to such sequestrations as well as sequestrations awarded under the current legislation. According to figures supplied by the Accountant in Bankruptcy, as at 31 December 2001 there were 25 sequestrations under the Bankruptcy (Scotland) Act 1913 still extant.

422   Tainted gifts

(1) This section applies if a person whose estate is sequestrated in Scotland has made a tainted gift (whether directly or indirectly).

(2) No decree may be granted under the Bankruptcy Act 1621 (c. 18) or section 34 or 36 of the 1985 Act (gratuitous alienations and unfair preferences), or otherwise, in respect of the making of the gift at any time when—

     (a) any property of the recipient of the tainted gift is subject to a restraint order under section 41, 120 or 190, or

     (b) there is in force in respect of such property an order under section 50, 52, 128(3), 198 or 200.

(3) Any decree made under the Bankruptcy Act 1621 (c. 18) or section 34 or 36 of the 1985 Act, or otherwise, after an order mentioned in subsection (2)(a) or (b) is discharged must take into account any realisation under Part 2, 3 or 4 of this Act of property held by the recipient of the tainted gift.

(4) A person makes a tainted gift for the purposes of this section if he makes a tainted gift within the meaning of Part 2, 3 or 4.

DEFINITIONS

"tainted gift": subs. 4.
"the 1985 Act": s. 434(1)(c).

GENERAL NOTE

This section is based on para. 1(5) of Sched. 2 of the Proceeds of Crime (Scotland) Act 1995 and sets out the relationship between the provisions on tainted gifts contained in this Act and the various statutory and common law provisions allowing the challenge of prior transactions of a debtor on his or her subsequent sequestration. The effect of the section is to give precedence to the provisions on tainted gifts: it provides that if a person whose estate has been sequestrated in Scotland has, directly or indirectly, made a tainted gift as defined in this Act and any property of the recipient of that tainted gift is subject to a restraint order made in Scotland, England, Wales or Northern Ireland or an enforcement or Director's receiver in England, Wales or Northern Ireland or an enforcement administrator in Scotland has been appointed in respect of any such property, no decree under the provisions for challenging prior transactions of a debtor on sequestration may be granted in relation to the making of that gift. The purpose of the section is "to ensure that a gift made by the defendant is treated as a tainted gift under the confiscation legislation, rather than as a voidable gift under the insolvency legislation" (Explanatory Notes accompanying the Bill).

It should be noted that para. 1(5) of Sched. 2 of the Proceeds of Crime (Scotland) Act 1995 referred only to the relationship between the provisions of that Act and the statutory provisions on gratuitous alienations and unfair preferences contained in ss. 34 and 36 of the Bankruptcy

(Scotland) Act 1985 respectively. This did not take account of the fact that prior transactions of the debtor could also be challenged under other provisions, in particular at common law. The section remedies these previous omissions.

A decree under the provisions for challenging prior transactions of a debtor on insolvency may be granted following the discharge of the relevant order under this Act. Subsection (3) provides that in such circumstances, the court granting the decree must take account of any realisations of the property of the person to whom the gift was given under this Act.

Subs. (1)

The section applies only where the donor of a tainted gift has been sequestrated. It is possible, however, for prior transactions of a debtor to be challenged even where there has been no sequestration. For example, the statutory provisions on gratuitous alienations and unfair preferences contained in ss. 34 and 36 of the Bankruptcy (Scotland) Act 1985 respectively may be invoked not only on sequestration but, *inter alia*, where the debtor has granted a protected trust deed for creditors, while the common law provisions require the debtor to absolutely insolvent and to have been so since the date of the transaction being challenged, but do not require him to have been sequestrated as such. Such challenges are not, however, affected by this section.

Subs. (2)

This subsection sets out the basic rule that the provisions on tainted gifts under this Act take precedence over the provisions for challenging prior transactions of a debtor on sequestration.

The Bankruptcy Act 1621. The Bankruptcy Act 1621 was repealed by the Bankruptcy (Scotland) Act 1985 with effect from 1 April 1986, but in theory a transaction which took place before that date could still be challenged under the Bankruptcy Act 1621.

Or otherwise. This includes a decree granted under the provisions of the common law.

Bankruptcy in Northern Ireland

423   **Modifications of the 1989 Order**

(1) This section applies if a person is adjudged bankrupt in Northern Ireland.

(2) The following property is excluded from his estate for the purposes of Part 9 of the 1989 Order—

  (a) property for the time being subject to a restraint order which was made under section 41, 120 or 190 before the order adjudging him bankrupt;

  (b) any property in respect of which an order under section 50 or 52 is in force;

  (c) any property in respect of which an order under section 128(3) is in force;

  (d) any property in respect of which an order under section 198 or 200 is in force.

(3) Subsection (2)(a) applies to heritable property in Scotland only if the restraint order is recorded in the General Register of Sasines or registered in the Land Register of Scotland before the order adjudging the person bankrupt.

(4) If in the case of a debtor an interim receiver stands at any time appointed under Article 259 of the 1989 Order and any property of the debtor is then subject to a restraint order made under section 41, 120 or 190, the powers conferred on the receiver by virtue of that Order do not apply to property then subject to the restraint order.

DEFINITION

"1989 Order" : s. 434(1)

GENERAL NOTE

Bankruptcy in Northern Ireland is regulated by the Insolvency (Northern Ireland) Order 1989 which in effect introduced the 1986 reforms into Northern Ireland with minor local modifications in October 1991.

Subss (1) and (2)
These provisions mirror s. 417 (1) and (2).

Subs. (3)
This deals with Scottish property held by a Northern Irish bankrupt and parallels s. 417(3).

Subs. (4)
This adapts s. 417(4) to the Northern Irish context.

424　Restriction of powers

(1) If a person is adjudged bankrupt in Northern Ireland the powers referred to in subsection (2) must not be exercised in relation to the property referred to in subsection (3).
(2) These are the powers—
　(a) the powers conferred on a court by sections 41 to 67 and the powers of a receiver appointed under section 48, 50 or 52;
　(b) the powers conferred on a court by sections 120 to 136 and Schedule 3 and the powers of an administrator appointed under section 125 or 128(3);
　(c) the powers conferred on a court by sections 190 to 215 and the powers of a receiver appointed under section 196, 198 or 200.
(3) This is the property—
　(a) property which is for the time being comprised in the bankrupt's estate for the purposes of Part 9 of the 1989 Order;
　(b) property in respect of which his trustee in bankruptcy may (without leave of the court) serve a notice under Article 280 or 281 of the 1989 Order (after-acquired property etc);
　(c) property which is to be applied for the benefit of creditors of the bankrupt by virtue of a condition imposed under Article 254(2)(c) of the 1989 Order;
　(d) in a case where a confiscation order has been made under section 6 or 156 of this Act, any sums remaining in the hands of a receiver appointed under section 50, 52, 198 or 200 of this Act after the amount required to be paid under the confiscation order has been fully paid;
　(e) in a case where a confiscation order has been made under section 92 of this Act, any sums remaining in the hands of an administrator appointed under section 128 of this Act after the amount required to be paid under the confiscation order has been fully paid.
(4) But nothing in the 1989 Order must be taken to restrict (or enable the restriction of) the powers mentioned in subsection (2).
(5) In a case where a petition in bankruptcy was presented or an adjudication in bankruptcy was made before 1 October 1991 (when the 1989 Order came into force) this section has effect with these modifications—
　(a) for the reference in subsection (3)(a) to the bankrupt's estate for the purposes of Part 9 of that Order substitute a reference to the property of the bankrupt for the purposes of the Bankruptcy Acts (Northern Ireland) 1857 to 1980;
　(b) omit subsection (3)(b);
　(c) for the reference in subsection (3)(c) to Article 254(2)(c) of the 1989 Order substitute a reference to Articles 28(4), (5)(c) and (11) and 30(6)(c) of the Bankruptcy Amendment (Northern Ireland) Order 1980 (S.I. 1980/561 (N.I. 4));

(d) for the reference in subsection (4) to the 1989 Order substitute a reference to the Bankruptcy Acts (Northern Ireland) 1857 to 1980.

Definitions
"powers" : subs. (2)
"property" : subs. (3)
"1989 Order" : s. 434(1)

General Note
This duplicates s. 418 by applying it in a Northern Irish context.

Subss (1)-(3)
See the General Note to s. 418(1)-(3).

Subs. (4)
This replicates s. 418(4).

Subs. (5)
This might have more significance that the comparable provision in English law for the simple reason that the new regime for bankruptcy enacted in the 1989 Order was not introduced into Northern Ireland until 1991.

425   Tainted gifts

(1) This section applies if a person who is adjudged bankrupt in Northern Ireland has made a tainted gift (whether directly or indirectly).
(2) No order may be made under Article 312, 313 or 367 of the 1989 Order (avoidance of certain transactions) in respect of the making of the gift at any time when—
    (a) any property of the recipient of the tainted gift is subject to a restraint order under section 41, 120 or 190, or
    (b) there is in force in respect of such property an order under section 50, 52, 128(3), 198 or 200.
(3) Any order made under Article 312, 313 or 367 of the 1989 Order after an order mentioned in subsection (2)(a) or (b) is discharged must take into account any realisation under Part 2, 3 or 4 of this Act of property held by the recipient of the tainted gift.
(4) A person makes a tainted gift for the purposes of this section if he makes a tainted gift within the meaning of Part 2, 3 or 4.
(5) In a case where a petition in bankruptcy was presented or an adjudication in bankruptcy was made before 1 October 1991 (when the 1989 Order came into force) this section has effect with these modifications—
    (a) for a reference to Article 312 of the 1989 Order substitute a reference to section 12 of the Bankruptcy Amendment Act (Northern Ireland) 1929 (c. 1 (N.I.));
    (b) for a reference to Article 367 of the 1989 Order substitute a reference to section 10 of the Conveyancing Act (Ireland) 1634 (c. 3).

Definitions
"tainted gift": subs (4) and s.225
"1989 Order": s. 434(1)

General Note
This adapts s. 419 and its technical provisions on tainted gifts to Northern Ireland. The drafting of what is now s. 425 was initially less elegant than its English counterpart but at a late stage in the passage of the Bill the two provisions were linguistically assimilated.

Subss (1)-(3)

See the comment on s. 419(1)-(3)

Subs. (4)

This refers us to Pts 2, 3 and 4 for clarification as to what is a tainted gift.

Subs. (5)

Again this refers to old bankruptcies under Northern Irish law.

Winding up in England and Wales and Scotland

426   Winding up under the 1986 Act

(1) In this section "company" means any company which may be wound up under the 1986 Act.

(2) If an order for the winding up of a company is made or it passes a resolution for its voluntary winding up, the functions of the liquidator (or any provisional liquidator) are not exercisable in relation to the following property—

  (a) property for the time being subject to a restraint order which was made under section 41, 120 or 190 before the relevant time;

  (b) any property in respect of which an order under section 50 or 52 is in force;

  (c) any property in respect of which an order under section 128(3) is in force;

  (d) any property in respect of which an order under section 198 or 200 is in force.

(3) Subsection (2)(a) applies to heritable property in Scotland only if the restraint order is recorded in the General Register of Sasines or registered in the Land Register of Scotland before the relevant time.

(4) If an order for the winding up of a company is made or it passes a resolution for its voluntary winding up the powers referred to in subsection (5) must not be exercised in the way mentioned in subsection (6) in relation to any property—

  (a) which is held by the company, and

  (b) in relation to which the functions of the liquidator are exercisable.

(5) These are the powers—

  (a) the powers conferred on a court by sections 41 to 67 and the powers of a receiver appointed under section 48, 50 or 52;

  (b) the powers conferred on a court by sections 120 to 136 and Schedule 3 and the powers of an administrator appointed under section 125 or 128(3);

  (c) the powers conferred on a court by sections 190 to 215 and the powers of a receiver appointed under section 196, 198 or 200.

(6) The powers must not be exercised—

  (a) so as to inhibit the liquidator from exercising his functions for the purpose of distributing property to the company's creditors;

  (b) so as to prevent the payment out of any property of expenses (including the remuneration of the liquidator or any provisional liquidator) properly incurred in the winding up in respect of the property.

(7) But nothing in the 1986 Act must be taken to restrict (or enable the restriction of) the exercise of the powers referred to in subsection (5).

(8) For the purposes of the application of Parts 4 and 5 of the 1986 Act (winding up) to a company which the Court of Session has jurisdiction to wind up, a person is not a creditor in so far as any sum due to him by the company is due in respect of a confiscation order made under section 6, 92 or 156.

(9) The relevant time is—

(a) if no order for the winding up of the company has been made, the time of the passing of the resolution for voluntary winding up;

(b) if such an order has been made, but before the presentation of the petition for the winding up of the company by the court such a resolution has been passed by the company, the time of the passing of the resolution;

(c) if such an order has been made, but paragraph (b) does not apply, the time of the making of the order.

(10) In a case where a winding up of a company commenced or is treated as having commenced before 29 December 1986, this section has effect with the following modifications—

(a) in subsections (1) and (7) for "the 1986 Act" substitute "the Companies Act 1985";

(b) in subsection (8) for "Parts 4 and 5 of the 1986 Act" substitute "Parts 20 and 21 of the Companies Act 1985".

DEFINITIONS
"1986 Act" : s. 434(1)
"restraint orders": ss. 41 and 120
"powers" : subs (5)

GENERAL NOTE
Restraint orders can be made under this Act against companies. Therefore it is necessary to deal with the potential clash between the confiscation machinery and the rules relating to the realisation/ distribution of assets of companies undergoing liquidation.

This provision merges a series of provisions which are comparable to ss. 417 and 418.

It applies both to the law in England and Wales and in Scotland.

For statutory predecessors see Criminal Justice Act 1988 s. 86 and Drug Trafficking Act 1994 s. 34.

Subss (1) and (2)
These apply rules similar to those embodied in s. 417 and prevent the liquidator from realising property that is already the subject of a restraint order or similar order made under this Act.

Subs. (3)
This deals with Scottish property owned by the company in question; a restraint order will only be effective against a liquidator if registered.

Subss (4)–(6) and (9)
These provisions restrict recovery powers under the 2002 Act where the liquidation is already afoot—see subs (9) for timing. In effect we have a corporate equivalent of s.418, though why these provisions were not placed in a discrete section is unclear.

Subs. (7)
This is a saving provision generally confirming the primacy of the 2002 Act. Presumably this primacy would apply as a matter of statutory interpretation.

Subs. (8)
This is a technical interpretation provision relevant to Scottish winding up cases.

Subs. (10)
This deals with "old" liquidations commenced prior to December 29, 1986.

427   Tainted gifts

(1) In this section "company" means any company which may be wound up under the 1986 Act.

(2) This section applies if—

(a) an order for the winding up of a company is made or it passes a resolution for its voluntary winding up, and

(b) it has made a tainted gift (whether directly or indirectly).

(3) No order may be made under section 238, 239 or 423 of the 1986 Act (avoidance of certain transactions) and no decree may be granted

under section 242 or 243 of that Act (gratuitous alienations and unfair preferences), or otherwise, in respect of the making of the gift at any time when—

(a) any property of the recipient of the tainted gift is subject to a restraint order under section 41, 120 or 190, or

(b) there is in force in respect of such property an order under section 50, 52, 128(3), 198 or 200.

(4) Any order made under section 238, 239 or 423 of the 1986 Act or decree granted under section 242 or 243 of that Act, or otherwise, after an order mentioned in subsection (3)(a) or (b) is discharged must take into account any realisation under Part 2, 3 or 4 of this Act of property held by the recipient of the tainted gift.

(5) A person makes a tainted gift for the purposes of this section if he makes a tainted gift within the meaning of Part 2, 3 or 4.

(6) In a case where the winding up of a company commenced or is treated as having commenced before 29 December 1986 this section has effect with the substitution—

(a) for references to section 239 of the 1986 Act of references to section 615 of the Companies Act 1985 (c. 6);

(b) for references to section 242 of the 1986 Act of references to section 615A of the Companies Act 1985;

(c) for references to section 243 of the 1986 Act of references to section 615B of the Companies Act 1985.

DEFINITIONS
"1986 Act": s. 434(1)
"tainted gift" : s. 77

GENERAL NOTE
This section translates rules similar to those contained in s. 419 on tainted gifts (see subs,(5)) to a corporate insolvency context.

Subss (1)–(2)
These define the parameters of this provision.

Subss (3), (5)
Transaction avoidance provisions under corporate insolvency law cannot come into play in respect of what might be a tainted gift under this Act (identified in subs. (5)) if proceedings under the 2002 Act against the company have already been started.

Subs. (4)
This deals with transaction avoidance orders under corporate insolvency law made after the discharge of a recovery order under the 2002 Act; again the law seeks to prevent the consequence of double recovery by introducing an accounting mechanism.

Subs. (6)
This makes provision for liquidations commenced under the pre 1986 law.

Winding up in Northern Ireland

428   Winding up under the 1989 Order

(1) In this section "company" means any company which may be wound up under the 1989 Order.

(2) If an order for the winding up of a company is made or it passes a resolution for its voluntary winding up, the functions of the liquidator (or any provisional liquidator) are not exercisable in relation to the following property—

(a) property for the time being subject to a restraint order which was made under section 41, 120 or 190 before the relevant time;

(b) any property in respect of which an order under section 50 or 52 is in force;

      (c) any property in respect of which an order under section 128(3) is in force;

      (d) any property in respect of which an order under section 198 or 200 is in force.

(3) Subsection (2)(a) applies to heritable property in Scotland only if the restraint order is recorded in the General Register of Sasines or registered in the Land Register of Scotland before the relevant time.

(4) If an order for the winding up of a company is made or it passes a resolution for its voluntary winding up the powers referred to in subsection (5) must not be exercised in the way mentioned in subsection (6) in relation to any property—

      (a) which is held by the company, and

      (b) in relation to which the functions of the liquidator are exercisable.

(5) These are the powers—

      (a) the powers conferred on a court by sections 41 to 67 and the powers of a receiver appointed under section 48, 50 or 52;

      (b) the powers conferred on a court by sections 120 to 136 and Schedule 3 and the powers of an administrator appointed under section 125 or 128(3);

      (c) the powers conferred on a court by sections 190 to 215 and the powers of a receiver appointed under section 196, 198 or 200.

(6) The powers must not be exercised—

      (a) so as to inhibit the liquidator from exercising his functions for the purpose of distributing property to the company's creditors;

      (b) so as to prevent the payment out of any property of expenses (including the remuneration of the liquidator or any provisional liquidator) properly incurred in the winding up in respect of the property.

(7) But nothing in the 1989 Order must be taken to restrict (or enable the restriction of) the exercise of the powers referred to in subsection (5).

(8) The relevant time is—

      (a) if no order for the winding up of the company has been made, the time of the passing of the resolution for voluntary winding up;

      (b) if such an order has been made, but before the presentation of the petition for the winding up of the company by the court such a resolution has been passed by the company, the time of the passing of the resolution;

      (c) if such an order has been made, but paragraph (b) does not apply, the time of the making of the order.

(9) In a case where a winding up of a company commenced or is treated as having commenced before 1 October 1991, this section has effect with the substitution for references to the 1989 Order of references to the Companies (Northern Ireland) Order 1986 (S.I. 1986/1032 (N.I. 6)).

Definitions

   "1989 Order": s. 434(1)

   "powers": subs. (5)

General Note

   This translates s.426 into a Northern Irish context.

Subss (1), (2) and (8)

   Compare s. 426(1), (2) and (9)

Subs. (3)

   This is the equivalent of s. 426(3) and it deals with Scottish real property held by a Northern Irish company.

Subss (4)-(6)
These subordinate actions in respect of recovery proceedings under this Act to the primacy of liquidation law if the winding up has already commenced.

Subs. (7)
Generally the 2002 Act prevails over the 1989 Order.

Subs. (9)
This deals with liquidations commenced prior to October 1, 1991.

429 Tainted gifts

(1) In this section "company" means any company which may be wound up under the 1989 Order.
(2) This section applies if—
   (a) an order for the winding up of a company is made or it passes a resolution for its voluntary winding up, and
   (b) it has made a tainted gift (whether directly or indirectly).
(3) No order may be made under Article 202, 203 or 367 of the 1989 Order (avoidance of certain transactions) in respect of the making of the gift at any time when—
   (a) any property of the recipient of the tainted gift is subject to a restraint order under section 41, 120 or 190, or
   (b) there is in force in respect of such property an order under section 50, 52, 128(3), 198 or 200.
(4) Any order made under Article 202, 203 or 367 of the 1989 Order after an order mentioned in subsection (3)(a) or (b) is discharged must take into account any realisation under Part 2, 3 or 4 of this Act of property held by the recipient of the tainted gift.
(5) A person makes a tainted gift for the purposes of this section if he makes a tainted gift within the meaning of Part 2, 3 or 4.

Definitions
  "1989 Order" : s. 434(1)
  "tainted gift" : subs. (5) and s. 225

General Note
  This applies the rules on tainted gifts (see the reference in subs (5)) made by insolvent companies to the Northern Irish context. It therefore largely replicates s. 427. The initial version of this provision was more clumsy than it presently appears; again the Bill was amended at a late stage to provide greater comparability with s. 427.

Subss (1) and (2)
These define the scope of the provision.

Subss (3) and (4)
These are the basic "mechanical" provisions. Again subs (4) is intended to forestall the possibility of double recovery.

Subs. (5)
This provides a circular definition of tainted gifts.

Floating charges

430 Floating charges

(1) In this section "company" means a company which may be wound up under
   (a) the 1986 Act, or
   (b) the 1989 Order.

(2) If a company holds property which is subject to a floating charge, and a receiver has been appointed by or on the application of the holder of the charge, the functions of the receiver are not exercisable in relation to the following property—

    (a) property for the time being subject to a restraint order which was made under section 41, 120 or 190 before the appointment of the receiver;

    (b) any property in respect of which an order under section 50 or 52 is in force;

    (c) any property in respect of which an order under section 128(3) is in force;

    (d) any property in respect of which an order under section 198 or 200 is in force.

(3) Subsection (2)(a) applies to heritable property in Scotland only if the restraint order is recorded in the General Register of Sasines or registered in the Land Register of Scotland before the appointment of the receiver.

(4) If a company holds property which is subject to a floating charge, and a receiver has been appointed by or on the application of the holder of the charge, the powers referred to in subsection (5) must not be exercised in the way mentioned in subsection (6) in relation to any property—

    (a) which is held by the company, and

    (b) in relation to which the functions of the receiver are exercisable.

(5) These are the powers—

    (a) the powers conferred on a court by sections 41 to 67 and the powers of a receiver appointed under section 48, 50 or 52;

    (b) the powers conferred on a court by sections 120 to 136 and Schedule 3 and the powers of an administrator appointed under section 125 or 128(3);

    (c) the powers conferred on a court by sections 190 to 215 and the powers of a receiver appointed under section 196, 198 or 200.

(6) The powers must not be exercised—

    (a) so as to inhibit the receiver from exercising his functions for the purpose of distributing property to the company's creditors;

    (b) so as to prevent the payment out of any property of expenses (including the remuneration of the receiver) properly incurred in the exercise of his functions in respect of the property.

(7) But nothing in the 1986 Act or the 1989 Order must be taken to restrict (or enable the restriction of) the exercise of the powers referred to in subsection (5).

(8) In this section "floating charge" includes a floating charge within the meaning of section 462 of the Companies Act 1985 (c. 6).

DEFINITIONS
"1986 Act" : s. 434(1)
"1989 Order" : s. 434(1)
"floating charge" : subs (8) and Insolvency Act 1986 s. 251
"restraint order" : ss. 41, 120 and 190
"powers" : subs. (5)

GENERAL NOTE
    This deals with the position of company receivers appointed under a "floating charge". Why receivers appointed under fixed charges are not covered is unclear. This may cause difficulties in the future as the boundaries between fixed and floating charge are problematic - see for example *Agnew v. IRC* [2001] 3 WLR 454.

    The floating charge, that archetypal security in English law, was first acknowledged by the courts in *Re Panama* (1870) 5 Ch App 318. The classic description is to be found by Romer LJ in

Re Yorkshire Woolcombers Association Ltd [1903] 2 Ch 284- confirmed on appeal sub nomine *Illingworth v Houldsworth* [1904] AC 355.

The floating charge in England, Wales and Northern Ireland is largely governed by case law principles. Whereas in Scotland the floating charge was introduced by statute in 1961 and its basic characteristics are governed by ss. 462-466 of the Companies Act 1985.

Section 430 introduces priorities comparable to s.426 but applicable not to cases of liquidation but rather receivership. This provisions applies both in England and Wales, Scotland and also in Northern Ireland.

The long term utility of this provision must remain in doubt as the Enterprise Bill 2002 proposes to abolish most forms of receivership prospectively, though with a saving concession for the enforcement of existing floating charges. Receivership will in many cases be subsumed by a more expansive notion of company administration. In view of this change it is surprising that the 2002 did not seek to deal with the interface between recovery proceedings and administration proceedings. Presumably some amendment to the 2002 Act will be required in the near future.

Subss (1), (8)
These define "company" and "floating charge" (the latter to cover the position in Scotland). Note that at present the floating charge is only available for use as security by a corporate debtor and not by private individuals.

Subs. (2)
A receiver appointed under a floating charge cannot exercise powers of enforcement in relation to property that is already subject to a restraint order or similar order made under this Act.

Subs. (3)
This again deals with the problem of heritable property in Scotland; the restraint order must have been registered in order to be effective against a receiver.

Subss (4)-(6)
These deal with the converse scenario and exclude recovery powers under this Act where a receiver has already been appointed by a floating charge holder.

Subs. (7)
This is the standard saving provision used throughout Pt.9.

Limited liability partnerships

431   Limited liability partnerships

(1) In sections 426, 427 and 430 "company" includes a limited liability partnership which may be wound up under the 1986 Act.

(2) A reference in those sections to a company passing a resolution for its voluntary winding up is to be construed in relation to a limited liability partnership as a reference to the partnership making a determination for its voluntary winding up.

DEFINITIONS
"1986 Act" : s. 434(1)
"limited liability partnership": Limited Liability Partnerships Act 2000 s. 1(2)

GENERAL NOTE
Limited liability partnerships (LLPs) were introduced by the Limited Liability Partnerships Act 2000. To all intents and purposes they are treated as companies for the purposes of insolvency. The 2002 Act maintains that tradition.

Subs. (1)
This makes it clear that ss.426, 427 and 430 apply to LLPs.

Subs. (2)
This is a necessarily modification to cater for the fact that LLPs do not formally resolve to have themselves wound up - see LLP Regulations 2001 (SI 2001/1090) Schedule 3 amending s. 84 of the Insolvency Act 1986.

432 Insolvency practitioners

(1) Subsections (2) and (3) apply if a person acting as an insolvency practitioner seizes or disposes of any property in relation to which his functions are not exercisable because—

   (a) it is for the time being subject to a restraint order made under
section 41, 120 or 190, or

   (b) it is for the time being subject to an interim receiving order made
under section 246 or an interim administration order made under
section 256,

and at the time of the seizure or disposal he believes on reasonable
grounds that he is entitled (whether in pursuance of an order of a court
or otherwise) to seize or dispose of the property.

(2) He is not liable to any person in respect of any loss or damage resulting
from the seizure or disposal, except so far as the loss or damage is
caused by his negligence.

(3) He has a lien on the property or the proceeds of its sale—

   (a) for such of his expenses as were incurred in connection with the
liquidation, bankruptcy, sequestration or other proceedings in
relation to which he purported to make the seizure or disposal,
and

   (b) for so much of his remuneration as may reasonably be assigned to
his acting in connection with those proceedings.

(4) Subsection (2) does not prejudice the generality of any provision of
the 1985 Act, the 1986 Act, the 1989 Order or any other Act or Order
which confers protection from liability on him.

(5) Subsection (7) applies if—

   (a) property is subject to a restraint order made under section 41, 120
or 190,

   (b) a person acting as an insolvency practitioner incurs expenses in
respect of property subject to the restraint order, and

   (c) he does not know (and has no reasonable grounds to believe) that
the property is subject to the restraint order.

(6) Subsection (7) also applies if—

   (a) property is subject to a restraint order made under section 41, 120
or 190,

   (b) a person acting as an insolvency practitioner incurs expenses
which are not ones in respect of property subject to the restraint
order, and

   (c) the expenses are ones which (but for the effect of the restraint
order) might have been met by taking possession of and realising
property subject to it.

(7) Whether or not he has seized or disposed of any property, he is entitled
to payment of the expenses under—

   (a) section 54(2), 55(3), 56(2) or 57(3) if the restraint order was made
under section 41;

   (b) section 130(3) or 131(3) if the restraint order was made under
section 120;

   (c) section 202(2), 203(3), 204(2) or 205(3) if the restraint order was
made under section 190.

(8) Subsection (10) applies if—

   (a) property is subject to an interim receiving order made under section 246 or an interim administration order made under section
256,

   (b) a person acting as an insolvency practitioner incurs expenses in
respect of property subject to the order, and

    (c) he does not know (and has no reasonable grounds to believe) that the property is subject to the order.

  (9) Subsection (10) also applies if—

    (a) property is subject to an interim receiving order made under section 246 or an interim administration order made under section 256,

    (b) a person acting as an insolvency practitioner incurs expenses which are not ones in respect of property subject to the order, and

    (c) the expenses are ones which (but for the effect of the order) might have been met by taking possession of and realising property subject to it.

  (10) Whether or not he has seized or disposed of any property, he is entitled to payment of the expenses under section 280.

DEFINITIONS

  "insolvency practitioner" : s. 433

  "1986 Act" : s. 434(1)

  "1989 Order": s. 434(1)

GENERAL NOTE

  This provision, which applies throughout the UK, offers relief to insolvency practitioners (as defined by s. 433) who mistakenly seize or dispose of assets in breach of the aforementioned rules in Part 9. Such a concession is not new in this context - see Criminal Justice Act 1988 s. 87 and Drug Trafficking Act 1994 s. 35.

Subss (1), (2)

  An insolvency practitioner who reasonably believes that he is entitled to seize or dispose of property notwithstanding the existence of a restraint order or similar order made under this Act is protected from civil liability except insofar as he has been negligent. Compare Insolvency Act 1986 s. 234.

Subs. (3)

  Furthermore the insolvency practitioner's right to a lien in respect of remuneration and expenses is maintained.

Subs. (4)

  This is a saving provision preserving any other statutory safe harbours for an insolvency practitioner (e.g. Insolvency Act 1986 s. 234).

Subss (5)-(7)

  These preserve the insolvency practitioner's rights to expenses in certain defined situations where property covered by a restraint order is mistakenly dealt with.

Subss (8)-(10)

  This is a similar preservation mechanism though operating in different circumstances (i.e. where the property is subject to an interim receivership or administration order).

433   Meaning of insolvency practitioner

  (1) This section applies for the purposes of section 432.

  (2) A person acts as an insolvency practitioner if he so acts within the meaning given by section 388 of the 1986 Act or Article 3 of the 1989 Order; but this is subject to subsections (3) to (5).

  (3) The expression "person acting as an insolvency practitioner" includes the official receiver acting as receiver or manager of the property concerned.

  (4) In applying section 388 of the 1986 Act under subsection (2) above—

    (a) the reference in section 388(2)(a) to a permanent or interim trustee in sequestration must be taken to include a reference to a trustee in sequestration;

    (b) section 388(5) (which includes provision that nothing in the section applies to anything done by the official receiver or the Accountant in Bankruptcy) must be ignored.

(5) In applying Article 3 of the 1989 Order under subsection (2) above, paragraph (5) (which includes provision that nothing in the Article applies to anything done by the official receiver) must be ignored.

DEFINITIONS
"1986 Act" : s. 434(1)
"1989 Order" : s. 434(1)

GENERAL NOTE

Subs. (1)
This aids the operation of s. 432 by defining the term "insolvency practitioner".

Subs. (2)
This refers us to the definition in s. 388 of the Insolvency Act 1986 and Art. 3 of the 1989 Order for Northern Ireland.

Subs. (3)
This clarifies the position with regard to public sector official receivers.

Subs. (4)
These add a gloss to the standard definition to deal with official receivers and insolvency practitioners in Scotland.

Subs. (5)
This is only relevant to Northern Ireland.

Interpretation

434   Interpretation

(1) The following paragraphs apply to references to Acts or Orders—
　　(a) the 1913 Act is the Bankruptcy (Scotland) Act 1913 (c. 20);
　　(b) the 1914 Act is the Bankruptcy Act 1914 (c. 59);
　　(c) the 1985 Act is the Bankruptcy (Scotland) Act 1985 (c. 66);
　　(d) the 1986 Act is the Insolvency Act 1986 (c. 45);
　　(e) the 1989 Order is the Insolvency (Northern Ireland) Order 1989 (S.I. 1989/2405 (N.I. 19)).
(2) An award of sequestration is made on the date of sequestration within the meaning of section 12(4) of the 1985 Act.
(3) This section applies for the purposes of this Part.

GENERAL NOTE
This is a dedicated interpretation provision relevant for Pt. 9.

Subs. (1)
This identifies the key insolvency legislation operating in the UK and relevant to this Part.

Subs. (2)
This explains the timing of an award of sequestration for the purposes of personal insolvency law in Scotland.

Subs. (3)
This is purely explanatory.

PART 10

INFORMATION

INTRODUCTION TO PART 10
Part 10 regulates the exchange of information between the Director of the ARA and other law enforcement agencies, but without compromising the protections offered by the Data Protection Act 1998 and the Regulation of Investigatory Powers Act 2000.

Given the sensitive nature of the information, whether personal, business or commercial, which can be collected under this Act, this part makes provision for the regulating the exchange of information between the Agency and government departments and law enforcing agencies.

England and Wales and Northern Ireland

435 Use of information by Director

Information obtained by or on behalf of the Director in connection with the exercise of any of his functions may be used by him in connection with his exercise of any of his other functions.

DEFINITION
"Director": s.1(2)

GENERAL NOTE
This section allows the Director to use information obtained, for example, in relation to a confiscation investigation to be used in, for example, a civil recovery investigation.

436 Disclosure of information to Director

(1) Information which is held by or on behalf of a permitted person (whether it was obtained before or after the coming into force of this section) may be disclosed to the Director for the purpose of the exercise by the Director of his functions.

(2) A disclosure under this section is not to be taken to breach any restriction on the disclosure of information (however imposed).

(3) But nothing in this section authorises the making of a disclosure—
   (a) which contravenes the Data Protection Act 1998 (c. 29);
   (b) which is prohibited by Part 1 of the Regulation of Investigatory Powers Act 2000 (c. 23).

(4) This section does not affect a power to disclose which exists apart from this section.

(5) These are permitted persons—
   (a) a constable;
   (b) the Director General of the National Criminal Intelligence Service;
   (c) the Director General of the National Crime Squad;
   (d) the Director of the Serious Fraud Office;
   (e) the Commissioners of Inland Revenue;
   (f) the Commissioners of Customs and Excise;
   (g) the Director of Public Prosecutions;
   (h) the Director of Public Prosecutions for Northern Ireland.

(6) The Secretary of State may by order designate as permitted persons other persons who exercise functions which he believes are of a public nature.

(7) But an order under subsection (6) must specify the functions in respect of which the designation is made.

(8) Information must not be disclosed under this section on behalf of the Commissioners of Inland Revenue or on behalf of the Commissioners of Customs and Excise unless the Commissioners concerned authorise the disclosure.

(9) The power to authorise a disclosure under subsection (8) may be delegated (either generally or for a specified purpose)—
   (a) in the case of the Commissioners of Inland Revenue, to an officer of the Board of Inland Revenue;
   (b) in the case of the Commissioners of Customs and Excise, to a customs officer.

DEFINITION
"Director": s.1(2)

GENERAL NOTE

Where disclosure of information is otherwise prohibited by, for example, a duty of confidentiality or a court order or a statutory obligation, its disclosure to the Director will not breach any such restrictions, by subs.(2). However, the assumption in this section is that any exchange of information will be on a voluntary basis. The Director cannot demand information from permitted persons. Nevertheless, while subs.(4) covers any arrangements between government departments or agencies, it also implies that, in the unlikely event of non-cooperation, the Director could seek orders for disclosure under Pt. 8 of this Act.

The major constraints on the exchange of information are the Data Protection Act 1998 and Part I of the Regulation of Investigatory Powers Act 2000. Part I of the 2000 Act deals with communications, placing restrictions on their unlawful and authorised interception, and providing safeguards, notably in ss.15 and 16, on the use of authorised material that is acquired lawfully. It also imposes restrictions on the acquisition and disclosure of communications data.

The 1998 Act, to be amended by the Freedom of Information Act 2000, sets out the principles that must be applied in processing personal data. The Act will not prevent information from being disclosed to the Director but any disclosure must comply especially with the conditions set out in Schs. 1-4. In summary, personal data must be obtained and processed fairly and lawfully, it must be held only for lawful purposes and not used or disclosed in a manner incompatible with those purposes, and it must be accurate, relevant and retained for no longer than is necessary. In addition, subject access rights must be respected and the data must be held securely. Generally, personal data may only be processed with the subject's consent unless one of the necessity requirements, in Scheds. 2 or 3 of the Act, applies. Generally, where the material is relevant only to a proceeds of crime investigation proper, the exemption for crime and taxation matters in s.29 of the 1998 Act will not apply.

Should the list of permitted persons be extended by the Secretary of State, by subss.(6) and (7), their functions must be narrowly defined; it will not be sufficient simply to designate, for example, a Secretary of State of a Government Department.

437   Further disclosure

(1) Subsection (2) applies to information obtained under section 436 from the Commissioners of Inland Revenue or from the Commissioners of Customs and Excise or from a person acting on behalf of either of them.

(2) Such information must not be further disclosed except—
   (a) for a purpose connected with the exercise of the Director's functions, and
   (b) with the consent of the Commissioners concerned.

(3) Consent under subsection (2) may be given—
   (a) in relation to a particular disclosure;
   (b) in relation to disclosures made in circumstances specified or described in the consent.

(4) The power to consent to further disclosure under subsection (2)(b) may be delegated (either generally or for a specified purpose)—
   (a) in the case of the Commissioners of Inland Revenue, to an officer of the Board of Inland Revenue;
   (b) in the case of the Commissioners of Customs and Excise, to a customs officer.

(5) Subsection (6) applies to information obtained under section 436 from a permitted person other than the Commissioners of Inland Revenue or the Commissioners of Customs and Excise or a person acting on behalf of either of them.

(6) A permitted person who discloses such information to the Director may make the disclosure subject to such conditions as to further disclosure by the Director as the permitted person thinks appropriate; and the information must not be further disclosed in contravention of the conditions.

DEFINITIONS
  "Director": s.1(2)
  "permitted person": s.436(5)

GENERAL NOTE

This section applies to the further disclosure of information received by the Director. Reflecting the sensitive nature of the material that they hold, there is a presumption that it cannot be further disclosed without explicit approval from the Commissioners of Inland Revenue and Customs and Excise. In the case of other permitted persons, provision is made for them to impose conditions on further disclosure and a duty on the Director to comply with them.

438   Disclosure of information by Director

(1) Information obtained by or on behalf of the Director in connection with the exercise of any of his functions may be disclosed by him if the disclosure is for the purposes of any of the following—

  (a) any criminal investigation which is being or may be carried out, whether in the United Kingdom or elsewhere;

  (b) any criminal proceedings which have been or may be started, whether in the United Kingdom or elsewhere;

  (c) the exercise of the Director's functions;

  (d) the exercise by the prosecutor of functions under Parts 2, 3 and 4;

  (e) the exercise by the Scottish Ministers of their functions under Part 5;

  (f) the exercise by a customs officer or a constable of his functions under Chapter 3 of Part 5;

  (g) safeguarding national security;

  (h) investigations or proceedings outside the United Kingdom which have led or may lead to the making of an external order within the meaning of section 447;

  (i) the exercise of a designated function.

(2) Subsection (1) does not apply to information obtained by the Director or on his behalf in connection with the exercise of his functions under Part 6.

(3) But such information may be disclosed by the Director—

  (a) to the Commissioners of Inland Revenue;

  (b) to the Lord Advocate for the purpose of the exercise by the Lord Advocate of his functions under Part 3.

(4) Information disclosed to the Lord Advocate under subsection (3)(b) may be further disclosed by him only to the Scottish Ministers for the purpose of the exercise by them of their functions under Part 5.

(5) If the Director makes a disclosure of information for a purpose specified in subsection (1) he may make any further disclosure of the information by the person to whom he discloses it subject to such conditions as he thinks fit.

(6) Such a person must not further disclose the information in contravention of the conditions.

(7) A disclosure under this section is not to be taken to breach any restriction on the disclosure of information (however imposed).

(8) But nothing in this section authorises the making of a disclosure—

  (a) which contravenes the Data Protection Act 1998 (c. 29);

  (b) which is prohibited by Part 1 of the Regulation of Investigatory Powers Act 2000 (c. 23).

(9) A designated function is a function which the Secretary of State thinks is a function of a public nature and which he designates by order.

DEFINITIONS
  "customs officer": s.454
  "Director": s.1(2)

GENERAL NOTE
This section mirrors ss.436 and 437 in regulating the flow of information from the Director to other agencies. There are similar constraints imposed by the Data Protection Act 1998 and Part I of the Regulation of Investigatory Powers Act 2000 (for which, see the note to s.436, above). In addition, however, subss.(2)-(4) limit the disclosure of information in respect of the Director's revenue functions under Pt. 6 of the Act.

Scotland

439   Disclosure of information to Lord Advocate and to Scottish Ministers

(1) Information which is held by or on behalf of a permitted person (whether it was obtained before or after the coming into force of this section) may be disclosed to the Lord Advocate in connection with the exercise of any of his functions under Part 3 or to the Scottish Ministers in connection with the exercise of any of their functions under Part 5.

(2) A disclosure under this section is not to be taken to breach any restriction on the disclosure of information (however imposed).

(3) But nothing in this section authorises the making of a disclosure—
   (a) which contravenes the Data Protection Act 1998;
   (b) which is prohibited by Part 1 of the Regulation of Investigatory Powers Act 2000.

(4) This section does not affect a power to disclose which exists apart from this section.

(5) These are permitted persons—
   (a) a constable;
   (b) the Director General of the National Criminal Intelligence Service;
   (c) the Director General of the National Crime Squad;
   (d) the Director of the Serious Fraud Office;
   (e) the Commissioners of Inland Revenue;
   (f) the Commissioners of Customs and Excise;
   (g) the Director of Public Prosecutions;
   (h) the Director of Public Prosecutions for Northern Ireland.

(6) The Scottish Ministers may by order designate as permitted persons other persons who exercise functions which they believe are of a public nature.

(7) But an order under subsection (6) must specify the functions in respect of which the designation is made.

(8) Information must not be disclosed under this section on behalf of the Commissioners of Inland Revenue or on behalf of the Commissioners of Customs and Excise unless the Commissioners concerned authorise the disclosure.

(9) The power to authorise a disclosure under subsection (8) may be delegated (either generally or for a specified purpose)—
   (a) in the case of the Commissioners of Inland Revenue, to an officer of the Board of Inland Revenue;
   (b) in the case of the Commissioners of Customs and Excise, to a customs officer.

440   Further disclosure

(1) Subsection (2) applies to information obtained under section 439 from the Commissioners of Inland Revenue or from the Commissioners of Customs and Excise or from a person acting on behalf of either of them.

(2) Such information must not be further disclosed except—

    (a) for a purpose connected with the exercise of the functions of the Lord Advocate under Part 3 and of the Scottish Ministers under Part 5, and

    (b) with the consent of the Commissioners concerned.

(3) Consent under subsection (2) may be given—

    (a) in relation to a particular disclosure;

    (b) in relation to disclosures made in circumstances specified or described in the consent.

(4) The power to consent to further disclosure under subsection (2)(b) may be delegated (either generally or for a specified purpose)—

    (a) in the case of the Commissioners of Inland Revenue, to an officer of the Board of Inland Revenue;

    (b) in the case of the Commissioners of Customs and Excise, to a customs officer.

(5) Subsection (6) applies to information obtained under section 439 from a permitted person other than the Commissioners of Inland Revenue or the Commissioners of Customs and Excise or a person acting on behalf of either of them.

(6) A permitted person who discloses such information to the Lord Advocate or to the Scottish Ministers may make the disclosure subject to such conditions as to further disclosure by the Lord Advocate or by the Scottish Ministers as the permitted person thinks appropriate; and the information must not be further disclosed in contravention of the conditions.

441   Disclosure of information by Lord Advocate and by Scottish Ministers

(1) Information obtained by or on behalf of the Lord Advocate in connection with the exercise of any of his functions under Chapter 3 of Part 5 may be disclosed to the Scottish Ministers in connection with the exercise of any of their functions under that Part.

(2) Information obtained by or on behalf of the Lord Advocate in connection with the exercise of any of his functions under Part 3 or by or on behalf of the Scottish Ministers in connection with the exercise of any of their functions under Part 5 may be disclosed by him or by them if the disclosure is for the purposes of any of the following—

    (a) any criminal investigation which is being or may be carried out whether in the United Kingdom or elsewhere;

    (b) any criminal proceedings which have been or may be started, whether in the United Kingdom or elsewhere;

    (c) the exercise of the functions of the Lord Advocate under Part 3;

    (d) the exercise of the functions of the Scottish Ministers under Part 5;

    (e) the exercise by the prosecutor of functions under Parts 2, 3 and 4;

    (f) the exercise of the Director's functions;

    (g) the exercise by a customs officer or a constable of his functions under Chapter 3 of Part 5;

    (h) safeguarding national security;

    (i) investigations or proceedings outside the United Kingdom which have led or may lead to the making of an external order within the meaning of section 447;

    (j) the exercise of a designated function.

(3) If the Lord Advocate makes a disclosure of information for a purpose specified in subsection (2) he may make any further disclosure of the information by the person to whom he discloses it subject to such conditions as he thinks fit.

(4) If the Scottish Ministers make a disclosure of information for a purpose specified in subsection (2) they may make any further disclosure of the information by the person to whom they disclose it subject to such conditions as they think fit.

(5) A person mentioned in subsection (3) or (4) must not further disclose the information in contravention of the conditions.

(6) A disclosure under this section is not to be taken to breach any restriction on the disclosure of information (however imposed).

(7) But nothing in this section authorises the making of a disclosure—
   (a) which contravenes the Data Protection Act 1998 (c. 29);
   (b) which is prohibited by Part 1 of the Regulation of Investigatory Powers Act 2000 (c. 23).

(8) This section does not affect a power to disclose which exists apart from this section.

(9) A designated function is a function which the Scottish Ministers think is a function of a public nature and which they designate by order.

Overseas purposes

442   Restriction on disclosure for overseas purposes

(1) Section 18 of the Anti-terrorism, Crime and Security Act 2001 (c. 24) (restrictions on disclosure of information for overseas purposes) applies to a disclosure of information authorised by section 438(1)(a) or (b) or 441(2)(a) or (b).

(2) In the application of section 18 of the Anti-terrorism, Crime and Security Act 2001 by virtue of subsection (1) section 20 of that Act must be ignored and the following subsection is substituted for subsection (2) of section 18 of that Act—

   "(2) In subsection (1) the reference, in relation to a direction, to a relevant disclosure is a reference to a disclosure which—
      (a) is made for a purpose authorised by section 438(1)(a) or (b) or 441(2)(a) or (b) of the Proceeds of Crime Act 2002, and
      (b) is of any such information as is described in the direction.".

PART 11

This Part contains provisions empowering the Queen in Council to make Orders in Council enabling orders made in one part of the United Kingdom to be enforced in another part, and for external requests, orders and investigation.

CO-OPERATION

443   Enforcement in different parts of the United Kingdom

(1) Her Majesty may by Order in Council make provision—
   (a) for an order made by a court under Part 2 to be enforced in Scotland or Northern Ireland;
   (b) for an order made by a court under Part 3 to be enforced in England and Wales or Northern Ireland;
   (c) for an order made by a court under Part 4 to be enforced in England and Wales or Scotland;
   (d) for an order made under Part 8 in one part of the United Kingdom to be enforced in another part;
   (e) for a warrant issued under Part 8 in one part of the United Kingdom to be executed in another part.

(2) Her Majesty may by Order in Council make provision—
   (a) for a function of a receiver appointed in pursuance of Part 2 to be exercisable in Scotland or Northern Ireland;

  (b) for a function of an administrator appointed in pursuance of Part
   3 to be exercisable in England and Wales or Northern Ireland;
  (c) for a function of a receiver appointed in pursuance of Part 4 to be
   exercisable in England and Wales or Scotland.
 (3) An Order under this section may include—
  (a) provision conferring and imposing functions on the prosecutor
   and the Director;
  (b) provision about the registration of orders and warrants;
  (c) provision allowing directions to be given in one part of the United
   Kingdom about the enforcement there of an order made or warrant issued in another part;
  (d) provision about the authentication in one part of the United
   Kingdom of an order made or warrant issued in another part.
 (4) An Order under this section may—
  (a) amend an enactment;
  (b) apply an enactment (with or without modifications).

444 External requests and orders

 (1) Her Majesty may by Order in Council—
  (a) make provision for a prohibition on dealing with property which
   is the subject of an external request;
  (b) make provision for the realisation of property for the purpose of
   giving effect to an external order.
 (2) An Order under this section may include provision which (subject to
  any specified modifications) corresponds to any provision of Part 2, 3
  or 4 or Part 5 except Chapter 3.
 (3) An Order under this section may include—
  (a) provision about the functions of the Secretary of State, the Lord
   Advocate, the Scottish Ministers and the Director in relation to
   external requests and orders;
  (b) provision about the registration of external orders;
  (c) provision about the authentication of any judgment or order of an
   overseas court, and of any other document connected with such a
   judgment or order or any proceedings relating to it;
  (d) provision about evidence (including evidence required to establish whether proceedings have been started or are likely to be
   started in an overseas court);
  (e) provision to secure that any person affected by the implementation of an external request or the enforcement of an external
   order has an opportunity to make representations to a court in the
   part of the United Kingdom where the request is being
   implemented or the order is being enforced.

445 External investigations

 (1) Her Majesty may by Order in Council make—
  (a) provision to enable orders equivalent to those under Part 8 to be
   made, and warrants equivalent to those under Part 8 to be issued,
   for the purposes of an external investigation;
  (b) provision creating offences in relation to external investigations
   which are equivalent to offences created by Part 8.
 (2) An Order under this section may include—
  (a) provision corresponding to any provision of Part 8 (subject to any
   specified modifications);
  (b) provision about the functions of the Secretary of State, the Lord
   Advocate, the Scottish Ministers, the Director, the Director General of the National Criminal Intelligence Service, the Director of
   the Serious Fraud Office, constables and customs officers;

    (c) provision about evidence (including evidence required to estab-
lish whether an investigation is being carried out in a country or
territory outside the United Kingdom).

(3) But an Order under this section must not provide for a disclosure
order to be made for the purposes of an external investigation into
whether a money laundering offence has been committed.

446   Rules of court

Rules of court may make such provision as is necessary or expedient
to give effect to an Order in Council made under this Part (including
provision about the exercise of functions of a judge conferred or
imposed by the Order).

447   Interpretation

(1) An external request is a request by an overseas authority to prohibit
dealing with relevant property which is identified in the request.

(2) An external order is an order which—

    (a) is made by an overseas court where property is found or believed
to have been obtained as a result of or in connection with criminal
conduct, and

    (b) is for the recovery of specified property or a specified sum of
money.

(3) An external investigation is an investigation by an overseas authority
into—

    (a) whether property has been obtained as a result of or in connec-
tion with criminal conduct, or

    (b) whether a money laundering offence has been committed.

(4) Property is all property wherever situated and includes—

    (a) money;

    (b) all forms of property, real or personal, heritable or moveable;

    (c) things in action and other intangible or incorporeal property.

(5) Property is obtained by a person if he obtains an interest in it.

(6) References to an interest, in relation to property other than land,
include references to a right (including a right to possession).

(7) Property is relevant property if there are reasonable grounds to
believe that it may be needed to satisfy an external order which has
been or which may be made.

(8) Criminal conduct is conduct which—

    (a) constitutes an offence in any part of the United Kingdom, or

    (b) would constitute an offence in any part of the United Kingdom if
it occurred there.

(9) A money laundering offence is conduct carried out in a country or
territory outside the United Kingdom and which if carried out in the
United Kingdom would constitute any of the following offences—

    (a) an offence under section 327, 328 or 329;

    (b) an attempt, conspiracy or incitement to commit an offence speci-
fied in paragraph (a);

    (c) aiding, abetting, counselling or procuring the commission of an
offence specified in paragraph (a).

(10) An overseas court is a court of a country or territory outside the
United Kingdom.

(11) An overseas authority is an authority which has responsibility in a
country or territory outside the United Kingdom—

    (a) for making a request to an authority in another country or terri-
tory (including the United Kingdom) to prohibit dealing with relevant property,

    (b) for carrying out an investigation into whether property has been
obtained as a result of or in connection with criminal conduct, or

    (c) for carrying out an investigation into whether a money launder-
       ing offence has been committed.
(12) This section applies for the purposes of this Part.

PART 12

MISCELLANEOUS AND GENERAL

INTRODUCTION TO PART 12

   Part 12 contains various miscellaneous provisions, in particular those concerned with commencement and transitional provisions. The Act is to come into effect in accordance with provision made by the Secretary of State by order. The Act contains no transitional provisions, but
provision is made for transitional provisions to be included in subordinate legislation.

Miscellaneous

448   Tax

   Schedule 10 contains provisions about tax.

449   Agency staff: pseudonyms

  (1) This section applies to a member of the staff of the Agency if—
    (a) he is authorised (generally or specifically) by the Director to do
       anything for the purposes of this Act, and
    (b) it is necessary or expedient for the purpose of doing the thing for
       the member of the staff of the Agency to identify himself by
       name.
  (2) The Director may direct that such a member of the staff of the Agency
     may for that purpose identify himself by means of a pseudonym.
  (3) For the purposes of any proceedings or application under this Act a
     certificate signed by the Director which sufficiently identifies the
     member of the staff of the Agency by reference to the pseudonym is
     conclusive evidence that that member of the staff of the Agency is
     authorised to use the pseudonym.
  (4) In any proceedings or application under this Act a member of the staff
     of the Agency in respect of whom a direction under this section is in
     force must not be asked (and if asked is not required to answer) any
     question which is likely to reveal his true identity.
  (5) Section 1(6) does not apply to anything done by the Director under
     this section.

450   Pseudonyms: Scotland

  (1) This section applies to—
    (a) any person named by the Scottish Ministers for the purpose of a
       civil recovery investigation under Part 8, or
    (b) any person authorised by the Scottish Ministers for the purpose
       of such a civil recovery investigation to receive relevant infor-
       mation under section 391,
    if it is necessary or expedient for the person to identify himself by
    name for that purpose.
  (2) The Scottish Ministers may direct that such a person may for that pur-
     pose identify himself by means of a pseudonym.
  (3) For the purposes of any proceedings or application under this Act, a
     certificate signed by the Scottish Ministers which sufficiently identifies
     the person by reference to the pseudonym is conclusive evidence that
     the person is authorised to use the pseudonym.
  (4) In any proceedings or application under this Act a person in respect of
     whom a direction under this section is in force must not be asked (and
     if asked is not required to answer) any question which is likely to
     reveal his true identity.

451   Customs and Excise prosecutions

(1) Proceedings for a specified offence may be started by order of the Commissioners of Customs and Excise (the Commissioners).

(2) Such proceedings must be brought in the name of a customs officer.

(3) If the customs officer in whose name the proceedings are brought—

(a) dies,

(b) is removed or discharged, or

(c) is absent,

the proceedings may be continued by a different customs officer.

(4) If the Commissioners investigate, or propose to investigate, any matter to help them to decide—

(a) whether there are grounds for believing that a specified offence has been committed, or

(b) whether a person is to be prosecuted for such an offence,

the matter must be treated as an assigned matter within the meaning of the Customs and Excise Management Act 1979 (c. 2).

(5) This section—

(a) does not prevent any person (including a customs officer) who has power to arrest, detain or prosecute a person for a specified offence from doing so;

(b) does not prevent a court from dealing with a person brought before it following his arrest by a customs officer for a specified offence, even if the proceedings were not started by an order under subsection (1).

(6) The following are specified offences—

(a) an offence under Part 7;

(b) an offence under section 342;

(c) an attempt, conspiracy or incitement to commit an offence specified in paragraph (a) or (b);

(d) aiding, abetting, counselling or procuring the commission of an offence specified in paragraph (a) or (b).

(7) This section does not apply to proceedings on indictment in Scotland.

452   Crown servants

(1) The Secretary of State may by regulations provide that any of the following provisions apply to persons in the public service of the Crown.

(2) The provisions are—

(a) the provisions of Part 7;

(b) section 342.

453   References to financial investigators

(1) The Secretary of State may by order provide that a specified reference in this Act to an accredited financial investigator is a reference to such an investigator who falls within a specified description.

(2) A description may be framed by reference to a grade designated by a specified person.

454   Customs officers

For the purposes of this Act a customs officer is a person commissioned by the Commissioners of Customs and Excise under section 6(3) of the Customs and Excise Management Act 1979 (c. 2).

455   Enactment

In this Act (except in section 460(1)) a reference to an enactment includes a reference to—

(a) an Act of the Scottish Parliament;

(b) Northern Ireland legislation.

General

456 Amendments

Schedule 11 contains miscellaneous and consequential amendments.

457 Repeals and revocations

Schedule 12 contains repeals and revocations.

458 Commencement

(1) The preceding provisions of this Act (except the provisions specified in subsection (3)) come into force in accordance with provision made by the Secretary of State by order.

(2) But no order may be made which includes provision for the commencement of Part 5, 8 or 10 unless the Secretary of State has consulted the Scottish Ministers.

(3) The following provisions come into force in accordance with provision made by the Scottish Ministers by order after consultation with the Secretary of State—

(a) Part 3;

(b) this Part, to the extent that it relates to Part 3.

459 Orders and regulations

(1) References in this section to subordinate legislation are to—

(a) any Order in Council under this Act;

(b) any order under this Act (other than one falling to be made by a court);

(c) any regulations under this Act.

(2) Subordinate legislation—

(a) may make different provision for different purposes;

(b) may include supplementary, incidental, saving or transitional provisions.

(3) Any power to make subordinate legislation is exercisable by statutory instrument.

(4) A statutory instrument is subject to annulment in pursuance of a resolution of either House of Parliament if it contains subordinate legislation other than—

(a) an order under section 75(7) or (8), 223(7) or (8), 282, 292(4), 309, 364(4), 377(4), 436(6), 438(9) or 458;

(b) subordinate legislation made by the Scottish Ministers;

(c) an Order in Council made under section 443 which makes provision only in relation to Scotland.

(5) A statutory instrument is subject to annulment in pursuance of a resolution of the Scottish Parliament if it contains—

(a) subordinate legislation made by the Scottish Ministers other than an order under section 142(6) or (7), 293(4), 398(4), 410(4), 439(6), 441(9) or 458;

(b) an Order in Council made under section 443 which makes provision only in relation to Scotland.

(6) No order may be made—

(a) by the Secretary of State under section 75(7) or (8), 223(7) or (8), 282, 292(4), 309, 364(4), 377(4), 436(6) or 438(9) unless a draft of laid before Parliament and approved by a resolution of each House;

(b) by the Scottish Ministers under section 142(6) or (7), 293(4), 398(4), 410(4), 439(6) or 441(9) unless a draft of the order has been laid before and approved by a resolution of the Scottish Parliament.

(7) The Scottish Ministers must lay before the Scottish Parliament a copy of every statutory instrument containing an Order in Council made under section 444 or 445.

460   Finance

(1) The following are to be paid out of money provided by Parliament—
  (a) any expenditure incurred by any Minister of the Crown under this Act;
  (b) any increase attributable to this Act in the sums payable out of money so provided under any other enactment.
(2) Any sums received by the Secretary of State in consequence of this Act are to be paid into the Consolidated Fund.

461   Extent

(1) Part 2 extends to England and Wales only.
(2) In Part 8, Chapter 2 extends to England and Wales and Northern Ireland only.
(3) These provisions extend to Scotland only—
  (a) Part 3;
  (b) in Part 8, Chapter 3.
(4) Part 4 extends to Northern Ireland only.
(5) The amendments in Schedule 11 have the same extent as the provisions amended.
(6) The repeals and revocations in Schedule 12 have the same extent as the provisions repealed or revoked.

462   Short title

This Act may be cited as the Proceeds of Crime Act 2002.

SCHEDULES

Section 1   SCHEDULE 1

ASSETS RECOVERY AGENCY

Director's terms of appointment

1   (1) The Director holds office for the period determined by the Secretary of State on his appointment (or re-appointment) to the office.
     (2) But—
          (a) the Director may at any time resign by giving notice to the Secretary of State;
          (b) the Secretary of State may at any time remove the Director from office if satisfied that he is unable or unfit to exercise his functions.
2   Subject to that, the Director holds office on the terms determined by the Secretary of State with the approval of the Minister for the Civil Service.

Staff

3   (1) The members of staff of the Agency must include—
          (a) a deputy to the Director who is to act as Director during any vacancy in that office or if the Director is absent, subject to suspension or unable to act, and
          (b) an assistant to the Director with responsibilities in relation to the exercise of the Director's functions in Northern Ireland.

(2) But the Director must not appoint a person under sub-paragraph (1)(b) unless he first consults the Secretary of State.

4   The members of staff of the Agency hold office on the terms determined by the Director with the approval of the Minister for the Civil Service.

Finances

5   (1) These amounts are to be paid out of money provided by Parliament—
      (a) the remuneration of the Director and the staff of the Agency;
      (b) any expenses incurred by the Director or any of the staff in the exercise of his or their functions.
      (2) Subject to anything in this Act any sums received by the Director are to be paid into the Consolidated Fund.

Annual plan

6   (1) The Director must, before the beginning of each financial year apart from the first, prepare a plan setting out how he intends to exercise his functions during the financial year (an annual plan).
      (2) The annual plan must, in particular, set out how the Director intends to exercise his functions in Northern Ireland.
      (3) The annual plan must also include a statement of—
      (a) the Director's objectives for the financial year;
      (b) any performance targets which he has for the financial year (whether or not relating to his objectives);
      (c) his priorities for the financial year;
      (d) the financial resources expected to be available to him for the financial year;
      (e) his proposed allocation of those resources.
      (4) Once the annual plan has been prepared the Director must send a copy to the Secretary of State for his approval.
      (5) If the Secretary of State does not approve the annual plan—
      (a) he must give the Director his reasons for not approving it, and
      (b) he may require the Director to revise it in the manner specified by the Secretary of State.
      (6) The Director must revise the annual plan, but if sub-paragraph (5)(b) applies he must do so in the manner specified by the Secretary of State.
      (7) The Director must send a copy of the revised annual plan to the Secretary of State for his approval.

Annual report

7   (1) The Director must, as soon as possible after the end of each financial year, prepare a report on how he has exercised his functions during the financial year.
      (2) The report for any financial year apart from the first must include—
      (a) the Director's annual plan for the financial year, and
      (b) an assessment of the extent to which it has been carried out.
      (3) The Director must send a copy of each report to the Secretary of State who must—
      (a) lay a copy of it before each House of Parliament, and
      (b) arrange for it to be published.

Meaning of "financial year"

8   In this Schedule "financial year" means—
      (a) the period beginning with the day on which section 1 comes into force and ending with the next 31 March (which is the first financial year), and
      (b) each subsequent period of twelve months beginning with 1 April.

Section 75   SCHEDULE 2

LIFESTYLE OFFENCES: ENGLAND AND WALES

Drug trafficking

1   (1) An offence under any of the following provisions of the Misuse of Drugs Act 1971
       (c. 38)—
          (a) section 4(2) or (3) (unlawful production or supply of controlled drugs);
          (b) section 5(3) (possession of controlled drug with intent to supply);
          (c) section 8 (permitting certain activities relating to controlled drugs);
          (d) section 20 (assisting in or inducing the commission outside the UK of an offence
              punishable under a corresponding law).
      (2) An offence under any of the following provisions of the Customs and Excise Manage-
          ment Act 1979 (c. 2) if it is committed in connection with a prohibition or restriction on
          importation or exportation which has effect by virtue of section 3 of the Misuse of
          Drugs Act 1971—
          (a) section 50(2) or (3) (improper importation of goods);
          (b) section 68(2) (exploration of prohibited or restricted goods);
          (c) section 170 (fraudulent evasion).
      (3) An offence under either of the following provisions of the Criminal Justice (Inter-
          national Co-operation) Act 1990 (c. 5)—
          (a) section 12 (manufacture or supply of a substance for the time being specified in
              Schedule 2 to that Act);
          (b) section 19 (using a ship for illicit traffic in controlled drugs).

Money laundering

2   An offence under either of the following provisions of this Act—
          (a) section 327 (concealing etc criminal property);
          (b) section 328 (assisting another to retain criminal property).

Directing terrorism

3   An offence under section 56 of the Terrorism Act 2000 (c. 11) (directing the activities of
        a terrorist organisation).

People trafficking

4   An offence under section 25(1) of the Immigration Act 1971 (c. 77) (assisting illegal
        entry etc).

Arms trafficking

5   (1) An offence under either of the following provisions of the Customs and Excise Man-
         agement Act 1979 if it is committed in connection with a firearm or ammunition—
          (a) section 68(2) (exportation of prohibited goods);
          (b) section 170 (fraudulent evasion).
      (2) An offence under section 3(1) of the Firearms Act 1968 (c. 27) (dealing in firearms or
          ammunition by way of trade or business).
      (3) In this paragraph "firearm" and "ammunition" have the same meanings as in section 57
          of the Firearms Act 1968 (c. 27).

Counterfeiting

6   An offence under any of the following provisions of the Forgery and Counterfeiting
        Act 1981 (c. 45)—
          (a) section 14 (making counterfeit notes or coins);
          (b) section 15 (passing etc counterfeit notes or coins);
          (c) section 16 (having counterfeit notes or coins);
          (d) section 17 (making or possessing materials or equipment for counterfeiting).

Intellectual property

7   (1) An offence under any of the following provisions of the Copyright, Designs and Patents
         Act 1988 (c. 48)—
          (a) section 107(1) (making or dealing in an article which infringes copyright);

(b) section 107(2) (making or possessing an article designed or adapted for making a copy of a copyright work);

(c) section 198(1) (making or dealing in an illicit recording);

(d) section 297A (making or dealing in unauthorised decoders).

(2) An offence under section 92(1), (2) or (3) of the Trade Marks Act 1994 (c. 26) (unauthorised use etc of trade mark).

Pimps and brothels

8   (1) An offence under any of the following provisions of the Sexual Offences Act 1956 (c. 69)—

(a) section 2 (procuring a woman by threats);

(b) section 3 (procuring a woman by false pretences);

(c) section 9 (procuring a defective woman to have sexual intercourse);

(d) section 22 (procuring a woman for prostitution);

(e) section 24 (detaining a woman in a brothel);

(f) section 28 (causing or encouraging prostitution etc of girl under 16);

(g) section 29 (causing or encouraging prostitution of defective woman);

(h) section 30 (man living on earnings of prostitution);

(i) section 31 (woman exercising control over prostitute);

(j) section 33 (keeping a brothel);

(k) section 34 (letting premises for use as brothel).

(2) An offence under section 5 of the Sexual Offences Act 1967 (c. 60) (living on the earnings of male prostitute).

Blackmail

9   An offence under section 21 of the Theft Act 1968 (c. 60) (blackmail).

Inchoate offences

10   (1) An offence of attempting, conspiring or inciting the commission of an offence specified in this Schedule.

(2) An offence of aiding, abetting, counselling or procuring the commission of such an offence.

Section 137   SCHEDULE 3

ADMINISTRATORS: FURTHER PROVISION

General

1   In this Schedule, unless otherwise expressly provided—

(a) references to an administrator are to an administrator appointed under section 125 or 128(3);

(b) references to realisable property are to the realisable property in respect of which the administrator is appointed.

Appointment etc

2   (1) If the office of administrator is vacant, for whatever reason, the court must appoint a new administrator.

(2) Any property vested in the previous administrator by virtue of paragraph 5(4) vests in the new administrator.

(3) Any order under section 125 or 128(7) in relation to the previous administrator applies in relation to the new administrator when he gives written notice of his appointment to the person subject to the order.

(4) The administration of property by an administrator must be treated as continuous despite any temporary vacancy in that office.

(5) The appointment of an administrator is subject to such conditions as to caution as the accountant of court may impose.

(6) The premium of any bond of caution or other security required by such conditions must be treated as part of the administrator's expenses in the exercise of his functions.

Functions

3   (1) An administrator—

(a) may, if appointed under section 125, and

(b) must, if appointed under section 128(3),

as soon as practicable take possession of the realisable property and of the documents mentioned in sub-paragraph (2).

(2) Those documents are any document which—

    (a) is in the possession or control of the person ("A") in whom the property is vested (or would be vested but for an order made under paragraph 5(4)), and

    (b) relates to the property or to A's assets, business or financial affairs.

(3) An administrator is entitled to have access to, and to copy, any document relating to the property or to A's assets, business or financial affairs and not falling within sub-paragraph (2)(a).

(4) An administrator may bring, defend or continue any legal proceedings relating to the property.

(5) An administrator may borrow money so far as it is necessary to do so to safeguard the property and may for the purposes of such borrowing create a security over any part of the property.

(6) An administrator may, if he considers that it would be beneficial for the management or realisation of the property—

    (a) carry on any business of A;

    (b) exercise any right of A as holder of securities in a company;

    (c) grant a lease of the property or take on lease any other property;

    (d) enter into any contract, or execute any deed, as regards the property or as regards A's business.

(7) An administrator may, where any right, option or other power forms part of A's estate, make payments or incur liabilities with a view to—

    (a) obtaining property which is the subject of, or

    (b) maintaining,

the right, option or power.

(8) An administrator may effect or maintain insurance policies as regards the property on A's business.

(9) An administrator may, if appointed under section 128(3), complete any uncompleted title which A has to any heritable estate; but completion of title in A's name does not validate by accretion any unperfected right in favour of any person other than the administrator.

(10) An administrator may sell, purchase or exchange property or discharge any security for an obligation due to A; but it is incompetent for the administrator or an associate of his (within the meaning of section 74 of the Bankruptcy (Scotland) Act 1985 (c. 66)) to purchase any of A's property in pursuance of this sub-paragraph.

(11) An administrator may claim, vote and draw dividends in the sequestration of the estate (or bankruptcy or liquidation) of a debtor of A and may accede to a voluntary trust deed for creditors of such a debtor.

(12) An administrator may discharge any of his functions through agents or employees, but is personally liable to meet the fees and expenses of any such agent or employee out of such remuneration as is payable to the administrator on a determination by the accountant of court.

(13) An administrator may take such professional advice as he considers necessary in connection with the exercise of his functions.

(14) An administrator may at any time apply to the court for directions as regards the exercise of his functions.

(15) An administrator may exercise any power specifically conferred on him by the court, whether conferred on his appointment or subsequently.

(16) An administrator may—

    (a) enter any premises;

    (b) search for or inspect anything authorised by the court;

    (c) make or obtain a copy, photograph or other record of anything so authorised;

    (d) remove anything which the administrator is required or authorised to take possession of in pursuance of an order of the court.

(17) An administrator may do anything incidental to the powers and duties listed in the previous provisions of this paragraph.

Consent of accountant of court

4   An administrator proposing to exercise any power conferred by paragraph 3(4) to (17) must first obtain the consent of the accountant of court.

Dealings in good faith with administrator

5   (1) a person dealing with an administrator in good faith and for value is not concerned to enquire whether the administrator is acting within the powers mentioned in paragraph 3.

     (2) Sub-paragraph (1) does not apply where the administrator or an associate purchases property in contravention of paragraph 3(10).

     (3) The validity of any title is not challengeable by reason only of the administrator having acted outwith the powers mentioned in paragraph 3.

     (4) The exercise of a power mentioned in paragraph 3(4) to (11) must be in A's name except where and in so far as an order made by the court under this sub-paragraph vests the property in the administrator (or in a previous administrator).

     (5) The court may make an order under sub-paragraph (4) on the application of the administrator or on its own motion.

Money received by administrator

6   (1) All money received by an administrator in the exercise of his functions must be deposited by him, in the name (unless vested in the administrator by virtue of paragraph 5(4)) of the holder of the property realised, in an appropriate bank or institution.

     (2) But the administrator may at any time retain in his hands a sum not exceeding £200 or such other sum as may be prescribed by the Scottish Ministers by regulations.

     (3) In sub-paragraph (1), "appropriate bank or institution" means a bank or institution mentioned in section 3(1) of the Banking Act 1987 (c. 22) or for the time being specified in Schedule 2 to that Act.

Effect of appointment of administrator on diligence

7   (1) An arrestment of poinding of realisable property executed on or after the appointment of an administrator does not create a preference for the arrester or poinder.

     (2) Any realisable property so arrested or poinded, or (if the property has been sold) the proceeds of sale, must be handed over to the administrator.

     (3) A poinding of the ground in respect of realisable property on or after such appointment is ineffectual in a question with the administrator except for the interest mentioned in sub-paragraph (4).

     (4) That interest is—

       (a) interest on the debt of a secured creditor for the current half-yearly term, and

       (b) arrears of interest on that debt for one year immediately before the commencement of that term.

     (5) On and after such appointment no other person may raise or insist in an adjudication against realisable property or be confirmed as executor-creditor on that property.

     (6) an inhibition on realisable property which takes effect on or after such appointment does not create a preference for the inhibitor in a question with the administrator.

     (7) This paragraph is without prejudice to sections 123 and 124.

     (8) In this paragraph, the reference to an administrator is to an administrator appointed under section 128(3).

Supervision

8   (1) If the accountant of court reports to the court that an administrator has failed to perform any duty imposed on him, the court may, after giving the administrator an opportunity to be heard as regards the matter—

       (a) remove him from office,

       (b) censure him, or

       (c) make such other order as it thinks fit.

     (2) Section 6 of the Judicial Factors (Scotland) Act 1889 (c. 39) (supervision of judicial factors) does not apply in relation to an administrator.

Accounts and remuneration

9   (1) Not later than two weeks after the issuing of any determination by the accountant of court as to the remuneration and expenses payable to the administrator, the administrator or the Lord Advocate may appeal against it to the court.

(2) The amount of remuneration payable to the administrator must be determined on the basis of the value of the work reasonably undertaken by him, regard being had to the extent of the responsibilities involved.

(3) The accountant of court may authorise the administrator to pay without taxation an account in respect of legal services incurred by the administrator.

Discharge of administrator

10 (1) After an administrator has lodged his final accounts under paragraph 9(1), he may apply to the accountant of court to be discharged from office.

(2) A discharge, if granted, frees the administrator from all liability (other than liability arising from fraud) in respect of any act or omission of his in exercising his functions as administrator.

Section 142   SCHEDULE 4

LIFESTYLE OFFENCES: SCOTLAND

Money laundering

1   An offence under either of the following provisions of this Act—
         (a) section 327 (concealing etc. criminal property);
         (b) section 328 (assisting another person to retain criminal property).

Drug trafficking

2 (1) An offence under any of the following provisions of the Misuse of Drugs Act 1971 (c. 38)—
         (a) section 4(2) or (3) (unlawful production or supply of controlled drugs);
         (b) section 5(3) (possession of controlled drug with intent to supply);
         (c) section 8 (permitting certain activities relating to controlled drugs);
         (d) section 20 (assisting in or inducing the commission outside the UK of an offence punishable under a corresponding law).

(2) An offence under any of the following provisions of the Customs and Excise Management Act 1979 (c. 2) if it is committed in connection with a prohibition or restriction on importation or exportation which has effect by virtue of section 3 of the Misuse of Drugs Act 1971—
         (a) section 50(2) or (3) (improper importation of goods);
         (b) section 68(2) (exploration of prohibited or restricted goods);
         (c) section 170 (fraudulent evasion).

(3) An offence under either of the following provisions of the Criminal Justice (International Co-operation) Act 1990 (c. 5)—
         (a) section 12 (manufacture or supply of a substance for the time being specified in Schedule 2 to that Act);
         (b) section 19 (using a ship for illicit traffic in controlled drugs).

Directing terrorism

3   An offence under section 56 of the Terrorism Act 2000 (c. 11) (directing the activities of a terrorist organisation).

People trafficking

4   An offence under section 25(1) of the Immigration Act 1971 (c. 77) (assisting illegal entry etc).

Arms trafficking

5 (1) An offence under either of the following provisions of the Customs and Excise Management Act 1979 if it is committed in connection with a firearm or ammunition—
         (a) section 68(2) (exportation of prohibited goods);

(b) section 170 (fraudulent evasion).
(2) An offence under section 3(1) of the Firearms Act 1968 (c. 27) (dealing in firearms or ammunition by way of trade or business).
(3) In this paragraph "firearm" and "ammunition" have the same meanings as in section 57 of the Firearms Act 1968 (c. 27).

Counterfeiting

6   An offence under any of the following provisions of the Forgery and Counterfeiting Act 1981 (c. 45)—
        (a) section 14 (making counterfeit notes or coins);
        (b) section 15 (passing etc counterfeit notes or coins);
        (c) section 16 (having counterfeit notes or coins);
        (d) section 17 (making or possessing materials or equipment for counterfeiting).

Intellectual property

7   (1) An offence under any of the following provisions of the Copyright, Designs and Patents Act 1988 (c. 48)—
        (a) section 107(1) (making or dealing in an article which infringes copyright);
        (b) section 107(2) (making or possessing an article designed or adapted for making a copy of a copyright work);
        (c) section 198(1) (making or dealing in an illicit recording);
        (d) section 297A (making or dealing in unauthorised decoders).
   (2) An offence under section 92(1), (2), or (3) of the Trade Marks Act 1994 (c. 26) (unauthorised use etc of trade mark).

Pimps and brothels

8   An offence under either of the following provisions of the Criminal Law (Consolidation) (Scotland) Act 1995 (c. 39)—
        (a) section 11(1) (living on earnings of prostitution or soliciting for immoral purposes);
        (b) section 11(5) (running of brothels).

Blackmail

9   An offence of blackmail or extortion.

Inchoate offences

10   (1) An offence of conspiring or inciting the commission of an offence specified in this Schedule.
   (2) An offence of aiding, abetting, counselling or procuring the commission of such an offence.

Section 223   SCHEDULE 5

Lifestyle offences: Northern Ireland

Drug trafficking

1   (1) An offence under any of the following provisions of the Misuse of Drugs Act 1971 (c. 38)—
        (a) section 4(2) or (3) (unlawful production or supply of controlled drugs);
        (b) section 5(3) (possession of controlled drug with intent to supply);
        (c) section 8 (permitting certain activities relating to controlled drugs);
        (d) section 20 (assisting in or inducing the commission outside the UK of an offence punishable under a corresponding law).
   (2) An offence under any of the following provisions of the Customs and Excise Management Act 1979 (c. 2) if it is committed in connection with a prohibition or restriction on importation or exportation which has effect by virtue of section 3 of the Misuse of Drugs Act 1971—
        (a) section 50(2) or (3) (improper importation of goods);
        (b) section 68(2) (exportation of prohibited or restricted goods);
        (c) section 170 (fraudulent evasion).
   (3) An offence under either of the following provisions of the Criminal Justice (International Co-operation) Act 1990 (c. 5)—

    (a) section 12 (manufacture or supply of a substance for the time being specified in Schedule 2 to that Act);

    (b) section 19 (using a ship for illicit traffic in controlled drugs).

Money laundering

2   An offence under either of the following provisions of this Act—

    (a) section 327 (concealing etc. criminal property);

    (b) section 328 (assisting another to retain criminal property).

Directing terrorism

3   An offence under section 56 of the Terrorism Act 2000 (c. 11) (directing the activities of a terrorist organisation).

People trafficking

4   An offence under section 25(1) of the Immigration Act 1971 (c. 77) (assisting illegal entry etc.).

Arms trafficking

5   (1) An offence under either of the following provisions of the Customs and Excise Management Act 1979 if it is committed in connection with a firearm or ammunition—

    (a) section 68(2) (exportation of prohibited goods);

    (b) section 170 (fraudulent evasion).

    (2) An offence under Article 4(1) of the Firearms (Northern Ireland) Order 1981 (S.I. 1981/155 (N.I. 2)) (dealing in firearms or ammunition by way of trade or business).

    (3) In this paragraph "firearm" and "ammunition" have the same meanings as in Article 2(2) of that Order.

Counterfeiting

6   An offence under any of the following provisions of the Forgery and Counterfeiting Act 1981 (c. 45)—

    (a) section 14 (making counterfeit notes or coins);

    (b) section 15 (passing etc counterfeit notes or coins);

    (c) section 16 (having counterfeit notes or coins);

    (d) section 17 (making or possessing materials or equipment for counterfeiting).

Intellectual property

7   (1) An offence under any of the following provisions of the Copyright, Designs and Patents Act 1988 (c. 48)—

    (a) section 107(1) (making or dealing in an article which infringes copyright);

    (b) section 107(2) (making or possessing an article designed or adapted for making a copy of a copyright work);

    (c) section 198(1) (making or dealing in an illicit recording);

    (d) section 297A (making or dealing in unauthorised decoders).

    (2) An offence under section 92(1), (2) or (3) of the Trade Marks Act 1994 (c. 26) (unauthorised use etc of trade mark).

Pimps and brothels

8   (1) An offence under any of the following provisions of the Criminal Law Amendment Act 1885 (c. 69)—

    (a) section 2 (procuring a woman or girl);

    (b) section 3 (procuring a woman or girl by threats or false pretences);

    (c) section 8 (detaining a woman in a brothel);

    (d) section 13(3) (letting premises for use as a brothel).

    (2) An offence under section 1(1) of the Vagrancy Act 1898 (c. 39) (man living on the earnings of prostitution).

    (3) An offence under that Act as extended by section 7(4) of the Criminal Law Amendment Act 1912 (c. 20) (woman exercising control over prostitute).

    (4) An offence under section 21 of the Children and Young Persons Act (Northern Ireland) 1968 (c. 34) (causing or encouraging prostitution etc of girl under 17).

    (5) An offence under Article 8 of the Homosexual Offences (Northern Ireland) Order 1982 (S.I. 1982/1536 (N.I. 19)) (living on the earnings of male prostitute).

    (6) An offence under Article 122(1)(b) or (c) of the Mental Health (Northern Ireland) Order 1986 (S.I. 1986/595 (N.I. 4)) (procuring or causing prostitution by woman suffering from severe mental handicap).

    (7) An offence of keeping a bawdy house.

Blackmail

9   An offence under section 20 of the Theft Act (Northern Ireland) 1969 (c. 16) (blackmail).

Inchoate offences

10 (1) An offence of attempting, conspiring or inciting the commission of an offence specified in this Schedule.

    (2) An offence of aiding, abetting, counselling or procuring the commission of such an offence.

Section 247 and 257   SCHEDULE 6

POWERS OF INTERIM RECEIVER OR ADMINISTRATOR

Seizure

1   Power to seize property to which the order applies.

Information

2 (1) Power to obtain information or to require a person to answer any question.

    (2) A requirement imposed in the exercise of the power has effect in spite of any restriction on the disclosure of information (however imposed).

    (3) An answer given by a person in pursuance of such a requirement may not be used in evidence against him in criminal proceedings.

    (4) Sub-paragraph (3) does not apply—

      (a) on a prosecution for an offence under section 5 of the Perjury Act 1911, section 44(2) of the Criminal Law (Consolidation) (Scotland) Act 1995 or Article 10 of the Perjury (Northern Ireland) Order 1979 (false statements), or

      (b) on a prosecution for some other offence where, in giving evidence, he makes a statement inconsistent with it.

    (5) But an answer may not be used by virtue of sub-paragraph (4)(b) against a person unless—

      (a) evidence relating to it is adduced, or

      (b) a question relating to it is asked,

    by him or on his behalf in the proceedings arising out of the prosecution.

Entry, search, etc.

3 (1) Power to—

      (a) enter any premises in the United Kingdom to which the interim order applies, and

      (b) take any of the following steps.

    (2) Those steps are—

      (a) to carry out a search for or inspection of anything described in the order,

      (b) to make or obtain a copy, photograph or other record of anything so described,

      (c) to remove anything which he is required to take possession of in pursuance of the order or which may be required as evidence in the proceedings under Chapter 2 of Part 5.

    (3) The order may describe anything generally, whether by reference to a class or otherwise.

Supplementary

4 (1) An order making any provision under paragraph 2 or 3 must make provision in respect of legal professional privilege (in Scotland, legal privilege within the meaning of Chapter 3 of Part 8).

    (2) An order making any provision under paragraph 3 may require any person—

      (a) to give the interim receiver or administrator access to any premises which he may enter in pursuance of paragraph 3,

      (b) to give the interim receiver or administrator any assistance he may require for taking the steps mentioned in that paragraph.

Management

5   (1) Power to manage any property to which the order applies.
     (2) Managing property includes—
         (a) selling or otherwise disposing of assets comprised in the property which are perish-
             able or which ought to be disposed of before their value diminishes,
         (b) where the property comprises assets of a trade or business, carrying on, or arrang-
             ing for another to carry on, the trade or business,
         (c) incurring capital expenditure in respect of the property.

Section 267   SCHEDULE 7

POWERS OF TRUSTEE FOR CIVIL RECOVERY

Sale

1   Power to sell the property or any part of it or interest in it.

Expenditure

2   Power to incur expenditure for the purpose of—
         (a) acquiring any part of the property, or any interest in it, which is not vested in him,
         (b) discharging any liabilities, or extinguishing any rights, to which the property is
             subject.

Management

3   (1) Power to manage property.
     (2) Managing property includes doing anything mentioned in paragraph 5(2) of Schedule
         6.

Legal proceedings

4   Power to start, carry on or defend any legal proceedings in respect of the property.

Compromise

5   Power to make any compromise or other arrangement in connection with any claim
         relating to the property.

Supplementary

6   (1) For the purposes of, or in connection with, the exercise of any of his powers—
         (a) power by his official name to do any of the things mentioned in sub-paragraph (2),
         (b) power to do any other act which is necessary or expedient.
     (2) Those things are—
         (a) holding property,
         (b) entering into contracts,
         (c) suing and being sued,
         (d) employing agents,
         (e) executing a power of attorney, deed or other instrument.

Section 325   SCHEDULE 8

FORMS OF DECLARATIONS

The Director

"I, A.B., do solemnly declare that I will not disclose any information received by me in
carrying out my functions under Part 6 of the Proceeds of Crime Act 2002 except for the
purposes of those functions or for the purposes of any prosecution for an offence relating to
inland revenue, or in such other cases as may be required or permitted by law."

Members of the staff of the Agency

"I, A.B., do solemnly declare that I will not disclose any information received by me in
carrying out the functions under Part 6 of the Proceeds of Crime Act 2002 which I may from

time to time be authorised by the Director of the Assets Recovery Agency to carry out except for the purposes of those functions, or to the Director or in accordance with his instructions, or for the purposes of any prosecution for an offence relating to inland revenue, or in such other cases as may be required or permitted by law."

GENERAL NOTE

This Schedule contains the forms of declarations which are, by s.325, required to be made as soon as practicable after appointment by the Director, and by every member of the staff of the Assets Recovery Agency who is authorised to carry out any of the Revenue functions from time to time vested in the Director. They both require that the Director, or Agency staff member, will not disclose any information received in carrying out the Revenue functions (the functions under Pt. 6 of the Act) except for the purposes of those functions, or for the purposes of any inland revenue prosecution or in such other cases as may be required or permitted by law. Additionally, the declaration to be made by a member of the Agency staff permits the disclosure of information received in carrying out the Revenue functions to the Director, or in accordance with his instructions.

Section 330   SCHEDULE 9

REGULATED SECTOR AND SUPERVISORY AUTHORITIES

PART 1

REGULATED SECTOR

Business in the regulated sector

1   (1) A business is in the regulated sector to the extent that it engages in any of the following activities—
(a) accepting deposits by a person with permission under Part 4 of the Financial Services and Markets Act 2000 (c. 8) to accept deposits (including, in the case of a building society, the raising of money from members of the society by the issue of shares);
(b) the business of the National Savings Bank;
(c) business carried on by a credit union;
(d) any home-regulated activity carried on by a European institution in respect of which the establishment conditions in paragraph 13 of Schedule 3 to the Financial Services and Markets Act 2000, or the service conditions in paragraph 14 of that Schedule, are satisfied;
(e) any activity carried on for the purpose of raising money authorised to be raised under the National Loans Act 1968 (c. 13) under the auspices of the Director of Savings;
(f) the activity of operating a bureau de change, transmitting money (or any representation of monetary value) by any means or cashing cheques which are made payable to customers;
(g) any activity falling within sub-paragraph (2);
(h) any of the activities in points 1 to 12 or 14 of Annex 1 to the Banking Consolidation Directive, ignoring an activity described in any of sub-paragraphs (a) to (g) above;
(i) business which consists of effecting or carrying out contracts of long term insurance by a person who has received official authorisation pursuant to Article 6 or 27 of the First Life Directive.
(2) An activity falls within this sub-paragraph if it constitutes any of the following kinds of regulated activity in the United Kingdom—
(a) dealing in investments as principal or as agent;
(b) arranging deals in investments;
(c) managing investments;
(d) safeguarding and administering investments;
(e) sending dematerialised instructions;
(f) establishing (and taking other steps in relation to) collective investment schemes;
(g) advising on investments.

(3) Paragraphs (a) and (i) of sub-paragraph (1) and sub-paragraph (2) must be read with section 22 of the Financial Services and Markets Act 2000, any relevant order under that section and Schedule 2 to that Act.

2 (1) This paragraph has effect for the purposes of paragraph 1.

(2) "Building society" has the meaning given by the Building Societies Act 1986 (c. 53).

(3) "Credit union" has the meaning given by the Credit Unions Act 1979 (c. 34) or the Credit Unions (Northern Ireland) Order 1985 (S.I. 1985/1205 (N.I. 12)).

(4) "European institution" means an EEA firm of the kind mentioned in paragraph 5(b) or (c) of Schedule 3 to the Financial Services and Markets Act 2000 (c. 8) which qualifies for authorisation for the purposes of that Act under paragraph 12 of that Schedule.

(5) "Home-regulated activity" in relation to a European institution, means an activity—

   (a) which is specified in Annex 1 to the Banking Consolidation Directive and in respect of which a supervisory authority in the home State of the institution has regulatory functions, and

   (b) if the institution is an EEA firm of the kind mentioned in paragraph 5(c) of Schedule 3 to the Financial Services and Markets Act 2000, which the institution carries on in its home State.

(6) "Home State", in relation to a person incorporated in or formed under the law of another member State, means that State.

(7) The Banking Consolidation Directive is the Directive of the European Parliament and Council relating to the taking up and pursuit of the business of credit institutions (No. 2000/12 EC).

(8) The First Life Directive is the First Council Directive on the co-ordination of laws, regulations and administrative provisions relating to the taking up and pursuit of the business of direct life assurance (No. 79/267/EEC).

Excluded activities

3 A business is not in the regulated sector to the extent that it engages in any of the following activities—

   (a) the issue of withdrawable share capital within the limit set by section 6 of the Industrial and Provident Societies Act 1965 (c. 12) by a society registered under that Act;

   (b) the acceptance of deposits from the public within the limit set by section 7(3) of that Act by such a society;

   (c) the issue of withdrawable share capital within the limit set by section 6 of the Industrial and Provident Societies Act (Northern Ireland) 1969 by a society registered under that Act;

   (d) the acceptance of deposits from the public within the limit set by section 7(3) of that Act by such a society;

   (e) activities carried on by the Bank of England;

   (f) any activity in respect of which an exemption order under section 38 of the Financial Services and Markets Act 2000 has effect if it is carried on by a person who is for the time being specified in the order or falls within a class of persons so specified.

PART 2

SUPERVISORY AUTHORITIES

4 (1) Each of the following is a supervisory authority—

   (a) the Bank of England;

   (b) the Financial Services Authority;

   (c) the Council of Lloyd's;

   (d) the Director General of Fair Trading;

   (e) a body which is a designated professional body for the purposes of Part 20 of the Financial Services and Markets Act 2000 (c. 8).

(2) The Secretary of State is also a supervisory authority in the exercise, in relation to a person carrying on a business in the regulated sector, of his functions under the enactments relating to companies or insolvency or under the Financial Services and Markets Act 2000.

(3) The Treasury are also a supervisory authority in the exercise, in relation to a person carrying on a business in the regulated sector, of their functions under the enactments relating to companies or insolvency or under the Financial Services and Markets Act 2000.

PART 3

POWER TO AMEND

5   The Treasury may by order amend Part 1 or 2 of this Schedule.

Section 448   SCHEDULE 10

TAX

PART 1

GENERAL

1   Sections 75 and 77 of the Taxes Management Act 1970 (c. 9) (receivers: income tax and
         capital gains tax) shall not apply in relation to—
         (a) a receiver appointed under section 48, 50 or 52;
         (b) an administrator appointed under section 125 or 128;
         (c) a receiver appointed under section 196, 198 or 200;
         (d) an interim receiver appointed under section 246;
         (e) an interim administrator appointed under section 256.

PART 2

PROVISIONS RELATING TO PART 5

INTRODUCTORY

2   (1) The vesting of property in the trustee for civil recovery or any other person by a recov-
         ery order or in pursuance of an order under section 276 is referred to as a Part 5 transfer.
     (2) The person who holds the property immediately before the vesting is referred to as the
         transferor; and the person in whom the property is vested is referred to as the
         transferee.
     (3) Any amount paid in respect of the transfer by the trustee for civil recovery, or another,
         to a person who holds the property immediately before the vesting is referred to (in
         relation to that person) as a compensating payment.
     (4) If the recovery order provides or (as the case may be) the terms on which the order
         under section 276 is made provide for the creation of any interest in favour of a person
         who holds the property immediately before the vesting, he is to be treated instead as
         receiving (in addition to any payment referred to in sub-paragraph (3)) a compensating
         payment of an amount equal to the value of the interest.
     (5) Where the property belongs to joint tenants immediately before the vesting and a com-
         pensating payment is made to one or more (but not both or all) of the joint tenants, this
         Part has effect separately in relation to each joint tenant.
     (6) Expressions used in this paragraph have the same meaning as in Part 5 of this Act.
     (7) "The Taxes Act 1988" means the Income and Corporation Taxes Act 1988 (c. 1), and
         "the Allowances Act 2001" means the Capital Allowances Act 2001 (c. 2).
     (8) This paragraph applies for the purposes of this Part.

CAPITAL GAINS TAX

3   (1) If a gain attributable to a Part 5 transfer accrues to the transferor, it is not a chargeable
         gain.
     (2) But if a compensating payment is made to the transferor—
         (a) sub-paragraph (1) does not apply, and
         (b) the consideration for the transfer is the amount of the compensating payment.
     (3) If a gain attributable to the forfeiture under section 298 of property consisting of—
         (a) notes or coins in any currency other than sterling,
         (b) anything mentioned in section 289(6)(b) to (d), if expressed in any currency other
              than sterling, or

(c) bearer bonds or bearer shares,

accrues to the person who holds the property immediately before the forfeiture, it is not a chargeable gain.

(4) This paragraph has effect as if it were included in Chapter 1 of Part 2 of the Taxation of Chargeable Gains Act 1992 (c. 12).

INCOME TAX AND CORPORATION TAX

Accrued income scheme

4   If a Part 5 transfer is a transfer of securities within the meaning of sections 711 to 728 of the Taxes Act 1988 (transfers with or without accrued interest), sections 713(2) and (3) and 716 of that Act do not apply to the transfer.

Discounted securities

5   In the case of a Part 5 transfer of property consisting of a relevant discounted security (within the meaning of Schedule 13 to the Finance Act 1996 (c. 8)), it is not to be treated as a transfer for the purposes of that Schedule.

Rights to receive amounts stated in certificates of deposit etc.

6   In the case of a Part 5 transfer of property consisting of a right to which section 56(2) of the Taxes Act 1988 applies, or a right mentioned in section 56A(1) of that Act, (rights stated in certificates of deposit etc.) it is not to be treated as a disposal of the right for the purposes of section 56(2) of that Act.

Non-qualifying offshore funds

7   In the case of a Part 5 transfer of property consisting of an asset mentioned in section 757(1)(a) or (b) of the Taxes Act 1988 (interests in non-qualifying offshore funds etc.), it is not to be treated as a disposal for the purposes of that section.

Futures and options

8   In the case of a Part 5 transfer of property consisting of futures or options (within the meaning of paragraph 4 of Schedule 5AA to the Taxes Act 1988), it is not to be treated as a disposal of the futures or options for the purposes of that Schedule.

Loan relationships

9   (1) Sub-paragraph (2) applies if, apart from this paragraph, a Part 5 transfer would be a related transaction for the purposes of section 84 of the Finance Act 1996 (c. 8) (debits and credits brought into account for the purpose of taxing loan relationships under Chapter 2 of Part 4 of that Act).

(2) The Part 5 transfer is to be disregarded for the purposes of that Chapter, except for the purpose of identifying any person in whose case any debit or credit not relating to the transaction is to be brought into account.

Exception from paragraphs 4 to 9

10   Paragraphs 4 to 9 do not apply if a compensating payment is made to the transferor.

Trading stock

11 (1) Sub-paragraph (2) applies, in the case of a Part 5 transfer of property consisting of the trading stock of a trade, for the purpose of computing any profits of the trade for tax purposes.

(2) If, because of the transfer, the trading stock is to be treated for that purpose as if it had been sold in the course of the trade, the amount realised on the sale is to be treated for that purpose as equal to its acquisition cost.

(3) Sub-paragraph (2) has effect in spite of anything in section 100 of the Taxes Act 1988 (valuation of trading stock at discontinuance).

(4) In this paragraph, trading stock and trade have the same meaning as in that section.

CAPITAL ALLOWANCES

Plant and machinery

12 (1) If there is a Part 5 transfer of plant or machinery, Part 2 of the Allowances Act 2001 is to have effect as if a transferor who has incurred qualifying expenditure were required to

bring the disposal value of the plant or machinery into account in accordance with section 61 of that Act for the chargeable period in which the transfer occurs.

(2) But the Part 5 transfer is not to be treated as a disposal event for the purposes of Part 2 of that Act other than by virtue of sub-paragraph (1).

13 (1) If a compensating payment is made to the transferor, the disposal value to be brought into account is the amount of the payment.

(2) Otherwise, the disposal value to be brought into account is the amount which would give rise neither to a balancing allowance nor to a balancing charge.

14 (1) Paragraph 13(2) does not apply if the qualifying expenditure has been allocated to the main pool or a class pool.

(2) Instead, the disposal value to be brought into account is the notional written-down value of the qualifying expenditure incurred by the transferor on the provision of the plant or machinery.

(3) The notional written-down value is—

$$QE - A$$

where—

QE is the qualifying expenditure incurred by the transferor on the provision of the plant or machinery,

A is the total of all allowances which could have been made to the transferor in respect of the expenditure if—

(a) that expenditure had been the only expenditure that had ever been taken into account in determining his available qualifying expenditure, and

(b) all allowances had been made in full.

(4) But if—

(a) the Part 5 transfer of the plant or machinery occurs in the same chargeable period as that in which the qualifying expenditure is incurred, and

(b) a first-year allowance is made in respect of an amount of the expenditure,

the disposal value to be brought into account is that which is equal to the balance left after deducting the first year allowance.

15 (1) Paragraph 13 does not apply if—

(a) a qualifying activity is carried on in partnership,

(b) the Part 5 transfer is a transfer of plant or machinery which is partnership property, and

(c) compensating payments are made to one or more, but not both or all, of the partners.

(2) Instead, the disposal value to be brought into account is the sum of—

(a) any compensating payments made to any of the partners, and

(b) in the case of each partner to whom a compensating payment has not been made, his share of the tax-neutral amount.

(3) A partner's share of the tax-neutral amount is to be determined according to the profit-sharing arrangements for the twelve months ending immediately before the date of the Part 5 transfer.

16 (1) Paragraph 13 does not apply if—

(a) a qualifying activity is carried on in partnership,

(b) the Part 5 transfer is a transfer of plant or machinery which is not partnership property but is owned by two or more of the partners ("the owners"),

(c) the plant or machinery is used for the purposes of the qualifying activity, and

(d) compensating payments are made to one or more, but not both or all, of the owners.

(2) Instead, the disposal value to be brought into account is the sum of—

(a) any compensating payments made to any of the owners, and

(b) in the case of each owner to whom a compensating payment has not been made, his share of the tax-neutral amount.

(3) An owner's share of the tax-neutral amount is to be determined in proportion to the value of his interest in the plant or machinery.

17 (1) Paragraphs 12 to 16 have effect as if they were included in section 61 of the Allowances Act 2001.

(2) In paragraphs 15 and 16, the tax-neutral amount is the amount that would be brought into account as the disposal value under paragraph 13(2) or (as the case may be) 14 if the provision in question were not disapplied.

Industrial buildings

18 (1) If there is a Part 5 transfer of a relevant interest in an industrial building, Part 3 of the Allowances Act 2001 is to have effect as if the transfer were a balancing event within section 315(1) of that Act.

(2) But the Part 5 transfer is not to be treated as a balancing event for the purposes of Part 3 of that Act other than by virtue of sub-paragraph (1).

19 (1) If a compensating payment is made to the transferor, the proceeds from the balancing event are the amount of the payment.

(2) Otherwise—

(a) the proceeds from the balancing event are the amount which is equal to the residue of qualifying expenditure immediately before the transfer, and

(b) no balancing adjustment is to be made as a result of the event under section 319 of the Allowances Act 2001.

20 (1) Paragraph 19 does not apply to determine the proceeds from the balancing event if—

(a) the relevant interest in the industrial building is partnership property, and

(b) compensating payments are made to one or more, but not both or all, of the partners.

(2) Instead, the proceeds from the balancing event are the sum of—

(a) any compensating payments made to any of the partners, and

(b) in the case of each partner to whom a compensating payment has not been made, his share of the amount which is equal to the residue of qualifying expenditure immediately before the Part 5 transfer.

(3) A partner's share of that amount is to be determined according to the profit-sharing arrangements for the twelve months ending immediately before the date of the Part 5 transfer.

21 Paragraphs 18 to 20 have effect as if they were included in Part 3 of the Allowances Act 2001.

Flat conversion

22 (1) If there is a Part 5 transfer of a relevant interest in a flat, Part 4A of the Allowances Act 2001 is to have effect as if the transfer were a balancing event within section 393N of that Act.

(2) But the Part 5 transfer is not to be treated as a balancing event for the purposes of Part 4A of that Act other than by virtue of sub-paragraph (1).

23 (1) If a compensating payment is made to the transferor, the proceeds from the balancing event are the amount of the payment.

(2) Otherwise, the proceeds from the balancing event are the amount which is equal to the residue of qualifying expenditure immediately before the transfer.

24 (1) Paragraph 23 does not apply to determine the proceeds from the balancing event if—

(a) the relevant interest in the flat is partnership property, and

(b) compensating payments are made to one or more, but not both or all, of the partners.

(2) Instead, the proceeds from the balancing event are the sum of—

(a) any compensating payments made to any of the partners, and

(b) in the case of each partner to whom a compensating payment has not been made, his share of the amount which is equal to the residue of qualifying expenditure immediately before the transfer.

(3) A partner's share of that amount is to be determined according to the profit-sharing arrangements for the twelve months ending immediately before the date of the transfer.

25 Paragraphs 22 to 24 have effect as if they were included in Part 4A of the Allowances Act 2001.

Research and development

26 If there is a Part 5 transfer of an asset representing qualifying expenditure incurred by a person, the disposal value he is required to bring into account under section 443(1) of the Allowances Act 2001 for any chargeable period is to be determined as follows (and not in accordance with subsection (4) of that section).

27 (1) If a compensating payment is made to the transferor, the disposal value he is required to bring into account is the amount of the payment.

(2) Otherwise, the disposal value he is required to bring into account is nil.

28 (1) Paragraph 27 does not apply to determine the disposal value to be brought into account if—

(a) the asset is partnership property, and

(b) compensating payments are made to one or more, but not both or all, of the partners.

(2) Instead, the disposal value to be brought into account is equal to the sum of any compensating payments.

29 Paragraphs 26 to 28 have effect as if they were included in Part 6 of the Allowances Act 2001.

EMPLOYEE ETC. SHARE SCHEMES

Share options

30 Section 135(6) of the Taxes Act 1988 (gains by directors and employees) does not make any person chargeable to tax in respect of any gain realised by the trustee for civil recovery.

Conditional acquisition of shares

31 Section 140A(4) of the Taxes Act 1988 (disposal etc. of shares) does not make the transferor chargeable to income tax in respect of a Part 5 transfer of shares or an interest in shares.

Shares acquired at an undervalue

32 Section 162(5) of the Taxes Act 1988 (employee shareholdings) does not make the transferor chargeable to income tax in respect of a Part 5 transfer of shares.

Shares in dependent subsidiaries

33 Section 79 of the Finance Act 1988 (c. 39) (charge on increase in value of shares) does not make the transferor chargeable to income tax in respect of a Part 5 transfer of shares or an interest in shares.

Section 456   SCHEDULE 11

AMENDMENTS

Introduction

1 The amendments specified in this Schedule shall have effect.

Parliamentary Commissioner Act 1967 (c. 13)

2 (1) The Parliamentary Commissioner Act 1967 is amended as follows.

(2) In Schedule 2 (Departments etc. subject to investigation) at the appropriate place insert—

"Director of the Assets Recovery Agency."

(3) In the Notes to that Schedule before paragraph 1 insert—

"A1 In the case of the Director of the Assets Recovery Agency an investigation under this Act may be conducted only in respect of the exercise of functions vested in him by virtue of a notice served on the Commissioners of Inland Revenue under section 317(2), 321(2) or 322(2) of the Proceeds of Crime Act 2002 (Inland Revenue functions)."

Police (Scotland) Act 1967 (c. 77)

3 (1) The Police (Scotland) Act 1967 is amended as follows.

(2) In section 38(3B)(liability of Scottish Ministers for constables on central service) after "central service" insert "or on temporary service as mentioned in section 38A(1)(aa) of this Act".

(3) In section 38A(1) (meaning of "relevant service") after paragraph (a) insert—

"(aa) temporary service with the Scottish Ministers in connection with their functions under Part 5 or 8 of the Proceeds of Crime Act 2002, on which a person is engaged with the consent of the appropriate authority;".

Criminal Appeal Act 1968 (c. 19)

4 (1) The Criminal Appeal Act 1968 is amended as follows.

(2) In section 33 (appeal to House of Lords) after subsection (1) insert—

"(1A) In subsection (1) above the reference to the prosecutor includes a reference to
the Director of the Assets Recovery Agency in a case where (and to the extent
that) he is a party to the appeal to the Court of Appeal."

(3) In section 50(1) (meaning of sentence) after paragraph (c) insert—

"(ca) a confiscation order under Part 2 of the Proceeds of Crime Act 2002;

(cb) an order which varies a confiscation order made under Part 2 of the Proceeds of Crime Act 2002 if the varying order is made under section 21, 22
or 29 of that Act (but not otherwise);".

Misuse of Drugs Act 1971 (c. 38)

5   (1) Section 27 of the Misuse of Drugs Act 1971 (forfeiture) is amended as follows.

(2) In subsection (1) for "a drug trafficking offence, as defined in section 1(3) of the Drug
Trafficking Act 1994" substitute "an offence falling within subsection (3) below".

(3) After subsection (2) insert—

"(3) An offence falls within this subsection if it is an offence which is specified in—

(a) paragraph 1 of Schedule 2 to the Proceeds of Crime Act 2002 (drug trafficking offences), or

(b) so far as it relates to that paragraph, paragraph 10 of that Schedule."

Immigration Act 1971 (c. 77)

6   In section 28L of the Immigration Act 1971, in paragraph (c) for the words "33 of the
Criminal Law (Consolidation) (Scotland) Act 1995" substitute "412 of the Proceeds of
Crime Act 2002".

Rehabilitation of Offenders Act 1974 (c. 53)

7   In section 1 of the Rehabilitation of Offenders Act 1974 (rehabilitated persons and
spent convictions) after subsection (2A) insert—

"(2B) In subsection (2)(a) above the reference to a fine or other sum adjudged to be
paid by or imposed on a conviction does not include a reference to an amount
payable under a confiscation order made under Part 2 or 3 of the Proceeds of
Crime Act 2002."

Rehabilitation of Offenders (Northern Ireland) Order 1978 (S.I. 1978/1908 (N.I. 27))

8   In Article 3 of the Rehabilitation of Offenders (Northern Ireland) Order 1978
(rehabilitated persons and spent convictions) after paragraph (2) insert—

"(2A) In paragraph (2)(a) the reference to a fine or other sum adjudged to be paid by
or imposed on a conviction does not include a reference to an amount payable
under a confiscation order made under Part 4 of the Proceeds of Crime Act
2002."

Criminal Appeal (Northern Ireland) Act 1980 (c. 47)

9   (1) The Criminal Appeal (Northern Ireland) Act 1980 is amended as follows.

(2) In section 30(3) (meaning of sentence) omit "and" after paragraph (b) and after paragraph (c) insert—

"(d) a confiscation order under Part 4 of the Proceeds of Crime Act 2002;

(e) an order which varies a confiscation order made under Part 4 of the Proceeds of Crime Act 2002 if the varying order is made under section 171,
172 or 179 of that Act (but not otherwise)."

(3) In section 31 (appeal to House of Lords) after subsection (1) insert—

"(1A) In subsection (1) above the reference to the prosecutor includes a reference to
the Director of the Assets Recovery Agency in a case where (and to the extent
that) he is a party to the appeal to the Court of Appeal."

Legal Aid, Advice and Assistance (Northern Ireland) Order 1981 (S.I. 1981/228 (N.I. 8))

10 (1) Part I of Schedule 1 to the Legal Aid, Advice and Assistance (Northern Ireland) Order
1981 (proceedings for which legal aid may be given under Part II of the Order) is
amended as follows.

(2) After paragraph 2 insert—

"2A. (1) The following proceedings in the Crown Court under the Proceeds of
Crime Act 2002—

(a) proceedings which relate to a direction under section 202(3) or
204(3) as to the distribution of funds in the hands of a receiver;

    (b) applications under section 210 relating to action taken or proposed to be taken by a receiver;

    (c) applications under section 211 to vary or discharge an order under any of sections 196 to 201 for the appointment of or conferring powers on a receiver;

    (d) applications under section 220 or 221 for the payment of compensation;

    (e) applications under sections 351(3), 362(3), 369(3) or 375(2) to vary or discharge certain orders made under Part 8.

  (2) But sub-paragraph (1) does not apply in relation to a defendant (within the meaning of Part 4 of that Act) in the following proceedings—

    (a) proceedings mentioned in head (b) of that sub-paragraph;

    (b) an application under section 221 for the payment of compensation if the confiscation order was varied under section 179."

  (3) In paragraph 3 (courts of summary jurisdiction), after sub-paragraph (i) insert—

    "(j) proceedings under sections 295, 297, 298, 301 and 302 of the Proceeds of Crime Act 2002".

  (4) The amendments made by this paragraph are without prejudice to the power to make regulations under Article 10(2) of the Legal Aid, Advice and Assistance (Northern Ireland) Order 1981 amending or revoking the provisions inserted by this paragraph.

Civil Jurisdiction and Judgments Act 1982 (c. 27)

11   In section 18 of the Civil Jurisdiction and Judgments Act 1982 (enforcement of United Kingdom judgments in other parts of the United Kingdom) in subsection (3) (exceptions) insert after paragraph (c)—

    "(d) an order made under Part 2, 3 or 4 of the Proceeds of Crime Act 2002 (confiscation)."

Civic Government (Scotland) Act 1982 (c. 45)

12 (1) The Civic Government (Scotland) Act 1982 is amended as follows.

  (2) In section 86A(3) (application of Part VIIA) for "sections 21(2) and 28(1) of the Proceeds of Crime (Scotland) Act 1995" substitute "section 21(2) of the Proceeds of Crime (Scotland) Act 1995 and Part 3 of the Proceeds of Crime Act 2002".

  (3) In paragraph 8 of Schedule 2A (interpretation) for the definition of "restraint order" substitute—

    " "restraint order" means a restraint order made under Part 3 of the Proceeds of Crime Act 2002".

Criminal Justice Act 1982 (c. 48)

13   In Part 2 of Schedule 1 to the Criminal Justice Act 1982 (offences excluded from early release provisions) after the entry relating to the Drug Trafficking Act 1994 insert—

    "PROCEEDS OF CRIME ACT 2002

Section 327 (concealing criminal property etc).

Section 328 (arrangements relating to criminal property).

Section 329 (acquisition, use and possession of criminal property)."

Police and Criminal Evidence Act 1984 (c. 60)

14 (1) The Police and Criminal Evidence Act 1984 is amended as follows.

  (2) In section 56 (right to have someone informed when arrested) for subsection (5A) substitute—

    "(5A) An officer may also authorise delay where he has reasonable grounds for believing that—

    (a) the person detained for the serious arrestable offence has benefited from his criminal conduct, and

    (b) the recovery of the value of the property constituting the benefit will be hindered by telling the named person of the arrest.

    (5B) For the purposes of subsection (5A) above the question whether a person has benefited from his criminal conduct is to be decided in accordance with Part 2 of the Proceeds of Crime Act 2002."

  (3) In section 58 (access to legal advice) for subsection (8A) substitute—

    "(8A) An officer may also authorise delay where he has reasonable grounds for believing that—

(a) the person detained for the serious arrestable offence has benefited from his criminal conduct, and

(b) the recovery of the value of the property constituting the benefit will be hindered by the exercise of the right conferred by subsection (1) above.

(8B) For the purposes of subsection (8A) above the question whether a person has benefited from his criminal conduct is to be decided in accordance with Part 2 of the Proceeds of Crime Act 2002."

(4) In section 116 (meaning of serious arrestable offence) in subsection (2) for paragraph (c) and the word "and" immediately preceding it substitute—

"(c) any offence which is specified in paragraph 1 of Schedule 2 to the Proceeds of Crime Act 2002 (drug trafficking offences),

(d) any offence under section 327, 328 or 329 of that Act (certain money laundering offences)."

Bankruptcy (Scotland) Act 1985 (c. 66)

15 (1) The Bankruptcy (Scotland) Act 1985 is amended as follows.

(2) In section 5(4) (meaning of "qualified creditor") for the words from "has the meaning" to "1995" substitute "means a confiscation order under Part 2, 3 or 4 of the Proceeds of Crime Act 2002".

(3) In section 7(1) (meaning of "apparent insolvency") for the words from "has the meaning assigned" where second occurring to "said Act of 1994" where second occurring substitute " "confiscation order" and "restraint order" mean a confiscation order or a restraint order made under Part 2, 3 or 4 of the Proceeds of Crime Act 2002".

(4) After section 31 (vesting of estate at date of sequestration) insert—

"31A Property subject to restraint order

(1) This section applies where—

(a) property is excluded from the debtor's estate by virtue of section 420(2)(a) of the Proceeds of Crime Act 2002 (property subject to a restraint order),

(b) an order under section 50, 52, 128, 198 or 200 of that Act has not been made in respect of the property, and

(c) the restraint order is discharged.

(2) On the discharge of the restraint order the property vests in the permanent trustee as part of the debtor's estate.

(3) But subsection (2) does not apply to the proceeds of property realised by a management receiver under section 49(2)(d) or 197(2)(d) of that Act (realisation of property to meet receiver's remuneration and expenses).

31B Property in respect of which receivership or administration order is made

(1) This section applies where—

(a) property is excluded from the debtor's estate by virtue of section 420(2)(b), (c) or (d) of the Proceeds of Crime Act 2002 (property in respect of which an order for the appointment of a receiver or administrator under certain provisions of that Act is in force), and

(b) a confiscation order is made under section 6, 92 or 156 of that Act,

(c) the amount payable under the confiscation order is fully paid, and

(d) any of the property remains in the hands of the receiver or administrator (as the case may be).

(2) The property vests in the permanent trustee as part of the debtor's estate.

31C Property subject to certain orders where confiscation order discharged or quashed

(1) This section applies where—

(a) property is excluded from the debtor's estate by virtue of section 420(2)(a), (b), (c) or (d) of the Proceeds of Crime Act 2002 (property in respect of which a restraint order or an order for the appointment of a receiver or administrator under that Act is in force),

(b) a confiscation order is made under section 6, 92 or 156 of that Act, and

(c) the confiscation order is discharged under section 30, 114 or 180 of that Act (as the case may be) or quashed under that Act or in pursuance of any enactment relating to appeals against conviction or sentence.

(2) Any property in the hands of a receiver appointed under Part 2 or 4 of that Act or an administrator appointed under Part 3 of that Act vests in the permanent trustee as part of the debtor's estate.

(3) But subsection (2) does not apply to the proceeds of property realised by a management receiver under section 49(2)(d) or 197(2)(d) of that Act (realisation of property to meet receiver's remuneration and expenses)."

(5) In section 55 (effect of discharge) after subsection (2) insert—

"(3) In subsection (2)(a) above the reference to a fine or other penalty due to the Crown includes a reference to a confiscation order made under Part 2, 3 or 4 of the Proceeds of Crime Act 2002.".

Insolvency Act 1986 (c. 45)

16 (1) The Insolvency Act 1986 is amended as follows.

(2) In section 281 (effect of discharge) after subsection (4) insert—

"(4A) In subsection (4) the reference to a fine includes a reference to a confiscation order under Part 2, 3 or 4 of the Proceeds of Crime Act 2002."

(3) After section 306 insert—

"306A Property subject to restraint order

(1) This section applies where—

  (a) property is excluded from the bankrupt's estate by virtue of section 417(2)(a) of the Proceeds of Crime Act 2002 (property subject to a restraint order),

  (b) an order under section 50, 52, 128, 198 or 200 of that Act has not been made in respect of the property, and

  (c) the restraint order is discharged.

(2) On the discharge of the restraint order the property vests in the trustee as part of the bankrupt's estate.

(3) But subsection (2) does not apply to the proceeds of property realised by a management receiver under section 49(2)(d) or 197(2)(d) of that Act (realisation of property to meet receiver's remuneration and expenses).

306B Property in respect of which receivership or administration order made

(1) This section applies where—

  (a) property is excluded from the bankrupt's estate by virtue of section 417(2)(b), (c) or (d) of the Proceeds of Crime Act 2002 (property in respect of which an order for the appointment of a receiver or administrator under certain provisions of that Act is in force),

  (b) a confiscation order is made under section 6, 92 or 156 of that Act,

  (c) the amount payable under the confiscation order is fully paid, and

  (d) any of the property remains in the hands of the receiver or administrator (as the case may be).

(2) The property vests in the trustee as part of the bankrupt's estate.

306C Property subject to certain orders where confiscation order discharged or quashed

(1) This section applies where—

  (a) property is excluded from the bankrupt's estate by virtue of section 417(2)(a), (b), (c) or (d) of the Proceeds of Crime Act 2002 (property in respect of which a restraint order or an order for the appointment of a receiver or administrator under that Act is in force),

  (b) a confiscation order is made under section 6, 92 or 156 of that Act, and

  (c) the confiscation order is discharged under section 30, 114 or 180 of that Act (as the case may be) or quashed under that Act or in pursuance of any enactment relating to appeals against conviction or sentence.

(2) Any such property in the hands of a receiver appointed under Part 2 or 4 of that Act or an administrator appointed under Part 3 of that Act vests in the trustee as part of the bankrupt's estate.

(3) But subsection (2) does not apply to the proceeds of property realised by a management receiver under section 49(2)(d) or 197(2)(d) of that Act (realisation of property to meet receiver's remuneration and expenses)."

Criminal Justice Act 1988 (c. 33)

17 (1) The Criminal Justice Act 1988 is amended as follows.

    (2) The following provisions shall cease to have effect—

        (a) sections 71 to 102;

        (b) Schedule 4.

    (3) In section 151(4) (Customs and Excise power of arrest) omit "and" after paragraph (a), and after paragraph (b) insert—

        "(c) a money laundering offence;"

    (4) In section 151(5) for the words after "means" substitute "any offence which is specified in—

        (a) paragraph 1 of Schedule 2 to the Proceeds of Crime Act 2002 (drug trafficking offences), or

        (b) so far as it relates to that paragraph, paragraph 10 of that Schedule."

    (5) In section 151 after subsection (5) insert—

        "(6) In this section "money laundering offence" means any offence which by virtue of section 415 of the Proceeds of Crime Act 2002 is a money laundering offence for the purposes of Part 8 of that Act."

    (6) In section 152(4) (remands of suspected drugs offenders to customs detention) for the words after "means" substitute "any offence which is specified in—

        (a) paragraph 1 of Schedule 5 to the Proceeds of Crime Act 2002 (drug trafficking offences), or

        (b) so far as it relates to that paragraph, paragraph 10 of that Schedule."

Extradition Act 1989 (c. 33)

18 (1) The Extradition Act 1989 is amended as follows.

    (2) In section 22 (extension of purposes of extradition for offences under Acts giving effect to international conventions) in subsection (4)(h)—

        (a) for sub-paragraph (i) substitute—

            "(i) any offence which is specified in—

                (a) paragraph 1 of Schedule 2 to the Proceeds of Crime Act 2002 (drug trafficking offences), or

                (b) so far as it relates to that paragraph, paragraph 10 of that Schedule;

            (ia) any offence which by virtue of section 415 of the Proceeds of Crime Act 2002 is a money laundering offence for the purposes of Part 8 of that Act;";

        (b) for sub-paragraph (ii) substitute—

            "(ii) any offence which is specified in—

                (a) paragraph 2 of Schedule 4 to the Proceeds of Crime Act 2002, or

                (b) so far as it relates to that paragraph, paragraph 10 of that Schedule;

            (iia) any offence which by virtue of section 415 of the Proceeds of Crime Act 2002 is a money laundering offence for the purposes of Part 8 of that Act;";

        (c) omit "and" after sub-paragraph (ii) and for sub-paragraph (iii) substitute—

            "(iii) any offence which is specified in—

                (a) paragraph 1 of Schedule 5 to the Proceeds of Crime Act 2002 (drug trafficking offences), or

                (b) so far as it relates to that paragraph, paragraph 10 of that Schedule; and

            (iv) any offence which by virtue of section 415 of the Proceeds of Crime Act 2002 is a money laundering offence for the purposes of Part 8 of that Act;".

    (3) In paragraph 15 of Schedule 1 (deemed extension of jurisdiction of foreign states)—

        (a) for paragraph (j) substitute—

            "(j) any offence which is specified in—

                (i) paragraph 1 of Schedule 2 to the Proceeds of Crime Act 2002 (drug trafficking offences), or

                (ii) so far as it relates to that paragraph, paragraph 10 of that Schedule;

            (ja) any offence which by virtue of section 415 of the Proceeds of Crime Act 2002 is a money laundering offence for the purposes of Part 8 of that Act;";

(b) for paragraph (k) substitute—
   "(k) any offence which is specified in—
        (i) paragraph 2 of Schedule 4 to the Proceeds of Crime Act 2002, or
        (ii) so far as it relates to that paragraph, paragraph 10 of that Schedule;
   (ka) any offence which by virtue of section 415 of the Proceeds of Crime Act 2002 is a money laundering offence for the purposes of Part 8 of that Act;";
(c) for paragraph (m) substitute—
   "(m) any offence which is specified in—
        (i) paragraph 1 of Schedule 5 to the Proceeds of Crime Act 2002 (drug trafficking offences), or
        (ii) so far as it relates to that paragraph, paragraph 10 of that Schedule;
   (ma) any offence which by virtue of section 415 of the Proceeds of Crime Act 2002 is a money laundering offence for the purposes of Part 8 of that Act;".

Police and Criminal Evidence (Northern Ireland) Order 1989 (S.I. 1989/1341 (N.I. 12))

19 (1) The Police and Criminal Evidence (Northern Ireland) Order 1989 is amended as follows.
   (2) In Article 57 (right to have someone informed when arrested) for paragraph (5A) substitute—
      "(5A) An officer may also authorise delay where he has reasonable grounds for believing that—
            (a) the person detained for the serious arrestable offence has benefited from his criminal conduct, and
            (b) the recovery of the value of the property constituting the benefit will be hindered by telling the named person of the arrest.
      (5B) For the purposes of paragraph (5A) the question whether a person has benefited from his criminal conduct is to be decided in accordance with Part 4 of the Proceeds of Crime Act 2002."
   (3) In Article 59 (access to legal advice) for paragraph (8A) substitute—
      "(8A) An officer may also authorise delay where he has reasonable grounds for believing that—
            (a) the person detained for the serious arrestable offence has benefited from his criminal conduct, and
            (b) the recovery of the value of the property constituting the benefit will be hindered by the exercise of the right conferred by paragraph (1).
      (8B) For the purposes of paragraph (8A) the question whether a person has benefited from his criminal conduct is to be decided in accordance with Part 4 of the Proceeds of Crime Act 2002."
   (4) In Article 87 (meaning of serious arrestable offence) in paragraph (2) for sub-paragraph (aa) substitute—
      "(aa) any offence which is specified in paragraph 1 of Schedule 5 to the Proceeds of Crime Act 2002 (drug trafficking offences);
      (ab) any offence under section 327, 328 or 329 of that Act (certain money laundering offences);".

Insolvency (Northern Ireland) Order 1989 (S.I. 1989/2405 (N.I. 19))

20 (1) The Insolvency (Northern Ireland) Order 1989 is amended as follows.
   (2) In Article 255 (effect of discharge) after paragraph (4) insert—
      "(4A) In paragraph (4) the reference to a fine includes a reference to a confiscation order under Part 2, 3 or 4 of the Proceeds of Crime Act 2002."
   (3) After Article 279 insert—

   "279A Property subject to restraint order

      (1) This Article applies where—
         (a) property is excluded from the bankrupt's estate by virtue of section 423(2)(a) of the Proceeds of Crime Act 2002 (property subject to a restraint order),
         (b) an order under section 50, 52, 128, 198 or 200 of that Act has not been made in respect of the property, and

(c) the restraint order is discharged.

(2) On the discharge of the restraint order the property vests in the trustee as part of the bankrupt's estate.

(3) But paragraph (2) does not apply to the proceeds of property realised by a management receiver under section 49(2)(d) or 197(2)(d) of that Act (realisation of property to meet receiver's remuneration and expenses).

279B Property in respect of which receivership or administration order made

(1) This Article applies where—

(a) property is excluded from the bankrupt's estate by virtue of section 423(2)(b), (c) or (d) of the Proceeds of Crime Act 2002 (property in respect of which an order for the appointment of a receiver or administrator under certain provisions of that Act is in force),

(b) a confiscation order is made under section 6, 92 or 156 of that Act,

(c) the amount payable under the confiscation order is fully paid, and

(d) any of the property remains in the hands of the receiver or administrator (as the case may be).

(2) The property vests in the trustee as part of the bankrupt's estate.

279C Property subject to certain orders where confiscation order discharged or quashed

(1) This Article applies where—

(a) property is excluded from the bankrupt's estate by virtue of section 423(2)(a), (b), (c) or (d) of the Proceeds of Crime Act 2002 (property in respect of which a restraint order or an order for the appointment of a receiver or administrator under that Act is in force),

(b) a confiscation order is made under section 6, 92 or 156 of that Act, and

(c) the confiscation order is discharged under section 30, 114 or 180 of that Act (as the case may be) or quashed under that Act or in pursuance of any enactment relating to appeals against conviction or sentence.

(2) Any such property in the hands of a receiver appointed under Part 2 or 4 of that Act or an administrator appointed under Part 3 of that Act vests in the trustee as part of the bankrupt's estate.

(3) But paragraph (2) does not apply to the proceeds of property realised by a management receiver under section 49(2)(d) or 197(2)(d) of that Act (realisation of property to meet receiver's remuneration and expenses)."

Criminal Justice (International Co-operation) Act 1990 (c. 5)

21 In section 13(6) of the Criminal Justice (International Co-operation) Act 1990 (information not to be disclosed except for certain purposes)—

(a) omit "the Drug Trafficking Act 1994 or the Criminal Justice (Scotland) Act 1987";

(b) at the end insert "or of proceedings under Part 2, 3 or 4 of the Proceeds of Crime Act 2002".

Pension Schemes Act 1993 (c. 48)

22 (1) The Pension Schemes Act 1993 is amended as follows.

(2) In section 10 (protected rights and money purchase benefits), after subsection (5) insert—

"(6) Where, in the case of a scheme which makes such provision as is mentioned in subsection (2) or (3), any liability of the scheme in respect of a member's protected rights ceases by virtue of a civil recovery order, his protected rights are extinguished or reduced accordingly."

(3) In section 14 (earner's guaranteed minimum), after subsection (2) insert—

"(2A) Where any liability of a scheme in respect of an earner's guaranteed minimum pension ceases by virtue of a civil recovery order, his guaranteed minimum in relation to the scheme is extinguished or reduced accordingly."

(4) In section 47 (further provisions relating to guaranteed minimum pensions), in subsection (6), after "but for" insert "section 14(2A) and".

(5) In section 68B (safeguarded rights), at the end insert "including provision for such rights to be extinguished or reduced in consequence of a civil recovery order made in respect of such rights".

(6) In section 181(1) (general interpretation), after the definition of "Category A retirement pension" insert—

" "civil recovery order" means an order under section 266 of the Proceeds of Crime Act 2002 or an order under section 276 imposing the requirement mentioned in section 277(3)."

Pension Schemes (Northern Ireland) Act 1993 (c. 49)

23 (1) The Pension Schemes (Northern Ireland) Act 1993 is amended as follows.

    (2) In section 6 (protected rights and money purchase benefits), after subsection (5) insert—

        "(6) Where, in the case of a scheme which makes such provision as is mentioned in subsection (2) or (3), any liability of the scheme in respect of a member's protected rights ceases by virtue of a civil recovery order, his protected rights are extinguished or reduced accordingly."

    (3) In section 10 (earner's guaranteed minimum), after subsection (2) insert—

        "(2A) Where any liability of a scheme in respect of an earner's guaranteed minimum pension ceases by virtue of a civil recovery order, his guaranteed minimum in relation to the scheme is extinguished or reduced accordingly."

    (4) In section 43 (further provisions relating to guaranteed minimum pensions), in subsection (6), after "but for" insert "section 10(2A) and".

    (5) In section 64B (safeguarded rights), at the end insert "including provision for such rights to be extinguished or reduced in consequence of a civil recovery order made in respect of such rights".

    (6) In section 176(1) (general interpretation), after the definition of "Category A retirement pension" insert—

        " "civil recovery order" means an order under section 266 of the Proceeds of Crime Act 2002 or an order under section 276 imposing the requirement mentioned in section 277(3)."

Criminal Justice and Public Order Act 1994 (c. 31)

24   In section 139(12) of the Criminal Justice and Public Order Act 1994 (search powers) in paragraph (b) of the definition of "items subject to legal privilege" for "section 40 of the Criminal Justice (Scotland) Act 1987" substitute "section 412 of the Proceeds of Crime Act 2002".

Drug Trafficking Act 1994 (c. 37)

25 (1) The Drug Trafficking Act 1994 is amended as follows.

    (2) The following provisions shall cease to have effect—

        (a) sections 1 to 54;

        (b) in sections 55(4)(a) (orders to make material available) and 56(3)(a) and (4)(a) (authority for search) the words "or has benefited from";

        (c) in section 59 (disclosure of information held by government departments), subsections (1) to (10) and in subsection (11) the words "An order under subsection (1) above, and,";

        (d) in section 60(6) (Customs and Excise prosecution powers), in the definition of "specified offence", in paragraph (a) the words "Part III or" and paragraph (c) and the word "or" immediately preceding it;

        (e) in section 60(6) the words from "and references to the institution of proceedings" to the end;

        (f) in section 60, subsections (7) and (8);

        (g) in section 61 (extension of certain offences to the Crown), subsections (2) to (4);

        (h) sections 62, 63(1), (2) and (3)(a) and 64 (interpretation);

        (i) in section 68(2) (extent—Scotland), paragraphs (a) to (c) and in paragraph (g) the words "1, 41, 62" and "64";

        (j) in section 68(3) (extent—Northern Ireland), paragraph (a) and in paragraph (d) the word "64".

    (3) In section 59(12)(b) for the words "referred to in subsection (1) above" substitute "specified in an order under section 55(2)".

    (4) After section 59 insert the following section—

"59A Construction of sections 55 to 59

      (1) This section has effect for the purposes of sections 55 to 59.

(2) A reference to a constable includes a reference to a customs officer.

(3) A customs officer is a person commissioned by the Commissioners of Customs and Excise under section 6(3) of the Customs and Excise Management Act 1979 (c. 2).

(4) Drug trafficking means doing or being concerned in any of the following (whether in England and Wales or elsewhere)—

    (a) producing or supplying a controlled drug where the production or supply contravenes section 4(1) of the Misuse of Drugs Act 1971 or a corresponding law;

    (b) transporting or storing a controlled drug where possession of the drug contravenes section 5(1) of that Act or a corresponding law;

    (c) importing or exporting a controlled drug where the importation or exportation is prohibited by section 3(1) of that Act or a corresponding law;

    (d) manufacturing or supplying a scheduled substance within the meaning of section 12 of the Criminal Justice (International Co-operation) Act 1990 where the manufacture or supply is an offence under that section or would be such an offence if it took place in England and Wales;

    (e) using any ship for illicit traffic in controlled drugs in circumstances which amount to the commission of an offence under section 19 of that Act.

(5) In this section "corresponding law" has the same meaning as in the Misuse of Drugs Act 1971."

(5) In section 60 after subsection (6) insert—

"(6A) Proceedings for an offence are instituted—

    (a) when a justice of the peace issues a summons or warrant under section 1 of the Magistrates' Courts Act 1980 (issue of summons to, or warrant for arrest of, accused) in respect of the offence;

    (b) when a person is charged with the offence after being taken into custody without a warrant;

    (c) when a bill of indictment is preferred under section 2 of the Administration of Justice (Miscellaneous Provisions) Act 1933 in a case falling within paragraph (b) of subsection (2) of that section (preferment by direction of the criminal division of the Court of Appeal or by direction, or with the consent, of a High Court judge).

(6B) Where the application of subsection (6A) would result in there being more than one time for the institution of proceedings they must be taken to have been instituted at the earliest of those times."

(6) In section 61(1) for "sections 49(2), 50 to 53 and 58" substitute "section 58".

(7) In section 68(2)(d), for "59(10)" substitute "59(11)".

Criminal Justice (Northern Ireland) Order 1994 (S.I. 1994/2795 (N.I. 15))

26   In Article 16 of the Criminal Justice (Northern Ireland) Order 1994 in paragraph (a) after "Proceeds of Crime (Northern Ireland) Order 1996" insert "or Part 4 of the Proceeds of Crime Act 2002".

Proceeds of Crime Act 1995 (c. 11)

27   Section 15(2) and (3) of the Proceeds of Crime Act 1995 (investigation into benefit to be treated as the investigation of an offence for the purposes of sections 21 and 22 of the Police and Criminal Evidence Act 1984) shall cease to have effect.

Proceeds of Crime (Scotland) Act 1995 (c. 43)

28 (1) The Proceeds of Crime (Scotland) Act 1995 is amended as follows.

    (2) The following provisions in the Act shall cease to have effect—

    (a) Part I, except section 2(7);

    (b) in section 28, subsections (1)(a) and (2) and in subsection (5) the words "(including a restraint order made under and within the meaning of the 1994 Act)";

    (c) section 29;

    (d) in section 31, subsection (2) and in subsection (4) the words "or (2)";

    (e) sections 35 to 39;

    (f) in section 40, subsections (1)(a), (2) and (4);

    (g) in section 42, subsections (1)(a) and (b);

    (h) in section 43, in subsection (1) the words ", confiscation order" and subsection (2);

    (i) in section 45, subsection (1)(a);

   (j) section 47;
   (k) in section 49, in subsection (1) the definitions of "the 1988 Act", "the 1994 Act" and "confiscation order" and subsection (4).
 (3) The following provisions in Schedule 1 to the Act shall cease to have effect—
   (a) in paragraph 1(1)(b) the words "or a confiscation order", in paragraph 1(2)(a) the words "subject to paragraph (b) below", paragraph 1(2)(b) and in paragraph 1(3)(a)(i) the words "or confiscation order";
   (b) in paragraph 2(1)(a) the words ", and if appointed (or empowered) under paragraph 1(1)(b) above where a confiscation order has been made";
   (c) paragraph 4;
   (d) in paragraph 5(1) the words "Part I of";
   (e) in paragraph 8(2) the words ", unless in a case where a confiscation order has been made there are sums available to be applied in payment of it under paragraph 4(4)(b) above,";
   (f) in paragraph 10(1) the words "or the recipient of a gift caught by Part I of this Act or an implicative gift" and paragraphs 10(2) and 10(3);
   (g) in paragraph 12(1)(a) the words "paragraph (a) or (b) of section 4(1) or".
 (4) The following provisions in Schedule 2 to the Act shall cease to have effect—
   (a) in paragraph 1(2) the words "and 35 to 38";
   (b) in paragraph 2, in sub-paragraph (1) the words "realisable or", in sub-paragraph (2) the words "and 35 to 38", sub-paragraph (5);
   (c) in paragraph 3(2) the words "and 35 to 38" and paragraphs 3(4) and (5);
   (d) in paragraph 4(2) the words "and 35 to 38";
   (e) paragraph 6(2)(a).
 (5) In section 28(9) (restraint orders) for "Subsections (2)(a) and" substitute "Subsection".
 (6) In section 42 (enforcement) in subsections (2)(a), (c) and (d) for "Part I," substitute "Part".

Criminal Procedure (Scotland) Act 1995 (c. 46)

29 (1) The Criminal Procedure (Scotland) Act 1995 is amended as follows.
 (2) In section 109(1) (intimation of appeal) for "section 10 of the Proceeds of Crime (Scotland) Act 1995 (postponed confiscation orders)" substitute "section 99 of the Proceeds of Crime Act 2002 (postponement)".
 (3) In section 205B(5) (minimum sentence for third drug trafficking offence) for the definition of "drug trafficking offence" substitute—
           " "drug trafficking offence" means an offence specified in paragraph 2 or (so far as it relates to that paragraph) paragraph 10 of Schedule 4 to the Proceeds of Crime Act 2002;".
 (4) In section 219(8)(b) (fines: imprisonment for non-payment) for "14(2) of the Proceeds of Crime (Scotland) Act 1995" substitute "118(2) of the Proceeds of Crime Act 2002".

Police Act 1996 (c. 16)

30 (1) Section 97 of the Police Act 1996 (police officers engaged on service outside their force) is amended as follows.
 (2) In subsection (1) after paragraph (cc) insert—
    "(cd) temporary service with the Assets Recovery Agency on which a person is engaged with the consent of the appropriate authority;".
 (3) In subsection (6)(a) after "(cc)" insert "(cd)".
 (4) In subsection (8) after "(cc)" insert "(cd)".

Proceeds of Crime (Northern Ireland) Order 1996 (S.I. 1996/1299 (N.I. 9))

31 (1) The Proceeds of Crime (Northern Ireland) Order 1996 is amended as follows.
 (2) Parts II and III shall cease to have effect.
 (3) The following provisions shall also cease to have effect—
   (a) in Article 2 (interpretation) in paragraph (2) from the definition of "charging order" to the definition of "external confiscation order" and from the definition of "modifications" to the definition of "restraint order" and paragraphs (3) to (10) and (12);
   (b) Article 3 (definition of "property" etc.);

(c) in Article 49 (additional investigation powers), in paragraph (1) sub-paragraph (c) and the word "and" immediately preceding it, in paragraph (1A) sub-paragraph (c) and the word "and" immediately preceding it, paragraph (4) and in paragraph (5) the definitions of "customs officer" and "relevant property";

(d) in Article 52 (supplementary provisions) in paragraph (2) sub-paragraph (b) and the word "and" immediately preceding it, and paragraph (3);

(e) in Article 54 (disclosure of information held by government departments) paragraphs (1) to (10) and (13) and in paragraph (11) the words "An order under paragraph (1) and,";

(f) in Article 55 (Customs and Excise prosecution powers), in paragraph (6) in the definition of "specified offence" in paragraph (a) the words "Part III or" and paragraph (c) and the word "or" immediately preceding it, and paragraph (7);

(g) Article 56(2) to (4) (extension of certain offences to the Crown);

(h) in Schedule 2 paragraph 3.

(4) In Article 49(1) (additional investigation powers)—

(a) for "county court" substitute "Crown Court";

(b) in sub-paragraph (a) for the words from "an investigation" to the end of head (ii) substitute "a confiscation investigation";

(c) in sub-paragraph (b) after "and who is" insert "an accredited financial investigator".

(5) In Article 49(1A)—

(a) after "application made by" insert "the Director of the Assets Recovery Agency or";

(b) for "county court" substitute "Crown Court";

(c) in sub-paragraph (a) for the words from "an investigation" to the end of head (ii) substitute "a confiscation investigation";

(d) in sub-paragraph (b) after "if" insert "the Director or";

(e) after "authorise" insert "the Director or";

(f) for "paragraphs 3 and 3A" where it twice occurs substitute "paragraph 3A".

(6) In Article 49(5) insert at the appropriate place in alphabetical order—

" "accredited financial investigator" has the meaning given by section 3(5) of the Proceeds of Crime Act 2002;

"confiscation investigation" has the same meaning as it has for the purposes of Part 8 of that Act by virtue of section 341(1);".

(7) In Article 50(1) (order to make material available)—

(a) for sub-paragraphs (a) and (b) substitute "drug trafficking";

(b) for "county court" substitute "Crown Court".

(8) In Article 50(4)(a), for heads (i) to (iii) substitute "has carried on drug trafficking".

(9) In Article 50(8) for "county court" substitute "Crown Court".

(10) In Article 51(1) (authority for search)—

(a) for sub-paragraphs (a) and (b) substitute "drug trafficking";

(b) for "county court" substitute "Crown Court".

(11) In Article 51(3)(a) for heads (i) to (iii) substitute "has carried on drug trafficking".

(12) In Article 51(4)—

(a) in sub-paragraph (a) for heads (i) to (iii) substitute "has carried on drug trafficking";

(b) in sub-paragraph (b)(i) for the words from "the question" to the end substitute "drug trafficking".

(13) In Article 52(1)(a) (supplementary provisions), for heads (i) to (ii) substitute "drug trafficking".

(14) In Article 54 (disclosure of information held by government departments) in paragraph (12)(b) for "referred to in paragraph (1)" substitute "specified in an order under Article 50(2)".

(15) After Article 54 insert the following Article—

"54A Construction of Articles 49 to 54

(1) This Article has effect for the purposes of Articles 49 to 54.

(2) A reference to a constable includes a reference to a customs officer.

(3) A customs officer is a person commissioned by the Commissioners of Customs and Excise under section 6(3) of the Customs and Excise Management Act 1979.

(4) Drug trafficking means doing or being concerned in any of the following (whether in Northern Ireland or elsewhere)—

    (a) producing or supplying a controlled drug where the production or supply contravenes section 4(1) of the Misuse of Drugs Act 1971 or a corresponding law;

    (b) transporting or storing a controlled drug where possession of the drug contravenes section 5(1) of that Act or a corresponding law;

    (c) importing or exporting a controlled drug where the importation or exportation is prohibited by section 3(1) of that Act or a corresponding law;

    (d) manufacturing or supplying a scheduled substance within the meaning of section 12 of the Criminal Justice (International Co-operation) Act 1990 where the manufacture or supply is an offence under that section or would be such an offence if it took place in Northern Ireland;

    (e) using any ship for illicit traffic in controlled drugs in circumstances which amount to the commission of an offence under section 19 of that Act.

    (5) In this Article "corresponding law" has the same meaning as in the Misuse of Drugs Act 1971."

(16) In Article 55 after paragraph (6) insert—

"(6A) Proceedings for an offence are instituted—

    (a) when a summons or warrant is issued under Article 20 of the Magistrates' Courts (Northern Ireland) Order 1981 in respect of the offence;

    (b) when a person is charged with the offence after being taken into custody without a warrant;

    (c) when an indictment is preferred under section 2(2)(c), (e) or (f) of the Grand Jury (Abolition) Act (Northern Ireland) 1969.

(6B) Where the application of paragraph (6A) would result in there being more than one time for the institution of proceedings they must be taken to have been instituted at the earliest of those times."

(17) In Article 56(1) (extension of certain offences to the Crown), for "Articles 44, 45, 46, 47(2), 48 and" substitute "Article".

(18) In Schedule 2 (financial investigations) in paragraph 3A—

    (a) in sub-paragraph (1) for "any conduct to which Article 49 applies" substitute "his criminal conduct";

    (b) after that paragraph insert—

"(1A) For the purposes of sub-paragraph (1) the question whether a person has benefited from his criminal conduct is to be decided in accordance with Part 4 of the Proceeds of Crime Act 2002."

Crime (Sentences) Act 1997 (c. 43)

32 (1) The Crime (Sentences) Act 1997 is amended as follows.

    (2) In section 35 (fine defaulters) in subsection (1)(a) after "Drug Trafficking Act 1994" insert "or section 6 of the Proceeds of Crime Act 2002".

    (3) In section 40 (fine defaulters) in subsection (1)(a) after "Drug Trafficking Act 1994" insert "or section 6 of the Proceeds of Crime Act 2002".

Crime and Punishment (Scotland) Act 1997 (c. 48)

33   The following provisions of the Crime and Punishment (Scotland) Act 1997 shall cease to have effect—

    (a) section 15(3),

    (b) in Schedule 1, paragraph 20.

Police (Northern Ireland) Act 1998 (c. 32)

34 (1) Section 27 of the Police (Northern Ireland) Act 1998 (members of the Police Service engaged on other police service) is amended as follows.

    (2) In subsection (1) after paragraph (c) insert—

"(ca) temporary service with the Assets Recovery Agency on which a member of the Police Service of Northern Ireland is engaged with the consent of the Chief Constable;".

    (3) In subsection (5)(b) after "(c)" insert "(ca)".

    (4) In subsection (7) for "or (c)" there is substituted "(c) or (ca)".

Crime and Disorder Act 1998 (c. 37)

35   In Schedule 8 to the Crime and Disorder Act 1998 paragraphs 115 and 116 shall cease to have effect.

Access to Justice Act 1999 (c. 22)

36   (1)   Schedule 2 to the Access to Justice Act 1999 (services excluded from the Community Legal Service) is amended as follows.

     (2)   In paragraph 2(2), after paragraph (d) insert "or

           (e)   under the Proceeds of Crime Act 2002 to the extent specified in paragraph 3,"

and omit the "or" at the end of paragraph (c).

     (3)   In paragraph 2(3) (magistrates courts), after "2001" insert—

           "(l)   for an order or direction under section 295, 297, 298, 301 or 302 of the Proceeds of Crime Act 2002,"

and omit the "or" at the end of paragraph (j).

     (4)   After paragraph 2 insert—

       "3   (1)   These are the proceedings under the Proceeds of Crime Act 2002—

           (a)   an application under section 42(3) to vary or discharge a restraint order or an order under section 41(7);

           (b)   proceedings which relate to a direction under section 54(3) or 56(3) as to the distribution of funds in the hands of a receiver;

           (c)   an application under section 62 relating to action taken or proposed to be taken by a receiver;

           (d)   an application under section 63 to vary or discharge an order under any of sections 48 to 53 for the appointment of or conferring powers on a receiver;

           (e)   an application under section 72 or 73 for the payment of compensation;

           (f)   proceedings which relate to an order under section 298 for the forfeiture of cash;

           (g)   an application under section 351(3), 362(3), 369(3) or 375(2) to vary or discharge certain orders made under Part 8.

       (2)   But sub-paragraph (1) does not authorise the funding of the provision of services to a defendant (within the meaning of Part 1 of that Act) in relation to—

           (a)   proceedings mentioned in paragraph (b);

           (b)   an application under section 73 for the payment of compensation if the confiscation order was varied under section 29."

Powers of Criminal Courts (Sentencing) Act 2000 (c. 6)

37   (1)   The Powers of Criminal Courts (Sentencing) Act 2000 is amended as follows.

     (2)   In section 110(5) (minimum sentence for third drug trafficking offence) for the definition of "drug trafficking offence" there is substituted—

       " "drug trafficking offence" means an offence which is specified in—

           (a)   paragraph 1 of Schedule 2 to the Proceeds of Crime Act 2002 (drug trafficking offences), or

           (b)   so far as it relates to that paragraph, paragraph 10 of that Schedule."

     (3)   In section 133 (review of compensation orders) in subsection (3)(c) after "Criminal Justice Act 1988" insert ", or Part 2 of the Proceeds of Crime Act 2002,".

Financial Services and Markets Act 2000 (c. 8)

38   In Schedule 1 to the Financial Services and Markets Act 2000 (provisions relating to the Financial Services Authority) after paragraph 19 insert—

       "19A   For the purposes of this Act anything done by an accredited financial investigator within the meaning of the Proceeds of Crime Act 2002 who is—

           (a)   a member of the staff of the Authority, or

           (b)   a person appointed by the Authority under section 97, 167 or 168 to conduct an investigation,

must be treated as done in the exercise or discharge of a function of the Authority."

Terrorism Act 2000 (c. 11)

39   (1)   Schedule 8 to the Terrorism Act 2000 (detention) is amended as follows.

     (2)   In paragraph 8 (authorisation of delay in exercise of detained person's rights) for sub-paragraph (5) substitute—

"(5) An officer may also give an authorisation under sub-paragraph (1) if he has reasonable grounds for believing that—

   (a) the detained person has benefited from his criminal conduct, and

   (b) the recovery of the value of the property constituting the benefit will be hindered by—

      (i) informing the named person of the detained person's detention (in the case of an authorisation under sub-paragraph (1)(a)), or

      (ii) the exercise of the right under paragraph 7 (in the case of an authorisation under sub-paragraph (1)(b)).

(5A) For the purposes of sub-paragraph (5) the question whether a person has benefited from his criminal conduct is to be decided in accordance with Part 2 of the Proceeds of Crime Act 2002."

(3) In paragraph 17(3) (grounds for authorising delay or requiring presence of senior officer), in paragraph (d) for "Part VI of the Criminal Justice Act 1988, Part I of the Proceeds of Crime (Scotland) Act 1995" substitute "Part 2 or 3 of the Proceeds of Crime Act 2002".

(4) For paragraph 17(4) (further grounds for authorising delay in exercise of detained person's rights) substitute—

"(4) This sub-paragraph applies where an officer mentioned in paragraph 16(4) or (7) has reasonable grounds for believing that—

   (a) the detained person has benefited from his criminal conduct, and

   (b) the recovery of the value of the property constituting the benefit will be hindered by—

      (i) informing the named person of the detained person's detention (in the case of an authorisation under paragraph 16(4)), or

      (ii) the exercise of the entitlement under paragraph 16(6) (in the case of an authorisation under paragraph 16(7)).

(4A) For the purposes of sub-paragraph (4) the question whether a person has benefited from his criminal conduct is to be decided in accordance with Part 3 of the Proceeds of Crime Act 2002."

(5) In paragraph 34 (authorisation for withholding information from detained person) for sub-paragraph (3) substitute—

"(3) A judicial authority may also make an order under sub-paragraph (1) in relation to specified information if satisfied that there are reasonable grounds for believing that—

   (a) the detained person has benefited from his criminal conduct, and

   (b) the recovery of the value of the property constituting the benefit would be hindered if the information were disclosed.

(3A) For the purposes of sub-paragraph (3) the question whether a person has benefited from his criminal conduct is to be decided in accordance with Part 2 or 3 of the Proceeds of Crime Act 2002."

Criminal Justice and Police Act 2001 (c. 16)

40 (1) The Criminal Justice and Police Act 2001 is amended as follows.

   (2) In section 55 (obligation to return excluded and special procedure material) in subsection (5) (powers in relation to which section does not apply as regards special procedure material) omit "and" after paragraph (b), and after paragraph (c) insert—

"and

   (d) section 352(4) of the Proceeds of Crime Act 2002,".

   (3) In section 60 (cases where duty to secure seized property arises) in subsection (4) (powers in relation to which duty does not arise as regards special procedure material) omit "or" after paragraph (b), and after paragraph (c) insert—

"or

   (d) section 352(4) of the Proceeds of Crime Act 2002,".

   (4) In section 64 (meaning of appropriate judicial authority) in subsection (3) after paragraph (a) omit "and" and insert—

"(aa) the power of seizure conferred by section 352(4) of the Proceeds of Crime Act 2002, if the power is exercisable for the purposes of a civil recovery investigation (within the meaning of Part 8 of that Act);".

   (5) In section 65 (meaning of "legal privilege")—

(a) in subsection (1)(b) for the words "33 of the Criminal Law (Consolidation) (Scotland) Act 1995 (c. 39)" substitute "412 of the Proceeds of Crime Act 2002";

(b) after subsection (3) insert—

"(3A) In relation to property which has been seized in exercise, or purported exercise, of—

(a) the power of seizure conferred by section 352(4) of the Proceeds of Crime Act 2002, or

(b) so much of any power of seizure conferred by section 50 as is exercisable by reference to that power,

references in this Part to an item subject to legal privilege shall be read as references to privileged material within the meaning of section 354(2) of that Act."

(6) In Part 1 of Schedule 1 (powers of seizure to which section 50 applies) at the end add—

"Proceeds of Crime Act 2002 (c. 00)

73A The power of seizure conferred by section 352(4) of the Proceeds of Crime Act 2002 (seizure of material likely to be of substantial value to certain investigations)."

(7) In Part 3 of Schedule 1 (powers of seizure to which section 55 applies) at the end add—

"Proceeds of Crime Act 2002 (c. 00)

110 The power of seizure conferred by section 352(4) of the Proceeds of Crime Act 2002 (seizure of material likely to be of substantial value to certain investigations)."

Section 457   SCHEDULE 12

REPEALS AND REVOCATIONS

Short title and chapter	Extent of repeal or revocation
Misuse of Drugs Act 1971 (c. 38)	In section 21 the words "or section 49 of the Drug Trafficking Act 1994". In section 23(3A) the words "or section 49 of the Drug Trafficking Act 1994".
Criminal Appeal (Northern Ireland) Act 1980 (c. 47)	In section 30(3) the word "and" after paragraph (b).
Police and Criminal Evidence Act 1984 (c. 60)	In section 65— (a) the definitions of "drug trafficking" and "drug trafficking offence"; (b) the words from "references in this Part" to "in accordance with the Drug Trafficking Act 1994".
Criminal Justice Act 1988 (c. 33)	Sections 71 to 102. In section 151(4) the word "and" after paragraph (a). In section 172— (a) in subsection (2) the words from "section 76(3)" to "extending to Scotland"; (b) in subsection (4) the words from "sections 90" to "section 93E". Schedule 4.
Housing Act 1988 (c. 50)	In Schedule 17, paragraphs 83 and 84.
Extradition Act 1989 (c. 33)	In section 22(4)(h) the word "and" after sub-paragraph (ii).
Police and Criminal Evidence (Northern Ireland) Order 1989 (S.I. 1989/1341 (N.I. 12))	In Article 53— (a) the definitions of "drug trafficking" and "drug trafficking offence"; (b) the words from "References in this Part" to "Order 1996".
Criminal Justice (International Co-operation) Act 1990 (c. 5)	In section 13(6) the words "the Drug Trafficking Act 1994 or". Section 14. In Schedule 4, paragraph 1.

Short title and chapter	Extent of repeal or revocation

Criminal Justice (Confiscation) (Northern Ireland) Order 1990 (S.I. 1990/2588 (N.I. 17))	In Article 37—
	  (a) paragraph (2);
	  (b) in paragraphs (3) and (4) sub-paragraph (b) and the word "and" before it;
	  (c) paragraph (5).

Criminal Justice Act 1993 (c. 36)	Section 21(3)(e) to (g). Sections 27 to 35. In Schedule 4, paragraph 3. In Schedule 5, paragraph 14.
Criminal Justice and Public Order Act 1994 (c. 33)	In Schedule 9, paragraph 36.
Drug Trafficking Act 1994 (c. 37)	Sections 1 to 54. In sections 55(4)(a) and 56(3)(a) and (4)(a) the words "or has benefited from". In section 59, subsections (1) to (10) and in subsection (11) the words "An order under subsection (1) above, and". In section 60(6), in the definition of "specified offence", in paragraph (a) the words "Part III or" and paragraph (c) and the word "or" immediately preceding it. In section 60(6), the words from "and references to the institution of proceedings" to the end. Section 60(7) and (8). Section 61(2) to (4). Sections 62, 63(1), (2) and (3)(a) and 64. In section 68(2), paragraphs (a) to (c) and in paragraph (g) the words "1, 41, 62" and "64". In section 68(3), paragraph (a) and in paragraph (d) the word "64". In Schedule 1, paragraphs 3, 4(a), 8, 21 and 26.
Proceeds of Crime Act 1995 (c. 11)	Sections 1 to 13. Section 15(1) to (3). Section 16(2), (5) and (6). Schedule 1.
Criminal Law (Consolidation) (Scotland) Act 1995 (c. 39)	Part V.
Criminal Procedure (Consequential Provisions) (Scotland) Act 1995 (c. 40)	In Schedule 3, paragraph 4(2). In Schedule 4, paragraphs 69 and 94.
Private International Law (Miscellaneous Provisions) Act 1995 (c. 42)	Section 4(3).
Proceeds of Crime (Scotland) Act 1995 (c. 43)	Part I, except section 2(7). In section 28, subsections (1)(a) and (2) and in subsection (5) the words "(including a restraint order made under and within the meaning of the 1994 Act)". Section 29. In section 31, subsection (2), in subsection (4) the words "or (2)". Sections 35 to 39. In section 40, subsections (1)(a), (2) and (4). In section 42, subsections (1)(a) and (b). In section 43, in subsection (1) the words "confiscation order", subsection (2). Section 45(1)(a). Section 47. In section 49, in subsection (1) the definitions of "the 1988 Act", "the 1994 Act" and "confiscation order" and subsection (4). In Schedule 1, in paragraph 1, in sub-paragraph (1)(b) the words "or a confiscation order", in sub-paragraph (2)(a) the words "subject to paragraph (b)

Short title and chapter	Extent of repeal or revocation
Proceeds of Crime (Scotland) Act 1995 (c. 43)—*cont.*	below", sub-paragraph (2)(b), in sub-paragraph (3)(a)(i) the words "or confiscation order". In Schedule 1, in paragraph 2, in sub-paragraph (1)(a) the words ", and if appointed (or empowered) under paragraph 1(1)(b) above where a confiscation order has been made", paragraph 4, in paragraph 5(1) the words "Part I of", in paragraph 8(2) the words from ", unless in a case where a confiscation order has been" to "4(4)(b) above,". In Schedule 1, in paragraph 10(1) the words "or the recipient of a gift caught by Part I of this Act or an implicative gift", paragraphs 10(2) and (3), in paragraph 12(1)(a) the words "paragraph (a) or (b) of section 4(1) or". In Schedule 2, in paragraph 1(2) the words "and 35 to 38", in paragraph 2(1) the words "realisable or", in paragraph 2(2) the words "and 35 to 38", paragraph 2(5), in paragraph 3(2) the words "and 35 to 38", paragraphs 3(4) and (5), in paragraph 4(2) the words "and 35 to 38", paragraph 6(2)(a).
Proceeds of Crime (Northern Ireland) Order 1996 (S.I. 1996/1299 (N.I. 9))	Parts II and III. In Article 2 in paragraph (2) from the definition of "charging order" to the definition of "external confiscation order" and from the definition of "modifications" to the definition of "restraint order" and paragraphs (3) to (10) and (12). Article 3. In Article 49, in paragraph (1) sub-paragraph (c) and the word "and" immediately preceding it, in paragraph (1A) sub-paragraph (c) and the word "and" immediately preceding it, paragraph (4) and in paragraph (5) the definitions of "customs officer" and "relevant property". In Article 52 in paragraph (2) sub-paragraph (b) and the word "and" immediately preceding it, and paragraph (3). In Article 54 paragraphs (1) to (10) and (13) and in paragraph (11) the words "An order under paragraph (1) and,". In Article 55, in paragraph (6) in the definition of "specified offence" in paragraph (a) the words "Part III or" and paragraph (c) and the word "or" immediately preceding it, and paragraph (7). Article 56(2) to (4). In Schedule 2— (a) in paragraph 1(3) "3 or"; (b) paragraph 3; (c) in paragraphs 4(2), 5(1) and 6(1) "3". In Schedule 3, paragraphs 1 to 3 and 18.
Justices of the Peace Act 1997 (c. 25)	In Schedule 5, paragraphs 23 and 36.
Crime and Punishment (Scotland) Act 1997 (c. 48)	Section 15(3). In Schedule 1, paragraph 20.
Crime and Disorder Act 1998 (c. 37)	Section 83. In Schedule 1, paragraphs 115 and 116. In Schedule 8, paragraph 114. In Schedule 9, paragraph 8.
Access to Justice Act 1999 (c. 22)	In Schedule 2— (a) in paragraph 2(2) the word "or" at the end of paragraph (c); (b) in paragraph 2(3) the word "or" at the end of paragraph (j). In Schedule 13, paragraphs 139 and 172.

Short title and chapter	Extent of repeal or revocation
Powers of Criminal Courts (Sentencing) Act 2000 (c. 6)	In Schedule 9, paragraphs 105 to 113 and 163 to 173.
Terrorism Act 2000 (c. 11)	In Schedule 15, paragraphs 6, 10 and 11(2).
Criminal Justice and Police Act 2001 (c. 16)	In section 55(5) paragraph (a) and the word "and" after paragraph (b).
	In section 60(4) paragraph (a) and the word "or" after paragraph (b).
	In section 64(3) the word "and" after paragraph (a).
	In Schedule 1, paragraphs 47 and 105.
Financial Investigations (Northern Ireland) Order 2001 (S.I. 2001/1866 (N.I. 1))	Articles 3(2)(b) and 4(1)(a) and (c), (2), (3) and (5).
Land Registration Act 2002 (c. 9)	In Schedule 11, paragraphs 22 and 32.
This Act	Section 248(2)(a) and (4).

INDEX

References are to sections and Schedules

THOMSON
SWEET & MAXWELL
™

Thank you for purchasing **Proceeds of Crime Act: A Current Law Statutes Guide**.

To order any option of **Current Law**, please complete and return this FREEPOST order form.

YES, PLEASE SEND ME THE FOLLOWING:

QTY	TITLE		PRICE	POSTAGE	TOTAL
	Current Law A Service	0011-362X	£929		
	Current Law B Service	0011-362X	£769		
	Current Law C Service	0011-362X	£599		
	Current Law D Service	0011-362X	£840		
	Current Law Week	0968-879X	£225		
	European Current Law	0964-0037	£685		
	Please keep me informed of any new **Current Law Statutes Guide** to new legislation.				

ORDER SOURCE No.: 6505 A

Postage and Packing: UK – please add £3.50 for this order. *Europe* – please add £7 for first item, £2.50 for each additional item. *Rest of world* – please add £30 for first item, £15 for each additional item

MY PERSONAL DETAILS ARE:

PLEASE COMPLETE IN BLOCK LETTERS

TITLE: _____ FIRST NAMES: _____

SURNAME: _____

JOB TITLE: _____

DEPARTMENT: _____

TELEPHONE: _____

E-MAIL ADDRESS: _____

MY ORGANISATION DETAILS ARE:

NAME: _____

ADDRESS: _____

TOWN: _____

COUNTY: _____

POSTCODE: _____

COUNTRY: _____

DX: _____

FAX: _____

PAYMENT OPTIONS:

Using my Sweet & Maxwell Account:

Please charge my credit card:

☐ AMEX ☐ Visa

☐ Mastercard ☐ Diners Club

Expiry Date: _____

Card No.: _____

Or

☐ I enclose a cheque payable to Sweet & Maxwell Group

☐ Please send under your 30 days' Satisfaction Guarantee (UK & Europe)

EU MEMBER STATES: CAT, TVA, MWST, IVA, BTW, FPA, MOMS will be charged to your order if applicable. **Please state your number:**

_____

Signature: _____

Date: _____

Your order is not valid unless signed

HOW TO RETURN YOUR REQUEST

☎ **BY PHONE**

UK: 020 7449 1111
International Customer Services:
   +44 1264 342906
International Subscriptions:
   +44 1264 342795
Quoting Order Source No. 4411

➥ **BY DX**

Sweet & Maxwell
DX 38861 Swiss Cottage

✉ **BY MAIL**

Smeena Khan, Sweet & Maxwell Group, FREEPOST LON 12091, London NW3 4YS

➟ **BY FAX**

UK: 020 7393 7030
International: +44 1264 342706

✒ **BY INTERNET**

http://www.sweetandmaxwell.co.uk

Or contact your local Representative

Please allow up to 28 days for delivery in the UK. Prices, specifications and details are subject to change without prior notification.

Registered offices: Sweet & Maxwell Group, 100 Avenue Road, Swiss Cottage, London NW3 3PF.

Registered No. 28096 (England). Sweet & Maxwell VAT REGISTRATION No. GB 198 9232 09.

Sweet & Maxwell Group goods and services are supplied subject to our terms of sale and supply. Copies of our terms are available upon request.

Sweet & Maxwell Group is a member of the Thomson Corporation and is a registered data user. Data supplied may be used to inform you about other related Thomson Corporation services.

Data Protection Act 1998 Registration No. K4119392.

☐ Please tick if you do not wish to receive marketing information from Sweet & Maxwell Group

☐ Sweet & Maxwell Group is a member of the Thomson corporation. Please tick if you do not wish to be informed of other related Thomson products and services.

THOMSON
™
SWEET & MAXWELL

11.2003 / SK / ID / -

LEGAL BUSINESS UNIT

SWEET & MAXWELL LTD

FREEPOST LON 12091

LONDON

NW3 4YS

UNITED KINGDOM